土木与交通类专业双语教学专用教材

Introduction to Tunnel Engineering
隧道工程导论

马建秦　著

人民交通出版社股份有限公司
北　京

Outline(内容提要)

This textbook generally presents the contemporary theoretical themes of tunnel design, construction and operation, and also the practical side of work on the tunnel structural design, the construction site such as tunnel supporting and surrounding rock reinforcement, ground water control and management, tunneling process with conventional and mechanical methods.

The general themes of cut and cover tunnels, and immersed tunnels are presented in a self – governed chapter, respectively. The tunnel operational facilities and management, and tunnel operational environments and safety control are shown, with special reference to road tunnel ventilation and lighting. A chapter of risk management is devoted to underline the importance of risk control in tunnel projects.

本教材将现代隧道设计、施工与运营管理理念贯穿于全书始终,从勘测设计、隧道施工方法、技术和管理、隧道运营设施与管理,以及隧道工程风险识别与管理的角度,介绍了隧道工程的主要理论、技术与方法。本书内容全面、涵盖了山岭、城市及水下隧道工程的基本内容。在系统介绍隧道工程相关知识的基础上,注重其工程适用性,并将欧美规范、设计指南的部分要点贯穿于其中,有助于培养学生解决实际问题的能力。

本书可作为培养具有国际视野的道路、桥梁与渡河工程、交通工程专业本科生及研究生隧道工程课程的教材,也可供隧道及地下工程领域工程技术人员参考。

图书在版编目(CIP)数据

隧道工程导论 = Introduction to Tunnel Engineering:英文 / 马建秦著. — 北京:人民交通出版社股份有限公司,2020.8

ISBN 978-7-114-16658-7

Ⅰ. ①隧… Ⅱ. ①马… Ⅲ. ①隧道工程—高等学校—教材—英文 Ⅳ. ①U45

中国版本图书馆 CIP 数据核字(2020)第 150860 号

土木与交通类专业双语教学专用教材
Suidao Gongcheng Daolun

书　　名:	隧道工程导论
著 作 者:	马建秦
责任编辑:	钱　堃　卢　珊
责任校对:	刘　芹
责任印制:	刘高彤
出版发行:	人民交通出版社股份有限公司
地　　址:	(100011)北京市朝阳区安定门外外馆斜街 3 号
网　　址:	http://www.ccpcl.com.cn
销售电话:	(010)59757973
总 经 销:	人民交通出版社股份有限公司发行部
经　　销:	各地新华书店
印　　刷:	北京虎彩文化传播有限公司
开　　本:	787×1092　1/16
印　　张:	36.5
字　　数:	955 千
版　　次:	2020 年 8 月　第 1 版
印　　次:	2020 年 8 月　第 1 次印刷
书　　号:	ISBN 978-7-114-16658-7
定　　价:	85.00 元

(如有印刷、装订质量问题的图书,由本公司负责调换)

Preface

We have a long history of using underground structures for living, defense, religion, transportation, storage, etc. Over time, the utilizations of underground structures have developed from primarily shelter to space for a wide range of functional facilities. Nowadays, tunnels and underground space can be used for a variety of purposes, such as for infrastructure, services and transport, recreation, entertainment and commercial uses.

In modern times, the requirements for infrastructures due to industrialization and business boom have propelled the construction of new infrastructures and the improvement of the existing ones. Since the 1970s, tunnel and underground space are an area of special interest to the world, as we have recognized that we must develop underground space to insure a sustainable world.

Tunnels are parts of infrastructures, such as in the field of transportation, public works, common utilities and facilities. With the developing of economy, society and technology, more tunnels will be built in the future, especially in the developing countries. At the same time, the tasks of operation, maintenance, rehabilitation and improvement of the existing tunnels become an important and challenging issue. The planning, design, construction, operation and maintenance of tunnels are therefore the main issues of Tunnel Engineering.

Tunnels are unique structures mainly due to that they are built in various grounds. For a mined tunnel, the surrounding rock(ground) is not only the host medium for the structures, but also the part of structures of the excavation. The properties of the surrounding rock and the stability of the excavation have a direct relationship to the type and dimensions of tunnel supporting measures required. The stability of a tunnel structure are related to various factors, such as the features of the tunnel, the properties of the surrounding rock, hydrological condition of the ground, construction method and supporting measures applied, as well as the interaction between the surrounding rock and supporting measures.

It is well recognized that the interaction between the tunnel supporting system and surrounding rock is one of the key considerations in tunnel design and construction. For example, excavations lead to the surrounding rock disturbance, which may undergo a period of adjustment after the excavation. Whether the surrounding rock can come back to an equilibrium and stable condition, depends strongly on the properties of the surrounding rock, the three dimensions of the tunnel structures, construction method, as well as the time effect of the surrounding rock. So the influence of the changing characteristics of the surrounding rock during the adjustment period, must be accounted for in tunnel design and construction.

Since the host ground plays an active role in the stability of a tunnel, the features of the ground as surrounding rock should be approximated in tunnel planning, design and construction, such as in terms of strength, structures (or integrality), permeability, in-situ stress, ground water conditions and their chemical characteristics, which may have strong influence on the behaviors of both surrounding rock and tunnel structures, as well as the durability of the tunnel structures. Of the approximation of the ground conditions of a tunnel, much difficulty is related to the uncertainties of the adverse geology, which may cause unacceptable risks, such as accidents or damages to equipments and personnel, time schedule delay, cost overrun, etc. Risk control, related to the uncertainty of the ground features approximating, is therefore vital to the success of a tunnel project.

The tunnels in a line of road or railway are enclosed underground passageway except for entrance and exit, commonly at each end. This situation makes the environment in a tunnel may be significantly different from that of an open road or railway, such as in terms of lighting, ventilation and safety control during an accident, especially for a long and super long tunnel, of which special considerations are required for the tunnel operation in design and construction. This also makes a tunnel or underground structure unique in terms of design, construction and operation, in comparison to a ground structure.

Practices in the field of tunnel and underground structures have indicated that the safety of the tunnel construction and operation, as well as the risk control of the tunnel project, depends heavily on a good planning and design. The subject, focusing on the planning, design, construction, operation and management, rehabilitation of tunnels, is the main topics of tunnel engineering. The wide field of this subject tells its own story. Tunnel engineering has the features of both complicacy and syntheses, in terms of knowledge and techniques.

There are numbers of old tunnels in operation, but the requirements of tunnels will increase with the development of the society to pass through the obstacles in the way of a planned transportation line. Tunnel engineering is still one of the most interesting and challenging engineering disciplines, since a qualified tunnel engineer depends not only on theoretical knowledge but also practical experience.

We live in a fast changing world, at least, in terms of knowledge and economy. Although certain basics of engineering will be almost same in the future, the explosion of knowledge and the change of the global economy will be reflected by our working and living ways. The way engineers work will reflect an ongoing evolution. In the field of industry and commercial business, internationalization is a general trend. If we want to share the world economic situation and be able to share international jobs in the future, we must prepare for this wave of change. Information is food for thought and is keen to develop innovative ideas further. The importance of making the learning experience more meaningful to students will never be over-strengthened. The activities at a university are required to enrich and broaden engineering education, and then graduates will be well prepared to work in a constantly changing world.

This textbook is written on the base of the lecture notes, which have been used in the course of Tunnel Engineering in bilingual style for those, who want to be involved in a tunnel project of international feature in the future, at the Highway School, Chang'an University. The accent will be on the fundamental knowledge, principles, and working procedures, in terms of design, construction and operation. Also, an important function of this book is to provide engineers with a pantoscopic vision in the field of Tunnel Engineering.

The book is a reference resource document for professional learning in the field of Road, Bridge and Tunnel Engineering. The emphasis of the book is on why and how. The author hopes this is a step in the right direction. However, it is not intended to override or replace the necessary use of good judgment, common sense and the research of current best practices, such as design codes, manuals, handbooks and guidelines. Hereby, the book is titled as *Introduction to Tunnel Engineering*, considering numerous contents left for presenting in this field.

The preparation of this book was accomplished under the direction of the administrative department of both Chang'an University and School of Highway. Colleagues in the department of Geotechnical and Tunnel, professors Wang Yongdong and Ye Fei, Innovative Center, professor Yang Guanghui, Liu Yu, gave their time, knowledge and suggestions to successfully completing this book. The author would like to thank them for their helps and constructive comments. The ordinary words "thank you" are entirely inadequate to express my appreciation, but the author acknowledge professor Chen Jianxun, Chen Yu and Li Yao, who reviewed the book manuscript and gave constructive comments, which is indispensable to this book.

The author trusts that the contents of this book may meet the current needs of the students to accomplish their duties, but there is a long way to make it good.

Any comments and suggested improvements are welcome. These should be sent through telephone (+86)(0)29-82334854 or E-mail: majq@ gl. chd. edu. cn.

Ma Jianqin
Chang'an University
2017. 7

Contents

1 **Introduction** 1
   1.1 Requirement of tunnel and underground space 1
   1.2 Philosophy of tunnel 5
   1.3 Brief history of tunneling 8
   1.4 Types of tunnels 9
   1.5 Utilization of tunnels 16
   1.6 Content and layout of this book 18
   1.7 Critical thinking problems 20
   1.8 References 20

2 **Structures of a Tunnel** 21
   2.1 Introduction 21
   2.2 Supports and structures 21
   2.3 Main structures of a tunnel 22
   2.4 Auxiliary structures of a tunnel 33
   2.5 Critical thinking problems 36
   2.6 References 36

3 **Planning of a Tunnel** 37
   3.1 Introduction 37
   3.2 Alternative analysis 41
   3.3 Tunnel type studies 50
   3.4 Geometry design of a tunnel 62
   3.5 Operational and financial planning 81
   3.6 Risk analysis and management 84
   3.7 Comments on the planning of a tunnel project 85
   3.8 Critical thinking problems 86
   3.9 References 87

4 **Site Investigation in a Tunnel Project** 88
   4.1 Introduction 88
   4.2 Site investigation in general 88
   4.3 Site investigation in a tunnel project 97

4.4	Ground characteristic parameters	111
4.5	Ground (rock mass) classification	133
4.6	Site investigation reports	161
4.7	Critical thinking problems	167
4.8	References	168

5　Tunnel Location Optimization　174

5.1	Introduction	174
5.2	General principles	174
5.3	Location optimization of a tunnel	180
5.4	Comments on the tunnel location study	192
5.5	Critical thinking problems	192
5.6	References	193

6　Preliminary Analysis for Tunnel Design　194

6.1	Introduction	194
6.2	Behavior of surrounding rocks in general	197
6.3	Analysis tools for tunnel design	205
6.4	Preliminary stress pattern in surrounding rocks	212
6.5	Critical thinking problems	229
6.6	References	229

7　Design of Tunnel Structures　232

7.1	Introduction	232
7.2	Design considerations	233
7.3	Methods of predicting lining loads	246
7.4	Choice of lining types	262
7.5	Critical thinking problems	268
7.6	References	269

8　Tunnel Support and Surrounding Rocks Reinforcement　272

8.1	Support and surrounding rocks reinforcement in general	272
8.2	Ground improvement and pre-support	275
8.3	Primary support	280
8.4	Support and reinforcement design	297
8.5	Critical thinking problems	298
8.6	References	299

9　Tunnel Construction Techniques in General　302

9.1	Introduction	302
9.2	Features of tunneling	302

9.3	Types of construction methods	307
9.4	Excavations in conventional tunneling	311
9.5	New Austrian Tunneling Method	316
9.6	Observational Method in design and construction	320
9.7	Instrumentation and monitoring in tunneling	321
9.8	Choice of tunneling methods	324
9.9	Critical thinking problems	330
9.10	References	330

10 Drill and Blast Tunneling — 332

10.1	Introduction	332
10.2	Drill and blast in tunneling	334
10.3	Material handing	344
10.4	Critical thinking problems	345
10.5	References	346

11 Mechanical Tunneling in Rocks — 347

11.1	Introduction	347
11.2	Types of mechanical methods	347
11.3	Excavation with a roadheader	354
11.4	TBM tunneling in rocks	355
11.5	Risks of TBM tunneling	366
11.6	Critical thinking problems	368
11.7	References	369

12 Shield Tunneling in Soft Ground — 372

12.1	Introduction	372
12.2	System of soft ground tunneling shield TBMs	374
12.3	Tunnel segment lining	380
12.4	Ground displacements	382
12.5	Risks of shield tunneling in urban areas	384
12.6	Critical thinking problems	385
12.7	References	386

13 Cut and Cover Tunnels — 388

13.1	Introduction	388
13.2	Construction methodology	389
13.3	Excavation method and supporting system	393
13.4	Design considerations	406
13.5	Risks of construction	418

13.6	Critical thinking problems	420
13.7	References	421

14 Immersed Tunnels ... 423

14.1	Introduction	423
14.2	Features and applications	424
14.3	Structures of immersed tunnels	426
14.4	Construction	436
14.5	Critical thinking problems	446
14.6	References	446

15 Tunnel Operational Facilities and Management ... 448

15.1	Introduction	448
15.2	Facilities for a road tunnel in general	449
15.3	Design of operational facilities for a tunnel	451
15.4	Safety control of a tunnel	456
15.5	Case histories	464
15.6	Critical thinking problems	468
15.7	References	468

16 Ventilation in Tunnel Engineering ... 470

16.1	Introduction	470
16.2	Ventilation for construction	471
16.3	Tunnel operation ventilation	475
16.4	Fresh air requirement	495
16.5	Choice of ventilation system	507
16.6	Critical thinking problems	512
16.7	References	513

17 Tunnel Lighting ... 515

17.1	Introduction	515
17.2	Lighting of a road tunnel in general	515
17.3	Daytime lighting levels of long tunnels	523
17.4	Determination of night-time lighting levels	531
17.5	Design of lighting system	532
17.6	Remarks on tunnel lighting	546
17.7	Critical thinking problems	546
17.8	References	548

18 Risk Management in Tunnel Engineering ... 549

18.1	Introduction	549

18.2	Risk management in general	549
18.3	Main components of risk management in a tunnel project	554
18.4	Risk control in tunneling	560
18.5	Comments on risk management	567
18.6	Critical thinking problems	568
18.7	References	568

19 Appendix-Frequently Used Tunneling Terms 571

1 Introduction

1.1 Requirement of tunnel and underground space

Expansion reading 1-1

Tunnels are parts of the infrastructures of a society. In recent years, developing countries are building new infrastructure, and developed countries are rehabilitating and expanding their infrastructure to meet the demands of increasing urban population, energy efficiency, and the environmental awareness of the public. Urban problems and underground solutions have been the focuses in sustainable development blueprints of the world for a long time. The functions and advantages of tunnels are one of the considerations to meet the requirements of sustainable development. For example, the Working Group No. 20 of the International Tunnelling Association (ITA) has continued examining the use of underground space in the urban environment as it evolves with expanding cities and urban densification. ITA[1] issued its special edition of the tribune entitled *Why Go Underground——Contribution of the Use of Underground Space to Sustainable Development*.

In general, the consumption of energy and space occupation per capita increases with the development of a society. There appears contradiction between the increasing space occupation requirement and the limited space available on the ground of the earth. Effective and sustainable infrastructures are one of the indispensable conditions of a modern society to cope with this situation. Tunnels and underground space are an area of special interest to the world's, as we have no choice but to develop underground space in order to become sustainable in both the developed and developing countries. Tunnels and underground space can be used for a variety of purposes, such as infrastructure, services and transport, entertainment and commercial uses [2].

Urbanization is a world tendency for a long period. Urbanization means the increasing number of people will live in urban areas. In 2007, our planet became predominantly urban as for the first time and more than half of the world's population lived in cities. In the second half of the last century, the number of people living in urban areas increased from 750 million to 2.86 billion; by 2030, this proportion is estimated to rise to 60% of the world's population, or nearly 5 billion people, as shown in Figure 1-1❶. Figure 1-1 also shows that, by 2050, about 64% and 86% of the population in developing and developed countries, respectively, will be urbanized❷.

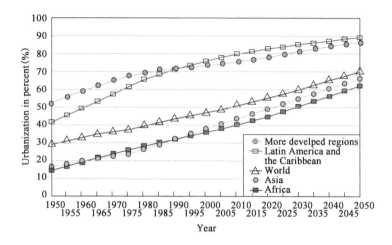

Figure 1-1 Necessities of tunnels and underground space

Urbanization predominantly results in the physical growth of urban areas, in horizontal and vertical dimensions. At the same time, sustainable connections between the cities and the parts in the cities are accordingly required, in terms of shortcut, economy, efficiency and safety. Tunnels are always parts of the connections, especially in the lines of railways and roadways. In this term, during the urbanization process of a country, underground space is not only a very valuable resource, but also one of the potential solutions.

In the sense of regional difference in urbanization, it is unbalance in the world❸, as shown in Figure 1-2. There are many factors which have influence on the development of a region or country. Urbanization is necessary to sustain growth in developing countries before reaching middle income status[3]. The higher productivity in cities and persistent geographical advantage are shown in Figure 1-3, which demonstrates China's coastal cities enjoy quick development and a large income advantage. The features of the strong geographic and cumulative urban agglomeration advantages in the cities often mean the significant productivity advantage of urban areas over rural areas in China. Accordingly, different sorts of tunnels and underground structures should be built in the future, to meet the requirements of a region or country. For example, in the inland, most of the tunnels

---

❶ UN State of the World Population. UNFPA. 2007.
❷ Urban life: Open-air computers. The Economist. 27 October 2012.
❸ Word Urbanization Prospects 2018, https://esa.un.org/unpd/wup/Publications/.

are mountain tunnels, while in the coast areas, more underwater tunnels and urban tunnels are necessary. There is a proposal of a 260 billion (RMB) tunnel project, building the world's longest undersea tunnel from Dalian to Yantai across the Bohai Strait in the future. The planned tunnel will be more than twice the length of the Channel Tunnel and shorten 1280 km off the current along coast route between Dalian and Yantai[❶].

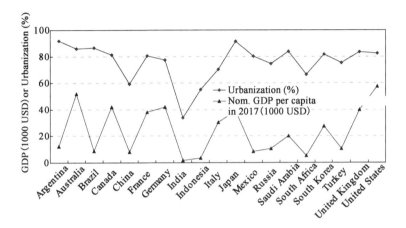

Figure 1-2 Urbanization-degree and Nom. GDP per capita of the World's Major Economics[❷]

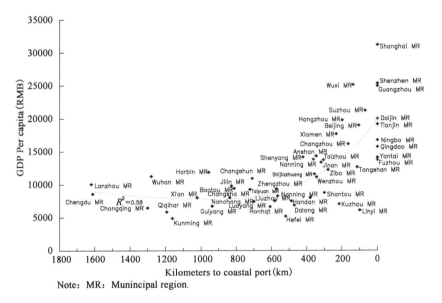

Note: MR: Municipal region.

Figure 1-3 Income advantages of coastal metropolitan regions in China, 2000[3]

---

❶ World Urbanization Prospects 2018, https://esa.un.org/unpd/wup/Publications/.

❷ GDP per capita data from http://www.imf.org/external/pubs/ft/weo/2018/01/weodata/index.aspx;
Urbanization Data from https://www.cia.gov/library/publications/the-world-factbook/fields/2212.html.

In history, the uses for underground structures have developed from primary shelter to space of a wide range of functional facilities. The uses may be categorized into several primary groups, such as infrastructure for transit and utilities, storage, and the protection of environment. For example, in large cities, the public increasingly demands a higher quality environment with respect to ITA[2]: ①reliable and safe transport of people and goods; ②water distribution and sewerage systems; ③ sustainability of the environment and containing sprawl control; ④more green space and recreational areas; ⑤reduced use of fuel and fuel emissions; ⑥noise control; ⑦aesthetics; ⑧efficient use of real-estate.

These demands[2] call for continuous improvement of sustainable and resource-efficient urban planning and development. This situation can be facilitated by the use of tunnels and underground structures. Advanced underground construction technologies can provide solutions for reducing congestion and other environmental problems while contributing to energy efficiency. One of the aims of underground space use in an urban environment may be to free surface space for other human needs and to improve the living conditions of citizens. The tunnel and underground structures may offer better natural protection against environmental elements, including destructive weather, noise, and seismic events. At the same time, the space created for underground structures has the advantage of allowing use of the surface for other functions.

The cost of road congestion in OECD❶ countries is estimated to be equivalent to about 2 percent of the GDP[4]. Time saving during rush hours by using grade separated rail systems saves hundreds of hours per year per worker. The urban "problems" are well documented and those that may be solved through use of the underground space include[2]: ① crowding and lack of space for work and recreation; ② traffic congestion; ③ aging infrastructure and distribution of resources; ④ environmental conditions such as noise and air pollution; ⑤ esthetic qualities and image of our urban environment quality; ⑥ safety, security, and protection against natural disasters; ⑦ flooding; ⑧ sewage conveyance and treatment; ⑨ synergy effects of the above.

In a sense of efficient transportation system, selecting a tunnel solution may be justified due to some of the following factors[2]: ① providing new routes under densely developed urban areas, where land acquisition costs are high; ② being through mountains to avoid steep grades and longer routes; ③ providing new routes under rivers and large bodies of water to keep shipways clear; ④ avoiding impact on cultural heritage or environmentally sensitive areas; ⑤ where clearance requirements or land use prevent construction of bridges.

---

❶ Organization for Economic Cooperation and Development (OECD), an international economic organisation of 34 countries founded in 1961 to stimulate economic progress and world trade.

1.2 Philosophy of tunnel

1.2.1 Definition and meanings in general

As a noun, tunnel means an underground or underwater passage, or a passage through or under a barrier in a way. A tunnel may be a cave or underground structure, which is an engineering production or a natural underground space. As a verb, tunnel means to make a space in the form of a tunnel by excavating or digging, usually with the help of supports to stabilize the excavations. In engineering, tunneling means to make a space or build a structure underground. This is similar to penetrating, driving, drilling or boring underground. A typical case is mining by Tunnel Boring Machine (TBM). In general, the process of constructing a tunnel is presented by the word tunneling in the field of civil engineering and the word tunnel is always used as a noun, meaning an underground or underwater structure.

1.2.2 Tunnels in civil engineering

A tunnel is a closed or roofed structure carrying a way through or under an obstacle. The obstacle may be anything in the path of a preferred way alignment, such as a mountain, a body of water, a building or an existing structure. A transportation tunnel is an underground passageway, completely enclosed except for entrance and exit, commonly at each end. A road or railway tunnel is of relatively long and narrow features. Although various shorter excavations may be constructed, the length of a tunnel is often much greater than twice of its diameter.

The definition of what constitutes a tunnel is not universally agreed upon. For example the definition of a road tunnel in the United Kingdom is defined by DB[5] as "a subsurface highway structure enclosed for a length of 150 m or more"; anything shorter than this should be called an underpass. The requirement of the length magnitude in the National Fire Protection Association (in the USA) is greater than 23 m, with diameter greater than 1.8 m❶. However, as a general guideline a minimum length of 100 m is used in defining a tunnel for inventory purposes in the USA. This length is primarily to exclude long underpass, but other reasons for using the tunnel classification may exist such as the presence of lighting or a ventilation system, which could override the length limitation. PIARC❷ defines a

---

❶ National Fire Protection Association (NFPA) Standard for Safeguarding Construction, Alteration, and Demolition Operations.
❷ The Permanent International Association of Road Congresses (PIARC) was founded in 1909, with about 142 member countries a round the world. Its head office is located in Paris.

road tunnel as an enclosed road structure with a length of at least 5 times the width of one tube, intended for use by authorized traffic on the carriageway. In China, there is no corresponding number for the length presented definitely. Similarly, the FHWA[1] explained that tunnel is an enclosed passageway, as for trains, automobiles and so on, through or under an obstruction, such as a city, mountain, river, or harbor; or in simplicity, tunnel is an underground passage.

It is beneficial bearing in mind that various definitions or concepts are acceptable in different fields in the world. For example, in the United Kingdom a pedestrian tunnel or other underpass beneath a road is called a subway. In the Glossary of Transportation Terms[1], subway is explained as: ① the portion of a transportation system that is constructed beneath the ground surface, regardless of its method of construction; ② an underground rail rapid transit system or the tunnel through which it runs; ③ in local utilization, sometimes used for the entire rail rapid transit system, even if it is not all beneath the ground surface; ④ a pedestrian underpass, respectively. Tunnels that bring water from reservoirs to cities may be called aqueducts. Mass-transit railway tunnels constructed under cities to relieve crowded streets are also known as subway or metro in the world.

Several related concepts include passage, shaft, underpass, subway and adit. A passage is a structure between rooms or buildings. Shaft is a long vertical or steeply inclined passage sunk into the earth, as for a mine or tunnel. Underpass is an underground tunnel or passage enabling pedestrians to cross a road or railway. Adit is a entrance or exit to a tunnel other than portals.

In simplicity, tunnels are presented as being excavated underground, with the overlying material left in place, and then lined as necessary to support the adjacent ground. An entrance to the inside of the tunnel is called a portal. A nearly horizontal passage, with one end connecting to the inside of a tunnel and the other end being an entrance at a hillside, is called a transverse passage or duct. The entrance at the hillside, except portals, is usually called an adit or access, which is often used for accessing the tunnel during tunnel construction.

Artificial tunnel is usually referred to the structure covering or shedding a road or river or railway. For example, there are many cases that the structures may be used for crossing over or protecting a railway, road or canal. Accordingly, they may be called overbridges, sheds or canal tunnes. Sheds are a kind of artificial tunnels built to protect a railway or road from avalanches, rockfalls, etc.

---

[1] Glossary of Transportation Terms. U. S. Department of Transportation, Federal Highway Administration, 1994.

1.2.3 Natural tunnels

A nearly horizontal underground passageway may be produced by excavation or occasionally by natural action in dissolving a soluble rock, such as limestone. A vertical opening is usually called a sinkhole. In China, natural tunnel are usually called caves, sinkhole, passage or cavern.

A natural tunnel means a hole or passage developed by natural force or dynamic geological processes in a geological formation, such as loess, limestone, snow or ice. For example, in the USA, the natural tunnel is referred to the natural limestone cave at the Natural Tunnel State Park, near Duffield, Virginia, USA. The natural tunnel, for which this park was named, is believed to be over one million years old❶. The tunnel is carved through limestone and dolomite, where there are various holes and caves in sizes and shapes. Both a train and a river share the same natural limestone cave, measuring 255 m long. The railway has used this tunnel since 1890. In recent years, the tunnel attracts hundreds of visitors each year.

In general, a natural tunnel is not as regular as a tunnel by engineering construction. A natural tunnel may be longer than 100 m, however, the width and height of the tunnel is usually relatively variable along length. On the other hand, a natural tunnel may be short but wide enough; or a natural tunnel is narrow like a horizontal chimney.

1.2.4 Tunnel engineering as a subject

Tunnels are built in grounds varying from soft clay to hard rock or partially in water. The methods of tunnel construction depend on such factors as the ground conditions, the length and diameter of the tunnel, the depth of the tunnel, the logistics of supporting the tunnel excavation, the final use and shape of the tunnel.

Similarly to the other civil engineering, to make a structure from a plan into a practical building, unique design and construction techniques are involved in this process. Many people, representing different parties, will be involved in the project. The planning, design, and construction of the project should be executed

---

❶ Natural Tunnel began forming during the early Pleistocene Epoch and was fully formed by about one million years ago. The Glenita fault line running through the tunnel, combined with moving water and naturally forming carbonic acid may have formed Natural Tunnel through the surrounding limestone and dolomitic bedrock. After the tunnel formed and the regional water table lowered, Stock Creek diverted underground, then later took the path of least resistance through the Natural Tunnel, flowing south to join the Clinch River.

in a planned procedure. And therefore project management is part of the project implementation procedure. When the construction of a tunnel project is finished and open to use, operation and maintenance are required, in terms of safety and durability. For some old tunnels, rehabilitation may be conducted to maintain or improve the operation conditions.

In general, tunnel engineering is a subject which focuses on the planning, design, construction, operation and rehabilitation of tunnels or underground structures.

1.3 Brief history of tunneling

It is a probable underground space use process that prehistoric people first lived in some natural caves, and then learned to enlarge their caves with simple tools. Later, they could excavate caves in soils. In civilizations, tunnels are used for mining, transportations, water diversion, housing underground installations such as power plants, storages, etc. The utilizations of the tunnels and underground structures have been expanding with time. The ancient art of tunneling has evolved throughout history with occasional periods of impressive development, which is corresponding to the applications of the new techniques of the times. For example, the applications of metal tools made it possible to excavate tunnel or mining in rocks. The excavation efficiency could be improved with the application of black powder in mining. However, these developments were significantly surpassed by the new techniques appeared in the period of Industrial Revolution. The list of drivers for tunneling can be simply considered as: ① thanks to the Industrial Revolution, the productivity was greatly increased and more commercial activities were required; ② safe and convenient transportation system would be built to meet the social and economical development requirements, with the application of the new industrial techniques. For example, many mountain railway tunnels were built in the late half 19th century. The demands on tunneling increased as rapidly as the population growth, rapid urbanization, and development of national and international rapid transportation networks. The well developed urbanization has made a growing realization that many transportation system and utility facilities built traditionally above ground can be located to advantage underground. Nowadays, tunnel projects become more and more ambitious, though new important problems appear, challenging the capabilities of the tunnel and engineers in related fields.

In general, the brief history of tunneling can be presented with the typical ancient tunnels, canal and railway tunnels, underwater tunnels, machine-mined tunnels, as well as the design principles, technology and materials applied in tunneling, with era features. The new tunnels in the future are to meet various

Expansion reading 1-2

requirements. The presentations in details for these items are in the Expansion reading 1-2.

1.4 Types of tunnels

As the above shown, tunnels have many utilizations. The types of tunnel develop with the expending of its utilizations. In general, the utilizations of an engineering structure depend strongly on the requirements in history, the capacity of construction, such as, the techniques available and economic situation. The purpose of this section is to look at the types that are commonly used in Tunnel Engineering.

Mainly due to the long history of the development of tunnel, in terms of construction method, dimension of tunnels, as well as the techniques of excavating and supporting, there is no universally agreed type or classification system. A classification of tunnels usually focuses on one or several key factors, which have a strong influence on the design, construction or operation of the tunnels in considerations. For example, the tunnels in the field of highway and rail transit tunnels, their types are usually described by their shape, liner and invert types, construction methods, as well as tunnel finishes. It should be noted that other types may exist currently or be constructed in the future as new technologies become available.

1.4.1 Types based on construction method

Tunnels are built in grounds varying from soft clay to hard rock. There are three basic types of tunnel, in terms of construction method:

(1) Cut and cover tunnel, constructed in a shallow trench and then covered over.

(2) Bored tunnel, constructed in situ, without removing the ground above. They are usually of circular or horseshoe cross-section.

(3) Immersed (tube or box) tunnel, sunk into a body of water and sit on, or are buried just under its bed.

Some tunnel types named, with special reference to a construction method, such as excavation with drill and blast method, TBM, construction with pipe or box jacking, are widely used in the modern time.

For a specific tunnel, the choice of construction method is determined by the features of the tunnel and the construction conditions. The former includes the geotechnical conditions, the ground water conditions, the length and diameter of the tunnel drive, the depth of the tunnel, the final use and shape of the tunnel, etc. The construction conditions are related to not only the features of the tunnel project, but also the techniques and materials available, the logistics conditions of construction, qualified people available, social and environmental conditions so on.

It is noted that several methods may be used in a tunnel project. For example, the approach sections of an immersed tube tunnel are often built with cut and cover method.

1.4.2 Types of bored tunnels

A tunnel may be bored by drill and blast, TBM and roadheader. Some tunnels are excavated with method of pipe or box jacking. Accordingly, a tunnel, bored with a special or typical mechanical construction method, especially with a system of machine, such as TBM, is often named after the special machine. For example, in China, we use the name of TBM tunnel, shield tunnel, jacked pipe tunnel.

1.4.3 Types based on the properties of surrounding rocks

Ground stability is one of the key focuses in the field of tunnel and underground structure engineering. As a tunnel being built, excavation induces stress redistribution around the excavation. The redistributed stress will lead to ground deformation and degeneration in properties. As the magnitude of the redistributed stress is large enough, the deformation of the surrounding rocks will be unacceptable and collapse may come to heel.

The ground is not only the medium in which a tunnel will be built, but also part of the structures of the tunnel. The types and the features of surrounding rocks have a strong influence on the stability of a planned tunnel. For example, for the tunnels in rocks, the strength of rocks and the structures in the rock mass are the key parameters of the geotechnical features of the surrounding rocks. The properties of the surrounding rocks of planned tunnel are one of the key parameters in the tunnel design and construction.

Based on the types of surrounding rocks, a tunnel is often named as rock tunnel or soil tunnel. The rock tunnels are also sub-divided as hard rock tunnels and soft rock tunnels. Rocks, with uniaxial compressive strength more than 30 MPa, are generally considered hard, though whether the rock mass is hard or soft depends on the stress state thrust on it during and after construction.

Sometimes, in order to underline the geotechnical properties of the grounds, in which a tunnel will be built, the type of a tunnel is put into a special one, for example, loess tunnel, soft soils tunnel, frost soil tunnel.

1.4.4 Types based on geography or locations

Based on geography characteristics or the locations of a tunnel, it can be called urban tunnel, underwater (subaqueous) tunnel, or mountain tunnels. Some tunnels are built in special geographic units, such as loess plateau, the tunnels are named after its geographic unit, such as, loess tunnel, karst tunnel.

For a mountain tunnel, tunnel may be designed to pass through the ridge, pass area or nek, mountainside or hillside in a mountain area. Where a tunnel is located at mountainside or hillside, it is called mountainside or hillside tunnel. This kind of tunnel is usually designed in a transportation line along a river or valley. Some typical locations of tunnels in a mountain area are sketched in Figure 1-4.

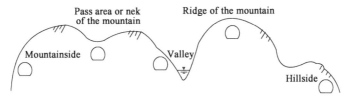

Figure 1-4 Sketch showing the geographical locations of tunnels in a mountain area

1.4.5 Types based on utilization

As above discussed, tunnels have many utilizations. A tunnel for a special use, is usually named after its utilization. For example, a tunnel in a transportation system may be called road tunnel, railway tunnel, canal tunnel, and mining tunnel. Some tunnels have a special name, for example, shaft, and underground structures: power plants, ore-processing plants, pumping stations, vehicle parking, storage of oil and water, water-treatment plants, warehouses; also command centers and other special military needs.

Secret tunnels are built for military purposes, or by civilians for smuggling of weapons, contraband, or illegal immigration. Special tunnels, such as wildlife crossings, are built to allow wildlife to cross human-made barriers safely.

1.4.6 Types based on shapes or dimensions

The shape of the tunnel is largely dependent on the applied construction method and on the ground conditions of the tunnel. For example, rectangular tunnels are often constructed by either the cut and cover method, by the immersed method or by jacked box tunneling. Circular tunnels are generally constructed by using either TBM or mined in soft grounds. Horseshoe configuration tunnels are generally constructed using drill and blast method in rocks or other conventional construction methods. The common sections of tunnels are shown in Figure 1-5.

There are three main shapes of road tunnels, i.e., circular, rectangular, and horseshoe or curvilinear. The tunnels, with these shape characteristics, are accordingly named as circular tunnel, rectangular tunnel, and horseshoe or curvilinear sidewall tunnel, respectively.

Of same shape in cross section, the stability of the tunnel is closely related to the dimension of the section. For a road tunnel, the dimension of a cross section is usually described in terms of span or width. A tunnel may designed for one lane or more. The names of the tunnel are accordingly called single lane tunnel, two-lane tunnel, three-lane tunnel, or even four-lane tunnel. A tunnel, with no less than three lanes, is usually called large cross section tunnel, or large span tunnel in China. In general, of the equivalent sectional area, tunnels are classified according to the size of excavation area into very large (sectional area of 100 m^2 or greater), large (50-100 m^2), medium (10-50 m^2), small (3-10 m^2) and very small (3 m^2 or less) tunnels. However, there is a trend of increasing tunnel sectional areas in a classification.

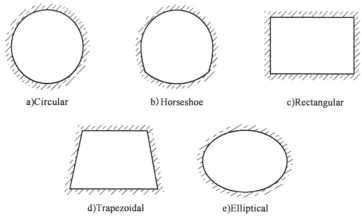

a) Circular b) Horseshoe c) Rectangular

d) Trapezoidal e) Elliptical

Figure 1-5 Shapes of tunnel in a cross section

The length of tunnels varies from few meters to more than 50 km. The difficulty of the design, construction and operation of a tunnel, with large length, is different from that of few meters. The types of tunnels, in Chinese railway and road systems, are classified as: short tunnel, medium tunnel, long tunnel and extra-long tunnel, in terms of length, as shown in Table 1-1.

Table 1-1 The classification of road and railway tunnels in length in China

The types of tunnels	Road tunnel	Railway tunnel
	In length, $L(m)$	
Short tunnel	$L < 500$	$L \leq 500$
Medium tunnel	$500 \leq L < 1000$	$500 < L \leq 3000$
Long tunnel	$1000 < L \leq 3000$	$3000 < L \leq 10000$
Extra-long tunnel	$L > 3000$	$L > 10000$

1.4.7 Variant types of tunnels

With the development of the utilizations of tunnel and underground structures, some "new" types (variant types) appeared. In the field of transportation, double-deck tunnel was innovated in the 1930s. In recent years, the first multipurpose tunnel was built in Malaysia.

1.4.7.1 Double-deck tunnel

Double-deck tunnels were first built in the USA in the 1930s. The utilizations of the decks are of project specific feature. For example, the Queensway Tunnel under the river Mersey between Liverpool and Birkenhead in the UK was originally to have road vehicles running on the upper deck and trains on the lower. During construction the train utilization was cancelled. The lower section is now used for cables, pipes and emergency accident refuge enclosures. The two major segments of the San Francisco-Oakland Bay Bridge (completed in 1936) are linked by the 160-m-long double-deck tunnel, the largest diameter bore tunnel in the world at that time. The tunnel was built for the combination of bidirectional rail and truck pathway on the lower deck, with automobiles above. The tunnel is now converted to one-way road vehicle traffic on each deck.

In China, the first case of double-deck tunnel with both decks for motor vehicles is the Fuxing Road Tunnel in Shanghai. The tunnel was opened to use in 2004, with cars on the two-lane upper deck and heavier vehicles on the single-lane lower deck. In recent years, three double-deck tunnels have been opened to use and other three are under construction, as shown in Table 1-2.

Table 1-2 Double-deck tunnels in China

No.	Tunnels	Location	Features of the main tunnel				Year of completion
			Structure	Length[m]	Traffic	Construction method	
1	Fuxindonglu Tunnel	Shanghai	Two tubes, underwater	1214	Two-lane (2.6-m-high) on upper deck and one lane (4-m-high) on lower deck	Shield TBM, with diameter 10.04 m of cutterhead	2004
2	Shanghai Yangtze River Tunnel	Shanghai	Two tubes, underwater	7500	Three-lane on upper deck and one reserved track rail transit on lower deck	Shield TBM, with diameter 15.43 m of cutterhead	2009
3	Shouxihu Tunnel	Yangzhou	One tube, underwater (partially)	1280	Two-lane on each deck	Shield TBM, with diameter 14.93 m of cutterhead	2014
4	Nanjing Yangtze River Tunnel (Ⅲ)	Nanjing	Two tubes, underwater	3357(4135 south line)	Two-lane on each deck	Shield TBM, with diameter 14.93 m of cutterhead	2015
5	WuhanSanyanglu Yangtze River Tunnel	Wuhan	Two tubes, underwater	2599	Three-lane on upper deck and one track rail transit on lower deck	Shield TBM, with diameter 15.76 m of cutterhead	2017
6	Daluoshan Tunnel	Wenzhou	Two tubes	1400	Two-lane on each deck	NATM, with the area of the excavation profile 180 m^2	2018
7	Chunfeng Tunnel	Shenzhen	One tube	2700	Two-lane on each deck	Shield TBM, with diameter 15.76 m of cutterhead	2020

1.4.7.2 Multipurpose tunnel

Multipurpose tunnels are the ones that have more than one purpose. The SMART tunnel in Malaysia is the first multipurpose tunnel in the world, as it is used for both controlling traffic and flood in Kuala Lumpur (KL). The SMART stands for Stormwater Management and Road Tunnel. The SMART's purpose is to solve the flooding caused by heavy rains at the confluence of Sg Klang and Sg Ampang in the city and to relieve traffic congestion heading into and out of the KL-Seremban Highway [Figure 1-6a)], which is one of the artery to the city downtown.

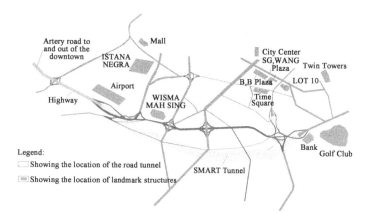

Note: ① The 9.7-km-long "Stormwater Management and Road Tunnel" is called "SMART Tunnel", a storm drainage and road structure in Kuala Lumpur, Malaysia. ② The main objective of this tunnel is to solve the problem of flash floods in Kuala Lumpur and also to reduce traffic jams along Jalan Sungai Besi and Lok Yew flyover at Pudu during rush hour. ③ The 4-km-long double-deck motorway is within stormwater tunnel, and quick and direct access to and out of the city center. ④ It is the longest multi-purpose tunnel in the world.

a) Map showing the location and route of the SMART Tunnel

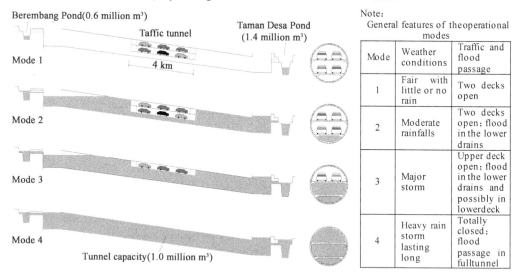

Note:
General features of the operational modes

Mode	Weather conditions	Traffic and flood passage
1	Fair with little or no rain	Two decks open
2	Moderate rainfalls	Two decks open; flood in the lower drains
3	Major storm	Upper deck open; flood in the lower drains and possibly in lowerdeck
4	Heavy rain storm lasting long	Totally closed; flood passage in fulltunnel

b) Operational modes of the SMART Tunnel

Figure 1-6　Features of the SMART Tunnel in Kuala Lumpur, Malaysia[1]

---

[1] http://smarttunnel.com.my.

The SMART tunnel is the longest stormwater tunnel in South East Asia and longest multi-purpose tunnel in the world. The tunnel consists of 9.7-km-long stormwater by-pass tunnel and 3-km double-deck motorway within the stormwater tunnel. The motorway tunnel is suitable for light vehicles only, with two-lane and one emergency lane on each deck, while motorcycles and heavy vehicles are not allowed. The project commenced in Dec 2003 and was completed in June 2007.

In April and October of 2001, and again in June 2003, massive floods in KL caused serious damage, because the rivers flowing through the city were unable to hold the water and space constraints did not permit river improvement work. So a tunnel plan was initiated to alleviate flood problems in KL, as well as the financial, business and commercial hub of Malaysia. However, at the design stage of the SMART, the dual purpose concept was born from the ingenuity of the project proponents and the motorway tunnel was integrated into the system to relieve traffic congestion at the main Southern Gateway to the city centre [Figure 1-6a)].

The unique feature of this project is the 3-km double-deck motorway within the stormwater tunnel at the centre of tunnel [Figure 1-6b)]. In the event of a flood, the operation of the highway in the SMART system would work on a planned principle mode[6]. The information from the tunnel management deparment shows that the following four modes possibly be applied during operation, respectively.

Mode 1: When weather is fair with little or no rain and traffic is allowed in the tunnel.

Mode 2: Activated when moderate rainfalls and the flow rate recorded at the confluence of upper (Sg. Klang)/(Sg. Ampang) (L4 flow station) is 70-150 m^3/s. Only 50 m^3/s is allowed to flow downstream and excess flood water will be diverted to SMART storages and only the lower drains of tunnel is used for conveying flood flow to the Desa attenuation pond. A set of twin gates has been installed at either end of the tunnel and is kept shut at all times in order to keep traffic safe in the tunnel. The road tunnel will still be open to traffic.

Mode 3: Activated when major storm event occurs and flood model forecasts a flow rate of 150 m^3/s or more at L4. Traffic will be evacuated from the road tunnel. This normally takes about one hour. Only 10 m^3/s is allowed to flow downstream. If heavy rain storm stops early or due to some specific circumstances, then the traffic tunnel will not be flooded. Road tunnel will be re-opened to traffic within 2-8 hours after closure.

Mode 4: Activated if heavy rain storm prolongs, usually will be confirmed 1-2 hours after Mode 3 is declared. Road tunnel will be used for the passage of flood after traffic evacuation completed. Only 10 m^3/s is allowed to flow downstream. Road tunnel will be re-opened within 4 days of closure.

1.4.7.3 Covered passageways

Covered passageway is constructed due to an over-bridge covering a road or river or railway. Similarly, sheds are a kind of artificial tunnels built to protect a railway or road from avalanches of snow, or from rockfalls. For road tunnels, it is generally effective to reduce the amount of direct sunlight reaching the road surface and walls at the portal area using daylight louvre or screen structures over the tunnel entrance, and then it is a means of reducing energy consumption of threshold zone lighting. Also, where two road tunnels in a line is such near that the distance between the two tunnels from the exit portal of one tunnel to the entrance portal of the other is less than a safety stop distance, a daylight louvre or screen structure may be built to reduce the amount of direct sunlight reaching the road between the two tunnels.

1.5 Utilization of tunnels

In the old times, underground structures, either natural or man-made, have been used for shelter and producing raw materials. Today, underground structures have various types, such as tunnels, caverns and other underground space. Tunnels have many uses: for mining ores, for transportation, including road vehicles, trains, subways, and for conducting water and sewage. Underground chambers, often associated with a complex of connecting tunnels and shafts, are increasingly used for such things as underground hydroelectric-power plants, ore-processing plants, pumping stations, vehicle parking, storage of oil and water, water-treatment plants, warehouses, and light manufacturing; also defense works, such as command centers and other special military needs.

In the field of transportation as infrastructure, tunnels may be used for road, railway or metro, canal, pedestrians or cyclists passages. The central part of a rapid transit network is usually built in tunnels. Rail stations with much traffic usually provide pedestrian tunnels from one platform to another.

Some tunnels are aqueducts, constructed purely for carrying water, such as for consumption, hydroelectric purposes or sewers, while others carry other services such as telecommunications cables. In urban area, to guarantee consumers, the distribution of fresh water, gas, district heating, electricity and telecommunication, pipeline and cable systems may use more complex underground solutions, such as bundling all components in service ducts or tunnels. Cable tunnels carry high voltage cables across bodies of water, consolidate conduits, and reduce the disruption of conventional cut and cover method for individually installed conduits and the consequent impact on city streets.

Nowadays, as community development and improvement, such as underground cultural and amusement facilities, underground parking, are key facilities for a modern city.

There are even tunnels designed as wildlife crossings, such as for endangered or protected species. Some secret tunnels have also been made as a method of entrance or escape from an area, such as the Cu Chi Tunnels❶ or the tunnels connecting the Gaza Strip to Egypt❷ Some tunnels are not for transport at all but are fortifications, for example, Mittelwerk and Cheyenne Mountain❸.

Today, underground infrastructure is a diverse field and can be categorized in several ways. Some of the uses involve access by the general public; others involve storage or are for protection of the materials from exposure or access. Some representative examples of tunnel and underground utilizations in society are shown in Figure 1-7, including transportation, mining, hydropower engineering, urban underground structure and tunnels, storage, water supply and drainage, defense works.

---

❶ The tunnels of Cu Chi, located about 72 km northwest of Ho Chi Minh City in Vietnam, are an elaborate, underground system stretching over 120 km. It played host to barracks, medical facilities, storage rooms, classrooms, even a small movie theater all underground. At one time, it was part of the Ho Ch Minh Trail, a veritable pipeline of arms, supplies and fighters smuggled from North Vietnam to the South.

❷ Gaza Strip smuggling tunnels are smuggling tunnels that have been dug under the Egypt-Gaza Strip separation barrier, which separates Egypt from the Gaza Strip. The barrier runs along the international border along the Philadelphi a corridor, which is a buffer zone along the border created by the Israel-Egypt Peace Treaty. In late 2009 Egypt commenced construction of an underground barrier with the aim of blocking existing tunnels and making it more difficult to create new ones, because they would have to be deeper.

❸ The Cheyenne Mountain nuclear bunker (colloq. NORAD cave, etc.) is one of several United States subterranean sites of the Cold War. The bunker is the location of military centers which are in warm standby including a backup for the operational NORAD-NORTHCOM Command Center at nearby Peterson Air Force Base, including other standby centers: Air Warning Center, Missile Correlation Center, Systems Center, and Weather Center. The bunker includes a "main excavation" with buildings for the centers; support tunnels with structures for water storage, backup generators, etc.; a 1.4-km-long-north-south tunnel between portals to the outside; and access tunnels to the main excavation from the north blast door in the wall of the portal tunnel.

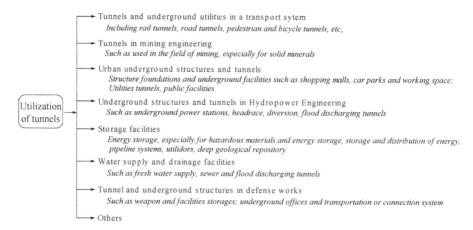

Figure 1-7　Sketch showing the utilizations of tunnels

1.6　Content and layout of this book

Tunnels in transportation lines are often parts of a infrastructure system. The demand for tunnels increases with the development of the society. A tunnel is generally planned to pass through the obstacles in the way of a transportation line. The design and construction of a tunnel project can be challenging, since the tunnel may be built under difficult ground conditions and rigorous environmental restrictions. On the other hand, each tunnel is unique, in terms of ground conditions, utilization and dimension features. Although there are numbers old tunnels in operation, Tunnel Engineering is still one of the most interesting and challenging engineering disciplines. This subject depends not only on theoretical knowledge but also practical experience in geology, geomechanics, structural design, concrete construction, machine technology, construction process technology and management. When a tunnel is open to use, it is then put into the operation and maintenance accordingly.

The framework of this textbook is to present the general knowledge of Tunnel Engineering. After a brief introduction of the tunnel and tunnel engineering in Chapters 1 and 2, the main points of the tunnel engineering will be presented in terms of planning, survey and design, construction and operation in chapters, respectively. The tunnel rehabilitation will not be included in this book.

Chapter 3 provides a general overview of the planning process of a transportation tunnel project including alternative route study, geometry design of a tunnel, tunnel type and tunneling method study, operation and financial planning, and risk analysis and management.

Chapter 4 is for the site investigation of tunnel design. After a general introduction on the procedure and main points of site investigation, the approaches of approximating ground characteristic parameters, as well as some typical values for both soils and rocks, are presented, to describe rock mass properties. Several commonly used rock mass classification schemes are quoted to show their applications in tunnel and underground structure designs. The main points of a site investigation report, including the Geotechnical Baseline Report (GBR), are presented to meet the requirements of the design, construction and management of a tunnel project.

Chapter 5 discusses the general issues of tunnel location optimization. The main factors, which are usually considered in tunnel location optimization, such as major geological units, in-situ stress and slope features of tunnel portals, are discussed, in terms of the avoiding adverse geological units or the risk control of a tunnel project.

Chapter 6 deals with the features of the stress changes that are induced when tunnels or caverns are excavated in grounds. The presentation is intended to cover only those topics which are essential for the reader to know about when dealing with the analysis of stress induced instability and the design of support to stabilize the surrounding rocks under these conditions.

Chapter 7 presents the design of tunnel linings, in terms of general procedures, often used methods in conventional design, the requirements of linings, the methods of ground pressure approximation, as well as some cases of excavation design. The factors influencing the load on the liner and available design methods to estimate the lining loads are also discussed, including the consideration on the ground response to tunneling.

Chapter 8 presents the principles and major techniques used in support and reinforcement practice for tunneling excavations, with special reference to the components of a composite lining system, including pre-supports and yield supports for squeezing ground.

Chapter 9 presents the construction techniques in general for tunnels and underground structures, in terms of construction procedures, excavation methods and construction management. The factors considered in construction method choosing are also presented in general.

The general issues of the tunnel construction with the applications of drill and blast method, mechanical excavation methods in rocks, shield tunneling in soft ground, are shown in Chapter 10 to Chapter 12, respectively.

The general points of the cut and cover tunnels and immersed tunnels are presented in Chapter 13 and Chapter 14, respectively, in terms of design and construction.

For the tunnel operation, the Chapter 15 will give a general presentation of tunnel operation and management, including tunnel operation and management facilities; the ventilation in tunnel engineering and tunnel lighting will be presented in Chapter 16 and Chapter 17, respectively.

The last but not the least, Chapter 18 presents the main points of the risk management in a tunnel project, in terms of the identification, assessment, allocation and control of risks throughout a tunnel project development.

For the convenience of the execution of this bilingual course, some frequently used terms in tunnel engineering are listed as an appendix in Chapter 19.

1.7 Critical thinking problems

The types of tunnels are classified or named according to varying indexes. Consider: ①the key features of a tunnel; ②the situations of various tunnel types, such as in terms of design, construction and operation; ③main features of the tunnels in both historical periods and modern times; ④the application situations of tunnel engineering in both developing and industrialized nations.

1.8 References

[1] ITA Executive Council. Why go underground contribution of the Use of Underground Space So Sustainable Development[J]. Tribune, special issue, 2002:1-22.

[2] Thewes M, Godard J P, Kocsonya F P, et al. Report on Underground Solutions for Urban Problems[J]. ITA Report, No.11, April 2012, 2012.

[3] Annez P C, Buckley R M. Urbanization and growth: Setting the context[J]. Urbanization and growth, 2009, 1: 1-45.

[4] Godard J P. Should we/can we avoid underground urban mass transit systems[J]. WTC 2008-Agra, India, 2008.

[5] The Department for Transport. Design Manual for Roads and Bridges: Volume 2: Section 2: Part 9: BD 78/99: Design of Road Tunnels[M]. TSO, 2014.

[6] Kamis A, Setan H, Fung P L C. The Applications of Surveying Techniques in Kuala Lumpur Smart Tunnel Project[C]//International Symposium and Exhibition on Gps/Gnss. 2007, 5: 7.

2 Structures of a Tunnel

2.1 Introduction

Expansion reading 2-1

In the field of transportation, a tunnel can be considered as an enclosed road or railway for traffic, with vehicle access limited to portals. Tunnels are the structures that require, based on the owner's determination, special design considerations including the structures of tunnel itself, construction methods, the facilities for operations and management, such as lighting, ventilation, fire protection systems and emergency egress capacity. All these factors may have influence on the requirements and features of the tunnel structures.

From the above discussion, we can say that the structures of a tunnel should be designed, at least, to meet the requirements of the client, functions of the tunnel, stability of both the structures and the ground around the tunnel, constructability of the tunnel, adaptation of the proposed construction method, as well as the operation and management of the tunnel.

2.2 Supports and structures

The term "support" is generally used for describing the procedures and materials used for improving the stability and maintaining the load-carrying capability of the ground near the boundaries of excavations. The parts of the ground, which are related to or have influence on the stability of a tunnel or underground excavation, is called surrounding rocks. In letter, the support seems meaning a passive action of bearing the surrounding rocks pressures or confining the deformation of the surrounding rocks. However, in modern tunneling practice, the primary objective of a support for a tunnel or underground structure is to mobilize or conserve the inherent strength of the surrounding rocks so that it will be, at least partially, self-supporting, especially for the cases in which the surrounding rocks are partially in plastic state due to the disturbance of the excavation.

In accord with modern tunneling practice, a distinction between the terms support and reinforcement was given by Windsor and Thompson[1]. *Support* is the application of a reactive force to the surface of an excavation and includes techniques and devices such as timber, fill, shotcrete, steel mesh, steel or concrete sets and liners. *Reinforcement*, on the other hand, is a means of conserving or improving the overall rock mass properties from within the rock mass by techniques such as grouting, soil mixing, rock bolts, cable bolts and ground anchors.

Expansion reading 2-2

Supports may be described as temporary or permanent ones. Support or reinforcement may also be classified as being either active or passive. In general, the support or reinforcement of permanent excavations is described as primary or secondary ones. In practice, a lining system may or may not be built in a tunnel. In some cases, a tunnel is of single lining or monolithic lining.

The supporting and surrounding rock reinforcement measures that commonly applied in tunnel and underground engineering will be presented in details in Chapter 8.

2.3 Main structures of a tunnel

For a tunnel in a transportation line, there are, at least, two portals for access. The portals and the channels between the portals are generally called the main structures of a tunnel. The main structures are mainly designed to meet the functional requirements of a planned tunnel. For example, the main structures of a road or railway tunnel are to provide a channel across the obstacle in the line. However, for a long tunnel in a transportation line, additional structures may be required to meet the requirements of tunnel operation and management, such as for providing lighting, ventilation, fire protection systems, transverse connections or passages between the two neighbor tubes, emergency egress passage. A pilot tunnel, access passage or shaft may be designed and built for site investigation or construction reason in some mega projects. The structures designed and built for these considerations are called auxiliary structures. These auxiliary structures for site investigation or construction reason may also be used for tunnel operation, such as for ventilation, safety and smoke control during fires in the tunnel.

2.3.1 Structures in longitudinal alignment

A tunnel may have one tube or two tubes. Each tube has two or more portals. Between the portals of a tube, the main structures may be constructed by cut and cover method or/and mined or bored method. Accordingly, the structures of a tunnel, for example, in mountain area, can be classified as portals, cut and cover section, and mined or bored section. A typical longitudinal alignment of the structures of a mountain tunnel is shown in Figure 2-1. It should be noted that there may be one cut and cover section, two cut and cover sections or none of it in the longitudinal alignment of a tunnel.

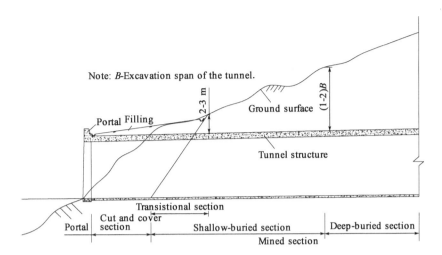

Figure 2-1 Typical longitudinal alignment of the structures of a mountain tunnel

2.3.2 Structures in cross section

It is well accepted that the stability of a tunnel is related to various factors, including the strength of the surrounding rocks, the structures in the rock mass, the dimension of the tunnel, the excavation method applied, supporting system being installed, as well as the interaction between installed supporting system and surrounding rocks in the project-specific construction sequence. The ground is not only the medium, in which a tunnel will be built, but also part of the structures of the tunnel. However, for the simplicity of presentation, the structures of a tunnel are usually narrowly referenced to tunnel supporting system, especially to linings.

Lining is a temporary or permanent structure made of concrete or other materials to secure and finish the tunnel interior or to support an excavation. In practice, a tunnel may be lined or unlined. Tunnel liner types can be described using the following classifications[2]: ①unlined rock; ②rock reinforcement systems; ③shotcrete; ④ribbed (steel set or girder) systems; ⑤segmental linings; ⑥placed concrete; ⑦slurry walls.

In a project, two or more of the above liner types may be built or installed at a tunnel, or the sections of a tunnel. For example, a composite lining system of ribbed systems, shotcrete, rockbolts, cast-in-place concrete, together with a water drainage and proofing system between the primary and final linings, are applied in a tunnel designed and built in accordance to the principles of the NATM.

2.3.2.1 Unlined tunnels

Tunnels in very sound rocks are usually stable. There is no need of lining in terms of Stability. Where the surrounding rocks are not affected by exposure to air, humidity, or freezing, and there is no special requirement for appearance, the excavations of the tunnel may be left unlined. In the early times of railway system, there are many cases of unlined tunnels. One of the examples is the Donner Pass Summit tunnel❶ in the USA (Figure 2-2).

In general, an unlined tunnel is one where no lining is built for the majority of the tunnel length. Linings of various types may exist at portals or at limited sections, such as in weak rock zones. For example, in Norway, the hydropower tunnels in good crystalline rock are often unlined for most of their length and are called unlined rock tunnels. This type of liner is common in older railway tunnels and tunnels in low grade roads. Figure 2-3 is a case of unlined tunnel in a road of grade Ⅲ in the south part of Shaanxi Province, China. The majority of the tunnel is unlined, except the two portal sections and a short mined section.

Figure 2-2　The west portal of the Donner Pass Summit tunnel showing the unlined feature

Figure 2-3　A mainly unlined tunnel in a low grade road

The surrounding rocks of an unlined tunnel may be reinforced locally by rock reinforcement measures to add additional stability to rock blocks. Where there are some structural defects in the surrounding rocks, the application of rockbolts are effective to prevent small rock fragments or blocks from sliding or falling off their original positions.

2.3.2.2　Lined tunnels

The types of tunnel linings depend on the requirement of the tunnel stability control, the materials available to build, the construction condition and techniques,

---

❶ The Donner Pass Summit tunnel in the Central Pacific Railroad, USA, is 506-m-long, with the greatest overburden 38 m. The surrounding rocks are mainly granite, of medium quality, with seams in every direction. The tunnel was mined by painstakingly hand drilling then blasting with black powder and newly invented nitroglycerine. The tunnel was in service from 1868 to 1993. Details see: http://www.cprr.org/Museum/index.html.

time schedule and so on. The types of linings are usually classified in terms of construction materials or construction methods. In the old times, tunnels and underground structures were lined with timbers, masonry structures of bricks, stones and so on. Later, cast iron lining was also sometimes used. When the cement was rediscovered, concrete linings took the most of their places. At present, the rock reinforcement systems, ribbed systems, shotcrete linings, segmental linings and cast-in-place concrete linings are most widely used, such as in a single or composite lining system. For the cut and cover tunnels, which are built in soft soils in urban area, slurry walls may be used.

2.3.2.2.1 Shotcrete lining

Where the surrounding rocks of a tunnel are sound but may deteriorate through contact with water or atmospheric conditions, or get loose due to deformation after excavation, the excavation surface can be protected or confined by coating with shotcrete (sprayed concrete)❶, reinforced with steel meshes or fibers, or not. The shotcrete lining may be applied together with rock reinforcement measures. Shotcrete is also applied only as a local solution to the instabilities in a rock tunnel.

Shotcrete can be used as a temporary application or primary lining prior to a final lining. For example, shotcrete lining is generally considered as a temporary measure in terms of design in some nations; however, shotcrete lining is designed as a bearing structure, which is the primary lining of composite lining system, in China. For a composite lining system, the primary lining is a thin, active rather than passive support; and the surrounding rocks can be strengthened by a flexible combination of shotcrete shell, rock bolts, wire mesh and steel sets.

Shotcrete is appealing as a lining type due to its ease of application, short concreting time, and supporting or protecting the excavations in time.

Where shotcrete is used as a final lining for a tunnel, the structures of the tunnel is often called single lining. This kind of structure system is popular in the North Europe. Where this is the case, it is typically placed in layers and can have steel or randomly oriented, synthetic fibers as reinforcement. The inside surface can be finished smoothly as with regular concrete. Where the finished structures are applied as water and frost protection systems, it is called inner linings[3], as shown in Figure 2-4.

---

❶ Shotcrete is concrete (or mortar) conveyed through a hose and pneumatically projected at high velocity onto a surface, as a construction technique. Shotcrete is usually called sprayed concrete, for example in the UK. In the filed of tunnel engineering, Shotcrete is an all-inclusive term that can be used for both wet-mix and dry-mix versions. In the construction trade however, the term "shotcrete" refers to wet-mix and "gunite" refers to dry-mix. Shotcrete undergoes placement and compaction at the same time due to the force with which it is projected from the nozzle. The additive of accelerator in the concrete or mortar mixture makes the concrete coagulated in a short time. It can be impacted onto any type or shape of surface, including vertical or overhead areas.

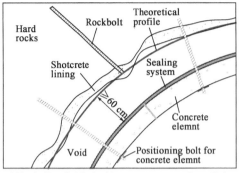 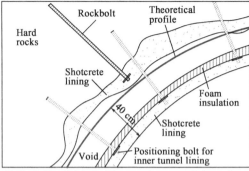

a) Single ling finished with precast concrete inner lining

b) Single ling finished with sprayed concrete lining and insulated with foam plate

Figure 2-4　Single lining finished with so-called inner linings applied in Norwegian tunnels[4]

It is noted that there is no enough safety margin for the stability of the tunnel with single lining if a heavy rockfall or large cave-in occurs at the crown of the tunnel, such as the incident occurred in the Hanekleiv Road Tunnel[5], because the so-called inner linings are not able to withstand the dynamic load by the falling rocks.

In recent years, a new technique of sprayed waterproof membrane has applied in some tunnels[6]. In the cases, where a sprayed waterproof membrane is application, the shotcrete inside the waterproof membrane is in contact with the shotcrete outside the membrane in terms of supporting action. There is no void between the two layers of shotcrete and both of the layers are a structural part of the tunnel, as shown in Figure 2-5. And therefore, this new single lining system, with sprayed waterproof membrane in the shotcrete lining, has a relatively higher safety margin for the stability of the tunnel structures in comparison to the conventional single lining system.

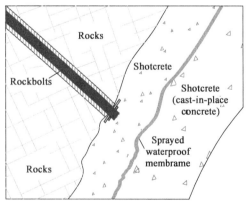 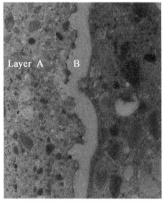

Note
①The layers:
A-sprayed concrete;
B-sprayed waterproof membrane;
C-inner (final) lining, sprayed concrete or cast-in-place concrete.
②The layers A and C are partially shown.

a) The sprayed waterproof membrane in a tunnel lining system

b) Sprayed waterproof membrane in practical case

Figure 2-5　Sketch showing single lining with sprayed waterproof membrane

2.3.2.2.2 Rock reinforcement systems

Rock reinforcement is a means of conserving or improving the overall rock mass properties by techniques such as rockbolts, cable bolts and ground anchors. Rock reinforcement systems are used for adding stability to rock or soil tunnels, especially for the tunnels where the properties of the surrounding rocks are mainly controlled by the structural defects in the rocks. The intent of reinforcement systems is to unify the rock pieces to produce a composite resistance to the outside forces.

Rockbolts are the most commonly used measure of rock reinforcement systems. Rockbolts are often applied in conjunction with shotcrete. And therefore, rockbolts and shotcrete supporting system are frequently referred in the field of tunnel and underground engineering. In practice, to prevent small fragments of rock from spalling off, wire mesh may be applied in shotcrete layers; while to provide structural stability to an excavation, ribbed systems may be required to closely follow the excavation face. The elements of the ribs nowadays are steel sets or girders. Where the ribbed systems are the parts of the primary lining of a tunnel, they are embedded in shotcrete layers to meet the requirement of durability.

Rock reinforcement can be applied as pre-supports or pre-reinforcements, such as forespiles and forepoles.

2.3.2.2.3 Concrete lining

Tunnels in soft ground usually require a solid lining with high stiffness. Stone or brick masonry was used in the past, but currently concrete is popular. The thickness of the permanent concrete lining is mainly determined by the magnitude and features of the ground pressures, and the stress state of the surrounding rocks of a tunnel.

A concrete lining is either reinforced or not. Where a concrete lining is designed to protect the rock and provide a smooth interior surface, or where the concrete lining is exposed to compression stresses only, it is often unreinforced. For the tunnels in hard rocks, for example, road tunnels are always lined for appearance and better lighting and ventilation conditions.

In some cases, the concrete lining is reinforced with steel meshes, where the predicted surrounding rocks deformation of the excavations is large, such as the tunnels in squeezing ground or soft ground, or the concrete lining may be thrusted by large moment forces due to non-uniform ground pressures. In some special cases, the reinforced concrete lining is strengthened by prestressed stress, for example, in some pressure tunnels[1].

---

[1] Pressure tunnels are tunnels used to divert water from a reservoir, usually to a hydropower house. They take their name due to the fact that, instead of most common tunnels in which the main load is geostatic (pointing inwards the tunnel), pressure tunnels are submitted to high water pressures pointing outwards the tunnel.

According to the construction methods of concrete structures, the concrete lining is classified as cast-in-place concrete and precast concrete lining. On the other hand, the concrete lining is classified as unreinforced concrete lining and reinforced concrete lining, as shown in Figure 2-6.

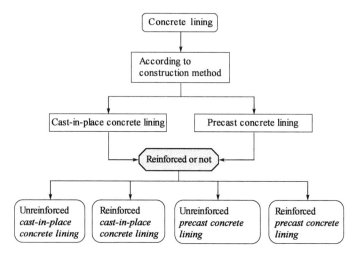

Figure 2-6 Types of concrete linings based on construction methods and reinforcements

2.3.2.2.3.1　Cast-in-place concrete

Cast-in-place concrete is used for building final linings or monolithic lining for tunnels. They can be used as a cover layer over the primary liner to provide a finished surface within the tunnel or to sandwich a waterproofing membrane. In terms of supporting, the cast concrete linings can be designed as a non-structural finish element or as the main structural support for the tunnel. The concrete lining can be reinforced or unreinforced.

2.3.2.2.3.2　Precast concrete

Segmental linings are mainly used in conjunction with a shield TBM in soft ground conditions. The prefabricated lining segments are erected within the cylindrical tail shield of the TBM. These prefabricated segments can be made of steel, concrete or cast iron and are usually bolted together to compress gaskets for preventing water penetration.

Expansion reading 2-3

2.3.2.2.4　Slurry walls

Slurry walls are often used as retaining walls at a deep excavation in soft soils to provide both supporting and cutting off ground water. Slurry wall construction types vary, but typically they consist of excavating a trench that matches the proposed wall profile. This trench is continually kept full with a drilling fluid during excavation, which stabilizes the sidewalls. After a reinforcing cage is lowered into the slurry or soldier piles are driven at a predetermined interval, tremie concrete is finally placed into the excavation. This procedure is repeated in specified panel lengths, which are separated with watertight joints.

For a cut and cover tunnel, the slurry walls may be designed as the outer part of tunnel structures, or even main structures, such as sidewalls. The details of slurry walls will be presented in Chapter 13.

2.3.2.3 Invert structure and floor slab

In some cases of tunnel project, where the surrounding rocks is soft or under high stress state, the tunnel lining is required to be closed by a curved invert, as shown in Figure 2-7. The curved invert of a tunnel, which is designed and constructed according to the principles of the NATM, is considered as an effective measure to control the ground deformation upon excavation, through closing the primary lining or/and final lining.

There are cases, where there is no need for an invert structure, such as the tunnels in sound rocks, in terms of stability or excavation deformation control. In some tunnels, floor slab may be built as roadway, as shown in the right part of Figure 2-7b), or to support track bed. Similarly, floor slab may also be built because the ductwork under the slab should be used by the ventilation systems of the tunnel. In this case, the slab is to span the roadway between sidewalls to provide duct space under the roadway or railway.

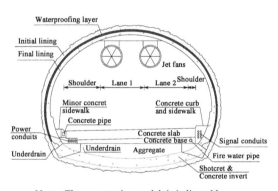

Note: The concrete invert slab is indicated by dashed lines since the slab was not needed for the entire length of the tunnel[1].

a) A cross-sectional of view of the Fourth Bore of the Caldecott Tunnel[1]

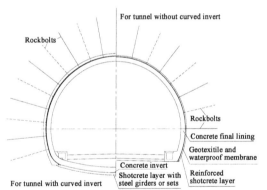

Note: ①The shotcrete invert is indicated by dashed lines since the slab was not needed for the entire length of the tunnel.
②In the right half, the invertstructure may be only for final lining or for both initiallining and final lining.

b) The cross sectional of a tunnel, with or without invert

Figure 2-7 Tunnel structures with or without curved invert

---

[1] http://www.ucmp.berkeley.edu/exhibits/caltrans/index.php.

2.3.2.4 Pipe in tunnel

For some utility tunnels, for example, water and sewer tunnels up to 3.5 m in diameter are often provided with an internal pipe that forms the inner lining. After the pipe is secured against movement, the space between the initial ground support and the pipe is filled with cellular or mass concrete. Sewer pipes may require a further interior lining to protect against corrosive liquids and gases. In practice, the pipe in the tunnel can be a composite lining system, which will be discussed in the following section.

Water tunnels with a high internal pressure exceeding the expected external pressures are usually provided with a steel lining if a reinforced concrete lining is insufficiently strong. It is noted that the tunnel must also be designed for the external pressure, since the pipe may be dewatered. If the pipe has leakes, the external pressure may equal the internal pressure.

2.3.3 Waterproofing and drainage system

The waterproofing and drainage system of a tunnel may include water deviating system on the ground surface around or above the tunnel, and waterproofing and drainage system in the tunnel. The ground surface water deviating system is to prevent the surface water, such as the water from surface precipitation, influxing into the tunnel, especially around the portal of a tunnel. This is similar to the water deviating system of ground structure.

The waterproofing and drainage system in a mined tunnel usually needs specifically designed, such as according to the ground water conditions, the functions, and environment restrictions of the tunnel. Where a tunnel is located above groundwater table, waterproofing is usually applied to ceilings in transportation tunnels to prevent dripping. For most tunnels below groundwater table, a waterproofing membrane enveloping the tunnel is used between the initial ground support and the final lining. To handle any water that does appear, circumferential drainage paths may be provided along arch and sidewalls of the tunnel; and longitudinal drainage paths along the base of the walls, as shown in Figure 2-8. The drainage paths can also be provided by geotextile sheets or pipes.

In terms of tunnel structure design, if the tunnel lining is undrained, the final lining will carry the full groundwater pressure and should be designed accordingly. Where drainage is provided outside the waterproofing membrane, the final lining may be designed for a reduced groundwater pressure.

A tunnel can be waterproofed with membranes and coatings to protect structural. Waterproofing is a fundamental aspect of creating an envelope which is a controlled environment. For a tunnel, its arch, sidewalls, and invert all may need to be water-resistant and sometimes waterproof. Many types of waterproof membrane systems are available including felt paper or tar paper with asphalt, other bituminous waterproofing, EPDM (Ethylene-Propylene-Diene Monomer) rubber, hypalon, polyvinyl chloride(PVC) and more. Waterproofing membranes may also need to resist deleterious gases or corrosive groundwater expected to be present. Figure 2-8 shows the typical structures of the waterproofing and drainage system of a mined tunnel, with composite lining.

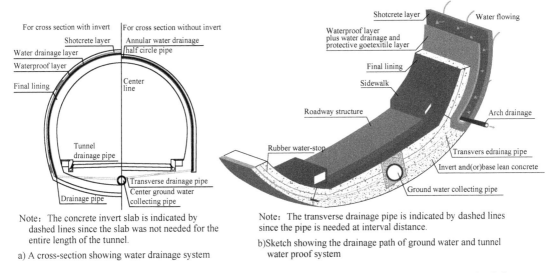

Figure 2-8 Structures of the waterproofing and drainage system sandwiched in composite linings

For a cut and cover tunnel, a waterproofing membrane can be applied onto the outside of the tunnel structures. However, for mined tunnel or section, the waterproofing layer, such as waterproofing coating, or sprayed waterproofing membranes, can be applied onto the inner surface of the tunnel lining, or sandwiched between two layers of shotcrete. In recent years, the advantages of a sprayed membrane applied as a waterproofing layer become well recognized in the world[6] and the practical cases are increasing. However, the conventional waterproofing and drainage system, sandwiched between the primary lining and the final lining in a composite lining system, is commonly the measure of this issue, especially in the mountain tunnels or the tunnels with difficult ground conditions.

2.3.4 Tunnel finishes

The interior finish of a tunnel is very important to the overall tunnel function. The finishes must ensure tunnel safety and the ease of maintenance, such as being: ①designed to enhance tunnel lighting and visibility; ②fire resistant; ③precluded from producing toxic fumes during a fire; ④able to attenuate noise; ⑤easy to clean.

The typical types of tunnel finishes that exist in highway tunnels are ceramic tile, porcelain-enameled metal panels, epoxy-coated concrete and miscellaneous finishes (e.g., coated cement board panels, pre-cast concrete panels, metal tiles, etc.). In general, the running tunnels of a metro system often do not have an interior finish because the public is not exposed to the tunnel lining except as the tunnel approaches the stations or portals. For some tunnels, false walls with finishes are often used for hiding tunnel sidewalls, where leakage is expected, or some facilities and utilities pipes installed along the tunnel sidewalls.

2.3.5 Composite linings

Composite lining system is popular in tunnels, mined with conventional methods, such as tunnels driven by drill and blast method. The composite lining system of a tunnel is typically composed of the primary lining of a rockbolts and shotcrete system, final lining, and a waterproofing and drainage system sandwiched between the linings. A composite lining system, with pre-supports, applied in a large span mountain tunnel in soft rocks[7] is shown in Figure 2-9.

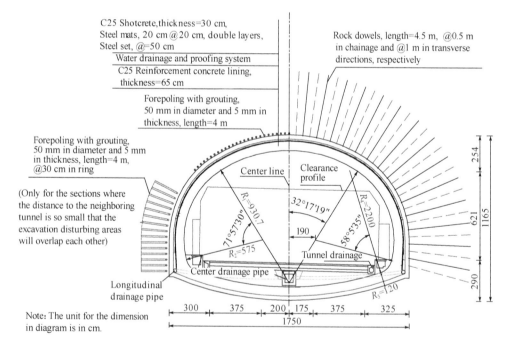

Figure 2-9 Composite lining and pre-supports applied in a large span mountain tunnel in soft rocks

A composite lining system may also be made of a precast segmental concrete lining and a cast-in-place concrete final lining (Figure 2-10).

For some existing tunnels, their supporting system may degenerated in strength or durability, due to, such as the system eroded by corrosive ground water; or the original supporting system can not meet the requirements of stability, such as the bearing capacity of supporting system is relatively low in terms of designed safety margin. Under these situations, the tunnels may need reinforced or rehabilitated in structures. When an additional lining layer is applied to a tunnel, a kind of "new" composite lining system is formed; and this kind of reinforced or rehabilitated is accordingly called inside lining method.

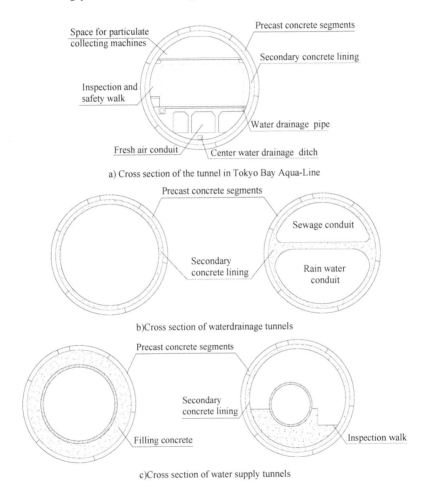

Figure 2-10 Composite linings of precast and cast-in-place concrete structures

2.4 Auxiliary structures of a tunnel

Auxiliary structures of a tunnel are built for site investigation, construction access and transportation, operation environment and safety. For example, a pilot tunnel may be excavated before the main tubes to investigate the geotechnical conditions of the surrounding rocks, as well as to test the proposed structures and construction plan.

For a super long tunnel, a temporary access shaft is sometimes necessary during the excavation. Shafts are usually circular and go straight down until they reach the level at which the tunnel is going to be built. Shafts are the main entrance in and out of the tunnel until the project is completed. For some TBM tunnels, shafts are starting points. Once the access shafts are complete, TBMs are lowered to the bottom and excavation can start. A tunnel may be so long that several shafts at various locations may be bored to provide excavating faces. A shaft normally has concrete walls and is usually built to be permanent. Once construction is complete, construction access shafts are often used as ventilation shafts and may also be used as emergency exits.

For a long or super long tunnel, some auxiliary structures should also be designed and built to meet the requirements of operational environments and safety. For example, for long road tunnels with heavy traffic, facilities and structures to provide ventilation, lighting, water supply pipes for firefighting, signals and signs above roadway lanes, are often designed and built, according to design requirements. Some additional facilities and structures to provide CCTV surveillance cameras, emergency telephones, communication antennae equipment, monitoring equipment of noxious emissions and visibility, are always necessary, for a super long tunnel with large traffic volumes. In some cases, a control center or office, operation and management center, buildings for fire fighting team and vehicles are also built, especially for fire and safety control. Where a long tunnel with two tubes, some pedestrian passageways and vehicle passageways are situated at certain intervals between the tubes, and each passage has an airtight and fire resistant door.

To provide the above mentioned facilities and make their operation efficient, some auxiliary tunnels or shafts are also designed and built, such as the service tunnel between the main tubes of the Channel Tunnel(Figure 2-11), the ventilation shafts for the Qinling Zhongnanshan Highway tunnel(Figure 2-12)in China.

Figure 2-11 shows the typical tunnel cross section of the Channel Tunnel, with the service tunnel between twin rail tunnels. The duct linking the rail tunnels is a piston relief duct to manage pressure changes due to the movement of trains. The ducts connecting the two running tunnels allow air to flow from one to the other, reducing the trains' power consumption and air turbulence. The ducts can be closed remotely as required, for example to prevent the spread of fire. There are passages connecting the running tunnels with the service tunnel, with a door connecting the running tunnels to the cross passages. Passages are situated at 375-m intervals; each passage has an airtight and fire resistant door. For the trains, there is crossover, where a section of track is built to combine the two running tunnels to enable a train to pass from one running tunnel to the other in either direction. The two crossovers in the tunnel are situated 17 km from each portal.

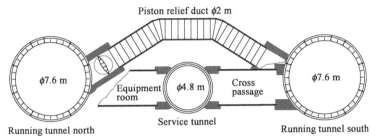

Note: Piston relief duct is a duct connecting the 2 running tunnels allowing air to flow from one to the other, reducing the trains' power consumption and air turbulence. They can be closed remotely as required, for example to prevent the spread of fire.

Figure 2-11 Typical tunnel cross section of the Channel tunnel[8]

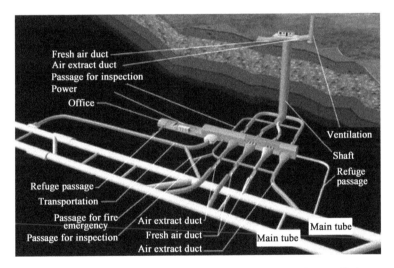

Figure 2-12 Sketch showing the shafts and rooms for the ventilation at the Qinling Zhongnanshan Highway tunnel

Three ventilation shafts were built at the Qinling Zhongnanshan Highway tunnel. Each shaft has two ducts for fresh air supplying and polluted air discharging. The maximum diameter of the shafts is 11.5 m and the maximum length is 661 m. The ventilation system connecting to a shaft is sketched in Figure 2-12❶.

---

❶ http://www.qltunnel.com/SitePage.aspx? ID=294.

2.5 Critical thinking problems

C1: There are varying types of tunnel structures in practice. Consider:①What are the commonly used types in history and at present, respectively? ②Are there regional features in tunnel structures? ③What are the general features of the tunnel structures of mountain tunnels, urban tunnels and underwater tunnels, respectively?

C2: In general, the structures of a tunnel should be preliminarily determined in planning stage of a tunnel project and designed in details in design stage. Consider:①What are the dominated factors in the determination of types of tunnel structures of a planned or designed tunnel? ②What are the dominated factors of project-specific feature?

C3: A tunnel may be built with or without auxiliary structures in a project. Consider:①How to determine the indispensable auxiliary structures for a tunnel? ②What are the commonly built auxiliary structures for a long and super long road tunnel, respectively?

C4: What are the components of a composite lining system? and what are the functions of these components?

2.6 References

[1] Windsor C R, Thompson A G. Rock reinforcement—technology, testing, design and evaluation[J]. Comprehensive rock engineering, 1993, 4: 451-484.

[2] Kuesel T R, King E H, Bickel J O. Tunnel engineering handbook[M]. Springer Science & Business Media, 2012.

[3] Broch E, Grøv E, Davik K I. The inner lining system in Norwegian traffic tunnels[J]. Tunnelling and underground space technology, 2002, 17(3): 305-314.

[4] Ramoni M, Matter J. Inner lining in traffic tunnels[J]. Strait Crossings 2013, 16-19 June, Bergen, Norway, 2013.

[5] Mao D, Nilsen B, Lu M. Numerical analysis of rock fall at Hanekleiv road tunnel[J]. Bulletin of Engineering Geology and the Environment, 2012, 71(4): 783-790.

[6] Ma J Q. Application of spray-on waterproofing membrane in tunnels [C]//Advanced Materials Research. Trans Tech Publications, 2011, 168: 822-826.

[7] Ma J Q. Construction of a Large-Span Tunnel with Small Overburden in Soft Rocks[M]// GeoCongress 2012: State of the Art and Practice in Geotechnical Engineering. 2012: 3295-3304.

[8] Carvel R. Fire dynamics during the Channel Tunnel fires [C]// Fourth International Symposium on Tunnel Safety and Security, 2010.

3 Planning of a Tunnel

3.1 Introduction

Tunnels are built for various purposes. Road and railway tunnels are built to cross barriers, including mountains, existing structures (such as roads, railways buildings and facilities) or a water body; to satisfy environmental or ecological requirements. For example, in urban areas, tunnels are practical means to minimize potential environmental impact such as traffic congestion, pedestrian movement, air quality, noise pollution or visual intrusion. A tunnel may be also one of the feasible alternatives, such as to protect the areas of special cultural or historical districts, buildings; or for sustainability reasons to avoid the impact on natural landscape or to reduce disturbance to the surface land.

There are innumerable tunnels in use in the world. We can say that there are few designed tunnels are not finished in construction; however, some projects are partially failed, such as due to lack of foresight and proper planning. A well planned project will give a broad understanding of how underground space can be utilized effectively, and ensure that any negative impacts of underground development are properly mitigated or controlled to an acceptable level. In general, the experience gained from many tunneling projects is presented in codes and guidelines that can be of help for those starting a project[1].

3.1.1 General procedures of a tunnel project

In general, a tunnel project is executed through a few stages, such as planning, design, construction to operation and management, as shown in Figure 3-1. The planning is the first stage of a tunnel project procedure.

Expansion reading 3-1

In brief, tunnel project planning is to determine the most economic and beneficial solutions for the utilization, construction, operation and maintenance of the tunnels. The planning of a tunnel project can be considered as an optimization process of the evaluation of variant factors, such as : ①the planned use of the structure; ②the functional requirements for the equipment; ③the requirements for user safety; ④the designed working life; ⑤the requirements for waterproofing;

⑥the safety, serviceability and environmental requirements in the execution and operation phases;⑦the social and regional benefits of the project, especially in a long run.

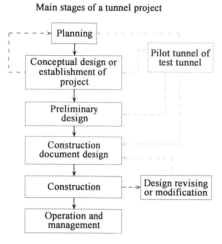

Figure 3-1 The main stages of a tunnel project implementation

It is noted that the information of supporting the decision-making in the tunnel project procedure, such as, in terms of tunnel planning, structure design and construction method choosing, increases generally from the planning stage to the construction and operation[2]. And therefore, an iterative approach is often applied in this procedure, as shown in Figure 3-1. For example, tunnels are built in ground and the geological and hydrological conditions may have a vital influence on the success of a tunnel project. In theory, an adequate geological-geotechnical exploration and a thorough description of the ground earlier will make the planning and design more reasonable, since the ground conditions may be decisive not only for the shape of the cross section and the method of construction but also for the tunnel system and the alignment. However, for a project, there need a balance of cost, time schedule, and the efficiency of the site investigation. In practice, the information for approximating the properties of the ground conditions may from desk working, site investigation and tunnel construction. At the stage of project planning, the decision is mainly based on the results of desk working and preliminary site investigation. When the tunnel is designed, some of the ground conditions are also based on predicted models. And therefore, the final design is usually revised during construction. The construction method, including excavation method and sequence, ground reinforcement measures and supporting system installation, should be tuned according to the monitored results of the behaviors of both ground and supporting system. In this sense, the design of a tunnel or underground structure will not be finished until the end of construction.

3.1.2 Design standards

A tunnel should be planned and designed according to the functional classifications, such as defined in standards, codes and guidelines, which provide the general design considerations, in terms of tunnel structures, service level, cross section elements and the requirements of facilities for the tunnel operation and management in the planned transportation line. For example, the publications of the American Association of State Highway and Transportation Officials (AASHTO), the Federal Highway Administration (FHWA) for roadways in the USA, and *the Technical Standard of Highway Engineering* (JTG B01—2014) and *Specifications for Design of Highway Tunnels: Section 1 Civil Engineering* (JTG 3370.1—2018) in China, provide concepts, criteria, and procedures for tunnel planning and design.

3.1.2.1 Tunnel or open trench

When a tunnel is planned to pass through an obstacle in a transportation line, at least, these factors should be comprehensively considered, such as the functions of the tunnel and its contribution to the social and economic development, ground conditions of the planned tunnels, and the cost of the project.

In general, where the depth of a planned open trench for open road is more than 30 m in a line, an alternative between the open trench and a tunnel should be studied, in terms of the cost and risk of construction, safety of operation and management, the cost of maintenance, etc. On the other hand, a tunnel may also be planned to pass through the ground under water (such as river, lake and strait) or existing buildings.

3.1.2.2 Classes of roads and vehicle sizes

A road tunnel is designed to accommodate planned road and vehicles, such as presented in the *Standard* (JTG B01—2014) in China. The features of a tunnel, in terms of alignments, dimensions, and the clearance for vehicle sizes are often determined by the responsible authority, mainly based on the classifications of the road (i.e. state, province, county or local roads). The current design codes and standards, such as the *Specification* (JTG 3370.1—2018) in China, provide regulations in terms of engineering solutions. At the same time, economic evaluation should be considered in order to meet the intention of the project.

The determination of the tunnel clearance is the result of optimization, with various factors as considerations. For example, the size and type of vehicles to be considered depend mainly upon the aim of the project. On the other hand, the tunnel geometrical configuration should generally accommodate all potential vehicles that use the roads, such as the over-height vehicles and military vehicles if it is needed. Under these situations, however, it is necessary to consider the cost because designing a tunnel facility to accommodate only a very few extraordinary oversize vehicles may not be optimum if feasible alternative routes are available.

The lane width and clearance of a tunnel should match that of the approach roads. Often, allowance for repaving is provided in determining the headroom or clearance of the tunnel. In addition, pedestrian and cyclist use of the tunnel may be required and a special duct(or passage) is often encouraged for such utilizations.

3.1.2.3 Traffic capacity

Road tunnels should have at least the same traffic capacity as that of surface roads. In general, the traffic in a tunnel will slow down, where the lane width is less than standards(too narrow), and will shy away from tunnel walls if insufficient lateral clearance is provided inside the tunnel. Also, very low ceilings give an impression of speed and tend to slow traffic. Therefore, it is important to provide adequate lane width and headroom comparable to those of the approach road. It is recommended that traffic lanes for new tunnels should meet the required road geometrical requirements (e. g. 3.75 m or 3.5 m wide for each lane). It is also recommended to have a reasonable edge distance between the lane and the tunnel walls or barriers.

Road tunnels, especially those in urban areas, or super long tunnels, often have cargo restrictions. These may include hazardous materials, flammable gases and liquids, and over-height or wide vehicles. Provisions should be made in the approaches to the tunnels for detection and removal of such vehicles.

3.1.2.4 Tunnel shape and internal elements

There are three main shapes of highway tunnels—circular, rectangular, and horseshoe (or curvilinear). The shape of the tunnel is largely dependent on the method used for building the tunnel and on the ground conditions. The planned shape should meet the clearance requirements of a transportation line and the space requirements for interior elements. For example, the road tunnels are usually equipped with various operation facilities, such as for ventilation, lighting, communication, fire-life safety, traffic operation and control.

Road tunnels are often finished with interior finishes, such as for good operation environment, safety and maintenance requirements. The interior finishes, which usually are mounted or adhered to the final lining, consist of ceramic tiles, epoxy coated metal panels, porcelain enameled metal panels or various coatings, to provide enhanced tunnel lighting and visibility, fire protection for the lining, a surface easy to clean, or to attenuate noise. Tunnel walls and ceilings often receive a finish surface and the roadway is often paved with asphalt pavement.

3.2 Alternative analysis

3.2.1 Route studies

A tunnel in a transportation system is an alternative vehicular way to a ground line, a bridge or a viaduct. Tunnels are considered to shorten the travel time and distance or to add extra travel capacity through barriers such as mountains, water bodies or existing structures. Tunnels are also considered to avoid surface congestion, improve air quality, reduce noise, or minimize surface disturbance. Often, a tunnel is proposed as a sustainable alternative to a bridge or a surface way.

In a tunnel route study, the following issues should be considered: ①subsurface, geological and hydrological conditions; ②constructability; ③long-term environmental impact; ④seismicity; ⑤land use restrictions; ⑥potential air right developments; ⑦design life; ⑧economical benefits and life cycle cost; ⑨operation and maintenance; ⑩security; ⑪sustainability.

At the stage of route studies, such as alternative analysis, two or more proposals(schemes) are usually presented by a planning team, based on preliminary studies on the above factors. For example, during the route alternative analysis and tunnel types studies of the Channel tunnel crossing the English Channel, the "Tunnel-Only Schemes" was chosen mainly due to the following considerations[3]:

"Carries the lowest technical risks that might prevent it from proceeding to completion."

"Is the safest project from the traveller's point of view."

"Presents no problems to maritime traffic in the Channel."

"Is the one that is least vulnerable to sabotage and terrorist action."

"Has an environmental impact that can be contained and limited."

"Offers the best prospect of attracting the necessary finance."

Expansion reading 3-2

3.2.2 Financial studies

The financial viability of a tunnel depends on its life cycle cost analysis. In the west countries, tunnels are traditionally designed for a life of more than 100 to 125 years. In China, a tunnel in a high grade road should be designed for at least 100 years. There is a trend to design tunnels for 150 years life[4].

In evaluating the life cycle cost of a tunnel, the costs of the project should include construction, operation and maintenance and financing. In addition, a cost-benefit analysis should be performed with considerations given to intangible factors, such as environmental benefits, aesthetics, noise and vibration, air quality, right of way, real estate, potential air right developments, etc.

The financial evaluation should also take into account construction and operation risks. These risks are often expressed as financial contingencies or provisional cost items. The level of contingencies would be decreased as the project design level advances. The risks are then better quantified and provisions to reduce or manage them are identified.

3.2.3 Types of tunnels

The selection of the type of tunnel is an iterative process taking into account many factors, including the depth of the tunnel, number of traffic lanes, type of ground traversed, and available construction methodologies. For example, a two-lane tunnel can fit easily into a circular tunnel to be bored by a TBM. However, the requirement for four lanes may be met by a larger span tunnel, a two-tube tunnel or another method of construction such as cut and cover. In recent years, practices in the application of TBM have proved that bored tunnels of mega dimensions of 15-17 m and more in diameter are possible and a TBM tunnel would be for a multi-mode transportation tunnel. One of the cases is the combined three-lane highway and metro crossing of the Yangtze River in the city of Wuhan, China. The TBM tunnel is believed to be the first case of multi-mode in China using the 15.76 m diameter mixshield TBM order from Herrenknecht[1]. The twin bore double deck tunnel will feature a three-lane highway on the upper level, and Wuhan metro line 7 on the lower one, as sketched in Figure 3-2a). A similar case is in Shanghai [Figure 3-2b)].

a) A shield tunnel in Wuhan[2]   b) A shield tunnel in Shanghai[3]

Figure 3-2 Sketch showing the section of the multi-mode tunnel crossing the Yangtze river in China

---

[1] Mega-TBMs for China double-deck link. http://www.tunneltalk.com(2014-9-15).
[2] http://www.crcc.cn/g282/s913/t29226.aspx.
[3] http://sh.people.com.cn/BIG5/138654/10292168.html.

The features of the planned tunnel and its construction conditions, as well as the geography features, where the planned the tunnel will be located, are generally important factors to be considered in tunnel types study. For example, when larger and deeper tunnels are needed, either different type of construction methods, or tunnels of multiple shapes are usually used. If the ground is suitable, the tunnel cross section can be made to accommodate multiple lanes. The result will be cost effective in a long run.

For tunnels below water bodies, immersed method can be used. The unique features of the construction of an immersed tunnel are of dominant factor. For example, the immersed tunnel section of the Hong Kong-Zhuhai-Macao Bridge (HZMB) consists of 33 precast concrete tunnel elements❶. The length of a standard tunnel elements is 180 m long, with its top surface area about 7000 m² and self-weight almost 80000 t. Figure 3-3 shows the tunnel elements next to the west artificial island during construction.

a)Towing of precast tunnel element to west artificial island❶   b)Placement of the first precast tunnel element next to west artificial island

Figure 3-3 Construction of the immersed tunnel section of the HZMB main bridge

Shallow tunnels would most likely be constructed using cut and cover method. In special circumstances where existing surface traffic cannot be disrupted, jacked precast tunned is an alternative. In addition to the variety of tunneling methods, non-conventional techniques have been used for constructing large cross section in soft ground, such as the Mt. Baker Ridge Tunnel, 19 m in diameter, Washington. It is said the world's largest diameter soft earth tunnel, having been bored through clay❷. During the tunnel construction, multiple overlapping drifts were constructed and filled with concrete to form a circular envelop that provided the overall support system of the ground. Then the space within this envelop was excavated and the tunnel structure was constructed within it[4], as shown in Figure 3-4.

---

❶ http://www.hzmb.hk/eng/media_publications.html (2014-9-15).
❷ http://en.wikipedia.org/wiki/Mount_Baker_Tunnel (2014-9-15).

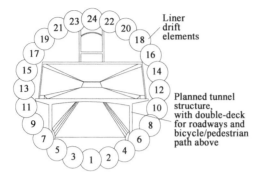

a) Sketch of the planned tunnel structures and 24 drifts[4]   b) Excavation inside the 24 drifts❷

Note: The newest Mount Baker Tunnel was built north of the original tunnels and opened in June 1989. The tunnel has a double-decked roadway with the bicycle/pedestrian path above the traffic lanes. During the tunnel construction, multiple overlapping drifts were constructed and filled with concrete to form a circular envelop that provided the overall support system of the ground and the tunnel structure was constructed within it. The numbers in the small drifts showing the construction sequence of the drift boring and concrete casting. At 19 m in diameter, it is the world's largest diameter soft earth tunnel, having been bored through clay. The note is based on https://en.wikipedia.org/wiki/Mount_Baker_Tunnel (2017/9/18)

Figure 3-4 Stacked drift and final Mt baker tunnel, I-90, Seattle, WA, USA

For the tunnels to pass through problematic ground or adverse geological unit, such as mixed face (rock and soft ground), squeezing rock, hard rocks with high in-situ stress or other difficult ground conditions, the structures or the supporting system of the tunnels should usually be designed with special considerations, such as in terms of construction and material properties.

3.2.4 Geotechnical investigations

Geotechnical investigations are critical for the proper planning and design of a tunnel[5,6]. The selections of the tunnel alignment, cross section and construction method are influenced by the geological and geotechnical conditions, as well as other site constraints, such as the restriction from the third party and environment. The good knowledge of the expected geological conditions is essential. The type of the ground encountered along the alignment would affect the selection of the tunnel type and construction method. For example, where TBM is applied in tunnel construction, the mixed ground conditions or unrecognized objects can add complications to the TBM performance and may result in the inability or breakdown of the TBM. A great lesson can be learned from the mega TBM applied in Seattle tunnel❷, where the giant Hitachi TBM, with 17.5 m in diameter, bores the double deck highway tunnel in Seattle, Washington, USA. The TBM came to a standstill in early 2013 and lasted for a long period due to the serious damage, which may be related to unrecognized objects in the boring way.

---

❶ Tunneling in Seattle-A history of Innovation. http://www.discovery.org/scripts/viewDB/filesDB-download.php?command=download&id=3901
❷ Tracking the world's mega-TBMs. http://www.tunneltalk.com/Discussion-Forum-Mega-TBMs.php (2014-9-15).

In general, the geotechnical investigations during the stage of tunnel project planning are preliminary. For most of the cases, the main information on the geotechnical conditions of the planned tunnels is based on desk working, such as analysis on the regional geological and hydrological conditions, information from nearby projects, and site reconnaissance, with help of shallow digs or excavations, such as wells or trenches. However, of the investigations on the site geotechnical conditions, where the proposed tunnels will pass through, it is important to meet the basic requirements, including: ①to identify the major formation of the ground, such as in terms of the types of the geological units, the structures of rock mass, weathering conditions; ②to approximate the hydrological conditions of the ground, such as in terms of ground water table, water pressures and the permeability of the major geological units; ③to predict the features of the in-situ stress of the surrounding rocks of the tunnels, such as based on the maximum overburden of the tunnels, regional geological stress features; ④to predict the potential adverse geological zones or hazards along the proposed tunnel, as well as their related risks during and after the tunnel construction.

Geotechnical issues such as the soil or rock properties, the ground water regime, the ground cover over the tunnel, the presence of contaminants along the alignment, the presence of underground utilities and obstructions such as boulders or buried objects, and the presence of sensitive surface facilities should be taken into consideration when evaluating tunnel alignment. Tunnel alignment is sometimes changed based on the results of the geotechnical conditions to minimize construction cost or to reduce risks.

The effect of the impact of geological features on the tunnel alignment may be related to the distribution of the major geological units and the features of the adverse geological zones. An ideal result is that the proposed tunnel is located in sound geological units and all of the adverse geological zones or conditions are avoided or well coped with. For example, where there is a large fault, it is recommended to avoid crossing a fault zone and preferred to avoid being in a close proximity of an active fault. However, if avoidance of a fault cannot be achieved, then proper measures for crossing it should be considered, such as to cope with the predicted ground water inflowing, high in-situ stress, weak rocks and so on.

If the route selection is limited, it is beneficial that the geotechnical investigation start as early as possible during the initial planning phase of the project. The properties of the surrounding rocks and their behavior during construction will have a strong influence on the construction method choosing for the planned tunnels. For example, where the conventional method is planned, ground stand-up time is critical for its success. If the ground does not have sufficient stand-up time, pre-support or ground improvement such as grouting should be provided. For soft ground TBM tunneling, the presence of boulders for example would affect the selection of TBM type and its excavation tools. Similarly, the selection of a rock TBM would require knowledge of the rock unconfined compressive strength, its abrasivity and its jointing characteristics. The investigation should also address groundwater. For the tunnels in soft ground, the stability of the excavated face is greatly dependent on control of the groundwater. Dewatering, pre-draining, grouting, or freezing may be required to stabilize the excavation. For a shallow tunnel, especially in urban area, the potential settlements on the surface and nearby structures and facilities are closely related to the ground behavior during tunneling. Measures to minimize settlements by using suitable tunneling methods or by preconditioning the ground to improve its properties would be required.

The selection of a tunnel alignment should take into consideration site specific constraints such as the presence of contaminated materials, special existing buildings and surface facilities, existing utilities, or the presence of sensitive installations such as historical landmarks, educational institutions, cemeteries, or houses of worship. If certain site constraints cannot be avoided, construction methodologies, and special provisions should be provided. For example, if the presence of contaminated materials near the surface cannot be avoided, a deeper alignment and/or the use of mined tunnel would be more suitable than cut and cover method. Similarly, if sensitive facilities exist at the surface and cannot be avoided, special provisions to minimize vibration, and potential surface settlement should be provided in the construction methods.

Sometimes, modifications in the tunnel structure or configurations would provide benefits for the overall tunnel construction and cost. For example, locating the tunnel ventilations ducts on the side, rather than at the top would reduce the tunnel height, raise the profile of the tunnel and consequently reduce the overall length of an urban or underwater tunnel. Obviously, all these measures should be based on the results of the site geotechnical investigation.

The earlier implementing site investigation, the more chance of improving the tunnel planning and design may be available, especially for a mega tunnel project, where the tunnel is the only key structure of the project. For these tunnel projects, with the mega features in terms of structure dimensions, cost, social and political influence, the geotechnical investigations will last a long period. The results of the geotechnical investigation are vital to the success of the project. For example, the site investigation of the Channel tunnel project is one of the successful case histories. In the 1880s, nearly 2 km of tunnel was bored beneath Dover directed by Colonel Beaumont. The work was soon stopped by the British Parliament, concerned about strategic implications. However, the Beaumont tunnel still exists in an unlined and good condition[3]. In 1958-1960, a detailed investigation of the geology of the site was conducted under the direction of the Channel Tunnel Study Group. During 1958-1959, geophysical surveys were completed and overwater borings were carried out producing chalk cores from the geology. At the same time, examination of the old Beaumont tunnel showed it to be in excellent condition and practically dry after standing unlined for nearly 80 years. In 1964-1965 further site investigations took place but on a much larger scale. Work again included geophysical surveys and both land and overwater borings. Additionally, hydraulic and hydrographic studies and laboratory testing of rock samples were undertaken. In-situ tests in boreholes to check the permeability of the various chalk strata were also completed. Those studies constituted the best investigation to date for a fixed link and confirmed that a bored tunnel within the Lower Chalk stratum appeared to be wholly feasible[3]. The alignment of the Channel Tunnel in the Chalk stratum is shown in Figure 3-5. The great success in the construction of the Channel Tunnel have spoken for itself that what a great contribution can the geotechnical site investigation make to a well designed project.

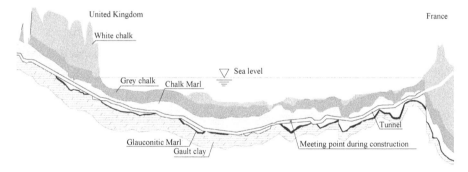

Figure 3-5　Sketch showing the geological profile of the Channel Tunnel❶

3.2.5　Environmental and community issues

Tunnels are more environmentally friendly than other surface facilities. For example, in urban area, traffic congestion would be reduced from the local streets. Air quality would be improved because traffic generated pollutants are captured and disposed of away from the public. Similarly, noise would be reduced and visual aesthetic and land use would be improved. By placing traffic underground, property values would be improved and communities would be less impacted in the long term. Furthermore, tunnels will provide opportunities for land development

---

❶ https://en.wikipedia.org/wiki/File:Channel_Tunnel_geological_profile_1.svg (2016-2-19).

along and over the tunnel alignment adding real estate properties and potential economical development potential. One of the world famous case histories is the Central Artery/Tunnel Project(CA/T), known unofficially as the Big Dig in the USA. The Big Dig is a megaproject in Boston that rerouted the Central Artery (Interstate 93), which is the chief highway through the heart of the city, into a 5.6-km-long tunnel. The project also includes the construction of the Ted Williams Tunnel(extending Interstate 90 to Logan International Airport), the Leonard P. Zakim Bunker Hill Memorial Bridge over the Charles River, and the Rose Kennedy Greenway in the space vacated by the previous I-93 elevated roadway.

In planning for an urban tunnel, the construction impact on the community and the environment is sensitive and must be addressed. Issues such as impact on traffic, businesses, infrastructure facilities, installations and utilities, and residences should be addressed. Construction noise, dust, vibration, water quality, aesthetic, and traffic congestion are important issues to be addressed and any potentially adverse impact should be mitigated. For example, where a cut and cover tunnel is proposed, the disturbance to the surface traffic and activities, and the nearby utilities and facilities may be significant and unacceptable, especially in the downtown. Sometimes, top-down construction rather than bottom-up construction should be used for improving the disruption and reduce its duration. At the same time, rigid excavation support systems and ground improvement techniques may be required to minimize potential settlements and lateral ground deformations, and their impact on adjacent structures. On the other hand, dewatering is also required to be limited to control the induced settlement of the retained soil.

Similarly, for immersed tunnels, the impact on underwater bed level and the water body should be assessed. Dredging will generate bottom disturbance and create solid turbidity or suspension in the water. Be sure that excavation methods are available that can limit suspended solids in the water to acceptable levels. Existing fauna and flora and other ecological issues should be investigated to determine whether environmentally and ecologically adverse consequences are likely to ensue. For example, the assessment of the construction on fish migration and spawning periods should be made and measures to deal with them should be developed. Similarly, the potential impact of construction wetlands should be investigated and mitigated.

Excavation may encounter or produce contaminated soils or ground water. The contaminated materials may need to be processed or disposed in a contained disposal facility, which may also have to be capped to meet the environmental regulations. Provisions would need to address public health and safety and meet regulatory requirements. It is noted that tunneling produced environmental problem can be a

3   Planning of a Tunnel   49

disaster in practice. For example, the 8.7-km-long twin railway Hallandsås tunnel project in the south of Sweden, was supposed to be completed in 1996 but later was scheduled to open in 2015. One of the main reasons on the delayed schedule is the environmental disaster due to the use of the chemical grout (Rhoca-Gil) when cement grout did not succeed in sealing the fractured rock from leaking large amounts of water into the tunnels[1].

3.2.6   Operational issues

In planning a tunnel, provisions should be made to address the operational and maintenance aspects of the tunnel and its facilities. Issues such as traffic control, ventilation, lighting, life safety systems, equipment maintenance, tunnel cleaning and the like, should be identified and provisions should be made for them during the planning phases. For example, items requiring more frequent maintenance, such as light fixtures, should be arranged to be accessible with minimal interruption to traffic. On the other hand, the water drainage system may need dredging or cleaning in the designed life period. The structures of the drainage ducts should be designed easy to access without disturbing normal operation.

3.2.7   Sustainability

Tunnels are of sustainable features including longer life, land use saving, favorable to environment. In general, tunnels have longer life expectancy than a surface facility. Since the tunnels are built in ground, the surface land will be spared for land development for residential, commercial, or recreational facilities, especially in the downtown of an urban area. When a metro system is built in an area, there is a potential increase of the property values of the real estate nearby. Tunnels also enhance community connections and protect residents from traffic pollutants, noise and bad weather in an urban area. The construction of a mountain tunnel can be designed to the minimum disturbance to the natural environment.

In a long run, the being sustainable means that the construction of the tunnel should consider the future development of the region, where the tunnel is located, during the planning of a tunnel. A good case history is the route alternative analysis on the Dayaoshan tunnel in the south of China. The Dayaoshan tunnel is in the line of the realignment section of the Hengyang to Guangzhou double-track project at the end of 1980s. The chosen route had made allowance for the developing of the hydroelectricity

---

[1] Information provided by Rolf Kindbom, 5013 Tenth Line Erin. to the OMB Public Hearing on April 12 2010 regarding the Rockford Quarry.

power station, as shown in Figure 3-6. With the site of a power dam considered, the Dayaoshan tunnel was designed 14.295-km-long. The Lechang Gorge hydro project was fully in operation in 2013.

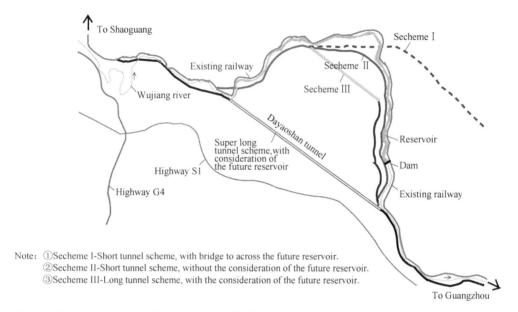

Note: ①Secheme I-Short tunnel scheme, with bridge to across the future reservoir.
②Secheme II-Short tunnel scheme, without the consideration of the future reservoir.
③Secheme III-Long tunnel scheme, with the consideration of the future reservoir.

Figure 3-6 Route alternative analysis on the Dayaoshan tunnel in the line of Guangzhou to Shaoguan

3.3 Tunnel type studies

3.3.1 General description of tunnel types

3.3.1.1 Types by construction method

In terms of construction method, the principal types in use are cut and cover tunnels, bored or mined tunnels, immersed tunnels and jacked tube tunnels. Where the planned tunnel is shallow-buried and there is space for open cut, cut and cover tunnel can be better answer. In a tunnel, cut and cover section may be built between the mined part and portal of the tunnel.

Bored or mined tunnels may be built in soft ground or hard rocks with conventional methods or TBMs. For example, in terms of excavating methods applied, soft ground tunnels are excavated in soil using a shield or pressurized face TBM (principally earth pressure balance or slurry types), or by conventional mining methods. Similarly, the rock tunnels may be excavated by drill and blast method, mechanized excavators or TBMs, respectively.

An immersed tunnel may be optimum for an underwater tunnel, while jacked tunnels are often used where they are very shallow but the surface must not be disturbed, for example beneath road or railway embankments.

The selection of a tunnel type depends on the geometrical configurations, the ground conditions, the type of crossing, and environmental requirements. For example, an immersed tunnel may be most suitable for crossing a water body; however, environmental and regulatory requirements might make this method very expensive or infeasible. Therefore, it is important to perform the tunnel type study as early as possible in the planning process and select the most suitable tunnel type to meet the particular project requirements. Preliminary road tunnel type selection for conceptual study in the route studies can be dictated by the general ground condition[4], as shown in Figure 3-7.

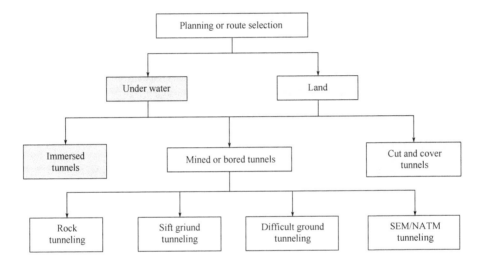

Figure 3-7 Preliminary road tunnel type selection process[4]

3.3.1.2 Types in special cases

Tunnels are planned as underground sections to pass through the obstacles in the planned line during the planning of a route for a transportation system. The locations and types of the tunnels should be considered in companion with the connecting structures, e. g., approach open road, bridges, or tunnels. In some special cases, the locations of the planned tunnels may be mainly determined by the connecting structures. For example, in mountain area, multi-arch tunnel, branch tunnels may be required by the whole line alignment. Figure 3-8 shows the alignment of a branch tunnel, Baziling tunnel, which connects to a large span bridge across a deep valley. The branch tunnel is composed of multi-arch section, neighborhood tunnel section and separate tunnel sections, which have the general features of the corresponding tunnel types, as shown in Table 3-1.

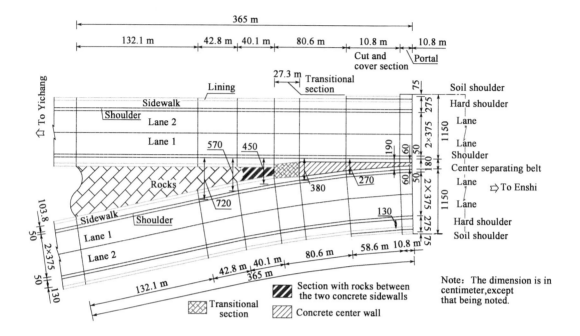

Figure 3-8 Plan of the linings of the branch section of the Baziling tunnel in Hubei Province, China

Table 3-1 Types of tunnels according to the alignment of tubes

Types	Description of the features or main applications of the tunnel
Single tube tunnel with bidirectional traffic	Single tube, mainly built in the lines of grade II, III and IV roads.
Tunnel with two separated tubes	Tunnels with two tubes, mainly used in the lines of grade I road or freeway, and with their net spacing of the two tubes no less than the values in the Table 3.0.3 of the *Guidelines* (JTG/T D70—2010); the influence of the one tube tunneling on the other is generally not significant.
Neighborhood tunnel	Tunnels with two tubes and their net spacing of the two tubes less than the values in the Table 3.0.3 of the *Guidelines* (JTG/T D70—2010); the influence of the one tube tunneling on the other is so significant that special consideration is required in both design and construction.
Multi-arch tunnel	Tunnels with two tubes and the inner sidewalls of the two tubes being designed and built as a single structure.
Branch tunnel	Tunnels, under a special circumstance, successively composed of super-large span arch or (and) multi-arch, neighborhood and separated tunnel sections from one portal to another one; mainly built in the lines of grade I road or freeway.

In recent years, large span tunnels have often been built to alleviate transportation congestion. The tunnels, especially for the underwater tunnels, are usually key structures in the lines. As a result, the tunnel is a "bottle-neck" in the transportation line nets, where each tube of the tunnel has been designed usually with one entrance and exit, respectively. However, when an underwater tunnel is designed with additional entrances and exits, the functions of the tunnel can be the same as an interchange bridge. Figure 3-9 shows the alignments of the main tunnel tubes and their branch tunnel ramps of the Xiangjiang tunnel along the Yinpan road in Changsha, China.

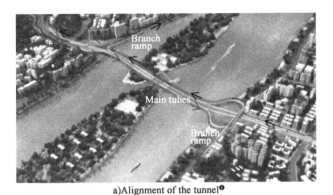
a) Alignment of the tunnel❶

b) Main tunnel tube and it's branch ramp❷

Figure 3-9 Alignment of the Xiangjiang tunnel along the Yinpan road in Changsha, China

3.3.2 Design process

The basic process used in the design of a road tunnel is to[4]: ①define the functional requirements, including design life and durability requirements; ②carry out the necessary investigations and analyses of the geologic, geotechnical and hydrological data; ③conduct environmental, cultural, and institutional studies to assess how they impact the design and construction of the tunnel; ④perform tunnel type studies to determine the most appropriate method of tunneling; ⑤establish design criteria and perform the design of the various tunnel elements, including appropriate initial and final ground support and lining systems, with the considerations of both ground conditions and the proposed method of construction; ⑥establish tunnel alignment, profile and cross-section; ⑦determine potential modes of failure, including construction events, unsatisfactory long-term performance, and failure to meet environmental requirements; ⑧perform risk analysis and identify mitigation measures and how to implement those measures in the design; ⑨prepare project documents including construction plans, specifications, time schedules, estimates. The design of a tunnel is often excuted in stages and the main points of the design stages are shown in Figure 3-1.

---

❶ http://www.cmct.cn/Item/2331.aspx.
❷ http://news.hexun.com/2011-10-29/134693238.html.

3.3.3 Tunnel cross-section

In dimensions, the tunnel cross section geometrical configuration must satisfy the required traffic lanes, shoulders or safety walks, as well as suitable space for ventilation, lights, traffic control system, fire/life safety systems, etc. In shapes, the cross section of a tunnel is closely related to the tunnel construction method applied and ground conditions. For example, a TBM bored tunnel usually results in circular configuration, while cut and cover construction results in rectangular shape. The structural systems will also vary accordingly. The available space in a circular cross section can be used for housing tunnel operational systems, such as the ventilation duct or fans, lighting, traffic control systems and signs, close circuit TV and the like. For rectangular sections the various systems can be placed overhead, invert or adjacent to the traffic lanes if overhead space is limited. On the other hand, the designed shape and structures layout for the tunnel should be favorable to the easy inspection and maintenance of tunnel structures and equipments installed for tunnel operation and management.

The tunnel structural systems depend on the type of tunnel, the geometrical configuration of the cross section and method of construction. For example, in cut and cover tunnel of rectangular cross section, cast in place concrete is often the selected structural system, while for a mined tunnel with conventional methods, a composite lining system is well used in practice. For soft ground tunnels using shield TBM, the structural system is often a precast segmental one pass lining. Sometimes, the excavation support system can be used as the final tunnel structural system such as the case in top down construction in a cut and cover tunnel.

3.3.4 Groundwater control and management

Building a dry tunnel is a primary concern of the owner, user, and operator alike. A dry tunnel appears a safer and friendlier environment and means lower operation and maintenance costs. The advancements in tunneling technology and in the waterproofing field have facilitated the implementation of strict water infiltration criteria and the ability to build dry tunnels. The ground water infiltration criteria recommended by the ITA are the followings: ①Allowable Infiltration: Tunnels ≤ 0.002 gal/sq. ft/day(0.082 L/m^2/day); Underground public space ≤0.001 gal/sq. ft/day(0.041 L/m^2/day). ②In addition no dripping or visible leakage from a single location shall be permitted.

In China, the water infiltration criteria for a tunnel is required by the *Technical Code for Waterproofing of Underground Works* (GB 50108—2008) as the following: ① No dripping but visible leakage from a single location shall be permitted; ②The total wet area should be less than 2/1000, and the numbers of the single wet location less than 3 per 100 m², the area of each wet location should be no more than 0.2 m²; ③Allowable Infiltration: tunnels ≤0.05 L/(m² · day), and ≤0.15 L/(100 m² · day) for waterproof area; underground public space, e.g., metro stations no dripping and visible leakage being permitted.

Tunnel waterproofing systems are used for preventing groundwater inflow into an underground opening. They consist of a combination of various materials and elements, such as waterproof membrane, water-stop belt, waterproof concrete ling. The design of a waterproofing system is based on the understanding of the ground and hydrological conditions, geometry and layout of the structure and construction methods to be used. A waterproofing system should always be an integrated system that takes into account intermediate construction stages, final conditions of structures and their ultimate utilization including maintenance and operations.

There are two basic types of waterproofing systems: undrained (closed) and drained (open), as shown in Figures 3-10 and 3-11, respectively. Various waterproofing materials are available for these systems in market.

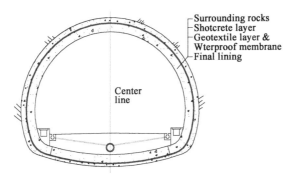

Figure 3-10 Undrained(closed) **waterproofing systems for a tunnel**

Closed waterproofing systems (Figures 3-10), often referred to as closed or tanked systems, extend around the entire tunnel perimeter and aim at excluding the groundwater from flowing into the tunnel drainage system completely. Thus no groundwater drainage is provided. The secondary lining therefore has to be designed for full hydrostatic water pressures. These systems are often applied in permeable soils, where groundwater discharge into the tunnels would be significant and would otherwise cause a lowering of the groundwater table and possibly cause surface settlements, as a drained system applied.

Open waterproofing systems allow groundwater inflow into a tunnel drainage system (Figures 2-10 and 3-11). Typically, the tunnel vault area is equipped with a waterproofing system forming an umbrella-like protection that drains the water seeping towards the cavity around the arch into a drainage system that is located at the bottom of the tunnel sidewalls and in the tunnel invert. The open system is commonly used in tunnels where water infiltration rates are low. Groundwater inflow is typically localized to distinct locations such as joints and fractures and the overall permeability is such that a groundwater draw-down in soil layers overlying the rock mass will not be affected. This system is commonly installed between an initial tunnel support (initial lining) and the secondary or final support (permanent lining). The open waterproofing system generally allows for a more economical secondary lining and invert design as the hydrostatic load of water is greatly reduced or eliminated.

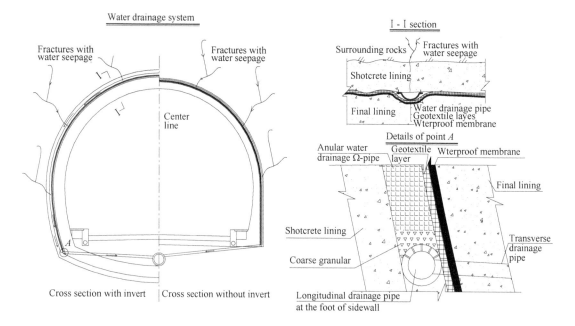

Figure 3-11 Drained (open) waterproofing systems for a tunnel

For precast segmental lining, the segments are usually equipped with gaskets to seal the joints between segments and thus provide a watertight tunnel. For cut and cover tunnels under the groundwater table and for immersed tunnels, waterproofing membranes encapsulating the structures and water stops at joints are recommended.

The waterproofing system should be addressed as early as possible and design criteria for water infiltration should be established during the design process. This issue is usually discussed in the design of tunnel linings.

Where an open waterproofing system is planned for a tunnel, the related drainage system is therefore required, with the outlet of the drainage under consideration, especially in cold region or in the situation, where the the water is corrosive or unfavorable to environment. Accumulation of ice must be avoided for the drainage system.

Good design anticipates drainage needs. Usually sump-pump systems are provided at the portals and at low points. Roadway drainage throughout the tunnel using drain inlets and drainage pipes should be provided. The drainage system should be designed to deal with surface drainage as well as any groundwater infiltration into the tunnel. Other areas of the tunnels, such as ventilation ducts and potential locations for leakage, should have provision for drainage.

3.3.5 Tunnel portals

Portals are the "gate" of entering and exiting a tunnel. The location of tunnel portal is vital to the safety of operation, especially for the tunnels in mountain regions, where is readily subjected to seism, flood, gravity flow (e. g., debris flow, earthflow), landslide, rockfall, etc. It is required to predict the stability of portal excavation, in terms of the geotechnical features (e. g., lithology, morphology, tectonics and structure) of the slop to be entered, the behaviour of the slope after tunnel construction.

Tunnel portals may require special design considerations in terms of the stability of the slope at the portal. Portal sites need to be located in stable ground with sufficient space for construction. Otherwise, the normal operation of the road or railway may be abruptly halted, e. g., due to heavy raining or earthquake. Figure 3-12 shows the collapse of the slope at the north portal of Angou tunnel in the highway Xi'an-Ankang, Shaanxi Province, China. From the picture we may deduce that the collapse is related to the structures in the rock mass. The structures of the rock bedding partings and the joints cutting the beddings should have a significant influence on the stability of the slope. The collapse is said being induced by the heavy and lasting raining.

Figure 3-12 Collapse of the slope at the north portal of the Angou tunnel, in Shaanxi Province, China

The portal should be located at a point, where the depth of the tunnel is suitably covered. The dimension of the overburden depends on the type of construction, the crossing configuration, and the geometry of the tunnel. For example, in a cut and cover tunnel, the portal can be as close to the surface as the roof of the tunnel can be placed with sufficient clearance for traffic. On the other hand, in TBM mined tunnels, the portal will be placed at a location where there is sufficient ground cover to start the TBM. On the other hand, an optimized portal location is also beneficial to the construction of the tunnel, such as in terms of constructing access and mucking deposit. In mountain tunnels the portal can be as close to the face of the mountain as practically feasible.

The locations of tunnel portals should also be considered in terms of flood influence and ground surface water drainage, especially at the slope around the portals. In determining portal locations and where to end the approach structure and retaining walls, protection should be provided against flooding resulting from high water levels near bodies of water and tributary watercourses, or from storm runoff. The height of the portal end wall and the approach retaining wall toes should be set to a level at least 0.6 m higher than the design flood level. Alternatively a flood gate can be provided. Adequate provision should be made for immediate and effective removal of water from rainfall, drainage, groundwater seepage, or any other source. Portal cross drain and sump-pump should be provided, especially for the urban tunnels.

Portals and ventilation shafts should be located such that they satisfy environmental and air quality requirements, as well as the geometrical configuration of the tunnel. The environmental restriction can be a key factor of choosing the location of a tunnel portal or ventilation shaft. For a tunnel of two tubes, it may be necessary to extend the dividing wall between traffic traveling in opposite directions to reduce recirculation of pollutants from the exit tunnel into the entry tunnel. In safe of ventilation, a central dividing wall sometime is extended some distance out from the portal to prevent recirculation of polluted air, i.e., vented polluted air from one traffic duct is prevented from entering an adjacent duct as "clean" air.

For the safe driving, portals should be oriented to avoid drivers being blinded by the rising or setting sun. Special lighting requirements at the portal are needed to address the "black hole" effect. Orientation of the portals should avoid if possible direct east and west to avoid blinding sunlight. Light reducing measures, such as louver, should be taken where drivers might otherwise be blinded by the rising or setting sun.

3.3.6 Fire-life safety systems

Safety in the event of a fire is of paramount importance in a long tunnel. The catastrophic consequences of the tunnel fires [e. g. , the Mont Blanc tunnel (1999) and the Swiss St. Gotthard tunnel (2001)] resulted in loss of life and severe property damages. The devastating fire of 1999 at the Mont Blanc tunnel caused 39 deaths. The tunnel was then shut for three years. During the fire, the temperature reportedly reached about 1000 ℃ in few minutes, thick smoke and combustible product propagated over 4. 6 km within 45 minutes. The damage of the fire to the concrete lining was serious at about 100-m-long section, as shown in Figure 3-13. The cases of fire in tunnels raise the concerns of the fire-life safety protection in road tunnels.

Figure 3-13　The damage situation of the lining and vehicles aftermath of the 1999 fire at the Mont Blanc tunnel❶

For planning purposes, it is important to understand the fire-life safety issues of a road tunnel and consider their impacts on the alignments, tunnel cross section, emergency exits, ventilation provisions, geometrical configuration, right-of-way, and conceptual cost estimates. For example, in the USA, the *National Fire Protection Association (NFPA) 502-Standard for Road Tunnels, Bridges, and Other Limited Access Highways* provides the following fire protection and life safety requirements for road tunnels: ①protection of structural elements; ②fire detection; ③communication systems; ④traffic control; ⑤fire protection (i. e. , standpipe, fire hydrants, water supply, portable fire extinguisher, fixed water-base fire-fighting systems, etc,); ⑥ tunnel drainage system; ⑦ emergency egress; ⑧ electric; ⑨emergency response plan.

---

❶ Mont Blanc Tunnel at age 46. http://tunneltalk. com.

Based on researches and case studies in European, it is recommended that conducting research on tunnel emergency management that includes ① human factors;②developing tunnel design criteria that promote optimal driver performance during incidents;③developing more effective visual, audible, and tactile signs for escape routes;④using a risk-management approach to tunnel safety inspection and maintenance.

3.3.6.1 Emergency egress

It is beneficial that a road tunnel with more than one traffic tube, so that in the event that one tube is shut down, the traffic can be carried in the other. For reasons of safety, it is not recommended that tunnels are designed for bi-directional traffic. For bored and mined long tunnels, where separate tubes are constructed for traffic in each direction, there are transverse passageways built for vehicles and person emergency egress. For cut and cover, jacked and immersed tunnels, it is preferable for the traffic tubes for the two directions to be constructed within a single structure. Emergency egress should be provided in the structure for a long or important tunnel.

For super long tunnels, emergency egress for persons using the tunnel to a place of refuge, as shown in Figure 3-14❶, should be provided at regular intervals. Throughout the tunnel, functional, clearly-marked escape routes should be provided for use in an emergency. The exits should be clearly marked and the spacing of exits into escape routes should not exceed 300 m. The emergency egress walkways should be a minimum of 1.1 m wide and should be protected from oncoming traffic. Signage indicating both direction and distance to the nearest escape door should be mounted above the emergency walkways at reasonable intervals(e. g. ,30 to 45 m) and be visible in an emergency. The emergency escape routes should be provided with adequate lighting level and connected to the emergency power system.

a) Emergency exit to shelter door　　　　　b) Interior of a safe shelter

Figure 3-14　Emergency exit to shelter door and the interior of a safe shelter at the Mont Blanc tunnel

---

❶ http://www.tunnelmb.net/v3.0/gb/equipement_gb.asp.

Where tunnels are provided in twin tubes, cross passages to the adjacent tube can be considered safe haven. The cross passage should be of at least two-hour fire rating construction, should be equipped with self closing fire rated doors that open in both directions or sliding doors, and the cross passages should be located not more than, e. g. ,300 m apart. An emergency walkway at least 1.1-m-wide should be provided on each side of the cross-passageways. In China, the cross passage between the two tubes of a tunnel is required at an interval of 250 m or no more than 500 m for walkway.

In long tunnels, breakdown emergency stop site(local widening) or lay-by for vehicles, as shown in Figure 3-15, should be provided. Some European tunnels also provide at intervals an emergency turn-around for vehicles into the adjacent roadway duct which turn-around would normally be closed by doors. In China, the cross passage for vehicles is at an interval of 750 m.

Figure 3-15 Emergency parking area at the Mont Blanc tunnel[1]

3.3.6.2 Emergency ventilation, lighting and communication

An emergency ventilation system should be provided to control smoke and to provide fresh air for the evacuation of passengers and for support to the emergency responders. The emergency ventilation system is often the normal ventilation system operated ata special mode. Emergency ventilation scenarios should be developed and the operation of the fans would be based on the location of the fire and the direction of the tunnel evacuation. For super long tunnels, there are standby power for the fans and emergence lighting and signal signs.

Emergency tunnel lighting, fire detection, fire lines and hydrants should be provided. In certain installations, fire suppression measures such as foam or deluge system have been used. The risk of fire spreading through power cable ducts should be eliminated by dividing cable ducts into fireproof sections, placing cables in cast-in

---

[1] http://www.tunnelmb.net/v3.0/gb/equipement_gb.asp.

ducts, using fireproof cables where applicable and other preventative measures. Vital installations should be supplied with fire-resistant cables. Materials used should not release toxic or aggressive gases such as chlorine. Water for fire-fighting should be protected against frost. Fire alarm buttons should be provided adjacent to every cross-passage. Emergency services should be able to approach a tunnel fire in safety.

Emergency telephones should be provided in the tunnels and connected to the emergency power supply. When such a telephone is used, the location of the caller should be identified both at the control center and by a warning light visible to rescuing personnel. Telephones should be provided at cross-passage doors and emergency exits. Communication systems should give the traveling public the possibility of receiving instructions for rescue.

In super long tunnels, radio coverage for police, fire and other emergency services and staff should extend throughout the tunnel. It is necessary for police, fire and emergency services to use their mobile radios within tunnels and cross-passages. Radio systems should be connected to the emergency power supply to communicate with each other. It is also recommended that mobile telephone coverage be provided in tunnels.

3.4 Geometry design of a tunnel

The layout and tunnel geometry of tunnel is determined according to the design data and operation requirements of a tunnel. The space of the tunnel should meet the basic requirements for specified carriageway widths and traffic clearances, with additional space for the operation and management, as well as the space for the installations of equipments and facilities, such as for ventilation, lighting, signaling, maintenance, lay-bys for emergencies, etc. According to the circumstances at each tunnel, a detailed consideration in tunnel geometry design is always as the followings:①traffic composition and design flows;②design speed; ③sight distances and the relations between alternative tunnel cross-sections and minimum horizontal radii;④scope for tunnel widening at curves;⑤basis of tunnel operation(one way, two way, contra flow);⑥tunnel cross section;⑦approach road geometry and traffic measurements (lane merge, diverge, climbing lane, proximity of junctions);⑧any other aspects peculiar to a planned tunnel.

3.4.1　Choice of tunnel system and alignment

The tunnel system comprises all underground structures and facilities that are necessary to achieve the planned use and ensure the safety of persons. Besides the main structures, the tunnel system may comprise, e.g., cross-passages, adits and shafts as escape routes or other auxillary structures for operation and safety control, such as ventilation shafts or caverns for technical equipments. The choice of the tunnel system is based mainly on operational, organizational and safety considerations and the ground conditions and the topography, where the layout of the access tunnels and shafts may also have an influence on the selection of the tunnel system. For example, for a railway tunnel, these factors may have dominated influence on planning a tunnel with two tubes or a double-track tunnel, with construction time and cost risks under consideration.

The vertical and horizontal alignment of the tube(s) also depends on several factors, such as: ①the use of the tunnel (maximum longitudinal gradient, minimum curvature); ②the drainage considerations during construction and operation; ③the accessibility and natural hazards in the portal areas; ④the ground conditions. If possible, the alignment should be adapted to the ground conditions in an early phase of the project, as hazards and the construction time and cost risks can be avoided or reduced by the choice of a different alignment.

Aspects of operation and safety (such as the necessity of intermediate adits, ventilation shafts or escape adits) may also influence the choice of the alignment. This is particularly true for super long tunnels.

The ground conditions may have strong influence on determining the selection of the location and axis orientation of the tunnels, the spacing between two adjacent tubes, alignment of the tubes, such in the case of branching and portal region.

3.4.2 Tunnel layout

Internal clearances and overall alignment are common considerations to the tunnels, including road, railway, and rapid transit. Limitations on the tunnel layout are imposed by operating requirements and by factors inherent in certain construction methods. For example, the layout of an underwater tunnel generally admits a greater variety of approaches than mountain tunnels. In general it can be concluded that the design elements of tunnels should be in harmony with the function and category of the roads in which tunnels are situated[7].

3.4.2.1 Clearances for road tunnels

The clearance of a tunnel is the least and necessary space for the normal operation of the planned traffics. The minimum tunnel inner dimensions are determined by adding the structure gauge with the space for the installations of designed facilities in a cross section, such as the space for ventilation ducts and fans. The structure gauge diagram is based on all potential vehicles envelopes and also should take into consideration potential future vehicle heights, vehicle mounting on curbs, construction tolerances, and any potential ground and structure settlement. Any facilities, such as ventilation equipment, lighting, guide signs, and other equipment, should not encroach within the clearance diagram. Figures 3-16 shows how the terminology applies where the tunnel cross section above the carriageway level differs markedly as for approximately circular and rectangular cross sections[7].

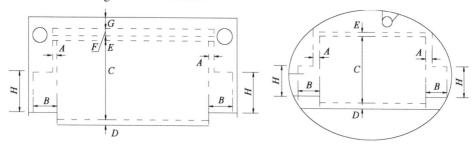

a) Clearances and allowances for box profiles

b) Clearances and allowances for arch profiles

Note: A-Lateral clearance between the edges of the roadway and fixtures such as detection equipment, fans, signs etc. ;

B-Walkway;

C-Maintained headroom;

D-Additional allowance to provide for road resurfacing;

E-Vertical clearance between the maintained headroom and fixtures such as detection equipment, fans, signs etc. ;

F-Allowance due to construction of the roof;

G-Vertical clearance for fixtures such as detection equipment, fans, signs etc. ;

H-Walkway headroom.

Figure 3-16 Clearances and allowances for box and arch profiles

In China, the *Specification* (JTG 3370.1—2018) has established standard horizontal and vertical clearances for various classes of roads, as shown in Figure 3-17. The technical specifications for the structure gauge of both unidirectional and bidirectional road tunnels are presented in the *Guidelines* (JTG/T D70—2010), as shown in Table 3-2 and Table 3-3, respectively.

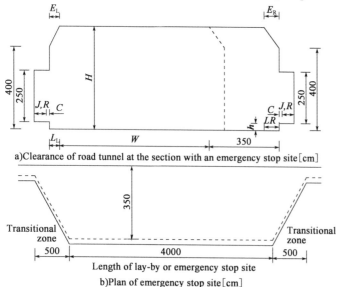

a) Clearance of road tunnel at the section with an emergency stop site [cm]

b) Plan of emergency stop site [cm]

Note:
H-Height of structure gauge for roadway;
W-Width of the roadway;
L_L, L_R-Left, right additional width for the roadway, respectively;
C-Lateral clearance between the edges of the roadway and fixtures such as detection equipment, fans, signs etc.;
J, R-Width of the walkway;
E_L-Width of left top angle of the clearance, $E_L = L_L$;
E_R-Width of right top angle of the structure gauge, where $L_R \leqslant 1$ m, $E_R = L_R$, and as $L_R > 1$ m, $E_R = 1$ m.
For express highway tunnels, a 5-m vertical clearance is required, while a 4.5-m vertical structure gauge is for tunnels in low-grade roads.

Figure 3-17 Clearance for a two-lane tunnel and its emergency parking area ($H = 5$ m)

Table 3-2 Technical specifications for the clearances of unidirectional road tunnels

Design speed [km/h]	Width of carriageway lanes [m]	Additional width for the carriageway [m]		Lateral clearance, C [m]	Width of maintaining way, J [m]		Total width [m]
		Lift side, L_L	Right side, L_R		Lift side	Right side	
120	3.75 ×2	0.75	1.25	0.50	1.00	1.00	11.50
100	3.75 ×2	0.75	1.00	0.25	0.75	1.00	11.00
80	3.75 ×2	0.50	0.75	0.25	0.75	0.75	10.25
60	3.50 ×2	0.50	0.75	0.25	0.75	0.75	9.75

Note: ①C is for the lateral clearance between the edges of the roadway and fixtures such as detection equipment, fans, signs etc.
②For the tunnel with three or four lanes, more lanes can be added to the width of the carriageway lanes and the other parameters are same.
③The width of the lateral clearance C is included in the width of the width of maintaining way J.
④The unit is in meter.

Table 3-3 Technical specifications for the clearances of bidirectional road tunnels

Design speed [km/h]	Width of carriageway lanes [m]	Additional width for the lift side of carriageway, L_L [m]	Lateral clearance, C [m]	Width of walkway, R [m]	Total width [m]	
					With walkway	Without walkway
80	3.75 ×2	0.75	0.25	1.00	11.00	
60	3.50 ×2	0.50	0.25	1.00	10.00	
40	3.50 ×2	0.25	0.25	0.75	9.00	
30	3.25 ×2	0.25	0.25			7.50
20	3.00 ×2	0.50	0.25			7.50

Note: The width of the lateral clearance C is included in the width of the width of walkway R.

The headroom of different lanes may be not same in a tunnel. In some tunnels, a lane for over-height vehicles is available. The situation is dependent on the classification of the road. Additional height may be required on vertical curves to allow for long trucks. Additional space may be required for ventilation, ventilation equipment, and ventilation ducts. The vertical clearance shall also take into consideration for future resurfacing of the roadway. In horizontally curved tunnels, provisions must be made to accommodate superelevation of the roadway, and superelevation transitions at the ends of alignment curves. The accepted values usually 4.5-5.0 m for the headroom of a clearance.

Since construction costs of tunnels are high, clearance requirements are usually somewhat reduced. Although some older 2-lane tunnels have used roadway widths of 6.5 m between curbs for unidirectional traffic and 7.0 m for bi-directional traffic, usually with speed restrictions, these widths no longer meet current standards for 3.75-m lanes. Where full width shoulders are not provided due to cost, at least an additional 30 cm is provided adjacent to each curb. Wider shoulders may be required around horizontal curves to comply with sight distance requirements. A minimum distance between walls of 9.0 m is a common requirement for the width of a road tunnel.

Followings are the recommendations on traffic lanes and carriageway by PIARC [7]: ①The width of traffic lanes in tunnels with design speed of 100 km/h be not less than 3.50 m; ②When it is acceptable/necessary to impose restricted speed limits(80 or even 60 km/h) in road tunnels(i.e., when sharp curves are unavoidable, noise reduction in built-up areas, limited capacity necessary, cost reduction) a restriction of the width of traffic lanes(to for instance 3.25 m) may help drivers to reduce speed and thus act as a psychological support of the speed limit; ③In the design stage of two tubes consideration should be given to traffic management during maintenance and repair works requiring the replacement of normal width lanes by temporary narrower width traffic lanes; ④Wherever possible to maintain the same width of traffic lanes and off-carriageways in road tunnels as on the adjoining carriageways in the open air; ⑤If the width of traffic lanes in tunnels is restricted by comparison with the adjoining carriageways in the open air and a restricted design speed is applied, this restriction should commence at least 150 m from the entrance of the tunnel.

Tunnel ventilation ducts, if required, can be provided above or below the traffic lanes, or to the sides of them. Where clearances to the outside of the tunnel at a particular location are such that by moving ventilation from overhead to the sides can reduce the tunnel gradients or reduce its length, such an option should be considered.

The designated structure gauge should be provided throughout the approaches to the tunnel. Over-height warning signals and diverging routes should be provided before traffic can reach the tunnel entrances.

3.4.2.2 Alignment and gradient for tunnels

3.4.2.2.1 Line in plan

Alignment should be straight, if possible. Alignment of a tunnel, both horizontal and vertical, generally consists of straight lines connected by curves. If curves are required, the minimum radius is determined by safety stopping sight distances and acceptable superelevation in relation to design speed.

Radii of curvature should match tunnel design speed. Small radii require superelevation and some widening of roadway to provide for overhang space and sight distance. Superelevation in track construction is the design vertical distance that the outer rail is set above the inner rail on a curve. In road construction, supere-levation is by the banking of the roadway on a curve.

In some cases, a curve section or even curve tunnel may be proper in comparison to a straight line. For example, a spiral(sometimes called a spiral loop or just loop) is a technique employed by railways to ascend steep hills. A railway spiral❶ rises on a steady curve until it has completed a loop, passing over itself as it gains height, allowing the railway to gain vertical elevation in a relatively short horizontal distance. It is an alternative to a zig-zag, and avoids the need for the trains to stop and reverse direction while ascending. It is clear that one curve tunnel, at least, is needed in a spiral line, as shown in Figure 3-18❶.

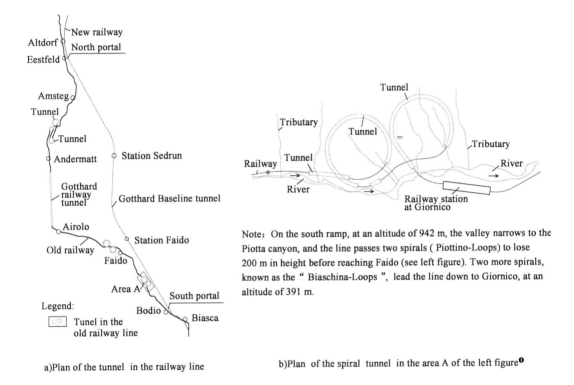

a) Plan of the tunnel in the railway line

b) Plan of the spiral tunnel in the area A of the left figure❶

Figure 3-18 Spiral tunnels on the north and south ramps to the Gotthard tunnel in the Gotthard railway

In recent years, spiral curves are also designed for tunnels in highway engineering in China. For example, Figure 3-19 shows the alignment of tunnels in a spiral curve at Laobaoshan in Shui-Ma highway.

In China, spiral tunnels have also been used for avoiding adverse geological units, such as active faults, which are susceptible earthquake, as shown in Figure 3-20. During the route alternative analysis on the highway in Tuowushan area, the line with double spiral tunnels were chosen to avoid passing through the active faults.

---

❶ http://en.wikipedia.org/wiki/Spiral_(railway)#mw-navigation.

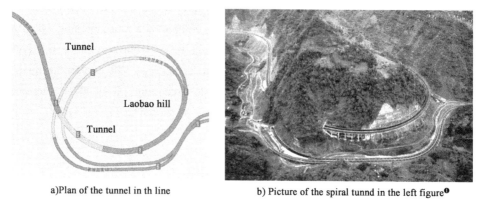

a) Plan of the tunnel in th line
b) Picture of the spiral tunnd in the left figure❶

Figure 3-19　Tunnels in a spiral curve at Laobaoshan in Shui-Ma highway

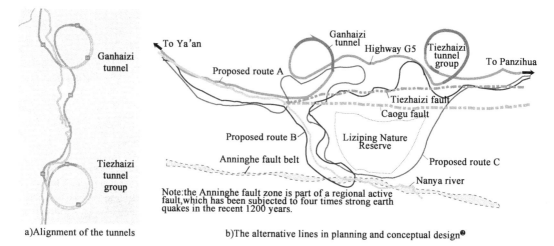

a) Alignment of the tunnels
b) The alternative lines in planning and conceptual design❷

Figure 3-20　An line with double spiral tunnels to avoid active faults

3.4.2.2.2　Vertical alignment and longitudinal gradient

For tunnels, the penalties of steep gradients are more severe than on open roads and will include higher ventilation costs, due to increased vehicle emissions. Also traffic speeds may be reduced unacceptably with large proportions of HGVs. Trunk road tunnels with gradients exceeding 6% is unlikely to be practical. A climbing lane is not normally a practical provision within a tunnel. In a steeply graded bidirectional tunnel, for example, a climbing lane might be provided by a 3-lane-carriageway, two lanes up and one down. Where adequate alternative routes can be provided, it may be advantageous to prohibit heavy vehicles from steeply graded tunnels. Where a large gradient, such as around 6%, is required, a cost-benefit study is needed, in terms of operation cost and safety, as well as construction cost.

---

❶ https://www.ynjtt.com/Item/9201.aspx.
❷ http://blog.sina.com.cn/s/blog_632b78fb01015ipm.html.

The minimum gradients are established to ensure adequate drainage. The maximum grades depend on the purpose of the tunnel. Construction of a tunnel in the upgrade direction is preferred whenever possible, since this permits water to drain away from the face under construction.

For road tunnels, gradients are limited between 0.3% and 3.0%. For tunnels under navigable water carrying heavy traffic, grades about 4% are acceptable. For lighter traffic volumes, grades up to 6% have been used for economy's sake in construction. Between governing navigation clearances, grades are reduced to a minimum adequate for drainage, preferably not less than 0.3% longitudinally and a cross slope of 1.0%. For long rock tunnels with two-way traffic, the maximum grade of 3% is desirable to maintain reasonable truck speeds. Additional climbing lanes for slower traffic may be required when grades exceed 4%.

At crests, visibility may be obstructed by the intervening road. Details of crest curve and visibility requirements are usually given in related design codes or guidelines. On the other hand, to accommodate long full height vehicles at sag curves, additional headroom clearance for sag radii of 6000 m, or less should be considered accordingly.

Stopping Sight Distances(SSD) shall be checked for a driver's eye height of 2.0 m. If the minimum values are not achieved either the tunnel headroom should be increased, or, if practical, the speed limit reduced.

3.4.2.2.3　Superelevation

To provide comfortable levels of lateral acceleration, it is desirable to provide superelevation for certain levels of horizontal curvature. The superelevation may have an adverse effect on the tunnel cross section and on the provision of service ducts under the roadway. In general, the full recommended levels of superelevation provide only small compensation for lateral acceleration. So, superelevation is not recommended for road tunnels in some nations, such as in China.

For tunnels, the need to drain the road surface arises from routine wall washing, flushing away accidental spillage and any seepage. The normal cross-fall, such as 1.5% to 2.5%, is often provided throughout the tunnel.

PIARC[7] recommended the off-carriageway as the followings. ①In heavy congested tunnels(e.g., in cities) the off-carriageways adjacent to the overtaking lane should be wide enough to enable safe parking of broken down vehicles. ②It is recommended to avoid sudden changes in characteristic features at the entrance of tunnels. And such changes should where required be introduced at a minimum distance of 150 m from the tunnel portal. ③It is recommended during maintenance work in one way tunnel tubes to close at least one lane for traffic adjacent to the place of action. This favors the safety of maintenance workers more than walkways. ④It is recommended wherever possible to put cables and ducts outside the tunnel tube. Especially the connections which require most access should be separated from the traffic area. This decreases the need to close lanes during maintenance works.

3.4.2.3 Controls on layout of tunnels

The limitations on the layout of tunnels are always imposed by design and operating considerations, and by present construction capabilities. The relative suitability of the present construction methods will depend primarily on the hydrological and geotechnical conditions of the proposed project site. On the other hand, the layout of a tunnel is also influenced by the operational conditions, features of the neighbor structures of the tunnel.

3.4.2.3.1 Construction conditions

The construction limitations are generally related to the stability of the ground and the capability to control the inflow of groundwater into the tunnel, especially for an underwater tunnel. These limitations are also considered in tunneling method choosing and tunnel type design. One of the basic requirements for tunneling is free air. For super long tunnels, construction ventilation may also have influence on the layout of the tunnel. On the other hand, the construction access sometimes also is a factor to be considered in tunnel layout design.

The construction conditions should be accomplished first by seeking the most favorable geology for the tunnel alignment and profile. In this process, the types of the tunnel and the proposed construction method are of important considerations. For example, there no inherent limits on the depth of mined rock tunnels in mountain area in terms of construction conditions. Although at great depth and in some geological units, ground heat may become a problem. However, for an urban or underwater tunnel, the influence of the tunnel depth can be significant in tunnel layout, especially in the length of the tunnel and the requirements for operational structures.

The construction method of the underwater tunnels depends heavily on the geological conditions and the overburden of the proposed tunnel. For example, shield methods for underwater tunnel construction are generally limited to shallow depths under estuaries and coastal sites. They are most suited to sites with deep deposits of moderately soft, impervious clay. Under such conditions, the excavation may be accomplished in free air, although it may be necessary to pressurize the face of the tunnel heading if the clay is very soft and highly stressed and tends to squeeze into the tunnel. Shield tunnels through pervious ground are generally limited to the depth at which the groundwater pressure may be balanced by internal air pressure. Under this situation, medical limits for worker safety give an absolute limit of about 3 atm degassers, corresponding to 30 m below the water surface. However, if these conditions exist over a substantial length, the economic limit is likely to be 20 m. However, where the ground is relatively impervious strata, the air pressure balanced shield can be applied in much deep underwater tunnels. For example, the Tokyo Bay tunnel is at depth of 50 m and Demark's Great Belt Railway Tunnel is a depth of 75 m below the sea surface.

Immersed tubes are generally suited to crossing of soft-bottomed water body, where trenches may be excavated by floating equipment. The deepest trench for an existing tunnel extends more than 60 m below sea level, for the Marmaray Crossing, Bosporus, Turkey. Immersed tubes are usually buried beneath the level of the existing sea bed, although short projections above the bottom across deep natural trenches may be mounded over for protection. Other limitations on immersed tube construction include the followings[4]: ①there must be sufficient duration of slack tidal current to permit lowering the tube, preferably less than 1 m/s over a duration of 2 hours; ②the bottom must not be so soft and unstable that trench cannot be kept open; ③the site must be reasonably free from rapid deposition of fluid silts, which can alter the density of water in the trench and affect the balance of buoyancy at tube placement.

3.4.2.3.2 Operational requirements

For long road tunnels, ventilation is a prime consideration in the layout of the tunnels. For heavy traffic volumes, it is desirable to adopt a limit of 4% upgrade because the ventilation requirements rise rapidly for higher gradients. In general, tunnels with lengths between ventilation points exceeding about 3 km require special ventilation measures if they carry substantial traffic volumes. For heavily traveled urban tunnels, the requirement for ventilation capacity is much significant. The electric power required to ventilate a tunnel of given total length varies in proportion to the sums of the power of the distances between vent points. And therefore, the maximum distance between vent points can be important factors in the evaluation of operating costs and economic feasibility.

Shafts of a super long tunnel may be required by operational ventilation. The locations of the shafts should be considered in terms of construction, cost, as well as the environmental effects of the ventilation tower, especially the polluted air exiting tower, on the ground residents and buildings. On the other hand, an air tower may be designed with the consideration of a landmark building or special design. One of the cases is the wind tower of the Trans-Tokyo Bay Highway, as shown in Figure 3-21. At this tunnel, fresh air is supplied to the tunnel by the distinctive wind tower in the middle of the tunnel. The wind tower is not only distinctive in shape, but also using the bay's almost-constant winds as a power source.

3.4.2.3.3 Design speed, SSD and overtaking

The SSD of a tunnel is determined from the design speed, the driver's reaction time and the average deceleration rate to stop. The desirable SSD is usually based on a 2-second reaction time and $0.25g$ deceleration, where g is the acceleration of gravity.

The tunnel design speed shall be the same as the approach road design speed. However, as the design speed is high, such as for highway, the lighting cost will quickly increase. And therefore, speed limit is usually used in highway tunnel design. Few tunnels are designed with speed limit more than 100 km/h (Figure 3-21).

Figure 3-21 The Tower of Wind at Kawasaki artificial island above the Trans-Tokyo Bay Highway[1]

In a design code for tunnels, the recommended relationship between the speed limit, the design speed and SSD, as well as the relationship between the design speed and the horizontal curvature, is usually provided based upon alignment standards.

In a road tunnel, overtaking is often unallowed.

3.4.2.3.4 Approach

A tunnel is connected to open road, bridge or another tunnel by an approach section. The length of approach road from the portal equals to 1.5 times the open road SSD. In China, the length of the approach should be designed to travel for 3 seconds at a design speed for road tunnels.

For the safe of traveling, the design standards of the approach of a tunnel should not be lower than the tunnel, in terms of geometry, especially in width and curve radii.

---

[1] http://en.wikipedia.org/wiki/File:Kawasaki_artificial_island.jpg.

For some special cases, the approach zone may be designed in considering the construction method of the tunnel, the operational features of the project, as wells as landscape environment and site visiting. For example, at the crossover point of 4.4-km-bridge and the 9.6-km-tunnel of the Tokyo Bay Aqua-Line in Japan, there is an artificial island called Umihotaru(literally meaning "sea firefly"), with a rest area consisting of restaurants, shops and amusement facilities, as shown in Figure 3-22.

Figure 3-22 Umihotaru Parking Area-Tokyo Bay Aqua Line Highway❶

3.4.2.3.5 Elevations of portals and accesses

In addition to structural requirements, inundation of the tunnel by floods, surges, tides and waves, or combinations thereof resulting from storms must be prevented. The height and shape of walls surrounding tunnel entrances, the elevation of access road surfaces and any entrances, accesses and holes must be designed such that entry of water is prevented. For example, it is recommended that water level with the probability of being exceeded no more than 0.005 times in any one year(the 500-year flood level) be used as the design water level for the road tunnels in the USA. In China, the water level with the probability of being exceeded no more than 0.01 times in any one year is recommended for the tunnels in highways and class-1 road.

3.4.2.3.6 Spatial relationship between tunnels

A tunnel may be alone in line, such as the tunnels in a low grade road. There may be no existing tunnel neighbor to a planned tunnel. The tunnels in a highway line, two tubes are usually designed for vehicles in one-way traveling. The spatial relationship between the two tubes may change from a few meters to several tens meters, or even more.

---

❶ http://en.wikipedia.org/wiki/File:Umihotaru200508-1.jpg.

For a tunnel in urban area, for example, tunnels under passing existing road or buildings, the two tubes of the tunnel is usually separated by a center wall, as shown in Figure 3-23. These tunnels can be constructed by cut and cover method or jacked box method.

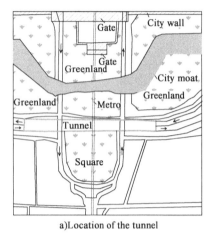 

a)Location of the tunnel   b)The east portal of the tunnel and the nearby city wall

Figure 3-23   Yongningmen tunnel underpassing existing road in Xi'an, China

For the tunnels in mountains, the relationship between the two tubes of a planned tunnel is usually controlled not only by the features of the tunnel and ground conditions, but also by the features of its connecting structures. Where the net space between the two tubes of a planned tunnel is such large that the construction effect of one tube has no influence on the other tube, the two tubes are separated tunnels in terms of stability. Otherwise, where the net distance between the two tubes is so small that the disturbance due to one tube construction will have influence on the other tube, the two tubes are neighborhood tunnels. When a tunnel is planned connecting to a large structure, e. g. a large span bridge across a deep valley, the two tubes of the tunnel may only be separated by a center wall. These two tubes are multi-arch tunnels. Figure 3-24 shows the alignment of the multi-arch tunnel, Yuehuquan tunnel, connecting with the large span bridge, Shenxianhe bridge, with the pier of the bridge tower 150 m high.

It is noted that the separated tunnels are advantage in comparison to the neighborhood tunnels and multi-arch tunnels, in terms of structures stability, construction and even maintaining. The maximum length of a multi-arch tunnel and neighborhood tunnel is recommended, for example, by the *Guideline* (JTG/T D70—2010) in China, as shown in Tables 3-4 and 3-5, respectively. Where the geological condition is sound, the smaller one can be used for the net distance, otherwise, the larger one is recommended for the net distance.

Figure 3-24 Multi-arch tunnels connecting to a large span bridge with high pier

Table 3-4 Maximum length of a neighborhood tunnel and the net space between the two tubes

Type of tunnels	Rational maximum length of the tunnel [m]	Net spacing between the two tubes [m]
Two-lane tunnel	750-1000	5-15
Three-lane tunnel	500-750	8-20

Table 3-5 Maximum length of a multi-arch tunnel

Features of tunnels	Rational maximum length of the tunnel [m]
Two lane for each tube	400-750
Three lane for each tube	300-500

3.4.3 Geometry of a tunnel

The cross section shapes of the inner profiles of road tunnels are typically rectangular, circular, horseshoe or modified horseshoe, respectively, as shown in Figure 3-25. The shape of a tunnel depends mostly on the method of construction. The typical cross sections and corresponding construction methods, commonly applied in practice, are indicated in Table 3-6.

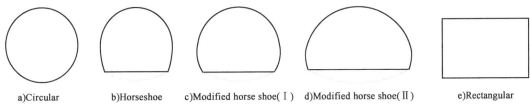

a) Circular   b) Horseshoe   c) Modified horse shoe (Ⅰ)   d) Modified horse shoe (Ⅱ)   e) Rectangular

Figure 3-25 Common shapes of road tunnels

Table 3-6　Cross sections of road tunnels and typical construction methods

Cross Section	Typical construction method	Comments
Circular	Shield TBMs, Open TBMs	Recently extended in Japan to rectangular cross section.
Rectangular/Circular	Immersed tube/box	Mainly concrete box, but circular steel tubes.
	Cut and cover method	Often rectangular box, but sometimes leads with precast circular cross sections above the carriageway.
Horseshoe	Conventional/mining method	Drill and blast method applied in hard rocks.
Modified horse shoe	Conventional/mining method	Drill and blast method applied in hard rocks.

3.4.3.1　Shape

The shapes and the dimensions of the cross section of underground openings are determined essentially by ITA[2]: ①he serviceability requirements associated with the use of the underground works; ②the geological-geotechnical conditions; ③construction aspects.

The space of the cross section necessary for traffic may vary due to[7,8]: ①traffic volumes and the importance of the tunnel; ②design speeds, safe stopping distances and sight distances; ③space for in-tunnel equipment, such as signs, traffic and environment monitoring; ④cost of the facility balanced against the required safety standards; ⑤the traffic management required to respond to an incident in the tunnel; ⑥the usual local norms and the financial possibilities.

The required clearance profile is a key factor in the determination of the cross section of the underground opening. The clearance profile is mainly defined according to the scope of the structures or the usage of the tunnel. Besides the scope of the structure, further serviceability criteria required by the client can be decisive for the choice of cross section.

The shape of a tunnel or underground structure is also influenced by rock mass properties, the features of in-situ stress, selected construction methods, estimated ground load and the redistribution features during construction, the lining and reinforcement measures. In practice, one of the common shapes (Figure 3-25) can be determined, in terms of the stability of the tunnel structure. For example, weak rock zones, squeezing or swelling rock and soft ground (soils) require a circular cross section or at least a horseshoe-shaped cross section including an invert arch to control the surrounding rocks deformation. For some special situations, such as under high in-situ stress state, an ellipse shape is chosen, as the major axis of the ellipse is usually based on the direction of major principal stress. For the tunnels in structural controlled rock mass, certain directions and cross-sectional shapes of tunnels and underground excavations will always be better than the others provided that the discontinuities do not occur at random orientations.

Economic considerations and the availability of the necessary equipment may be decisive for the construction method and have, therefore, a considerable influence on the shape of the cross section. In contrast to TBM or shield tunneling, the cross section of tunnels excavated by conventional methods can be freely chosen within the constraints of the geological conditions. Also, when an invert is needed for the tunnels in soft ground, the tunnel shape is usually horseshoe or modified horseshoe.

3.4.3.2　Size of cross section

The size of a tunnel or underground structure is determined by the functional requirements of its capacity, geotechnical condition, construction method and features of supporting system. For example, the capacity of a road tunnel defined by its structure gauge (Figures 3-16 and 3-17), the section space required for the installations of operational and safety controlling facilities, which must be complied with related codes, such as the *National Fire Protection Association (NFPA) 502-Standard for Road Tunnels, Bridges, and Other Limited Access Highways* in the USA, the Section 2 (Traffic Engineering and Affiliated Facilities of the Specifications) of Design of Highway Tunnels in China. The position of a specific facility is often optimized according to the shape of tunnel.

The design of tunnel cross section sizes should take into account costs, traffic volumes, safety requirements, right of way, socioeconomic and environmental impacts, without compromising safety considerations. A road tunnel cross section must be able to accommodate the horizontal and vertical traffic clearances, as well as the other required elements. The typical cross section elements include: ①travel lanes; ② shoulders; ③ sidewalks/curbs; ④ tunnel drainage; ⑤ tunnel ventilation; ⑥tunnel lighting; ⑦ tunnel utilities and power; ⑧ water supply pipes for firefighting; ⑨cabinets for hose reels and fire extinguishers; ⑩ signals and signs above roadway lanes; ⑪ CCTV surveillance cameras; ⑫ emergency telephones; ⑬communication antennae/equipment; ⑭ monitoring equipment of noxious emissions and visibility; ⑮emergency egress illuminated signs at low level (so that they are visible in case of a fire or smoke condition).

Carriageway and shoulder width, sidewalks/emergency egress, drainage, ventilation, lighting and traffic control are usually basic requirements for a long road tunnel. Additional elements may be needed under certain design requirements and should be taken into consideration when developing the tunnel geometrical configuration. Figure 3-26 shows the layout of the facilities elements in the Shueshan tunnel, Taiwan, China.

Inadmissible reduction in size of the opening due to ground convergence must be avoided by means of additional excavation to account for ground deformations and corresponding support measures.

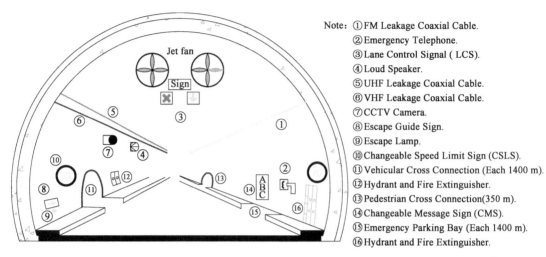

Figure 3-26 Sketch showing facilities layout in the Shueshan tunnel in Taiwan, China[1]

In the determination of the shape and dimensions of the cross section attention must be given to tolerances with respect to driving accuracy, construction tolerances and surveying tolerances.

It is always beneficial to allow some additional dimensions for future. For example, the clearance of a tunnel often designed larger than the limit value given by code requirements. Additional 10-15 cm dimensional allowance may extend the life of a tunnel 50 years.

3.4.3.3 Design of cross section

The shape of a tunnel lining cross section is also called profile. Various profiles are used in practice. The shapes of circular, rectangular and horseshoe profiles are common. The choice of the profile aims at accommodating the space requirements of a planned tunnel. For example, the inner profile of the lining should be such large that it can contain both tunnel structure gauge and the space for the installation of the auxiliary structures (e. g., structures and facilities for ventilation) of the planned tunnel, as well as with additional space in redundancy, which should include the allowance deformation of the excavation profile or surrounding rocks. On the other hand, a proper shape of the profile is beneficial to minimize bending moments in the lining, the costs for excavation and the construction of the lining. The durability of the lining structure and the accessibility and cost of maintenance are also the considerations in the choice of the profile shape. In the following, a horseshoe profile is exemplified, in terms of lining profile design.

---

[1] Lin, B.-P. 2005. Introduction of Hsuehshan Tunnel Traffic Control System. Proc. of the World Long Tunnels 2005, Taipei, 405-416.

A horseshoe profile may be composed of several circular sections, such as with the radii of r_1, r_2 and r_3, respectively, as shown in Figure 3-27a). When the sizes of the radii of r_1, r_2 and r_3 are proposed, the following parameters of the geometry of the cross section, as shown in Figure 3-27a), can be calculated accordingly:

$$\sin\beta = \frac{r_1 - r_2}{r_3 - r_2}, c = \sqrt{r_3^2 - 2r_2(r_3 - r_1) - r_1^2} = (r_3 - r_2)\cos\beta;$$

Cross section area:

$$A = \frac{\pi}{2}r_1^2 + \left(\frac{\pi}{2} - \beta\right)r_2^2 + \beta r_3^2 - (r_1 - r_2)c, \beta \text{ in radian};$$

Height: $H = r_1 + r_3 - c$;

Span: $D = 2r_1$.

The horseshoe profile can be presented by using the parameters of r_1, r_2, r_3 and angle of β, as shown in Figure 3-27b). The parameters of the rectangle space, $a \times b$ as shown in Figure 3-27b), which can be fitted into the horseshoe profile, and can be calculated as: $b = 2r_3\sin\beta$, $H_1 = r_2\cos\beta = r_3\cos\beta - c$, $H_2 = \sqrt{r_1^2 - \frac{b^2}{4}}$ and $a = H_1 + H_2$. In practice, the clearance area, $a \times b$ rectangle space, is first defined, then the parameters of r_1, r_2 and r_3, are chosen such as using the method of trial and error.

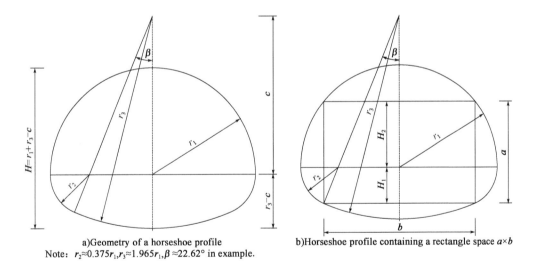

a) Geometry of a horseshoe profile b) Horseshoe profile containing a rectangle space $a \times b$

Note: $r_2 \approx 0.375r_1, r_3 \approx 1.965r_1, \beta \approx 22.62°$ in example.

Figure 3-27 Geometry of a horseshoe profile and its parameter

The method of presenting the inner lining profile may vary in different fields of civil engineering. Besides professional custom, the other reasons may be attributed to the features of the clearance and the utilization of the space outside of the structure gauge of the planned tunnels. For example, in the field of road tunnel engineering in China, considering features of the clearance of a road tunnel (Figure 3-17), the horseshoe profile of a tunnel is usually composed of half circle in crown, circular sections for both sidewalls, with or without invert circular section, with radii of R_1, R_2 and R_4, respectively, as shown in Figure 3-28a). The sections of sidewall and invert are connected by a circular section with small radii, R_3. The parameters for the profile presenting include the heights of H_1, H_2 and H'_2, and angle of θ for the transitional circular section, as shown in Figure 3-28. For the section with emergency stop site, the width of profile should be increased, by inserting a 90° circular section with a radii of R_5 as shown in Figure 3-28b). The typical parameters of highway and class-1 two-lane road tunnel profiles suggested in the *Specification* (JTG 3370.1—2018) are quoted in Table 3-7.

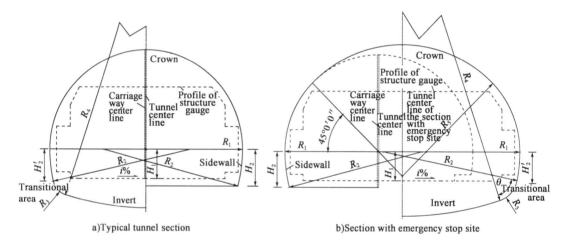

Figure 3-28 Example of a horseshoe profile for road tunnel

Table 3-7 Parameters of highway and class-1 two-lane road tunnel profiles suggested in the Specification

Design speed [km/h]		R_1 [cm]	R_2 [cm]	R_3 [cm]	R_4 [cm]	H_1 [cm]	H_2 [cm]	H'_2 [cm]	R_5 [cm]	Clearance [cm]		$\theta [°]$
										Height	Width	
120	Typical section	612	862	100	1500	160.4	200	144			1100	59.54
	Section with lay-by	612	862	150	1800	162.1	200	136	789		1400	59.52
100	Typical section	570	820	100	1500	160.6	200	164.5			1050	59.56
	Section with lay-by	570	820	150	1800	162.4	200	151.5	747	500	1350	59.52
80	Typical section	543	793	100	1500	160.2	200	176.1			1025	59.47
	Section with lay-by	543	793	150	1800	162.3	200	159.1	745		1325	59.29
60	Typical section	514	764	100	1500	170.0	200	188.4			975	59.54
	Section with lay-by	514	764	150	1800	162.3	200	184.1	708.5		1275	59.97

3.5 Operational and financial planning

3.5.1 Potential funding sources and cash flow requirements

In general, government and local funds are the main funding sources for the tunnels in an infrastructure system. However, private enterprises and public-private partnership (PPP) are recently becoming more attractive potential sources for funding tunnel projects. Various forms of financing have been applied in the World. Tolls are often levied on users to help repay construction costs and to pay operating costs, especially where the roads are financed by private sources. In some cases, bond issues have been used for raising funds for the project.

In developing the funds strategy, it is important to consider and secure the cash flow required to complete the project. In assessing the cash flow analysis, escalation to the year of expenditure should be used. It is recommended that escalation rates comparable to this type of construction and for the area of the project should be used. Factors such as work load in the area, availability of materials, availability of skilled labor, specialty equipment and the like, should be taken into consideration. Repayment of loans and the cost of the money should be considered. They may continue for a substantial number of years while the operation and maintenance costs of the tunnel also have to be covered.

3.5.2 Conceptual level cost analysis

At the conceptual level, cost analyses are often based upon the costs per unit measurement for a typical section of tunnel. The historical cost data updated for inflation and location is also commonly used as a quick check. However, such data should be used with extreme caution since in most cases, the exact content of such data and any special circumstances are not known. The results from case histories show that cost underestimating is almost common in public works projects, especially for megaprojects[10].

When a cost analysis is carried out, the following factors, at least, should be considered in a comprehensive mode:①construction conditions, e.g., construction method planned and techniques available, experience of labors and managers, etc.; ②features of the planned tunnel, e.g., the length and span, features of the ground, depth and locations of the tunnel, etc.; ③the requirements of third party and environmental constrictions, e.g., allowance of the transportation interfering, deformation of the ground and neighbor buildings, noising, etc. For example, the tunnel being a linear structure, its cost is highly dependent on the advance rate of construction, which in turn is dependent on the labor force, the geological conditions, the suitability of equipment, the contractor's means and methods, and the experience of the workers. On the other hand, tunneling is highly dependent on the labor cost. The issues such as advance rates, construction schedule, number of shifts, labor union requirements, local regulations(e. g. ,permissible time of work), environmental factors (e. g., noise and vibrations), should be taken into considerations when construction cost estimates are made. The use of experience from other similar projects in the area is usually used in predicting labor force and the advance rates.

At the conceptual level, substantial contingencies may be required at the early stages of a project. As the design advances and the risks identified and dealt with, contingencies would be reduced gradually as the level of detail and design increases. Soft costs such as engineering, program and construction management, insurance, owner cost, third party cost, right of way costs should be also considered. The cost estimate should progressively become more detailed as the design is advanced in stages(Figure 3-1).

3.5.3 Project delivery method

Generally, two categories of delivery methods, i. e., Design-Bid-Build and Design-Build (D-B), are well used in tunnel and underground structure constructions, with various levels of success. The contractual terms of these two delivery methods vary widely. The most common is the fixed price approach, although for tunneling, the unit price approach is the most suitable.

The traditional project delivery model is the design-bid-build. In this method, the client finances the project and develops an organization to deal with project definition, legal, commercial, and land access/acquisition issues. It appoints a consulting engineer under a professional services contract to act on its behalf to undertake certain design, procurement, construction supervision, and contract administration activities. The client places construction contracts following a competitive tendering process for a fixed price, with the selection are often based on low bid. This type of contract is simple, straight forward and familiar to public owners. However, in this process, the majority of construction risk is passed to the contractor, who often uses higher contingency factors to cover the potential construction risks. The client effectively pays the contractor for taking on the risk, irrespective of whether the risk actually transpires.

Whilst the traditional type of contract has its advantages, its shortfalls particularly on large infrastructure projects could be significant. Adversarial

Expansion reading 3-3

relationships between project participants, potential cost overruns, and delays to project schedules are by no means unusual. With the traditional contract forms, there is significant potential for protracted disputes over responsibility for events, to the detriment of the progress of the construction works. The client and the contractors are subject to different commercial risks and potentially conflicting commercial objectives.

The allocation of risk between the owner and the contractor will have a direct relationship to the contractor contingency as part of the contractor's bid. Therefore, it is important to identify a risk sharing mechanism that is fair and equitable and that will result in a reasonable contingency by the contractor and sufficient reserve fund to be provided by the owner to address unforeseen conditions. For example unforeseen conditions due to changes in the anticipated ground conditions are paid for by the owner if certain tests are met; while the means and methods are generally the contractor's responsibility and his inability to perform under prescribed conditions are risks to be absorbed by the contractor. With proper contracting form and equitable allocation of risks between the owner and the contractor, the contractor contingency, which is part of its bid price, will be reduced. Similarly, the owner's reserve fund will be used only if certain conditions are encountered, resulting in an overall lesser cost to the owner.

Most claims in tunnel construction are related to unforeseen ground conditions. Risk sharing is especially useful if anticipated conditions can be defined within certain limits and the client takes the risk if the limits are exceeded. Examples of conditions that might not be expected include soil behavior, the hardness of rock, flood levels, extreme winds and currents. Considerable use is currently made of Geotechnical Baseline Report(GBR)to define anticipated ground conditions in this way. The details of GBR will be presented in Chapter 4.

In practice, it is important to establish a selection process by which only qualified contractors can bid on tunneling projects, with fair contracts that would allocate risks equitably between the owner and the contractor, in order to have safe, on time, and high quality underground projects at fair costs.

3.5.4 Operation and maintenance cost planning

The cost of operation and maintenance of a tunnel may be related to the expense related to the duty operation and management, the maintenance of the structure and facilities, staff wages, fund repayment, etc. Operations are divided into three main areas, i.e., traffic and systems control, toll facility (if any) and emergency services, though not all of these are provided for any particular tunnel. The staff needed in these areas would vary according to the size of the facility, the location, and the needs. For 24-hour operation, staff would be needed for three shifts and weekends; weekend and night shifts would require sufficient staff to deal with traffic and emergency situations.

The day-to-day maintenance of the tunnel generally requires a dedicated operating unit. Tunnel cleaning and roadway maintenance are important and essential for safe operation of the tunnel. Special tunnel cleaning equipment may be required, especially for super long tunnels or tunnels with heavy traffics.

Mechanical, electrical, communication, ventilation, monitoring, and control equipment for the tunnel must be kept operational and in good working order, since faulty equipment could compromise public safety. Regular maintenance and 24-hour monitoring is essential, since failure of equipment such as ventilation, lights and pumps is unacceptable and must be corrected immediately. Furthermore, vehicle breakdowns and fires in the tunnel need immediate response.

Generally most operational work can be carried out during normal working hours including mechanical and electrical repair and traffic control. However, when the maintenance work involves traffic lane closure, such as changing lighting fixtures, roadway repairs, and tunnel washing, partial or full closure of the tunnel may be required, though this is usually done at night or weekends. The related cost should also considered in planning.

3.6 Risk analysis and management

Risk is always in companion to a tunnel project, especially to megaprojects[9]. Major risk categories include construction failures, public impact, schedule delay, environmental commitments, failure of the intended operation and maintenance, technological challenges, unforeseen geotechnical conditions, and cost escalation. And therefore, risk analysis and management is essential for a tunnel and underground project.

A risk analyses and management should be issued as early as possible in the project development. A risk register would identify potential risks, their probability of occurrence and their consequences. Then a risk management plan should be established to deal with the various risks either by eliminating them or reducing their consequences by planning, design, or by operational provisions. For risks that cannot be mitigated, provisions must be made to reduce their consequences and to manage them. An integrated risk management plan should be regularly updated to identify all risks associated with the design, execution and completion of the tunnel. The plan should include all reasonable risks associated with design, procurement and construction. It should also include risks related to health and safety, the public and to the environment.

Risk assessment is an important factor in selecting a tunnel alignment. Construction risks include risks related the construction of the tunnel itself, or related to the impact of the tunnel construction on existing facilities. Some methods of tunneling are inherently more risky than others or may cause excessive ground movements. Sensitive existing structures may make use of such construction methods in their vicinity undesirable. Therefore, it is important to conduct risk analysis as early as possible to identify potential risks due to the tunnel alignment and to identify measures to reduce or manage such risks.

The object of risk analysis and management in a tunnel project is to eliminate or control the related risk to an acceptable level. The main points of this issue will be presented in Chapter 18.

3.7 Comments on the planning of a tunnel project

The planning is the first stage of a tunnel project execution procedure. It may be finished in a short period for a short tunnel, which can be design and constructed with commonly used approaches. However, when a tunnel has the features of mega project, the planning of the tunnel project may be time consuming and challenge task. Various factors, such as cost, time schedule, techniques available, environmental restrict, public policy, may dominate the procedure of the project, since the resources that will be required to the project are gigantic. Table 3-8 presents some features of the Fehmarnbelt Fixed Link tunnel between Germany and Denmark, with special reference to the approximated main resources required to construct the Fehmarnbelt Fixed Link tunnel.

Table 3-8　Some features of the Fehmarnbelt Fixed Link tunnel[❶]

Items			Quantities
Period of proposal, planning and design			2007-2014
Features of the tunnel	Length of the immersed tunnel		17.6km
	Traffic capacity of the four lane motorway in two tubes		110 km/h
	Traffic capacity of twin track railway	Passenger rail traffic	200 km/h
		Freight rail traffic	140 km/h
Construction time schedule in plan			2014-2020
Cost of the project in plan			5.6 billion(EUR)
Resource requirements for construction	Concrete in tunnel elements		2.5 million m^3
	Reinforcement		300000 tonnes
	Ballast concrete		0.4 million m^3

❶ http://www.femern.com.

	Items	Quantities
Resource requirements for construction	Structural concrete, portal buildings, ramps and cut and cover	0.2 million m^3
	Total volume dredged from tunnel trench, access channel, harbours	19 million m^3
	Trench backfill volume	6.4 million m^3
	Total reclamation area	350 ha
	Total area Production site	120 ha

Note: 1 ha = 10^4 m^2.

Every coin has two sides. When a mega tunnel is well planned, a challenging factor may be utilized as resource, which has dual benefits of cutting costs and conserving natural resources. A recent tunnel project case history is the 57-km-long Gotthard Base Tunnel in Switzerland. The excavation of the long tunnel will produce huge quantities of excavated rock 13.3 million m^3. At the same time, it is becoming increasingly difficult quarrying high quality gravels in the Swiss midlands. Based on four years of research in laboratories and tests on construction sites, it was finally proved that the rock chips from the TBMs can indeed be used for producing high-quality concrete. Around 5 million tonnes of concrete aggregate is being converted from the high-quality excavated rock at the working site and the by-product of the conversion process, about 0.8 million tonnes of extremely fine slurry, can be used in the brick-making industry❶.

It is feasible, with the features of a proposed tunnel project being considered, the well planned project will give a broad understanding of how underground space can be utilized effectively, and ensure that any negative impacts of underground development are properly mitigated.

3.8 Critical thinking problems

C1: It is generally necessary to start a tunnel project from planning. Consider: ①What are the main functions of the planning of a tunnel project or why is the planning important for a mega project? ② What are the main factors to be considered in the planning of a tunnel project.

C2: Alternative analysis is critical to a mega tunnel project. Consider: ①Why is the route alternative analysis of a tunnel project important? ②What are the main factors to be considered in the alternative analysis?

❶ AlpTransit Gotthard Ltd. The new Gotthard Rail Link. https://www.alptransit.ch.

C3: During the planning stage of a tunnel project, the type and geometry of the tunnel profile should be preliminarily determined. What are the main factors to be considered to reach a reasonable scheme?

C4: A horseshoe shape cross section is often designed for a tunnel driven with conventional method, such as drill and blast method. For a planned mined tunnel, with composite lining system, consider: ①What are the parameters required to determined the inner profile of the final lining and the design excavation excavation profile of planned tunnel? ②Choose one group of the parameters, listed in Table 3-7, to draw the inner profile of the final lining.

C5: Of the tunnel project management, risk control is one of the tasks. Risk analysis and management are necessary and beneficial, especially for a mega tunnel project. Consider: ①What are the possible main sources of risks in a tunnel project? ②Is the risks of project-specific feature? ③What are the commonly used measures to control the risks of a tunnel project at the tunnel planning stage?

3.9 References

[1] ITA. Guidelines for the design of tunnels [J]. Tunnelling and underground space technology, 1988, 3(3): 237-249.

[2] ITA Working Group Conventional Tunnelling. General Report on Conventional Tunnelling Method: ITA REPORT No. 002 [R/OL]. http://tunnel.ita-aites.org/media/k2/attachments/public/ITA_Report_N2_WG19_P.pdf.

[3] Sargent J H. Channel tunnel project [J]. Journal of professional issues in engineering, 1988, 114(4): 376-393.

[4] Hung C J, Monsees J, Munfah N, et al. Technical manual for design and construction of road tunnels—civil elements [J]. US Department of Transportation, Federal Highway Administration, National Highway Institute, New York, 2009.

[5] Kuesel T R, King E H, Bickel J O. Tunnel engineering handbook [M]. Springer Science & Business Media, 2012.

[6] Parker H W. Planning and site investigation in tunneling [C]//Congresso Brasileiro de Túneis e Estructuras Subterrâneas, Seminário Internacional South American Tunneling. 2004.

[7] Flyvbjerg B, Bruzelius N, Rothengatter W. Megaprojects and risk: An anatomy of ambition [M]. Cambridge University Press, 2003.

[8] Flyvbjerg B, Holm M S, Buhl S. Underestimating costs in public works projects: Error or lie? [J]. Journal of the American planning association, 2002, 68(3): 279-295.

[9] Gransberg D D, Koch J E, Molennar K R. Preparing for design-build projects: A primer for owners, engineers, and contractors [C]. American Society of Civil Engineers, 2006.

[10] Andersen J, Iversen C Putten, E. V. Marine works operations and environmental considerations when building the Fehmarnbelt tunnel [J]. Terra et Aqua, 2012 (127).

4 Site Investigation in a Tunnel Project

4.1 Introduction

Expansion reading 4-1

A tunnel is built in ground, which may be composed of rocks or soils, or both of them. The geological units formations, around a tunnel or underground excavation and having influence on the stability of the tunnel or excavation during and after construction, are usually called surrounding rocks.

4.2 Site investigation in general

The required site investigation of a tunnel project vary with the project's features, such as the dimension of the planned tunnel, the complexity of the ground, and information available and engineering experience on the ground. The specific works of the site investigation will also vary with the project proceeding. The required efforts at any stage depend upon the complexity of the project and the investigation results will have a direct impact on risk mitigation and project cost[2,3]. The strategy for site investigations is to maximize the benefit in acquiring knowledge at a right project stage, in terms of investigation effort, responsibility, time schedule and cost.

4.2.1 Components of site investigations

Typical components of site investigations for a tunnel project include desk study, site reconnaissance, field investigations, laboratory tests, exploratory/investigation tunnel or shaft, as well as the presentation of the results.

4.2.1.1 Desk study

Expansion reading 4-2

Desk study is also called literature research and the collection of information available. After gaining a thorough understanding of the project requirements, all relevant information available on the project site should be collected and reviewed. Information may consist of: ①reports, regional maps, technical literature, aerial photographs about ground conditions; ②data related to neighboring and/or similar projects; ③existing land use and environmental factors; ④seismic, meteorologic and hydrological data.

For the tunnels in transportation system, there are many cases that a road line is planned nearly parallel to an existing railway line, or near to the railway line. The project information of the railway tunnels is helpful to the route alternative analysis and structure design by applying analogical method. One of the case histories is the application of the project information of the Qinling tunnel in railway line from Xi'an to Ankang in the planning and design of the Qinling Zhongnanshan Highway tunnel, which is nearly parallel to the railway tunnel, in China. The two tunnels, with two tubes each, are located within around 200 m wide corridor in plan.

4.2.1.2 Site reconnaissance

Site reconnaissance is generally performed by a group of geotechnical and geological experts, together with tunnel engineers, through site visiting, observation on key outcrops and structural mapping. The main points of site reconnaissance include the appreciation of the topographic, geologic and geotechnical conditions at the project site. Sometimes, the excavations, such as pit and trench, are used for discovering key outcrops for the development of geologic profile. In general, the following factors at the site should be defined by the field reconnaissance.

(1) *Stratigraphy and structures*: Identify geological formations and major structures, such as in terms of types, features and their distributions. It is also important to identify the document information to the site formations.

(2) *Existing slopes around planned tunnel portals*: Assess the stability factors of major slope-forming geologic units, in which the planned tunnel portals will be located. Natural slopes and any existing soil or rock slope failures should be evaluated and documented.

(3) *Ground and surficial water*: Estimate the general nature of surface water and groundwater regimes at the project site, and develop plan for future investigations.

(4) *Geologic constraints*: Identify adverse geologic conditions, which are unfavorable to project development plans and devise methods of investigating the degree of potential impact.

(5) *Explorations*: Based on the information and the kinds of samples that may be required, determine the type(s) of exploration that would best accomplish the project needs.

(6) *Drilling logistics*: Define the type, approximate locations and depths of geotechnical borings and determine approximate routes of access to each drilling location.

(7) *Environmental considerations*: Identify potential impacts that the project may have on subsurface materials, landforms, and the surrounding area, and

determine if project areas are governed by special regulations.

The reconnaissance plan and results are will be helpful to the following investigations.

4.2.1.3 Field investigations

Field investigations include the works of investigations, surveys and monitoring. The investigations can be grouped into direct investigations and indirect investigations. The former includes: trial pits, boring and sampling, in-situ testing (i.e., in-situ stress tests, Lugeon or permeability tests, etc.), while the latter is related to geophysical methods, airborne and remote sensing surveys. The main points of surveys are the information on topography, building conditions and foundations, utilities, environment and water wells. The monitoring may be used for assessing geotechnical and hydrological conditions, and the response of existing surface and underground structures to the project activities.

The main contents of field investigations for a tunnel project, in terms of providing knowledge to design and construction, will be presented in details in the followings.

4.2.1.4 Laboratory tests

The laboratory tests of the site investigation for a tunnel project may include: ①identification and classification tests, such as mineralogical and petrographic tests; ②rock/soil mechanical laboratory tests to define strength and deformability properties, time-dependent behavior, hardness, abrasivity; ③hydrochemistry test.

4.2.1.5 Exploratory/investigation(tunnel or shaft)

Expansion reading 4-3

A tunnel project is executed in various phases, such as through planning, feasibility studies, preliminary design, detailed design and construction, then putting into operation. The related site investigation is accordingly implemented in stages. The working procedure and the main points of each stage of site investigation are suggested in guidelines and handbooks, such as *Guidelines for the Design of Tunnels*[4] and *Strategy for Site Investigation of Tunneling Projects*[2], as shown in Figure 4-1.

With tunnel construction period as reference point, the site investigation may be conducted before and during construction. Before the construction, the site investigation is generally considered design phases, i.e., feasibility studies, preliminary/basic design, detailed/final design. In terms of design, the feasibility studies may include pre-feasibility, technical feasibility and conceptual design for some important and mega projects. Specific site investigations can be carried out during the construction stage, such as pre-face prospecting. The main tasks at each phase of the site investigation is briefly tabulated in Table 4-1.

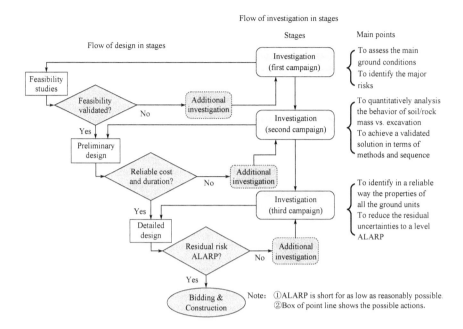

Figure 4-1 Relation of the site investigations and design stages of a tunnel project[2]

Table 4-1 Main tasks of site investigation

Project phase	Stages	Main tasks
Pre-design	Feasibility studies	To collect enough data to confirm the feasibility of the project.
Design	Preliminary design	To determine quantitative characteristics of the ground so that technical solutions may be developed to a point where reliable costs and duration.
Design	Detailed design	To reduce the residual uncertainty and inherent risks to a level as low as reasonably practicable.
Construction	and iterative design during construction	Mainly an iterative process of data collection, assessment, re-evaluation and redefinition of investigations.

The goals, expected results and related investigation means of site investigation are tabulated in Table 4-2 to Table 4-4 for the feasibility studies, preliminary design and detailed design, respectively. An iterative process of data collection, assessment, re-evaluation and redefinition of investigations may be required within the same design phase, since the information is accumulated with excution of the project. For example, in complex projects, where exploratory tunnel/shafts are required, the results from such investigations become available progressively during the preliminary and detailed design phases.

Table 4-2 Investigations for feasibility studies

Goals	Expected results	Investigation means
①To assess the general suitability of the location of the site/tunnel; ②To achieve the best interpretation of the ground conditions based on existing data; ③To assess the technical and economic merits of alternative alignments and their respective ground conditions; ④To make conceptual level estimates of cost and schedule; ⑤To identify major risks and/or fatal flaws and propose a Risk Register; ⑥To assess the ground conditions and risks, if any, which could determine the feasibility itself.	Geological and hydrogeological maps.	Regional topographic, geological, hydrogeological/groundwater, seismic hazard maps.
	Natural risk map, when appropriate.	Information from field surveys and/or adjacent similar projects.
	Longitudinal geological profile.	
	Longitudinal geotechnical and geomechanical profile with the qualitative identification of ground behavior classes and the identification of the major hazards (with qualitative assessment).	Geophysics may provide useful information.
		Limited site investigations to confirm extremely critical geological or groundwater conditions e.g., faults, karsts, aquifer, if needed.
	Preparation of Risk Register.	

Table 4-3 Investigations for preliminary design

Goals	Expected results	Investigation means
①To develop a 3D model of geological conditions which quantitatively characterizes the ground and the hydrogeological regime to a level that permits; ②To define the extent of the zone of influence and to estimate the impact this may have on adjacent structures or land forms; ③To quantitatively identify the risks, to assess their impact on the cost and potential delays to the schedule, and to decide on design measures to reduce the risk; ④To give a reasonable range of probable cost and duration; ⑤To assess the level of residual uncertainty so that the need for additional ground investigation can be identified; ⑥To provide information for the EIA, depending on the legal requirements.	Longitudinal geological profile (1/5000 to 1/2000).	Geophysics and boreholes at the portals and shafts.
	Longitudinal geotechnical-geomechanical profile (1/5000 to 1/2000) with the quantitative characterization of ground behavior classes and identified hazards.	Boreholes along the alignment.
		Water sources and groundwater monitoring.
		Laboratory tests.
	Geological and geotechnical cross-sections at the portals (1/500 to 1/200).	Outcrop and surface mapping.
	Geological and geotechnical sections at access/ventilation shafts.	In-situ stress measurements and permeability tests, when appropriate.
	Preliminary characterization of the hydrogeological regime.	Exploratory galleries / shafts, if needed.
	Update of Risk Register.	

Note: EIA is short for Environmental Impact Assessment.

In general, the earlier the exploration is made, the greater the potential for savings and for cheaper and better project. The practices in this field indicate that field mapping and desk studies are relatively inexpensive and yet they yield much information, such as in terms of the "knowledge vs. cost curve", as shown in Figure 4-2. In practice, during preliminary design phase, the general information should be available for: ①the selection of the most suitable alignment; ②preparation of an adequate and economical design, together with preliminary cost estimate; ③selection of appropriate construction methods with as low as reasonably practicable inherent risk, such as through predicting the behavior of the ground versus excavation method, determining the different temporary support classes and their distribution along the tunnel alignment, together with a possible range of variation, and designing the ancillary works and portals.

Table 4-4　Investigations for detailed design

Goals	Expected results	Investigation means
①to reduce the residual uncertainty to a ALARP level; ②to plan and execute the field and laboratory investigations to confirm the geotechnical and hydrogeological properties of the various ground units; ③to develop a reliable 3-dimensional geotechnical and hydrological model so that the construction method(s) can be validated and justified by calculation and detailed in terms of specifications; to obtain the full set of design parameters (including their potential range of variation) in order to finalize the dimensioning of all elements of the design; ④to achieve a final, accurate assessment of cost and duration; ⑤to update the risk register, re-assess the level of residual risk, and confirm mitigation measures in order to reduce the nonacceptable risks to a ALARP level; ⑥to identify requirements for the collection of additional geological, hydrogeological and geotechnical information during the construction phase, including the necessary full scale field trials, if any.	Longitudinal geological profile (1/2000 to 1/1000).	Additional boreholes both at the portals and along the alignment.
	Longitudinal detailed geotechnical and geomechanical profile (1/2000 to 1/1000) with the quantitative characterization of ground behavior and support classes, identified hazards, distribution of support sections and controls during construction.	Laboratory and field tests.
		In specific cases/locations, geophysics may provide useful information.
	Geological and geotechnical cross-sections at the portals, shafts and along the tunnel (1/200 to 1/100).	Excavation of experimental sections along the tunnel alignment, if needed.
	Definition of detailed set of design parameters and their variability.	Continue the monitoring program of water sources and groundwater.
	Detailed characterization of the hydrogeological regime.	
	Update of the Risk Register.	
	Specifications for investigations during construction.	

Note: ALARP is short for as low as reasonably possible.

During the detailed investigation phases, there is still a lot of important information to be obtained for tunnel design and risk management. The cost to obtain the information is generally higher than that in the previous stage, but it makes a significant contribution to improving the reliability of the knowledge of the ground conditions.

The site investigations during the construction phase may be carried out for the purposes[2] to: ① validate the 3-dimensional (3D) geotechnical and hydrological

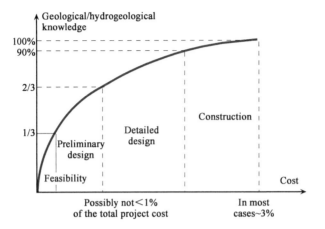

Figure 4-2　Schematic knowledge vs cost curve[2]

model using face mapping, investigations ahead of the tunnel face (e. g. , probe drilling, geophysics), TBM performance data, etc. ; ②monitor the surrounding rocks, ground support and groundwater behavior; ③systematically update the 3D ground model in order to predict ground behavior of the subsequent sections, and to adjust the design/construction method accordingly; ④analyze the excavated material and assess its potential reuse, or spoil influence on environments; ⑤ record or monitor the response of the nearby ground, facilities, structures/buildings to the construction activities.

4.2.2　Site investigation for tunnel design and construction

In terms of design, engineers promise that the designed structure will be safe and filling function requirements during its planned lifetime. Ground behavior models, based on the site investigation, are necessary for tunnel design in order to predict the behavior of a tunnel during the excavation and its lifetime. The stability of the tunnel partially or totally depends on the participating strength of the ground. The designer may begin by applying estimated and simple behavioral models. Adjustments based on actual experiences during the tunnel excavation, such as excavating the initial section in the same ground conditions or driving a pilot tunnel, will bring the model closer to reality and refine it. The interpretations of in-situ measurements and back analyses also may assist designers in making these adjustments. The functions of site investigation in the design flow-chart of a tunnel project is shown in Figure 4-3, considering the tunnel design is a step-by-step iterative process. The main points of the site investigation for tunnel design and construction are the following.

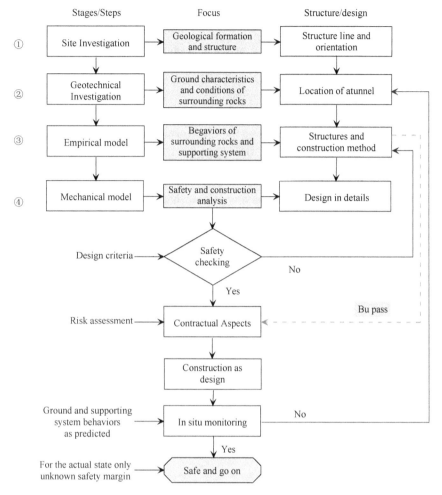

Figure 4-3   Site investigation in the design of a tunnel

At stage①, geology and site investigations must confirm the line, orientation, depth, etc., of the tunnel.

At stage②, ground probing and soil or rock mechanics must be applied to determine the ground characteristics, e.g., in-situ stresses, soil or rock strength, faults, groundwater conditions.

At stage③, experience and preliminary estimates or calculations are used for determining the cross-section required and the the excavation method, as well as the measures of surrounding rocks supporting and behavior controlling.

Based on the information from the stages①to③, tunneling engineer proposes a ground behavior model for tunnel design of each section along the planned tunnel, including deciding construction method, ground supporting and behavior controlling measures. Special attention should be paid to the sections of potential adverse geological condition.

The bypass in Figure 4-3 indicates that for many underground structures, as in self-supporting hard rock, no design models at all are applied, the design and construction can be managed by analogy approach. In such cases, past experiences alone may be sufficient. The construction is straight forward and generally as design.

For most of the tunnel project, where uncertainty is involved, risk assessment by the contractor as well as by the owner is needed at the time of contract negotiations. Risks may involve structural failures of the tunnel support and lining, functional failures after completion of work, and financial risks. It is beneficial to make the contract of the features of risk sharing.

In-situ monitoring can be applied only after the tunneling has begun. If the displacements stop increasing over time, it generally may be assumed that the structure is designed safely. Yet monitoring provides only part of the answer to the question of safety, for it does not tell how close the structure may be to sudden collapse or nonlinear failure modes. The results of field measurements and experiences during excavation may compel the engineer to change the design model by adjusting it to real behavior.

All of the elements of the procedure (Figure 4-3) should be considered an interacting unity, in terms of design model propose and modification. Inaccuracy in one part of the model will affect the accuracy of the model as a whole. And therefore, proper site investigation and reasonable application of the results are simultaneously required in this process.

4.2.3 Challenges of site investigation

It is almost impossible to predict all information through ordinary site investigation. The underground always poses some challenges to the geotechnical and tunnel design teams[1,5], as quoted in Figure 4-4.

The geotechnical engineer must appreciate the fact that such imprecision is contrary to the customary data precision to a designer. It is important that this uncertainty and its associated risk should be fully appreciated by all involved parties, especially the management and legal staff of the owner.

Owners and designers should evaluate risks in terms of cost and potential time schedule delays in the planning process and much more comprehensively. Preparation for this work should begin in the planning stage. The identification of the potential risks at this stage is important because it gives time for planners and decision makers to understand the uncertainties associated with the project. The proper measure may be applied to cope with the risks.

> ① Underground projects have vast uncertainty.
> ② The cost, and indeed feasibility, of the project is dominated by geology.
> ③ Every aspect of the geologic investigation for tunnels is more demanding than investigations for traditional foundation engineering projects.
> ④ Regional geology and hydrogeology must be understood.
> ⑤ Groundwater is the most difficult condition/parameter to predict and the most troublesome during construction.
> ⑥ The range of permeability is significantly greater than the range of any other engineering parameter (roughly 10^{-7} to 10^3 a factor of 10000000000).
> ⑦ Even comprehensive exploration programs recover a relatively minuscule drill core volume that is less than 0.0005 percent of the future excavated volume of the tunnel.
> ⑧ Engineering properties change with a wide range of conditions, such as time, seasons, rate and direction of loading, etc. ; sometimes drastically.
> ⑨ It is guaranteed that the actual stratigraphy, groundwater flow, and behavior observed during construction will be compared to your predictions.

Figure 4-4 Challenges possibly posing to geotechnical and tunnel design teams[1,5]

4.3 Site investigation in a tunnel project

4.3.1 In general

An important step in site investigation is to have an adequate subsurface exploration program. The number, depth, spacing, and type of borings, sampling, and testing in an exploration program are so dependent on site conditions and the project features, that no uniform rule can be established for a exploration plan. The general requirements of site investigation for a cut and cover tunnel and mined tunnel are briefly presented, respectively.

4.3.1.1 Cut and cover tunnels

For a cut and cover tunnel, the main focus of site investigation is on the information for the retaining wall design and the ground water control.

At retaining wall locations, borings should be taken at a maximum interval of one per 30 m of the wall with a minimum of two borings and as close to the wall alignment as possible. Retaining structures with tiebacks or soil nails will need an additional borings at the sites, where the anchor load zone is anticipated.

Borings should be continued to depths that all unsuitable founding materials are penetrated. The boring depth is generally referenced from the proposed length of the walls. During the boring, core loggings, in-situ test and test samples recovering are continuously required. For example, for the application of the Standard Penetration Test(SPT), split-spoon samples should be made within the upper 10 m of any boring, and then every 2 m down to 20 m. For cohesive soils, undisturbed samples should be obtained at 2-m intervals in at least one boring. Undisturbed samples should be obtained from more than one boring where possible. In-situ vane shear tests are recommended where soft clay, peat or other soft or highly organic materials are encountered. Representative undisturbed samples should be obtained in these materials for index testing and possible laboratory shear strength testing. Chemical tests are required on all new tunnel projects. As a minimum, one test should be conducted on each soil that will be in contact with structural steel elements.

For rocks, successive core runs should be made with the objective of obtaining the best possible core recovery. The RQD should be determined from rock cores. SPT's should be performed between core runs in soft rock, typically at 2-m intervals.

The works are varying with project and ground condition features. For example, in the case of a water crossing, samples of streambed materials and each underlying stratum should be obtained for determination of the median particle diameter, D_{50}, for scour analysis.

4.3.1.2 Mined tunnels

Tunnels are of linear features. The boring programs for the site investigation should concentrate in the areas of great potential difficulty. In general, borings should not be arbitrarily spaced at some given distance from each other along the alignment. Some of the areas requiring more detailed exploration are: portals, topographic lows above the tunnel, rocks with deep weathering potential, water bearing horizons and shear or fracture zones.

The geological conditions may vary greatly along the planned tunnel. The investigation criteria for tunnels should be established according to tunnel project feature. Good borings layout should produce a much complete picture of the geological situation and be effort and cost efficient. Some borings even do not reach the tunnel grade. Figure 4-5 give an example showing the poorly, fairly and well-located borings for site investigation, respectively. Alignments of drill holes are often adjusted with depth. The number of borings required is a function of the geological complexity of the area. The more complex in geological formations, the more borings are required. For example, soft ground can be encountered at any depth of cover in a tunnel due to large shear zones, hydrothermal alteration, poor cementation in sedimentary beds and so on. Some special investigation considerations are required due to excavation size and construction methods. The recommended tunnel depth depends on the likelihood that there may be strata at some depth that might permit cheaper or safer tunneling. Once a depth is selected, exploration depths of 1 to 2 times diameters below the invert of the tunnel are common.

4 Site Investigation in a Tunnel Project

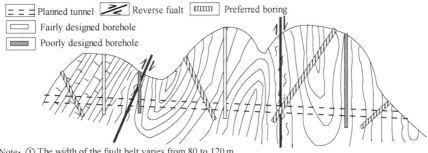

Note: ① The width of the fault belt varies from 80 to 120 m.
② The surrounding-rocks are mainly slightly weathered sedimentary rocks, with two sets of joints.

Figure 4-5 Sketch showing poorly, fairly and preferred boring layout along a planned tunnel

Field-developed cross-sections are useful to nearly all types of site-specific geotechnical investigations. Although the cross-sections is lack of the precision at the stages of planning, feasibility studies and preliminary design, they provide an excellent opportunity to observe the project area and apply the scientific method in resolving surface and subsurface relationships and other field observations. Another advantage is that the sections are developed and plotted during the reconnaissance, so discrepancies can be identified and resolved immediately.

The cross-sections developed from the site investigation generally condense the relevant data for the ground description and for the tunnel design along the tunnel axis. For example, from the borehole results and associated testing it is possible to obtain a geological section along the tunnel and in a plan showing the layering, i.e., a geological model along the route of the tunnel (Figure 4-6). It may also be useful to conduct some shorter angled drillings to help develop the stratigraphic section and produce a more complete picture (Figure 4-5). This is important if the strata are highly dipping and relatively thin, as the vertical boreholes are not effective.

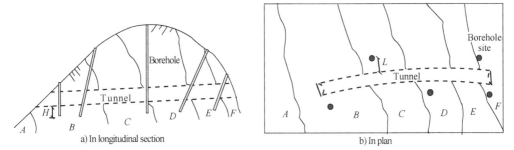

Figure 4-6 Possible borehole locations for a mountain tunnel

4.3.2 Subsurface exploration methods

Methods of observing the rock mass below the surface, obtaining samples, and determining physical properties of the soils and rock include test pits, trenching (particularly for locating faults and slide planes), borings, and cone penetration tests(CPT) or SPT and drilling.

4.3.2.1 Test pits and trenches

Test pits and trenches are the simplest methods of discovering subsurface outcrops. They consist of excavations performed by hand, backhoe or dozer. Test pits and trenches offer the advantages of speed and ready access for sampling. They are hampered by limitations of depth and cannot be used in soft soils or boulders.

4.3.2.2 Soil drilling

A wide variety of equipment is available for performing borings and obtaining soil samples. The method used for advancing the boring should be compatible with the soil and groundwater conditions to assure that soil samples of suitable quality are obtained. For example, below the groundwater level, drilling fluids are often needed to stabilize the sidewalls and bottom of the boring in soft clays or cohesionless soils. Soil borings are usually advanced with solid stem continuous flight, hollow-stem augers or rotary wash boring methods.

4.3.2.3 Rock drilling

Where borings must extend into rock formations, rock drilling and sampling procedures are required. The use of ISRM Commission on Standardization of Laboratory and Field Tests[1] guidelines are recommended for detailed guidance for rock drilling, coring, sampling, and logging of boreholes in rock masses.

4.3.2.3.1 Types of core drilling

Types of core barrels may be single-tube, double-tube, or triple-tube. The standard is a double-tube core barrel, which offers better recovery by isolating the rock core from the drilling fluid stream and consists of an inner and outer core barrel, as shown in Figure 4-7. The inner tube can be rigid or fixed to the core barrel head and rotate around the core or it can be mounted on roller bearings, which allow the inner tube to remain stationary while the outer tube rotates.

The diameter of borehole and diameter of core vary among regions. The size of about 75 mm in borehole diameter is the most frequently used for engineering explorations. In general, a larger core size will produce greater recovery and less mechanical breakage.

Clear water is commonly used as the drilling fluid in rock coring. If drilling mud is required to stabilize collapsing holes or to seal zones the type of drilling mud should be designed. Drilling mud will clog open joints and fractures, which adversely affects permeability measurements and piezometer installations.

---

[1] http://www.isrm.net/gca/? id = 177.

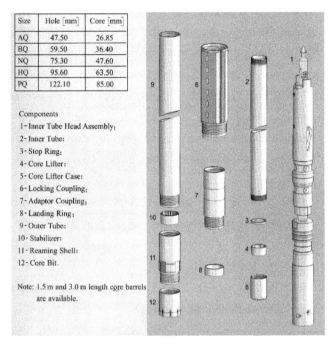

Figure 4-7　Geological Q series core barrels[1]

4.3.2.3.2　Observation during core drilling

For core drilling, the following parameters should be described in details during drilling cores logging.

(1) Drilling rate/time. The drilling rate should be monitored and recorded on the boring log in the units of minutes per 0.3 m. Only time spent advancing the boring should be used for determining the drilling rate.

(2) Core photographs. Cores in the split core barrel should be photographed immediately upon removal from the borehole. A label should be included in the photograph to identify the borehole, the depth interval and the number of the core runs.

(3) Optical borehole explorations, if possible. Optical explorations are ideal not only for monitoring and petrographic assessment of borehole walls but also for measuring the spatial position of layer and fissure surfaces and for determining the width of fissure openings and the degree of planar separation. At present, optical borehole explorations are possible in several ways[2].

(4) Rock classification. The rock type and its inherent discontinuities, joints, seams, and other facets should be documented. Rock classification and other information should be recorded for rock core.

---

[1] http://www.alibaba.com/product detail/Geological-Q-Series-Core-Burrels-GBBQ_442061518.html.
[2] Geotechnical Testing, GIF, 2004. http://www.gif-ettlingen.de/engl/html/geotechnical_testing.html-2008-8-25.

(5) Recovery. The core recovery is the length of rock core recovered from a core run, and the recovery ratio is the ratio of the length of core recovered to the total length of the core drilled on a given run, expressed as either a fraction or a percentage. Core length should be measured along the core centerline. When the recovery is less than the length of the core run, the non-recovered section should be assumed to be at the end of the run unless there is reason to suspect otherwise (e.g., weathered zone, drop of rods, plugging during drilling, loss of fluid, and pieces of core). Non-recovery should be marked, such as NCR (no core recovery), on the boring log.

(6) Core handling and labeling. Rock cores from geotechnical explorations should be properly stored and handled, since they may be used later for examining or test sampling.

4.3.2.3.3 Rock quality designation (RQD)

The Rock Quality Designation (RQD) index was developed by Deere in 1964 and well accepted after the publication in 1967[6,7]. The RQD now is a tool of quantitative estimate of rock mass quality from drill core logs. RQD is defined as the percentage of intact core pieces longer than 100 mm in the total length of core, in terms of quantity. The core should be at least NX size (54.7 mm in diameter) and should be drilled with a double-tube core barrel. The correct procedures for measurement of the length of core pieces and the calculation of RQD are presented in Figure 4-8.

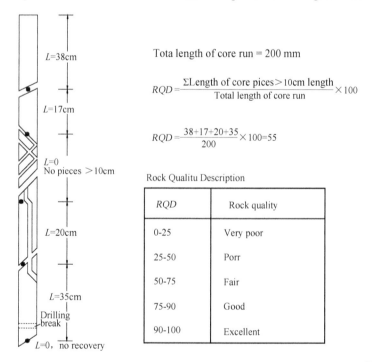

Figure 4-8 Procedure for measurement and calculation of RQD[7]

The *RQD* is an index of rock quality in that problematic rock that is highly weathered, soft, fractured, sheared, and jointed typically yields lower *RQD* values. Thus, *RQD* is simply a measurement of the percentage of "good" rock recovered from an interval of a borehole. The reported experience[7] indicates that cores with diameters both slightly larger and smaller than *NX* may be used for computing *RQD*. However, the smaller core sizes are discouraged because of a higher potential for core breakage and loss.

RQD is intended to represent the rock mass quality in situ. When using diamond drill core, care must be taken to ensure that fractures, which have been caused by handling or the drilling process, are identified and ignored when determining the value of *RQD*. *RQD* is a directionally dependent parameter and its value may change significantly, depending upon the borehole orientation. The value of *RQD* measured from drill core can be an unreliable predictor of discontinuity frequency due to that: ①it relies on the ability of the logger to discriminate between natural fractures and those caused by drilling disturbance; ②it may be influenced by the strength of the rock material being drilled; ③good core recovery depends on the drilling practice used; ④in an anisotropic rock mass, the measured *RQD* will be influenced by drilling orientation.

Expansion reading 4-4

4.3.3 Geophysical methods

Geophysical exploration is used for subsurface exploration, such as through the measurement of seismic (elastic) waves, using surface-wave methods and/or downhole methods, and electromagnetic surveys (magnetometer, resistivity, and ground-penetrating radar). Exploration geophysics is the practical application of physical methods (such as seismic, gravitational, magnetic, electrical and electromagnetic methods) to measure the physical properties of grounds to detect the measurable physical differences between ground units in properties. Takahashi[9] grouped geophysical methods into two categories: land geophysics and borehole geophysics, which are conducted from the ground surface, in or between boreholes, respectively.

Geophysical exploration methods can provide subsurface profile information, such as the depth to bedrock, depth to groundwater, and the extent of granular/rock areas, peat deposits, or subsurface anomalies. Geophysical exploration methods are one of the rapid and economical means of supplementing subsurface borings and test pits. These exploration techniques are most useful for extending the interpretation of subsurface conditions beyond what is determined from small diameter borings. A limitation of these techniques is that no samples are recovered.

The reliability of geophysical exploration results can be limited by several factors, including the presence of groundwater, nonhomogeneity of soil stratum thickness, gradation or density, and the range of wave velocities within a particular stratum. It is difficult to distinguish subsurface strata that have similar physical properties, with geophysical exploration methods. In practice, geophysics are considered a secondary exploration method to drillings. The field data should be interpreted by an expert, such as with the information from conventional boring.

Geophysical exploration methods commonly used for transportation engineering purposes include: seismic refraction and reflection, electrical resistivity, and Ground Penetrating Radar(GPR) methods.

4.3.3.1 Seismic refraction and reflection

The seismic refraction and reflection methods rely on the fact that shock waves typically travel at different velocities through different materials. The times required for an induced shock wave to travel from the energy source to vibration detectors (geophones) after being refracted or reflected by the various subsurface materials are measured. The measured seismic velocities are used for interpreting certain material properties and the thickness of the units that comprise the subsurface profile. Seismic refraction is limited to profiles in which velocities increase with depth. Seismic investigations can be performed from the surface or from various depths within borings. Seismic refraction and reflection may be effective to detect geological units, as shown in the Table 4-5.

Table 4-5 **Applications of seismic refraction and reflection methods in site investigation**

Method	Seismic refraction	Seismic reflection
Applications	Map bedrock topography; Map faults in bedrock; Estimate depth to groundwater; Estimate bedrock rippability; Evaluate rock properties, etc.	Map subsurface stratigraphy; Map lateral continuity of geologic layers; Map buried paleo-channels; Map faults in sedimentary layers; Map basement topography, etc.

QR code 4-1

Seismic reflection is often used in site investigation, especially at the early stage of design and pre-face prospecting. A seismic reflection profile provides a visualization of subsurface boundaries where acoustic impedance (or velocity) contrasts occur as the reflection events. However, in order to obtain the geological section, the seismic reflection profile should be interpreted in comparison with surface and borehole geological information as well as well logs if available. The QR code 4-1 below shows an example of the interpreted depth section indicating faults from the results of a seismic reflection survey profile, where the rock layers and the buried faults are clearly indicated in terms of the distributions of geological units.

4.3.3.2 Electrical resistivity

Electrical resistivity method is based on the differences in electrical conductivity between subsurface strata. When an electric current is passed through the ground between electrodes, the resistivity of the subsurface materials is measured and correlated to material types. This method is often used for detecting a geological unit, which is full of water or of high water content. A good case history is the application of electrical resistivity method in the site investigation of the Hsuehshan tunnel in Taiwan. The results of the resistivity image profiling (RIP) survey for the Hsuehshan tunnel, where the investigation depth is about 900 m, are shown in QR code 4-2[10]. The results of the RIP technique provided the tunnel engineers to know where the groundwater was. Before dealing with the more complex types of surveys, RIP provide briefly at the resistivity values of some rocks and soils that is rich-jointed. At the site, the joint zone, fault zone and fracture zone are rich of groundwater. However, experience from this project showed that it's important to use the RIP result, together with geological prognosis and drilling.

QR code 4-2

4.3.3.3 Ground penetrating radar

The velocity of electromagnetic radiation is dependent upon the material through which it is traveling. GPR uses this principle to analyze the reflections of radar signals transmitted into the ground by a low frequency antenna. Signals are continuously transmitted and received as the antenna is towed across the area of interest. The interpreted results yield a profile of the subsurface material interfaces. The depth of signal penetration is limited, e.g., about 50 m. And therefore, the GPR is usually used for detecting the soils layers near to ground surface or the distribution of the bedrock topography, as shown in Figure 4-9.

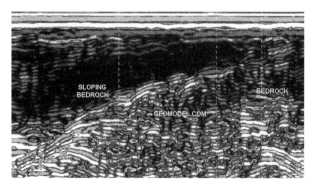

Figure 4-9 Distribution of the bedrock topography in GPR map[❶]

---

❶ http://www.geomodel.com.

4.3.4 In-situ tests

In-situ tests are useful for projects, where obtaining representative samples suitable for laboratory testing is difficult, such as those involving soft clays, loose sands and/or soils below the water table. Some benefits of in-situ tests include avoidance of soil disturbance (and changes in stress) and large scale testing when size requirements exceed common sample dimensions. Common in-situ tests are performed in conventional drilled borings, whereas specialized tests require a separate borehole or different insertion equipment.

4.3.4.1 Tests for soils investigations

Several in-situ tests are often used for defining the geostratigraphy and obtain direct measurements of soil properties and geotechnical parameters. The tests include: standard penetration (SPT), cone penetration test (CPT), piezocone (CPTu), flat dilatometer (DMT), pressuremeter (PMT), and vane shear (VST). Each test applies different loading schemes to measure the corresponding soil response in an attempt to evaluate material characteristics, such as strength and/or stiffness. Figure 4-10 depicts these various devices and simplified procedures mainly used for soil investigations, the details are presented in Mayne et al[11].

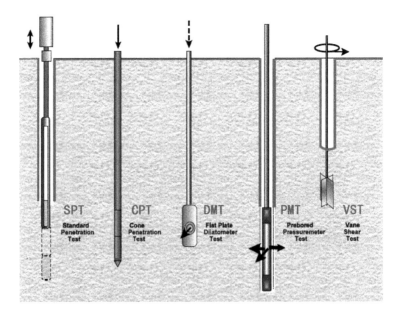

Figure 4-10 Common in-situ tests for geotechnical site characterization of soils[11]

4.3.4.2 Permeability tests

Hydraulic conductivity, also referred to as permeability, is the measure of the rate of water seepage in grounds or through samples. In-situ hydraulic conductivity test results are more representative of the actual geotechnical material property than test results obtained in laboratory, since the former is performed on the entire hydraulic system, with all its variables including joints, sand seams, and small fissures, while the laboratory tests samples are so small that they not be truly representative of field conditions. Pumping test, slug test, and Lugeon test are commonly used in-situ methods.

One means of determining the in-situ permeability is conducted in test boreholes. Three types of tests are in common use: falling head, rising head, and constant water level methods. One of the pre-conditions for the tests is that the permeability is low enough to permit accurate determination of the water level in the boreholes.

In the falling level test, the flow is from the hole to the surrounding soil and there is danger of clogging of the soil pores by sediment in the test water used. This danger does not exist in the rising level test, where water flows from the surrounding soil to the hole, but there is the danger of the soil at the bottom of the hole becoming loosened or quick if too great a gradient is imposed at the bottom of the hole. The rising level test is generally the preferred test. In those cases where the permeability is so high as to preclude accurate measurement of the rising or falling water level, the constant level test is used.

4.3.4.2.1 Falling water level method

In this test, the casing is filled with water, which is then allowed to seep into the soil. The rate of drop of the water surface in the casing is observed by measuring the depth of the water surface at 1, 2 and 5 minutes after the start of the test and at 5-minute intervals thereafter. These observations are made until the rate of drop becomes negligible or until sufficient readings have been obtained to satisfactorily determine the permeability.

4.3.4.2.2 Rising water level method

Rising water level method consists of bailing the water out of the casing and observing the rate of rise of the water level in the casing at intervals until the rise in the water level becomes negligible. The rate is observed by measuring the elapsed time and the depth of the water surface below the top of the casing. The intervals at which the readings are required will vary somewhat with the permeability of the soil. The total elapsed time for the readings should longer than 5 minutes. A rising level test should always be followed by a sounding of the bottom of the hole, such as with drill rods, to determine whether heaving of the bottom has occurred.

4.3.4.2.3 Constant water level method

In constant water level method, water is added to the casing at a rate sufficient to maintain a constant water level at or near the top of the casing for a period of no less than 10 minutes. The data recorded should consist of the amount of water added to the casing at 5 minutes after the start of the test, and at 5-minute intervals thereafter until the amount of added water becomes constant.

During rock drilling investigation, the hydraulic conductivity of rock mass usually testes with the Lugeon test, which is named after Maurice Lugeon, a Swiss geologist who first formulated the method in 1933. The Lugeon test, also called Packer test, is widely used for estimating the average hydraulic conductivity of rock mass. Basically, the Lugeon test is a constant head permeability type test carried out in an isolated part of a borehole. The results provide information about hydraulic conductivity of the rock mass including the rock matrix and the discontinuities. The Lugeon value is defined as the loss of water in liters per minute and per meter borehole at an over-pressure of 1 MPa.

The unit Lugeon value can quantify the water permeability of bedrock and the hydraulic conductivity resulting from fractures. Considering a homogenous and isotropic condition, one Lugeon will be equal to 1.3×10^{-7} m/s [1]. Contrary to the continuum media, the hydraulic conductivity of the rock mass is very much influenced by the rock discontinuities. Therefore, the Lugeon value could represent not only the conductivity but also the rock jointing condition. Typical range of Lugeon values and the corresponding rock permeability conditions are indicated in Table 4-6.

Table 4-6　Conditions of rock mass discontinuities associated with different Lugeon values [2]

Lugeon value	Conductivity classification	Rock discontinuity condition
<1	Very low	Very tight
1-5	Low	Tight
5-15	Moderate	Few partly open
15-50	Medium	Some open
50-100	High	Many open
>100	Very high	Open closely spaced or voids

4.3.4.2.4　Slug Tests

As an alternative to aquifer pump tests, slug tests can be preformed to determine the hydraulic conductivity of the formation in the immediate vicinity of a monitoring well. During a slug test a small volume of water is suddenly removed or added to the well and the rise and/or fall of the water level is measured. Also, a

---

[1] Fell R, MacGregor P, Stapledon D, Bell G. 2005. Geotechnical Engineering of Dams. Taylor & Francis. London. UK.

[2] Camilo Quiñones-Rozo, Lugeon test interpretation, revisited, http://ussdams.com/proceedings/2010Proc/405-414.pdf.

solid body can also be submerged into the well to displace the water. In this method, enough water is removed or displaced to raise or lower the water level, such as by about 10 to 50 cm. No pumping, or piezometers are needed, and the slug test can be completed within a few minutes, or at the most a few hours. And also slug tests are less expensive and time consuming, they are more popular than pump tests. However they should not be regarded as a substitute for conventional pump tests. Slug tests only determine the characteristics of a small volume of aquifer material surrounding the well, and this volume may have been disturbed during well drilling and construction.

In the Slug tests, the water level in the well is assumed to return to the equilibrium level exponentially. The forces of inertia in both the aquifer and the well are neglected. In deed, the effect of the inertia is significant in highly permeable aquifers or in deep wells[11].

4.3.4.3 In-situ stress measurement

In-situ stresses are essential conditions for tunnel design and analysis. Knowledge of the in-situ stress state in rock mass is essential for the proper planning and design of tunnel, such as to optimize tunnel alignment. As a tunnel may be built in greater depth, stress conditions can have adverse influence on the tunneling.

The in-situ stress in rock mass can be determined by direct measurement. Since the 1950's, significant researches have bee done on the methods of in-situ stress measurement[16]. Recently, one of the the new methods of in-situ stress measurement is the use of Kaiser effect❶ gauging, with the Kaiser effect change point being determined by means of acoustic emission monitoring.

With the test results, the general situation of the in-situ stress of the world and some regions are proposed accordingly. Stress estimation using the existing in-situ stress database and the observations of rock behavior around openings is an alternative way, as the the indirect techniques[12]. Routine stress mapping by rock engineering and geological method will provide additional on-going valuable information, and will be of benefit to tunnel stability evaluation. Back analysis of stresses is also valuable provided that suitable deformation monitoring data are available.

---

❶ Kaiser effect is an absence of acoustic emission at loads not exceeding the previous maximum load level when material undergoes repetitive loading patterns. Discontinuities created in material during previous steps do not move or expand until former stress is exceeded resulting in Kaiser effect. http://dict.youdao.com/eng/kaiser%20effect/(2014-9-23).

4.3.4.3.1 Rock stress prior to excavation

Generally, the in-situ stress in rock mass prior to excavation is the resultant of the following components[13]:

(1) *Gravitational stresses*. The magnitude of the total vertical stress may be identical with the magnitude of the gravitational vertical component. The horizontal stress induced by gravity may constitute only a small part of the total vertical stress.

(2) *Topographic stresses*. The topography can influence considerably on the rock stress situation when the surface is not horizontal. In high valley sides, where underground excavations often are located, the stress situation will often be dominated by the topographic effects. Near the surface in such cases, major stress will be more or less parallel to the slope of the valley, and minor stress will be approximately perpendicular to the slope.

(3) *Tectonic stresses*, which are responsible for incidents like faulting and folding. Plate tectonics are the main cause of tectonic stress. Due to the existence of tectonic stresses, the total horizontal stress is in most cases much higher than the horizontal stress induced by gravitation. This is particularly the case at shallow and moderate depths. The relationship between horizontal and vertical stress may vary within very wide ranges, and hence underlines the importance of measurements.

(4) *Residual stresses*, also referred to as remanent stresses, are stresses, locked in the rock material during earlier stages of its geological history, such as contraction during the cooling of a rock melt (magma), the compression of tectonic movement and overburden. Measured vertical stresses, which are abnormally high, are often explained by residual stresses.

The occurrence of major weakness zones may influence considerably on the in-situ stress situation. As many such zones are only able to transform shear stress to a minor extent, the principal stresses will often be parallel or perpendicular to the zones, respectively. Hence, a tunnel through a major weakness zone may experience extensive rock spalling on one side of the zone, while the stresses are reduced to a moderate or low level on the other side.

4.3.4.3.2 Methods of in-situ stress measurement

The in-situ stress in rock mass can be determined by direct or indirect measurement. Most of the methods of in-situ stress measurement involve the observation of a change in deformation or stress resulting from a change in the geometry of an opening in the rock, and the subsequent calculation of the stresses from those measured changes. In tunnel engineering, the most widely used methods are: hydraulic fracturing method, strain relief method and flat jack stress measurement technique.

The strain relief method and flat jack stress measurement technique can only be applied around surface or excavation face. For deep tunnel site investigation, most of the methods are associated with boreholes as the "opening" in the rock mass and hydraulic fracturing method is often used during survey drilling.

For the borehole-based methods, borehole deformation (strain) and stress change may be measured. Methods that measure borehole deformation (strain) are common types. As the closed form theoretical solution relating the elastic stresses and strains around the borehole or borehole end is known, stresses are calculated from these deformations or strains using elastic theory[16].

Expansion reading 4-5 [18-22]

The application of the borehole-basedmethods requires high quality diamond core drilling, with associated equipment, facilities and devices and a special device for centering of the pilot hole. Success with the method is also dependent on good quality rock such that intact cores at least 300 mm long can be obtained. Since elastic theory is used for the calculation of the in-situ stresses from the measured deformations, it is important that no failure of the rock occurs around the borehole, since the failure might lead to non-elastic behavior. The elastic material parameters of the rock material also need to be obtained from laboratory testing.

4.4 Ground characteristic parameters

Geotechnical materials description is essential so that users of the information can properly understand and interpret the subsurface conditions. Material descriptions are mainly based on the visual-manual method, which uses visual observations and simple manual index tests to estimate the physical and behavioral properties of the material. Material classifications are based on more detailed, visual-manual observations and inspections, as well as the results of specific laboratory and in-situ tests. Material classifications, and information obtained during the subsurface explorations, also have significant importance in resolving claims disputes. It is therefore necessary for the method of reporting this data to be standardized. Records of subsurface explorations should follow a specified format as presented in certain guidelines or codes.

4.4.1 Geotechnical material description

4.4.1.1 Soil

Soil classifications are based on the distribution and behavior of fine-grained (passing No. 200 sieve) and coarse-grained (retained No. 200 sieve) soil constituents. Visual examination and simple manual tests are used for identifying soil characteristics. Manual tests for dry strength, dilatancy, toughness and plasticity indicate the type of fine-grained soil. Organics are generally identified by their color, odor and spongy feel. The following items are usually included on the exploration logs: soil name and classification, color plasticity, moisture, consistency/relative density, texture, cementation, structure, as well as its origin.

4.4.1.1.1 Soil type

To describe a soil, the geotechnical engineer should determine whether the soil is predominantly fine or coarse grained. A mixed-grained soil, which contains both fine and coarse-grained constituents, is categorized by determining its predominant engineering behavior. The estimated percent and type of organic material present should be included as part of the visual sample description. The percentage of organics or any other constituent in a sample can be estimated visually by comparing the sample to standardized volume percentage charts. Based on the percentage of organics present, the material classification is specified accordingly.

The parameters to describe fine-grained soils include dilatancy, dry strength, toughness, dispersion and plasticity. Coarse-grained soils are described based on an estimation of particle-size distribution. If the soil contains no discernable fines, then the soil is described as "clean". Where the secondary or additional constituent is fine-grained, the term "clay" or "silt" is selected based on the predominant plasticity characteristics from tests.

Organics can generally be identified by their distinctive dark color and by their spongy feel. Fresh, wet organic soils usually have a distinctive odor of decomposed organic matter.

4.4.1.1.2 Color

The color of a soil is of minor importance except to provide a clue as to its origin, presence of organics, or for correlation with adjacent boreholes.

4.4.1.1.3 Plasticity

Plasticity is a significant indicator property for cohesive soils. Field estimates of plasticity should be based on dry strength and toughness tests, as described in Table 4-7. An accurate measurement of plasticity is typically made in laboratory by means of the Atterberg limits test, to confirm visual-manual soil descriptions.

Table 4-7　Characteristics of silt and clay [11]

Characteristics	Silt	Clay
Dilatancy (Movement of water in voids due to shaking) None Slow Rapid	Rapid reaction. Water appears on the surface to give a livery appearance when shaken. Squeezing the soil causes water to disappear rapidly.	Sluggish or no reaction. Surface of the samples remain lustrous. Little or no water appears when hand is shaken. Sample remains lustrous during squeezing.

continue

Characteristics	Silt	Clay
Dry strength(cohesiveness in dry state) None Low Medium High Very high	None to low. Even oven-dry strength is low. Powder easily rubs off surface of the sample. Little or no cohesive strength—will crumble and slake readily.	High to very high. Exceptionally high if oven-dry. Powder will not rub off the surface. Crumbles with difficulty. Slakes slowly.
Toughness(plasticity in moist state) Low Medium High	Plastic thread has little strength. Dries quickly. Crumbles easily as it dries below plastic range. Seldom can be rolled to 1/8″ thread without cracking.	Plastic thread has high strength. Dries slowly. Usually stiff and tough as it dries below plastic range. Can easily be rolled to 1/8″ thread without cracking.
Dispersion(settlement in water)	Settles out of suspension in 15 to 60 minutes. (Sands settle in 30 to 60 seconds).	Settles in several hours or days, unless it flocculates(rapidly precipitates out in small clumps).
Visual inspection and feel	Only coarsest individual silt grains are visible to the naked eye. Feels slightly gritty when rubbed in fingers. Dries quickly and dusts off easily.	Individual grains cannot be observed by the naked eye. Feels smooth and greasy when rubbed in fingers. Dries slowly and does not dust off; must be scraped off.
Bite test	Gritty feeling between the teeth, does not stick to the teeth.	No gritty feeling between the teeth; tends to stick to the teeth.

4.4.1.1.4 Moisture

A visual estimation of the relative moisture content of a soil sample is usually required for the field description. The in-situ moisture content of a soil should be described as dry, damp, moist or wet(Table 4-8). An accurate natural moisture contents is determined in the laboratory from soil samples.

Table 4-8 Moisture designations of soils[11]

Term	Field Identification
Dry	Absence of moisture. Dusty. Dry to the touch.
Damp	Soil has moisture. Cohesive soils are below plastic limit(BPL) and usually moldable.
Moist	Grains appear darkened, but no visible water. Silt/clay will clump. Sand will bulk. Soils are often at or near plastic limit.
Wet	Visible water on larger grain surfaces. Sand and cohesionless silt exhibit dilatancy. Cohesive silt/clay can be readily remolded. Soil leaves wetness on the hand when squeezed. "Wet" indicates that the soil is much wetter than the optimum moisture content and above plastic limit.

4.4.1.1.5 Relative density and consistency

Relative density refers to the degree of compactness of a coarse-grained soil. SPT N-values (blows per foot) are typically used for defining the relative density and consistency. Nonplastic silt soils that exhibit the general properties of a granular soil are given a relative density description.

4.4.1.1.6 Texture

Texture refers to the actual size, shape and gradation of the constituent grains, such as following the gradation definitions in Table 4-9. Where the soil is predominantly coarse grained, the grain nature, such as the parent rock type(s) and hardness (soft or hard), weathering condition (fresh, weathered or decomposed), should be described.

Table 4-9 Gradation categories of soils[11]

Gradation Term	Description	Example
Well-graded	Full range and even distribution of grain sizes present	Coarse to fine sand with trace silt
Poorly-graded	Narrow range of grain sizes present	Fine to medium sand
Uniformly-graded	Consists predominantly of one grain size	Clean fine sand
Gap-graded	Within the range of grain sizes present, one or more sizes are missing	Fine sand with some coarse gravel

4.4.1.1.7 Cementation

Cementation is the bonding of grains by secondary minerals (e.g., calcium carbonate, iron oxide) or degradation products (e.g., clay). The presence of calcium carbonate cementation can be detected by its reaction to hydrochloric acid. The relative degrees of cementation of undisturbed soil are defined, such as in Table 4-10.

Table 4-10 Relative degrees of cementation of undisturbed soils[11]

Term	Field Identification
Weak	Crumbles or breaks with handling or light finger pressure and rubbing.
Moderate	Crumbles or breaks with considerable finger pressure and rubbing.
Strong	Will not crumble or break with finger pressure and rubbing.

4.4.1.1.8 Structure

Structural features include stratifications, varves, lenses, fissures, seams, slickensides, striations, blocky structure, relict rock structure, and voids (root or worm holes, cavities). The thickness, frequency, and inclination of these features should be noted. Table 4-11 presents criteria for describing structures.

Table 4-11 Criteria for describing soil structure[11]

Term	Field Identification
Stratified	Alternating layers of varying material or color with layers at least 0.25-inch (0.62 mm).
Laminated	Alternating layers of varying material or color with layers less than 0.25-inch (0.62 mm).
Fissured	Contains shears or separations along planes of weakness.
Blocky	Cohesive soil that can be broken down into small angular lumps which resist further breakdown.
Lensed	Inclusion of small pockets of different soils, such as small lenses of clay; note thickness.
Homogeneous	Same color and appearance throughout.

4.4.1.1.9 Sensitivity

Sensitivity refers to the significant loss of strength when a fine-grained soil is remolded. Sensitivity is a function of the primary structure of the soil, strength of grain bonding and water content. A sensitive soil may be highly compressible as the natural moisture content is above its liquid limit. A measure of the sensitivity (S_t) is the ratio of the undrained shear strength (S_u), or unconfined compressive strength (q_u) of the undisturbed sample to that of the remolded sample.

4.4.1.1.10 Origin

The origin of the soil is generally interpreted based on knowledge of geologic site conditions and the soil description. A generic name for soil origin may be provided at the end of the soil description in parentheses, such as alluvium, colluvium, terrace deposit, decomposed and fill. All soils should be examined to see if they contain nonnative materials indicative of man-made fills. Manmade items such as glass, brick, dimensioned lumber, concrete, metal, plastics; plaster in fills should be listed in each of the soil descriptions. The limits (depth range) of fill material should be determined and identified at each exploration location.

4.4.1.2 Rock

Rock descriptions for engineering purposes are to present intact and in-situ characters of the rock mass. Intact character is of the description of the intact rock, in terms of its origin, mineralogical makeup, texture, degree and nature weathering, and strength. In-situ character, mainly presenting structures in rock mass, includes the nature and orientation of its constituent interlocking blocks, plates, or wedges formed by bounding discontinuities such as bedding, foliation planes, fractures, joints, shear planes, shear zones and faults.

4.4.1.2.1 Intact character

Expansion reading 4-6

The main points of intact rock material descriptions include formation name, rock name, color, degree of weathering, relative hardness, structure/discontinuities (joints, stratification, faults, separation, infilling, continuity), core recovery and *RQD*, other characteristics, such as mineralization, slaking, unit weight, discontinuity surface condition and voids.

4.4.1.2.2 In-situ character

The in-situ character of rock mass is one of the parameters, which may control how the surrounding rocks perform in tunneling. The intact strength rarely controls the stability of an excavation in structurally controlled rock mass, in which the structural discontinuities divide nearly all rock bodies into discrete planar, wedge or block-shaped pieces. For example, one joint set may yield slabs, two intersecting joint sets may yield wedges, and three or more intersecting joint sets may yield blocks or highly fragmented rock. The stability or movement along these discontinuities usually control the stability of rock mass. Most structural information is obtained from outcrops. Additional information can be obtained from borings and excavation faces.

4.4.2 Soil properties interpretation

Soil properties can be deduced from their types and the measured data from laboratory and in-situ tests. The assessment of data quality and the selection of properties are vital to design, especially where multiple methods are available to obtain a property. The soil properties are usually presented in terms of: ①subsurface stratigraphy; ②in-situ stress state; ③deformation properties; ④shear strength; ⑤hydraulic conductivity.

Expansion ading 4-7[23-28,31-41]

These topics are often indicated as: properties interpretation in a profile, in-situ stress state, consolidation properties of soil, stiffness properties, soil shear strength and hydraulic conductivity properties, respectively. The presentations in details for these items are in the Expansion reading 4-7.

4.4.3 Rock mass properties interpretation

The intact blocks of rock between the discontinuities are usually sufficiently strong, except in the case of weak & porous rocks. The engineering behavior of most rock mass under loading is determined primarily by the structures or discontinuities and the planes of weakness. For the tunnels in rocks, the characteristics of the intact rock and the features of structures should be approximated in site investigations.

4.4.3.1 Rock types and properties

The properties of the rocks are related to their types, structures and weathering grade. In general, more attention should be paid to weak rocks and the ones related adverse geology.

4.4.3.1.1 Unit weight of rocks

The specific gravity of solids (G_s) of different rock types depends upon the minerals present and their relative percentage of composition. Very common minerals include quartz, feldspar, calcite, chlorite, mica, and the clay mineral group. The bulk value of these together gives a representative average value of $G_s \approx 2.7 \pm 0.1$.

The unit weight of rock is needed in calculating overburden stress profiles in problems involving rock slopes and tunnel support system design. The unit weight is an indicator of the degree of induration of the rock unit and is thus an indirect indicator of rock strength. Strength of the intact rock material tends to increase proportionally to the increase in unit weight. Representative dry unit weights for moderately weathered to unweathered rocks are shown in Table 4-12. The wide range in unit weights of shale, sandstone, and limestone represents effect of variations in porosity, cementation, grain size, depth and age.

Table 4-12 Representative range of dry unit weights[11]

Rock Type	Unit Weight Range[kN/m³]	Rock Type	Unit Weight Range[kN/m³]
Sandstone	18-26	Schist	23-28
Limestone	19-27	Gneiss	23-29
Shale	20-25	Granite	25-29
Basalt	20-30		

The dry unit weight (γ_{dry}) can be calculated from the bulk specific gravity of solids and porosity (n) according to: $\gamma_{dry} = \gamma_{water} G_s (1-n)$, Where the unit weight of water is $\gamma_{water} = 9.81$ kN/m³. The saturated unit weight (γ_{sat}) of rocks can be expressed: $\gamma_{sat} = \gamma_{water} [G_s(1-n) + n]$. The unit weight decreases with increasing porosity, as presented in Figure 4-11, for some rocks and a selected range of specific gravity values.

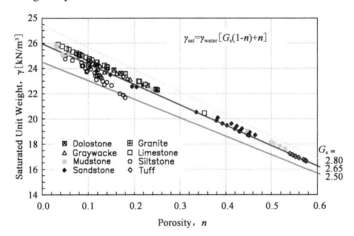

Figure 4-11 Saturated rock unit weight in terms of porosity and specific gravity[11]

4.4.3.1.2 Strength of rocks

The compressive strength serves as an initial index on the competency of intact rock. The strength magnitude implies excavatability issues and stability of rock mass.

4.4.3.1.2.1 Compressive strength

The compressive strengths of intact rocks are obtained from tests conducted in laboratory on samples. The stress (σ)-strain (ε)-strength behavior of intact rock specimens can be measured during a uniaxial compression test, or triaxial test. The peak stress of the σ-ε curve during unconfined loading is the uniaxial compressive strength, σ_u. The value of σ_u can be estimated from the point load index (I_s) that is easily conducted in the field. Representative values of compressive strengths for a variety of intact rock specimens are given by Goodman[45], as quoted in Table 4-13. In this database, the compressive strengths ranged from 11 to 355 MPa. A wide range in compressive strength can exist for a particular geologic rock type, depending upon porosity, cementation, degree of weathering, formation heterogeneity, grain size angularity and degree of interlocking of mineral grains. The compressive strength also depends upon the orientation of load application with respect to microstructure(e. g. ,foliation and bedding planes). For schist rock, the uniaxial compressive strength of this material varies by a factor of about 5, depending upon the direction of loading, and the rock mass properties are dependent upon the strength parallel to schistosity rather than that normal to it[46].

Table 4-13　Representative measured parameters on intact rock specimens[45]

Intact Rock Material	Uniaxial compressive strength, σ_u [MPa]	Point Load Index, T_0 [MPa]	Young's modulus E_R (MPa)	Poisson's Ratio, ν	Ratio σ_u/T_0	Ratio E_R/σ_u
Baraboo Quartzite	320.0	11.0	88320	0.11	29.1	276
Bedford Limestone	51.0	1.6	28509	0.29	32.3	559
Berea Sandstone	73.8	1.2	19262	0.38	63.0	261
Cedar City Tonalite	101.5	6.4	19184	0.17	15.9	189
Cherokee Marble	66.9	1.8	55795	0.25	37.4	834
Dworshak Dam Gneiss	162.0	6.9	53622	0.34	23.5	331
Flaming Gorge Shale	35.2	0.2	5526	0.25	167.6	157
Hackensack Siltstone	122.7	3.0	29571	0.22	41.5	241
John Day Basalt	355.0	14.5	83780	0.29	24.5	236
Lockport Dolomite	90.3	3.0	51020	0.34	29.8	565
Micaceous Shale	75.2	2.1	11130	0.29	36.3	148
Navajo Sandstone	214.0	8.1	39162	0.46	26.3	183
Nevada Basalt	148.0	13.1	34928	0.32	11.3	236
Nevada Granite	141.1	11.7	73795	0.22	12.1	523
Nevada Tuff	11.3	1.1	3649.9	0.29	10.0	323
Oneota Dolomite	86.9	4.4	43885	0.34	19.7	505
Palisades Diabase	241.0	11.4	81699	0.28	21.1	339
Pikes Peak Granite	226.0	11.9	70512	0.18	19.0	312
Quartz Mica Schist	55.2	0.5	20700	0.31	100.4	375
Solenhofen Limestone	245.0	4.0	63700	0.29	61.3	260
Tavernalle Limestone	97.9	3.9	55803	0.30	25.0	570
Taconic Marble	62.0	1.2	47926	0.40	53.0	773
Statistical Results — Mean	135.5	5.6	44613	0.29	39.1	372.5
Statistical Results — S. Dev.	93.7	4.7	25716	0.08	35.6	193.8

An estimate of the compressive strength of rock can be made using available correlation information based on the point load strength test. It has been found that, on average, the uniaxial compressive strength, σ_c, is about 20 to 25 (average is approximately 24) times the point load strength index. Tests on many different types of rock, however, show that the ratio can vary between 15 and 50[11]. The point load strength test is not recommended for very weak rocks, with uniaxial compressive strength less than 25 MPa.

In the point load strength test, if the fracture runs across some other plane or if the loading points sink into the rock surface causing excessive crushing or deformation, the test result should be rejected[47].

When laboratory tests results are not available, Table 4-14, quoted from Hoek[46] for a field estimates of uniaxial compressive strength, will be useful to approximating σ_u.

Table 4-14　Field estimates of uniaxial compressive strength[46]

Grade	Term	Uniaxial Comp. Strength [MPa]	Point Load Index [MPa]	Field estimate of strength	Examples
R6	Extremely strong	>250	>10	Specimen can only be chipped with a geological hammer	Fresh basalt, chert, diabase, gneiss, granite, quartzite
R5	Very strong	100-250	4-10	Specimen requires many blows of a geological hammer to fracture it	Amphibolite, sandstone, basalt, gabbro, gneiss, granodiorite, limestone, marble, rhyolite, tuff
R4	Strong	50-100	2-4	Specimen requires more than one blow of a geological hammer to fracture it	Limestone, marble, phyllite, sandstone, schist, shale
R3	Medium strong	25-50	1-2	Cannot be scraped or peeled with a pocket knife, specimen can be fractured with a single blow from a geological hammer	Claystone, coal, concrete, schist, shale, siltstone
R2	Weak	5-25	* *	Can be peeled with a pocket knife with difficulty, shallow indentation made by firm blow with point of a geological hammer	Chalk, rocksalt, potash
R1	Very weak	1-5	* *	Crumbles under firm blows with point of a geological hammer, can be peeled by a pocket knife	Highly weathered or altered rock
R0	Extremely weak	0.25-1	* *	Indented by thumbnail	Stiff fault gouge

Note: * Grade according to Brown.　* * Point load tests on rocks with a uniaxial compressive strength below 25 MPa are likely to yield highly ambiguous results.

4.4.3.1.2.2 Influence of sample size

In a uniaxial test, the specimen should be selected to provide a length/diameter ratio of at least 2 but less than 2.5 and the ends must be smooth, parallel and perpendicular to the long axis of the core. It is also noted that for a given rock mass, as the size of the tested rock core increases, the uniaxial compression strength decreases, due primarily to the fact that as the specimen size increases there is a higher likelihood of encountering discontinuities in the rock core. Hoek and Brown[17] have suggested that the uniaxial compressive strength σ_{cd} of a rock specimen with a diameter of d mm is related to the uniaxial compressive strength σ_{c50} of a 50 mm diameter sample by the relationship: $\sigma_{cd} = \sigma_{c50} \times \left(\dfrac{50}{d}\right)^{0.18}$, as shown in Figure 4-12, which implies that as more fractures are included in the test samples the strength reaches a constant value.

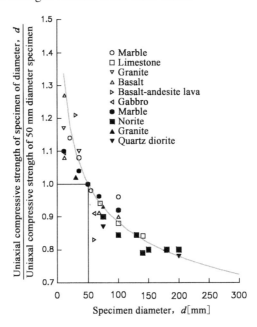

Figure 4-12   Influence of specimen size on the strength of intact rock[17]

4.4.3.2   Rock mass structure

The properties of rock mass are different from that of intact rocks. This is mainly because the structures in the rock mass. The term rock mass is the total in-situ medium containing the intact rock elements, discontinuities, and their structures. Rock masses are of discontinuous, heterogeneous and anisotropic engineering properties.

The properties of discontinuities in rock mass were well studied in the period of 1960s-1970s. And then it is well accepted that the features and properties of the discontinuities may have a strong influence on the engineering behavior of rock masses[42]. The document "Suggested methods for the quantitative description of discontinuities in rock masses" prepared by the Commission on Standardization of Laboratory and Field Tests, International Society for Rock Mechanics, subsequently referred to as the ISRM Commission, are guideline of this field. The main parameters, used for describing the properties of rock mass discontinuities, include orientation, spacing, persistence, roughness, aperture and filling. The main points of these parameters are briefly presented here. The parameters usually used in the site description of discontinuities are shown in Figure 4-13.

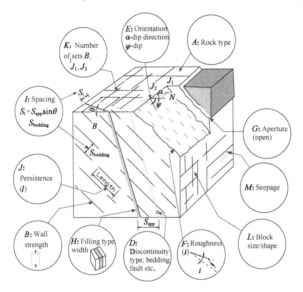

Figure 4-13 Factors & parameters affecting geologic mapping of rock mass features[44]

4.4.3.2.1 Orientation

Orientation shows the occurrence of a discontinuity in space, and is described by the dip of the line of maximum declination on the discontinuity surface measured from the horizontal, and the dip direction or azimuth of this line, measured clockwise from true north, such as orientation data in the form of dip direction (three digits) ∠dip (two digits), 035∠70 (or 035/70). The orientations of discontinuities relative to the faces of excavations have a dominant effect on the potential for instability due to rock block falling or slip on the discontinuities. The mutual orientations of discontinuities will determine the shapes of the blocks, into which the rock mass is divided.

4.4.3.2.2 Spacing

Spacing is the perpendicular distance between adjacent discontinuities. The spacing of discontinuities determines the sizes of the blocks making up the rock mass. Table 4-15 gives the terminology used by the ISRM[98].

Table 4-15 Classification of discontinuity spacing[99]

Description	Spacing[mm]	Description	Spacing[mm]
Extremely close spacing	<20	Wide spacing	600-2000
Very close spacing	20-60	Very wide spacing	2000-6000
Close spacing	60-200	Extremely wide spacing	>6000
Moderate spacing	200-600		

The mechanism of deformation and failure can vary with the ratio of discontinuity spacing to excavation size. Rock mass permeability also varies with discontinuity spacing.

Discontinuity spacing is also a factor used in many rock mass classification schemes. In classifying rock masses for engineering purposes, it is common practice to quote values of RQD to quantify discontinuity spacing. Priest & Hudson[43] found that an estimate of RQD could be obtained from discontinuity spacing measurements made on core or an exposure using the equation $RQD = 100e^{-0.1\lambda}(0.1\lambda + 1)$, where $\lambda \approx 1/x_a$ is the mean discontinuity frequency of a large discontinuity population and x_a is the mean spacing of a given discontinuity spacing value.

4.4.3.2.3 Persistence

Persistence is used for describing the extent or size of a discontinuity within a plane. It can be crudely quantified by observing the trace lengths of discontinuities on exposed surfaces. The ISRM[99] uses the most common or modal trace lengths of each set of discontinuities measured on exposures to classify persistence according to Table 4-16. The persistence of discontinuities will have a major influence on the shear strength developed in the plane of the discontinuity and on the fragmentation characteristics, cavability of an excavation and permeability of the rock mass.

Table 4-16 Classification of discontinuity persistence[98]

Description Modal	Trace length[m]	Description Modal	Trace length[m]
very low persistence	<1	high persistence	10-20
low persistence	1-3	very high persistence	20
medium persistence	3-10		

4.4.3.2.4 Roughness

Roughness is a measure of the inherent surface unevenness and waviness of the discontinuity relative to its mean plane. The wall roughness of a discontinuity has a potentially important influence on its shear strength, especially in the case of undisplaced and interlocked features (e.g., unfilled joints). The importance of roughness declines with increasing aperture, filling thickness or previous shear displacement.

When the properties of discontinuities are being recorded from observations made on either drill core or exposures, it is usual to distinguish between small-scale surface irregularity or unevenness and larger-scale undulations or waviness of the surface(Figure 4-14). Each of these types of roughness may be quantified on an arbitrary scale of, say, one to five. The classification of the roughness of discontinuities suggested by ISRM[98], as illustrated in Figure 4-15, may be used for describing roughness on two scales: the small scale(several centimeters) and the intermediate scale(several meters).

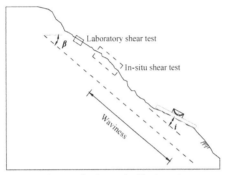

Note: Waviness can be characterised by the angle i.

Figure 4-14 Different scales of discontinuity roughness sampled by different scales of shear test[98]

Class	Sketch	Description
I	Stepped rough	rough or irregular, stepped
II	smooth	smooth, stepped
III	slickensided	slickensided, stepped
IV	Undulating rough	rough or irregular, undulating
V	smooth	smooth, undulating
VI	slickensided	slickensided, undulating
VII	Planar rough	rough or irregular, planar
VIII	smooth	smooth, planar
IX	slickensided	slickensided, planar

Note: Profile lengths are in the range 1 to 10 m; Vertical and horizontal scales are equal.

Figure 4-15 Typical roughness profiles and suggested nomenclature[98]

4.4.3.2.5 Aperture

Aperture is the perpendicular distance separating the adjacent rock walls of an open discontinuity, in which the space is filled with air or water. Aperture is thereby distinguished from the width of a filled discontinuity (Figure 4-16). Large apertures can result from shear displacement of discontinuities having appreciable roughness, from outwash of filling materials (e. g., clay), from solution or from extensile opening. The apertures of discontinuities usually vary widely along the orientation of the discontinuity.

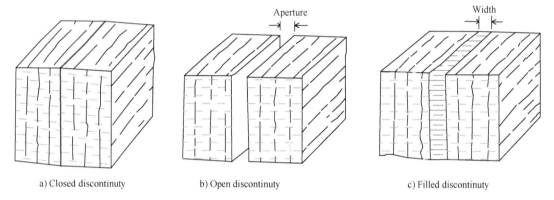

a) Closed discontinuty b) Open discontinuty c) Filled discontinuty

Figure 4-16　The aperture of open discontinuities and the width of filled discontinuities[98]

The width of aperture and its spatial variation will have an influence on the shear strength of the discontinuity, and also on the permeability or hydraulic conductivity of the discontinuity and of the rock mass. For laminar flow, the hydraulic conductivity of a single discontinuity with plane, parallel sides is given[42] by $k = \dfrac{ge^3}{12v}$, where k = hydraulic conductivity [m/s], g = acceleration due to gravity [m/s^2], e = discontinuity aperture [m] and v = kinematic viscosity of the fluid [m^2/s] (= 1.01 × 10^{-6} m^2/s for water at 20 ℃). If e = 0.05 mm, for example, k = 1.01 × 10^{-7} m/s for water at 20 ℃, but if e is increased to 0.5 mm, k is increased by a factor of 1000 to 1.01 × 10^{-4} m/s.

4.4.3.2.6 Filling

The commonly seen filling materials include calcite, chlorite, clay, silt, fault gouge, breccia, quartz or pyrite. Filling materials will have a major influence on the shear strengths of discontinuities. With the exception of those filled with strong vein materials (calcite, quartz, pyrite), filled discontinuities will generally have lower shear strengths than comparable clean, closed discontinuities. The behavior of filled discontinuities will depend on a wide range of filling materials properties, which mainly depend on the followings: ① mineralogy of the filling material, especially low-friction materials such as chlorite and illite; ② grading or particle size; ③ water content and permeability; ④ previous shear displacement; ⑤ wall roughness; ⑥ width of filling; ⑦ fracturing, crushing or chemical alteration of wall rock.

4.4.3.3 Shear strength of jointed rock mass

For the rock mass with joints or fractures, the shear strength behavior of infillings, the rough ness of discontinuities are critical to the deformation of fractured rock masses. Direct shear testing method (laboratory or in situ) is commonly used for evaluating the shear strength of infillings and discontinuity surfaces (Figure 4-16). Shear strength for fractured rock mass can also be evaluated with back analysis methods or semi-empirically methods based on rock types and rock mass classification.

4.4.3.3.1 Mohr-Coulomb materials

For tunnel design analyses, intact rock and jointed rock masses are preliminarily assumed to be a Mohr-Coulomb material, of which the shear strength of the rupture surface is expressed in terms of the cohesion intercept (c) and the friction angle (φ). When an effective normal stress σ' acts on the rupture surface, the shear stress (τ) developed is: $\tau = c + \sigma' \tan\varphi$. It is clear, as the shear strength approximating method, $\tau = c + \sigma' \tan\varphi$, is applied, the occurrence and condition of the rupture surface will present a significant influence on the magnitude of the rock shear strength, especially when the gravity effect is considered in design analysis. Figure 4-17 illustrates the relationship between the typical shear strength parameters of the rupture surface for five geological conditions, considered as five modes [44,52].

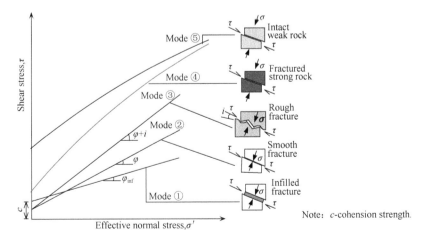

Figure 4-17 Sketch showing the modes of shear strength along a rock rupture surface

Mode ①-Infilled discontinuity: If the infilling is a weak clay or fault gouge, the friction angle of the infilling is likely to be low, and there may be some cohesion if the infilling is undisturbed. Alternatively, if the infilling is strong (e.g. a healed surface) then the cohesive strength and the friction angle may be large.

Mode ②-Smooth discontinuity: A smooth, clean discontinuity in the parent rock will have little or no cohesion, and the friction angle will be that of the parent rock.

Mode ③-Rough discontinuity: Clean, rough discontinuity surfaces will have little or no cohesion, and the friction angle will be made up of the rock material friction angle (φ), and a component related to the roughness, or asperities, of the surface.

Mode ④-Fractured rock mass: The shear strength of a fractured rock mass, in which the rupture surface lies partially on discontinuity surfaces and partially passes through intact rock, can be expressed as a curved envelope. At low normal stresses where individual fragments may move and rotate, the cohesion is low but the friction angle is high because the sliding surface is effectively rough and may involve non-frictional material. In addition, at the low normal stresses, the response may be dilative. At higher normal stresses, dilation is reduced and crushing of the rock fragments begins to take place and the friction angle reduces. The shape of the strength envelope is related to the degree of fracturing and the strength of the intact rock.

Mode ⑤-Weak intact rock: The shear strength of weak, but intact, rock is governed by the combination of cohesion and parent rock friction. Some rock comprises finegrained material that has a low friction angle. However, due to its intact nature, the cohesion can be higher than that of a closely fractured well hard rock.

Expansion reading 4-8[48-51]

4.4.3.3.2 Shear strength of discontinuities

If discontinuities are identified within a rock mass, it will be necessary to evaluate the friction angle and cohesion intercept along the potential rupture surface to perform design analyses. The investigation should focus on the information on the discontinuity characteristics, water occurrence, as well as the effect of water on the properties of the infilling.

4.4.3.3.3 Post-failure behavior of rock mass

Expansion reading 4-9[51-60]

The geotechnical materials around tunnel or excavation may be partially in plastic state. For design analysis, such as with numerical method, it is often required to study the progressive failure of surrounding rocks or retained soils. The parameters of the post-peak or post-failure are therefore sometimes required in design analysis. These parameters can be conducted by laboratory tests or by empirical methods. At present, no definite rules for dealing with this problem is well accepted. Based upon experience in numerical analysis of a variety of practical problems, Hoek[46] suggested using the post-failure characteristics illustrated in Figure 4-18 as a starting point. Three types of rock masses, i. e., very good quality hard rock masses, average and very poor quality rock masses, are shown as a typical example, respectively. The typical properties of both peak strength and post-peak characteristics for these three types rock mass are exemplified by Hoek and Brown[62], as shown in Table 4-17.

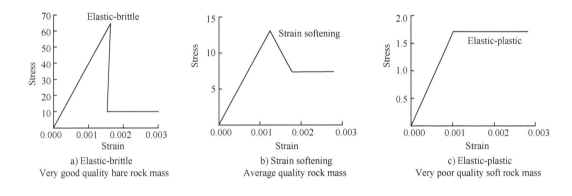

Figure 4-18 Post failure characteristics for different quality rock masses[46]

Table 4-17 Typical properties of rock masses[62]

Parameters		Magnitude of rock masses		
		very good quality	average	very poor quality
Intact rock strength	σ_{ci}	150 MPa	80 MPa	20 MPa
Hoek-Brown constant	m_i	25	12	8
Geological Strength Index	GSI	75	50	30
Friction angle	φ'	46°	33°	24°
Cohesive strength	c'	13 MPa	3.5 MPa	0.55 MPa
Rock mass compressive strength	σ_{cm}	64.8 MPa	13 MPa	1.7 MPa
Rock mass tensile strength	σ_{tm}	-0.9 MPa	-0.15 MPa	-0.01 MPa
Deformation modulus	E_m	42000 MPa	9000 MPa	1400 MPa
Poisson's ratio	ν	0.2	0.25	0.3
Dilation angle	α	$\varphi'/4 = 11.5°$	$\varphi'/8 = 4°$	0
(Post-peak characteristics)				
Friction angle	φ_f'	38°	-	-
Cohesive strength	c_f'	0	0	0
Broken rock mass strength	σ_{fcm}	-	8 MPa	1.7 MPa
Deformation modulus	E_{fm}	10000 MPa	5000 MPa	1400 MPa

4.4.3.4 Rock deformation modulus

4.4.3.4.1 Intact rock modulus

The deformation modulus of intact rock, E_R, can be evaluated by uniaxial compression tests on pieces of rock core obtained from drilling using a diamond core barrel, as shown in Figure 4-19. With the axial and diameter strain measured, the stress-strain behavior of the intact rock can be approximated in the laboratory[44].

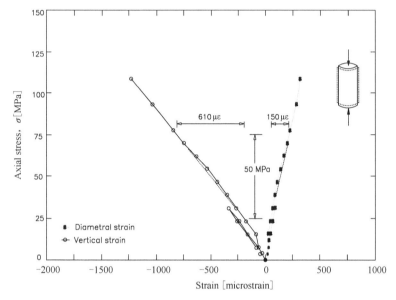

Figure 4-19 Axial and diametral stress-strain curves for intact rock under uniaxial compression[44]

Wyllie[44] compiled the results of uniaxial compression tests carried out to determine the elastic constants of a variety of rock types, as quoted in Table 4-18. The Young's modulus for intact rock is significantly rock formation specific, with the magnitude of 0.1 to 100 GPa.

Table 4-18 Typical elastic constants for intact rock[44]

Rock Type	Young's modulus, E [GPa]	Poisson's Ratio, ν	Reference
Andesite, Nevada	37.0	0.23	Brandon(1974)
Argillite, Alaska	68.0	0.22	Brandon(1974)
Basalt, Brazil	61.0	0.19	Ruiz(1966)
Chalk, USA	2.8	-	Underwood(1961)
Chert, Canada	95.2	0.22	Herget(1973)
Claystone, Canada	0.26	-	Brandon(1974)
Coal, USA	3.45	0.42	Ko and Gerstle(1976)
Diabase, Michigan	68.9	0.25	Wuerker(1956)
Dolomite, USA	51.7	0.29	Haimson and Fairhurst(1970)

continue

Rock Type	Young's modulus, E [GPa]	Poisson's Ratio, ν	Reference
Gneiss, Brazil	79.9	0.24	Ruiz(1966)
Granite, California	58.6	0.26	Michalopoulos and Triandafilidis(1976)
Limestone, USSR	53.9	0.32	Belikov(1967)
Salt, Ohio	28.5	0.22	Sellers(1970)
Sandstone, Germany	29.9	0.31	Van der Vlis(1970)
Shale, Japan	21.9	0.38	Kitahara et al. (1974)
Siltstone, Michigan	53.0	0.09	Parker and Scott(1964)
Tuff, Nevada	3.45	0.24	Cording(1967)

Expansion reading 4-10

Expansion reading 4-11

4.4.3.4.2　Rock mass modulus

It is noted that the deformation of surrounding rocks will be controlled by the deformation modulus of the related rock mass but not by the deformation modulus of intact rock. The magnitude of the Young's modulus from intact rock may be much larger that that from overall rock mass. The selection of rock mass deformation modulus in a design generally is through two ways. First, the empirical method, which is based on the parameters either RMR (Rock Mass Rating) or RQD. If the design analyses predict deformations that exceed target values for a specific structure, then it may be appropriate to perform in-situ tests to develop a more accurate assessment of the in-situ modulus.

4.4.4　Selecting soil and rock properties

During surrounding rocks behavior analysis, the results of both in-situ and laboratory tests for soils and rocks properties may be used as parameters. In general, the values of the parameters should be properly evaluated before a value is specified for a soil or rock mass properties. This means choosing a design value for a specific parameter, which should be conducted according to a well designed procedure, such as the flow chart of Figure 4-20. In Figure 4-20, the aspects include recommendations for planning and executing a subsurface investigation, such as selecting drilling and sampling techniques, sampling intervals and number of samples, developing the field and laboratory testing programs, and conducting and interpreting the field and laboratory tests. At the end of this flow chart, one of the key aspects related to design is specifically identified as "Select Material Properties and Finalize Subsurface Model". At this stage, a designer potentially finds out following two questions to be solved:①there are inconsistencies between the results of selected tests;②there is a significant variability in a selected parameter within the assumed relatively "uniform" subsurface model?

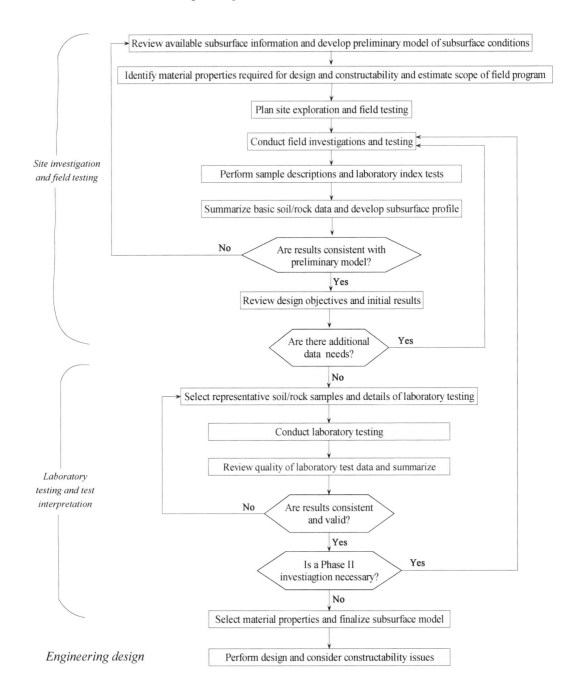

Figure 4-20　Soil and rock property selection flowchart[54]

To resolve these two issues, engineers need assess the available data and ultimately apply judgment to select the appropriate values for the design. In practice, it is not an easy task to define what "good or bad" judgment in a decision making procedure. Some suggestions are presented by Sabatini et al. [54]

4.4.4.1 Resolving inconsistencies

Inevitably, in practice, there are inconsistencies between test results on the properties of surrounding rocks. One of the common facts is the variability of data. This may be because of the inherent variability of the geotechnical material itself, the variations due to laboratory and field testing conditions, and the variation inherent in engineering property correlations. It is often that the calculated/estimated results will not be entirely consistent. Sabatini et al. [54] provides a step-by-step summary of how the engineer may resolve these differences, through: data validation, historical and performance comparison, correlation calibration, and assessing influence of test complexity.

The ultimate goal of this activity is to confirm that the data are valid for the test considered and to provide a summary of valid data that is representative of the surrounding rocks at the site. In many cases, after considering all of these steps, it may be found that the actual anticipated range of properties is much less than originally reported. However, it is also common to find that the results of this work will indicate that all of the data are apparently valid and, thus, the material at the site is inherently variable; this by itself is a significant finding.

4.4.4.2 Estimating variability of parameters

In practice, variability (or uncertainty) may be characteristic of the geotechnical materials. The variability includes the combination of both inherent material variability and testing variability. The inherent material variability should also be assessed, such as by the application of judgment, to estimate the variability for each of the selected parameters that will be considered in the design. In this way, the approaches, such as experience and statistics, are helpful to estimate the parameters variability.

Duncan[92] presented an accumulation of experience regarding the coefficient of variation for several soil parameters, as presented in Table 4-19. The values for the coefficient of variation are defined as the standard deviation divided by the average value. These values can be used as reference ranges for test parameters.

Table 4-19 Values of coefficient of variation for geotechnical properties and in-situ tests[92]

Measured or interpreted parameter value	Coefficient of variation, $V(\%)$
Unit weight, γ	3-7
Buoyant unit weight, γ_b	0-10
Effective stress friction angle, φ'	2-13
Undrained shear strength, s_u	13-40
Undrained strength ratio, s_u/σ_v'	5-15
Compression index, C_c	10-37
Preconsolidation stress, σ_p'	10-35

continue

Measured or interpreted parameter value	Coefficient of variation, $V(\%)$
Hydraulic conductivity of saturated clay, k	68-90
Hydraulic conductivity of partly-saturated clay, k	130-240
Coefficient of consolidation, c_v	33-68
Standard penetration blowcount, N	15-45
Electric cone penetration test, q_c	5-15
Mechanical cone penetration test, q_c	15-37
Vane shear test undrained strength, s_{uVST}	10-20

One of the way of using experience is to establish best-case and worst-case scenarios for the design parameters. Relying on the experience of the engineer, it may be possible to establish not only the average value for a selected parameter, but also an "absolute" upper-bound and a lower-bound(i. e. ,best-case and worst case) estimate for the parameter. Once these extreme values are defined, it is possible to define the highest conceivable value (HCV) and the lowest conceivable value (LCV) for the parameter[92], in terms of statistics.

The results of approximating the variability of the parameters should be checked with the other information, such as from the previous section, to confirm that the coefficient of variability resulting from this step encompasses the actual variability for the parameter as measured(or estimated)from the data[54].

4.4.4.3　Final selection of design parameters

Based on a combination of judgment, experience and actual data evaluation, the validity of the data and the anticipated variability of the data that are assessed for design. This final step again involves judgment and the use of information from the previous two sections to select the appropriate design parameters. As discussed by Sabatini[54], the semi-deterministic techniques are recommended to be used only when the individual engineer has extensive experience in the project area and with the materials involved in the design. In this case, experience is extensively relied upon and should only be considered for non-critical applications.

For some key parameters in a critical project, sensitivity analyses will be necessary if the engineer determines that the design calculation results are marginal or that the results are sensitive to the selected parameter. Probabilistic analyses, as Duncan[92] presented, are approach of combining variability in the design calculations and the concepts of probability to estimate the potential for failure(or poor performance), to consider the significance of parameter variability. The results will help to select parameter values. Probabilistic techniques should be considered whenever the variability in the parameters is large or where the consequence of failure is high, and when the costs of acquiring additional confirming data are large[54].

4.5 Ground (rock mass) classification

4.5.1 General

Tunnels may be built in different rock masses, which are of varying quality in terms of geotechnical properties. There is no single parameter that can fully designate the properties of rock masses. Various parameters have different significance and only in an integrated form can describe a rock mass satisfactorily. In practice, during the feasibility and preliminary design stages of a tunnel project, when very little detailed information is available on the rock mass and its stress and hydrologic characteristics, tunneling rock mechanics problems can not be totally solved using the analytical tools and engineering mechanics-based approaches[46]. One of the reasons is that the determining the behaviour of the surrounding rocks is sometimes much complex[29]. In these cases, design decisions should take account of previous experience, such as those gained in the mining, tunneling or elsewhere[30].

Expansion
eading 4-12[67-71]

4.5.2 Rock load classification method

The rock load classification method is one of the first methodologies for rock mass classification for engineering. Karl von Terzaghi developed the methodology for tunnels supported by steel sets in the 1940s[70]. Based on the descriptions of the rock mass properties approximating, a parameter of *Rock Load Factor* on the planned supporting system, e. g., steel sets, can be evaluated, as shown in Table 4-20. The meaning of the parameters for the *Rock Load Factor* approximating is shown in Figure 4-21.

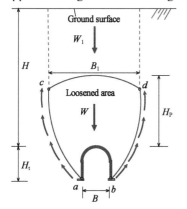

Note: B=span of the tunnel;
H_t=Height of the excavation;
H=Overburden of the tunnel with design excavation profile crown as reference;
B_1=The maximum width of the loosened area;
The envelop *a-b-c-d* showing the boundary of the loosened area;
H_p=Rock load factor;

Figure 4-21 Sketch showing the meaning of the parameters for the Terzaghi's Rock Load Factor approximating

Table 4-20 Rock Load Factor in Terzaghi's classification system

Rock class	Definition	Rock Load Factor H_p [feet] (B and H_t in feet)	Remark
①Hard and intact	Hard and intact rock contains no joints and fractures. After excavation the rock may have popping and spalling at excavated face.	0	Light lining required only if spalling or popping occurs.
② Hard stratified and schistose	Hard rock consists of thick strata and layers. Interface between strata is cemented. Popping and spalling at excavated face is common.	0 to 0.5B	Light support for protection against spalling. Load may change between layers.
③ Massive, moderately jointed	Massive rock contains widely spaced joints and fractures. Block size is large. Joints are interlocked. Vertical walls do not require support. Spalling may occur.	0 to 0.25B	Light support for protection against spalling.
④ Moderately blocky and seamy	Rock contains moderately spaced joints. Rock is not chemically weathered and altered. Joints are not well interlocked and have small apertures. Vertical walls do not require support. Spalling may occur.	0.25B to 0.35 ($B+H_t$)	No side pressure.
⑤Very blocky and seamy	Rock is not chemically weathered, and contains closely spaced joints. Joints have large apertures and appear separated. Vertical walls need support.	(0.35 to 1.1) ($B+H_t$)	Little or no side pressure.
⑥Completely crushed but chemically intact	Rock is not chemically weathered, and highly fractured with small fragments. The fragments are loose and not interlocked. Excavation face in this material needs considerable support.	1.1($B+H_t$)	Considerable side pressure. Softening effects by water at tunnel base. Use circular ribs or support rib lower end.
⑦ Squeezing rock at moderate depth	Rock slowly advances into the tunnel without perceptible increase in volume. Moderate depth is considered as 150-1000 m	(1.1 to 2.1) ($B+H_t$)	Heavy side pressure. Invert struts required. Circular ribs recommended.
⑧Squeezing rock at great depth	Rock slowly advances into the tunnel without perceptible increase in volume. Great depth is considered as more than 1000 m.	(2.1 to 4.5) ($B+H_t$)	
⑨Swelling rock	Rock volume expands (and advances into the tunnel) due to swelling of clay minerals in the rock at the presence of moisture.	up to 76 m (250 feet), irrespective of B and H_t	Circular ribs required. In extreme cases use yielding support.

4.5.2.1 Main points

Terzaghi's descriptions[70] (quoted directly from his paper) are the followings:

(1) *Intact rock contains neither joints nor hair cracks.* Hence, if it breaks, it breaks across sound rock. On account of the damage to the rock due to blasting, spallings may drop off the roof several hours or days after blasting. This is known as a spalling condition. Hard, intact rock may also be encountered in the popping condition involving the spontaneous and violent detachment of rock slabs from the sides or roof.

(2) *Stratified rock consists of individual strata with little or no resistance against separation along the boundaries between the strata.* The strata may or may not be weakened by transverse joints. In such rock the spalling condition is quite common.

(3) *Moderately jointed rock contains joints and hair cracks, but the blocks between joints are locally grown together or so intimately interlocked that vertical walls do not require lateral support.* In rocks of this type, both spalling and popping conditions may be encountered.

(4) *Blocky and seamy rock consists of chemically intact or almost intact rock fragments which are entirely separated from each other and imperfectly interlocked.* In such rock, vertical walls may require lateral support.

(5) *Crushed but chemically intact rock has the character of crusher run.* If most or all of the fragments are as small as fine sand grains and no recementation has taken place, crushed rock below the water table exhibits the properties of a water-bearing sand.

(6) *Squeezing rock slowly advances into the tunnel without perceptible volume increase.* A prerequisite for squeeze is a high percentage of microscopic and sub-microscopic particles of micaceous minerals or clay minerals with a low swelling capacity.

(7) *Swelling rock advances into the tunnel chiefly on account of expansion.* The capacity to swell seems to be limited to those rocks that contain clay minerals such as montmorillonite, with a high swelling capacity.

4.5.2.2 Comments

The *Rock Load Factor* classification system provides reasonable support pressure estimates for small tunnels with diameter up to 6 meters. However, it generally gives over-estimates for large tunnels with diameter above 6 meters. The estimated support pressure has a wide range for squeezing and swelling rock conditions, and it is usually not an easy job for a designer to approximate the pressures in terms of a meaningful application. It is noted that the *Rock Load Factor* classification system was based on the case histories of tunnels, mined with conventional method and first supported with temporary elements, such as steel sets and timber lagging. This construction situation is different from where modern tunneling methods applied, such as using shotcrete and rock bolts as primary supports. In this term, the *Rock Load Factor* classification system generally gives a conservative result of the ground pressures and support requirements.

4.5.3 Stand-up time classification

Stand-up time is the amount of time a tunnel or excavation will support itself without any added structures. The support itself here means that the magnitude of the deformation or the movement of the surrounding rocks is in the allowance range, which will not induce the excavations and construction to adverse conditions.

4.5.3.1 Main points

The stand-up time classification was developed by Lauffer❶ and modified by a number of authors, notably Pacher et al❷. The significance of the stand-up time concept is that an increase in the span of the tunnel leads to a significant reduction in the time available for the installation of support or structure. The ideas of this system are incorporated in modern rock mechanics science. In practice, a small pilot tunnel may be successfully constructed with minimal support, while a larger span tunnel in the same rock mass may not be stable without the immediate installation of support.

Lauffer[46] proposed that the stand-up time for an unsupported span is related to the quality of the rock mass, in which the space is excavated. In a tunnel, the unsupported span is defined as the span of the tunnel or the distance between the face and the nearest support, if this is greater than the tunnel span[17], also called active span, as shown in Figure 4-22.

Knowing the stand-up time allows the engineers to determine how much can be excavated before support is needed. The longer the stand-up time is the faster the excavating will go. Generally, hard and intact rocks, well cemented or consolidated soils, such as stiff clay, will have relatively long stand-up time, while incompact sand will have a much lower stand-up time. Figure 4-23 shows the stand-up times of tunnels in varies rock mass, from very good to very poor rocks, which are presented as

---

❶ Lauffer H. 1958. Gebirgsklassifizierung für den Stollenbau. Geol. Bauwesen 24(1), 46-51.
❷ Pacher F, Rabcewicz L, Golser J. 1974. Zum der seitigen Stand der Gebirgsklassifizierung in Stollen-und Tunnelbau. Proc. XⅫ Geomech. colloq., Salzburg, 51-58.

A, B, $\cdots$, G belts, respectively. The shaded areas in Figure 4-23 are the locations, where the stand-up times of the cases histories are plotted into.

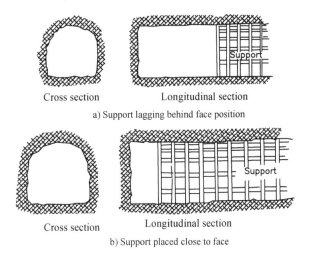

Figure 4-22 Meaning of active span[17]

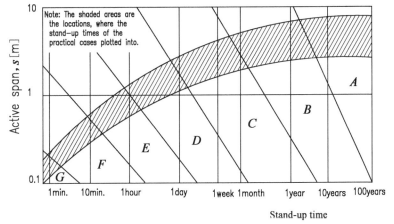

Note:
① The cases plotted in the belts of A, B, ..., G presents the cases of the tunnels in different rocks, with the features of
  a. stable, intact or massive rocks;
  b. blocky rocks, with possibility of block falling;
  c. very blocky rocks, with high possibility of rock block falling;
  d. disintegrated and fractured rocks;
  e. fragmentized rocks;
  f. soft or weak rocks;
  g. very soft or weak rocks.
② The shaded areas are the locations, where the stand-up times of the case histories are plotted into.

Figure 4-23 Stand-up times of some case histories in various rocks

4.5.3.2 Comments

The stand-up time system provides tunnel and underground structure designers a useful tool of approximating the time period between the end of the excavating and finishing time of installing supporting system for a planned construction. This is very vital to safe tunneling, where the stand-up time is limited before failure occurs. In these conditions, the use of smaller headings and benching or the use of multiple drifts to form a reinforced ring inside which the bulk of the tunnel can be excavated, since the length of the stand-up time depends not only the features of the surrounding rock, but also the size of the active span of the excavation.

It is noted that the design method based on the stand-up time classification scheme is applicable to the tunnels, of which the stability is controlled by stress state, such as the tunnels in soft rocks such as shales, phyllites and mudstones, in which the squeezing and swelling problems are likely to occur; as well as tunnelling in excessively broken rock. However, great care should be taken in attempting to apply these techniques to excavations in hard rocks in which different failure mechanisms occur.

For the tunnels or excavations in hard rocks, their stability is often not time-dependent, but usually structure or discontinuities controlled. For example, if a structurally defined wedge is exposed in the roof of an excavation, it will fall as soon as the rock supporting it is removed. This can occur at the time of the blast or during the subsequent scaling operation. If it is required to keep such a wedge in place, or to enhance the margin of safety, it is essential that the support be installed as early as possible, preferably before the rock supporting the full wedge is removed. On the other hand, in a highly stressed rock, failure will generally be induced by some change in the stress field surrounding the excavation. The failure may occur gradually and manifest itself as spalling or slabbing or it may occur suddenly in the form of a rock burst. In either case, the support design must take into account the change in the stress field rather than the "stand-up" time of the excavation. So, it is prudent to assume that the stability or failure of the rock mass surrounding the excavation in hard rocks may be also controlled by other factors in design, instead of merely depending on the stand-up time classification scheme.

4.5.4　Rock quality designation(*RQD*)

4.5.4.1　Main points

The *RQD* system is developed by Deere in the 1960s to classify the quality of a rock mass based on the integrity of borehole cores. *RQD* represents fracturing degree of the rock mass. It partially reflects the rock mass quality. The main points of *RQD* as a rock mass classification scheme are presented in Figure 4-8. Nowadays the *RQD* system is used in many rock mass classification systems, such as *RMR*, *Q*-system, and the *BQ*-system in China.

In practice, it is very difficult to relate *RQD* to other jointing measurements[72], because *RQD* is a one-dimensional, with averaged measurement based solely on core pieces longer than 0.1 m. Simulations using blocks of the same size and shape penetrated by a line(i. e., borehole) at different angles have been used for such estimations. The first attempts when the volumetric joint count (J_v) was introduced were made by Palmstrom[9,73] as: $RQD = 115 - 3.3J_v$ ($RQD = 0$ for $J_v > 35$, and $RQD = 100$ for $J_v < 4.5$).

As was shown by Palmstrom[73], it is a rather poor correlation between RQD and J_v, especially, where many of the core pieces have lengths around 0.1 m. Under this situation, it is difficult to calculate RQD indeed. However, when J_v is the only joint data available, the RQD has alternative finding way from J_v. When no cores are available, another the simple way of determining RQD, by Priest and Hudson[74] is from joint spacing (λ [joints/meter]) measurements made on an exposure by using $RQD = 100e^{-0.1\lambda}(0.1\lambda + 1)$.

4.5.4.2 Comments

The range covered by RQD represents the most important part of blocky ground with respect to single rock falls, which is where classification systems generally work best. However, the RQD system has limitations in areas where the joints contain clay fillings[75]. The clay fillings would reduce the joint friction and the RQD would be high despite the fact that the rock is unstable. In addition, the RQD covers only a limited part of the range of jointing, which reduces the applicability of RQD in characterizing the whole span of jointing.

The RQD is not scale dependent. There is a big difference between a short, narrow tunnel compared to a large water storage reservoir. For excavations with large spans, the RQD may give questionable value, as unlikely that all defects found in the boreholes would be of significance to the rock mass stability[80].

RQD is not a good parameter in the case of a rock mass with joint distances near 100 mm. For example, if the distance between continuous joints is 105 mm (core length), the RQD value gives 100%; while if the distance between continuous joints is 95 mm, the RQD value is 0%. However, if the parameter J_v[76] is used, its value would be close to 10 joints/meter for both of the cases[78].

RQD is relatively insensitive to changes in intact block size[79]. For example, a rock mass with a calculated RQD of 100% may have 3 joint sets with an average spacing of 0.4 meters or 1 joint set with a spacing of several meters[79].

The RQD value may change significantly depending on the borehole orientation relative to the geological structure. Under this situation, the use of the parameter J_v is useful[77].

4.5.5 Rock Structure Rating(RSR)

The RSR system is a quantitative method for describing quality of a rock mass and appropriate ground support, in particular, for steel-rib support, developed by

Wickham et al.[81] in the 1970s.

4.5.5.1　Main points

Wickham et al.[81] described a quantitative method for describing the quality of a rock mass and for selecting appropriate support on the basis of their *RSR* classification. The *RSR* concept introduced a rating system for rock masses. It was the sum of weighted values in this classification system. There are considered two general categories: ① *geotechnical parameters*: rock type, joint pattern, joint orientations, type of discontinuities, major faults, shears and folds, rock material properties, weathering or alteration; ② *construction parameters*: size of tunnel, direction of drive, method of excavation. The significance of the *RSR* system is that it introduced the concept of rating each of the components listed below to arrive at a numerical value of *RSR* = *A* + *B* + *C*.

(1) *Parameter A*, *Geology*: General appraisal of rock strength and geological structure on the basis of:

①Rock type origin (igneous, metamorphic and sedimentary).

②Rock hardness (hard, medium, soft and decomposed).

③Geologic structure (massive, slightly faulted/folded, moderately faulted/folded, intensely faulted/folded).

(2) *Parameter B*, *Geometry*: Effect of discontinuity pattern with respect to the direction of the tunnel drive on the basis of:

①Joint spacing.

②Joint orientation (strike and dip).

③Direction of tunnel drive.

(3) *Parameter C*: Effect of groundwater inflow and joint condition on the basis of:

①Overall rock mass quality on the basis of *A* and *B* combined.

②Joint condition (good, fair, poor).

③Amount of water inflow (in gallons per minute per 1000 feet of tunnel).

Three tables by Wickham et al.[81] can be used for evaluating the rating of each of these parameters to arrive at the *RSR* value. The *RSR* value is a numerical value in the interval of 0 to 100. The values for parameters *A*, *B* and *C* are as the followings:

Parameter *A*: Rock type with strength index + Geologic structures, maximum value, $A_{max} = 30$.

Parameter *B*: Rock joint spacing + Orientation with respect to tunnel drive, maximum value, $B_{max} = 45$.

Parameter *C*: Joint condition + Groundwater inflow, maximum value, $C_{max} = 25$.

Parameter *A* is to combine the generic rock type with an index value for rock strength along with the general type of structure in the studied rock mass. Parameter *B* relates the joint pattern with respect to the direction of drive. Parameter *C* considers the overall rock quality with respect to parameters *A* and *B* and also the degree of joint weathering and alteration and the amount of water inflow.

4.5.5.2 Comments

Most of the case histories, used in the development of the *RSR* system, were for relatively small tunnels supported by means of steel sets, although historically this system was the first to make reference to shotcrete support. In spite of this limitation, the *RSR* system demonstrates the logic involved in developing a quasi-quantitative rock mass classification system. Although the *RSR* classification system is not widely used today, Wickham et al.[81] work played a significant role in the development of the other classification schemes, in terms of comprehensive features.

4.5.6 *RMR* system-Geomechanics classification

Bieniawski[63,64] developed his scheme using data obtained mainly from the excavations in sedimentary rocks in South Africa. Over the years, this system has been successively refined as more case records have been examined. The following presentation is based upon the 1989 version of the classification[65]. Both 1989 version and the 1976 version deal with estimating the strength of rock masses.

4.5.6.1 Main points

The following five parameters (Table 4-21) are used for classifying a rock mass using the *RMR* system:

(1) *Strength of the intact rock material.* The uniaxial compressive strength of the intact rock may be measured on cores. Alternatively, for all but very low-strength rocks, the point load index may be used.

(2) *Rock Quality Designation (RQD).*

(3) *Spacing of joints.* In this context, the term joints are used for describing all discontinuities.

(4) *Condition of joints.* This parameter accounts for the separation or aperture of discontinuities, their continuity or persistence, their surface roughness, the wall condition (hard or soft) and the nature of any in-filling materials present.

(5) *Groundwater conditions.* An attempt is made to account for the influence of groundwater pressure or flow on the stability of underground excavations in terms of the observed rate of flow into the excavation, the ratio of joint water pressure to major principal stress, or by a general qualitative observation of groundwater conditions.

Table 4-21 Rock Mass Rating System[65]

① Classification parameters and their ratings

Qualitative Description		Exceptionally Strong	Very Strong	Strong	Average	Weak	Very weak	Extremely weak
a. Strength of intact rock materials	Point Load Strength [MPa]	>10	4-10	2-4	1-2	5-25	1-5	Use of uniaxial compressive strength is preferred
	Compressive Strength [MPa]	>250	100-250	50-100	25-50	5-25	1-5	<1
Rating		15	12	7	4	2	1	0
b. RQD [%]		90-100	75-90	50-75	25-50	<25		
Rating		20	17	13	8	3		
c. Spacing of discontinuities [m]		>2	0.6-2	0.2-0.6	0.06-0.2	<0.06		
Description Spacing		Very wide	Wide		Moderate	Close	Very close	
Rating		20	15		10	8	5	
d. Condition of discontinuities		Very rough surfaces and unweathered, wall rock. Not continuous, no separation	Slightly rough surfaces and slightly weathered walls. Separation <1 mm	Slightly rough surfaces and highly weathered walls. Separation <1 mm	Slickensided surfaces or <5 mm thick gouge or 1-5 mm separation, continuous discontinuity	Soft gouge >5 mm thick, Separation >5 mm continuous discontinuity		
Rating		30	25	20	10	0		
e. Ground water condition	Inflow per10 m tunnel length [litre/min]	None	<10	10-25	25-125	>125		
	$\frac{\text{Joint water pressure}}{\text{Major principal stress}}$	0	<0.1	0.1-0.2	0.2-0.5	>0.5		
	General description	Completely dry	Damp	Wet	Dripping	Flowing		
Rating		15	10	7	4	0		

② Adjustment for joint orientation

Strike and dip orientation of joints		Very favorable	Favorable	Fair	Unfavorable	Very Unfavorable
Rating	Tunnels & mines	0	-2	-5	-10	-12
	Foundations	0	-2	-7	-15	-25
	Slopes	0	-5	-25	-50	-60

③ Rock mass classes determined from total ratings

Parameter/properties of rock mass	Rock Mass Rating (Rock class)				
Ratings	100-81	80-61	60-41	40-21	<20
Classification of rock mass	Very Good	Good	Fair	Poor	Very Poor

④ Meaning of rock mass classes

Average stand-up time	10 years for 15 m span	6 months for 8 m span	1 week for 5 m span	10 hours for 2.5 m span	30 minutes for 1 m span
Cohesion of the rock mass	>400 kPa	300-400 kPa	200-300 kPa	100-200 kPa	<100 kPa
Friction angle of the rock mass	>45°	35°-45°	25°-35°	15°-25°	<15°

continue

Each of the five parameters is assigned a value corresponding to the characteristics of the rock (Table 4-21). These values are derived from field surveys.

The way in which these parameters are incorporated into Bieniawski's geomechanics classification for jointed rock masses is shown in Part ① of Table 4-21. For various ranges of each parameter, a rating value is assigned. The allocation of these rating values allows for the fact that all parameters do not necessarily contribute equally to the behaviour of the rock mass. The overall *RMR* is obtained by adding the values of the ratings determined for the individual parameters. This *RMR* value may be adjusted for the influence of discontinuity orientation by applying the corrections given in Part② of Table 4-21. The terms used for this purpose are explained in Table 4-22. Part③ of Table 4-21 sets out the class and description assigned to rock masses with various total ratings. The interpretation of these ratings, in terms of stand-up times of underground excavations and rock mass strength parameters, is given in Part④ of Table 4-21. The sum of the six parameters is the "*RMR* value", which lies between 0 and 100. The final *RMR* values are grouped into five rock mass classes, where the rock mass classes are in groups of twenty ratings each. Higher rock mass rating indicates better rock mass condition/quality, as shown in Table 4-23.

Table 4-22 The effects of joint strike and dip in tunnelling (after Bieniawski)[65]

Strike perpendicular to tunnel axis				Strike parallel to tunnel axis		Dip 0°-20° irrespective of strike
Drive with dip		Drive against dip		Dip 45°-90°	Dip 20°-45°	
Dip 45°-90°	Dip 20°-45°	Dip 45°-90°	Dip 20°-45°			
very favorable	Favorable	Tair	Very unfavorable	Unfavorable	Fair	Fair

4.5.6.2 Applications

In practice, the rating of each of the five parameters are summarised to give a value of *RMR* for rock mass. All parameters are measurable in the field and some of them may also be obtained from borehole data. The calculated *RMR* value may be used for finding which of five pre-defined rock mass classes the rock mass belongs to, going from very good rock to very poor rock, as shown in Table 4-21.

In applying this classification system, the rock masses are divided into a number of structural regions. The boundaries of the structural regions usually coincide with major structural features [65]. However, from the practical point of view, the rating is also related to length of the blasting round or the recently excavated tunnel section.

Bieniawski[65] published a set of guidelines for estimating the stand-up time, as shown in Figure 4-24, and for selecting rock support in tunnels, based on the *RMR* value, as shown in Table 4-23. However, Bieniawski[65] strongly emphasizes that a great deal of judgment is needed in the application of rock mass classification to support design. The *RMR* value has also been used for estimating rock mass properties, e. g., rock mass deformation modulus, the *m* and *s* factors in the Hoek-Brown failure criterion, as discussed in the above section. However, these are only empirical relations and have nothing to do with rock engineering classification in its true sense.

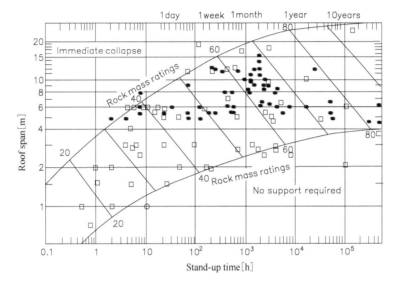

Figure 4-24   Estimating the stand-up time with parameters of *RMR* and active span[65]

Table 4-23   Guidelines for excavation and support of 10 m span rock tunnels based on the *RMR* system[65]

Rock mass class	Excavation	Rock bolts (20 mm diameter, fully grouted)	Shotcrete	Steel sets
①Very good rock *RMR*: 81-100	Full face, 3 m advance.	Generally no support required except spot bolting.		
②Good rock *RMR*: 61-80	Full face, 1-1.5 m advance. Complete support 20 m from face.	Locally, bolts in crown 3 m long, spaced 2.5 m with occasional wire mesh.	50 mm in crown where required.	None.
③Fair rock *RMR*: 41-60	Top heading and bench, 1.5-3 m advance in top heading. Commence support after each blast. Complete support 10 m from face.	Systematic bolts 4 m long, spaced 1.5-2 m in crown and walls, with wire mesh in crown.	50-100 mm in crown and 30 mm in sides.	None.

Rock mass class	Excavation	Rock bolts (20 mm diameter, fully grouted)	Shotcrete	Steel sets
④Poor rock RMR: 21-40	Top heading and bench, 1.0-1.5 m advance in top heading. Install support concurrently with excavation, 10 m from face.	Systematic bolts 4-5 m long, spaced 1-1.5 m in crown and walls with wire mesh.	100-150 mm in crown and 100 mm in sides.	Light to medium ribs, spaced 1.5 m where required.
⑤Very poor rock RMR: <20	Multiple drifts 0.5-1.5 m advance in top heading. Install support concurrently with excavation. Shotcrete as soon as possible after blasting.	Systematic bolts 5-6 m long, spaced 1-1.5 m in crown and walls with wire mesh. Bolt invert.	150-200 mm in crown, 150 mm in sides, and 50 mm on face.	Medium to heavy ribs spaced 0.75 m with steel lagging and forepoling if required. Close invert.

Bieniawski[65] published a set of guidelines for the selection of support in tunnels in rock for which the value of *RMR* has been determined. These guidelines are reproduced in Table 4-24. Note that these guidelines have been published for a 10 m span horseshoe shaped tunnel, constructed using drill and blast method, in a rock mass subjected to a vertical stress < 25 MPa (equivalent to a depth below surface of <900 m).

4.5.6.3 Comments

The *RMR* system is one of the well accepted rock mass classification scheme in the world, in the fields of tunnel and underground engineering. In general, the system works well to classify the rock mass quality, since it is relatively well defined and the rating for each parameter can be estimated with acceptable precision. The *RMR* system has been used in many tunnel projects as one of the indicators to define the support or excavation classes. However, *RMR* cannot be used as the only indicator, especially when rock stresses or time dependent rock properties are of importance for the rock engineering issue.

4.5.7 Rock mass quality rating-the *Q* system

On the basis of an evaluation of a large number of case histories of tunnel projects of hydro-power related tunneling, underground power houses, and of road and rail tunnels, Barton et al.[55] of the Norwegian Geotechnical Institute (NGI) proposed a Tunneling Quality Index (*Q*) as a classification system for estimating rock support in tunnels. It is a quantitative classification system based on a numerical assessment of the rock mass quality. Later, Barton et al.[83-85] have published several papers on the *Q* system aiming at extending its applications. The original parameters of the Q system have not been changed, but the rating for the stress reduction factor SRF has been altered by Grimstad and Barton[83]. Some new Q value correlations were presented by Barton[82], which also included new footnotes for the existing parameter ratings. The Q system has become a widely referenced and used method for characterizing rock mass conditions, and for assisting in the selection of temporary or permanent support for tunnels, shafts and caverns.

4.5.7.1 Main points

The numerical value of the index Q is defined by six parameters with the following equation:

$$Q = \frac{RQD}{J_n} \times \frac{J_r}{J_a} \times \frac{J_w}{SRF}$$

where, RQD is the rock quality designation; J_n is the joint set number, which represents the number of joint sets in the rock mass, varying from 0.5 for a massive rock mass with no or few joints to 20 for crushed or disaggregated rock; J_r is the joint roughness number, which represents the roughness of the structural features in the rock mass, varying from 0.5 for slickensided, planar surfaces to 5 for non-persistent structures with spacing larger than 3 m; J_a is the joint alteration number, representing the condition or degree of alteration of the structures in the rock mass, varying from 0.75 for wall-wall contact in unaltered rock or for joints containing tightly healed, hard, non-softening, impermeable filling to 20 for structures with thick fillings of clay gouge; J_w is the joint water reduction factor, representing the groundwater conditions, varying from 0.05 for exceptionally high inflows or for water pressure continuing without noticeable decay to 1.0 for dry conditions or minor inflows; SRF is the stress reduction factor, which is a coefficient representing the effect of stresses acting on the rock mass, varying from 0.5 for high stress but tight structure conditions in good quality rock to 400 for heavy squeezing rock pressures or heavy rock burst conditions and immediate dynamic deformations in massive rock.

In explaining the system and the use of the parameters to determine the value of Q, Barton et al.[55] have given the following explanations: ①the first quotient (RQD/J_n) represents roughly the block size of the rock mass; ②the second quotient (J_r/J_a) describes the frictional characteristics of the rock mass; ③the third quotient (J_w/SRF) represents the active stress situation. The third quotient is the most complicated empirical factor, which should be given special attention, as it represents 4 groups of rock masses: stress influence in brittle blocky and massive ground, stress influence in deformable (ductile) rock masses, weakness zones, and swelling rock.

The third quotient (J_w/SRF) consists of two stress parameters and is a complicated empirical factor describing the 'active stress'. SRF is a measure of:

①loosening load in the case of an excavation through shear zones and clay bearing rock;②rock stress in competent rock;③squeezing loads in plastic incompetent rocks. It can be regarded as a total stress parameter. The parameter J_w is a measure of water pressure, which has an adverse effect on the shear strength of joints due to a reduction in effective normal stress. Water may, in addition, cause softening and possible outwash in the case of clay-filled joints. It has proved impossible to combine these two parameters in terms of inter-block effective stress, because paradoxically a high value of effective normal stress may sometimes signify less stable conditions than a low value, despite the higher shear strength.

The Q system can be used as supervised classification❶ of rock mass quality. Possible Q values range from 0.001 to 1000 on a logarithmic scale. The system defines nine geotechnical classes of rock mass ranging from exceptionally poor($Q \leqslant 0.01$) to exceptionally good($Q \geqslant 400$), as shown in Table 4-24.

Table 4-24　Q value and rock mass quality[82]

Q value	Class	Group	Rock mass quality
400-1000	A$_1$	1	Exceptionally good
100-400	A$_2$		Extremely good
40-100	A$_3$		Very good
10-40	B		Good
4-10	C	2	Fair
1-4	D		Poor
0.1-1	E	3	Very poor
0.01-0.1	F		Extremely poor
0.001-0.01	G		Exceptionally poor

4.5.7.2　Applications

The Q system is normally used as an empirical design method for rock support. In relating the value of the index Q to the stability and support requirements of underground excavations, Barton et al. [55] defined an additional parameter which they called the Equivalent Dimension, D_e, of the excavation. This dimension is obtained by dividing the span, diameter or wall height of the excavation by a quantity called the Excavation Support Ratio, ESR. Hence:

D_e = (Excavation span, diameter or height) / [Excavation Support Ratio (ESR)]

---

❶ Supervised classification is based on a training of presenting with example inputs and their desired outputs. The goal of the training is to learn a general rule that maps inputs to outputs. Supervised classification needs enough prior knowledge, such as tunnel design and construction case histories. The method is a kind of analogical method in a practical case.

Together with the ratio between the span or height of the opening and an excavation support ratio (ESR), the Q value defines the rock support. The ESR was determined from investigations of the relation between existing maximum unsupported excavation span ($SPAN$) and Q around an excavation standing up for more than 10 years. The value of ESR is related to the intended use of the excavation and to the degree of security which is demanded of the support system installed to maintain the stability of excavation. Barton[82] gives suggested values for ESR according to Table 4-25. and the $SPAN$ is calculated as: $SPAN = 2Q^{0.66} = 2(ESR)Q^{0.4}$.

Table 4-25 Value of ESR for different excavation categories[82]

Excavation category	ESR
A-Temporary mine openings.	3-5
B-Permanent mine openings, water tunnels for hydro power(excluding high pressure penstocks), pilot tunnels, drifts and headings for large excavations.	1.6
C-Storage rooms, water treatment plants, minor road and railway tunnels, surge chambers, access tunnels.	1.3
D-Power stations, major road and railway tunnels, civil defence chambers, portal intersections.	1.0
E-Underground nuclear power stations, railway stations, sports and public facilities, factories.	0.8

The design information on rockbolt length, maximum unsupported spans and roof support pressures can be preliminarily presented with the recommendations of the Q system[86].

The length L of rockbolts can be estimated from the excavation width B and the Excavation Support Ratio ESR: $L = 2 + 0.15B/ESR$.

The maximum unsupported span can be estimated from: Maximum span (unsupported) = $2(ESR)Q^{0.4}$.

Based upon analyses of case records, Grimstad and Barton[83] suggest that the relationship between the value of Q and the permanent roof support pressure P_{roof} is estimated from:

$$P_{roof} = \frac{2\sqrt{J_n}Q^{-1/3}}{3J_r}$$

As mentioned earlier, the Q system has been modified due to changes in the stress reduction factor[83] and also due to new supporting methods, such as steel fibre reinforced shotcrete [$S(fr)$] and systematic bolting (B). Grimstad and Barton[83] presented an updated Q support chart for the new supporting methods, see Figure 4-25. The basic Q system reinforcement and support components $B + S(fr)$ meaning systematic rock bolting, and (since the 1993 update) fiber-reinforced shotcrete, were developed from challenging conditions, with weathered rock, clay-fillings, shear zones and fault zones. The area where the Q system works best was added by Palmstrom and Broch[66].

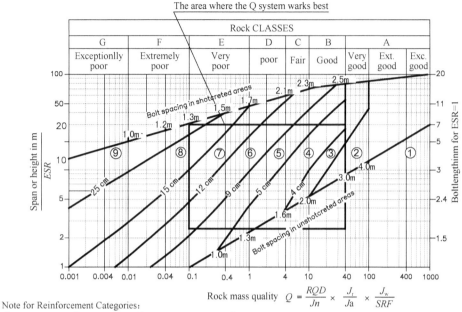

Figure 4-25 Chart for design of steel fibre reinforced shotcrete and systematic bolting support[66]

4.5.7.3 Comments

The Q system has become a widely referenced and used method for characterizing rock mass conditions, and for assisting in the selection of temporary support or permanent support for tunnels, shafts and caverns[87]. However, the accuracy of the estimation of rock support is very difficult to evaluate, especially in the poorer rock class (e.g., Q is less than 1)[46]. For example, the true nature of the rock mass, such as swelling, squeezing or popping ground, is essential for the determination of the support measures is not explicitly considered in the Q system. Nor are such issues as the timing for installation and the need for an invert strut. For the conditions in faults and weakness zones, the supports should be checked or designed by complimentary engineering methods[46,87].

The Q system was originally proposed for single-shell tunnels and caverns, where corrosion protected rock bolts and good quality fiber-reinforced shotcrete form the final permanent support. In these cases, water control using high pressure systematic pre-injection is the preferred method of ensuring dry excavations[87]. For the tunnels and caverns with composite lining system, the Q system can be used for the rock mass characterization and for the selection of temporary support, which is needed to ensure stability until a concrete lining has been completed, even for tunnels in bad rocks, such as, intensely jointed tuffs and sometimes deeply weathered granites[87].

Grimstad and Barton[83] have also presented an equation to use the Q value to estimate the rock mass deformation modulus (for values of $Q > 1$). The Q value is also used as one way to estimate the m and s factors in the Hoek-Brown failure criterion. Additional features of this empirical method have indicated the correlation of Q values with seismic velocity, deformation modulus, tunnel or cavern deformation, permeability, and the estimates of the cohesive and frictional strength of rock masses[87]. In this respect, it is only an empirical relationship and has nothing to do with engineering classification[46].

4.5.8 The GSI system

As part of the continuing development and practical application of the Hoek-Brown empirical rock mass strength criterion, Hoek et al.[61] introduced a new rock mass classification scheme known as the Geological Strength Index (GSI), to estimate the parameters s, a and m_b in the criterion. The GSI was developed to overcome some of the deficiencies that had been identified in using the RMR scheme with the rock mass strength criterion. The GSI system is a way to estimate the reduction in rock mass strength for different geological conditions, in comparison to the strength of intact rocks.

4.5.8.1 Main points

The strength of a jointed rock mass depends on the properties of the intact pieces of rock and upon the freedom of those pieces to slide and rotate under a range of imposed stress conditions. This freedom is controlled by the shapes of the intact rock pieces as well as by the condition of the surfaces separating them. The GSI seeks to account for these two features of the rock mass, its structure as represented by its blockiness and degree or interlocking, and the condition of the discontinuity surfaces. The GSI provides a system for estimating the reduction in rock mass strength for different geological conditions as identified by field observations. The rock mass characterisation is based on the visual impression of the rock structure, in terms of blockiness, and the surface condition of the discontinuities indicated by joint roughness and alteration. The combination of these two parameters provides a practical basis for describing a wide range of rock mass types.

The GSI may be estimated from visual exposures of the rock mass or borehole core. Visual determination of GSI parameters represents the return to quality descriptions instead of advancing quantitative input data as in the RMR and Q systems.

There are other two ways of calculating the *GSI*, by using the *RMR* for better quality rock masses (*GSI* > 25) as:

For $RMR'_{76} > 18$, $GSI = RMR'_{76}$; for $RMR'_{89} > 23$, $GSI = RMR'_{89} - 5$, where RMR'_{76} and RMR'_{89} are the values of the rock masses based on the the *RMR* system of 1976 vision and 1989 vision under dry condition, respectively.

In addition, no adjustments for joint orientation (very favourable) should be made, since the water conditions and joint orientation should be assessed during the rock mass analysis[61]. Hoek and Brown[62] recommended that *RMR* should only be used for estimating *GSI* for better quality rock masses (i.e., for *GSI* > 25 and values of $RMR'_{76} > 18$ and $RMR'_{89} > 23$).

For very poor quality rock masses, it is difficult to estimate *RMR* from the table provided by Bieniawski[64]. Hoek et al[61] suggested using the *Q* system[55] in these circumstances.

For all *Q* values: $GSI = 9\ln Q' + 44$, where both the joint water reduction factor (J_w) and the stress reduction factor (*SRF*) should be set to 1 in the *Q* system.

Five grades of rock mass quality are considered according to the *GSI* value, as shown in Table 4-26.

Table 4-26 **GSI and rock mass quality**[61]

GSI value	76-95	56-75	41-55	21-40	< 20
Rock mass quality	Very good	Good	Fair	Poor	Very poor

4.5.8.2 Applications

The main object of the *GSI* system is to estimate the parameters s, a and m_b for the Hoek-Brown empirical rock mass strength criterion. In this meaning, *GSI* is used for estimating input parameters (strength), it is only an empirical relation and has nothing to do with rock engineering classification.

4.5.8.3 Comments

The *GSI* system is mainly used for estimating the geotechnical parameters for the Hoek-Brown empirical rock mass strength criterion. *GSI* system is generally useful for weaker rock masses, such as with *RMR* < 20. Marinos and Hoek[68] present a series of indicative charts which show the most probable ranges of *GSI* values for rock masses of several generic rock types.

The aim of the *GSI* system is to determine the properties of the undisturbed rock mass; otherwise, compensation must be made for the lower *GSI* values obtained from such locations. When using a version older than the 2002 edition[88], one should move up one row in the *GSI* tables, if the rock face is blast damaged. When using the 2002 edition, the *m* and *s* value should be adjusted to a disturbance factor (*D*).

4.5.9 The rock mass classification system for road and railway tunnels in China

In China, the rock mass classifications systems used in the design of road and railway tunnels are similar. In these systems, the grade evaluation of the surrounding rocks of a rock tunnel is based on the *Standard for engineering classification of rock masses* (GB/T 50218—1994). The following grade evaluation of the surrounding rocks of rock tunnels is based on the 2014 revised edition.

Since a tunnel may be built in soils, the grade evaluation of the surrounding rocks of a soil tunnel is added into these systems. However, the indices of the properties of soils are generally different from that of the rocks, especially in terms of the stability of surrounding rocks, and the parameters of the geotechnical properties of rocks are generally different from that of soils. The evaluating of the grades of soils and rocks are conducted separately, since the main parameters being used in the classification are different for soils and rocks.

4.5.9.1 Main points

4.5.9.1.1 Tunnels in rocks

The grade of the surrounding rocks of a tunnel is determined in two steps: ①Determination of grade of rock mass basic quality; ②Rock mass classification in underground engineering. The former is to evaluate the basic quality (BQ) of the surrounding rocks, in terms of rock mass; while the latter to deter the features of rock mass in terms of surrounding rocks, showing the grade (class) of tunnel engineering rock mass. The general procedure and main points of the grade evaluation of the surrounding rocks of rock tunnels are shown in Figure 4-26 as a flow chart.

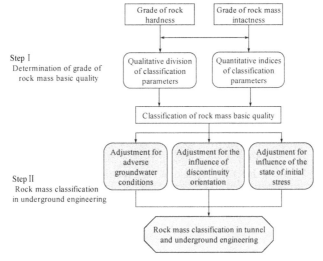

Figure 4-26 The general procedure and main points of the grade evaluation of the surrounding rocks of rock tunnels

The basic quality of rock masses is determined with two basic parameters, i. e., the hardness of rocks and the intactness of rock mass. Each of the two parameters is assigned a value corresponding to the characteristics of the rock mass. These values are derived from both field surveys and laboratory tests.

(1) *Hardness of rocks.* The hardness should be approximated in terms of description (qualitative data) and quantity. For the later, the parameter of *hardness of rock mass* is similar to the strength of the intact rock material. In terms of quantity, the uniaxial compressive strength of the saturated intact rock may be measured on cores. Alternatively, for all but very low-strength rocks, the point load index [$I_{s(50)}$] may be used. Five hardness grades have been considered in terms of strength, as shown in Table 4-27.

Table 4-27　Grade of intact rock strength

Grade of hardness	Hard rocks		Soft rocks		
	Hard rocks, I	Moderately hard rocks, II	Moderately soft rocks, III	Soft rocks, IV	Very soft rocks, V
Strength of rocks [MPa]	>60	60-30	30-15	15-5	≤5

The hardness of the rocks is related to the weathering grade of the rock masses. For the *weathering grade of rock masses*, five weathering grades have been considered: grade V (completely weathered rock), grade IV (highly weathered rock), grade III (moderately weathered rock), grade II (slightly weathered rock) and grade I (fresh rock).

(2) *Intactness of rock masses.* The intactness of the rock masses are described with the parameters of the numbers of joint sets or discontinuities, types of the discontinuities (e.g., joints, cleavages, fractures, faults, bedding partings), the space, aperture, roughness and fillings of the discontinuities. Based on these features of the rock mass intactness, five *intactness* grades have been considered as intact, moderately intact, moderately fractured, highly fractured, completely fractured.

In terms of quantity, the *intactness of rock masses* can be approximated with intactness index of rock mass, K_v, which is calculated as $K_v = (v_{rm}/v_r)^2$, where v_{rm} and v_r are the speed of primary elastic waves in rock mass and intact rocks, repectively; or with the volumetric joint count of rock mass (J_v), as shown in Table 4-28.

Table 4-28　Grade of rock mass intactness

Grade of rock mass intactness	Intact, I	Moderately intact, V	Moderately fractured, III	Highly fractured, IV	Completely fractured, V
J_v [count of joints/m³]	<3	3-10	10-20	20-35	≥35
K_v	0.75	0.75-0.55	0.55-0.35	0.35-0.15	≤0.15

4.5.9.1.2 Tunnels in soils

Expansion reading 4-13

Different parameters are used for classifying grainular soils and clayey soils in the codes for the design of railway and road tunnels, as shown in Table 4-29. For cohesive soils, plasticity or moisture is a significant indicator of property, while, relative density is usually used for describing the degree of compactness of a coarse-grained soil.

Table 4-29 Parameters for the grade evaluating of soils

Types of soils	Parameters	Index and description	
Clayey soils	Moisture	In description	Hard, plastic, liquid
		In qauntity	Index of liquidity, I_L
Sandy soils	Relative density	In description	loose, slightly dense, moderately dense, dense
		In qauntity	Standard Penetration Test(SPT) N-values
	Moisture	In description	damp, moist, wet(saturated)
		In qauntity	Saturation, S_t
Gravel soils	Relative density	In description	loose, slightly compacted, moderately compacted, close-grained
		In qauntity	Dynamic Penetration Test, N-values

Three grades of soil quality are considered, with clayey soils, sandy soils and gravel soils being presented separately, as shown in Tables 4-30 to 4-32, respectively. Three grades of the surrounding rocks of soils are considered as Ⅳ, Ⅴ and Ⅵ. The grade Ⅳ of soils is belonging to the sub-grade $Ⅳ_3$, which is corresponding to the grades of rocks. Similarly, the grade Ⅴ of soils is considered as two sub-grades, $Ⅴ_1$ and $Ⅴ_2$.

Table 4-30 Grades of clayey soils based on basic quality index

Grades of surrounding rocks		Index and description		Types of soils
Grade	Sub-grades	Moisture		
		In description	Index of liquidity, I_L	
Ⅳ	$Ⅳ_3$	Hard	≤ 0	Dense and hardy clayey soils, Q_1 and Q_2 loess
Ⅴ	$Ⅴ_1$	Hard ~ hard-plastic	≤ 0.25	hardy clayey soils, Q_3 loess
	$Ⅴ_2$	hard-plastic ~ plastic	0-0.75	Hard-plastic clayey soils, plastic clays, Q_4 loess
Ⅵ		Plastic ~ liquid-plastic	≥ 0.75	Soft-plastic clayey soils, plastic clayey soils

Note: Q_1, Q_2 and Q_3 are the lower, middle, upper Pleistocene series, respectively; Q_4 is Holocene series.

Table 4-31 Grades of sandy soils based on basic quality index

Grades of surrounding rocks		Index and description		Types of soils
Grade	Sub-grades	Relative density		
		In description	SPT, N-numbers	
IV	IV_3	Dense	>30	Dense sandy soils or sandy soils with diagenesis
V	V_1	Moderately dense-dense	>15	Dense damp sandy soils, or moderately cemented sandy soils
	V_2	Moderately-slightly dense	10-30	Moderately cemented sandy soils
VI		Loose	<10	Loose, saturated silts

Table 4-32 Grades of gravel soils based on basic quality index

Grades of surrounding rocks		Index and description		Types of soils
Grade	Sub-grades	Relative density		
		In description	Dynamic Penetration Test, N-numbers	
IV	IV_3	Dense	$N_{63.5}>20$, or $N_{120}>11$	Calcium, ferro-cemented gravel soils
V	V_1	Moderately dense	$N_{63.5}>10$, or $N_{120}>6$	Damp to moist gravel soils, pebble soils, breccia soils
	V_2	Moderately-slightly dense	$5<N_{63.5}\leqslant20$, or $3<N_{120}>11$	Damp to moist loose gravel soils, pebble soils, breccia soils

4.5.9.2 Applications

The parameters used for presenting a value of BQ are measurable in the field and some of them may also be obtained from laboratory tests. The calculated BQ or $[BQ]$ value may be used for finding which of five pre-defined rock mass classes the ground belongs to, going from very good rock, i.e., Grade I, to very poor rock, i.e., Grade VI.

In the design codes and guidelines for tunnels, the BQ-classification system are used for estimating the stand-up time, geotechnical parameters, and for selecting rock support in tunnel design, based on the grades of rock mass. The values for these design parameters are tabulated in design codes and guidelines, such as the *Specifications* (JTG 3370.1—2018) and the *Guidelines* (JTG/T D70—2010). For example, to help to evaluate the capacity of surrounding rocks to support tunnel excavation without support, the *Guideline* (JTG/T D70—2010) presents the features of the stand-up capacity of tunnel surrounding rocks, in terms of both tunnel span and the grade of rock mass, as shown in Table 4-33. The stand-up time of the surrounding rocks of a planned tunnel can be preliminarily estimated, provided that there is an approximation of the grade of the surrounding rocks.

Similarly, the features of the stand-up capacity of tunnel surrounding rocks can be used for preliminarily evaluating the requirement of pre-support or the difficulty of a planned construction method for a planned tunnel.

Table 4-33 Features of the stand-up capacity of tunnel surrounding rocks

Grade of surrounding rocks		Stand-up capacity of tunnel surrounding rocks without any support	
Grade	Sub-grade	Span of a tunnel, B [m]	Features of the stand-up capacity of the surrounding rocks
I	-	$B = 20$	Stable, but possibly rock block falling
II	-	$10 < B < 20$	Generally stable, but possibly rock block falling or small collapsing locally
		$B = 10$	Stable, but possibly rock block falling
III	III$_1$	$B > 18$	Possibly occurring intermediate to large collapse
		$10 < B < 18$	Being stable for a period, but possibly with small to intermediate collapse
		$B = 10$	Generally stable
	III$_2$	$B > 14$	Possibly occurring intermediate to large collapse
		$7 < B < 14$	Being stable for a period, but possibly occurring small to intermediate collapse
		$B = 7$	Generally stable
IV	IV$_1$	$B > 9$	Possibly occurring intermediate to large collapse
		$7 < B < 9$	Being stable for a period, but possibly with small collapse
		$B < 7$	Generally stable
	IV$_2$	$B > 7$	Possibly occurring intermediate to large collapse
		$6 < B < 7$	Being stable for a period, but possibly with small collapse
		$B < 6$	Generally stable
	IV$_3$	$B > 5$	Being stable for a period or unstable, but possibly with small collapse
		$B \leqslant 5$	Generally stable
V	V$_1$	$B > 6$	The tunneling excavation is unstable without proper pre-support
		$4 < B < 6$	Being stable for a period, but possibly with intermediate to large collapse
		$B < 4$	Generally stable
	V$_2$	$B > 4$	The tunneling excavation is unstable without proper pre-support
		$3 < B < 4$	Being stable for a period, but possibly with intermediate to large collapse
		$B < 3$	Generally stable
VI	-	The tunneling excavation is unstable without proper pre-support	

Note: A small collapse is the one with the height of the collapsing area in the surrounding rocks less than 3 m or the volume of falling debris less than 30 m^3. An intermediate collapse is the one with the height of the collapsing area in the surrounding rocks from 3 to 6 m or the volume of falling debris from 30 to 100 m^3. A large collapse is the one with the height of the collapsing area in the surrounding rocks more than 6 m or the volume of falling debris more than 100 m^3.

The suggested values for the typical geotechnical parameters of rock and soil are presented in the Tables 4-34 and 4-35, respectively.

Table 4-34 Suggested values for the typical geotechnical parameters of rock tunnels

Grade of surrounding rocks		γ [kN/m³]	k [MPa/m]	E [GPa]	ν	φ [°]	c [MPa]	φ_c [°]	f	v_p [km/s]
Grade	Sub-grade									
I	-	26-28	1800-2800	>33.0	<0.20	>60	>2.1	>78	15-20	>4.5
II	-	25-27	1200-1800	20.0-33.0	0.20-0.25	50-60	1.5-2.1	70-78	8-15	3.5-4.5
III	III₁	24-25	850-1200	10.7-20.0	0.25-0.26	44-50	1.1-1.5	65-70	6-8	3.2-4.0
III	III₂	23-24	500-800	7.0-10.7	0.26-0.30	39-44	0.7-1.1	60-65	3-6	2.5-3.2
IV	IV₁	22-23	400-500	3.8-7.0	0.30-0.31	35-39	0.5-0.7	57-60	2.3-3.0	2.5-3.0
IV	IV₂	21-22	300-400	2.4-3.8	0.31-0.33	30.-35	0.3-0.5	54-57	1.7-2.3	2.0-2.5
IV	IV₃	20-21	200-300	1.3-2.4	0.33-0.35	27-30	0.2-0.3	50-54	1.1-1.7*	1.5-2.0
V	V₁	18-20	150-200	1.3-2.0	0.35-0.39	22-27	0.12-0.20	45-50	1.1-1.5	1.4-2.0
V	V₂	17-18	100-150	1.0-1.3	0.39-0.45	20-22	0.05-0.12	40-45	0.8-1.1	1.0-1.4

Note: γ-Unit weight; k-Elastic resistance coefficient; E-Deformation modulus; ν-Poisson's Ratio; φ-Internal friction angle; c-Cohesion strength; φ_c-Apparent internal friction angle; f-Protodyakonov's coefficient; v_p-Elastic wave velocity.

Table 4-35 Suggested values for the typical geotechnical parameters of soil tunnels

Grade of surrounding rocks		Type of soils	γ [kN/m³]	k [MPa/m]	E [MPa]	ν	φ [°]	c [kPa]	φ_c [°]	f	v_p [km/s]
Grade	Sub-grade										
IV	IV₃	Clayey soils	20-23	200-300	30-45	0.25-0.33	30-45	60-250	50-54	1.0-1.7	1.5-2.0
IV	IV₃	Sandy soils	18-19	200-300	24-30	0.29-0.31	33-40	12-24	50-54	1.0-1.7	1.5-2.0
IV	IV₃	Gravel soils	22-24	200-300	50-70	0.15-0.30	43-50	19-30	50-54	1.0-1.7	1.5-2.0
V	V₁	Clayey soils	18-20	150-200	15-30	0.33-0.37	20-30	30-60	45-50	1.1-1.5	1.4-2.0
V	V₁	Sandy soils	16.5-18	150-200	9-24	0.31-0.33	30-33	6-12	45-50	1.1-1.5	1.4-2.0
V	V₁	Gravel soils	20-22	150-200	33-50	0.20-0.30	37-43	8-19	45-50	1.1-1.5	1.4-2.0
V	V₂	Clayey soils	16-18	100-150	5-15	0.37-0.43	15-20	15-30	40-45	0.8-1.1	1.0-1.4
V	V₂	Sandy soils	15-16.5	100-150	3-9	0.33-0.36	25-30	3-6	40-45	0.8-1.1	1.0-1.4
V	V₂	Gravel soils	17-20	100-150	10-33	0.25-0.35	30-37	<8	40-45	0.8-1.1	1.0-1.4
VI	-	Clayey soils	14-16	<100	<5	0.43-0.50	<15	<15	30-40	0.3-1.0	<1.0
VI	-	Sandy soils	14-15	<100	3-5	0.36-0.42	10-25	<3	30-40	0.3-1.0	<1.0

Note: γ-Unit weight; k-Elastic resistance coefficient; E-Deformation modulus; ν-Poisson's Ratio; φ-Internal friction angle; c-Cohesion strength; φ_c-Apparent friction angle; f-Protodyakonov's coefficient; v_p-Elastic wave velocity.

4.5.9.3 Comments

The *BQ* system can be used as supervised classification of rock mass quality in tunnel design. The system has been used in many tunnel projects as one of the indicators to define the support or excavation classes. However, BQ system should not be used as the only indicator, especially when rock stresses or time dependent rock properties are of importance for the rock engineering issue. For example, it is often in a quandary in the applications of the BQ system in tunnel design, when a narrow weak rock belt or structural belt appears in the rock masses along the planned tunnel axial. In general, the length of the rock unit, which can be considered as a separated grade or sub-grade, should be at least 20 m and 10 m, respectively. However, a section of surrounding rocks with 10 m in length is usually long enough to have a significant influence on the stability or construction of the tunnel, when a collapse or large deformation occurs in this section.

4.5.10 Comments on the rock mass classification

Based on case histories, the primary object of all rock mass classification systems is to quantify different engineering properties of the rock mass. One important use of the classification system today has therefore been to serve as a kind of checklist tool[13] in approximating surrounding rock behaviors. This enables the comparison of rock mass conditions throughout the site and the delineation of regions of the rock mass from 'very good' to 'very poor', thus providing a map of rock mass quality boundaries.

Empirical design methods based on characterization of rock masses is a matter of fact[13]. Major benefit from the use of rock mass classification systems is the empirical design with guidelines for tunnel support compatible with rock mass quality and the method of excavation. This approach is called analogical method in China.

In the early stages of a project, the existing quantitative rock mass classification systems (empirical design methods) can be applied as a useful tool to establish a preliminary design. It is necessary to adapt an existing classification system to the actual condition and problem, and calibrate the existing rock mass classification systems against the experience gained from a specific project[13]. However, classification systems are unreliable for rock support determinations during construction, as local geometric and geological features may override the rock mass quality defined by the classification system, as pointed out by Bieniawski[91]. In practice at least two systems should be applied[65].

It is noted that the index of the rock mass quality derived from the existing classification system should be used as indicator of sturcture design. For the situation, such as when unforeseen geological conditions have been encountered, and where the system has not been applicable, the observational method[90] should be used in order to form a system for classification that incorporates deformation measurements or visual inspections, especially of the typical conditions, such as swelling, squeezing, ravelling, or popping ground.

On the other hand, as already stated by Einstein et al.[89] that the accuracy of the existing empirical design methods is not established. The methods probably overestimate the support requirements and the relationships to the ground support pressure are often not very accurate[13]. The classification systems used today should, strictly speaking, either be described as rock mass characterization systems or empirical design methods, as long as the outcome is not organized into classes. The main requirements for a true classification system capable of solving rock-engineering problems are as follows[29]: ①the reliability of the classes to assess the given rock engineering problem must be estimated; ②the classes must be exhaustive (every object belongs to a class) and mutually exclusive (no object belongs to more than one class); ③the principles of division (rules) governing assignment into the classes must be based on suitable indicators (ground parameters, etc.) and must include the possibility of being updated during construction using the experience gained; ④these rules must also be so flexible that additional indicators can be incorporated; ⑤the uncertainties, or the quality, of the indicators must be established so that the probability of mis-classification can be estimated; ⑥the useful system should be practical and robust, and give an economic and safe design.

Since none of the existing classification systems fulfils the requirements for a true classification system for rock engineering problems, the following requirements can be put forward to build up such a system to be able to adequately solve rock engineering problems[13]: ①to use a supervised classification adapted to the specific project; ②the reliability of the classes to handle the given rock engineering problem must be estimated; ③ the classes must be exhaustive and mutually exclusive; ④to establish the principles of the division into classes based on suitable indicators; ⑤the indicators should be related to the different tools used for the design; ⑥the principles of division into classes must be so flexible that additional indicators can be incorporated; ⑦the principles of division into classes have to be updated to take account of experiences gained during the construction; ⑧the uncertainties or quality of the indicators must be established so that the probability of mis-classification can be estimated; ⑨the system should be practical and robust, and give an economic and safe design.

4.6 Site investigation reports

The contents of site investigation report may vary in different projects, mainly due to different purposes or requirements of the investigation. The report serves to summarize the investigations performed, interpret the geological conditions, establish the geotechnical design parameters for the various ground encountered, provide geotechnical features and recommendations for the design of the proposed tunnels, and identify the conditions that may influence construction.

Tunnel projects entail great uncertainty and risk in defining typically complex geological and groundwater conditions, and in predicting ground behavior during tunneling and operations. Even with extensive subsurface investigations, considerable judgment is required in the interpretation of the subsurface investigation data to establish geotechnical design parameters and to identify the adverse geological units. This situation is further complicated during tunneling since the behavior of the ground during construction is typically influenced by the contractor's selected means and methods for tunnel excavation and the type and installation of tunnel supports.

Using conventional geotechnical reports for tunnel projects would essentially assign the full risk of construction to the contractor since the contractor is responsible for interpreting the available subsurface information. Although this approach appears to protect the owner from the uncertainties and risks of construction, experience on underground projects has demonstrated that it results in high contingency costs being included in the contractors' bids, and does not avoid costly contractor claims for additional compensation when subsurface conditions vary from those that could reasonably be anticipated.

Current practice for tunnel and underground project sencourage obtaining a more equitable sharing of risks between the contractor and the owner. It is recognized that owners largely define the location, components and requirements of a project and the extent of the site investigations performed, and therefore should accept some of the financial risk as the differing site conditions, i.e., ground conditions encountered during construction differ significantly from those anticipated during design and preparation of the contract documents. The overall objectives of this risk sharing approach are to: ①reduce the contractors' uncertainty regarding the financial risks of tunneling projects to obtain lower bid prices; ② foster greater cooperation between the contractor and the owner; ③quickly and equitably resolve disputes between the contractor and the owner that may arise when ground conditions encountered during construction differ substantially from those reflected in the contract documents at the time of bidding; ④obtain the lowest final cost for the project.

To help achieve the above objectives, the site investigation report of a tunnel project generally include these reports, such as Geotechnical Data Reports (GDR), Geotechnical Design Memorandum (GDM), Geotechnical Interpretive Report (GIR) and GBR. The information on these reports for tunnel projects in details is provided by ASCE[93-96] and Brierley[97], as well as Chinese codes and guidelines in this field.

4.6.1　Geotechnical Data Report

The GDR is one complete assemblage of all geotechnical facts associated with the project. All subsurface facts about what was done, where it was done and what was learned from those activities must be assembled in one report. Each test boring, geophysical investigation, and laboratory test result must be described and the results of those activities summarized in tables, graphs, and plots.

The purpose of the GDR is to compile all factual geological, geotechnical, groundwater, and other data obtained from the geotechnical investigations for use by the various participants in the project, including the owner, designers, contractors and third parties that may be impacted by the project. It serves as a single and comprehensive source of geotechnical information obtained for the project.

The GDR should avoid making any interpretation of the data[98] since these interpretations may conflict with the data assessment subsequently presented in the GDM or other geotechnical interpretive or design reports, and the baseline conditions defined in the GBR[96]. Any such discrepancies could be a source of confusion to the contractors and open opportunities for claims of differing site conditions. In practice, it may not be possible to eliminate all data interpretation from the GDR. In such case, the data reduction should be limited to a determination of the properties obtained from that individual test sample, while avoiding any recommendations for the geotechnical properties for the stratum from which the sample was obtained.

The GDR should contain the following information[96]: ①descriptions of the geologic setting; ②descriptions of the site exploration program(s); ③logs of all borings, trenches, and other site investigations; ④descriptions/discussions of all field and laboratory test programs; ⑤results of all field and laboratory testing. If such additional information is limited in volume, consideration should be given to including these data in an appendix to the report. For example, the attachments and appendices would present the field and laboratory test records, and may also include helpful summary tables and plots that summarize the factual data obtained from the investigations. A typical outline for a GDR was presented by Brierley[97].

4.6.2 Key information for tunnel design and construction

For tunnel projects, one or more interpretive reports may be prepared to evaluate the available data as presented in the GDR, address a broad range of design issues, and communicate design recommendations for the design team's internal consideration. These interpretive reports are also used for evaluating design alternatives, assess the impact of construction on adjacent structures and facilities, focus on individual elements of the project, and discuss construction issues. The current guidelines recommend referring to such design reports as GDM, instead of GIR[96]. A sample outline for a GDM is presented in the guidelines[97].

The GDM should highlight the interpretive nature of the report[96,97]. In evaluating the engineering properties of the soil and rock materials, it is appropriate for the GDM to note the likely ranges for these properties and to recommend a value, or range of values, for use in design. The report should document the basis for selecting these parameters and discuss their significance to the design and construction of the proposed facilities. Presenting a range of parameters, along with a discussion of their consequences on the design, helps the owner and the design team understand and quantify the inherent uncertainty and risk associated with the proposed underground project. Such information allows the owner to determine the level of risk to be accepted, and the share of the risk to be borne by the contractor.

An example of this decision process would be a case where a tunnel must be constructed through relatively low strength rock that contains intrusive dikes of very hard igneous rock of unknown frequency and thickness. Based on limited geotechnical investigations, the geotechnical engineer determines that the amount of hard rock may range from 10 to 30 percent of the total length of the tunnel. This range, and possibly a best estimate percentage, would be reported in the GDM. During subsequent preparation of the GBR and other contract documents, a specific baseline value would be determined and referenced for contractual purposes and reflected in the design. If the owner, in an effort to get lower bid prices, is willing to accept the greater risk of cost increases during construction, a value closer to the lower end of the range would be selected as the baseline. However, if the owner wishes to reduce the risk of cost extras during construction, a value closer to the conservative end of the range would be selected. However, in choosing this second option, the owner needs to recognize that it will result in higher bid prices.

The GDM should include generalized subsurface profiles developed from an assessment of the available geotechnical and geological information. These subsurface profiles greatly facilitate a visualization and understanding of the existing subsurface conditions for design purposes. However, it must be recognized that such definition of subsurface conditions is highly dependent on the quantity and quality of the available geotechnical investigation data, and the judgment of the geotechnical engineer in interpreting these data and the relevant geological information. Accordingly, the report must emphasize that the profiles are based on an interpolation between widely spaced borings, and that actual subsurface conditions between the borings may vary considerably from those indicated on the profiles.

The GDM provides an interpretation of the available subsurface information to determine likely subsurface conditions for design and construction purposes. The GDM should present a general discussion of the appropriate methods of construction and the potential hazards that may be encountered during construction, as well as the possible measures that can be considered to mitigate these hazards. However, the GDM is not intended to be a definitive representation of the ground conditions and is not to be used as a baseline for contractual purposes.

4.6.3 Geotechnical baseline report

4.6.3.1 Purpose and objective

As above discussed, a fundamental principal in the current contracting practices for tunnel projects is the equitable sharing of risk between the owner and contractor, with the objectives of reducing contingency fees in contractor bids, achieving lower total cost for the project, and streamlining resolution of contractor claims for changed conditions during construction. Over the years, various forms and names have been given to the interpretive geotechnical report to be incorporated into the Contract Documents for underground projects in order to achieve the aforementioned objectives. Originally, this was called the Geotechnical Design Summary Report(GDSR). However, since 1997 and continuing with the current *Geotechnical Baseline Reports-Suggested Guidelines*[96] the industry has determined that the incorporated report be called GBR.

The primary purposes of the GBR include: ① to establish a contractual document that defines the specific subsurface conditions to be considered by contractors as baseline conditions in preparing their bids; ② to establish a contractual procedure for cost adjustments when ground conditions exposed during construction are poorer than the baseline conditions defined in the contract documents. Although it reflects the findings of the geotechnical investigations and design studies, a GBR is not intended to predict the actual geotechnical and geological conditions at a project site, or to accurately predict the ground behavior during construction. Rather, it establishes the bases for delineating the financial risks between the owner and the contractor.

ASCE[95] also noted the secondary purposes of the GBR as: ①it presents the geotechnical and construction considerations that formed the basis of design; ②it enhances contractor understanding of the key project issues and constraints, and the requirements of the contract plans and specifications; ③ it identifies important considerations that need to be addressed during bid preparation and construction; ④itassists the contractor in evaluating the requirements for tunnel excavation and support; ⑤ it guides the construction manager in administering the contract and monitoring contractor performance.

A common misconception of the GBR is that it represents a warranty of the existing site conditions by the geotechnical engineer and designer. In fact, since it principally serves as a contractual instrument for allocating risks, the GBR is not intended to predict or warranty actual site conditions. If the GBR were to become a warranty, it is reasonable to expect that the geotechnical engineer and designer would more conservatively define subsurface conditions and ground behavior, resulting in a higher cost for the project, a consequence clearly contrary to the primary motivation for adopting a risk-sharing approach to tunnel construction contracts.

It is also important to clearly differentiate the GBR from other interpretive reports may be prepared by the design team addressing a broad range of design issues for the team's internal consideration, as presented in a report of GDM.

The GBR should be the only final report prepared for use in bidding and constructing the project. The GBR should be limited to interpretive discussion and baseline statements, and should make reference to, rather than repeat or paraphrase, information contained in the GDR, drawings, or specifications[96].

4.6.3.2 General considerations

The various elements of the construction contract documents each serve a different purpose. The GDR provides the factual information used by the designer for designing the various components of the project, and by the contractor for developing appropriate means and methods of construction. The contract plans and specifications detail the specific requirements for the work to be performed, without providing an explanation or background information. The GBR is based on the factual information presented in the GDR as well as input from the owner regarding risk allocation, and provides an explanation for the project requirements as presented in the contract plans and specifications. The baseline information presented in the GBR must be coordinated with the GDR, contract plans and specifications, and contract payment provisions to assure consistency throughout the contract. However, the GBR should not repeat or paraphrase statements made in these other contract documents since even minor rewording of a statement may cause confusion or an unintended interpretation of the statement. Any inconsistency or confusion in the contract documents could lead to a successful contractor claim for additional compensation during construction since these are usually judged against the owner as the originator of the contract.

4.6.3.3　Guidelines for preparing a GBR

The GBR translates facts, interpretations and opinions regarding subsurface conditions into clear, unambiguous statements for contractual purposes. Items typically addressed in a GBR[96] include:①the amounts and distribution of different materials along the selected alignment;②description, strength, compressibility, grain size, and permeability of the existing materials;③description, strength and permeability of the ground mass as a whole;④groundwater levels and expected groundwater conditions, including baseline estimates of inflows and pumping rates;⑤anticipated ground behavior, and the influence of groundwater, with regard to methods of excavation and installation of ground support;⑥construction impacts on adjacent facilities;⑦ potential geotechnical and man-made sources of potential difficulty or hazard that could impact construction, including the presence of faults, gas, boulders, solution cavities, existing foundation piles and the like. A general checklist for a GBR preparation can refer to the guideline[96].

In general, a GBR should be brief and practical and avoid using ambiguous terminology, such as "may", "should", "can";rather, use definitive terms, such as "is", "are", "will". Whenever possible, refer baselines to properties and parameters that can be objectively observed and measured in the field. For the parameters that are anticipated to vary considerably, the GBR should note the potential range of values, but clearly state a specific baseline value for contractual purposes.

Since ground behavior is largely influenced by construction means and methods, statements of ground behavior in the GBR should also note the corresponding construction equipment, procedures and sequencing on which these statements were based. Individuals who prepare the GBR must be highly knowledgeable of both the design and construction of underground facilities, with construction experience particularly important for the necessary understanding of construction methods, equipment capabilities, ground behavior during tunnel excavation, and the potential hazards associated with the different ground conditions and methods of construction[96,98]. In addition, these individuals must be experienced in the preparation of a GBR and clearly understand its role as a contract document establishing reference baseline conditions. In general, to achieve greater consistency in the contract documents, the individuals preparing the GBR should belong to the same organization that prepares the contract plans and specifications.

4.7 Critical thinking problems

C1: The site investigation of a tunnel project is usually executed in stages. Consider: ①Why is the investigation in stages? ②What are the main tasks for the stages? ③The commonly used measures of the site investigation for the design in details.

C2: One of the objects of the site investigation in tunnel project is to approximate the geotechnical hydrological properties of the ground. The ground properties are usually first approximated by the test results of the related soils and rocks. Consider: ①The main parameters approximating the properties of soils and rocks, respectively; ②The typical magnitudes of (a) the strength of soils and rocks, in terms of soft, medium and hard; (b) the permeability of soils and rocks, in terms of being low and high, respectively.

C3: The properties of the surrounding rocks of a tunnel or underground structure can be evaluated with the application of a rock mass classification system, especially where an analogical method is used in tunnel design. In the application of a comprehensive rock mass classification system to grade the properties of surrounding rocks, the geological and hydrological conditions, such as ground in-situ stress, groundwater conditions, structural features of rock mass, are commonly used indexes, which are evaluated based on the results of the site investigation as a weighting factor. Consider: ①Main points and features of the well accepted rock mass classification systems, including Terzaghi's, *RQD* system, *RMR*, *Q* sytem, *GSI* and the system suggested in the design code in China (*BQ* system); ②How the weighting factors of the indexes, such as strength, intactness, in-situ stress, groundwater conditions, occurrence of the major structures, are evaluated in a rock mass classification system? ③The typical magnitudes of the geotechnical properties of the surrounding rocks presented in the rock mass classification system, such as *RMR*, *Q* sytem and *BQ* system, in terms of the grades of surrounding rocks; ④ The features and magnitudes of the suggested parameters of supporting system and stand-up time of a tunnel in the grades of surrounding rocks.

C4: The achievements of the site investigation of a tunnel project is presented in a report. Consider: ①Main points of a site investigation; ②Why has the GBR become increasingly recognized in the field of tunnel and underground engineering in recent years?

4.8 References

[1] Parker H W. Planning and site investigation in tunneling[C]//Congresso Brasileiro de Túneis e Estructuras Subterrâneas, Seminário Internacional South American Tunneling. 2004.

[2] ITA Working Group 2 Research. Strategy for Site Investigation of Tunnelling Projects [R/OL]. ITA, 2015. https://about.ita-aites.org/publications/wg-publications/download/1373_c23b267187260e75764d4a39728328aa.

[3] Eskesen S D, Tengborg P, Kampmann J, et al. Guidelines for tunnelling risk management: international tunnelling association, working group No. 2[J]. Tunnelling and Underground Space Technology, 2004, 19(3): 217-237.

[4] ITA. Guidelines for the design of tunnels[J]. Tunnelling and underground space technology, 1988, 3(3): 237-249.

[5] Kuesel T R, King E H, Bickel J O. Tunnel engineering handbook[M]. Springer Science & Business Media, 2012.

[6] Deere D U, Hendron A J, Patton F D, et al. Design of surface and near-surface construction in rock[C]//The 8th US symposium on rock mechanics (USRMS). American Rock Mechanics Association, 1966.

[7] Deere D U, Deere D W. Rock Quality Designation (RQD) after Twenty Years[R]. DEERE (DON U) CONSULTANT GAINESVILLE FL, 1989.

[8] Palmström A. The volumetric joint count-a useful and simple measure of the degree of rock jointing[J]. Proc. 4th Int. Cong. Int. Assoc. Eng. Geol, 1982, 5: 221-228.

[9] Takahashi T. ISRM suggested methods for land geophysics in rock engineering[J]. Int. J. Rock Mech. Min. Sci., 2004, 6(41): 885-914.

[10] Tsai D T, Hwang F L, Kao S C, et al. Application of Resistivity Image Profiling for the Hsuehshan Tunnel [J]. Proc. Of the World Long Tunnels 2005, Hsuehshan Tunnel, Taiwan, 165-170.

[11] Mayne P W, Christopher B R, Dejong J. Manual on Subsurface Investigations[R/OL]. National Highway Institute, Publication No. FHWA NHI-01-031, Federal Highway Administration, Washington, DC, 2001. https://www.fhwa.dot.gov/engineering/geotech/pubs/012546.pdf.

[12] Stacey T R, Wesseloo J. Application of indirect stress measurement techniques (non strain gauge based technology) to quantify stress environments in mines[R]. Safety in Mines Research Advisory Committee, University of the Witwatersrand & SRK Consulting, 2002.

[13] Stille H, Palmström A. Ground behaviour and rock mass composition in underground excavations[J]. Tunnelling and Underground Space Technology, 2008, 23(1): 46-64.

[14] Zoback M L. First-and second-order patterns of stress in the lithosphere: The World Stress Map Project[J]. Journal of Geophysical Research: Solid Earth, 1992, 97(B8): 11703-11728.

[15] Stacey T R, Wesseloo J. Evaluation and upgrading of records of stress measurement data in the mining industry[J]. Safety in Mines Research Advisory Committee, GAP 511, 1998:

1-53.

[16] Zang A, Stephansson O. Stress field of the Earth's crust[M]. Springer Science & Business Media, 2009.

[17] Hoek E, Brown E T. Underground excavations in rock[M]. CRC Press, 1980.

[18] Sheorey P R. A theory for In Situ, stresses in isotropic and transverseley isotropic rock [J]. Int. J. Rock Mech. Min. Sci., 1994, 31(1):23-34.

[19] Haimson B C. Borehole Breakouts-A new tool for estimating in situ stress[C]// Int. symp. conf. on Rock Stress & Rock Stress Measurements, Stockholm, 1986.

[20] Kusznir N J, Vita-Finzi C, Whitmarsh R B, et al. The Distribution of Stress with Depth in the Lithosphere: Thermo-Rheological and Geodynamic Constraints: Discussion [J]. Philosophical Transactions of the Royal Society A Mathematical Physical & Engineering Sciences, 1991, 337(1645):95-110.

[21] Dyke C G. In situ stress indicators for rock at great depth[D]. Doctoral Thesis London University, 1988.

[22] Mark C, Mucho T P. Longwall mine design for control of horizontal stress[C]// U. S. Bureau of Mines Technology Transfer Seminar, New Technology for Longwall Ground Control, Pittsburgh, 1994.

[23] Mayne P W, Kulhawy FH. K_0-OCR Relationships in soil[J]. Journal of the Geotechnical Engineering Division, 1982, 20(1): 851-872.

[24] Atkinson J H, Sällfors G. Experimental determination of stress-strain-time characteristics in laboratory and-in-situ tests, General report[C]// the tenth European Conference on Soil Mechanics and Foundation Engineering, Florence, 26-30 May 1991.

[25] Simpson B. Retaining structures: displacement and design[J]. Géotechnique, 1992, 42 (4): 541-576.

[26] Deere D U, Deere D W. The Rock Quality Designation (RQD) Index in Practice, Rock Classification System for Engineering Purpose[C]// Symposium on Rock Classification Systems for Engineering Purposes, 1987, Cincinnati, Ohio, USA, 1988.

[27] Lunardi P. The design and construction of tunnels using the approach based on the analysis of controlled deformation in rocks and soils[J]. Tunnels & Tunnelling International, 2000: 3-30.

[28] ITA Working Group Conventional Tunnelling. General Report on Conventional Tunnelling Method: ITA REPORT No. 002 [R/OL]. http://tunnel.ita-aites.org/media/k2/attachments/public/ITA_Report_N2_WG19_P.pdf.

[29] Stille H, Palmström A. Classification as a tool in rock engineering[J]. Tunnelling & Underground Space Technology Incorporating Trenchless Technology Research, 2003, 18 (4): 331-345.

[30] Palmstrom A, Stille H. Ground behaviour and rock engineering tools for underground excavations[J]. Tunnelling & Underground Space Technology Incorporating Trenchless Technology Research, 2007, 22(4): 363-376.

[31] Deere D U. Technical description of rock cores for engineering purposes[J]. Rock Mechanics and Engineering Geology, 1964, 1: 17-22.

[32] Takahashi T, Takeuchi T, Sassa K. ISRM Suggested Methods for borehole geophysics in

rock engineering[J]. International Journal of Rock Mechanics & Mining Sciences, 2006, 43(3): 337-368.

[33] Jamiolkowski M, Lancellotta R, Lo Presti D C F, et al. Stiffness of Toyoura Sand at Small and Intermediate Strain[C]// XIII ICSMFE, New Delhi, 1994.

[34] Woods Richard D. Laboratory measurement of dynamic soil properties[M]// ASTM Special Technical Publication 1213, 1994: 165-190.

[35] Larsson R, Mulabdi M. Shear Moduli in Scandinavian Clays-Measurement of initial shear modulus with seismic cones-Empirical correlations for the initial shear modulus in clay [R/OL]. Linköping: Swedish Geotechnical Institute, 1991. http://www.swedgeo.se/globalassets/publikationer/rapporter/pdf/sgi-r40.pdf.

[36] Larsson R. Consolidation of soft soils [R/OL]. Linköping: Swedish Geotechnical Institute, 1986. http://www.swedgeo.se/globalassets/publikationer/rapporter/pdf/sgi-r29.pdf.

[37] Larsson R, Åhnberg H. On the evaluation of undrained shear strength and preconsolidation pressure from common field tests in clay [J]. Canadian Geotechnical Journal, 2005, 42: 1221-1231.

[38] Burns S, Mayne P. Small and High-Strain Measurements of In Situ Soil Properties Using the Seismic Cone Penetrometer [J]. Transportation Research Record Journal of the Transportation Research Board, 1996, 1548(1):81-88.

[39] Mesri G, Abdel-Ghaffar M E M. Cohesion Intercept in Effective Stress-Stability Analysis [J]. Journal of Geotechnical Engineering, 1993, 119(8):1229-1249.

[40] Terzaghi K, Peck R B, Mesri G. Soil mechanics in engineering practice[M]. 3rd ed. New York: Wiley-Interscience, 1996.

[41] Holtz R D, Kovacs W D. An introduction to geotechnical engineering. Prentice-Hall Inc., Englewood Cliffs, N. J., 1981.

[42] Brady B HG, Brown E T. Rock Mechanics: For underground mining[M]. 3rd ed. Springer, 2006.

[43] Priest S D, Hudson J A. Discontinuityspacings in rock[J]. Int. J. Rock Mech. Min. Sci., 1976, 13(5):135-148.

[44] Wyllie D C. Foundations on Rock: 2nded[M]. New York: E&FN Spon, 1999.

[45] Goodman R E. Introduction to Rock Mechanics, 2ndedn[M]. New York. Wiley: 1989.

[46] Hoek E. Practical Rock Engineering[EB/OL]. 2007 ed. https://www.rocscience.com/assets/resources/learning/hoek/Practical-Rock-Engineering-Full-Text.pdf.

[47] Hoek E, Bray J W. Rock Slope EngineeringM], Institution of Mining and Metallurgy, London, U. K., 1977.

[48] Medhurst T, Brown E. Large Scale Laboratory Testing of Coal[C]// Institution of Engineers, Australia, 1996.

[49] Bieniawski Z T. Determining rock mass deformability: experience from case histories[J]. Int. J. Rock Mech. & Min. Sci., 1978, 15(5):237-247.

[50] Serafim J L, Pereira J P. Considerations of the geomechanics classification of Bieniawski [C]// The Int. Symposium of Engineering Geology on Underground Construction, Lisbon, 1983.

[51] Carter J P, Kulhawy F H. Analysis and design of drilled shaft foundations socketed into rock: Final report[R]. Electric Power Research Institute, Palo Alto, Calif., 1988.

[52] Barton N. Review of a new shear-strength criterion for rock joints[J]. Engineering Geology, 1974, 7(4):287-332.

[53] Jaeger J, Cook N G, Zimmerman R. Fundamentals of Rock Mechanics[M]. 4th ed. Blackwell Publishing, 2007.

[54] Sabatini P J, Bachus R C, Mayne P W, et al. Geotechnical Engineering Circular No. 5: Evaluation of Soil and Rock Properties [R]. Federal Highway Administration, Washington, D. C., 2002.

[55] Barton N, Lien R, Lunde J. Engineering classification of rock masses for the design of tunnel support[J]. Rock Mechanics, 1974, 6(4): 189-236.

[56] Barton N. The shear strength of rock and rock joints[J]. Int. J. Rock Mech. & Min. Sci., 1976, 13(9):255-279.

[57] Goodman R E. Methods of geological engineering in discontinuous rocks[M]. West Pub. Co. 1976.

[58] Hoek E, Brown E T. The Hoek-Brown criterion—a 1988 update[C]// 15th Can. Rock Mech. Symp., Toronto: Univ. Toronto Press, 1988.

[59] Hoek E. Strength of jointed rock masses[J]. Géotechnique, 1983, 33(3):187-223.

[60] Hoek E. Strength of rock and rock masses [J]. International Symposium on Rock Mechanics News Journal, 1994, 2(2): 4-16.

[61] Hoek E, Kaiser P K, Bawden W F. Support of Underground Excavations in Hard Rock [M]. A. A. Balkema: Rotterdam, 1995.

[62] Hoek E, Brown E T. Practical estimates of rock mass strength[J]. Int. J. Rock Mech. Min. Sci., 1997, 34(8): 1165-1186.

[63] Bieniawski Z T. Engineering classification of jointed rock masses[J]. Trans S. Afr. Inst. Civ. Engrs, 1973, 15(12): 335-344.

[64] Bieniawski Z T. Rock mass classifications in rock engineering [C]. Symposium on exploration for rock engineering, Johannesburg, 1976.

[65] Bieniawski Z T. Engineering rock mass classifications : a complete manual for engineers and geologists in mining, civil, and petroleum engineering [M]. Wiley-Interscience, 1989.

[66] Palmstrom A, Broch E. Use and misuse of rock mass classification systems with particular reference to the Q-system[J]. Tunnelling & Underground Space Technology Incorporating Trenchless Technology Research, 2006, 21(6):575-593.

[67] Brown E T. Block Caving Geomechanics [M]. Brisbane: Julius Kruttschnitt Mineral Research Centre, 2003.

[68] Marinos P, Hoek E. GSI-A geologically friendly tool for rock mass strength estimation [C]// GeoEng 2000, Melbourne, 2000.

[69] Goodman R E. Engineering Geology: Rock in Engineering Construction[M]. New York: Wiley, 1993.

[70] Terzaghi K. Rock defects and loads on tunnel supports[M]// Rock tunneling with steel supports, Commercial Shearing and Stamping Co., Youngstown, Ohio, 1946.

[71] Palmstrom A. Measurements of and correlations between block size and rock quality designation (RQD)[J]. Tunnelling and Underground Space Technology incorporating Trenchless Technology Research, 2005, 20(4): 362-377.

[72] Palmstrom A. RMi-A rock mass characterisation system for rock engineering purposes[D/OL]. University of Oslo, Norway, 1995. http://www.rockmass.net/phd/contents_all_text.pdf.

[73] Priest S D, Hudson J A. Discontinuity spacings in rock. Int. J. Rock Mech. Mm. Sci. and Geomech. Abstr.[J], 1976, 13(5): 135-148.

[74] Merritt A H. Geologic prediction for underground excavations[C]// N Am Rapid Excav & Tunnelling Conf Proc. 1972.

[75] Palmstrom A. The volumetric joint count—A useful and simple measure of the degree of jointing[C/OL]// The 4th International Congress IAEG, New Delhi, 1982. http://www.rockmass.net/ap/8_Palmstrom_on_Vol_joint_count_IAEG.pdf.

[76] Hoek E, Moy D. Design of large powerhouse caverns in weak rock[M]// Comprehensive rock engineering. Oxford: Pergamon, 1993.

[77] Helgstedt M D, Douglas K J, Mostyn G. A re-evaluation of in-situ direct shear tests, Aviemore Dam, New Zealand[J]. Australian Geomechanics, 1997,31: 56-65.

[78] Milne D, Germain P, Grant D et al. Field observations for the standardization of the NGI classification system for underground mine design[C]// The Seventh Congress of the International Society for Rock Mechanics, Aachen, Germany, 1991.

[79] Douglas K J, Mostyn G. Strength of large rock masses-Field verification[C]// The 37th US Rock Mechanics Symposium, Vail, Colorado, 1999.

[80] Wickham G E, Tiedemann H R, Skinner E H. Support determinations based on geologic predictions[C]// N Am Rapid Excav & Tunnelling Conf. ,1972.

[81] Barton N. Some new Q-value correlations to assist in site characterization and tunnel design [J]. Int. J. Rock Mech. & Min. Sci. , 2002, 39(2): 185-216.

[82] Grimstad E, Barton N. Updating the Q-System for NMT[C]// The International Symposium on Sprayed Concrete-Modern Use of Wet Mix Sprayed Concrete for Underground Support, 1993.

[83] Bhasin R, Barton N, Løset F. Engineering geological investigations and the application of rock mass classification approach in the construction of Norway's underground Olympic stadium[J]. Engineering Geology, 1993, 35(1-2): 93-101.

[84] Grimstad E. Barton N. ,Løset F. Rock mass classification and NMT support design using a new Q-system chart[J]. World Tunnelling,1993,9.

[85] Barton N R, Løset F, Lien R, et al. Application of the Q-system in design decisions concerning dimensions and appropriate support for underground installations[C]// Int. Conf. on Sub-Surface Space-Rockstore,1980.

[86] Barton N. Integrated empirical methods for the design of tunnels, shafts and caverns in rock, based on the Q-system[C]// 3rd Int. Symp. on Tunnels and Shafts in Soil and Rock, Mexico City, 2013.

[87] Hoek E, Carranza-Torres C T, Corkum B, et al. Hoek-Brown failure criterion-2002 Edition [C]// Narms-Tac Conference, Toronto, 2002.

[88] Einstein H H, Steiner W, Baecher G B. Assessment of empirical design methods for tunnels in rock[C]// Rapid Excavation and Tunnelling Conference, 1979.

[89] Peck R B. Advantages and limitations of the observational method in applied soil mechanics[J]. Geotechnique, 1969,19(2): 171-187.

[90] Bieniawski Z T. Quo vadis rock mass classifications? [J]. Felsbau, 1997,15(3): 177-178.

[91] Duncan J M. Factors of Safety and Reliability in Geotechnical Engineering[J]. Journal of Geotechnical & Geoenvironmental Engineering, 2000, 126(4):307-316.

[92] Technical Committee on Contracting Practices of the Underground Technology Research Council, ASCE Avoiding and resolving disputes in underground construction: Successful practices and guidelines[M]. ASCE, 1989.

[93] Technical Committee on Contracting Practices of the Underground Technology Research Council, ASCE. Avoiding and Resolving Disputes During Construction: Successful Practices and Guidelines[M]. New York:ASCE, 1991.

[94] Technical Committee on Contracting Practices of the Underground Technology Research Council, ASCE. Geotechnical Baseline Reports for Underground Construction: Guidelines and Practices[M]. New York:ASCE, 1997.

[95] Essex R J. Geotechnical Baseline Reports for Construction: Suggested Guidelines[M]. New York:ASCE, 2007.

[96] Brierly G S, Dobbels D, Howard A. Geotechnical report preparation [C]// North American Tunneling, 2000.

[97] Brierley G, Soule N. To GBR or Not to GBR: Is that the Question? [C]// Geo-Congress 2014, ASCE, 2014.

[98] ISRM. International society for rock mechanics commission on standardization of laboratory and field tests : Suggested methods for the quantitative description of discontinuities in rock masses[J]. Int. J. Rock Mech. & Min. Sci. , 1978, 15(6):319-368.

5 Tunnel Location Optimization

5.1 Introduction

Expansion reading 5-1

As discussed in Chapters 3 and 4, the typical stages of a road tunnel project from conception to completion include: planning, feasibility study, corridor and alignment alternative study, environmental impact studies (EIS) and conceptual design, preliminary design, final design and construction. Based on a preliminary survey and study on the geotechnical and hydrological conditions, together with the other aspects to be considered in tunnel design, the location of a tunnel and its dimensions should be preliminarily designed or proposed in an alternative design or during the planning stage. The position locating of a proposed tunnel is usually made as part of the work of alternative lines choosing. During the design of tunnels, location optimization is of part of the key works, which are often mainly based on the results of site investigation, as discussed in Chapter 4. It is not uncommon to take several decades for a tunnel project to be conceptualized, developed, designed, and eventually constructed. Under these situations, tunnel location choosing is a time taking process.

Expansion reading 5-2

5.2 General principles

At the alternative design stage of tunnel alignment, the alternative tunnel location depends on variety of dominant factors, including site geotechnical and hydrological conditions, cost, time schedule, construction techniques, risk, as well as social effect of the proposed line.

Expansion reading 5-3

The optimization of the locations of tunnels during survey and design is vital to the success of the project, in terms of safety, economy and environment favorable. In general, the following principles are beneficial to evaluate the locations of the tunnels in alternative line.

(1) Avoiding adverse geological units, such as fault, extensively fractured zone, soft layer, water containing layer, karst bearing layer and so on.

(2) If a tunnel is limited to cross an adverse geological unit, locate the tunnel as perpendicular as possible to the strike of the unit, in stead of parallel to it.

(3) If a tunnel will be located in a geological unit with large in-situ stress, the direction of the tunnel axis should be nearly parallel to the major horizontal principal stress.

(4) The location of tunnel portal is vital to the safety of operation, especially for the tunnels in mountain regions, where is readily subjected to seism, flood, gravity flow (e. g., debris flow, earthflow), landslide, rockfalls, etc. On the other hand, an optimized portal location is also vital to the construction of a tunnel project, in terms of constructing access and mucking deposit.

5.2.1 Avoiding adverse geology unit or conditions

The selection of the tunnel profile must take into account potential ground movements and avoid locations where such movements or settlements could cause surface problems to existing utilities or surface facilities, or mitigation measures should be provided. For example, during the planning phase, it is recommended to avoid crossing a fault zone and preferred to avoid being in a close proximity of an active fault. However, if avoidance cannot be achieved, then proper measures for crossing it should be implemented. Special measures may also be required when tunneling in a ground that may contain methane or other hazardous gasses or fluids. Here, only is the influence of site geotechnical and hydrological conditions on the alternative line choosing discussed in brief, with special reference to the stability of the tunnels in a proposed line.

Geotechnical investigations are critical for the proper design of a tunnel. Selection of the alignment, cross section, and construction methods is influenced by the geological and geotechnical conditions, as well as the site constraints. The good knowledge of the expected geological conditions is essential. The type of the ground encountered along the alignment would affect the selection of the tunnel type and its method of construction. For example, when the alternative study for the tunnel location optimization of the Kuixian Daban tunnel, a relatively short tunnel scenario (3400-m-long), the ACK line, was compared with a long tunnel one (6200-m-long), as shown in Figure 5-1. When the ACK line is chosen, most of the rocks are soft rocks, e. g., chlorite schist and phyllite, and glacial till. The section of the glacial till is in the range of the fluctuation of permanent frost line, as shown in Figure 5-2.

After the optimization of the alternatives, the 6200-m-long tunnel scenario was chosen as the final planned tunnel location to pass through the mountain ridge. In the longitudinal engineering geology cross section of the planned tunnel, the length of the section of granite and gneiss is more than half of the tunnel length. In this alternative, there are no glacial sediments, and the geological conditions is generally favorable to tunnel construction. However, just as every coin has two sides, there are another two tunnels would be buidt in this alternative line(Figure 5-1).

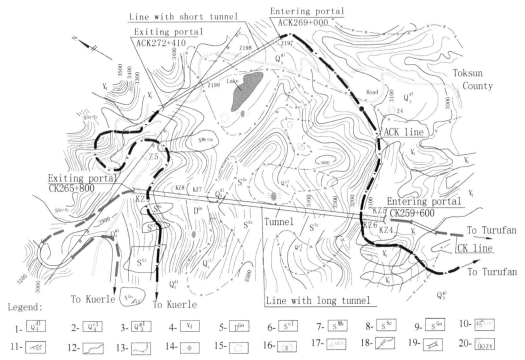

Figure 5-1 Engineering geology map of the Kuixian Daban tunnel[1]

1-Quaternary slope materials; 2-Quaternary relict sediments; 3-Quaternary glacial sediments; 4-Hercynian granite; 5-Devonian gneiss; 6-Silurian chlorite schist; 7-Silurian marble; 8-Silurian schist; 9-Silurian gneiss; 10-Reversed fault; 11-Strike and dip of rock layers; 12-Geological boundary; 13-Boundaries of the adverse geological units; 14-Frost soil swamp; 15-Thaw sinkhole; 16-Thaw slide; 17-Glacier till ridge; 18-Contour; 19-Tunnel; 20-Borehole and its number

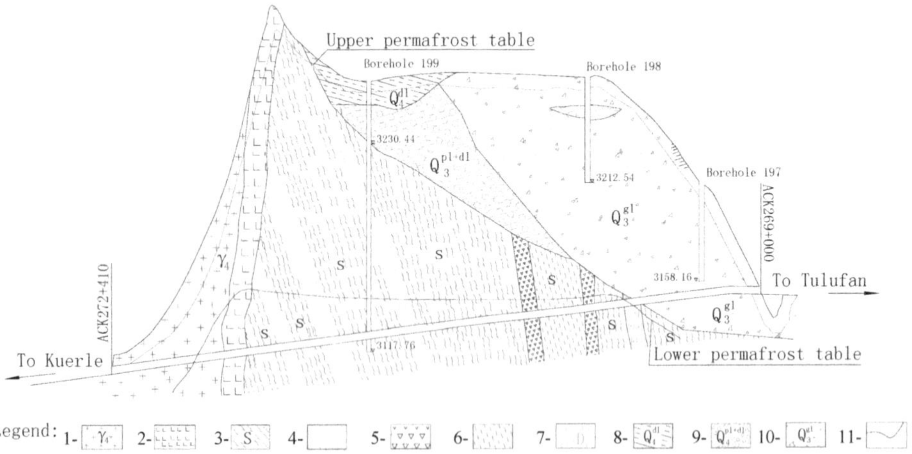

1-Hercynian granite; 2-Orthoclasite; 3-Silurian chlorite schist; 4-Marble; 5-Fault breccia; 6-Silurian phyllite; 7-Gneiss; 8-Quaternary slope materials; 9-Tertiary flood and slope sediments, glacial till; 10-Tertiary glacial sediments; 11-Geological boundary

Figure 5-2 Longitudinal geology cross section of the short tunnel alternative for the Kuixian Daban tunnel[1]

5.2.2 Safety distance for two tunnels

A tunnel may have two tubes or more. During the construction, the disturbance area in the surrounding rocks may be superimposed each other for the tubes. This situation is not favorable to the stability of the tunnel. In general, the tunnel should be located in a separated model. To meet this requirement, the minimum net distance between two tubes or tunnels should be no less than 0.8 to 2.0 times of the excavation span, as suggested by the design *Specifications* (JTG 3370.1—2018) for the better to worse ground conditions, respectively. However, a tunnel with two tubes may be a separated tunnel or neighborhood tunnel, multi-arch tunnel, branch tunnel in a limited situation. The safety distance or proper distance should be considered during tunnel location optimization.

Expansion reading 5-4

In practice, the locations of the tunnels or tubes may be confined to certain corridor, e.g., by approach structures, landscape, geological conditions and existing structures. In this condition, a neighborhood tunnel is usually applied in tunnel location optimization. The suggested net distance between the two tubes of a neighborhood tunnel is presented in the Expansion reading 5-4, for tunnels in the surrounding rocks of different grades.

Since the disturbance area of the two tubes of a neighborhood tunnel, multi-arch tunnel or branch tunnel, will be superimposed each other, the length of these type of tunnel should be limited in design optimization.

5.2.3 Minimum overburden or covering

In general, the magnitude of the overburden of a shallow tunnel is strongly related to the stability of the tunnel. For some special cases, the minimum overburden should be determined in design to meet the basic requirements of tunnel stability, construction and environmental control. For example, where a shield TBM tunnel is designed, especially in soft ground or underwater, the minimum overburden of the tunnel should be considered, in terms of anti-floating safety, uplifting of the ground during boring. In general, the minimum overburden should be about two times of the diameter of the tunnel. Otherwise, a checking calculation is always required in design to determine the minimum overburden. Similarly, where a hillside tunnel is designed, the thickness of the covering layers will have an influence on the location of the planned tunnel. For example, in China, the *Specifications* (JTG 3370.1—2018) recommends the minimum thickness of covering layers for hillside tunnels as presented in the Expansion reading 5-5.

Expansion reading 5-5

5.2.4 Tunnels in alignment

5.2.4.1 Relationship in line

There may be group of tunnels in a planned line. Where there are tunnels in a chain and the distance from the exit portal of a tunnel to the entrance portal of the following tunnel is such short that the influence of the two neighbor tunnels in a line on each other should be considered, such as in terms of the designs of tunnel alignment, ventilation and lighting. These neighbor tunnels are composed of tunnel group. The design considerations of road tunnel group under specified conditions are different.

Expansion reading 5-6

When two tunnels are neighbor in a line, the operational environment of the tunnels are closely related to the length of the tunnels and the net distance between the two tunnels, especially in terms of lighting condition. Whether the two tunnels are in group or not, in terms of lighting design, depends on the net distance between the two tunnels and the design speed of the line.

5.2.4.2 Tunnels in curve

As discussed in Chapter 3, the slope grade of a tunnel is generally limited to the range of 0.3%-3%, in terms of line alignment. At the same time, to meet the requirement of safety and sight, the geometry of the tunnels in curve should be considered in terms of horizontal curve and/or vertical curves features.

In a transportation line, a horizontal curve provides a transition between two tangent strips of roadway, allowing a vehicle to negotiate a turn at a gradual rate rather than a sharp cut. The design of the curve is dependent on the intended design speed for the roadway, as well as other factors including drainage and friction. These curves are semicircles as to provide the driver with a constant turning rate with radii determined by the laws of physics surrounding centripetal force. In China, it is often that no superelevation is designed for the roadway of a tunnel in horizontal curve. The minimum radii of the horizontal curve of a road tunnel should meet the requirements as suggested by the *Specifications* (JTG 3370.1—2018).

In terms of safety, the road tunnel design *Guidelines* (JTG/T D70—2010) presents the minimum requirement of stopping sight distance and intermediate sight distance for tunnels in curve line.

A vertical curve provides a transition between two sloped roadways, allowing a vehicle to negotiate the elevation rate change at a gradual rate rather than a sharp cut. Two types of vertical curves exist, i.e., sag curves and crest curves. Sag curves are used where the change in grade is positive, such as underwater tunnel or urban tunnels, while crest curves are used when the change in grade is negative, such as mountain tunnels. The design of the curve is dependent on the intended design speed for the roadway, as well as other factors including drainage, slope, acceptable rate of change, and friction. These curves are parabolic and are assigned stationing based on a horizontal axis. For example, in China, the minimum radii of the vertical curve of a road tunnel should meet the requirements as suggested by the *Specifications* (JTG 3370.1—2018).

Expansion reading 5-7

5.2.5 Risk control

Geotechnical issues such as the soil or rock properties, the ground water regime, the cover over the tunnel, the presence of contaminants along the alignment, the presence of underground utilities and obstructions such as boulders or buried objects, and the presence of sensitive surface facilities should be taken into consideration when evaluating tunnel alignment. Tunnel alignment is sometimes changed based on the results of the geotechnical conditions to minimize construction cost or to reduce the risks of the project.

5.2.6 Constructability

The tunnel profile can also be adjusted to improve constructability or accommodate construction technologies as long as the road geometrical requirements are not compromised. For example, for shield TBM tunnels in urban or underwater tunnel bored with shield TBM, the profile would be selected to ensure that sufficient cover is maintained for the TBM to operate satisfactorily over the proposed length of bore. However, this should not compromise the maximum grade required for the road.

5.2.7 Route selection in limited area

If the route selection is limited, then measures to deal with the poor ground in terms of construction method or ground improvement prior to excavation should be considered. It is recommended that the geotechnical investigation start as early as possible during the initial planning phase of the project. And therefore, the influence of the adverse geology unit or conditions can be well predicted in design and controlled during construction. For example, when a tunnel is planned in region with a regional fault occurred. The regional belt is often related to some adverse geological phenomena, such as soft and squeezing ground, high water pressure or water content, or even with large in-situ stress. The stability of the surrounding rocks of the fault zone is usually vital to the design and construction of a tunnel. The effect of the adverse geological conditions on the tunnel may last during tunnel operation. And therefore, it is generally designed that a tunnel transversely crossing the adverse geological unit or zone, so that the section of the tunnel in the adverse geological zone is as short as possible.

5.2.8 Being sustainable

It is noted that a tunnel is, to some extent, only part of a line. In a long run, the line is also part of the infrastructure system to a region or state. So, a planned tunnel is not only to be built, but the main object is its characteristics of social infrastructure. The construction of the planned tunnel should be favorable to environment, in terms of sustainable development of the related region.

For example, when a line is planned to build in mountain area, the line is often along a river side or across it. In order to make the line shorter and match the technical standard requirements, a tunnel is often a good choice. The site choosing should consider the effect of the tunnel construction on the hydrological development in the future. During the plan stage of the Dayaoshan tunnel, one of the key factors is to avoid a line with long distance along river, where is to build a dam and power station, as discussed in Chapter 3.

5.3 Location optimization of a tunnel

It is well accepted that the stability of a tunnel is mainly related to the factors, such as the properties of the surrounding rocks, and hydrological condition of the ground. During construction, surrounding rocks undergo a period of adjustment after an excavation is made. Whether the surrounding rocks can come back to an equilibrium and stable condition, depends strongly on the properties of the surrounding rocks. The interaction between the host rock and the underground structures plays a key role in the proper functioning of a tunnel. The host ground can play an active role in the stability of the ground of a tunnel. It is beneficial that a tunnel can be located in competent and water tight layers.

5.3.1 Control by major geological structures

Rock masses are natural material. The geological history of a rock mass will determine several key characteristics, such as the inhomogeneity (different properties at different locations), the anisotropy (different properties in different directions), the presence and mechanical characteristics of the discontinuities, and the hydraulic properties. In the location optimization of a tunnel, it is beneficial to consider the geological features of a major structure, where a tunnel will cross.

The nature and distribution of the major structures of the rock mass can have a dominate influence on the properties and the features of the hydrological conditions of the related rock mass. Obviously, the major geological structures of the rock mass can have a dominant effect on the response of a rock mass to tunneling operations. For example, large discontinuity can influence the choice of a tunneling method and the design of tunnel layouts because it can control stable excavation spans, support requirements, subsidence, cavability and fragmentation characteristics, since discontinuities have little or zero tensile strength, and the zone, with discontinuities, is often favorable to the penetrability of groundwater. The influence of major discontinuities, such as faults or other shear belt or zone, can be very significant to tunnel stability and constructability. At shallow depths and in de-stressed areas, structurally controlled failures may be the prime concern in excavation design. At depth and in the areas of high stress concentration, the influence of structure may be less marked, and the induced boundary stresses or energy release rates may be more important considerations.

Some of the major types of structural feature and their key engineering properties will be discussed in terms of tunnel design optimization.

5.3.1.1 Fold area

Folds are structures in which the attitudes of the beds are changed by flexure resulting from the application of post-depositional tectonic forces. The major effects of folds are that they alter the orientations of beds locally, and that certain other structural features are associated with them. In particular, well defined sets of joints may be formed in the crest or trough and in the limbs of a fold, as shown in Figure 5-3. Figure 5-4 shows three-dimensional fold growth controlling the along-strike variation in fold-related deformation in one stratum in an anticline[2]. During the folding, unique fracture networks in different structural positions may develop. On the other hand, anisotropy in permeability may be in spatial variation.

Expansion reading 5-8 [5-9]

During the stratum folding, the distribution of strain throughout a fold is related to the fold style and/or shape. In the context of isolated macroscopic folds, this is often related to whether a folded sequence of layers has continuous or discontinuous curvature[3], as shown in Figure 5-5. The evolving mechanical properties of the folded rocks not only control the number and distribution of fractures and other structures, but it also controls when these structures form during the folding process[4].

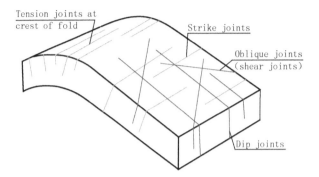

Figure 5-3 Jointing in a folded stratum[8]

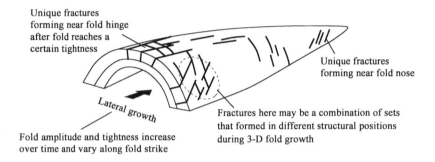

Figure 5-4 Fold growth controls spatio-temporal variation in fold-related deformation[2]

5.3.1.2 Fault and shear zone

Faults are defined when two adjacent blocks of rock have moved past each other in response to induced stresses. The features of a fault are that identifiable shear displacement has taken place between the rocks on opposite sides of the fault plane. In the fault zone, the responses of rocks to the induced stress may be brittle or ductile. Faults may be long and wide as a fault belt, which traverse a region or they may be of relatively limited local extent on the scale of meters. Fault width may vary from meters in the case of major, regional structures to millimeters in the case of local faults. The ground adjacent to the fault may be disturbed and weakened by associated structures such as drag folds or secondary faulting and fracturing. These factors result in faults being zones of low shear strength on which slip may readily occur. Figure 5-6 shows the folds beside a regional fault. The folds in Figure 5-6 can be considered as drag folds of a regional reverse fault, which is of the characteristic of strike-slip feature.

5 Tunnel Location Optimization   183

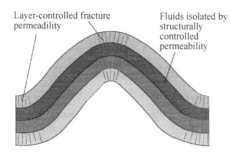
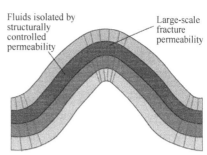

a) Structural and stratigraphic fluid compartmentalization resulting from localized fracturing; where the darker colors indicate modification of fluid chemistry during folding

b) Structural fluid compartmentalization in hinge zones spanning multiple stratigraphic levels

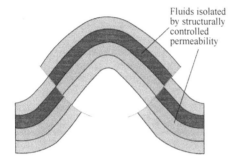
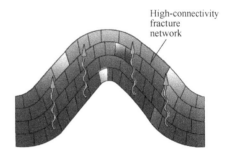

c) Fault bounded structural fluid compartmentalization; where isolated fluids evolve separately (darker colors)

d) Fluid flushing associated with the development of a high connectivity fracture network

Figure 5-5   Conceptual models of fractures, fault, and fluid distribution in folds[2]

Figure 5-6   Folds associated with a regional fault

With the influence of a fault or shear zone in consideration, it is generally beneficial to locate a tunnel following the principles: ①a tunnel should avoid faults or cross them in a nearly perpendicular mode, if it is possible; ②a fault zone is either being favorable to the storage of ground water or with a water tight layer in it, the favorable result of the tunnel location optimization is neither crossing a water bearing belt nor disturbing a water tight layer during tunnel construction.

Expansion reading 5-9[5-7]

Figure 5-7 shows the alternatives for the location optimization of the Guanjiao tunnel in the Qinhai-Tibet railway line. The optimized alternative location, ⑤-line in Figure 5-7, passed through eight faults, with five faults nearly perpendicular to the axial of the tunnel. The results of regional geological setting analysis showed that the maximum horizontal principal stress is in the direction of the tunnel axial.

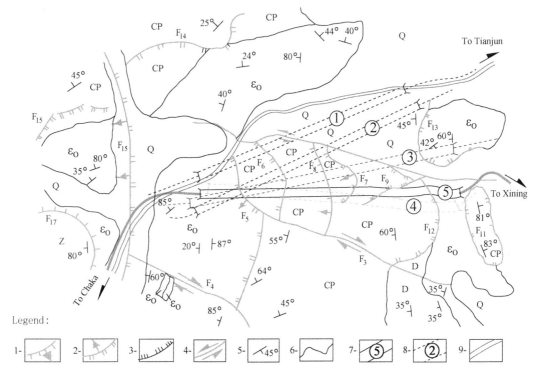

Q-Quaternary; CP-Carboniferous-Permian; D-Devonian; ε_O-Cambrian-Ordovician; Z-Sinian; 1-Normal fault; 2-Reversed fault; 3-Thrust fault; 4-Strike fault; 5-Occurrence of bedding and schist; 6-Boundary of stratum; 7-Optimized alternative; 8-Alternatives for comparison; 9-Road

Figure 5-7 Plan showing the distributions of geological units, faults and the optimized tunnel location[1]

5.3.1.3 Dykes

Dykes are long, narrow intrusions of generally fine-grained igneous rock with steep or vertical and approximately parallel sides. They may vary in width from a few centimeters to several meters and may appear as dyke swarms. Dykes may also be of considerable length. The Great Dyke of Rhodesia, for example, is some 500-km long. Some dyke rocks are more resistant to weathering than the country rock, but the basic igneous dyke rocks such as dolerite can weather to montmorillonite clays which are noted for their swelling characteristics. The dyke margins are often fractured and altered during the intrusion, as shown in Figure 5-8. They form potential seepage paths and the zones of low stiffness and shear strength, where movements will tend to be concentrated.

Figure 5-8 Fractures at the margin of a dyke

Expansion reading 5-10

Because of their high stiffness, unweathered dyke rocks can develop high stresses and so be susceptible to stress-induced failure. For example, in the deep-level gold mines of South Africa, hard and unweathered dyke rocks are associated with rockburst conditions. Figure 5-9 shows the effect of dyke proximity on rockburst incidence at the East Rand Proprietary Mines[10].

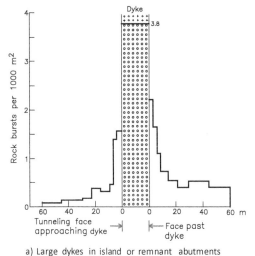

b) Large dykes in continent abutments

Note:

① High stiffness, unweathered dyke rocks can develop high stresses and so be susceptible to stress-induced failure.

② The effect of dyke proximity on rockburst incidence at the East Rand Proprietary Mines is significant, so is the difference of the influence of the dykes with different occurrences or from different locations.

a) Large dykes in island or remnant abutments

Figure 5-9 The effect of dyke proximity on rockburst incidence at a mine[11]

5.3.1.4 Layered strata

Layered stratum may be sedimentary rocks or metamorphic rocks. Here, it is referred to the rock mass, which is characteristics of a set of dominate discontinuities, such as sedimentary bedding planes, schistous planes in metamorphic rocks or even igneous rocks. The dominate planes or discontinuities are generally highly persistent features, though the layers may contain parting material of different grain size from the sediments forming the rock mass, or may have been partially healed by low-order metamorphism. In some cases, joints form parallel to bedding planes, foliations or slaty cleavage, when they may be termed bedding joints, foliation joints or cleavage joints.

In general, there would be some "cohesion" between the layers; otherwise, shear resistance on layer planes would be purely frictional. In mechanical properties, the strength of the rock mass in the direction parallel to the layer planes is much lower than in the direction perpendicular to the layer planes. This behavior of rock mass can have a strong influence on the stability of the tunnel, if the orientation of the layers is unfavorable to the stability of the tunnel excavations.

5.3.1.4.1 Horizontal layers

Horizontal layer rocks are often characteristics of changeable features in vertical direction, in terms of composition and properties. It is beneficial to locate a tunnel in competent and water tight layers. However, it is usually not an easy job. This is mainly because horizontal layered rocks, such as sedimentary rocks, often contain two sets of joints approximately orthogonal to each other and to the bedding planes. These joints sometimes end at bedding planes, but major joints may cross several bedding planes. In general, under same compressive regional geological stress field, joints occur in competent layers in a brittle mode, while weak layers deform in ductile mode. As a result, the competent layers are of high permeability while the weak layers may be water tight. This means that a tradeoff is often needed between stability and hydrogeological condition. Thick layers of competent layers are favorable to the crown stability of a tunnel, while the fractures, such as joints, may channel water into excavations. As shown in Figure 5-10, the location of the alternative Ⅱ(A-Ⅱ) will be perfect, in comparison to the others, especially in terms of stability. Of the others, the location of A-Ⅵ is relatively better, since competent rock layers are favorable to the stability of the crown of the planned tunnel.

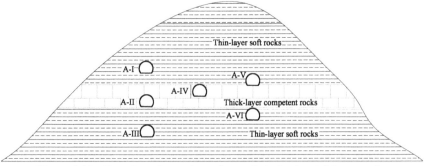

Figure 5-10 Location alternatives of tunnels in horizontal layer rocks

5.3.1.4.2 Inclined layers

In general, it is beneficial for a tunnel to cross inclined layers rather than to run parallel to the strikes of the layers. However, for the situation, where the layers are changeable greatly along their dip directions, a tunnel may totally be located in competent layers, provided that the thickness of the unit of the competent layers is wide enough. It is noted that, similar to the location optimization in horizontal layers, a tradeoff between stability and hydrogeological condition is also often needed. On the other hand, a boundary zone between weak layers and competent layers is often subjected to large deformation during tunnel construction. The boundary zone should neither to be excavated in a parallel mode nor to be nearby along whole tunnel.

For a tunnel located along slope side, the orientation of the rock layers to the slope may have strong influence on the stability of both the slope and the tunnel. In this situation, the favorable orientation of the rock layers is of the layers inclined down to the mountain, instead of being down to a river or valley.

Figure 5-11 shows the situation of location optimization in inclined and vertical layers. In general, the location of the alternative II (A-II) will be better than that of A-I.

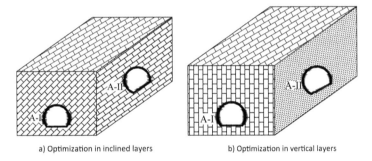

a) Optimization in inclined layers   b) Optimization in vertical layers

Figure 5-11   Location alternatives of tunnels in inclined or vertical layer rocks

5.3.1.4.3 Vertical layers

In general, vertical layered strata are much stable when a tunnel crosses through in a perpendicular mode, as the alternative II (A-II) shown the in Figure 5-11b). When a tunnel should run along the strikes of the layers, the location optimization is analogical to that in inclined layers.

5.3.2 Control by in-situ stress

The stability of a tunnel and the behavior of the surrounding rocks depend on the strength of rock mass and its stress state. The stress state of the surrounding rocks is related to the magnitude of in-situ stress in the rock mass and the features of the stress redistribution. The behaviors of the surrounding rocks during tunnel excavation depends on the stress state, in terms of magnitude and its loading mode on the surrounding rocks. The orientation of the major principal stress, especially the major horizontal in-situ stress, often has a strong influence on the stability of the excavation.

For a planned long tunnel, with large overburden, in a mountain area, in-situ stress is often one of the key geotechnical factors to be investigated during survey stage. Large in-situ stress is often related to hard rock mass, with excellent integrity and large overburden, or in a geological unit, which has been subjected to strong structural deformation in a compressive tress field during geological history. For the later situation, it is usually related to the fault belts or shear zones in young mountains.

In general, the major horizontal stress usually has a significant influence or the stability of the excavations. And therefore, it is usually beneficial to the stability of a tunnel to locate the axis of tunnel nearly parallel to the direction of major horizontal stress, as shown as alternative-II in Figure 5-12. Otherwise, once the magnitude of the major horizontal in-situ stress is relatively large and its orientation is nearly perpendicular to the tunnel axis, shown as alternative-I in Figure 5-12, the raveling condition of the surrounding rocks will have strong influence on the whole tunnel. In practice, the situation of alternative-III (Figure 5-12) is the common cases of tunnel design.

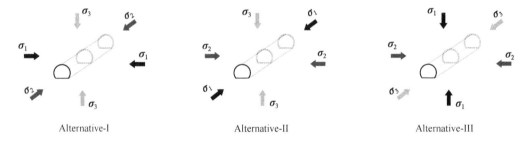

Figure 5-12 Location alternatives of tunnels under different in-situ stress field

5.3.3 Portal locations

The objective of tunnel portal location diagnosis is to predict the stress-strain response of the slope that is produced, in the absence of stabilization works, when excavation work commences to start the tunnel; and it will be safe enough not being subjected to adverse geological process, for example, landslide, rockfalls, earthflow, or natural disaster, flood, debris, or even earthquake.

5.3.3.1 Functions of tunnel portal structures

A tunnel is usually built in ground. Portals are the entering and exiting gates of the tunnel structures. The functions of tunnel portal structures may include the followings: ①entering and exiting passages of a tunnel; ②retaining and supporting the ground slope around the portals; ③a special structure to protect the line from natural disasters, e. g., snowslide, rockfalls; ④a special structure style being harmony with regional or local structures, environment, especially in aesthetics; ⑤a special structure to reduce the luminance at the tunnel portals; ⑥a special structure to reduce the air pressure at the high speed railway tunnel portals.

5.3.3.2 Structural types of tunnel portals

The design of the portals of a tunnel should meet the requirements of the functions of the planned tunnel portals. The structures of the portal accordingly vary among different tunnels. The types of portals, usually seen in transportation tunnels, as shown in Table 5-1, can be classified as conventional types, modified and special types. For the conventional types, circular frame, endwall type, post type and wing walls type are usually applied in the existing transportation tunnels. The modified types are the reformed structures of the conventional types. In terms of the relative position between the portal face of the tunnel and direction of tunnel axial, the strike of the tunnel portal face can be orthonormal to the tunnel axial or skew to the axial. The portals therefore may be orthonormal or skew ones.

Table 5-1 Types of tunnel portals and their main functions

Types		Main functions besides being part of tunnel structures					
		Alerting	Retaining	Protection	Luminance reducing	Air pressure reducing	Aesthetics
Conventional types	Circular frame type	Yes					
	Endwall type, stepped type	Yes	Yes				
	Post type	Yes	Yes				Yes
	Wing walls type	Yes	Yes				
Modified types	Skew tunnel portal	Yes	Yes				
	Arch wall type	Yes	Yes				
Special types	Shed	Yes		Yes	Yes		Yes
	Projected portal / Up bamboo-truncating	Yes		Yes	Yes		
	Projected portal / Down bamboo-truncating	Yes					
	Anti-slide-type open cut tunnel	Yes	Yes	Yes	Yes		
	Trumpet shape type	Yes		Yes		Yes	
	Ornamental portal	Yes					Yes

In recent years, tunnels in the field of transportation has witnessed great breakthrough and innovations in tunnel structures, such as the applications of bamboo-truncating type, trumpet shape type etc. These types blend the multiple functions of the portals, as well as the idea of environment favorable, into portal structures design.

5.3.3.3 Predicting the stability of portal excavation

The stability of a portal excavation in rocky ground characterized by joints and fractures is heavily influenced by the spatial orientation of the discontinuity families with respect to the free wall of the portal. The careful study of the geological structure of a rock mass will allow a fair initial estimate of the stability problem that will be encountered.

Expansion reading 5-11

The location optimization of the portal is to find how, with other factors remaining constant, a change in the position of a portal face affects the situation to be considered. To achieve this, thorough study of the following results of the survey phase must be conducted: ① the lithology, morphology, tectonics and structure of the slope to be entered; ② the hydrology, the pre-existing buildings and structures and the environmental constraints affecting the slope; ③ the geomechanical characteristics of the ground of which it is formed.

Expansion reading 5-12

Figure 5-13 shows a case history of tunnel location optimization in terms of avoiding adverse geological units around tunnel portal area, e.g., rockfalls, faulted and vertically jointed rock mass, rock piles, together with the relatively short karst section in the mined sections of the tunnel. At the preliminary design stage, the line ⅠDK was proposed to avoid building a long tunnel in limestone, which was considered an area with karst cavities. However, during the technical design, more rockfalls, faulted and vertically jointed rock mass, rock piles were identified around the portal areas of the planned tunnels along the line ⅠDK. At the same time, site investigation indicated that there is a long section without karst cavities along the alternative line ⅡDK, as shown in Figure 5-13. Finally, the line ⅡDK, with long tunnel, was built.

Forecasting the deformation behavior of the slope around a tunnel portal may be a tough job. The deformation behavior of the slope depends on the morphological, hydrogeological, stratigraphical, geomechanical and environmental situation of the ground. Some special factors may also need consideration in design optimization. For example, the force of earthquake may be a factor of inducing ground movement of the slope around the designed portal. What is difficult that when the earthquake will occur. In most of the time, the earthquake is a case of minor probability. It is noted that when the earthquake occurred, disaster usually followed. The rockfalls around the 109 Tunnel portal was due to the influence of the Wenchuan earthquake in 2008, in China. Coincidently, when the rockfalls occurred, a train transporting carbohydrate fuel partially ran out of the tunnel portal. The rockfalls not only stopped and damaged the train, but also induced fire of the carbohydrate fuel carried on the train. The disaster caused serious damage on both the train and the tunnel. The new tunnel was built at another site for the railway line in this section to avoid similar disaster.

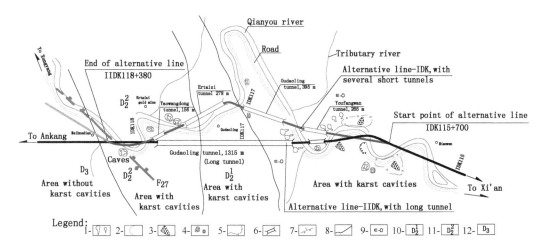

1-Rockfall; 2-Faulted or vertically jointed rock mass; 3-Rock piles; 4-Karst; 5-Boundaries of the adverse geological units; 6-Tunnel; 7-Reversed fault; 8-Geological boundary; 9-Cambrian-Ordovician limestone; 10-Middle Devoniansand-conglomerate, limestone; 11-Middle Devonian limestone; 12-Upper Devonian phyllite

Figure 5-13 Plan showing the distributions of geological units, faults and the optimized tunnel location[1]

Expansion reading 5-13

As noted by Lunardi[12], with the help of analysis, the design engineer must be able to establish:

(1) Whether excavation without confinement or support will be stable or unstable; ①if it is stable, whether the deformation suffered by the slope will be compatible with any pre-existing buildings and structures there may be; ②if it is unstable, what is the type of instability. More specifically, it is necessary to predict whether instability will occur as a result of slip along discontinuities or whether failure will occur in a fragile or ductile manner. In general, fragile behavior normally occurs each time the material is unable to develop sufficient residual strength(e.g., sand, stratified rock mass susceptible to landslide and characterized by discontinuities with poor shear strength). Ductile behavior normally occurs in material with a good reserve of residual strength(e.g., argillites, clays).

(2) The confinement or support action needed to contain potential instability.

(3) The design decisions to be taken in the structure design stage will be based

on these answers.

5.3.3.4 The condition of construction access

A tunnel is often with limited access to both construction and operation. When a tunnel is located in a specific site, the geotechnical conditions and geographical relief, such as the relationship to river, cliff, often have a strong influence on the condition of construction. The access condition to working site and the condition of transportation, such as mucking excavation spoils, and construction materials, are not only key factors to construction rate and time schedule, but also to the cost of the project. In a long run, the construction condition also has an influence on the quality of the construction.

It is also noted that the location of the portal of a tunnel will also have a strong influence on the cost of muck deposit and environmental effect. In general, the influence of the location of tunnel portal on the construction condition is much more significant for a long or super long tunnel than that for a short tunnel.

On the other hand, a good optimization of the portal location of a tunnel is related to the comprehensive consideration on the construction conditions of the approach structures, especially when the approach structure is a bridge. Under this situation, the interfering effect to both the tunnel and bridge is often important factors to be considered in construction plan.

5.4 Comments on the tunnel location study

During the alternative design and structure design of a tunnel, the location optimization is of significant importance, especially under complicated geological, geographical conditions, as well as environmental restriction. Many factors, such as site geotechnical conditions, constructability, cost, time schedule and risk of the tunnel project, operational and maintenance conditions, etc., should be considered in the location optimization. There may be variety of solutions to tunnels, but a proper location is the one, matched by the variety of site conditions, and other dominant factors. No one concept is superior for all situation or conditions. For each new proposed project, the full range of possible alternatives should be considered in order to develop a better solution.

5.5 Critical thinking problems

C1: During the preliminary design of a tunnel project, the location of the tunnel must be optimized with various factors under consideration. Consider: ①Why is the tunnel location optimization important for a tunnel project? ②What are the factors usually considered in the tunnel location optimization?

C2: As the task of tunnel location optimization is executed, what should the general principles be followed, such as in terms of: ①avoiding adverse geology unit or conditions; ②safety distance for two tunnels; ③tunnels in alignment, respectively.

C3: During the location optimization of a tunnel in details, the location and alignment of the planned tunnel should be determined, with several dominating factors under consideration. Consider the situations of: ①control by major geological structures, such as in fold structure, the relationship to fault and shear zone; ②control by in-situ stress, respectively.

C4: During the location optimization of the portals for a planned tunnel, various factors are under consideration. Consider these factors in details: ① the functions of tunnel portal structures; ② the structural types of tunnel portals and choosing; ③predicting the stability of portal excavation.

5.6 References

[1] The First Survey and Design Institute of China Railway (FSDICR). Case histories of railway engineering geology, Northwest and border upon area Fascicule[M]. Beijing: China Railway Press, 2002. (in Chinese).

[2] Evans M A, Fischer M P. On the distribution of fluids in folds: A review of controlling factors and processes[J]. Journal of Structural Geology, 2012, 44: 2-24.

[3] Hudleston P J, Lan L. Information from fold shapes[J]. Journal of Structural Geology, 1993, 15(3):253-264.

[4] Evans M A, Bebout G E, Brown C H. Changing fluid conditions during folding: An example from the central Appalachians[J]. Tectonophysics, 2012, s 576-577: 99-115.

[5] Eaton T T. On the importance of geological heterogeneity for flow simulation[J]. Sedimentary Geology, 2006, 184(3-4): 187-201.

[6] Sibson R H. Hinge-parallel fluid flow in fold-thrust belts: how widespread? [J]. Proceedings of the Geologists' Association, 2005, 116(3): 301-309.

[7] Haneberg W C, Mozley P S, Moore J C, et al. Fault-Fracture Networks and Related Fluid Flow and Sealing, Brushy Canyon Formation, West Texas[M]//Faults and Subsurface Fluid Flow in the Shallow Crust. American Geophysical Union, 2013: 69-81.

[8] Blyth F G H. A geology for engineers [M]. 7th ed. Edward Arnold, 1984.

[9] Gudmundsson A, Berg S S, Lyslo K B, et al. Fracture networks and fluid transport in active fault zones[J]. Journal of Structural Geology, 2001, 23(2-3):343-353.

[10] Cook N G W, Hoek E, Pretorius J P G, et al. Rock mechanics applied to the study of rockbursts[J]. Journal-South African Institute of Mining and Metallurgy, 1966, 66(10): 435-528.

[11] Brady B H G, Brown E T. Rock Mechanics: For underground mining [M]. 3rd ed. Springer, 2006.

[12] Lunardi P. Design and Construction of Tunnels, Analysis of controlled deformation in rocks and soils (ADECO-RS)[M]. Springer, 2008.

6 Preliminary Analysis for Tunnel Design

6.1 Introduction

Expansion reading 6-1

The in-situ stress in the surrounding rocks is disturbed due to tunneling and a new set of stresses are induced in the ground surrounding the opening. This process is also called stress redistribution in the surrounding rocks. The effect of the superimposition of the redistributed stress on the surrounding rocks depends strongly on the original properties of the surrounding rocks and the magnitude of the in-situ stress. Where the strength of the surrounding rocks is significantly exceeded and the resulting instability can have adverse consequences on the behaviors of the excavations.

The properties of the surrounding rocks are generally degenerated, such as due to the excavation disturbance, the effect of ground water, and the thrusting of the redistributed stress in the surrounding rocks. The magnitude of the degeneration of the surrounding rocks, i.e., the properties of the disturbed surrounding rocks, depends on the stress state of the surrounding rocks, ground water conditions and the effect of supporting and ground reinforcing measures.

Expansion reading 6-2

In terms of ground deformation control, the time effect of the surrounding rocks degeneration, and the interaction between the deformation of surrounding rocks and the actions of supporting measures, are key considerations in both design and construction. During design, it is always required to predict and give measures to control the mechanical performance of the surrounding rocks during tunneling and operation, such as in terms of safety and cost saving. And therefore, analysis on the behaviors of both the surrounding rocks and the support system of the planned tunnel, as well as their interaction, is parts of the steps of the design of a tunnel project, as shown in Figure 6-1.

6.1.1 Effects of tunneling on the ground

Stress redistribution in the surrounding rocks occurs due to tunneling. The pattern and the magnitude of the redistributed stress are related not only to the geotechnical properties of the ground and the state of the in-situ stress, but also the tunneling method and the features of the tunnel, such as its size and shape.

Figure 6-2 shows the effect of the tunneling on the surrounding rocks, in terms of stress redistribution[1]. In Figure 6-2, *A-B-C-D* represents section that is to be excavated. Prior to the excavation, the material within the envelope *A-B-C-D* exerts a set of support forces on the surrounding rocks. Excavation of the area of *A-B-C-D* to produce the rock configuration of Figure 6-2b) eliminates the support forces, i. e., the process of tunneling is statically equivalent to introducing a set of forces on the surfaces *A-B-C-D* equal in magnitude but opposite in sense to those acting originally. Under the action of these tunneling-induced forces, the following mechanical perturbations are imposed in the rock medium. Displacements of the adjacent surrounding rocks occur into the excavation space. Stresses and displacements are induced in the surrounding rocks. The final stresses in the surrounding rocks are derived from both the induced stresses and the initial state of stress in the ground.

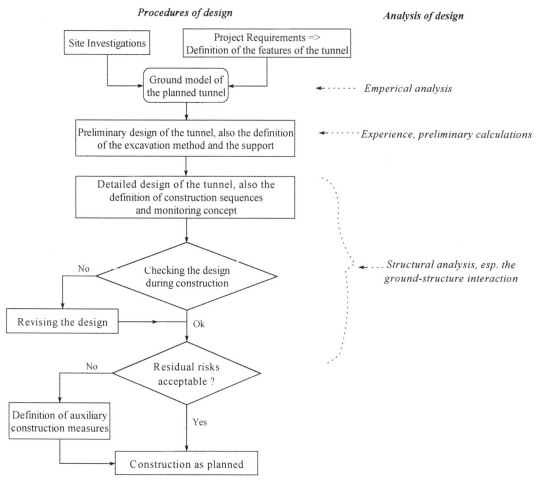

Figure 6-1 Analysis in tunnel design

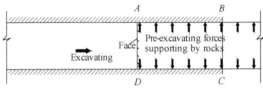
a) Pre-tunneling conditions around working face

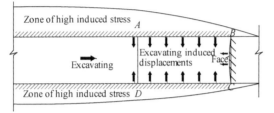
b) Mechanical consequences of tunneling excavations

Figure 6-2　Effect of tunneling excavation in rock mass[1]

Expansion reading 6-3

The effects of the stress redistribution, the strength degeneration and the increasing of the permeability of the surrounding rocks can cause instability or even collapse around the excavations, as well as water inflowing.

6.1.2　Analysis in tunnel design

As shown in Figure 6-1, an effective analysis, such as rock mechanics method, is required in tunnel design and the construction[2]. First, site characterization, mainly based on the result of site investigation, should be executed. Based on site characterization, a tunnel model representing the principal geomechanical features is formulated in tunnel design. In practice, this approach is proceeded as an empirical or analogical method.

At the later stages, having defined the prevailing conditions in the rock mass, the mechanical performance of planned excavating configurations and excavation geometries can be predicted using appropriate mathematical or numerical techniques. Recent rapid development of computational codes in power has improved the confidence of rock structural design analysis.

As shown in Chapter 4, uncertainty is often involved in the site characterization in a tunnel design. This is mainly due to the limited physical access, short time schedule, and limited cost of the site investigation for a specific project. A first-pass site characterization is intrinsically deficient[2]. To cope with this situation, tunnel design is itself an evolutionary process, in which engineering responses are formulated to reflect the observed performance of the surrounding rocks and supporting system during tunneling. And therefore, the analysis programme should be implemented via an iterative or multi-pass loop, as shown in Figures 6-1.

The objective of monitoring the surrounding rocks behavior during tunneling is to characterize the response of the ground to tunneling activity, such as through measuring the changing of the excavation profile, stress of the supporting system, the movement of the ground and neighbor structures, the fluctuation of ground water levels or pressures, etc. For example, the monitoring of the behaviors of both surrounding rocks and supporting system, as well as their interactions, is the components of the NATM, as proposed by Rabcewicz[3] and Pacher[4], including the whole sequence of rock tunneling aspects from investigation during design, engineering and contracting, to construction and monitoring[5].

In terms of design analysis, the results of monitoring should be analyzed to reassess and improve the knowledge of the in-situ mechanical properties of the surrounding rocks, as well as to review the adequacy of the postulated tunnel model in design, and to determine if a modification or adjusting is required in the design and construction. In this process, based on the analysis of the performance of the surrounding rocks and the identification of the key geomechanical parameters determining the deformational response of the medium, the design model, including detailed construction sequence and structure design criteria can be tuned or formulated, via the iterative loop(Figures 6-1), which is analogical to the principle of the observational method[6]. The monitoring and retrospective analysis are an engineering response to the problems posed by basic limitations in site characterization and conceptualization associated with excavation design in geologic media[7].

6.2 Behavior of surrounding rocks in general

Tunnels are located in various types of grounds, with specific behaviors. It is necessary to assess the surrounding rocks behavior, on which adequate excavating and support measures are based in design. Here are the general features of surrounding rocks presented as the followings.

6.2.1 Main parameters determining the behavior of surrounding rocks

The main parameters determining the behavior of the surrounding rocks are: the ground conditions, including rock mass compositions and structures, in-situ stresses and groundwater, and the project related features, e.g., size and shape of the tunnel, excavation method and the features of supporting system, as well as the interaction between the surrounding rocks and the supporting and reinforcing measures. The ground behavior can be assessed by combining relevant ground conditions with the project related features. The main parameters determining the behavior of tunnel surrounding rocks include[2]: ①the compositions and features of the surrounding rocks; ②the stress state of the surrounding rocks; ③the features of the project;④the assembled features of the project and surrounding rocks.

6.2.1.1 Compositions and structural features of surrounding rocks

The composition and structure of the rock mass have a strong influence on the tunnel surrounding rocks behaviors, because, for example, the compositions of the rocks, the degree of jointing in the rock mass, as well as the weathering degree of the rock mass, have dominative influence on the properties of the rock mass, as presented in the Chapter 4. Stille and Palmström[2] described the rock masses behavior modes with the following three groups, i. e., ①Group 1: General rock mass compositions occurring between weakness zones or faults; ② Group 2: Weakness zones and faults;③Group 3: Some minerals and rock types with special properties which may influence on ground behavior. For each of the three groups, the following classes for the degree of jointing are presented as Classes A, B, C, D and E(Figure 6-3), respectively. The main points of the Classes A, B, C, D and E are described as the followings[2].

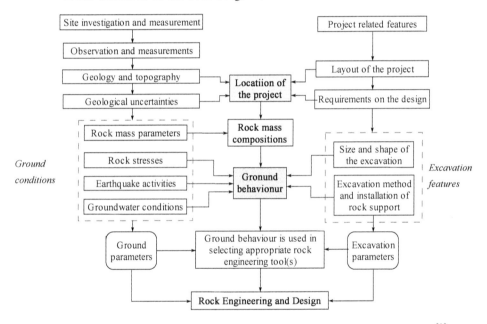

Figure 6-3　The principle process in identifying surrounding rocks behavior[2]

Classes A: *massive. Few joints or very wide joint spacing where the properties of the rock material dominate the behavior.*

Classes B and C: *jointed or blocky, i. e., slightly to strongly jointed rock masses. Here, the joints have the main influence on the behavior.*

Class D: *particulate rock mass. Includes heavily jointed or crushed rock, loose sedimentary(friable) rocks, and the materials of particles, grains or fragments with no or little bonding. The behavior in this group is a result of the interactions* between the blocks or fragments, as is the case in a bulk material.

Class E:rocks or rock masses with special properties different from the other four classes. An important feature is weathered and altered rocks are partly included (in class C, D or E). Such rocks may also occur in weakness zones(in group 2).

Expansion reading 6-4

6.2.1.2 Stress state of surrounding rocks

6.2.1.2.1 Effect of stress state

The in-situ stress state of rock mass can be approximated with the ratio of rock or rock mass strength and the in-situ stress, such as the ratio of intact rock strength and the maximum in-situ principle stress. The stress state of the surrounding rocks during construction is closely related to the stability and deformation features of the excavations. During tunneling, the stress redistribution of the surrounding rocks depends upon the magnitudes and directions of the in-situ principal stresses, the properties of the surrounding rocks, the geometry of the excavation, as well as the construction method of the tunnel. The behavior of the surrounding rocks under high stress state is different from that under low stress state. For example, under high stress state, the stress set up around the excavations may exceed the strength of the surrounding rocks. The deformation of the surrounding rocks can be remarkable and even induce collapse. However, under low stress state, instability may be induced by the low normal stresses on discontinuities in structurally controlled rock mass.

Hoek[9] showed a dimensionless plot from the results of parametric studies on rock mass strength, tunnel deformation and in-situ stress, as quoted in Figure 6-4, which shows the average trend of relationship between the surrounding rock deformation and the ratio of rock mass strength and in-situ stress. As shown in Figure 6-4, once the ratio of rock mass strength and in-situ stress is less than 0.2, deformations increase significantly and, unless these deformations are controlled, collapse or unacceptable deformation is likely to occur in the tunnel.

6.2.1.2.2 Effect of groundwater

The effect of groundwater on the stability of the surrounding rocks in two ways. According to the effective stress law, the groundwater pressure can have influence on the stability of the discontinuities in surrounding rocks, through reducing the normal effective stress between the discontinuity surfaces. The shear resistance, which can be mobilized by friction, decreases, and therefore, the effect of fissure or pore water under pressure is to reduce the ultimate strength of the surrounding rocks, when compared with the drained condition.

On the other hand, the effect of groundwater on rock mechanical properties may arise from the deleterious action of water on the rock mass strength for some particular rocks and minerals, such as the reduction of the strength of rock material and the reduced shear strength of discontinuities through slaking or swelling just due to moisture alteration. For example, in swelling clay, the adsorption of water significantly reduces friction and strength. Clay seams may soften in the presence of groundwater, reducing the strength and increasing the deformability of the rock mass. Argillaceous rocks, such as shale and argillite, also demonstrate marked reductions in material strength, such as groundwater infusing into weakness zones or layers.

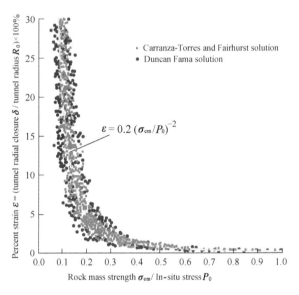

Figure 6-4　Tunnel deformation versus ratio of rock mass strength to in-situ stress[9]

Expansion reading 6-5

The groundwater pressure is also a kind of in-situ stresses. For example, groundwater pressure may contribute to instability in general, particularly in mixed rocks where ground water pressure may be built up behind layers of impermeable layer of weak ground.

6.2.1.3　Influence of project features

6.2.1.3.1　Effect of size and the shape of excavation

The stability and behavior of excavation is related to its size and shape. In principle, the deformations of an excavation will increase with increasing span or width. In over-stressed ground the strains and the loads thrusting on the support of the tunnel will also increase with the increasing span.

The effect of the shape to the stability of an excavation depends strongly on the in-situ stress features, such as the magnitude and the direction of the principle stresses. For example, when a tunnels is planned to be built in the ground, with hydrostatic in-situ stress, i.e. $\sigma_1 = \sigma_2 = \sigma_3$, a circle shape for the tunnel is usually favorable.

6.2.1.3.2 Effect of excavation method

The disturbance of surrounding rocks due to excavation depends greatly on the features of the chosen method. The disturbance is mainly presented by imposed cracks in the surrounding rocks and displacements, where is usually described as an excavation damaged and disturbed zone (EDZ) along the tunnel periphery. The magnitude of the EDZ will depend on both the chosen excavation method and the quality of the surrounding rocks. In general, drill and blast method will cause larger EDZ while it is less by TBM boring.

6.2.1.3.3 Effect of time and installation of supports

Tunnel may be built in hard rocks, where the surrounding rocks are in elastic state and the deformation induced by excavation will occur in time. However, it is noted that the instability of structurally controlled single block around the excavations of a tunnel in good rock mass will, however, have a very limited stand-up time, though the tunnel is generally stable.

Where a tunnel is excavated in incompetent ground, partial surrounding rocks will be in plastic state. Under this situation, the deformation will generally last for a relatively long period, which will depend on how soon after the excavation of a tunneling round the required supports will be installed and the effective ness of the deformation and strength degeneration being controlled by the support installation. The effect of time on the stability of the tunnels should be considered where there is a plastic area developing in the EDZ. The requirement of the support installation and the length of excavation round are governed by the stand-up time of the surrounding rocks.

6.2.1.4 Assembled features of the tunnel structures and surrounding rocks

6.2.1.4.1 Scale effect

Expansion reading 6-6[10]

Of the influence of intactness of the surrounding rocks on the stability of the planned tunnel, scale effect is of characteristics. Scale effect is illustrated schematically, where there is a transition from intact to a heavily jointed rock mass with increasing sample size. The behavior of the surrounding rocks may reflect the presence of discrete blocks of rock, whose stability is determined by frictional and other forces acting on their surfaces[9]. The most important factor to consider for design is the relative degree of jointing or fracturing.

6.2.1.4.2 The effect of major discontinuities

The effect of the occurrence of the major discontinuities on the stability of an excavation is strongly related to the space relationship between the occurrences of the major discontinuities and the axis of the tunnel. This effect is presented in some rock mass classification system, such as the *RMR* system in Chapter 4.

6.2.2 Ground behavior types of surrounding rocks

Tunnels are built in various rock masses. The behaviors of surrounding rocks are therefore various, in terms of stability and deformation mode. Schubert and Goricki[13] summarized the types of excavation instability (Table 6-1).

Table 6-1 Behavior types of rock mass as surrounding rocks[13]

No.	Basic behavior type	Description of potential failure modes/mechanics during excavation of the tunnel
1	Stable	Stable rock mass with the potential of small local gravity induced falling or sliding of blocks
2	Stable with the potential of discontinuity controlled block fall	Deep reaching, discontinuity controlled, gravity induced falling and sliding of blocks, occasional local shear failure
3	Shallow shear failure	Shallow stress induced shear failures in combination with discontinuity and gravity controlled failure of the rock mass
4	Deep seated shear failure	Deep seated stress induced shear failures and large deformation
5	Rock burst	Sudden and violent failure of the rock mass, caused by highly stressed, brittle rocks and the rapid release of accumulated strain energy
6	Buckling failure	Buckling of rocks with a narrowly spaced discontinuity set, frequently associated with shear failure
7	Shear failure under low confining pressure	Potential for excessive overbreak and progressive shear failure with the development of chimney type failure, caused mainly by a deficiency of side pressure
8	Ravelling ground	Flow of cohesionless dry or moist, intensely fractured rocks or soil
9	Flowing ground	Flow of intensely fractured rocks or soil with high water content
10	Swelling	Time dependent volume increase of the rock mass caused by physio-chemical reaction of rock and water in combination with stress relief, leading to inward movement of the tunnel perimeter
11	Frequently changing behavior	Rapid variation of stresses and deformations, caused by heterogeneous rock mass conditions or block-in-matrix rock situation of a tectonic melange (brittle fault zone)

Similarly, based on the works of Hoek[16] and Martin[14], Palmström and Stille[7] presented the behaviors of excavations with respect to the failure modes of surrounding rocks (Figure 6-5).

It is noted that, in some cases, the same rock mass and tunnel section may contain two or more possible types of failures. The combinations of behavior types may often occur, especially block falls in combination with, for example, swelling, rupturing, and plastic behavior.

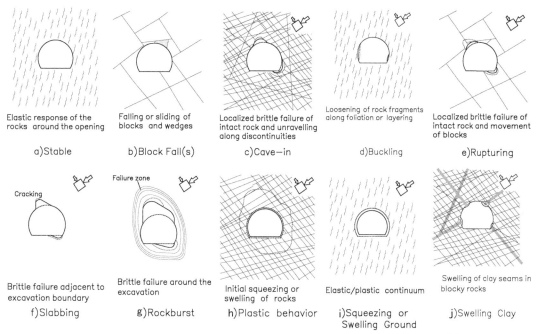

Figure 6-5 Types of surrounding rock behavior of underground openings[7]

Following the suggestions of two failure modes (instability) by Hoek and Brown[15] and by Hudson[16,17], Palmström and Stille[7] summarized the behavior types of surrounding rocks, with a third type being added to cover the influence of groundwater, as shown in Table 6-2. The main points are as followings.

Table 6-2 Behavior types in underground excavations[2]

Behavior types	Definition	Comments
Type 1-Gravity driven		
①Stable	The surrounding ground will stand unsupported for several days or longer	Massive, durable rocks at low and moderate depths
②Block fall(s)		
-of single blocks	Stable with potential fall of individual blocks	Discontinuity controlled failure
-of several blocks	Stable with potential fall of several blocks (slide volume <10 m^3)	Discontinuity controlled failure
③Cave-in	Inward, quick movement of larger volumes (>10 m^3) of rock fragments or pieces	Encountered in highly jointed or crushed rock
④Running ground	A particulate material quickly invades the tunnel until a stable slope is formed at the face. Stand-up time is zero or nearly zero	Examples are clean medium to coarse sands and gravels above groundwater level
Type 2-Stress induced		Brittle behavior
⑤Buckling	Breaking out of fragments in tunnel surface	Occurs in anisotropic, hard, brittle rock under sufficiently high load due to deflection of the rock structure

continue

Behavior types	Definition	Comments
⑥Rupturing from stresses	Gradually breaking up into pieces, flakes, or fragments in the tunnel surface	The time dependent effect of slabbing or rock burst from redistribution of stresses
⑦Slabbing	Sudden, violent detachment of thin rock slabs from sides or roof	Moderate to high overstressing of massive hard, brittle rock. Includes popping or spalling
⑧Rock burst	Much more violent than slabbing and involves considerably larger volumes. (Heavy rock bursting often registers as a seismic event)	Very high overstressing of massive hard, brittle rock
		Plastic behavior
⑨Plastic behaviour (initial)	Initial deformations caused by shear failures in combination with discontinuity and gravity controlled failure of the rock mass	Takes place in plastic (deformable) rock from overstressing. Often the start of squeezing
⑩Squeezing	Time dependent deformation, essentially associated with creep caused by overstressing. Deformations may terminate during construction or continue over a long period	Overstressed plastic, massive rocks and materials with a high percentage of micaceous minerals or of clay minerals with a low swelling capacity
Type 3-Water influenced		Hydratization
⑪Ravelling from slaking	Ground breaks gradually up into pieces, flakes, or fragments	Disintegration (slaking) of some moderately coherent and friable materials. Examples: mudstones and stiff, fissured clays
⑫Swelling		Swelling minerals
-of certain rocks	Advance of surrounding ground into the tunnel due to expansion caused by water adsorption. The process may sometimes be mistaken for squeezing	Occurs in swelling of rocks, in which anhydrite, halite(rock salt) and swelling clay minerals, such as smectite (montmorillonite) constitute a significant portion
-of certain clay seams or fillings	Swelling of clay seams caused by adsorption of water. This leads to loosening of blocks and reduced shear strength of clay	The swelling takes place in seams having fillings of swelling clay minerals(smectite, montmorillonite)
		Flowing water
⑬Flowing ground	A mixture of water and solids quickly invades the tunnel from all sides, including the invert	May occur in tunnels below groundwater table in particulate materials with little or no coherence
⑭Water ingress	Pressurized water invades the excavation through channels or openings in rocks	May occur in porous and soluble rocks, or along significant openings or channels in fractures or joints

(1) Type 1-Gravity driven: mostly discontinuity controlled failures (block falls), where pre-existing fragments or blocks in the roof and sidewalls become free to move once the excavation is made.

(2) Type 2-Stress induced: gravity assisted failures caused by overstressing, i.e., the stresses developed in the ground exceeding the local strength of the material. These failures may occur in two main forms, namely: ①as buckling, spalling, or rockburst in materials with brittle properties, i.e., massive brittle rocks; ②as plastic deformation, creep, or squeezing in materials having ductile or deformable properties, i.e., massive, soft/ductile rocks or particulate materials

(soils and heavy jointed rocks).

(3) Type 3-Water influenced: water pressure, an important load to consider in design especially in heterogeneous rock conditions. Groundwater initiated failures may cause flowing ground in particulate materials exposed to large quantities of water, and trigger unstable conditions, e. g. due to softening, swelling, slaking, etc. in some rocks. Water may also dissolve minerals like calcite in limestone.

As shown by Stille and Palmstrom[2], slaking is the breaking-up or disintegration of a rock or soil when exposed to moisture, saturated, or immersed in water; ravelling is a collective term for the breaking up and/or loosening of rock pieces; rupturing is the term for ravelling or breaking-up due to stress.

6.2.3 Methods to identify surrounding rocks behavior

In principle, the estimation of possible surrounding rocks behavior of a tunnel is based on the information, such as from desk works and site investigation. Stille and Palmstrom[2] proposed a schematic procedure of evaluating the surrounding rocks behaviors, in which the properties of the rock mass and the in-situ stresses in the ground are essential inputs to initially assess the surrounding rocks behaviors, and then with the additional parameters of the time after excavation, the way of the blocks move, and the presence of water under consideration, to determine the development of failure and the type of the behaviors.

Complex features, such as several types of behaviors, are also shown depending on the magnitude of stress and/or the content of special minerals. For example, under the situations of the mode of the stress state controlled surrounding rocks instability or damage, the behaviors of the surrounding rocks may appear as spalling, bursting or initial plastic deformation, in hard or soft rocks, respectively. The behavior mainly due to the effect of certain minerals or rocks, such as karst in limestones and swelling minerals in surrounding rocks should also be specially described, or measured, as well as treated individually[2].

6.3 Analysis tools for tunnel design

There are different types of tools, such as empirical method, analytical calculation, numerical modeling and observational methods, for option in tunnel design analysis. In some design codes, the principles of probabilistic approach are applied, in terms of the probability of failure, a safety index or a partial factor.

When choosing a tool for analysis, the predicted behavior of the surrounding rocks and the project related features, such as an acceptable standard or some other requirement, are key factors to be considered. A suitable tools for the design should be based on the actual surrounding rocks behavior and project requirements[2].

Sometimes, the behaviors of the surrounding rocks are project specific or unique and the prediction of the ground behaviors is difficult. The application of the observational method[6] is helpful and beneficial.

In practice, it is not an easy job to approximate the behavior of the tunnel surrounding rocks in complex geotechnical conditions. As Bieniawski[11] noted that "*provision of reliable input data for engineering design of structures in rock is one of the most difficult tasks facing engineering geologists and design engineers.*" So, tunnel design is frequently based on observations, experience and personal judgement, where rock engineering classification systems or empirical design methods play an important role[2].

Concerning choosing suitable tools for a tunnel project design analysis, Stille and Palmström[8] suggested an approach, which is based on actual ground behavior, in terms of a rock mass classification system and the rock engineering procedures.

6.3.1 Design tools and execution procedures

The tools often used in tunnel design analysis include empirical and classification methods, also called engineering judgement, calculations with numerical analysis or analytical method, observational methods. These methods may be applied together in tunnel design, such as in the mode shown in Figure 6-6.

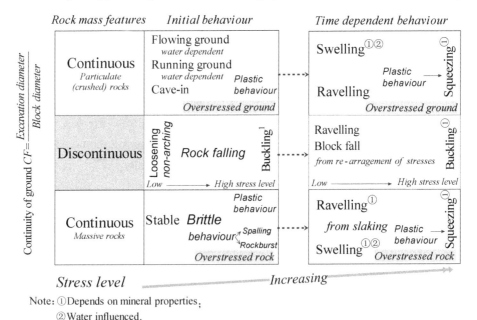

Figure 6-6 **The main principle types of tunnel surrounding rock behavior**[2]

The principles and procedures of executing design analysis, which is based on the assessments of tunnel surrounding rocks behaviors, from the pre-construction phase through to tunnel construction, are proposed by Schubert and Goricki[13]. The principles are mainly developed from experiences in Austria and presented in "Guidelines for geomechanical planning of underground works". Palmström and Stille [7] summarized them as followings (Figure 6-7).

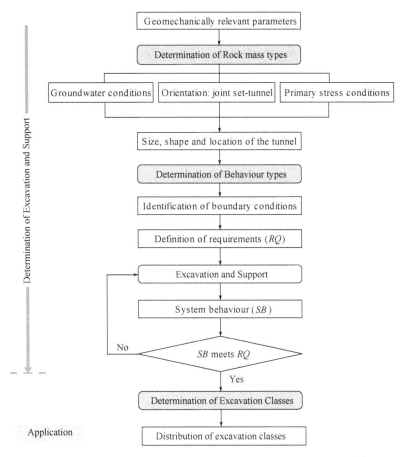

Figure 6-7 Flowchart of the basic procedure for tunnel design[13]

The first step in characterizing the rock mass is to define grade(s) of rock mass based on the information of lithology, laboratory tests and field observation data. From this, a parameter range is assigned for each grade.

The second step is to determine the type of behavior expected for the surrounding rocks. This is done in analysis by combining the previously defined rock mass grade with project related factors, such as stress conditions, orientation of discontinuities related to the tunnel axis, and the influence of groundwater, as well as the shape and size of the planned opening. From the results of the analysis, the potential failure modes are identified and the deformation magnitude of surrounding rocks is estimated. The identified types of behavior are used in construction method, and support requirements and measures scheme assessments.

During construction, monitoring and observation are applied to collect more information on the ground conditions and to verify the assumptions made during design. In this phase, the tunnel or system behavior(SB) is determined based on analysis of the rock mass/rock support interaction.

At the final step, the determined SB is compared to the required project goals to verify the design during construction. It can be done with the help of the subjective experiences called engineering judgement, or some existing empirical design rule(classification system) and calculation. It was noted by Palmström and Stille [7], that most of the issues related to serviceability and durability cannot be dealt with by calculations, and the design has to be based on experience and observations of the rock mass and its behavior in the tunnel. On the other hand, before the actual behavior can be observed, the complexity of the different issues related to the design process is widely recognized in the design codes. For the cases, in which uncertainties are involved in pre-calculations are so great that a design based on calculations may give a conservative design, or at least an unacceptably uncertain design is recognized, there is a consensus that the application of the observational method is preferable.

Expansion reading 6-7 [19-22]

6.3.2 Empirical methods

Empirical method in tunnel design is typically presented by the analogy method, which is mainly based on rock mass classification systems. The empirical method in tunnel design is therefore nearly almost referenced to the rock mass engineering classification method, of which some are listed in Figures 6-8 and 6-9 as empirical rock engineering design tools.

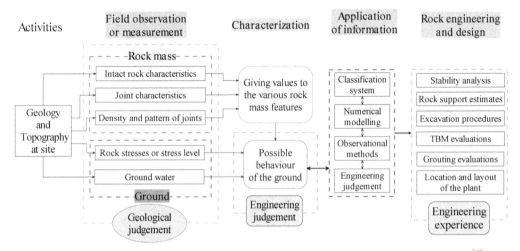

Figure 6-8 Methods and their applications in the procedures of tunnel design analysis[8]

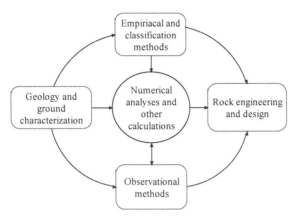

Figure 6-9 Main tools applied in the process of tunnel design[8]

When applying the empirical methods in tunnel design, it is important to keep in mind that there may be significant variation between the lowest and highest value of the geotechnical parameters, since all empirical systems based on experience have similar, inherent inaccuracies[8]. On the other hand, in terms of structure analysis, different types of analysis are appropriate for an intact rock mass, a blocky rock mass, or a crushed and heavily broken rock mass, respectively, as the behavior of an excavation will be fundamentally different[7].

Expansion reading 6-8

The main disadvantages of the application of the classification systems available today are that these systems generally cover the issue of structural resistance, with no consideration of the serviceability or durability of the structure, and do not allow the user to quantify the degree of safety in design[8].

6.3.3 Calculated solutions

6.3.3.1 Analytical calculations

Analytical method is often used in design for simplified situations, such as the behavior of a circular tunnel in an isotropic stress field, the block stability of surrounding rocks. One of the advantages of analytical solutions is to quantify the degree of safety in design. However, the dynamic behaviors of both surrounding rocks and supports, the interaction between the surrounding rocks and the supports, are generally too complex to be analyzed in a continuous process.

6.3.3.2 Numerical modeling

Expansion reading 6-9

Thanks to the robust computers, as well as the development of numerical analysis codes in geotechnical and tunnel fields, numerical methods become a usual tool for solving engineering problems in recent years. The most versatile classes of numerical analysis methods, such as finite element methods, discrete element methods, were originally developed in the field of structural analysis.

6.3.4 Judgement solutions

6.3.4.1 Engineering judgement

The ground conditions of a tunnel project may be complex and unique. Engineering judgement is always applied in design, as a check or verification mode, such as, acting as the judgement of an experienced designer, or the consultanting of an expert review board for particularly difficult issues or projects. In tunneling, a decision may have to be taken at the tunnel working face, especially under conditions, which are not readily calculable. Also, engineering judgement should be used in selecting a model for analyzing the overall stability, especially where there are two or more modes of behavior are acting, such as block falls and squeezing, or block falls and rupturing in the surrounding rocks of an excavation.

In practice, judgement may be used rather inconsistently in the various phases of planning or during construction. Einstein[18] gave the following comment on this issue: "*Judgement is required to set up the right lines of scientific investigation, to select the appropriate parameters for calculations, and to verify the reasonableness of the results. What we can calculate, enhances our judgement, allows us to make better judgements, permits us to arrive at better engineering solutions.*" Similarly, Peck[12] has written: "*Judgement is thus the intelligent use of experience or, more cautiously expressed, it is the recognition of the limitations of the methods one uses, and of the limitations and uncertainties of the materials one works with; and this brings us back to geology.*"

6.3.4.2 Observational method

The observational method[6] in geotechnical and tunnel engineering has been characterized as Terzaghi's "learn-as you-go" method. In terms of design, this method is also presented as "design as you go". The application of observational method in tunnel design and construction is mainly required for checking the design during construction. Where the prediction of the ground behavior is difficult, it may be appropriate to apply the observational method, which will be presented in Chapter 9.

6.3.5 Suitability of design tools

Every tunnel project is unique, such as in terms of ground conditions, structures features, construction, and environmental restriction. In general, the more complex of the planned tunnel project, the more design tools will be applied, such as empirical methods, engineering judgement, analytical and numerical methods. As stated by Stille and Palmström[2] that, for all types of rock mass behaviors, the assessments or calculations used in the design should be backed by engineering judgement, which requires the experience, skill and understanding of those involved in the projects.

Expansion reading 6-10

Every method has its advantage and disadvantage, based on the behavior of excavations in various ground conditions, the fitness of some of the rock engineering tools that are applicable to design studies is quoted, where it was suggested always to use more than one tool in the engineering design where individual tools have a higher fitness rating. Of the application of these tools in design, Stille and Palmström[2] suggested an engineering approach, based on the behavior of excavations, as shown in Figure 6-10.

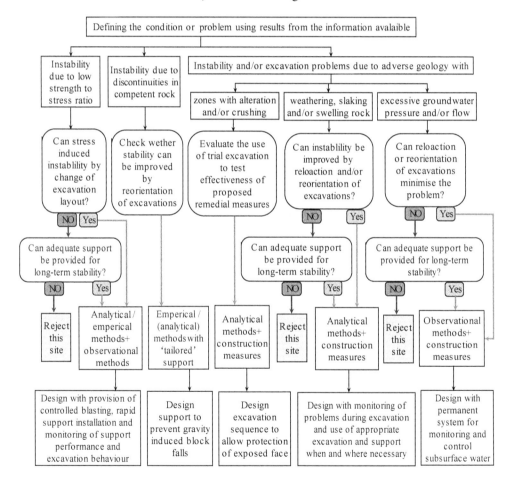

Note: Analytical methods include numerical modeling, physical modeling and failure criteria. Empirical methods include classification system and experience. Observational methods include in-situ monitoring and special geological observations. Construction measures include probing, grouting and special excavation procedures. "Tailored" support means support adapted to the local conditions encountered.

Figure 6-10 Simplified diagram for the selection of design methodology[7]

A method shown in Figure 6-10, in many situations, may be difficult to apply in any general or simplified system or calculation method[2]. For example, the rock engineering tools are poorly suited or not applicable relate to weakness zones or faults in rock mass[11].

6.4 Preliminary stress pattern in surrounding rocks

In tunnel stability analysis, the features of the stress redistribution due to tunneling are one of the considerations. The reaction of the ground to the excavation is related to the features of the ground conditions, the excavation method and its procedures, the features of supporting measures and their installation times. The analysis on the ground reaction and support behaviors are helpful to the tunnel design, since a good support design is one that will stabilize the excavation for the conditions to be expected, and is capable of being adapted to deal with changes from these conditions as they are revealed at the face during excavation, in which time effect is also a factor[26]. In the following section, the stress patterns around an excavation will presented, in terms of classical analysis method, which is one of the current design approaches.

6.4.1 Analytical solutions commonly used in tunnel design

As reviewed by Fairhurst and Carranza-Torres[26] that, some analytical solutions in continuum mechanics are commonly used in tunnel support design, such as the Lamé solution for the stress distribution around a cylindrical or spherical cavity in an elastic medium subjected to uniform internal and external pressure and the Kirsch solution for stresses around a circular hole in an elastic plate subjected to biaxial loading. Inglis effectively extended the Kirsch results in consideration of an elliptical hole in an elastic plate.

The distinct feature of these analytical or closed form solutions is that the results are expressed in dimensionless form. The stresses in surrounding rocks are seen to vary as the square of the dimensionless ratio of the "tunnel" radius (R) divided by the radial distance (r), or as the cube of this ratio in the case of a spherical cavity, while the deformations are proportional to the ratio of the applied stress ($\sigma_0, \sigma_1, \sigma_3$, respectively) to the elastic modulus (E) of the medium. The applied stresses can be considered as in-situ stresses. These general results, as summarized in Figure 6-11. The typical elastic and elasto-plastic analyses and convergence-confinement method in tunnel design will be presented in this section.

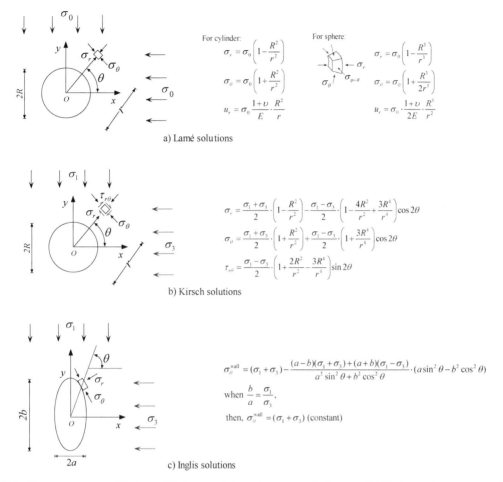

Note: The σ_r, σ_θ, $\tau_{r\theta}$-radial, tangential stress, and shear stress, respectively; u_r-radial displacement; σ_0, σ_1, σ_3-in-situ principal stresses, respectively; R-radii of excavation; a and b-small and large axis of elliptical excavations, respectively; r-radial distance from the centre of excavations; E, ν-elastic modulus of the surrounding rocks and their Poisson's ratio, respectively.

Figure 6-11 Some classical solutions for holes in elastic medium[26]

6.4.2 Elastic analysis

6.4.2.1 Excavations without suppor

Elastic analysis can provide considerable insight into tunnel support design. The expressions for elastic stress redistribution, for example, show that the stress concentrations in the surrounding rocks decrease as the ratio $(R/r)^2$, where R is the tunnel radius and r is the radial distance, in the case of a cylindrical tunnel, and as $(R/r)^3$ in the case of a spherical cavity. For example, for an excavation of radii, R, from the Lamé solution, the features of surrounding rocks stress disturbance with the radial distance, r, are presented in Table 6-3.

Table 6-3 The features of stress disturbance around excavation with the application of the Lamé solutions

Condition	Radial distance, r	$r=1.0R$	$r=1.5R$	$r=2.0R$	$r=3.0R$	$r=4.0R$	$r=5.0R$	$r=6.0R$
Anlysis as a cylinder under in-situ stress σ_0	Radial stress, σ_r	0.00	$0.56\sigma_0$	$0.75\sigma_0$	$0.89\sigma_0$	$0.94\sigma_0$	0.96	0.97
	Tangential stress, σ_θ	$2.00\sigma_0$	$1.44\sigma_0$	1.25	$1.11\sigma_0$	$1.06\sigma_0$	1.04	1.03
Anlysis as a sphere under in-situ stress σ_0	Radial stress, σ_r	0.00	$0.70\sigma_0$	$0.88\sigma_0$	$0.96\sigma_0$	$0.98\sigma_0$	0.99	1.00
	Tangential stress, σ_θ	$1.50\sigma_0$	$1.15\sigma_0$	$1.06\sigma_0$	$1.02\sigma_0$	$1.01\sigma_0$	1.00	1.00

The features of surrounding rocks stress disturbance in Table 6-3 shows that as the radial distance, $r = 2.0 R$, the stress "disturbance" around the excavation is 11% and 2%-4% for the analysis as a cylinder and as a sphere, respectively. This indicates that the influence of the neighbor excavation to a tunnel is insignificant provided their centers are several tunnel radii apart and can be considered to be independent of each other. For example, the application of the the Lamé solutions to the analysis on the stress redistribution of in-situ stress around the surrounding rocks of the English Channel tunnel, which is sketched in Figure 6-12, together with the smaller service tunnel. As the surrounding rocks is considered as elastic medium, using data $r = 30$ m and $R = 4.2$ m, the ratio $(R/r)^2$ is calculated as about 0.02. This implies that the excavation influence of the main tunnels on each other is insignificant. Similarly, the service tunnel will be subjected to an increase in loading of about 8% due to each larger tunnel, i.e., approximately 16% total increase in applied stress by the two main tubes excavations.

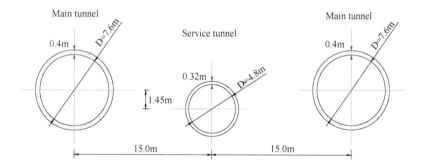

Figure 6-12 Typical cross-section of the railway tunnel system below the English Channel

The analysis of the elastic stress redistribution in the surrounding rocks can provide a reasonable indication of where inelastic deformation is likely to develop. The results can provide a simple and informative "first estimate" of the high stress regions, where potential inelastic deformation may occur around excavations. Figure 6-13 shows a practical case of the excavations at Kolar, where the extent of collapse is consistent with the shape of the high stress region behind the periphery.

After the collapse of the excavations in the Kolar gold mines, near Bangalore, India, elastic analysis was used for attempting to optimize the profile of excavations in competent rock. The elastic analysis results using the Inglis solution [Figure 6-11c)] shows that an elliptical opening in which the *major:minor* axis ratio was the same as the *major:minor* principal stress ratio was considered to be the most stable shape[26], since the tangential stress would be constant around the surrounding rocks. The analysis of the region of inelastic deformation indicates that rotation of the ellipse by 90° to the original orientation [Figure 6-13a)] would result in a reduction of the inelastic region. So when the tunnels were rehabilitated, their shapes are same as the overstressing and collapse areas of the excavations [Figures 6-13b) and 6-13c)]. The optimized shape of the excavation avoided future overloading region around the tunnel.

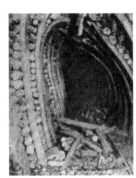

a) The original tunnel before collapse   b) The collapse of the tunnel   c) The collapse of the tunnel-2   d) Rehabilitated shape of the tunnel

Figure 6-13 Damage to steel-setted drives due to rockburst in Champion Reef Mine (about 87 level), **Kolar Gold Field, India**[26]

It is noted that, as stated by Carranza-Torres[24], in most of the practical situations, the high stress region behind the excavations due to stress redistribution is not constant. For example, as the surrounding rocks strength is lower than anticipated, inelastic deformation develops and then the region of failure will not be uniform.

6.4.2.2 Excavations with support

For the Lamé's solution, consider the situation of $R = 0$, where there is no excavation, we get $\sigma_r = \sigma_\theta = \sigma_0$, and $u_r = 0$. This means there is no excavation in the ground, no disturbance and no displacement occurs. Under the condition, as shown in Figure 6-14, where R is the radii of a circle excavation in elastic medium, and upon the excavation occurs, instant supports pressure p_i is applied in excavation, the radial and tangential stresses, σ_r, and σ_θ, at an unit with a radial distance r from the center of the excavation in the medium with in-situ stress σ_0 are[26]:

$$\sigma_r = \sigma_0 - (\sigma_0 - p_i)\left(\frac{R}{r}\right)^2 \qquad (6\text{-}1)$$

$$\sigma_\theta = \sigma_0 + (\sigma_0 - p_i)\left(\frac{R}{r}\right)^2 \qquad (6\text{-}2)$$

In a stressed medium under σ_0, when the excavation takes place, there is induced radial displacement u_r, generally in a convergence mode. The solution for the radial displacement is as the following[26]:

$$u_r = -\frac{1}{2G}(\sigma_0 - p_i)\frac{R^2}{r} \qquad (6\text{-}3)$$

Where G and E are the shear and elastic modulus of the ground, respectively, and $G = 0.5E/(1+\nu)$ and ν is the Poisson's ratio of the surrounding rocks.

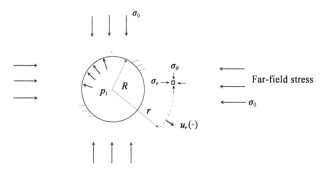

Figure 6-14 Model of excavation in elastic medium, loaded at infinity and inside the opening

6.4.3 Elasto-plastic analysis

Analytical extensions of Lamé's elastic solution to include plastic deformation around the cavity have been worked out by numerous authors for a variety of assumed models of the plastic behavior of the material. Most discussions of inelastic deformation around tunnels start from these solutions under uniform far-field stresses, i.e., the Lamé's case. A semi-analytical solution for the stress and displacements around a circular cavity is presented by Detournay[23], for the elasto-plastic extension of the Kirsch solution for the case where the far-field stresses are non uniform.

6.4.3.1 Elasto-plastic solution of a circular tunnel

When the support pressure is such less than a critical internal pressure, p_i^{cr}, or the installation of supporting measures being such late, that plastic region will develop around an excavation. This corresponding internal supporting pressure is called critical internal pressure. If $p_i \geq p_i^{cr}$, the problem is fully elastic. The solution is given by Lamé's solution.

If the support pressure $p_i < p_i^{cr}$, the problem is characterized by two regions

(Figure 6-15): ①elastic region: $r \geq R_p$; ②plastic region: $r \leq R_p$, where R_p is the radii the outer boundary of the plastic region.

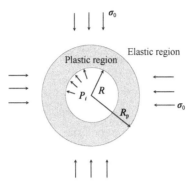

Figure 6-15 Pattern of plastic area developed around an excavation

The critical internal pressure p_i^{cr} can be found as the intersection of the failure envelope and Lamé's representation of the stress state. With σ_θ replaced by σ_1 and σ_r replaced by σ_3, Equations(6-1)and(6-2)are:

$$\sigma_1 = \sigma_0 + (\sigma_0 - p_i)\left(\frac{R}{r}\right)^2 \qquad (6-4)$$

$$\sigma_3 = \sigma_0 - (\sigma_0 - p_i)\left(\frac{R}{r}\right)^2 \qquad (6-5)$$

Equating the last part of the right-hand side of the equations above we have:

$$\sigma_1 = 2\sigma_0 - \sigma_3 \qquad (6-6)$$

The failure criterion of the material, which defines the relationship between the principal stresses σ_1 and σ_3 at failure, and can be written as:

$$\sigma_1 = f(\sigma_3) \qquad (6-7)$$

where f is a linear function in the case of Mohr-Coulomb material, or a parabolic function in the case of Hoek-Brown material[15].

Equating the right-hand side of Equations(6-6)and(6-7), making $\sigma_3 = p_i^{cr}$, the critical internal pressure p_i^{cr} is found from the solution of the following equation:

$$2\sigma_0 - p_i^{cr} = f(p_i^{cr}) \qquad (6-8)$$

Equation(6-8), which can be solved in closed-form for commonly used failure functions f, defines the critical internal pressure, below which the plastic zone develops around the tunnel. This critical internal pressure is also equal to the radial stress at the elasto-plastic boundary.

6.4.3.1.1 Solution for the elastic region($r \geq R_p$)

Consider the situation of the radius of the opening is R_p and the internal pressure is p_i^{cr}, the solutions for stresses and displacements in the elastic region is known from Lamé's solution as the followings:

$$\sigma_r = \sigma_0 - (\sigma_0 - p_i^{cr})\left(\frac{R_p}{r}\right)^2 \qquad (6-9)$$

$$\sigma_\theta = \sigma_0 + (\sigma_0 - p_i^{cr})\left(\frac{R_p}{r}\right)^2 \tag{6-10}$$

$$u_r = -\frac{1}{2G}(\sigma_0 - p_i^{cr})\frac{R_p^2}{r} \tag{6-11}$$

Note that the parameters in Equations (6-9) to (6-11) are the same as in Equations (6-1) to (6-3).

6.4.3.1.2 Solution for the plastic region ($r \leqslant R_p$)

(1) *Solutions for Mohr-Coulomb material*[26]

The Mohr-Coulomb yield condition is:

$$F = \sigma_1 - K_\varphi \sigma_3 - \sigma_c = 0 \tag{6-12}$$

where the coefficient K_φ is related to the friction angle φ according to:

$$K_\varphi = \frac{1+\sin\varphi}{1-\sin\varphi} \tag{6-13}$$

and the unconfined compression strength σ_c is related to the cohesion strength c, and the coefficient K_φ as:

$$\sigma_c = 2c\sqrt{K_\varphi} \tag{6-14}$$

The critical internal pressure p_i^{cr} is presented as:

$$p_i^{cr} = \frac{2}{K_\varphi + 1}\left(\sigma_0 + \frac{\sigma_c}{K_\varphi - 1}\right) - \frac{\sigma_c}{K_\varphi - 1} \tag{6-15}$$

The extent R_p of the failure zone is:

$$R_p = R\left[\frac{p_i^{cr} + \sigma_c/(K_\varphi - 1)}{p_i + \sigma_c/(K_\varphi - 1)}\right]^{\frac{1}{K_\varphi - 1}} \tag{6-16}$$

The solution for the radial stress field σ_r is given by the expression:

$$\sigma_r = \left(p_i^{cr} + \frac{\sigma_c}{K_\varphi - 1}\right)\left(\frac{r}{R_p}\right)^{(K_\varphi - 1)} - \frac{\sigma_c}{K_\varphi - 1} \tag{6-17}$$

The solution for the hoop stress field σ_θ is given by the expression:

$$\sigma_\theta = K_\varphi \left(p_i^{cr} + \frac{\sigma_c}{K_\varphi - 1}\right)\left(\frac{r}{R_p}\right)^{(K_\varphi - 1)} - \frac{\sigma_c}{K_\varphi - 1} \tag{6-18}$$

The solution for the radial displacement field u_r is given as:

$$u_r = \frac{1}{1-A_1}\left[\left(\frac{r}{R_p}\right)^{A_1} - A_1\frac{r}{R_p}\right]u_r(1) - \frac{1}{1-A_1}\left[\left(\frac{r}{R_p}\right)^{A_1} - \frac{r}{R_p}\right]u'_{r1} -$$

$$\frac{R_p}{2G}\frac{A_2 - A_3 K_\varphi}{(1-A_1)(K_\varphi - A_1)}\left(p_i^{cr} + \frac{\sigma_c}{K_\varphi - 1}\right)$$

$$\left[(A_1 - K_\varphi)\frac{r}{R_p} - (1 - K_\varphi)\left(\frac{r}{R_p}\right)^{A_1} + (1 - A_1)\left(\frac{r}{R_p}\right)^{K_\varphi}\right] \tag{6-19}$$

where the coefficients u_{r1} and u'_{r1} are:

$$u_{r1} = -\frac{R_p}{2G}(\sigma_0 - p_i^{cr}) \tag{6-20}$$

$$u'_{r1} = \frac{R_p}{2G}(\sigma_0 - p_i^{cr}) \qquad (6\text{-}21)$$

and for a linear flow rule,

$$A_1 = -K_\varphi, \quad A_2 = 1 - \nu - \nu K_\varphi, \quad A_3 = \nu - (1-\nu)K_\varphi \qquad (6\text{-}22)$$

$$K_\varphi = \frac{1 + \sin_\varphi}{1 - \sin_\varphi} \qquad (6\text{-}23)$$

where φ is the dilation angle of the surrounding rocks.

(2) *Solutions for Hoek-Brown material*[26]

Expansion reading 6-11

A closed-form solution is possible when the coefficient a is equal to 0.5 in the generalized Hoek-Brown criterion[15].

(3) *Solutions for Tresca material*[26]

Tresca material is a particular case of Mohr-Coulomb material, in which the friction angle φ is equal to zero. In such case the coefficient $K_\varphi = 1$, and singularities appear in the solution for stresses and displacements listed earlier [Equations (6-15) through (6-18)]. The solution for Tresca material can be obtained by taking the limit of the expressions for the Mohr-Coulomb failure criterion [Equations (6-15) through (6-18)] when $K_\varphi \to 1$.

Expansion reading 6-12

6.4.3.2 Influence zone of an excavation

The influence zone of a tunnel is used for defining a domain of the significant disturbance to the surrounding rocks, such as in terms of the pre-mining stress field, geotechnical and hydrological conditions, by tunneling. The influence zone due to tunneling is often considered in design, in terms of stress redistribution.

6.4.3.2.1 Stress around a circle hole in elastic medium

The magnitude of the redistributed stress around an excavation is related to both the radii of the excavation, R, and the features of the in-situ stress, σ_0, in the ground. For a circular hole in a hydrostatic stress field of magnitude σ_0, the radial stress σ_r, tangential stress σ_θ, and shear stress $\tau_{\theta r}$ at a unit, with a radial distance r, in the elastic surrounding rocks, are presented, with the Lamé solution for a cylinder, as:

$$\begin{aligned}\sigma_r &= \sigma_0\left(1 - \frac{R^2}{r^2}\right) \\ \sigma_\theta &= \sigma_0\left(1 + \frac{R^2}{r^2}\right) \\ \tau_{\theta r} &= 0\end{aligned} \qquad (6\text{-}24)$$

Equation (6-24) indicates that the stress redistribution is axisymmetric [Figure 6-16a)]. If a second excavation-II were generated outside the surface described by $r = 5R$ from the excavation-I, as shown in Figure 6-16b), the pre-excavating stress field would not be significantly different from the initial stress field. The boundary stresses for excavation-II are thus generally those for an isolated excavation. The excavations-I and II are considered separately and can be designed by ignoring the presence of each other. In general, for circular openings of the same radius, R, in a hydrostatic stress field, the mechanical interaction between the openings is insignificant if the distance $D_{I,II}$ between their centers is $D_{I,II} \geqslant 6R$.

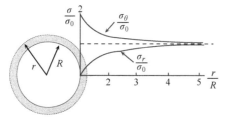

a) Axisymmetric stress distribution around a circular opening in a hydrostatic stress field

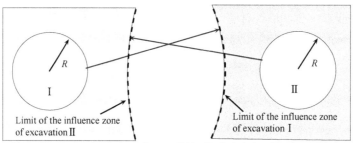

b) circular openings in a hydrostatic stress field, effectively isolated by virtue of their exclusion from each other's zone of influence

Figure 6-16 Stress redistribution around an excavation and the influence zones of two isolated excavations

Of the interaction between neighbor excavations, Figure 6-16b) illustrates the overlap of the influence zones of two circular openings, with same radii R and $D_{I,II} > 6R$. In the overlap region, the state of stress is produced by the pre-excavating stresses and the stress increments induced by each of the excavations I and II.

Figure 6-17 illustrates a case of a small-diameter excavation I is in the influence zone of a large-diameter excavation II, while the excavation II is outside the influence zone of the excavation I, and a fair estimate of the boundary stresses around the II is obtained from the stress distribution for a single opening. For excavation I, the field stresses are those due to the presence of excavation II. An engineering estimate of the boundary stresses around II can be obtained by calculating the state of stress at the centre of II prior to its excavation. This can be introduced as the far-field stresses in the Kirsch equations to yield the required boundary stresses for the smaller excavation I.

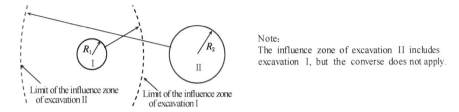

Note:
The influence zone of excavation II includes excavation I, but the converse does not apply.

Figure 6-17 Illustration of the effect of contiguous openings of different dimensions

6.4.3.2.2 Plastic zone around a circle hole

Plastic zone may develop around an excavation due to the stress redistribution in the influence zone of the excavation. The features of the plastic zone depend not only on the strength of the surrounding rocks, but also on the features of the in-situ stresses. Figure 6-18 gives general features of the plastic zones for different in-situ conditions, σ_{h0} and σ_{v0} for vertical and horizontal principal stresses, respectively, and as Case A for $\sigma_{v0} = \sigma_{h0}$, Case B for $\sigma_{v0} > \sigma_{h0}$, and Case C for $\sigma_{v0} >> \sigma_{h0}$.

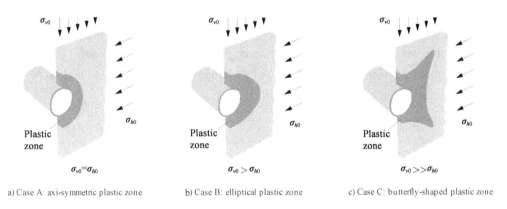

a) Case A: axi-symmetric plastic zone   b) Case B: elliptical plastic zone   c) Case C: butterfly-shaped plastic zone

Figure 6-18 Plastic zones developed around a circle hole under different in-situ stress conditions[23]

Detournay[23] showed that the elliptical pattern of inelastic deformation obtained under the condition of vertical pricinpal stress σ_{v0} is larger than the horizontal stress σ_{h0}, as quoted in Figure 6-19a). Detournay[23] found: ①that the mean radius (R) of the elliptical region is equal to the average of the major and minor semi-axes of the ellipse, b and c, $R = (b + c)/2$; ②that the major extension of the plastic zone is normal to the direction of the maximum far-field stress, σ_{v0}; ③that the point of maximum displacement[Figure 6-19b)] is located initially at the point B on the wall along the axis parallel to the maximum stress but changes to the point normal to the maximum stress direction as the radius R_0 increases, i.e., to the point A, as indicated in Figure 6-19a). Although the solution is limited to certain values of stress difference ($\sigma_{v0} - \sigma_{h0}$), characterized by the 'obliquity' m [Figure 6-19b)], numerical studies confirm the same general behavior under the conditions of greater field stress differences[26].

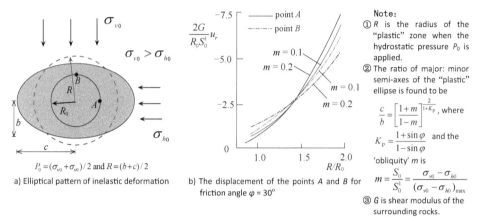

Figure 6-19 Inelastic zone around a circular tunnel under non-uniform far-field stresses[23]

Detournay and St. John[21] showed that features of the plastic zones developed around the excavations under the cases of various non-uniform far-field stresses (Figure 6-20), where P_0 is the mean far-field stress, $P_0 = (\sigma_{v0} + \sigma_{h0})/2$, and S_0 is the deviator far-field stress, $S_0 = (\sigma_{v0} - \sigma_{h0})/2$ and its maximum value is S_0^1. The chart is valid for a Mohr-Coulomb failure criterion with friction angle $\varphi = 30°$ and unconfined compressive strength σ_c.

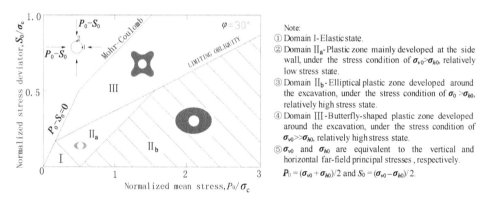

Figure 6-20 Plastic zone model under various non-uniform far-field stresses[21]

Similarly, Diederichs et al.[29] proposed a representation, in normalized principal stress space, of the fracture initiation, fracture extension, damage accumulation and shear failure envelopes, and the corresponding manifestations of the hard surrounding rocks failure, as shown in Figure 6-21. The several domains identified in Figure 6-21 may be defined by linear stress boundaries expressed by a generic form of the various "failure" criteria as[30]:

$$\sigma_1 = A\sigma_3 + B\sigma_{ci} \qquad (6-25)$$

The domain envelopes in Figure 6-21, defined using the equation, are explained as the followings.

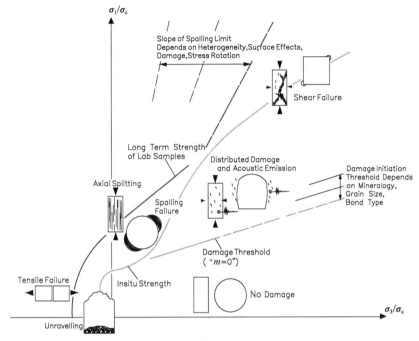

Figure 6-21 Modes of rock damage and failure and the composite in situ strength envelope for hard rock[29]

(1) The threshold for crack initiation and the onset of dispersed microseismic activity indicative of microscopic rock damage, is defined by $A = 1$-1.5 and $B = 0.4$-0.5. This approximates the maximum deviator stress criterion of Martin et al.[28]. It should be noted that the location of the damage threshold envelope depends on the mineralogy, grain size and bonding of the rock. The term $B\sigma_{ci}$ in equation is effectively the uniaxial compressive strength of the rock mass, UCS, which can be used for scaling other strength relations.

(2) A second threshold, described by $A = 2$, is identified with the onset of systematic fabric damage accumulation, and is represented by a transition from dispersed microseismic events to localised seismic clusters.

(3) The third threshold, given by $A = 3$-4, represents the conventional peak strength of the rock mass, corresponding to the interaction of damage zones and the localization of extension fractures into shear zones.

(4) A fourth threshold with $A = 0$, $B = 10$-20, applies close to excavation boundaries, under conditions where surface conditions tend to promote spalling.

6.4.4 Convergence-confinement method

The deformation of surrounding rocks and support system are often analyzed to evaluate the stability of excavation and the behaviors of surrounding rocks and support system, as well as the surrounding rock-support interaction. The results are used for approximating the required supports of the designed excavations and the time to install the supports. These problems can be preliminarily assessed by the convergence-confinement method.

6.4.4.1 Convergence-Confinement Method in general

The theoretical basis of convergence-confinement analysis has been described by Fenner[26] and others in tunnel support design. Later, this method has been applied in the NATM to develop practical tunneling support procedures, in which the support is optimized on site. Fairhurst and Carranza-Torres[26] presented Convergence-Confinement Method(CCM) as the following.

The convergence-confinement philosophy is illustrated by considering the simple case of a circular excavation in a homogeneous ground subject to uniform in-situ stress, as in the case of Lamé's solution. A uniform radial pressure (the support, σ_{ri}) is applied at the wall of the tunnel. Consider a wedge-shaped element of the ground bounded by two lines radiating from the center of the tunnel, line AB and CD and two circumferential lines, curve AD and BC, in the vicinity of the excavation, as shown in Figure 6-22.

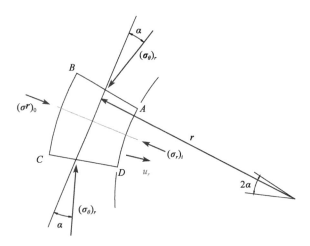

Figure 6-22 Forces acting on an elementary wedge in the vicinity of an excavation

Before excavation, each face of the wedge will be subject to the same uniform force acting normal to the face. Excavation of the tunnel will reduce the force acting radially outward on the inner face. The force on the outer face will be reduced also, but less so than on the inner face. The unbalanced radial force will cause the element to move radially towards the excavation. This will "tighten the wedge", i.e., the tangential force acting on the sides of the wedge will increase. A (small) component of the tangential force is directed radially outward, tending to reduce the net inward radial force. The wedge will tighten (i.e., displace towards the center of the tunnel), and the tangential stress will increase correspondingly until the wedge comes to equilibrium with the radial (support) pressure on the wall of the excavation. If the support pressure is reduced, the wedge will displace further towards the excavation until the forces are again in equilibrium. As long as the tangential stress continues to increase as the wedge displaces radially inwards, then the tunnel will find an equilibrium position as the support pressure is decreased. In this procedure, a lower rate of tangential stress increase with deformation simply implies that the radial displacement (convergence) will be greater before an equilibrium condition is reached. In some cases the tangential stress may reach an upper limit beyond which the wedge may "fail", such as reaching the shear strength of the material, slip along a joint traversing the wedge, etc. In such cases, the support pressure must be increased if the stability of the excavation is to be maintained.

Figure 6-23a) shows the typical form of the convergence-confinement diagram, which is usually derived for the case of a circular tunnel in homogeneous isotropic rock under uniform in-situ stress (P_0).

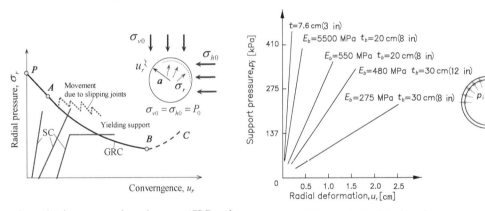

a) Interaction between ground reaction curve (GRC) and support characteristic (SC) around excavations

b) Support characteristics for various support systems

Note: The solid lines are for a wood-blocked steel support for various blocking conditions; the dotted line is the support characteristic for a 7.6 cm (3 in.) thick laye of shotcrete, with modulus $E = 21000$ MPa; the tunnel diameter ($2a$) = 5 m, steel support 15 cm × 10 cm light beam, 23.6 kg/m (16 1 bs/m), 61 cm (2 ft) spacing. Wood – block spacing = 1.05 m (41.9 in), E_b = block modulus (psi), t_b = block thickness (in).

How much stiffer the shotcrete support is than the steel-arch wood combinations? The shotrete will, in fact, not develop its full properties immediately, as assumed here, hence will have lower stiffness at early times.

Figure 6-23 Model of convergence-confinement analysis[26]

In Figure 6-23a), curve PB, often referred to as the Ground Reaction Curve, or GRC, indicates the radial deformation (u_r) that would develop when the tunnel came to equilibrium with a radial support pressure (σ_r). The initial segment PA

indicates elastic deformation; *AB* corresponds to stable inelastic deformation; piont *B* indicates the onset of unstable deformation(referred to by Austrian designers as the region of "loosening pressure"). Where there is at larger convergence, which is entirely possible, especially in the roof of a tunnel if the rock cohesion declines with deformation, and gravitational loads begin to dominate in determining the required support pressure[26]. Thus, the *BC* is an ascending portion of the curve.

The shape and magnitude of the Support Characteristic [SC, Figure 6-23a)] varies considerably depending on the type of support and the amount of convergence that has occurred prior to support installation. In the simplest case, of a uniform elastic ring installed around the tunnel periphery, the SC is a straight line as determined from the expression for the radial deformation (u_r) of a thin shell loaded externally(i. e. , at the rock-support interface) by the radial pressure (σ_r).

Figure 6-23b) shows a series of support characteristics for circular steel supports with various spacing of wood blocking between the rock and the steel ring. The relatively low stiffnes of the steel/wood block combinations arises due to the dominance of the low stiffness of the wood blocking in determining the overall SC. Although the intrinsic stiffness of the shotcrete is much lower than that of the steel, the fact that it is applied directly to the rock and results in a stiffer overall support. The procedure to estimate the stiffness of supporting system is presented in Hoek and Brown[15].

Figure 6-24 shows a series of GRCs, calculated for circular excavations in several hypothetical rock types under uniform loading conditions[26]. Two conditions are shown: ① where the rock cohesion is constant, independent of deformation; ②where the cohesion decreases linearly with deformation beyond the peak strength of the rock to a residual cohesion. It is seen that the support pressure required for equilibrium can increase considerably where cohesion decreases; or the amount of convergence may increase considerably if the support pressure is small. Loss of cohesion with inelastic deformation can be gradual in softer rocks or abrupt in more brittle rocks. It is also clear that, if the cohesion of the rock decreases to zero(this will occur first at the tunnel periphery), then the tunnel will inevitably collapse in theory.

Consider a small annulus Δr around the tunnel periphery where the cohesion has declined to zero. In a cohesionless material, the tangential stress will be proportional to the radial stress. If the radial stress is zero, i. e. , the tunnel is unsupported, then the tangential stress will also be zero. This annulus carries no load. It corresponds, in effect, to an enlargement of the tunnel. Since the tunnel is in an infinite medium, the stress redistribution around the tunnel, now of radius, $r + \Delta r$, will be the same as for the tunnel radius r. A new annulus will fail and the process is repeated without limit, i.e., the tunnel collapses totally. If, however, the annulus around the original tunnel retains some cohesion, albeit small, then a tangential stress will develop and the tunnel will be stable (although in some cases the convergence may be more than that is acceptable). This illustrates the importance of maintaining some integrity of the tunnel wall. This is especially true when rock bolts are the primary support. Special attention must be paid to the prevention of fallout and "unraveling" (e.g., by use of wire mesh between the bolts) especially in broken rock, prior to placing of additional support such as shotcrete.

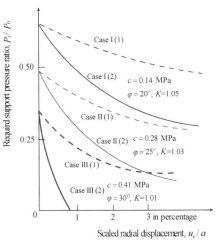

Note:
① Original isotropic stress P_0 = 2.8 MPa, Excavation radius a = 2.4 m (8 ft)
Based on the results Fairhurst, the support pressure P_i and radial displacement u_r are calculated as the following:

$$P_i = [P_0(1-\sin\varphi_i) - c_i \cos\varphi_i + c_r \cot\varphi_r] \cdot \left(\frac{a}{b}\right)^\alpha - c_r \cot\varphi_r, \text{ where}$$

$$\alpha = \frac{2\sin\varphi_r}{1-\sin\varphi_r};$$

$$(u_r^t)_{r=a} = \left(\frac{1+\nu}{E}\right)\left(\frac{b^2}{a}\right)(P_0 \sin\varphi_i + c_i \cos\varphi_i) + \frac{(b^2-a^2)(K-1)}{2a}$$

② The solid lines indicate the curves for the conditions where the rock strength is assumed to be represented by single Mohr envelop (i.e., $\varphi_i = \varphi_r; c_i = c_r$). The dotted lines represent cases where the rock strength drops progressively with deformation from the same initial values to the lower residual values (i.e., $\varphi_i > \varphi_r; c_i > c_r$).

③ In the diagram (and equations) above, K is a constant used for expressing in approximate form the dilation of the plastic zone. Thus K=1.01 implies 1% average (constant) dilation in the plastic region; K=1.05 implies 5% dilation. These values were based on field measurements in sandstones and shales (in coal mines) by Labasse.

Figure 6-24 Typical support pressure (P_i) versus radial displacement (u_r) curves based on elasto-plastic models[26]

The interaction between the surrounding rocks (i.e., the curve GRC) and the supporting (i.e., the curve SC) is represented in Figure 6-25a). The support starts to absorb load (i.e., it is installed in place) when the element of tunnel at the periphery has undergone a radial deformation, $(u_r)^c$. The rate at which the convergence will increase will be proportional to the difference in pressure (force) between the GRC and the SC. This rate will decline as the equilibrium convergence is approached. In the case of an inadequate support [the case of the "unstable" GRC in Figure 6-25a)], the rate will tend to increase beyond the minimum of the GRC. In practice, regular monitoring of convergence rates will thus allow the engineer to assess the adequacy of the support on site, even though the actual magnitudes of the GRC and the SC may not be known[26].

If a condition of impending instability is detected, as shown in dashed line in Figure 6-25b), then additional support, such as an additional layer of shotcrete, can be applied to "stiffen" (i.e., increase the slope of) the SC, in order to achieve stability.

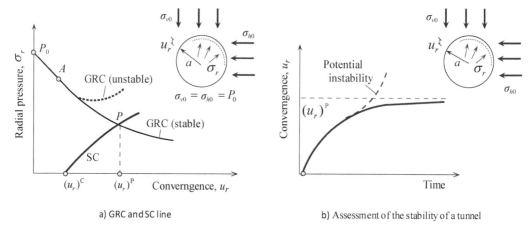

a) GRC and SC line

b) Assessment of the stability of a tunnel

Figure 6-25 Ground reaction curves as the basis for observation and assessment of the stability of a tunnel

6.4.4.2 Construction of GRC

Expansion reading 6-13[27]

The construction of the GRCs requires the consideration of a "failure" model for the surrounding rocks[25]. Non-linear models describing the failure of the rock are commonly used in tunnel engineering practice, such as the well accepted Hoek-Brown failure criterion, with the parabolic relationship between principal stresses. The fundamental parameters of the Hoek-Brown failure criterion are the unconfined compression strength σ_{ci} of the intact rock, and the parameters m_b, s and a[15].

6.4.5 Remarks on the analysis

Of tunnel surrounding rocks stability, the above discussion shows the importance of continuity of the tangential stress around an excavation. Frequently, in poor quality ground, the excavation may be carried out in several stages, e.g., heading and bench or several smaller profiles are excavated and supported separately before being connected to form the final section. So, under these conditions, it is vital applying the NATM principle of "*close the circle*" of the supporting system as soon as possible. Often this referred to early placement of the invert section of a lining to provide lateral stability to the vertical legs of the support, such as lining or steel sets. Just as stated by Fairhurst and Carranza-Torres[26] that to "*ensure continuity of tangential stresses in the rock and/or in the supports around the excavation*" is a simple practical guide to the application of the principles of the CCM. Loss of this continuity always means the risk of the onset of instability.

Although the analysis of the interaction between a tunnel support and the rock mass is considered a rational procedure in the CCM application and has been considered as standard[26], the successful application of the CCM is based on that the construction of the tunnel is capable of adapting quickly to ground conditions as they are revealed at the tunnel face to maintain the integrity of the tunnel periphery. To make the construction to be robust, in practice, the observational method is often in companion.

6.5 Critical thinking problems

C1: The behaviors of the surrounding rocks of a planned tunnel should be preliminarily approximated during the tunnel design, especially at the stage of planning and preliminary design. Consider: ① The parameters often used for determining the behavior of surrounding rocks; ② The main features of the surrounding rocks types, in terms of behaviors; ③ How is the behavior type of surrounding rocks determined, based on the information from site investigation?

C2: Analysis on the behaviors of the surrounding rocks and support system of a tunnel, as well as the interaction between the surrounding rocks and the support, is always required in tunnel design and construction. Consider: ①Commonly used tools for the tunnel design; ②Why are several tools or methods required by the design analysis of a mega project?

C3: During tunnel design, the surrounding rock stress redistribution induced by tunneling, the behaviors and stress patterns of surrounding rocks can be preliminarily approximated, such as in terms of elastic, elasto-plastic and convergence-confinement methods. Consider: ① What are the conditions for the application of the classical analysis solutions of Lamé, Kirsch and Inglis, respectively? ②The features of stress redistribution pattern around an excavation, in terms of Lamé, Kirsch and Inglis solutions, respectively; ③The conditions of plastic zone development in the excavation disturbance zone; ④The features of the plastic zones, developed under the in-situ stress field of $\sigma_{v0} > \sigma_{h0}$ and $\sigma_{v0} >> \sigma_{h0}$, respectively; ⑤The main functions of the internal support of an excavation, such as in terms of failure zone development control.

C4: The Convergence-Confinement Method (CCM) is well used in tunnel design analysis, especially when the principles of the NATM are applied in this process. Consider: ① The CCM in general; ② Time effect of the installation of support system in the CCM; ③The importance of maintaining some integrity of the tunnel surrounding rocks; ④ The parameters required for the construction of the GRC when the CCM is applied in tunnel design analysis.

6.6 References

[1] Brady B H G, Brown E T. Rock Mechanics: For underground mining [M]. 3rd ed.

Springer, 2006.

[2] Stille H, Palmström A. Ground behaviour and rock mass composition in underground excavations[J]. Tunnelling & Underground Space Technology, 2008, 23(1): 46-64.

[3] Rabcewicz L v. The new Austrian tunnelling method[J]. Water Power, Part 1, 1964: 511-515, Part 2, 1965: 19-24.

[4] Pacher F. The development of the New Austrian Tunnelling Method and the main features in design work and construction[C]//16th Symp. on Rock Mechanics, 1975.

[5] Brown E T. Putting the NATM into perspective[J]. Tunnels & Tunnelling International, 1981, 13(10): 13-17.

[6] Peck R B. Advantages and limitations of the observational method in applied soil mechanics [J]. Geotechnique, 1969, 19(2): 171-187.

[7] Palmström A, Stille H. Ground behaviour and rock engineering tools for underground excavations[J]. Tunnelling & Underground Space Technology Incorporating Trenchless Technology Research, 2007, 22(4): 363-376.

[8] Stille H, Palmström A. Classification as a tool in rock engineering[J]. Tunnelling & Underground Space Technology Incorporating Trenchless Technology Research, 2003, 18(4): 331-345.

[9] Hoek E. Practical Rock Engineering[EB/OL]. 2007 ed. https://www.rocscience.com/assets/resources/learning/hoek/Practical-Rock-Engineering-Full-Text.pdf.

[10] Palmstrom A. RMi-A rock mass characterisation system for rock engineering purposes[D/OL]. University of Oslo, Norway, 1995. http://www.rockmass.net/phd/contents_all_text.pdf.

[11] Bieniawski Z T. Rock mechanics design in mining and tunneling[M]. A A Balkema, Rotterdam, 1984.

[12] Peck R B. Where has all the judgment gone? [M]//Norwegian Geotechnical Institute Publication, Norwegian Geotechnical Institute, 1981.

[13] Schubert W, Goricki A. Probabilistic assessment of rock mass behaviour as basis for stability analyses of tunnels[C]//The Rock Mechanics Meeting, Stockholm, Sweden, 2004.

[14] Martin C D, Kaiser P K, Tannant D D, et al. Stress path and instability around mine openings[C]//The Nineth ISRM Congress on Rock Mechanics, 1999.

[15] Hoek E, Brown E T. Underground Excavations in Rock[M]. London: Institution of Mining and Metallurgy, 1980.

[16] Hoek E, Kaiser P K, Bawden W F. Support of Underground Excavations in Hard Rock [M]. A A Balkema: Rotterdam, 1995.

[17] Hudson J A. Rock mechanics principles in engineering practice[M]. CIRIA, 1989.

[18] Einstein H H. Observation, Quantification, and Judgment: Terzaghi and Engineering Geology[J]. Journal of Geotechnical Engineering, 1991, 117(11): 1772-1778.

[19] Hoek E. Big Tunnels in Bad Rock[J]. Journal of Geotechnical & Geoenvironmental Engineering, 2001, 127(9): 726-740.

[20] Carranza-Torres C, Fairhurst C. The elasto-plastic response of underground excavations in rock masses that satisfy the Hoek-Brown failure criterion[J]. Int. J. Rock Mech. Min. Sci. & Geomech., 1999, 36(6): 777-809.

[21] Detournay E, John C M S. Design charts for a deep circular tunnel under non-uniform loading[J]. Rock Mechanics & Rock Engineering, 1988, 21(2):119-137.

[22] Detournay E, Fairhurst C. Two-dimensional elastoplastic analysis of a long, cylindrical cavity under non-hydrostatic loading[J]. Int. J. Rock Mech. Min. Sci. & Geomech. Abstr., 1983, 24(4):197-211.

[23] Detournay E. Elastoplastic model of a deep tunnel for a rock with variable dilatancy[J]. Rock Mechanics & Rock Engineering, 1986, 19(2): 99-108.

[24] Carranza-Torres C. Dimensionless Graphical Representation of the ExactElasto-plastic Solution of a Circular Tunnel in a Mohr-Coulomb Material Subject to Uniform Far-field Stresses[J]. Rock Mechanics & Rock Engineering, 2003, 36(3):237-253.

[25] Brown E T, Bray J W, Ladanyi B, et al. Ground Response Curves for Rock Tunnels[J]. Journal of Geotechnical Engineering, 1983, 109(1): 15-39.

[26] Fairhurst C, Carranza-Torres C. Closing the Circle—Some Comments on Design Procedures for Tunnel Supports in Rock[C] // the University of Minnesota 50th Annual Geotechnical Conference, 2002.

[27] Carranza-Torres C, Fairhurst C. Application of the Convergence-Confinement method of tunnel design to rock masses that satisfy the Hoek-Brown failure criterion[J]. Tunnelling and Underground Space Technology incorporating Trenchless Technology Research, 2000, 15(2): 187-213.

[28] Martin C D, Kaiser P K, Mccreath D R. Hoek-Brown parameters for predicting the depth of brittle failure around tunnels[J]. Canadian Geotechnical Journal, 1999, 36(1): 136-151.

[29] Diederichs M S, Kaiser P K, Eberhardt E. Damage initiation and propagation in hard rock during tunnelling and the influence of near-face stress rotation[J]. Int. J. Rock Mech. Min. Sci. & Geomech., 2004, 41(5): 785-812.

[30] Brown E T. Estimating the Mechanical Properties of Rock Masses[C] // The 1st Southern Hemisphere International Rock Mechanics Symposium (SHIRMS), 2008.

7 Design of Tunnel Structures

7.1 Introduction

Expansion reading 7-1   Expansion reading 7-2

A tunnel is unique mainly because it is built in ground, which is considered as part of the structures of the tunnel. During the design of the tunnel lining or supporting system, the factors to be considered should include the properties of lining materials and the feature of ground pressures thrusting on the lining, construction procedures, and the interaction between the lining and ground[1]. These considerations will have a direct influence on choosing the type of tunnel supporting (lining) system.

7.1.1 Outline of the structural design process

Structure design is part of the tunnel design project, which is developed stepwise, beginning with the determination of zones with the similar ground behavior during construction and ending with the definition of the excavation and support classes.

Expansion reading 7-3

In the first step, the project area is subdivided into zones having similar conditions with respect to: ①geological and hydrogeological conditions; ②topographical conditions (e.g., depth of cover, slopes in the vicinity); ③environment and the third party aspects. These zones are corresponding to rock mass grades, respectively, as discussed in Chapter 4.

7.1.2 Features of tunnel surrounding rocks

Expansion reading 7-4

The recognition and the assessment of surrounding rock features are fundamental to the tunnel structure design. This work is based on the results of preliminary design, especially the geotechnical properties of the surrounding rocks from the site investigation, as discussed in Chapter 4. The assessment of project risk, including failure mechanisms or hazards, and the planning of appropriate mitigation measures are also parts of design jobs.

The detailed design should be based on the results of the analysis on the surrounding rocks behaviors. In terms of ground-structure interaction, the hazards and the design of the mitigation measures are generally considered based on the features of the surrounding rocks behaviors. With the commonly used design criteria and approach under consideration, the tunnel surrounding rock behaviors are generally approximated as the types of: ①stress controlled for high stress/strength ratio conditions, e. g., tunnels in soft ground or deep rock tunnel; ② structure controlled or block driven failure under low stress/strength ratio conditions; ③chemical, mineralogical effects dominate; ④ground water condition dominate; ⑤others, as shown in Figure 7-1.

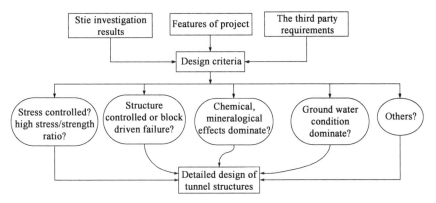

Figure 7-1 Identification of tunnel surrounding rocks behaviors types

7.2 Design considerations

In practice, it is impossible to avoid all risks related to tunneling. And therefore, the detailed design should be developed on the basis of reducing risks to "As Low As Reasonably Practical" (ALARP). Typically a design should be made to[1]: ①ensure that there are no inherent structural defects which could lead to catastrophic failure; ② have deformations contained so that the structure is not overstressed; ③have the material strengths of load-bearing elements maintained for the design life; ④ have support system capacity that is not exceeded if time-dependent behavior or other long-term effects are experienced; ⑤provide durability throughout the design life; ⑥control groundwater inflows and/or outflows from tunnels under internal pressure; ⑦evaluate constructability requirements.

Expansion reading 7-5

As suggested in the *Guidelines* (JTG/T D70—2010), the design of a tunnel should meet the general requirements, including: ①Structure safety and durability, i. e., during the design life, the tunnel structures, such as linings, work as expected by its designers e. g., within their specified parameters, or in other words, service normally in the design life expectancy of the item; ②Construction and operation safety, as well as favorable operation environment if it is possible; ③Environment favorable and energy saving, such as being in harmony with natural and human landscapes, especially for tunnel portal structure design.

In general, the following factors are considered to make the design of the tunnel structures functional, practical, safe and economic.

7.2.1 Structure safety grade

Given the uncertainty of the geotechnical condition parameters of the surrounding rocks, as well as the possible deviations of materials from what are expected and of construction from what is designed, a margin of safety is always necessary and considered in tunnel structure design. In general, the magnitude of the margin of safety depends on the features of the tunnel under consideration, such as in terms of importance to the project functionality, the significance or influence to the tunnel structure and society or third party if there is a structure damage in the tunnel. To be sure that the margin of safety is high enough, the structure of an important tunnel should be designed with robust methods and the design results should be checked in a rigorous procedure. On the other hand, for the tunnels, which are of the features of, such as short in length, small in width, simple and favorable in geotechnical and environmental conditions, an empirical or analogical method is usually enough to meet the design requirement. In practice, a new project is preliminarily specified to a grade of safety requirements, such as with a prescriptive approach. For example, based on the severity of influence due to structure damage, such as on the project functionality and society or third party, the grades of safety are designated for the types of tunnels in roadway.

Expansion reading 7-6

7.2.2 Design life and durability

A structure is designed durable in the working environment during its design life. The applied material is the features of maintaining its integrity and protecting other embedded materials or elements.

7.2.2.1 Design life

The design life of a tunnel is project specific. For example, in China, the design lives of 100 years are required for the tunnels in motorway, class-1 and 2 roads, while 50 years for the tunnels in low grade lines.

The durability of tunnel structures is related to lining types and applying environments. Where a structure is protected from aggressive agents, its life is determined by the structure characteristic. For example, the linings that receive annular grouting between the excavated bore and the extrados of the lining, or are protected by primary linings, such as sprayed concrete, may have increased resistance to any external aggressive agents[1]. For some composite lining systems, the final lining may be considered to be redundant in terms of design life.

The water tightness of a structure and fire-life safety are often considered in tunnel structure design. Linings may be exposed to various aggressive environments. The unprotected steel will corrode at a rate that depends upon the temperature, presence of water with reactive ions (from salts and acids) and availability of oxygen. A typical steel corrosion rate of 0.1 mm/year may considered in design. The factors influencing the durability of the concrete linings include operation environment, the shape and hulk of the concrete, cover to the embedded steel, the features of the concrete, e. g., the type of cement and aggregate, type and dosage of admixture, cement content and free water/cement ratio, workmanship, permeability, porosity and diffusivity of the final concrete.

7.2.2.2 Fire resistance

Expansion reading 7-7[2]

Tunnel structures should be of structural integrity under fire. There were a number of serious fires in tunnels in the recent two decades, for example the Channel tunnel fire in 1996, the Mont Blanc tunnel fire in 1999, the Tauern tunnel fire in 1999 and Gotthard road tunnels fires in 2001. Although the integrity of the tunnel structures was not affected in these cases, much of the material forming the permanent structural fabric was seriously damaged.

The influence of tunnel type and shape on the effects of fires should also be considered in design. The structural members of tunnels can be divided into two main types: flexural members and compression members. The form of a tunnel affects its ability to resist fire, such as the influence the loss of section under fire on the stability of the structure. In general, the influence of the damage of the reinforcement is more significant to a bending controlled member than to a structure under axial compression. Exposing the reinforcement, therefore, may not have the same significance and the reduction of capacity may only be governed by the amount and rate of spalling. For example, in 1996, the Channel Tunnel fire resulted in spalling up to 380-mm-deep (400-mm-thick units), where the spalling was deepest at the centre of the units, and was less pronounced at the four edges, with additional reinforcement.

7.2.2.3 Corrosion and physical processes

The three main aspects of attack that affect the durability of concrete linings are: the corrosion of metals, chloride-induced corrosion of embedded metals, and carbonation-induced corrosion of embedded metals. Chemical attack is by direct attack either on the lining material or on any embedded materials, caused by aggressive agents, which may be the part of the contents within the tunnel or in the ground in the vicinity of the tunnel. Damage to the material will depend on a number of factors including the concentration and type of chemical material in question, and the movement of the groundwater. In this respect static water is generally defined as occurring in ground having a mass permeability of $<10^{-6}$ m/s and mobile water of mass permeability $>10^{-6}$ m/s. Exchange reactions may occur between aggressive fluids and the components of the lining material, such as by sulphate attack, acid attack and alkali-silica reaction (ASR).

Expansion reading 7-8

Mechanical processes including freeze-thaw action, impact, abrasion and cracking can cause concrete damage by a physical process.

7.2.2.4 Protective systems

A high quality structure is achieved by the best of current practice in workmanship and materials. Protection of concrete surfaces is recommended in codes and standards when the level of aggression from chemicals exceeds the maximum specified limit. Surface protection can be coatings, waterproof barriers and a sacrificial layer for different situations.

7.2.3 Groundwater

7.2.3.1 Water pressures

The presence of groundwater and associated seepage pressures often adversely affects the stability and durability of tunnel linings. Lining designs often have to consider the long-term hydrostatic pressures. In deep tunnels, for example hydroelectric projects, where cover can exceed 1000 m, it is impractical to design linings for the full water pressure and pressure relief holes are required to avoid overstressing. In shallower tunnels, if seepage through the lining is unacceptable, a partial or full waterproofing system will be required. Full membranes are being used increasingly to control water inflows in new road and railway tunnels, such as in Germany and Switzerland. This is often driven by environmental concerns[4] and the maximum hydrostatic pressures designed for have been about 700 kPa[1]. When the designed hydrostatic pressure is too high, the lining become prohibitively expensive, and at higher pressures it is difficult to construct membranes that do not leak[1].

7.2.3.1.1 Watertight tunnel lining

For watertight tunnel lining system, the groundwater pressure, P_{w0}, which will thrust on the lining, can be approximated with the following method:

$$P_{w0} = \beta \gamma_w H \qquad (7\text{-}1)$$

Expansion reading 7-9

Where β is the reduction coefficient of groundwater pressures, which can be estimated following the *Guidelines* (JTG/T D70—2010); γ_w is the unit weight of water, kN/m^3; H is the head of groundwater pressure, m, and is equal to the elevation difference between the groundwater level and the elevation of tunnel center.

7.2.3.1.2 Partially watertight tunnel lining

Where the tunnel lining system is partially watertight, such as there are water seepage or drainage holes in the lining, the groundwater pressure, P, will be decreased due to the water drainage can be calculated as, P_{wd}:

$$P_{wd} = \beta_0 \beta \gamma_w H \qquad (7\text{-}2\text{-}1)$$
$$\beta_0 = 1 - Q/Q_0 \qquad (7\text{-}2\text{-}2)$$

Where β_0 is the reduction coefficient of groundwater pressure due to water drainage; Q is the designed discharge of the water drainage holes; Q_0 is the discharge of the groundwater from wallrocks without supporting or being unlined; the other parameters are same as in Equation (7-1).

In Equation (7-2), as $Q = 0$, the $\beta_0 = 1$, it means fully watertight lining; while $Q = 0$, the $\beta_0 = 0$, the $P_{wd} = 0$, this means the groundwater behind the lining is fully drained.

7.2.3.2 Waterproofing and drainage system

The strategy for achieving the function and operation of a tunnel will depend on the design requirements. The requirements of watertightness and permissible levels of leakage into sub-surface facilities are presented, such as by ITA and national codes as shown in Chapter 3. The water drainage and waterproof principles suggested in the design code or guideline provide a reasonable basis for an initial evaluation of design requirements, such as the summary of the effects of water ingress on different types of lining[1].

To control water inflow and seepage into a tunnel, there are a number of products available including membranes, gaskets, injected water stops, and annular and ground grouting. Membranes are available in two main types: ① sheet membranes that include materials such as PVC (polyvinylchloride), HDPE (high density polyethylene) and PO (polyolefin); ② spray-on membranes, which essentially consist of either cement-or rubber-based compounds. There are case histories of the applications of spray-on membranes in tunnel waterproof system. It is still not the time that all new tunnels to use spray-on membranes as waterproof system.

The measures, applied in a tunnel to cope with groundwater, belong to a drained or watertight system.

In the recent years, spray-on membranes have been applied in several tunnels. However, general considerations suggest that they are difficult to apply under wet conditions. At present, spray-on membranes can only be used as an alternative to

Expansion reading 7-10

PVC and only as part of a drained system.

7.2.3.3　Grouting for leakage or inflowing prevention

Leaks through sprayed concrete lining (SCL) and other linings can be prevented by grouting the surrounding ground with cement or chemical mixes. The close monitoring of the injection pressures and volumes, the movements of the surrounding soil/rock structure and the lining are necessary to prevent the lining being over stressed and possible damage.

For a shield tunneling tunnel, primary or secondary grouting of the annulus of a segmental ring may provide some short-term relief to leaks but will not provide a long-term seal against water penetration because the grout will crack as the ring deforms. However, grouting the surrounding ground is beneficial to the tunnel with segmental linings, to control the groundwater inflowing. Great care should be taken in order to prevent distortion or possible damage to the ring, such as through controlling grouting pressure close to the lining.

7.2.4　Ground-support interaction

Construction should be considered in the structure design, since the interaction between tunnel support system and surrounding rocks is strongly influenced by the applied construction method. The interaction are often analyzed with classical and numerical methods, but considerable judgment and experience are required in interpreting the results, mainly due to its complexity. To check whether the designs are sufficiently robust in analyzing the interaction, it is beneficial considering the following factors principles.

7.2.4.1　Factors

7.2.4.1.1　Stand-up time

The stand-up time of the surrounding rocks varies greatly, such as from the low grade of rock mass to high grade ones. This feature has been presented in Chapter 4, where the magnitude of surrounding rocks stand-up time is related to the grade of rock mass quality, such as in terms of the stability of a specific tunnel project.

When the ground-support interaction for a tunnel design is considered, the features of the stand-up time of the ground should be determined first. In the short term, the concept of stand-up time is used as a practical means of indicating the sensitivity of the ground to imposed stress changes. In terms of design, this influences both the support requirements and geometry of tunnel linings. Also, the magnitude of surrounding rocks stand-up time are dominating factor, which must be considered in construction method choosing, especially where the stand-up time is relatively short.

7.2.4.1.2　Ground pressures

The magnitude and features of the ground load acting on a tunnel depend on the geotechnical conditions of the surrounding rocks, such as in terms of the grade of rock mass, as well as the features of the degeneration of the surrounding rocks during tunneling. As a result, the pressures acting on a tunnel depend on the excavations and support sequence for any given set of ground conditions. In general, as much as 30%-50% of the deformation experienced during construction will occur ahead of the face. Depending on the extent of this deformation ahead of the face, the pressures acting on the lining will be significantly less than predicted from a simplistic two-dimensional "wished-in-place analysis" that assumes no stress relief. This is an important benefit in support design.

7.2.4.1.3　Deformation

In most cases, the bending strength and stiffness of structural linings are small compared to those of the surrounding ground. The ground properties therefore dictate the distortional deformations and changing the properties of the lining usually will not significantly alter this deformation. On the other hand, a completed lining resists uniform hoop deformation well. In general, what is required ideally, if it is possible, is a confined flexible lining that can redistribute stresses efficiently without significant loss of load-bearing capacity[1]. To realize this design object, certain support measures to control the ground deformation and the degeneration of the surrounding rocks are often necessary, such as pre-supports, rockbolts and shotcrete system, which are applied together with segmental or cast-in-place linings.

It is noted that the deformation, related to soil consolidation, swelling ground, squeezing ground, should be designed with special consideration of their specific geotechnical features.

7.2.4.1.4　Time of supports installation

Almost all ground properties are time dependent and strain controlled, both in the short and long term. Where the properties of the surrounding rocks change significantly with time increasing after the excavation, the time of supports installation is one of the dominant factors to be considered in tunneling. For example, when tunneling in weak or soft ground, the supports, when required, usually need to be installed as close to the face as possible because a large proportion of the deformation occurs ahead of the face. While there are a number of well-understood exceptions to this, such as tunneling in highly stressed hard rocks, if the installation of support is delayed, it could result in progressive deformations, such as tunneling in soft ground. Consequently there will be a need for additional support to control those deformations or the loosening and dead loads acting on the lining, and sometimes this could lead to instability.

7.2.4.2 The ground-support interaction process

As shown in Chapter 6, the ground-support interaction process can be modeled using Ground Reaction Curve (GRC), which uses an analytical approach to relate deformation in surrounding rocks with the supporting pressure acting outwards on the extrados of an excavation, resisting the inward deformation (Figure 7-2).

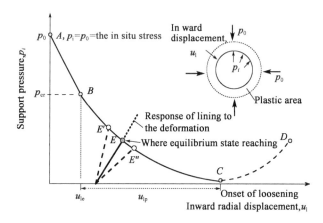

Note: A to B is elastic behavior; B to C is plastic behavior; u_{le} is elastic displacement; u_{lp} is plastic displacement; p_{cr} is critical support pressure defined by initiation of plastic failure of the rock surrounding the tunnel.

Figure 7-2 Typical GRC showing an elastic and non-linear ground response for a rock tunnel

Of the GRC, there is generally an elastic component (line AB) that will occur regardless of whether or when the support is installed. When the ground is relatively incompetent, such as in terms of strength, the amount of deformation related to non-linear behavior (curve BC) will be a function of the timing of installation of the support and the properties of the installed supports. In theory, support can be installed at different times to control the inward deformation of the surrounding rocks and, as long as the support resistance prevents the onset of loosening (curve CD), the system will achieve a new state of equilibrium, shown as the point E in Figure 7-2. During construction, the monitoring results of the ground and lining movements can be used for checking this design scenario. In practice, if the ground requires support, the full support should be installed without delay, unless there are special considerations related to time-dependent behavior or high ground stresses.

When the ground deformation or movement is not properly controlled, there is a potential for loosening conceptually, as shown in curve CD, though the simple theory behind the GRCs does not model this. Furthermore, the ground-support interaction is a dynamic process, so the point where the GRC and the support response line meet only represents an estimate of the required support pressure[1].

The analysis on the ground-support interaction is presented in Chapter 6 in terms of the CCM. It is noted that the real situation is more complex. A numerical method is usually required to deal with this interaction process.

7.2.4.3 Coping with variability in the ground

Very often it is not possible to predict accurately the geomechanical properties of the surrounding rocks and their behaviors. The difference between the predicted ground model and the real situation can be great or minor. Differing site conditions may appear during construction. Therefore the level of effort at design stage will depend on the likely impact of any potential ground condition variations on construction.

The measures to cope with the variability in the ground are project specific features. For example, a robust TBM, such as Mixshield TBM, may be chosen to tolerate wide variations in soft ground conditions. For most of the tunnel projects, the application of observational method[6], together with pre-face ground prospecting, is also often practical to address the potential variations of the surrounding rocks, during construction by ensuring that a range of suitable support systems is available. However, where the project is much sensitive to the unpredicted adverse ground conditions, such as in high-risk areas, shallow urban environments, a higher level of effort is required to evaluate the ground conditions and prove robust design[1].

7.2.5 Time-related behavior

Stress redistributions occur in response to tunneling and the effects on the radial and tangential stress redistributions are presented in Chapter 6, in terms of classical analysis method. As the plastic zone develops the peak tangential stress is transferred away from the edge of the excavation. It is noted that the stress redistributions of the surrounding rocks in response to tunneling is a three dimensional process and is related to the tunnel construction process[5,7]. For example, for tunnels in soft ground, equilibrium is generally established only after a heading has advanced approximately two diameters beyond the point in question. During this process, the deformation continue at a reasonably constant rate until the closed lining takes full effect and the movements soon cease. For example, this is about one diameter behind ring closure for a sprayed concrete lining (SCL) tunnel in London Clay[1].

7.2.5.1 Timely ring closure for soft ground

For tunneling in soft ground, the time of invert closing for a supporting system

Expansion reading 7-11

has strong influence on the surrounding rocks deformation control. It is therefore necessary in soft ground to specify that closure should be, such as within less than one diameter. Volume losses of less than 1.0% can be achieved in soft ground with SCLs[1].

Speed of closure of the invert is not applicable to most hard rock tunnels, where a solely elastic response is anticipated. There will be a finite amount of deformation, and depending on the stiffness of the rock mass and the depth of cover, volume losses of the order of 0.05%-0.5% will occur[1].

7.2.5.2 Special cases

7.2.5.2.1 Squeezing and swelling

The term *Squeezing* originates from the pioneering tunneling through the Alps[9], where residual tectonic stresses are locked into the rock mass and release occurs over relatively long periods of time during tunneling[11]. The squeezing of surrounding rocks of a tunnel refers to the reduction of the tunnel cross section that occurs as the tunnel is being excavated. *Squeezing of rock* stands for large time dependent convergence during tunnel excavation. Squeezing condition appears, when a particular combination of ground properties and induced stresses causes yielding in some zones around the tunnel, exceeding the limiting shear stress, at which creep starts. The deformation may terminate or continue over a long period of time[10].

Squeezing is essentially a time dependent behavior[11]. This originates from the fact that time dependent deformations are observed whenever face advancement is stopped and these are likely to take place during excavation, when it is difficult to distinguish the face effect from the time effect.

Expansion reading 7-12

The case study of the Saint Martin La Porte access adit along the Lyon-Turin Base Tunnel is quoted from Barla et al. [11], where time-dependent behavior imposes additional constraints on the excavation and support sequence, and much higher volume losses have to be allowed for. Volume losses of up to 10% required a very flexible support system to control deformations and maintain stability[1]. This can be achieved by means of yielding arch supports or by leaving longitudinal slots in the sprayed concrete lining.

Swelling ground conditions are typically related to marls, anhydrite and clay minerals, such as corrensite and montmorillonite. For example, volume losses can reach more than 13% for corrensite[12].

Swelling is a stress-dependent process and calls for construction methods that limit the exposure of the excavation surface to water, for example, the application of a sprayed concrete sealing layer. Water should be removed from the rock mass as quickly as possible. Where swelling is unavoidable, the linings should be designed specifically for the stress-dependent portion of volume change, as suggested in BTS[1].

7.2.5.2.2 Consolidation

Time-dependent behavior is also recorded in clays and a typical increase of 20%-30% in pressure on segmental linings has been recorded over a period of about 20 years in London Clay[13]. Most of this effect is related to consolidation and therefore there is considerable benefit in providing a full waterproof membrane or watertight gasket system in segmentally lined tunnels to prevent drainage, and so avoid attracting additional loads.

7.2.6 Construction method choice

The adopted method of excavation and the means of controlling face and excavation stability have a major influence on the design of the tunnel lining. During design, the construction method choice is based on the considerations of surrounding rock stability, the features of the project, the construction methods available as well as their productivity.

The choice of construction method for a tunnel project is generally considered at the planning of the project and specified during the detailed design of the project. The choice of method may be dictated by the degree of certainty to which potential geological problems may be identified and located, in terms of the risk control of the tunneling. Depending on the geological complexity, the extent of the geological pre-investigation and available experience from other projects in similar geological conditions, the information concerning the ground may be subject to uncertainties. If the structural behavior cannot be predicted with sufficient reliability based on site investigations, structural analysis and comparable experience, the design may permit or foresee construction method modifications during construction, provided that the relevant hazards can be detected and localized in time by observations and they do not lead to sudden or uncontrollable failure. Otherwise, constructional measures and suitable types of supports must reduce the potential hazards in order to comply with the safety requirements.

For the purpose of construction method modifications on site, the information gained during execution both on the ground properties and on the structural behavior shall be introduced into the current process of design and execution. In particular, the design should specify: ①relevant mechanisms endangering safety or impairing serviceability during construction; ②criteria for the selection of excavation, support or auxiliary measures; ③the actions to be taken for every foreseeable significant deviation of the observational findings from the expected ones. During construction, all relevant data, concepts, considerations and decisions shall be recorded in such a way that a review of the decision making process is possible.

It is essential that the above factors be considered early in the design process to ensure that tunnel production rates and tunnel lining integrity are not compromised[1]. The details of construction method choice will be presented in Chapter 9.

7.2.7 Performance requirements

The tunnel structure comprises the surrounding rocks and all temporary or permanent support elements necessary for the equilibrium or limitation of deformations. The successful construction of tunnels depends on the detailed consideration of structural behavior relevant factors including: ①ground structure and properties, hydrogeological conditions; ②in-situ stresses; ③the features of the tunnel project, such as size, location and alignment of the opening; ④excavation method; ⑤support measures and their installing time. The specific values of these parameters are defined according to the site investigation, structural analyses including ground-structure interaction, as well as engineer's own experience.

7.2.7.1 Features of ground response

Expansion reading 7-13

The performance of the tunnel surrounding rocks will depend on the geotechnical properties of the surrounding rocks and stress state, the properties of the supports and the timing of installation. The features of ground response to tunneling will provide an indication of whether a plastic zone could form and, and if so, radial confinement should be provided by the installed support to control the ground deformation and strength degeneration. In most cases a plastic zone is beneficial in re-distributing stresses providing that the yielding is controlled.

For the tunnels under low stress state, such as many rock tunnels, there will be an elastic response and therefore the strains in the surrounding rocks will be nominal. Stability under these conditions is related only to the ability of individual blocks or wedges to slide or fall. The influence of the failure of an individual block is usually local or limited for the tunnels in hard rocks, unless it is a key block that leads to a loss of arching action.

7.2.7.2 Lining flexibility

The relative stiffness between the surrounding rocks and supporting system has a significant influence on the behavior of tunnels. The research results of ISE[14] are quoted as the followings: ①*For ground-support modulus ratios of* 0.01 *or less, the support will carry as a hoop load, nearly all of the applied load from the overburden.* ②*For ratios greater than* 0.01, *the reduction in hoop load because of* *ground-support interaction is substantial.* ③ *Distortions of the opening will be determined by the properties of the ground, except at very small modulus ratios.* ④*If, for any reason, the support system is required to limit or resist distortions, the support capacity will have to be considerably increased.* The modulus ratio is defined as E_g/E, where E_g is the Young's Modulus of the ground and E is the Young's Modulus of the structure.

Expansion reading 7-14

7.2.7.3 Lining distortion

Of a flexible lining, such as most of segmental linings, the distortion occurs due to ground loading. Typical distortions of the flexible linings of circular tunnels in soft grounds due to ground loading are presented. These values can be used in design to check bending moments due to distortion and to assess performance during construction. The distortion is defined as the change in radius, δR, divided by the tunnel radius, R. The recommended distortion, for all situations, no more than 2% of the difference between the minimum and maximum diameters is provided in the BTS Specification[15].

Expansion reading 7-15

7.2.7.4 Critical strains in surrounding rocks

It is not easy defining practical limits of the performance of surrounding rocks of a tunnel. In terms of assessing the stability of excavations, Sakurai[16] suggested the concept of critical strain to define allowable displacements. Hazard warning levels for assessing the stability of tunnels given by Sakurai[16] are quoted. The critical strain is defined for rock masses as: $\varepsilon_{cr} = (m/n)\varepsilon_0$, where ε_0 is the critical strain for intact materials and m and n are reduction factors of uniaxial strength and Young's Modulus respectively for the rock mass. In general, the ratio of m/n varies from 1.0-3.0 depending on ground conditions[1]. The observational mothod is often used for tuning design input parameters and is combined with back-analysis from the performance of the structures to allow this ratio to be defined for the specific project.

Expansion reading 7-16

7.2.7.5 Allowable strain in primary lining

During tunnel construction, the deformation of the surrounding rocks may last for a long period, such as after the application of the primary lining and before the working of the final lining. Where the magnitude of the deformation of the primary lining, especially shotcrete lining, is such large that damage can occur in the supporting system, in forms of cracks, large distortion, to assure the bearing or supporting capacity of the primary lining, the radial deformation of the primary lining should be controlled to a specified range. For example, allowable strain in primary lining is suggested in *Technical code for engineering of ground anchorages and shotcrete support* (GB 50086—2015) in China, as quoted in Table 7-1.

Table 7-1　Suggested allowable radial strain in terms of the relative horizontal convergence of primary lining [%]

Grade of surrounding rocks	Overburden [m]			Note:
	<50	50-300	300-500	①For each of the value range, the larger value is for tunnels in soft rocks while the smaller one is for tunnels in hard rocks. ②For the excavations with $0.8 < H/L < 1.2$. ③From the *technical code* (GB 50086—2015)
Ⅲ, with $L_{hi} \leq 20$ m	0.10-0.30	0.20-0.50	0.40-1.20	
Ⅳ, with $L_{hi} \leq 15$ m	0.15-0.50	0.40-1.20	0.80-2.00	
Ⅴ, with $L_{hi} \leq 10$ m	0.20-0.80	0.60-1.60	1.00-3.00	

Expansion reading 7-17

On the other hand, the allowable strain of the primary lining of a tunnel also can be preliminarily considered as a warning deformation for the tunnel excavation and supports, with the implication of the instability of the surrounding rocks or the tendency of increasing deformation, provided the magnitude of the practical deformation is approximately equal to or beyond the specified warning value.

7.2.8　Ground improvement and pre-support

If the stand-up time of the surrounding rocks is minimal and/or the strengths of surrounding rocks are low, ground improvement measures or pre-supports ahead of the face may be needed. The commonly used pre-support measures, including forepoling and spiling, pipe-roof umbrellas/canopy, jet grouting, face sealing, will be presented in details in Chapter 8.

The effects of ground improvement or water management on linings should also be considered in design. The use of ground improvement techniques or groundwater control methods can have beneficial effects on the design of tunnel lining. Each technique can affect the loading on the lining or have direct effects on the lining construction.

7.3　Methods of predicting lining loads

Tunnel lining is designed to support the weight of the overburden and a pressure from the surrounding rocks. For a tunnel with a composite lining, the primary lining is usually designed to resist all transient loads developed during construction activities as well as the short-term ground loads; the final lining is used for ensuring a safe support of the tunnel for the any other additional loading resulting from future changes in the overall physical conditions and the possible increased long-term ground loads.

Expansion
eading 7-18[17-19]

The prediction of lining loads for the lining design has always been the goal of tunnel engineers. Peck [6] recommended four separate steps for tunnel design procedures: adequate ring loads, anticipate distortions due to bending, proper consideration to the possibility of buckling and allowance for any significant external conditions not included in previous steps.

7.3.1 Factors influencing the load on the liner

Tunnel linings seldom carry the full load of the overburden due to the arching effect of the ground. Many factors contribute to the features of loads on tunnel linings. It is beneficial to understand the influence of these factors on the prediction of the loads. In the following section, the factors influencing the load on the liner are presented, in terms of ground conditions, features of tunnel project, construction procedure and neighbors.

7.3.1.1 Ground conditions

7.3.1.1.1 Properties of surrounding rocks

The properties of surrounding rocks can be empirically evaluated in terms of rock mass classification. Based on the grade of the surrounding rocks, the loading of the surrounding rocks will thrust on the planned tunnel structures can be approximately specified through an empirical or semi-empirical approach. For example, Terzaghi[20] provided the approximate values of the loads on the roof of tunnel linings for each grade group. The ground loads are parameters to assess the support requirements for excavations. Similarly, the Q system and the RMR system, as presented in Chapter 4, also provided estimates of the appropriate support requirements for excavations. The Terzaghi[20] method indicates the increase of lining loads with the decrease of rock strength.

The lining loads are dependent on the stiffness of the lining but less than that corresponding to the overburden pressure. Ward and Pender[23] discussed the behavior of a tunnel in different soft ground conditions and their comments related to the lining loads are summarized as: ① Tunnels in dense sandy or gravelly materials with slight cohesion and proper drainage behave in a similar fashion to tunnels in hard ground or non-swelling rocks having much smaller lining load than those in clays and silts. ②The lining loads in till stabilize quickly after installation of the lining with the loads depending on the stiffness of the lining, but much less than that corresponding to the overburden pressure. ③Tunnels in heavily overconsolidated swelling clays have lining loads almost equivalent to the full overburden pressure even though the lining loads may only correspond to about 50% of the overburden pressure in the first year after construction. ④For tunnels in lightly overconsolidated silty clays, the lining loads tend to increase with time.

7.3.1.1.2 Groundwater conditions

The groundwater table is usually lowered during the construction of the tunnel to increase the stability of the unsupported excavations and to prevent flooding in the work space. The groundwater table may start to increase after the tunneling. Two different types of linings exist related to the handling of water, as shown in Chapter 3.

The tunnel lining can be either completely watertight or allow some controlled leakage. The effects of water pressure on the linings depend on the relative permeability of the tunnel structures with respect to that of the surrounding ground. Lining with complete watertight measures will have more loads than that with controlled leakage. The water pressure on the former case can be almost full hydrostatic pressure.

7.3.1.1.3 In situ stress

In situ stress is generally closely related to the behavior of the surrounding rocks and therefore should be considered in lining load assessing. The lining load is always likely to be considerably smaller than that corresponding to the overburden pressure. However, there are cases showing different situations. For example, Peck[6] presented several examples where the lining loads were higher than those corresponding to the overburden pressures due to the high in-situ stress ratios. Also, as suggested in the ASCE Guidelines for tunnel lining design[26], plastic behavior may lead to substantial inward displacements before the ground can mobilize enough shear strength to reduce lining loads in tunnels excavated under conditions of high in situ stress, especially in ground of relatively low strength. In such a case, the displacement of the ground causes an increase of the load on the lining because the ground cannot be stabilized by itself.

7.3.1.2 Features of the project

7.3.1.2.1 Shape of the excavations

The shape of the excavations has a significant influence on the surrounding rocks stress redistribution under a boundary stresses condition. The excavation aspect ratio and boundary curvature, can be used for developing a reasonable picture of the surrounding rocks stress state[3]. For an ellipse of major and minor axes $2a$ and $2b$, the boundary circumferential stresses in the sidewall (point A) and crown (point B) of the excavation, σ_A and σ_B respectively, are presented as the followings[3]:

$$\sigma_A = p\left(1 - K + \sqrt{\frac{2W}{r_A}}\right) \tag{7-3}$$

$$\sigma_B = p\left(K - 1 + K\sqrt{\frac{2H}{r_B}}\right) \tag{7-4}$$

where r_A and r_B are the radii of curvature at points A and B, with $r_A = b^2/a$, $r_B = a^2/b$; W is the excavation width, $W = 2a$ and H is the height, $H = 2b$; K is the ratio of the horizontal and vertical in-situ prinapal stresses. The relationships between the radii and stresses in the Equations (7-3) and (7-4) indicate that high boundary curvature (i.e., $1/r$) leads to high boundary stresses and that boundary curvature can be used in a semi-quantitative way to predict boundary stresses[3].

Expansion reading 7-19

Where it is not an effective approach to minimize the maximum boundary stress and the failure of boundary rock may be unavoidable under the local conditions of field stresses and rock mass strength, such as through orienting the major axis of the excavation parallel to the major principal field stress, other measures are expected to provide the optimal solution. Indeed, it has been proposed that, for an excavation subject to an extremely high vertical principal field stress and extensive sidewall failure in hard rocks, an elliptical excavation with the long horizontal axis may be the preferred excavation shape for the prevailing conditions of rock mass rupture and local instability[22]. This is applicable to the large span cave design in hard rocks.

7.3.1.2.2 Diameter and depth of the tunnel

As shown in Chapter 6, of the stress redistribution pattern around an excavation, the magnitude of the redistributed stresses will increase with increasing diameter, when there is plastic area development around the excavation. The construction difficulty and support costs will generally increase as the diameter of tunnel increases, especially for the tunnels in soft ground. The load on the lining increases if the ground is loosened or the strength is adversely degenerated during tunneling.

For the excavations in sound ground, the calculated stresses at the boundary of the excavation are independent of the tunnel diameter according to the elasticity theory. The features of the stress redistribution pattern depend on the conditions of in situ stresses and the geometrical features or shapes of the excavations.

The depth of the tunnel can affect the behavior of the lining. In general, where the tunnel is too shallow, the loading thrusting on the lining of a planned tunnel will be large, such as being near to the weight of the overburden of the tunnel. As the depth of the tunnel increase, the loading will decrease due surrounding rocks arching effect, until the overburden is such large that high stress state will dominate the behavior of the surrounding rocks. In empirical rule, the lining loads is almost constant when the overburden of the tunnel is about 2 to 3 times the excavation span (B), a condition which can be considered as a deep tunnel. For the tunnels in soft ground, the effect of gravitational stress of the overburden (H) is not negligible for the situation of the H/B ratio being greater than 5.

7.3.1.2.3 Relative rigidity of the lining

The lining loads are dependent not only on the properties of the ground but also on the stiffness of the lining. In general, a flexible lining will bear smaller loading in comparison to a stiff lining, provided that the ground deformation and degeneration of the ground are properly controlled. In simplicity, a flexible lining may be achieved by decreasing the thickness of the ling. However, it should be done carefully because the reduction of the liner thickness results in the increase of the circumferential stress in the liner due to the decrease of the cross sectional area of the liner. Too great of a reduction of the lining thickness can yield compressive stresses in excess of the compressive strength of the liner. In design, the concept of relative stiffness method is often in consideration. This concept is also explained by the CCM.

Expansion reading 7-20

7.3.1.3 Construction procedure

7.3.1.3.1 Ground response to tunneling

Tunneling significantly disturbs the surrounding rocks situ stress and induce the surrounding rocks deformation. The features of the ground response to tunneling are shown in Figure 7-3, which shows the longitudinal distribution of the radial displacements in response to the excavation, with reference to the excavation face, i.e., being ahead of, around and behind the face. The pre-convergence is the ground displacement that occurs ahead of the face, whereas convergence is the ground displacement that would have occurred totally. The ground deformation, e.g., convergence, will increase slower with the excavation face driven ahead, provided that the deformation of the surrounding rocks is properly controlled, such as with supports installation. Under these conditions, at the point, behind the face, is $1D$ to $1.5D$, where D is the diameter of the excavation, the convergence is generally near to its maximum magnitude. The features of the stress redistribution and the surrounding rocks displacements can be presented with CCM, which considers ground-support interaction.

Expansion reading 7-21

7.3.1.3.2 Excavation method

The preservation of the ground strength is beneficial to minimize lining loads. The influence of the excavation method on the ground loading, which will thrust on the planned tunnel structures, mainly depends on the damage of the surrounding rocks during the tunneling. In general, driving by blasting will cause more significant damage to the surrounding rocks in comparison to that by the TBM boring and manual excavation. The too much disturbance to the surrounding rocks would certainly have much negative effects on the stability of the opening. A proper construction method should be designed to make the surrounding rocks deformation and strength degeneration under control.

7.3.1.3.3 Length of the unsupported period of the cavity

During construction, radial displacements occur in surrounding rocks (Figure 7-3). For soft ground or the surrounding rocks under high stress state, the radial displacements will increase, even without the advance of the tunnel face, such as due to rock yielding with time. On the other hand, the deformation of the surrounding rocks should be properly controlled in order to maintain the wall rock strength, especially for soft or weak ground. For this reason, the supports or ground reinforcement measures should be applied in time, such as in the period of stand-up time of the surrounding rocks. Otherwise, much large degeneration will take place in the surrounding rocks. Where the degeneration of the surrounding rocks is such large that the loads on the lining can increase even though the face does not advance or is located far away from a reference point.

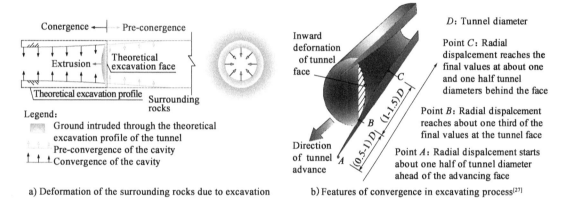

a) Deformation of the surrounding rocks due to excavation   b) Features of convergence in excavating process[27]

Figure 7-3　Sketch showing the ground response to tunneling

For the situation that surrounding rocks has yielded little and is stiff compared to a face that have been stationary for a long time, the surrounding rocks displacement is small. In other words, the displacement of the ground is less if the construction of the tunnel is progressed relatively quickly and the properties degeneration of surrounding rocks is well controlled. Therefore, the loads on the lining can vary depending on the rate of the tunnel construction.

The lining loads generally decrease as the support delay length, i.e., the distance between the tunnel face and the leading edge of the lining, increases because the lining will resist less displacement, provided that the degeneration of the ground strength is properly controlled. For example, the shorter excavation round length of the tunnels in hard rocks is, the higher stresses and more homogeneous stress distribution on the lining will develop in comparison to those of the longer excavation round length, through which the ground pressures can be properly released, such as due to the deformation and stress redistribution around the excavations. However, where support installation is too late, or the excavation round length is too large, the length of the unsupported period of the cavity is larger than the stand-up time, serious surrounding rocks properties degeneration will occur. The deformation and plastic area may be too large to be acceptable. And therefore, the excavation round length should be specified according to the stand-up time of surrounding rocks, features of supporting measures and construction procedures. In general, the longer of the stand-up time, the larger of the excavation round length is allowable.

7.3.1.3.4 Time effect

As the above section shown, of the tunnels in the ground of time-related behavior, the loading thrusting on the lining will increase with time. For example, the increase of the lining loads for tunnels in London clay, a process which is roughly proportional to the logarithm of time, although the lining load may increase at a decreasing rate depending on the nature of the soil due to the passage of time[6]. The increase of the lining load is also very obvious for swelling clays and soft plastic clays but quiet small for non-plastic grounds. In other words, the increase of the lining load mainly occurs in materials that have significant time-dependent behavior. The increase of the loads on the final lining can also is case as time passes either due to creep or deterioration of the initial lining.

7.3.1.3.5 Lining contact with the ground

In theory, the lining should contact to the surrounding rocks in perfect mode, where there is no void left between the outer edge of the lining and the excavation profile of the surrounding rocks. However, sometimes, it is not the case. For example, there are voids left behind the lining for shield tunneling, because the excavated diameter of the tunnel is usually bigger than the outer diameter of the lining. In design, the voids left behind the lining are filled with some kind of grout or can be closed by the expansion of the lining. For the tunnels, driven by drill and blast method, there is also chance of void left behind the lining, such as due to defect in construction.

If the ground has sufficient stand-up time and the gap is small, the lining will be in contact with the ground as the tunnel face advances, without the development of local instability or global ground collapse. In this case, the loads on the lining may be even smaller than that design predicts. However, either local instability or global ground collapse may occur, is a process which can cause a large increase of loads on the lining, if the gap between the lining and the excavation profile of the surrounding rocks is sufficiently large.

7.3.1.4 Influence of neighbor structures

Where the two tubes of a tunnel is in neighborhood or there is existing structure in the disturbance zone of the planned tunnel, the load on the lining of the first tunnel usually increases after construction of an adjacent second tunnel because the loads previously carried by the removed material are transferred to the surrounding ground and the existing lining of the first tunnel. Therefore, it is a common tunneling practice to delay placement of the cast-in-place concrete lining in the first tunnel until the second tunnel heading has passed to reduce bending stresses in the first tunnel lining, provided the surrounding rocks are stable.

In general, the interaction effect of the neighbor tubes is negligible when the two tubes are 3 to 4 times of the excavation diameter apart from centre to centre each other under a hydrostatic stress field, as shown in Chapter 6.

7.3.2 Types of surrounding rocks pressures

Before the excavation of a tunnel, the weight of the overlying ground layers will act as a uniformly distributed load on the deeper strata, where the planned tunnel will be excavated. When a space is excavated in the ground, the deformation of the loaded surrounding rocks is largely prevented by the adjacent ground. For the case that the surrounding rocks are such competent that the cavity will be self-stable, no support is needed, in terms of stability. Otherwise, in order to maintain the cavity the intrusion of the surrounding rocks must be prevented by support structures or reinforcements. The load acting on the supports is referred to ground ro surrounding rocks pressure. The determination of the magnitude of surrounding rocks pressure is required for tunnel lining or supporting system design. In general, surrounding rocks pressure is called or assumed the load acting on the supports.

It is difficult to determine the surrounding rocks pressures, which are related not only to the ground conditions, but also to the features of the tunnel, as well as the interaction between the tunnel structures and the surrounding rocks. The reasons may include: ①the inherent difficulty of predicting the in situ stress conditions, especially that prevailing in the interior of the non-uniform rock mass; ②the fact that, in addition to the strength properties of the rock, the magnitude of secondary pressures developing after excavation around the cavity is governed by a variety of factors, such as the size of the cavity, the method of its excavation, rigidity of support and the length of the period, during which the cavity is left unsupported.

The surrounding rocks pressures may develop around the tunnel structures due to: ①loosening of the surrounding rocks around the excavations; ②the weight of the overlying ground formation and redistribution of the in situ tectonic stresses in the ground; ③volume expansion of the ground, such as swelling due to physical or chemical action; ④load thrust due to rockbursting.

And therefore, the ground pressures are classified as four types, i. e., ①loosening pressure, the load by loosen ground or zone, may due to rock blocks or wedges falling (rockfalls), sliding along discontinuities, crown cave-in or collapse, wall buckling failure; ② swelling pressure, the load thrusting on the supports due to ground swelling, as the moisture of the surrounding rocks changing; ③ deformation pressure or squeezing pressure, the load due to the interaction between wall rock and supports, under the conditions of elastic, plastic or creeping state; ④pressure of rockbursting, the load thrusting on the supports due to rockbursting, as a kind of brittle failure of the surrounding rocks due to excavation.

7.3.3 Empirical methods

The lining loads can be calculated using the existing lining design methods, such as empirical and semi-empirical methods, ring and plate models, ring and spring models, and numerical models. A valid design methods must be capable of representing loads and deformations in accordance with the geologic and construction conditions and of correctly accounting for the ground-lining interaction[26]. Empirical methods are based on the in situ observations or measurements of completed tunnel supports or simply on past experiences. Earth pressure theories, Terzaghi's arching theory, and empirical techniques belong to these methods. Some commonly used empirical and semi-empirical methods of predicting lining loads are presented in the following sections.

7.3.3.1 Terzaghi's methods

7.3.3.1.1 Situation of shallow tunnel

To establish the method, Terzaghi considered the case of a rectangular tunnel (supported by wooden posts) excavated through "... a bed of sand..." as shown in Figure 7-4a) where the inclined boundaries of the zone of subsidence rise at an angle of $45° + \varphi/2$ and at the level of the roof of the tunnel, the width of the yielding strip is approximately equal to:

$$2B_1 = 2[B_0 + H\tan(45° + \varphi/2)] \qquad (7\text{-}5)$$

where, φ is internal frictional angle of the soils, B_0 and H are the width and height of the tunnel, respectively, as shown in Figure 7-4.

As Terzaghi[20] stated that *owing to the imperfect fit of the timbers at the joints and the compressibility of the supports of the footings of the vertical posts, the yield of the timbering is usually sufficient to reduce the pressure of the sand on the timbering almost to the value corresponding to the state of incipient shear failure in the sand. This state is similar to the state of stress in a mass of sand above a yielding strip. The sand adjoining the sides of the tunnel also subsides on account of the yield of its lateral support.*

It is assumed that the yielding region extends vertically upwards from points b_1-b_1 at the level of the roof [Figure 7-4a)] and from this situation, the vertical pressure on the horizontal section b_1-b_1 is calculated as:

$$\sigma_v = \frac{\gamma B_1}{K\tan\varphi} \cdot (1 - e^{-K\tan\varphi \cdot D/B_1}) \tag{7-6}$$

where K is an empirical coefficient he founds to be close to one, γ is the unit weight of the soils, D is the overburden [Figure 7-4a)] or the height of the loosening area above the tunnel, the other parameters see Figure 7-4a).

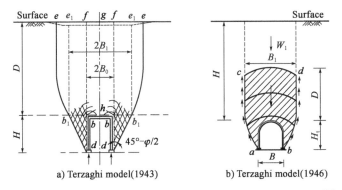

a) Terzaghi model(1943) b) Terzaghi model(1946)

Figure 7-4 **Terzaghi analysis models of the stability of tunnels**[7]

Expansion eading 7-22[24-25]

7.3.3.1.2 Rock load pressures

The Terzaghi[20] rock load design method has been a standard procedure for civil engineering tunnels in the U. S. since it was introduced over 60 years ago. The rock load pressures, of which Terzaghi's arching theory is applied, are related to the rock mass classification, as shown in Chapter 4.

7.3.3.2 Protodyakonov's coefficient

Protodyakonov's pressure arch theory has been applied to estimate the rock pressures in China. In this method, there is an assumed lossening area, which is bounded by Protodyakonov's pressure arch and fracture planes, as shown in Figure 7-5. The height of the lossening area is related to the width of lossening, B_m, and the features of the surrounding rocks, which can be evaluated with rock mass coefficient of strength, f_{kp}.

Based on the concept of rock mass coefficient of strength (also called coefficient of consistence in China), f_{kp}, which can be evaluated with rock mass parameters of the compressive strength of rocks (R_b), rock mass cohesion strength (c) and internal friction angle (φ_c), the vertical rock load pressures, q, can be calculated, as shown in the *Guidelines*(JTG/T D70—2010):

$$\left. \begin{array}{l} q = \gamma h_q \\ h_q = \dfrac{1}{2} \cdot \dfrac{B_m}{f_{kp}} \\ B_p = (H_t - H_0) \tan\left(45° - \dfrac{\varphi_c}{2}\right) \end{array} \right\} \quad (7\text{-}7)$$

where the meanings of the parameters in the Equation (7-7) are presented in Figure 7-5.

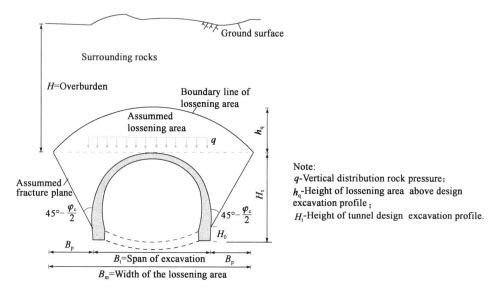

Figure 7-5　Parameters used in the rock load pressure evaluation with mass coefficient of strength

The coefficient of surrounding rock strength, f_{kp}, is empirically given as in the *Guidelines*(JTG/T D70—2010):

(1) For hard rock, $f_{kp} = \left(\dfrac{1}{12} - \dfrac{1}{15}\right) R_b$;

(2) For soft rock, $f_{kp} = \left(\dfrac{1}{8} - \dfrac{1}{10}\right) R_b$;

(3) For crashed rock and sand, $f_{kp} = \tan\varphi_c$;

(4) For clay or loess, $f_{kp} = \dfrac{c}{R_b} + \tan\varphi_c$, respectively.

7.3.3.3　Estimation based on rock mass grades

As the *RMR* value of the surrounding rocks of a tunnel is available, the following equation for the ground load, measured as the rock load height[21]:

$$H_b = (1 - RMR/100) B \quad (7\text{-}8)$$

where B is the tunnel width.

Similarly, based on the grade of the surrounding rocks of a tunnel, such as evaluated by the Q system (see Chapter 4), the supporting load for a tunnel in jointed rocks, P, can be calculated as [21]:

(1) Permanent support pressure, with three or more joint sets:
$$P = 2.0Q^{-1/3}/J_r \quad (7\text{-}9\text{-}1)$$

(2) Permanent support pressure, with less than three joint sets:
$$P = 2.0J_n^{-1/2}Q^{-1/3}/(3J_r) \quad (7\text{-}9\text{-}2)$$

where J_n is joint set number; J_r is joint roughness number; the Q value from the Q system of the rock mass classification, as shown in Chapter 4.

7.3.3.4 Semi-empirical methods in China

Semi-empirical methods are generally based on the properties evaluation results of the surrounding rocks of a planned tunnel, such as in terms of rock mass classification, as well as the features of the tunnel overburden, i. e., being shallow or deep tunnel. Since the stability and the behaviours of the surrounding rocks of a deep tunnel is generally different from these of a shallow tunnel.

7.3.3.4.1 Features of the overburden of a tunnel

In terms of the stability a tunnel or the disturbance due to excavation to the surrounding rocks, a deep tunnel is of the features that the boundary of the plastic zone of the disturbed area around the excavation is not near to the ground surface, as shown in Figure 7-6a). In other words, the overburden of the tunnel is large enough and an arching effect will be effective the the surrounding rocks. In other situations, where the overburden of a tunnel is relatively small and the boundary of the the plastic zone of the disturbed area of the tunnel will meet the ground surface, as shown in Figure 7-6b), the tunnel belongs to shallow type.

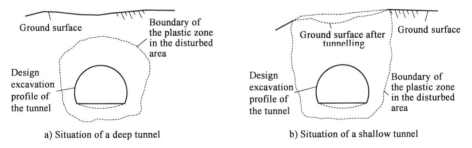

a) Situation of a deep tunnel   b) Situation of a shallow tunnel

Figure 7-6   Sketch showing the relationship between ground surface and the boundary of disturbance area

In tunnel design, the features of the overburden of a planned tunnel are preliminarily evaluated with a semi-empirical method, which is based on the results of the grade evaluation of the surrounding rocks and the geometrical features of the planned tunnel.

Based on the case histories of the collapses (cave-ins) of railway tunnels, which were built with traditional mining method, the height of the loosening or cave-in area at the crowns of the collapsed tunnels, as shown in Figure 7-7, are correlated to the grade of the tunnel surrounding rocks in a regression function. The factors of the span of the excavations and their geometrical features are also considered in this regression estimation. For the tunnels planned to be excavated with conventional method, the height of the loosening or cave-in area, h_q, can be estimated as:

$$h_q = 0.45 \times 2^{s-1} \omega \quad [\text{m}] \tag{7-10}$$

where, h_q is the height of the loosening or cave-in area, m; S is the grade of tunnel surrounding rocks, as the grade I, II, ..., IV being evaluated as 1, 2, ..., 6, respectively; ω-coefficient for the influence of excavation width, calculated by $\omega = 1 + i(B_t - 5)$; B_t is the width of the excavation, m; i is based on the width of B_t, when $B_t < 5$ m, $i = 0.2$; $B_t > 5$ m, $i = 0.1$.

The critical overburden for identifying a shallow or deep tunnel, H_p, is based on the following empirical equation:

$$H_p = (2 - 2.5) h_q \tag{7-11}$$

In the application of the Equation (7-11), H_p is equal to $2h_q$ for the surrounding rocks of grades I to III, while H_p is equal to $2.5h_q$ for the surrounding rocks of grades IV to VI.

Where the overburden of a tunnel or a section of the planned tunnel, D, is no less than the critical overburden, H_p, i.e., $D \geq H_p$, the tunnel or the section can preliminarily be considered deep one.

The requirements for the application of Equation (7-11), the planned tunnel should be with the characteristics of: ①$H_t/B_t < 1.7$, where H_t is the height of the tunnel, B_t is the width of the excavation; ②no significant unsymmetrical pressure and without swelling pressure in the surrounding rocks; ③excavated by drill and blast or conventional mining method.

7.3.3.4.2 Lining loads of a deep tunnel

7.3.3.4.2.1 Vertical loads

As assumed in the evaluation of the loosing area above the tunnel excavation profile in the above section, the designed surrounding rocks pressures of a tunnel is therefore approximated from the gravity of the predicted loosening material or the height of the cave-in, h_q. This method is recommended in the design codes for both road and railway tunnels. For example, in the "design code", the assumed vertical load pressure of a deep tunnel, q, is calculated with the following:

$$q = \gamma h_q = 0.45 \cdot 2^{s-1} \gamma \omega \tag{7-12}$$

where q is the vertical distribution load, kN/m²; h_q is the height loosening area, as calculated from Equation (7-10), γ is unit weight of the ground, kN/m³ and the other parameters are same as in Equation (7-10).

Except for being deep tunnel, the other pre-conditions of the application of Equation (7-12) is same as the requirements for the application of Equation (7-11).

7.3.3.4.2.2 Horizontal loads

Of the estimation of the horizontal load pressures for deep tunnels, two situations are considered, as presented in the *Guidelines* (JTG/T D70—2010) in China, i.e., for tunnels in competent rock mass and weak rocks or soils.

For the tunnels in competent rock mass, such as grades of Ⅰ, Ⅱ or Ⅲ, the horizontal (lateral) pressures, e, can be considered as distribution pattern and calculated as:

$$e = \lambda q \tag{7-13}$$

where e is the horizontal distribution pressures of the tunnel, kN/m^2; q is the vertical distribution pressures of the tunnel, kN/m^2; λ is the lateral pressure coefficient, calculating with $\lambda = \tan^2(45° - \varphi_c/2)$, where φ_c is the apparent internal friction angle of the surrounding rocks, or using the values in Table 7-2.

Table 7-2 Lateral load pressure coefficient for deep tunnels

Grade of the rock mass	Ⅰ, Ⅱ	Ⅲ	Ⅳ	Ⅴ	Ⅵ
Lateral load pressure coefficient, λ	0	<0.15	0.15-0.3	0.3-0.5	0.5-1.0

For the tunnels in weak rocks or soils, such as grades of Ⅳ, Ⅴ or Ⅵ, the horizontal distribution pressures, e, should be considered as trapezoid distribution pattern (Figure 7-7) and calculated as:

$$e_1 = \lambda q$$
$$e_2 = \lambda(q + \gamma H_t) \tag{7-14}$$

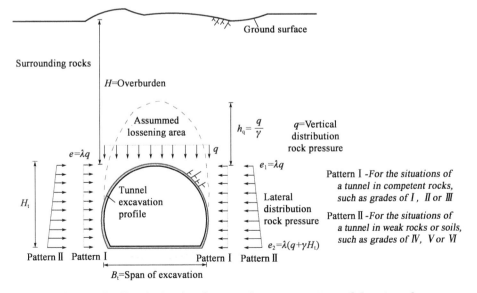

Figure 7-7 Sketch showing the ground pressure pattern of deep tunnels

where e_1 and e_2 are for the top and bottom pressures of the trapezoid distribution, respectively, kN/m^2; γ is the unit weight of surrounding rocks, kN/m^3; H_t is the height of the tunnel excavation profile, m; the λ and q are same as in Equation (7-13).

7.3.3.4.3 Lining loads of a shallow tunnel

For a shallow tunnel, the disturbance to the surrounding rocks due to excavation will reach the ground surface. However, the significance of the ground deformation, such as settlement, is closely related to the properties of the surrounding rocks and the features of the tunnel geometry and overburden. For a planned tunnel with its location being determined, the ground pressures of the tunnel is strongly influenced by the magnitude of the the overburden. Two situations of the lining loads evaluation are presented in the *Guidelines* (JTG/T D70—2010).

7.3.3.4.3.1 Tunnel with overburden less than the height of predicted loosing area

For the tunnels with small overburden (H), such as $H < h_q$, where h_q is calculated with Equation (7-10), the maximum vertical rock pressure is the total weight of the tunnel overburden and can be calculated as:

$$q = \gamma H \tag{7-15}$$

where q is the vertical distribution rock pressure, kN/m^2; γ is the unit weight of the surrounding rocks, kN/m^3; H is overburden of the tunnel, m, as shown in Figure 7-8.

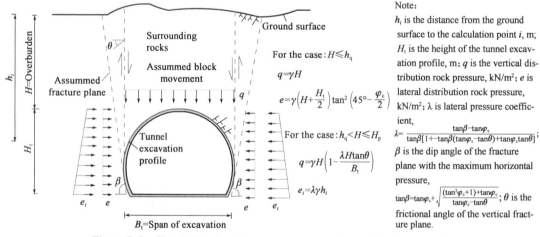

Figure 7-8 Sketch showing the rock pressure pattern of shallow tunnels

Under this situation, the lateral rock pressure, e, is considered as distribution pattern and can be calculated as:

$$e = \gamma \left(H + \frac{H_t}{2} \right) \tan^2 \left(45° - \frac{\varphi_c}{2} \right) \tag{7-16}$$

where e is the lateral distribution rock pressure, kN/m²; H_t is the height of the tunnel excavation profile, m; φ_c is the apparent internal friction angle of the surrounding rocks; the γ and H are same as in Equation(7-15).

7.3.3.4.3.2 Tunnel with overburden more than the height of predicted loosing area

For the shallow tunnels, but with relatively large overburden, such as $h_q < H \leq H_p$, where h_q and H_p are calculated with Equations (7-10) and (7-11), respectively, the movement of the rock mass block above the tunnel excavation profile is significantly constrained or resisted by the surrounding rock mass. The vertical rock load pressure of the tunnel can be calculated as:

$$q = \gamma H \left(1 - \frac{\lambda H \tan\theta}{B_t}\right) \quad (7\text{-}17)$$

where γ and H are same as in Equation (7-15); θ is friction angle along the vertical fracture plane, can be approximated with the suggested magnitude in Table 7-3; λ is the lateral pressure coefficient and can be calculated as: $\lambda = \dfrac{\tan\beta - \tan\varphi_c}{\tan\beta[1 + \tan\beta(\tan\varphi_c - \tan\theta) + \tan\varphi_c \tan\theta]}$, where β is the dip angle of the fracture plane corresponding to the maximum rock pressure, and the β can be determined from the following equation $\tan\beta = \tan\varphi_c + \sqrt{\dfrac{(\tan^2\varphi_c + 1)\tan\varphi_c}{\tan\varphi_c - \tan\theta}}$.

Table 7-3 Friction angles for the vertical fracture planes in the overburden of a shallow tunnel

Grade of surrounding rocks	I, II, III	IV	V	VI	Note: φ_c is the internal friction angle of the surrounding rocks, see Tables 4-34 and 4-35.
Friction angle for the fracture plane, θ	$0.9\varphi_c$	$(0.7\text{-}0.9)\varphi_c$	$(0.5\text{-}0.7)\varphi_c$	$(0.3\text{-}0.5)\varphi_c$	

The lateral rock pressure of the tunnel is considered as trapezoid distribution pattern(Figure 7-8) and calculated as:

$$e_i = \lambda \gamma h_i \quad (7\text{-}18)$$

where h_i is the distance the calculating point i to the ground surface, m; the λ and γ are same as in Equation (7-16).

7.3.4 Comments

The surrounding rocks (ground) pressures of a tunnel are related to the features of the surrounding rocks response to tunneling, as shown by the concept of the CCM. Factors influencing the lining load vary greatly, so does the ground load of a tunnel. The load thrusting on the liners would be close to zero, where the tunnels are built in sound ground, while the ground pressures may be near to the weight of the overburden, where the tunnels are built in soft ground. Under some

Expansion reading 7-23

special situations, such as where a tunnel is built in squeezing or swelling ground, the ground pressures can be much high in comparison to that of the usual cases. It is general true that the geotechnical conditions are the most important factor determining the features of the ground pressures, provided that the deformation of the surrounding rocks is well controlled during tunneling.

7.4 Choice of lining types

A lining system may be required for a tunnel or underground structure. The functions of lining include supporting, protection and aesthetic reason. Also, the design life and the use of the structure have a major impact on the choice of lining system. The lining system must be constructed in accordance with a specification that reflects best practice in this field. The final choice of lining system will be influenced by the expected ground conditions and cost, the contractor's preference or experiences available, and the chosen construction method.

7.4.1 Commonly used linings

7.4.1.1 Segmental linings

Circular prefabricated segments offer an economical and efficient method of tunnel linings, especially for shield TBM tunnels in soils and weak rocks. Modern segmental linings are generally a robust solution, such as in terms of construction safety. At present, segmental lining has been well used throughout the world. One-pass linings of precast concrete are popular. The segmental linings may be bolted or expanded. They may have one, two or no waterproofing gaskets, depending on watertightness criteria.

7.4.1.2 Sprayed concrete linings (SCLs)

SCLs are popular in the world. The linings may be used as temporary supports or permanent structures, in terms of design. Thanks to the features of sprayed concrete, SCLs may be used in tunnels in various grounds of both rocks and soils. Also, SCL is particularly cost effective for short tunnels and junctions.

Conventionally, the SCLs contain lattice girders and mesh for reinforcement. Voids behind the bars (shadowing) can raise the possibility of corrosion. This can be avoided by using steel-fibre reinforced SCLs with no lattice girders.

SCLs can be used in both one-pass and two-pass lining systems. In soft ground one-pass sprayed concrete linings have rarely been used because of concerns over the durability of the lining, except the single lining system with the application of wet-process. Two-pass systems have traditionally been used in tunnels where the ground is not largely self-supporting. In a composite lining system, the primary

Expansion reading 7-24

support systems including SCL are designed to maintain a stable excavation so that a final lining can be placed.

7.4.1.3 Cast in place concrete lining

Cast in place concrete linings are applied in both one-pass and two-pass lining systems. More recently, cast in place concrete linings are often used in the composite lining system of a tunnel excavated by the conventional tunneling method. The main functions of the final lining are to: ①meet the requirements of all the final load cases; ②fulfill the final safety margin; ③provide the necessary protection measures (e.g., water tightness, fire); ④guarantee the required service life time; ⑤meet the requirements of esthetics, ventilation, etc. In some design code and guidelines, the initial shotcrete lining is considered temporary support to secure the excavation, and the final linings are the permanent parts of many two-pass systems.

According to the requirements of the project, cast in place concrete lining is unreinforced or (steel bars or fibres) reinforced. The reinforcement fabric is designed to resist the tension stress or control the influence of distortions in the linings, and is also used in the circumstances of nonuniform loads. The reinforcement layer in linings with a single layer should be placed close to the inside face of the lining to resist temperature stresses and shrinkage. Multiple layers of reinforcement may be required due to large internal pressures or in a squeezing or swelling ground to resist potential nonuniform ground displacements with small distortion. The lining should remain basically undamaged for distortions up to 0.5 percent, measured as diameter change/diameter, and can remain functional for greater distortions.

Expansion reading 7-25

7.4.1.3.1 Monolithic concrete lining

In the recent years, one-pass cast in place concrete lining is usually applied in the portal sections or cut and cover sections of the tunnels, which are built with conventional method. In China, the lining applied in this situation is called monolithic lining.

7.4.1.3.2 Two-pass concrete lining

Where a large span tunnel is designed in weak rocks, the ground deformation control is one of the key points under considerations. For some cases, two-passcast-in-place concrete linings may be necessary for a composite lining system to meet the design requirements, such as in terms of both safety and ground deformation control. The composite lining under this situation can be considered as a three-layer lining. For example, two-pass concrete linings are suggested in the *Guidelines* (JTG/T D70—2010) for four-lane road tunnels in the surrounding rocks of grades Ⅳ or Ⅴ.

7.4.2 Failure modes of linings

Failure modes of concrete linings include collapse, excessive leakage, and accelerated corrosion. Compressive yield in reinforcing steel or concrete is also a failure mode. In general, tension cracks in concrete linings usually do not result in unacceptable performance.

As discussed in Chapter 6, a circular concrete liner under a uniform external load will experience a uniform compressive stress (hoop stress). If the lining is subjected to a nonuniform load or distortion, moments will develop resulting in tensile stresses at some parts of the lining. Tension cracks will occur if the moment is large enough to overcome the hoop compressive stress in the lining and the tensile strength of the concrete is exceeded. If the lining were free to move under the nonuniform loading, tension cracks could cause a collapse mechanism. Provided that the outward deformation of lining is confined by the surrounding rocks, the distortion intensity of the lining decreases as the lining is displaced in response to the loads toward the surrounding medium. A tension collapse mechanism, however, is generally not applicable to a concrete lining in rock. Howerver, tension cracks may add flexibility and encourage a more uniform loading of the lining.

Expansion eading 7-26[29-30]

In general, where the deformation and of the lining is outward deformation and is confined by surrounding rocks, the tension cracks in a concrete lining are not likely to penetrate the full thickness of the lining because the lining is subjected to radial loads and the net loads are compressive. However, if a tension crack is created at the section of the lining, the cross-section area is reduced resulting in higher compressive stresses at the residual part of these sections, arresting the crack. Under these situations, the thickness of the lining should be checked in design. In terms of stability, for a one-pass concrete lining, the shear bond between concrete and rock will tend to prevent a tension crack in the concrete, provided that the rock outside the concrete lining is in compression. Tension cracks have no consequence for the stability of the lining because they cannot form a failure mechanism until the lining also fails in compression.

It should be noted that the tension cracks in the concrete lining of noncircular openings (horseshoe-shaped, for example) must be examined for their contribution to a potential failure mode. The tension cracks are likely to create loose blocks, if the distortion of the concrete lining is not effectively confined by the surrounding rocks.

7.4.3 Structures of linings

7.4.3.1 Lining thickness and concrete cover over steel

In most cases, the thickness of concrete linings is determined by practical constructability considerations rather than structural requirements. For example, the minimum lining thickness is about 300 mm. Concrete clear cover over steel is usually taken as 30 mm to 50 mm. These thicknesses are greater than normally used for concrete structures and allow for misalignment during concrete placement, abrasion and cavitation effects, and long-term exposure to water. Tunnels exposed to aggressive corrosion or abrasion conditions may require additional cover.

Some deep tunnels under large external hydrostatic loads, or tunnels subjected to high, nonuniform loads or distortions, will govern structural requirements of the tunnel lining thickness.

7.4.3.2 Concrete mix design

Functional requirements for concrete linings and special constructability requirements should be considered in design. For most underground work, a 28-day compressive strength of 25 MPa and a water/cement ratio less than 0.45 is satisfactory. Higher strengths, up to about 35 MPa may be justified to achieve a thinner lining, better durability or abrasion resistance, or a higher modulus. One-pass segmental linings may require a concrete strength of 40 MPa or higher. In general, the concrete mixtures must be transported long distances into the tunnel to reach the location where it is pumped into the lining forms. A pumpable concrete mixture, with a slump of 100 mm to 125 mm up to 90 min after mixing, is often required for a long tunnel. Functionality, durability, and workability requirements may conflict with each other in the selection of the concrete mix. Some testing of trial mixes should be done to verify the designed requirements.

7.4.3.3 Reinforcing steel for crack control

The tensile strain in concrete due to curing shrinkage is about 0.05 percent[28]. Additional tensile strains can result from long-term exposure to the atmosphere (carbonization and other effects) and temperature variations. The cracks due to shrinkage occur at a few discrete locations, usually controlled by variations in concrete thickness or at steel rib locations. In tunnels, reinforcement for shrinkage control is usually 0.3 percent of the cross-sectional area and for highly corrosive conditions, up to 0.4 percent is used, such as suggested in the EM 1110-2-2901[28] in USA.

In general, no expansion joint is required in tunnel lining. So the reinforcing steel should be continued across construction joints, except the cases, where the construction joint is also of the function of settlement joint. A settlement joint is often design at the interval of 50 m to 80 m along the tunnel alignment, also for the transitional section of two different grade surrounding rocks.

7.4.3.4 Stress of the concrete linings under external hydrostatic load

For a circle tunnel concrete lining, under external hydrostatic load, such as concrete linings placed without provisions for drainage, should be designed for the full formation water pressure acting on the outside face, as shown in Figure 7-9a). If the lining thickness is less than one-tenth the tunnel radius ($t < 0.1R$), the concrete stress can be calculated as[28]:

$$N_c = pR/t \qquad (7\text{-}19)$$

where, N_c is stress in concrete lining; p is external hydrostatic pressure; R is radius to circumferential centerline of lining; t is lining thickness.

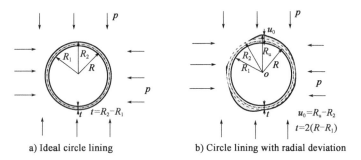

a) Ideal circle lining   b) Circle lining with radial deviation

Figure 7-9 Calculation models for final lining under external hydrostatic load

For a slender lining, with radial deviation from a circular shape u_0, as shown in Figure 7-9, the effect of the out-of-roundness on the features of the lining stress should be considered. The estimated value of u_0 should be compatible with specified roundness construction tolerances for the completed lining. The concrete stress will be calculated as[28]:

$$N_c = pR/t \pm 6pRu_0/[t^2(1 - p/p_{cr})] \qquad (7\text{-}20)$$

where p_{cr} is the critical buckling pressure determined by $p_{cr} = 3EI/R^3$, where E and I are elastic modulus and moment of inertia of the lining, respectively.

If the liningthickness is greater than one-tenth the tunnel radius ($t > 0.1R$), the maximum compressive stress at the inner surface of the concrete lining can be calculated as[28]:

$$N_c = 2pR_2^2/(R_2^2 - R_1^2) \qquad (7\text{-}21)$$

where R_2 is radius to outer surface; R_1 is radius to inner surface of lining.

7.4.3.5 Linings subject to bending and distortion

Expansion reading 7-27

In cases, where the surrounding rocks have been stabilized or reinforced at the time the concrete lining is placed, the lining will accept loads only from water pressure (internal, external, or both). Provided that the external water pressure is of hydrostatic feature, the circle lining will not be subjected to bending and distortion. Otherwise, reinforced concrete linings may be required to be designed for circumferential bending in order to minimize cracking and avoid excessive distortions.

Conditions causing circumferential bending in linings include: ①uneven support caused a thick layer of rock of much lower modulus than the surrounding rock, or a void left behind the lining; ②uneven loading caused by a volume of rock loosened after construction, or a localized water pressure trapped in a void behind the lining; ③displacements from uneven swelling or squeezing rock; ④construction loads, such as from nonuniform grout pressures; ⑤bending moment due to the shear zones or other zones of poor rock in the surrounding rocks.

Expansion reading 7-28

There are various methods available to assess tunnel linings for bending and distortion. The most important types can be classified as: ① free-standing ring subject to vertical and horizontal loads (no ground interaction); ② loaded ring supported by springs simulating ground interaction (e. g., in structural engineering codes); ③ continuum mechanics, numerical solutions; ④ continuum mechanics, closed solutions.

7.4.4 Special constructions

7.4.4.1 Lining of shafts

The linings of shafts are generally different from that of main tunnels, especially in terms of construction. The method of excavation and support adopted during shaft construction has a direct influence on the design of the shaft lining. In the permanent condition shafts are usually subject to uniform radial ground and groundwater loading, but in the temporary condition the imposed loads due to the construction operations may create a more adverse loading regime.

The designer of the shaft lining should be familiar with the different construction methods available and how they affect the design of the shaft lining. The possible methods of constructing the tunnel exits, passages or connections and their effects on the design of the tunnel lining should also be considered at an early stage to avoid costly delays during construction.

7.4.4.2 Junctions

The construction of a junction between the tunnel and another tunnel, a shaft, or other underground structure is often the critical operation in tunnel construction, in terms of the stability of the surrounding rocks and the structure. The designer must consider not only how the integrity of the structure is to be maintained in both the short and long term, but also how the stability of the surrounding rocks is to be maintained to prevent ingress and associated surface settlement or collapse. Due consideration must be given to the structural stability, surrounding rocks stability and constructability in design[1].

7.4.4.3 Portals, launch chambers and reception chambers

Portals present particular challenges because of the low cover and potentially poor nature of the ground, for example due to weathering. The lining usually must be designed to carry the entire weight of its overburden since the ground may not be able to arch over the tunnel. Additional measures such as canopy tubes may be required to guard against instability in the crown of the tunnel.

For TBM tunnels special measures may be required at the launch and reception points of each drive, either because of the low cover and inferior ground conditions or because of the need to maintain the pressure around a closed-face TBM. For example, where expanded segmental linings are used for the main tunnel, it is common practice to use bolted segmental rings within a distance of about two tunnel diameters of the portals, to safeguard against differential movements[1].

7.5 Critical thinking problems

C1: Tunnel structure design should be based on the results of the analysis on the surrounding rocks behaviors. Consider: ① How to determine the types of surrounding rocks behaviors for a planned tunnel? ② Of the types of tunnel surrounding rocks behaviors, such as stress controlled for high stress/strength ratio conditions, structure controlled or block driven failure under low stress/strength ratio conditions, chemical, mineralogical effects dominate and ground water condition dominate, what are the main performance requirements for each of these types of surrounding rocks behaviors, in terms of tunnel lining structure design, respectively?

C2: What are the main considerations in tunnel structure design? and how can the influence of geotechnical and hydrological conditions, project features and construction method choosing, be considered in a comprehensive method, such as in terms of surrounding rocks-tunnel structure interaction analysis?

C3: The shape of the excavations has a significant influence on the surrounding rocks stress redistribution under a boundary stresses condition. Consider the case: For the situation, the excavation width is $W = 2a$ and height is $H = 2b$, $a = b$; r_A and r_B are radii of the curve at the points A and B, $r_A = r_B = a$; $K = 0.5$. ①Using the Equations (7-3) and (7-4), calculate the sidewall boundary stress and the stress at the centre of the crown of an ellipse, σ_A and σ_B; ②Using the Kirsch solution to calculate the σ_A and σ_B.

C4: The lining loads are dependent on the stiffness of the lining but generally less than that corresponding to the overburden pressure. It is generally correct that a confined flexible ring works better than a stiff ring on the basis that there is no advantage in increasing lining thickness where the flexural capacity of the lining is not exceeded. Consider: ①How is the stiffness of the designed lining evaluated, in terms of being flexible or stiff? ②For the simple case, given $R = 6$ m, $t = 0.5$ m, $E_c = 30000$ MPa, $\sigma_v = 4$ MPa and $K_0 = 0.5$, calculate the maximum bending movement, M, and the maximum hoop force, N, in the lining, under the conditions presented in the following table, respectively.

Conditions						
	$E_r = 0$	$E_r = 300$ MPa, $\nu_r = 0.3$	$E_r = 600$ MPa, $\nu_r = 0.3$	$E_r = 12$ GPa, $\nu_r = 0.25$	$E_r = 96$ GPa, $\nu_r = 0.2$	$E_r = 240$ GPa, $\nu_r = 0.2$
	$E_r/E_c = 0$	$E_r/E_c = 0.01$	$E_r/E_c = 0.02$	$E_r/E_c = 0.40$	$E_r/E_c = 3.20$	$E_r/E_c = 8.00$
Calculated M						
Calculated N						

C5: The surrounding rocks (ground) pressures are often approximated for tunnel structures design. Consider: ①The factors influencing the load on the liner; ②The main points of the commonly used empirical methods to estimate the lining loads, such as Terzaghi's rock load pressure, the methods suggested in the *Specifications* (JTG 3370.1—2018) and the *Guidelines* (JTG/T D70—2010) in China.

C6: During the design of the tunnels in a planned highway, it is considered to use the semi-empirical method of approximating the deep tunnel surrounding rocks pressures, suggested in the *Specifications* (JTG 3370.1—2018), to approximate the surrounding rocks pressures for tunnel lining design. The tunnels are planned to be mined with conventional methods. Based on the preliminary analysis, the features of some planned deep tunnels or sections meet the pre-conditions of the application of the semi-empirical method. Determine the design parameters listed in the following table.

	Grade of the surrounding rocks	I	II	III	IV	V	VI
Features of the surrounding rocks	Unit weight of the surrounding rocks, γ [kN/m²]	27	26	25	24	24	23
Span of the tunnel design excavation profiles, B_t [m]		8.5	8.5	8.5	8.8	9.0	9.0
Height of the tunnel design excavation profiles, H_t [m]		14.5	14.5	15	15	15.5	16
Determine the critical overburden, H_p [m]							
Determine the surrounding rocks pressures for the deep tunnels or sections	Vertical pressure, q [kN/m²]						
	Horizontal load pressures, e [kN/m²]						

7.6 References

[1] The British Tunnelling Society (BTS), the Institution of Civil Engineers. Tunnel lining design guide[S]. London: Thomas Telford Publishing, Thomas Telford Ltd, 2004.

[2] Technical Committee 3.3 Road Tunnel Operation, PIARC. Design fire characteristics for road

tunnels[R/OL]. PIARC, 2016. https://www.piarc.org/ressources/publications/9/26494, 2017R01EN.pdf.

[3] Brady B H G, Brown E T. Rock Mechanics: For underground mining[M]. 3rd ed. Springer, 2006.

[4] Haack I A. Water leakages in subsurface facilities: Required watertightness, contractual matters, and methods of redevelopment[J]. Tunnelling & Underground Space Technology, 1991, 6(3):273-282.

[5] Hoek E, Brown E T. Underground Excavations in Rock[M]. London:. Institution of Mining and Metallurgy, 1980.

[6] Peck R B. Advantages and limitations of the observational method in applied soil mechanics[J]. Geotechnique, 1969, 19(2): 171-187.

[7] Fairhurst C, Carranza-Torres C. Closing the Circle—Some Comments on Design Procedures for Tunnel Supports in Rock[C]// the University of Minnesota 50th Annual Geotechnical Conference, 2002.

[8] Deane A P, Bassett R H. The Heathrow Express trial tunnel[J]. Geotechnical Engineering, 1995, 113(3):144-156.

[9] Barla G. Squeezing rocks in tunnels[J]. ISRM News Journal, 1995, 3/4: 44-49.

[10] Barla G B. Tunnelling under squeezing rock conditions[M]// Tunnelling Mechanics—Advances in Geotechnical Engineering and Tunnelling. 2002:169-268.

[11] Barla G, Bonini M, Debernardi D. Time Dependent Deformations in Squeezing Tunnels[J]. International Journal of Geoengineering Case Histories, 2010, 2(1): 40-65.

[12] Wittke W. Rock Mechanics: Theory and Application with Case Histories[M]. Berlin: Springer-Verlag, Berlin, 1990.

[13] Barratt D A, O'Reilly M P, Temporal J. Long-term measurements of loads on tunnel linings in overconsolidated clay[C]//Tunnelling'94 IMMG Conf. 1994.

[14] Institution of Structural Engineers (ISE). Soil-Structure Interaction: the Real Behaviour of Structures[M]. London: Institution of Structural Engineers, 1989.

[15] BritishTunnelling Society (BTS). Specification for Tunnelling[S]. London: Thomas Telford Publishing, Thomas Telford Ltd, 2000.

[16] Sakurai S. Lessons learned from field measurements intunnelling[J]. Tunnelling & Underground Space Technology, 1997, 12(4):453-460.

[17] Einstein H H, Schwartz C W. Simplified analysis for tunnel support[J]. J Geotech Eng Div. 1979, 105: 499-518.

[18] Hoek E, Marinos P. Predicting tunnel squeezing problems in weak heterogeneous rock masses. Tunnels &Tunnelling Internationul, 2000, Part 1 November: 45-51, Part 2 December: 33-36.

[19] Nicholson D, Tse C-M, Penny C. The Observational Method in Ground Engineering: Principles and Applicclrions[M]. London: CIRIA, 1999.

[20] Terzaghi K. Rock defects and loads on tunnel supports[M]// Rock tunneling with steel supports, Commercial Shearing and Stamping Co., Youngstown, Ohio, 1946.

[21] Unal E. Development of design guidelines and roof-control standards for coal-mine roofs[J]. Pennsylvania State Univ University Park Pa, 1983, 67(2): 309-312.

[22] Ortlepp W D, Gay N C. Performance of an experimental tunnel subjected to stresses ranging

from 50MPa to 230MPa[C]// ISRM Symposium, Cambridge, 1984.

[23] Ward W H, Pender M J. Tunneling in soft ground[C]// The 10th Conf. Soil Mech. Found. Eng., Stockholm, 1981.

[24] Deere D U, Peck R B, Parker H, et al. Design of tunnel support systems[M/OL]// Highway Research Record, Highway Research Board, 1970. http://onlinepubs.trb.org/Onlinepubs/hrr/1970/339/339-003.pdf.

[25] Carranza-Torres C, Fairhurst C. Application of the Convergence-Confinement method of tunnel design to rock masses that satisfy the Hoek-Brown failure criterion[J]. Tunnelling and Underground Space Technology incorporating Trenchless Technology Research, 2000, 15(2):187-213.

[26] O'Rourke T D. Guidelines for tunnel lining design[M]. New York: American Society of Civil Engineers(ASCE), 1984.

[27] Hoek E. Big Tunnels in Bad Rock[J]. Journal of Geotechnical & Geoenvironmental Engineering, 2001, 127(9):726-740.

[28] U. S. Army Corps of Engineers. Tunnels and shafts in rock-Engineer Manual [M]. Washington: U. S. Army Corps of Engineers, Department of the Army, 1997.

[29] U. S. Army Corps of Engineers. Strength Design for Reinforced Concrete Hydraulic Structures[M]. Washington: U. S. Army Corps of Engineers, Department of the Army, 1992.

[30] Morgan D R. Steel fiber reinforced shotcrete for support of underground openings in Canada [J]. Concrete International, 1991, Nov:56-64.

8 Tunnel Support and Surrounding Rocks Reinforcement

8.1 Support and surrounding rocks reinforcement in general

Expansion reading 8-1

Tunnel often needs supports or lining, though some rock tunnels are unlined except at the portals and in certain areas where the rock is less competent, or lined with concrete or internal finish surfaces, only for the conditions of lighting, ventilation and aesthetic feeling. In terms of stability or deformation control, rock reinforcements, such as rockbolts or steel dowels, are often needed in tunnels. To prevent small fragments of rock from spalling, wire mesh, shotcrete, or a thin concrete lining may be used, such as before the installation of a final lining. Where the surrounding rocks are so weak or the stand-up time of the surrounding rocks is so short that pre-supports or ground improvements are necessary for tunneling. Preface supports (pre-supports) are these ground improvement and reinforcement measures, which are applied ahead of the excavation face.

8.1.1 Support and reinforcement

The term support is widely used for describing the procedures and materials used for improving the stability and maintain the surrounding rocks load-carrying capability. The primary objective of support is to mobilize and conserve the inherent strength of the surrounding rocks to realize partially or fully self-supporting.

In the Engineering Manual of Rock Reinforcement[1], rock reinforcement is presented as *the placement of rock bolts, untensioned rock dowels, prestressed rock anchors, or wire tendons in a rock mass to reinforce and mobilize the rock's natural competency to support itself; rock support is that the placement of supports such as wood sets, steel sets, or reinforced concrete linings to provide resistance to inward movement of rock toward the excavation.* Windsor[2] stated that *support is the application of a reactive force at the face of the excavation, and includes techniques and devices, e. g. fill, timber, steel or concrete sets, shotcrete, etc.; and reinforcement is considered to be an improvement of the overall rock mass properties from within the rock mass and will therefore include all techniques, and devices that act within the rock mass, e. g. rock bolts, cable bolts and ground anchors*. In these terms, reinforcement devices, surrounding rocks and supports are considered a systems of the components of tunnel structures, with a consequence of the particular physical and mechanical characteristics of the components and their interactions[3].

In a composite lining system, the primary support, reinforcement or lining is applied during or immediately after excavation, to ensure safe working conditions during subsequent excavation, and to initiate the process of mobilizing and conserving rock mass strength by controlling boundary displacements. The primary support or reinforcement will form part, and may form the whole, of the total support or reinforcement required.

Support or reinforcement may be either active or passive[4], in terms of the surrounding rocks deformation control or the mobilization and conservation of the surrounding rocks inherent strength. Active support imposes a predetermined load to the rock surface at the time of installation. It can take the form of tensioned rock bolts or cables, hydraulic props, expandable segmented concrete linings. Active support is usually required when it is necessary to support the gravity loads imposed by individual rock blocks or by a loosened zone of surrounding rocks. Passive support or reinforcement is not installed with an applied loading, but rather, develops its loads as the rock mass deforms. Passive support may be provided by steel sets, timbered sets or composite packs, or by untensioned grouted rock bolts, reinforcing bars or cables. Untensioned, grouted rock bolts, reinforcing bars and cables are often described as dowels. It should be noted that, where the support or reinforcement is considered as a component of a system structure, together with the surrounding rocks, the meaning of being active or passive may be relative in the supporting system of a tunnel.

Ground reinforcement includes, the techniques of ground anchoring, cable bolting and rockbolting. Basically, all of these techniques seek to assure the stability of an artificial structure constructed within or on a soil or rock mass by the installation of structural elements within the ground. Ground anchors tend to be longer with the highest capacity, rockbolts tend to be shorter with the lowest capacities and cable bolts have evolved to address stability problems that lie between the two. Rockbolts are commonly used in tunnel engineering.

8.1.2 Support and surrounding rocks reinforcement principles

The safety of a tunnel should meet the requirements of both serviceability and structural safety. The design and construction of a tunnel should, at least, avoid the following failure or unacceptable cases. ①The structure loses its watertightness; ②The deformations are intolerably large; ③The tunnel is insufficiently durable for its projected life and use; ④ The material strength of the structural elements is exhausted locally, necessitating repair; ⑤ The support technique fails or causes damage; ⑥ Exhaustion of the material strength of the system causes structural failure, although the corresponding deformations develop in a restrained manner over time; ⑦ The tunnel collapses suddenly because of instability. Based on the yield criteria related to failure cases, the structural design model should be designed safely, with the safety margins for each of these failure cases, respectively.

In terms of safety and deformation control of a planned tunnel, the requirements of surrounding rocks supports and reinforcements depend on the surrounding rocks geotechnical conditions, the features of the tunnel project, planned construction method and the restrictions of environments so on. Of these influencing factors, the geotechnical condition is all-important factor to be considered in the design of the supports and reinforcements for a tunnel. The predicted behavior of surrounding rocks or the response of the ground to excavation, together with the objects of the surrounding rocks deformation control and safety requirements, is the base of the design.

The response of the ground to tunneling can vary widely. Based on the features of the tunnel type and structure, and the grade of surrounding rocks, the principal types of tunneling may be the following four cases.

(1) Case Ⅰ: Cut and cover tunnel, in most cases the ground acts only passively as a dead load on a tunnel structure erected like any above ground engineering structure.

(2) Case Ⅱ: Mined or bored tunnels in soft ground, immediate support must be provided by a stiff lining (e.g., in the case of shield-driven tunnels with prefabricated segments for ring support and pressurized slurry for face support). In such a case, the ground usually can confine the outward deformation of the lining.

(3) Case Ⅲ: Mined or bored tunnels in medium-hard rocks or in more cohesive soils, the ground may be strong enough to allow a certain open section at the tunnel face. Here, a certain amount of stress release may permanently be valid before the supporting elements and the lining begin acting effectively. In this situation only a fraction of the primary ground pressure is acting on the lining.

(4) Case Ⅳ: Mined or bored tunnels in hard rocks, the ground alone may preserve the stability of the opening so that only a thin lining, if any, will be necessary for surface protection.

It is well accepted that the behaviors of surrounding rocks or the response of the surrounding rocks to the tunneling are of dynamic characteristics, which is related to the properties of surrounding rocks and the tunneling procedure, as well as the interactions between the surrounding rocks and the applied structures or

8 Tunnel Support and Surrounding Rocks Reinforcement

Expansion reading 8-2[6]

supports and reinforcements. The disturbance of the excavation to the surrounding rocks generally changes with the tunneling. In this process, the in situ stresses in the surrounding rocks are being deviated by the opening of the cavity and channelled around it (arch effect) to create zones of increased stress in the surrounding rocks of around the excavation[5].

8.2 Ground improvement and pre-support

Expansion reading 8-3

In general, where a tunnel planned in the grounds, of which the stand-up time is minimal and/or material strengths are low, ground improvement techniques or pre-support is often needed, such as under the situation, where it is difficult to provide adequate support or reinforcement to the surrounding rocks sufficiently in time after the excavation has been made. The pre-reinforcement is also called auxiliary construction measures[8], which mainly include three categories: ①ground improvement; ②ground reinforcement; ③dewatering. In special cases, the excavation work can only be carried out with the help of additional auxiliary construction measures.

8.2.1 Ground improvement

Ground improvement means the application of methods that improve the mechanical or hydraulic properties of the ground. The commonly used methods are grouting, jet grouting and ground freezing.

Ground improvement has normally to be carried out alternately to the excavation, such as at the face, and leads to the interruptions of the excavation work. In special cases ground improvement can be carried out from the surface or pilot tunnels outside the future tunnel cross section.

8.2.1.1 Grouting

Grouting is generally used for filling voids or fissures in the ground with the aim to increase the geotechnical properties, such as cohesion, shear-strength and uniaxial compressive strength, and to reduce the ground permeability[9]. The most commonly used grout material is cement. In special cases chemical products such as resins or foams are also applied. In these cases the environmental and safety restrictions have to be considered specially. Grouting for ground improvement involves the pumping of a cementitious slurry or other setting fluid into the ground, usually at pressure. It is noted that, if this occurs during construction it can cause an increase in loading beyond that arising from overburden alone, either directly on the tunnel lining from the grout or by an increase in ground pressure on the tunnel lining.

Grouting includes permeation grouting, compaction grouting, hydro fracture

Expansion reading 8-4

grouting, jet grouting, rock grouting and compensation grouting and deep mixing method[10].

Compensation grouting is the responsive use of compaction, permeation or hydro fracture grouting as an intervention between an existing structure and tunnel excavations[11], such as to counteract tunneling-induced settlement. In compensation grouting, the risk of imposing additional loads on a tunnel is high since the grouting pressure must be greater than the overburden pressure. During construction, exclusion zones are often imposed around the tunnel face to reduce the probable risk to the tunnel.

Of rock grouting, the primary purpose of a pre-grouting in the surrounding rocks of a tunnel is to establish a zone around the tunnel periphery, where the hydraulic conductivity is reduced. The water pressure is gradually reduced through the grouted zone and the water pressure acting on the tunnel contour and the tunnel lining can be close to nil. In addition, pre-grouting may have the effect of improving the stability situation in the grouted zone. Grouting also serves as a permanent groundwater control in Norwegian tunnels, where a single lining system is applied. A commonly used figure in Norwegian tunnels is a maximum inflow to the tunnel of 30 litres per minute per 100 metres of tunnel. Many projects have been realized where the allowable inflow is in the range of 2-10 L/min/100 m, to avoid buildings settlements and impact on natural areas[14].

8.2.1.2 Jet grouting

Jet grouting is applied mainly horizontally or at a slightly upward or downward angle from within the face of the tunnel. An improvement of the roof arching behavior is achieved by applying one or more layers of jet grouting columns in stages corresponding to the excavation operations.

Expansion reading 8-5[12-13]

An improvement of the stability of the face is achieved by placing individual jet columns parallel to the direction of advance in the working face. Less common in tunneling is vertical or steeply inclined jet grouting, except in shallow tunnels where it is applied from the surface. From within the tunnel vertical or steeply inclined jet grouting is mainly applied to underpin the bottom of the roof arch.

8.2.1.3 Ground freezing

The ground freezing techniques are known to waterproof or stabilize temporarily the ground through: ①continuous frozen bodies which provide long-term load-bearing; ②short-term, immediately effective local freezing of damp zones close to the face or in the immediate vicinity outside the excavated cross section. The latter is usually achieved by means of injection lances with liquid nitrogen cooling.

8 Tunnel Support and Surrounding Rocks Reinforcement

A relatively long-term frozen body is produced along the top and side boundaries of the excavated cross section, and in some cases under the invert. The freezing is achieved by a drilled tube system, through which coolant is pumped. The frozen bodies can be installed alternately to the excavation work from the extended tunnel face in an overlapping way or in advance from separate adits or from ground surface for shallow tunnels.

Ground freezing is also developed to obtain access to working face in unfavorable ground conditions, especially to provide emergency support in unstable ground below the water table. Ground freezing involves the extraction of heat from the ground until the groundwater is frozen. Thus converting the groundwater into a cementing agent and the ground into a "frozen sandstone". The heat is extracted by circulating a cooling liquid, usually brine, in an array of pipes. Each pipe is actually two nested pipes, with the liquid flowing down the center pipe and back out through the annulus between the pipes. When the pipes are close enough and the time long enough, the cylinders of frozen soil formed at each pipe eventually coalesce into one solid frozen mass. This mass may be a ring as needed or a solid block of whatever shape necessary, such as umbrella for the working face.

Expansion reading 8-6[15]

8.2.2 Pre-reinforcement with elements

Ground reinforcement with elements involves the insertion of structural elements with one predominant dimension. Commonly used bolts, anchors, micro piles and spiles are such elements. The main methods of application or supporting patterns are pipe umbrellas and face bolting or radial bolting from a pilot bore.

In tunneling practice, pre-reinforcement is often provided by grouted rods or pipes that are not pre-tensioned and so may be described as being passive rather than active. Such pre-reinforcement is effective because it allows the surrounding rocks to deform in a controlled manner and to mobilize or protect its strength, such as through confining the amount of dilation and subsequent probably loosening. The role of this pre-reinforcement is critically dependent on the bonding between the reinforcing element and the grout, and between the grout and the ground.

8.2.2.1 Pipe umbrella

Pipe umbrellas are specified to supplement the vault structure and to stabilize the excavation face as a pre-support. Pipe-roof umbrellas (canopy) is commonly used, especially in form of canopy tube umbrellas, consisting of closely spaced and grouted steel tubes. The pipe-roof umbrella is effective in controlling deformations and volume losses for a wide range of ground conditions by reducing dilation, improving face stability and increasing surrounding rocks stand-up time.

To reduce the disturbance to the natural slope, pipe-roof umbrellas/canopy is often used at tunnel portals, where are of low cover and low strength, as shown in Figure 8-1. Portal pipe shields are drilled at the portal wall along the cross section parallel the direction of advance and serve to bridge zones of disturbance behind the walls. The starting points of the pipes are set on a steel and shotcrete arch or a cast in place concrete arch, with a circular spacing of around 0.4 m. With face driven ahead, the steel sets are installed at a space of, such as 0.6 m to 1.2 m, along the designed cross section profile. Fan-like, with an angle between the pipes and the tunnel axis less than 5°, overlapping pipe shields are installed in stages, alternately with the excavation for the tunnel driving. The length of the longitudinal overlapping of the pipes is at least 3.0 m. In general, the pipe umbrella shall extend at least 30% beyond the face of the next excavation, if the length of the pipes is around 10 m. It is also a way to improve the stiffness of the pipe canopy through grouting the pipes with cement mortar.

Figure 8-1 Application of pipe canopy at a loess tunnel portal

8.2.2.2 Spiles and forepoles

Spiles and forepoles are steel rods and pipes, respectively, installed in the ground for the local short-term stabilization of the roof section and at the working face on the boundary of the excavation. Spiles and forepoles are used interchangeably to describe support elements consisting of pipes or pointed boards or rods driven ahead of the steel sets or lattice girders. In generally, the length of forepoles is larger that of the spiles. Another difference between them is that the forepoles can be used for grouting the surrounding rocks.

The spiles rest on the first steel arch in front and should be at least 1.5 times as long as the subsequent advance round length in the excavation. Pre-supports of spiles and forepoles provide temporary overhead protection while excavation until the installation of the next set or girder is accomplished. Fan-like, or looking out, with a angle between the spiles or forepoles and the tunnel axis less than $30°$, overlapping steel bars or small diameter pipes shields are installed in stages alternately with the excavation for the tunnel driving. The length of the longitudinal overlapping of the spiles and forepoles should be no less than 0.5 m.

The design of spiles and forepoles is best described as "intuitive" as it must be kept flexible and constantly adjusted in the field as the ground behavior is observed during the construction. A preliminary approximation of design load might be a height of rock equal to $0.1B$ to $0.25B$, where B is the width of the opening[4].

Depending on the type of surrounding rocks, the spiles can be jacked, rammed or inserted in drill holes. After grouting, forepoles creates an optimum bond with the surrounding material.

8.2.2.3 Face dowels

Dowels can be utilized for stabilizing or reinforce the face in tunneling. Depending on the relevant hazard scenario, the relevant dowel type and length have to be determined in the design. As a protection against face collapse or intrusion, spot dowels may be sufficient, whereas in difficult ground conditions (e.g., squeezing rock and soils) systematic long dowels with a high number of long, overlapping steel or fibreglass may be necessary.

Under high stress and low ground strength environments, face dowels have been shown to be very effective in providing sufficient stability to allow full-face excavation, such as in Italy as part of the ADECO-RS (Analysis of Controlled Deformation in Rocks and Soils) full-face tunneling approach[5], of which the glass-fibre dowels have the advantage over steel dowels of being easier to cut during excavation.

8.2.2.4 Pre-cutting methods

Pre-cutting on the perimeter of the arch, with filling of the slot with concrete, provides a continuous load-bearing arch that pre-supports the ground. It is applied to weak relatively homogeneous materials having sufficient stand-up time to allow the slot to stay open[5]. A variation of this supporting measure is the jet grouting canopy or bored concrete pile canopy.

8.2.3 Dewatering and drainage

In some cases the tunnel construction is only possible with the application of special dewatering measures, such as conventional vertical or horizontal wells or vacuum drains.

In dewatering measures design, environmental aspects have to be considered, such as limits on lowering the ground water table, settlements. In the case of low overburden, dewatering measures can be carried out from the ground surface. Otherwise, dewatering has to be done from the tunnel face or from pilot tunnels.

Lowering the groundwater level will effectively reduce the pressures on a tunnel lining but may not be permitted for environmental reasons. On the cessation of the dewatering scheme the groundwater will be reintroduced into the ground. The main issue will be a change in stress regime surrounding the lining and the build up of water pressure. The latter could expose weaknesses in the quality of waterproofing of the lining, and also may introduce potential flotation problems.

8.2.4 Requirement of pre-supports

In tunnel design, it is necessary to consider the requirement of pre-supports for the tunnel, such as in terms of construction choosing and the stability of the surrounding rocks of the excavations. This issue can be preliminarily evaluated with empirical or analogical method, such as based on the grades of the surrounding rocks of the tunnel under consideration. For example, in terms of the magnitude of the stand-up time of the excavation of a tunnel in different grades of surrounding rocks, the requirement of pre-support for the tunnel excavation can be preliminarily determined with the recommendation in the *Guidelines*(JTG/T D70—2010).

Expansion reading 8-7

8.3 Primary support

In the modern tunneling, rockbolts and shotcrete system are commonly used as primary lining or single lining. The most common elements for the primary support are rockbolts, shotcrete, steel ribs or lattice girders, and meshes or steel fabric. These elements are applied individually or in combination.

The purpose of the primary support is to stabilize the underground opening until the final lining is installed. Thus the support design and construction is primarily a question of construction safety and the effect on surrounding rocks deformation control. The selection of the support elements has to consider the onset of effect and the dynamic process of the tunneling, as well as the interaction between the surrounding rocks and the installed supports.

8.3.1 Rockbolts and dowels

Rockbolts and dowels have been used for about 100 years for the support of underground excavations and were popularized in the 1970s. Nowadays they are extensively used as support in tunnels and a wide variety of bolt and dowel types have been developed to meet the different needs in practice. A rockbolt is a reinforcement system comprises four principal components: the surrounding rock, the element, the internal fixture and the external fixture[2], as shown in Figure 8-2.

Each component of the system is involved in two load transfer interactions.

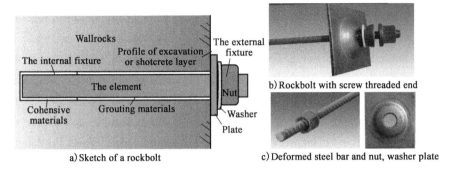

a) Sketch of a rockbolt   c) Deformed steel bar and nut, washer plate

Figure 8-2   The principal components of arockbolt reinforcing system

The bolts, utilized for connecting the anchorage to the bearing plate at the collar of the hole, are either smooth rods or deformed steel bars, with the features of solid or hollow (groutable), threaded one or both ends, or threaded one end and headed at the other, depending on the type of anchorage and the type of hardware at the collar. A single tensioned rockbolt usually consists of an anchorage, a steel rod or bar, a face plate, a tightening nut and sometimes a deformable plate. For short term applications, the bolt may be left ungrouted, but for permanent or long term applications, especially used in corrosive environments, rockbolts are usually fully grouted with cement or resin grout for improving both pull-out strength and corrosion resistance.

Dowels or anchor bars generally consist of deformed steel bars which are grouted into the rock. The load in the dowels is generated by differential movements in the surrounding rocks along the dowels. Dowels are usually grouted along their lengths on installation and develop their tension with deformation of the surrounding rocks in which they are installed.

The advantage of rockbolts and dowels applications is that they are very flexible and can be easily adapted to changing rock conditions during tunneling. For example to control excessive convergence, the number of rockbolts and/or their length can be systematically increased until the deformations are acceptable. This is also one of the reasons why rockbolts are used in tunnels constructed with conventional methods.

A distinction can be made between local reinforcement and general or systematic reinforcement. Local reinforcement is required when unstable blocks or wedges locally occur along the perimeter of the excavation. General or systematic reinforcement is needed when deformations occur for the entire tunnel sections.

8.3.1.1   Types

Adequate anchorage is critical to therequired performance of the reinforcement system. Rockbolts are often classified according to the nature of their anchorages, such as mechanical anchorages and grouted end anchorages (Table 8-1). The mechanical types make use of an expanding element that is forced against the walls of the borehole to deform the rock and to provide frictional resistance to pullout. Grouted end anchorages rely on a bonding medium between a portion of the reinforcing, element and the surrounding rock to develop the desired anchorage strength. Regardless of the anchorage type used, subsequent full length grouting after tensioning (if necessary) improves the reinforcement capability of the element and ensures permanence in a long run. Anchors formed from Portland cement or resin is generally more reliable and permanent.

Table 8-1　Types of rock bolts by anchorage methods[17]

Type	Anchorage	Description
Mechanical anchorages	Slot and wedge anchored	Anchorage is obtained by inserting the wedge into the slotted end of the bolt and expanding the slot by driving the wedge against the end of the drill hole.
	Expansion anchored	Anchorage device obtains its anchorage by the action of a wedge or cone moving against a shell (or fingers) and expanding the shell against the sides of the hole.
Grouted end anchorages	Resin anchored or cement grouting anchored	The length of element embedment varies with the type and condition of the rock and the bonding medium used. Portland cement, gypsum, and chemical grouts or mortars have been used successfully.

Split Set and Swellex bolts are commonly used mechanical rockbolts, which rely on the generation of friction at the rockbolt contact along their lengths for their anchorage and strength. As with mechanical anchors, friction bolts depend for their efficacy on the sizes and accuracy of the drilling of the holes in which they are installed. They are also susceptible to corrosion and blast-induced damage.

Grouted end anchorage rockbolts are used in tunnel engineering as a permanent reinforcement measure. When conditions are such that the installation of support can be carried out very close to an advancing face or in anticipation of stress changes that will occur at a later excavation stage, dowels can be used in place of rockbolts. The essential difference between the supporting effects of dowels and tensioned rockbolts is that tensioned rockbolts apply a positive force to the surrounding rocks, while dowels depend upon movement in the surrounding rocks to activate the reinforcing action. So, a tensioned or pre-stressed rockbolt is designed for the situation, where the deformation of the surrounding rocks should be strictly controlled upon the application of the rockbolt.

The simplest form of dowel in use today is the cement grouted dowel as illustrated in Figure 8-3. A thick grout (typically a 0.3-0.35 water/cement ratio grout) is used for bonding the surrounding rocks and the steel bar. The grout also protects bar from rusting. To restrain the movement of the surrounding rocks around the borehole collar, a faceplate and nut system may be used where it is necessary.

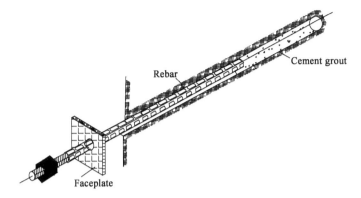

Figure 8-3 Grouted dowel using a deformed bar inserted into a grout-filled hole[17]

Where the supporting function is required in time, such as in tunnels in soft rocks, the bonding materials should be set in a short period. Fast-setting anchor cartridge or resin anchored rockbolt may be used in soft grounds. Figure 8-4 shows the details of the installation and grouting of a resin anchored and grouted bolt made from threaded bar. Resin encapsulated rockbolts are widely used for the reinforcement of soft rocks. In the recent years, fast-setting cartridges have generally taken the place of the grouting. The high unit cost of fast-setting cartridges is offset by the speed of installation.

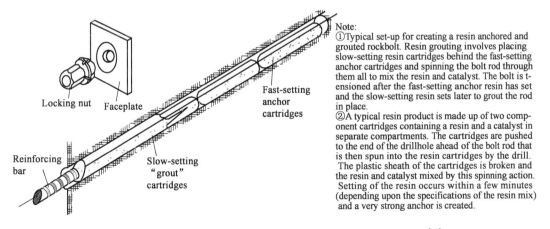

Figure 8-4 Installation of a resin anchored bolt, with cartridges[17]

Where it is difficult to bore a hole and then install the bolt, as the shape of the bored hole will be reshaped due to surrounding rocks deformation, a self-boring hollow injection bolt (Figure 8-5) is often applied in practice.

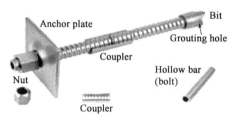

Figure 8-5　System of a self-boring hollow injection anchor bolt

A self-drilling anchor bolt is a unique anchoring system and is today's answer to the increasing demands of the tunneling industry and ground engineering for safer and faster production. The system provides advantages for all areas of its applications, where boreholes would require the time consuming drilling with casing systems in unconsolidated or cohesive soil. The main features and advantages of a self-drilling anchor bolt include: ①particularly suitable for difficult ground conditions; ②a high rate of installation since drilling, placing and grouting can be performed in one single operation; ③self drilling system eliminates the requirement for a cased borehole; ④installation with simultaneous drilling and grouting possible; ⑤easy installation in all directions, also upwards; ⑥suitable for working in limited space, height and in areas of difficult access; ⑦simple post grouting system; ⑧hot-dipped galvanizing for corrosion protection.

A self-drilling anchor bolt is used as radial bolting, forepoling, micro injection pile, to stabilize surrounding rocks around tunnel face or portal area. The system may be pre-stressed as a rockbolt or not, as a dowel or soil nail.

8.3.1.2　Structures of a bolt

The structures of a typical rockbolt may include[1]: bearing plate and mortar pad, bevel washers, hardened flat washer and thread lubricant, nut, grouting tubes, bond breaker, etc., as shown in Figure 8-6. A variety of other accessories such as angle washers, spherical washers, rubber bolt hole sealers, grout tube adapters, plastic washers for holding resin cartridges in place, and impact wrench adapters are available and described in related manufacturer's catalogs.

8.3.1.3　Installation of rockbolt

The success of rockbolt installation is largely dependent on the applied techniques and workmanship of the contractor. Conventionally, the installation procedure of a rockbolt includes: drilling hole and cleaning, grouting anchor or installing mechanical anchor, pre-stressing or tensioning the system, grouting the reinforcing elements.

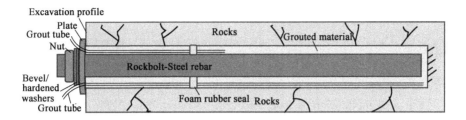

Note: ①Bearing plates and mortar pad are used for spreading out and transfer the concentrated bolt load to the rock around the collar of the hole. Bevel washers should be used between the bearing plate and the hardened washer to create a uniform bearing surface for the nut normal to the bolt axis.

②A hardened flat washer, with thread lubricant, should be used between the bevel washers and the nut in all cases. The nut should develop the ultimate strength of the bar; generally a heavy duty nut is required. Tubes installed in the drill holes for transmitting pumped liquid grout or for venting air should be semi-rigid. Bond breaker is used for preventing bond between the bar and the mortar of the bearing pad or grout seal and also to keep the threads clean of mortar. The volume of the grouted materials is intentionally overdrawn for indication.

Figure 8-6 Structure of a conventional grouted end anchorage, pumpable type

The control of hole drilling operations during the installation of rockbolts is extremely important for achieving successful rock reinforcement. Hole size, length, condition, location, and alignment are all factors which can significantly affect the installation results. Hole size is critical for most installations. Drill holes must be cleaned just prior to the installation of the bolt to remove sludge, rock dust and particles, and debris present in the hole. Cleaning can be accomplished by introducing compressed air at the bottom of the hole or by washing with water.

Rockbolt installation should be accomplished immediately after the drill hole is cleaned. Field tests are often conducted to determine embedment lengths, to determine required set or cure time of the bonding medium before tensioning of the element is attempted, and for establishing procedures to be used during the construction period.

For resin grouting anchor or fast-setting anchor, a typical resin product is made up of two component cartridges containing a resin and a catalyst in separate compartments. The cartridges are pushed to the end of the drillhole ahead of the bolt rod that is then spun into the resin cartridges by the drill. The sheath of the cartridges is broken and the resin and catalyst mixed by this spinning action. Setting of the resin occurs within a few minutes and a very strong anchor is created. In these applications, a number of slow-setting resin cartridges are inserted into the drillhole behind the fast-setting anchor cartridges. Spinning the bolt through all of these cartridges initiates the chemical reaction in all of the resins but, because the slow-setting "grout" cartridges are timed to set in up to 30 minutes, the bolt can be tensioned within several minutes of installation. This tension is then locked in by the later-setting grout cartridges and the result is a tensioned, fully grouted rockbolt.

There are two methods of tensioning. These are direct pull tensioning using a hydraulic system and torquing of the nut using a torque wrench. The direct pull tensioning can give a positive indication of the capacity of the anchorage within the range of the tensioning load for every bolt installed.

8.3.1.4 Support of rockbolts

The load transfer concept is critical to understand how fully encapsulated bolts stabilize an excavation. Windsor and Thompson[18] explain the concept by means of the three basic individual components (Figure 8-7) as: ①rock movement at the exposed excavation boundary, which causes load transfer from an unstable region (wedge or slab) to a reinforcing element; ②transfer of load via the reinforcement element from the unstable portion to a stable interior region within the rock mass; ③transfer of the reinforcing element load to the rock mass in the stable zone.

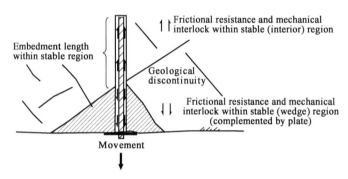

Figure 8-7 The load transfer concept for fully encapsulated reinforcement elements[19]

Expansion reading 8-8

As stated by Bobet and Einstein[16] that: ①the placement of the reinforcement while the surrounding rocks undergoes elastic deformations may not result in large reduction of tunnel convergence, while the stresses in the reinforcement can be substantial; ②it appears that best results can be obtained by placing the rockbolts while the surrounding rocks partially undergoes plastic deformations; ③when the distribution of rockbolts around the tunnel perimeter follows the distribution of the far-field stresses, smaller convergence and reduced reinforcement stresses are possible, for example, for $K_0 = 1$, a uniform reinforcement distribution seems appropriate, while for $K_0 = 0.5$ rockbolts concentrated around the springline seems a better strategy, where K_0 = the ratio of the horizontal and vertical principle stresses of the surrounding rocks.

In terms of supporting mechanism, the following functions are usually considered in the rockbolts design.

8.3.1.4.1 Rock block stability

When we consider the stability of an excavation, the gravity force cannot be ignored, especially in blocky surrounding rocks. Gravity is a direct contributor to instability immediately around the surface of an excavation, where relocation and permanent deformation has already taken place. As illustrated in Figure 8-8, slippage along joints could cause individual rock blocks to become separated from the host rock mass. Factors which would induce such conditions are that: ①the irregularities of joints are nominal; ②the resistance force against sliding along joints is low; ③the angle that the joints make with the surface of the excavation is small; ④the force of gravity tends to induce motion of the block. Blocks in the roof may be entirely free to fall, but blocks in the wall would have to slide or rotate along the joints at its sides and base before fallout could occur. The load transfer concept is often used for designing the rockbolts to make the rock blocks stable. The rockbolts are generally installed with a large angle to the major joint plane or in the direction of gravity at the tunnel crown.

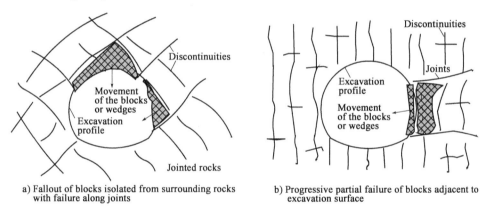

a) Fallout of blocks isolated from surrounding rocks with failure along joints

b) Progressive partial failure of blocks adjacent to excavation surface

Figure 8-8 Gravity effects on jointed or blocky rock mass stability

8.3.1.4.2 Rock beam reinforcement

Where excavations are made in horizontally stratified rocks, the crown of a tunnel is considered as a fixed end beam or slab or substantially uniform material, such as some rock or concrete, where rockbolts are applied in a pattern, as shown in Figure 8-9. The flexural tensile stresses are highest at the bottom in the center. This type of behavior is particularly apparent in materials which not only are horizontally stratified but also have joints, shears, or planes of weakness transverse to the axis of the beam. It is obvious that if the depth of such a beam is small relative to the span then the "arch" action cannot be effective and collapse will take place with very small deflections, since the tensile strength is less than the compressive strength of rocks.

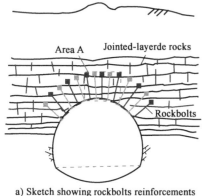
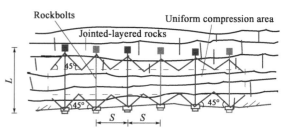

a) Sketch showing rockbolts reinforcements for layered rocks

b) Structural member concept of rock beam [1]

L=Length of rockbolt; s=rockbolt spacing in both the longitudinal and transverse directions
Note: Case for the crown area A shown in figure a).

Figure 8-9 Sketch showing the rock beam reinforcement mechanism

The applications of rockbolts in layered strata give rise to the concept that rockbolts created a beam or slab by clamping together a number of thin or incompetent horizontal strata. Rockbolts create a structural member in any jointed rock mass if a systematic pattern of bolts is used (Figure 8-9). The bolts, if prestressed, create a zone of uniform compression area. This zone is confined and acts effectively in stabilizing the rock excavations. Where untensioned grouted rebar is used instead of tensioned rockbolts a somewhat similar condition also develops after limited deformation has taken place. The "knitting" together the jointed rock layers between the ends of the bolts will increase the basic shear strength of the rock in this reinforced area.

At tunnel crown, the beam or slab tends to act at least partially as fixed ended and angling the bolts near the supports, as shown in Figure 8-9a), will increase their effectiveness[1]. The rockbolts also act as shear or diagonal tension reinforcement for the reinforced layers as a beam or slab, where steel channels or ties are used with angle bolts, with the action being analogous to the post tensioning in reinforced concrete practice.

The required length of the rockbolts is related not only to the geotechnical features of the surrounding rocks near the excavation profile but also to the span of the opening. The structural member created by the rockbolts near the opening surface should be relatively deep compared to the span. It is also related to the spacing chosen for the rockbolt pattern, as proposed in the *Guidelines* (EM110-1-2907)[1].

Expansion reading 8-9

8.3.1.4.3 Arch reinforcement

In tunnels or curved roof excavations, rock reinforcement stabilizes the roof by creating a structural arch within the rock between the ends of the bolts to develop a reinforced arch, of which the features are varying in bolts length and spacing.

In cases, where the occurrence of persistent well defined joints requires the use of relatively long bolts, it may be feasible to use a smaller number of these and provide shorter supplementary rock bolts between the longer bolts. This creates a more heavily reinforced zone near the surface and is effective in stabilizing closely fractured rock. The shorter bolts that are not anchored beyond the plastic area can also improve stability conditions of the surrounding rocks near the opening. In this model, the reinforced material is in triaxial compression rather than unconfined compression and hence is basically stronger. Also the reinforcement system, although not applying sufficient pressure to prevent the plastic deformation zone from forming, does prevent ravelling and fallout from the surface. This is favorable to the tunneling.

8.3.2 Shotcrete

Shotcrete is pneumatically applied concrete to provide supportand protection to the ground surface. It consists of a mixture of Portland cement, aggregates, water and a range of admixtures such as accelerators or retarders, plasticisers, microsilica and reinforcing fibres. Gunite, which pre-dates shotcrete in its use in underground construction, is pneumatically applied mortar. Shotcrete has been successfully used in tunnel construction in a wide variety of ground types since 1960s. Shotcrete is often used in conjunction with steel mesh or fibre and steel sets to provide primary support of excavations. The term shotcrete application refers to the engineering use to which shotcrete is put, the role it is intended to play, or the conditions in which it is used[22].

Expansion reading 8-10

8.3.2.1 Types

Shotcrete is prepared using either dry-mix or wet-mix process (Figure 8-10). In dry-mix process, dry or slightly dampened cement, sand and aggregate are mixed at the batching plant, and then entrained in compressed air and transported to the discharge nozzle. Water is added through a ring of holes at the nozzle. Accurate water control is essential to avoid excessive dust when too little water is used or an over-wet mix when too much water is added. In wet-mix process, the required amount of water is added at the batching plant, and the wet mixture is pumped to the nozzle where the compressed air is introduced.

For the application of dry mix machines, the shotcrete can be executed by hand-held nozzle, with sometimes even manually mixing the concrete on the tunnel invert. There are the integrated complete robotic systems mounted on different types of 4-wheel carriers. Where wet-mix process is applied, a robotic system is usually used for controlling the shotcreting process at the nozzle. On the other hand, the choice of accelerator type, such as liquid accelerators or powder products, may have a significant effect on the overall equipment solution.

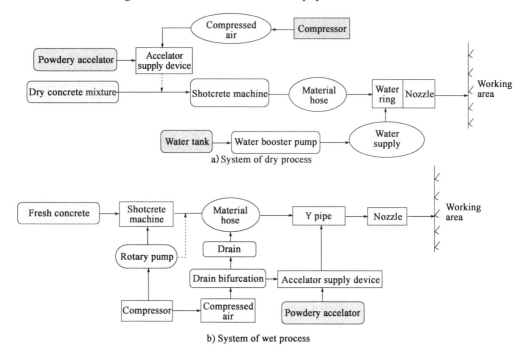

Figure 8-10 System flow of shotcrete

Until the 1990s dry-mix method was more widely used, mainly because the equipment required is lighter and less expensive, and because the dry material can be conveyed over longer distances, which is an important advantage in mining applications, especially for small diameter tunnel of long range. However, wet-mix methods have important advantages for tunneling applications in terms of being reduced dust levels, lower skill requirements and easy to obtain stable quality of shotcrete. Norway started using wet mix shotcrete already in the early 1970s. At the end of 2000, wet-mix methods have become an industry standard in Europe and North America. Table 8-2 gives a comparison of the dry-and wet-mix processes.

Table 8-2 Comparison of wet-and dry-mix shotcreting processes[22]

Wet process	Dry process
Little dust	Considerable dust
Low maintenance cost	High maintenance cost
High capital cost	Low capital cost
Low rebound, typically about 5% to 10%	High rebound, usually more than 25%
Moderate to high placement rate, between 4 and 25 m^3/hr	Low to moderate placement rate, up to 6 m^3/hr
Low transport distance, up to 200 m	High transport distance
Moderate to high placed quality	Moderate placed quality

The efficacy of the shotcreting process depends, to a large extent, on the skill of the operator. Shotcrete machine with discharge ability of over 20 m^3/h is adopted for spraying in the tunnels with large cross section. The nozzle should be kept as nearly perpendicular to the applying surface as possible and at a constant distance of about 1 m between the nozzle and the applied surface. A permanent shotcrete lining is usually between 50 mm and 500-mm-thick, with the larger thicknesses being placed in a number of layers.

The addition of 20-50-mm-long and 0.25 mm-0.8 mm diameter deformed steel fibres, or plastic fibres, has been found to improve the toughness, shock resistance, durability, and shear and flexural strengths of shotcrete, and to reduce the formation of shrinkage cracks. Fibre-reinforced shotcrete can accept larger deformations before cracking occurs than that of unreinforced shotcrete. However, after cracking has occurred, the reinforced shotcrete maintains its integrity and some load-carrying capability. On the other hand, fibre-reinforced shotcrete is more expensive and more difficult to apply than unreinforced shotcrete.

Air-less spraying devices, for which compressed air is not used for have been developed in order to reduce rebound and dust emission[22]. In the Air-less spraying devices, concrete is conveyed from the pump to the head of material hose by pumping pressure and throw out by the rotation force of impeller blade. The discharge abilities of the spraying devices are as same as usual pump type devices. It is reported that dust concentration is reduced into 1/4-1/2 by changing spraying device from usual one to these ones. On the other hand, they have problems of their operation and impeller exhaustion.

Feeder pocket type wet-process is used in small diameter tunnel, because the machine is compact. It has discharge ability of 10 m^3/h and materials conveyance ability of maximum 1000 m with horizontal distance.

8.3.2.1.1 Components

Shotcrete mix design is a difficult and complex process involving a certain amount of trial and error. The mix design must satisfy the following criteria[7]: ①shoot ability—the mix must be able to be placed overhead with minimum rebound; ②early strength—the mix must be strong enough to provide support to the ground at ages of a few hours; ③ long-term strength—the mix must achieve a specified 28 day strength with the dosage of accelerator needed to achieve the required shootability and early strength; ④durability—adequate long-term resistance to the environment must be achieved; ⑤ economy—low-cost materials must be used, and there must be minimum losses due to rebound.

A typical basic mix contains the following percentages of dry components by

Expansion reading 8-11

weight: ①cement 15%-20%; ②coarse aggregate 30%-40%; ③fine aggregate or sand 40%-50%; ④accelerator 2%-5%. The water/cement ratio for dry-mix shotcrete lies in the range 0.3-0.5 and is adjusted by the operator to suit local conditions. For wet-mix shotcrete, the water/cement ratio is generally between 0.4 and 0.5.

8.3.2.1.2　Method of reinforcement

Reinforcement of shotcrete has been a subject of discussion for decades[22]. The main questions are about: ①which kind of steel mesh to use; ②how to combine with bolts, steel beams or reinforcement ribs; ③shadow effects when spraying the concrete; ④a number of other details. These questions are still there[22], but now there is much more focus on fibre reinforcement. Today, the plastic fibres are also on the market (primarily polypropylene) and this is further complicating the picture as well as adding new possibilities.

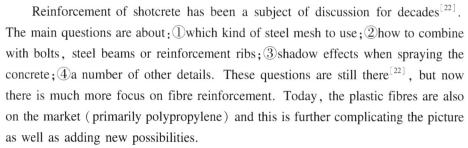
Expansion reading 8-12[23-24]

8.3.2.1.3　Accelerators

Accelerated wet mix shotcrete is increasingly the preferred choice for ground support in tunneling and other civil construction work in the world. In the majority of cases, alkali free accelerators are used due to the stringent Occupational Health and Safety practices. These accelerators belongs to two groups, i.e., the 2nd generation or normal performance alkali-free, and third generation high performance alkali free accelerators[22].

8.3.2.2　Support mechanisms

Holmgren[20] discussed the support functions, modes of failure and methods of design of shotcrete as a component of hard rock support and reinforcement systems. Hoek et al.[21] gave a set of detailed recommendations for the use of shotcrete in hard rock mining. The supporting effects arising from the placement of shotcrete in underground excavations was also presented by the South Africa cases[22]. The main support mechanisms of shotcrete applied on the peripheries of excavations include[4]: ①a single block; ②a beam anchored by bolts; ③a roof arch; ④a closed ring, as shown in Figure 8-11 and the Expansion reading 8-13.

8.3.3　Wire mesh

Expansion reading 8-13

Chain-link or welded steel mesh is used for restraining small pieces of rock between bolts or dowels, and to reinforce shotcrete. For the latter application, welded mesh is preferred to chain-link mesh because of the difficulty of applying shotcrete satisfactorily through the smaller openings in chain-link mesh. For tunnels, weld mesh typically has 6 mm to 8 mm diameter wires spaced at 100 mm to 150 mm. Fibres are increasingly used in wet-proccess shotcrete.

8 Tunnel Support and Surrounding Rocks Reinforcement   293

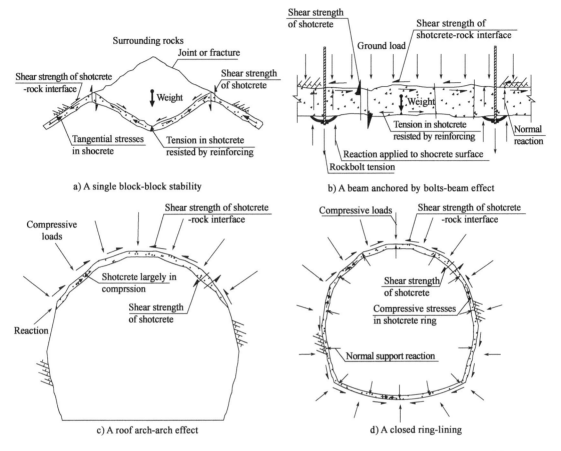

Figure 8-11 Support mechanisms of shotcrete applied on the peripheries of excavations[4]

8.3.4 Steel sets

Expansion reading 8-14

Steel arches or sets are used where high load-carrying capacity elements are required to support tunnels or confining the deformation of the surrounding rocks. A wide range of rolled steel sections are available for this application. Where the rock is well jointed, or becomes fractured after the excavation is made, the spaces between the sets may be filled with steel mesh, steel lagging, or steel plates.

Steel sets are applied in single lining system or as primary lining in a composite lining system. The application of steel sets nowadays is embedded in multiple layers of shotcrete. The ribs of the steel sets can be of formed steel, such as H-type and I-type beams or prefabricated reinforcing bar cages as a girder.

Steel sets provide support rather than reinforcement. They cannot be preloaded against the surrounding rocks face and, their efficacy largely depends on the quality of the blocking provided to transmit loads from the surrounding rocks to the steel set. And therefore, the voids behind the sets will have adverse influence on the function of the sets, as well as the lining system. It is required to fill these voids with shotcrete. In this term, a steel girder made of reinforcing bars is favorable to reduce the shading areas or voids when shotcrete is applied around the sets.

8.3.5 Micropiles

A tunnel may be excavated in top heading and bench sequence. The top heading is ahead of the bench and supporting and reinforcements are often followed in the crown or the up part of the tunnel cross section, as an arch structure. When the bench is excavated, parts of the feet of the arch structure may be hung in the air. In order to provide vertical supporting for the arch structure, the deformation of the feet should be controlled, such as installing inclined micropiles around the feet (Figure 8-12), which is analogical to an underpinning.

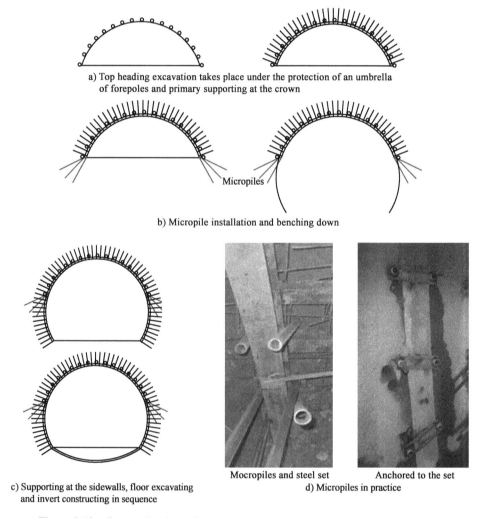

a) Top heading excavation takes place under the protection of an umbrella of forepoles and primary supporting at the crown

b) Micropile installation and benching down

c) Supporting at the sidewalls, floor excavating and invert constructing in sequence

Mocropiles and steel set   Anchored to the set
d) Micropiles in practice

Figure 8-12 Supporting including micropiles in top heading and bench sequence

As micropiles are applied to tunneling in soft ground or soils, they are essentially the same as soil dowels. The out ends of the micropiles should be well connected to the feet of the arch structure, such as bonding to the steel sets of the arch structure. In tunneling, steel rebars (rods) or pipes are typically used as piles because they are much easier to install. In soft ground, such as claystone, mudstone and loess, the micropiles can by pushed or driven into the surrounding rocks with an excavator or shovel.

8.3.6 Yielding supports

The surrounding rocks of squeezing ground feature will deform inward, such as much large convergence. Steel arches are widely used for supporting tunnels, where quite large deformations will occur. Yielding supports are often applied to accommodate these large deformations, such as in squeezing ground. The yielding arches containing elements, i.e., yielding joints, designed to slip at predetermined loads, or by permitting the splayed legs of the arches to punch into the floor to accommodate the surrounding rocks deformations.

The number of yielding joints are designed to provide the needs of the surrounding rocks currently being excavated[25] since all components are manufactured on site (Figure 8-13). It is essential to shotcrete the gaps, where there is a slot at each of the yielding joints (Figures 8-14 and 8-15), in time. Once the closure nears the limit allowed, the steel sections actually butting together[4]. Where the shotcrete is applied late, failure may occur when this butting has been allowed to happen.

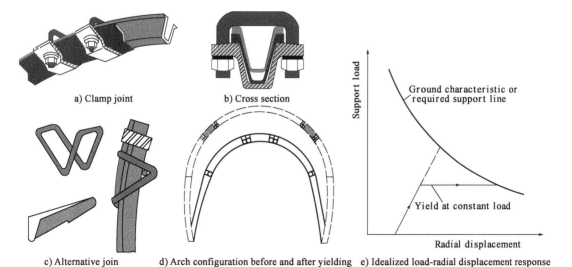

a) Clamp joint b) Cross section
c) Alternative join d) Arch configuration before and after yielding e) Idealized load-radial displacement response

Figure 8-13 Toussaint-Heintzmann yielding arch[4]

Figure 8-14　Circular steel arches (W6 × 20) with two sliding joints[25]

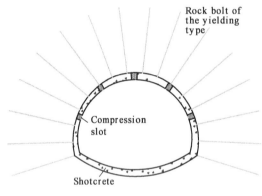

a) Cross section of a tunnel with compression slots[26]

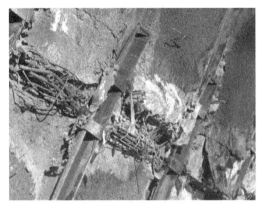

b) Detail of deformable element [11]

Figure 8-15　Cross section of a tunnel with compression slots applied in squeezing rock conditions

A closed ring is often required in a yielding supporting system. Brady and Brown[4] stated that allowing the invert to heave freely for twenty to thirty days before making an invert closure allows the total support system to resist all remaining loads with some reserve capacity for long term load increases.

As summarized by Brady and Brown[4], the yield support system provides a relatively low initial support pressure and permits almost uniform stress relief for the surrounding rocks in a controlled manner while preventing the rock from ravelling. The shotcrete is not damaged by the convergence because of the yielding joints (Figure 8-15) and so maintains its integrity, provided that timely closures are made. After allowing practically all of the stress relief required by the elasto-plastic stage of the planned surrounding rocks deformation, the support system is made rigid to deal with long term creep pressure.

8.4 Support and reinforcement design

Safety is required for a design, as the support and reinforcement are designed to resist static or dynamic loading, or both of them. The design may be based on precedent practice and experience or on observations such as at trial excavations or the early stages of tunneling[4]. Static design analyses are commonly used in tunnel design, such as in: ①local support and reinforcement to support individual blocks or loosened zones on an excavation boundary; ②general or systematic reinforcement to mobilize and conserve the inherent strength of the surrounding rocks. Here are these two applications briefly discussed.

8.4.1 Local support and reinforcement

Two types of design analysis will be presented here. The first type involves simple static limiting equilibrium analyses which essentially treat the system components as rigid bodies in a simplified model. The second is more rigorous and comprehensive analyses, which take into account the deformation and slip or yield of the support and reinforcing system elements[4].

8.4.2 Systematic reinforcement

Expansion reading 8-15[26-30]

In order to maintain the self-supporting capacity of the surrounding rocks or to mobilize and conserve the inherent strength of the rock mass itself, systematic reinforcement is always applied in tunneling. In the general case, it is expected that the surrounding rocks of an excavation will fracture or yield[4]. The design approaches that may be applied in this case are rock support interaction calculations, the application of empirical design rules, the use of rock mass classification-based design rules and numerical analyses[4,7].

8.4.2.1 Empirical design rules

Empirical design of support and reinforcement are based on precedent practice over the last 50 years. The design are geometrically based and do not account explicitly for the stress field induced around the excavation or for the quality of the surrounding rocks[4]. And therefore, cautions must be paid in the applications of these rules for making a preliminary estimate to surrounding rocks reinforcement requirements.

8.4.2.2 Rock mass classification schemes

Expansion reading 8-16

Support requirements for underground excavations are generally approximated based on the suggestion of a rock mass classification system, such as shown in Table 4-24, which is based on precedent practice. Barton et al. proposed 38 categories of support based on their tunneling quality index, Q, and the excavation support ratio, ESR, which varies with the use of the excavation and the extent to which some degree of instability is acceptable. Similarly, the *Guidelines* (EM 1110-1-2907)[1] presented the schemes of the support and reinforcement requirements for underground excavations.

In China, based on the grades of the surrounding rocks of a tunnel under considerations, with the application of analogical method, suggestions on the composite lining system of road and railway tunnels can be preliminarily used for designing the support and reinforcements of the tunnel, such as in the "Specifications" and the "guidelines". It is noted that the design of the supporting system for large span tunnels should be determined according to the results from the design calculation or trial tunnel construction of the project during that stage of design in details. The final design of the lining system should be checked or tuned according to the practical situations of both construction and the results of instrumentation.

Expansion reading 8-17

8.5 Critical thinking problems

C1: Supports and surrounding rocks reinforcements are often applied in a tunnel. Consider: ①The concepts of supports and surrounding rocks reinforcements; ②The general principles of the applications of supports and reinforcements in tunnel project.

C2: Ground improvements and pre-supports may designed for a tunnel project. Consider:①Situations, under which ground improvements or pre-supports are required, respectively; ②The commonly used types of ground improvements and pre-supports, respectively.

C3: Rockbolt and shotcrete system is well used in various fields, such as mining and civil engineering, underground defense works. In tunnel engineering, a rockbolt and shotcrete system is often applied as a lining, either single lining or primary lining. Consider: ①Why is rockbolt and shotcrete system well used in tunneling? ②What are the probable components of the primary lining in squeezing ground? ③The types of rockbolts and the probable support mechanism in a rock tunnel;④The types of shotcrete and the probable support mechanism in a rock tunnel;⑤Features of yielding supports applied in tunnels in in squeezing ground.

C4: During the design and construction of rockbolt and shotcrete support system for a planned tunnel, both the features of the surrounding rocks properties and the behaviors of the components of the planned support system, as well as the interaction between the surrounding rocks and the support system, should be considerd to mobilize the full self-support capacity of the tunnel surrounding rocks.

In this aim-oreinted approach, the realization of this fruit object depends strongly on applying a proper support or surrounding rocks reinforcement measure, such as with a proper stiffness, at a proper time. Consider: ①How to implement "applying a proper support or surrounding rocks reinforcement measure at a proper time", such as in terms of the CCM; ②Taking the application of shotcrete or rockbolts for example, to present the implementation of this principle.

C5: The design of rockbolts in tunnel engineering is often based on analogical method, such as the suggestions in design code and guidelines. For a key project, the empirical design parameters should be checked with calculation. For a deep road tunnel in moderately jointed rock mass, which is graded as III in the rock mass classification system of the specifications. The span of the design excavation profile is 12 m. Consider: ① Following the suggestions in the Appendix P of the *Specifications*(JTG 3370.1—2018), propose parameters for the rockbolts, planned to apply at the tunnel crown; ②If we can, using the Equations (7-11) and (7-12), for the unit weight of surrounding rocks $\gamma = 25$ kN/m^3, to evaluate the vertical stresses, σ_v, and the depth of the de-stressed zone, D, with the calculation method proposed by Lang and Bischoff[29], shown in the Expansion reading 8-15, respectively, and for $k = 0.5$, $\alpha = 1.0$, $\mu = \tan \varphi$, check the above proposed parameters for the rockbolts, applying the following cohesion strength c and internal friction angle φ for the surrounding rocks(Table C5-1), respectively.

Table C5-1 Parameters for the checking calculation in Critical thinking problem C5

Parameters	Values for case I	Values for case II	Values for case III	Values for case IV
c [kPa]	200	400	600	800
φ [°]	25	20	35	40

8.6 References

[1] U.S. Army Corps of Engineers. Engineering and Design, Rock Reinforcement[M]. U.S. Army Corps of Engineers, Department of the Army, 1980.

[2] Windsor C R. Rock reinforcement systems[J]. Int. J. Rock Mech. Min. Sci. & Geomech., 1996, 34(6): 919-951.

[3] Windsor C R, Thompson A G. Terminology in Rock Reinforcement Practice[C] // The 2nd North American Rock Mechanics Sympoosium, NARMS'96. Montreal, Canada, 1996.

[4] Brady B H G, Brown E T. Rock Mechanics: For underground mining[M]. 3rd ed. Springer, 2006.

[5] Lunardi P. The design and construction of tunnels using the approach based on the analysis of controlled deformation in rocks and soils[J]. Tunnels & Tunnelling International, 2000:3-30.

[6] Daemen J J K. Problems in tunnel support mechanics[J]. Underground Space, 1977, 1: 163-172.

[7] Hoek E, Brown E T. Underground Excavations in Rock[M]. London: Institution of Mining and Metallurgy, 1980.

[8] ITA Working Group Conventional Tunnelling. General Report on Conventional Tunnelling Method: ITA REPORT n°002 [R/OL]. ITA, 2009. http://tunnel.ita-aites.org/media/k2/attachments/public/ITA_Report_N2_WG19_P.pdf.

[9] Moseley M P, Kirsch K. Ground Improvement[M]. 2nd ed. Spon Press, 2004.

[10] Rawlings C G, Hellawell E E, Kilkenny W M. Grouting for grouting engineering[M]. London: CRIRIA press, 2000.

[11] Kobayashi S. Assessment and Comparison of Grouting and Injection Methods in Geotechnical Engineering[J]. European Journal of Scientific Research, 2009, 27(2): 234-247.

[12] Lunardi P. Design and Construction of Tunnels, Analysis of controlled deformation in rocks and soils (ADECO-RS)[M]. Springer, 2008.

[13] Croce P, Modoni G, Russo G. Jet-Grouting Performance in Tunnelling[C] // Geosupport Conference, 2004.

[14] NorwegianTunnelling Society (NTS). Grouting[M] // Introduction to Norwegian Tuunnelling, Norwegian Tunnelling Society, 2004.

[15] U. S. Department of Transportation, FHWA. Technical Manual for Design and Construction of Road Tunnels -Civil Elements[M/OL]. Books Express Publishing, 2009. http://www.fhwa.dot.gov/bridge/tunnel/pubs/nhi09010/tunnel_manual.pdf.

[16] Bobet A, Einstein H H. Tunnel reinforcement with rockbolts[J]. Tunnelling & Underground Space Technology Incorporating Trenchless Technology Research, 2011, 26(1):100-123.

[17] Hoek E. Practical Rock Engineering[EB/OL]. 2007 ed. https://www.rocscience.com/assets/resources/learning/hoek/Practical-Rock-Engineering-Full-Text.pdf.

[18] Windsor C R, Thompson A G. Rock Reinforcement-Technology, Testing, Design and Evaluation[M] // Excavation Support & Monitoring, Comprehensive Rock Engineering, Oxford: Pergamon, 1993.

[19] Hyett A J, Bawden W F, Reichert R D. The effect of rock mass confinement on the bond strength of fully grouted cable bolts[J]. Int. J. Rock Mech. Min. Sci. & Geomech., 1992, 29(5): 503-524.

[20] Holmgren J. Guidelines for Shotcrete Support in Hard Rock[C] // Shotcrete for Underground Support V. ASCE, 2010:85-89.

[21] Hoek E, Kaiser P K, Bawden W F. Support of Underground Excavations in Hard Rock[M]. A. A. Balkema: Rotterdam, 1995.

[22] ITA Working Group 12, Shotcrete for rock support[R/OL]. ITA, 2007. https://about.ita-aites.org/component/k2/download/156_5ad855b0d72cf0cbc39c3e7adc7e79bd.

[23] Stacey T R. Review of membrane support mechanisms, loading mechanisms, desired membrane performance, and appropriate test methods[J]. Journal of the South African Institute of Mining & Metallurgy, 2001, 101(7):343-351.

[24] Ortlepp W D, Stacey T R. Rockburst mechanisms in tunnels and shafts[J]. Tunnelling & Underground Space Technology, 1994, 9(1): 59-65.

[25] Hoek E, Carranza-Torres C, Diederichs M. The 2008 Kersten Lecture Integration of geotechnical and structural design in tunneling[C] // Geotechnical Engineering Conference,

2008.
- [26] Barla G B. Tunnelling under squeezing rock conditions[M]//Tunnelling Mechanics—Advances in Geotechnical Engineering and Tunnelling. 2002:169-268.
- [27] Barla G, Bonini M, Debernardi D. Time Dependent Deformations in Squeezing Tunnels[J]. International Journal of Geoengineering Case Histories, 2010, 2(1): 40-65.
- [28] Lang T A. Theory and Practice of Rock Bolting[J]. A. I. M. E. , Trans. , 1961, 220: 333-348.
- [29] Lang T A, Bischoff J A. Stabilization Of Rock Excavations Using Rock Reinforcement[C]//The 23rd U. S. Symp. Rock Mech. , Berkeley, 1982.
- [30] Sofianos A I, Nomikos P, Tsoutrelis C E. Stability of symmetric wedge formed in the roof of a circular tunnel: nonhydrostatic natural stress field [J]. Int. J. Rock Mech. Min. Sci. & Geomech. , 1999, 36(5): 687-691.

9 Tunnel Construction Techniques in General

9.1 Introduction

Expansion reading 9-1

In general, tunnel construction means building a tunnel. In a narrow meaning, tunnel construction or tunneling means the construction of the underground spaces of any shape with a cyclic process of excavating, mucking and supporting. The excavation can be made by drill and blast method, conventional mechanical excavators or full face TBM. After the mucking, the supports or lining, such as steel sets, rockbolts, sprayed or cast in place concrete, are applied in procedure. For some cases, pre-supports are applied ahead of the procedure.

In a broad sense, tunnel construction is a process, which is related to tunnel construction method, techniques, and management. In this procedure, the involved variables include not only substantial factors, such as the ground conditions of the tunnel, building materials and tools or machines applied in the constructions, but also the people, who and how apply these factors. These factors are interacting each other and management is therefore important to the success of the construction.

Expansion reading 9-2

In general, the construction of a tunnel, especially a mega and complex tunnel project, such as in terms of size, dimensions, environmental confinement, is a comprehensive application of certain theory and technology about tunnel construction method, techniques, and management.

9.2 Features of tunneling

Tunnel construction is simply considered a process of excavating, mucking and supporting. However, tunneling construction should not be considered a simple and straight procedure of these activities. The records of various accidents or difficulty, such as the collapse or uncontrolled deformation of excavations, ground water inrushing, schedule delay, cost overruns, are countless in world records. To make tunneling safe and economic, the features of tunneling should be fully understood by all of the involved groups, such as client, designer, contractor, construction supervisor and consultant, especially for a complex project.

9.2.1 A dynamic process

Tunnel construction can be a quite complex dynamic process, as much involved variables interact each other. As tunneling in ground, the stability of the excavations heavily depends on the geotechnical and hydrological conditions of surrounding rocks, the features of the tunnel project, as well as the in interaction between the surrounding rocks and the support system. During this process, the properties of the surrounding rocks is generally degenerated due to the excavation disturbance, the effect of groundwater, and the thrusting of the redistributed stress in the ground. The magnitude of the degeneration of the surrounding rocks and the features of the redistributed stresses in the surrounding rocks depend on the stress state of the surrounding rocks, groundwater conditions and the effect of supporting and ground reinforcing measures. The time effect of the interaction between the deformation of surrounding rocks and the actions of supporting measures is one of the key factors considered in both design and construction, especially for the case that the degeneration and deformation of the surrounding rocks should be properly controlled by applying ground reinforcing and supporting measures with proper stiffness at a proper time. In this dynamic process, to control surrounding rocks deformation or to mobilize the full self-support capacity of the surrounding rocks, time effect is quite significant in the degeneration of weak or soft ground, the behaviors of the surrounding rocks, the effects of supporting measures, as well as the interactions of these factors.

9.2.2 Construction as design or "design as you go"

In a conventional way, a structure is built as design, such as according to detailed design. This process is simply called construction as design. The success of this kind of project from design to construction depends strongly on the veracity of the design. However, tunnel construction is site specific. The quality of the tunnel design is strongly related to the veracity of the site investigation. The uncertainty in the site investigation will often make the design risk-bearing, such as the risk due to differing site.

It is well accepted that tunnel project is often in companion to risks. The degree of risks in a project is usually perceived differently by different parties involved in a project, especially where the risks are unquantifiable or from numerous unknowns to the owner, engineer and contractor. However, in terms of modern project management, the risks in a tunnel project should be distributed equitably among the involved parties, or shared in a proportionate mode. In deed, it is inherently difficult to assess the risks in a tunnel project well and truly at design stage. People, who do not perceive the same risk, do not want to assume a share of such risk, at least in intuition. In this sense, the straight process of construction as design is only applicable to a tunnel, with simple or well investigated ground conditions. When there seems uncertainty, which may have strong influence on the tunnel project, such as in terms of the stability of the structure, the safety of both the construction and environment of the tunnel, cost overrun, delay of time schedule, a procedure of "design as you go", as proposed by Peck[2], is always beneficial to the project execution.

9.2.3 Construction procedure in terms of project management

The planning of the construction of a tunnel starts from design, but to be tuned with the construction procedure going ahead. In terms of project management, the construction procedure includes three functions, i.e., construction plan, execution of construction plan and the observation of the behaviors of surrounding rocks and supporting system. The results of the observation in progress will be used for the tuning of the plan and will affect the execution of the project construction. As implied by Figure 9-1, the procedure of the plan, execution and observation is iterative to make the construction safe and economic, such as in terms of the risk and cost control. The procedure is conducted by involved groups, such as client, designer, contractor, site supervisor and consultant. The object of a tunnel project is achieved by the cooperation of these involved groups. The function of project management is always required to ensure balance between the contributions by the involved groups.

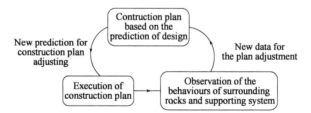

Figure 9-1 Iterative procedure of a tunnel construction[3]

9.2.3.1 Construction plan

Tunnel is site and project specific. The approximation of the surrounding rocks features and properties are based on the site investigation and related empirical evaluation. The ground to be excavated has been only partially bored or excavated during the site investigation. The design of the tunnel is partially based on the predicting the behavior of the surrounding rocks. In this term, the designer is a "predictor"[3]. One of the predicting approaches is the application of a rock mass classification system, as discussed in Chapter 4.

In a conventional construction and design process, the construction plan is fully based on the predicted ground conditions. The designer needs to specify clearly the features of construction details and conditions, which are essential for the success of the construction plan.

9.2.3.2 Construction in a dynamic mode

As the above discussion shown that the construction plan is often partially based on predicted information. During the construction, the plan should be tuned where the construction conditions are different enough from what is the prediction. For example, the properties of surrounding rocks have a strong influence on the tunnel construction procedure, in terms of building sequence, as well as safety, time schedule and cost control. The construction plan is accordingly tuned to accommodate the site condition change. The construction plan should be executed in a dynamic mode.

On the other hand, during excavation, the properties of the surrounding rocks are degenerated due to the disturbance of tunneling. During construction, where the predicted ground condition is adjusted, the construction plan, in terms of excavation and support measures application, is accordingly tuned to the requirements of the adjusted ground model or grade.

The tunnel construction methods applied in a complex project should be so robust, such as to accommodate the potential problems across variations of the ground. In other words, the construction method is applicable without major problems within a wide range of variation of the ground; and capable of modification, without appreciable cost or delay, to meet the foreseen variations of the ground. In terms of construction choosing, a proper construction method has such good adaptability that the features of excavation and supporting can be tuned in accordance with new construction plan and conditions.

9.2.3.3 Observation of the behaviors of surrounding rocks and supports

During tunneling, the behaviors of the surrounding rocks and supports, as well as their interaction, should be evaluated, at least, in terms of safety and risk control. In general, observation, which embraces inspection of the construction activities and quality of the built structures, is executed in the most general sense. Observation may also be required to provide data for the refinement of the design and construction plan. The construction observation generally include inspection, geological observation and performance observation[3].

Inspection is an ordinary route to ascertain that the work is conducted in full compliance with the related engineering specifications and other particular requirements, such as particularly for concealed works in tunnels.

Geological observation, being a methodical examination and recording of the surrounding rocks at working face, is vital to the tunneling. The results of geological observation are the fundamental information for reinterpreting surrounding rocks, warning of the unexpected, which may otherwise constitute an unforeseen hazard. Sometimes, pre-face prospecting is also conducted to predict or check the ground conditions.

Performance observation is to evaluate or approximate the behaviors of both the surrounding rocks and support system, as well as their interactions in tunneling, such as with application of the observational method(OM)[2]. Besides macroscopic observation, such as on the obvious characteristics of defects such as cracking or deformation, the observation based on instrumentation or monitoring on the behaviors of the surrounding rocks and supports is often applied in a complex tunnel project, such as instrumentation on the strains and stresses of the supports and surrounding rocks, groundwater levels and pore-water pressures in the surrounding rocks.

In practice, the application of the observational method implies that some remedial action may be taken if predetermined limits are exceeded. This means "design as you go" or an observational design approach in tunnel design and construction procedure. As Muir Wood[3] stated that the application of observational design or "informal support" is a practical and effective approach in tunneling.

9.2.4 Cooperation of the involved groups

There are several groups of people, representing client, designer, contractor, supervisor, consultant, respectively, are involved in a tunnel project. Tunnel project is analogical to a band playing an orchestral music. A good tune is the cooperation results of all involved players in the band. The success of tunnel project depends strongly on the balanced contributions of the involved groups, especially for a complex project. If the construction is not skillfully executed in an effective procedure, accident or risk, which is unbearable to any group, may occur. The overall success of the project is the shared goal, so it is beneficial to avoid the situation that one group's success is at the expense of the subdivided responsibility of another[3,4]. Cooperation of the involved groups is necessary.

The cooperation of the involved groups is also required, in terms of the risk sharing contract management mechanism. To control the quality of the tunnel project, people, involved in a mega or complex tunnel project, need not only to be charged with specific functions to perform but to be encouraged to consider the interdependence of the functions performed by each involved group.

9.3 Types of construction methods

We have a long history of tunnel use. Various tunnels have been built and the methods for construction accordingly developed with the increasing utilizations. There are often various methods available for the construction of a planned tunnel. However, the choosing of construction method depends strongly on the ground conditions, features of the tunnel, and construction environment restrictions and conditions. Tunnels are built in various grounds. The chosen construction method should be seasoned with the geotechnical conditions of the planned tunnel surrounding rocks. The features of the tunnel, such as size and dimension, overburden, the final use and shape of the tunnel, should also be considered, together with the construction conditions, including the logistics, accessibility, mucking and drainage conditions, and the confinement of the third party.

The choosing of construction method for a tunnel is also largely dependent on the cross section shape of the tunnel. Three construction methods, i. e., cut and cover method, bored or mined method and immersed method are in common use. A shallow tunnel in urban area and the cut and cover sections of mountain tunnels are often built with cut and cover method. A deep tunnel is often excavated with conventional method, such as excavating with manual tools, drill and blast method, partial face excavator or roadheader, or by full face tunnel boring machine (TBM). TBMs are usually used for the constructions of long tunnels and running tunnels in a metro system. Immersing method can be an option for shallow-buried underwater tunnels. Jacking tube or box is often applied in traversing the soft ground under existing structures in a planned line.

9.3.1 Cut and cover method

Cut and cover method involves excavating an open trench, in which the tunnel is constructed to the design finish elevation and subsequently covered with various compacted materials. The variations of this method include various retaining walls and horizontal supports at the excavations, different types of the tunnel structures and their construction sequences.

Cut and cover method is generally a simple construction procedure for shallow tunnels, which are located in rural regions or green lands in urban area. However, the construction of a cut and cover tunnel may be quite difficult and complicated. For example, a cut and cover tunnel in soft ground in urban area is often deep or large, such as underground metro stations, where two or more levels are generally required for the economical arrangements for ticket hall, station platforms, passenger access and emergency egress, ventilation and smoke control, staff rooms, and equipment rooms. Various factors, such as the safety of the construction, environmental restriction, the choosing of the temporary supporting system, are of considerations in details.

A major disadvantage of cut and cover is the widespread disruption generated at the surface level during construction. However, where the top-down method is applied, the disruption due to the excavation of the tunneling may be scheduled to an acceptable mode.

9.3.2 Conventional method

Conventional tunneling means that a tunnel or underground structure is built or excavated with commonly used methods. Since the oldest method in tunneling is mining method, which is originally learnt from the excavating and supporting method in mining engineering, conventional tunneling is often considered same as mining method, such as excavating with manual tools, partial face tunnel boring or excavating machine, drill and blast method.

It is noted that the definition of what is "conventional tunneling" is rather arbitrary, subject to variations, depending on the concept adopted. For example, if the concept is based on excavation equipment, the term conventional method could apply to any tunnel that is not excavated by a TBM. But today the TBM method has become very common and thus could also be regarded as "conventional"[1].

9.3.2.1 Manual or partial-face machine excavation

Tunnels in soft grounds can be excavated or driven with simple manual tools, such as shovel, pickaxe, mattock, etc. The manual tools may give their places to partial face machines, such as excavators and roadheaders, in long and large span tunnels.

9.3.2.2 Drill and blast method

Where the rocks are such hard that the efficiency of partial face machines is low or high cost, drill and blast (D-B) method can be an option for tunnel excavating. D-B method is an old approach but widely applied in tunnel and underground structure excavation. When powder was applied in mining, D-B method got well used. However, before the powerful and safe explosives, such as dynamite applied in mining, the utilization of D-B method is limited in infrastructure building. On the other hand, thanks to the development of drilling techniques during industrial times, the potential utilization of the D-B method was fully realized. Since then, D-B method was successfully used for building tunnels throughout the world. Before the advent of TBM, D-B method was the only economical way of excavating long tunnels through hard rock, where digging with simple tools is not possible. Even today, D-B method is still widely used in tunneling.

As the name suggests, D-B method works as follows: ①drilling a number of holes at the excavating face and charging the holes with explosives; ②detonating the explosive to break the planned rocks; ③ mucking the broken bits and applying reinforcements and supports onto the new tunnel surface (if they are applied); ④repeating these steps will eventually create a tunnel.

At present, where controlled blasting techniques are applied, the positions and depths of the holes and the amount of explosive each hole receives are determined by a carefully constructed pattern, which, together with the correct timing of the individual explosions, will guarantee that the excavations will have an approximately designed cross-section profile.

9.3.3 Boring with TBMs

A full face TBM, also known as a "mole", is a machine utilized for excavating tunnels, usually with a circular cross section, through a variety of soil and rocks. Tunnel diameters are from one metre (micro-TBMs) to near 20 m. In July 2011, Nevskaya Concession Company placed an order with TBM manufacturer Herrenknecht in Germany for the construction of a Mixshield, with a diameter of 19.25 m, which was planned to be used in the Orlovski Tunnel to link both halves of the center of St. Petersburg under the River Neva. Although this project is still under planning stage, the planned shield TBM indicated the tendency of TBM diameter increasing.

TBMs are used as an alternative to D-B method in rock tunneling and conventional mining in soil. TBMs have the advantages of limiting the disturbance to the surrounding ground and producing a smooth excavation profile. TBMs and associated back-up systems are used for highly automating the entire tunneling process. In tunneling, TBM can be a quick and cost effective alternative. In general, the application of TBMs can significantly reduce the lining cost of rock tunnels and shield TBMs are suitable to urban tunnels soft grounds. For example, four TBMs, with a diameter of about 9 m, were used for excavating the 57-km-long Gotthard Base Tunnel in Switzerland. The one of the world's largest TBM "Big Bertha", a 17.5-m-diameter machine built by Hitachi Zosen Corporation, is digging the Alaskan Way Viaduct replacement tunnel in Seattle, Washington, USA.

The major disadvantage of the TBM application is the high cost of the TBMs themselves and can be difficult to transport. The high cost of assembling the TBMs on-site is also factor limiting TBM application. However, as modern tunnels become longer and larger, the cost of TBMs may be balanced by other factors, such as tunneling efficient, shortened completion times, reduced temporary supporting or ground improvement measures, etc.

There are a variety of TBMs available for a variety of conditions, from hard rocks to soft water-bearing grounds. The details of the types of TBMs will be presented in Chapter 11. The open TBMs and shield TBMs are two typical types for hard rocks and soft ground, respectively.

9.3.4 Immersed method

An immersed tunnel is a kind of underwater tunnel composed of segments, constructed elsewhere and floated to the tunnel site to be sunk into place and then linked together, to cross rivers, estuaries and sea channels/harbors in the way of a road and railway. Immersed tunnels are often used in conjunction with other forms of tunnel at their end, such as a cut and cover or bored tunnel, which is usually necessary to continue the tunnel from near the water's edge to the portal at the land surface. The immersed method is for that of building an immersed tunnel.

The segments of the tube may be constructed in one of two methods. One way is to construct steel or cast iron tubes which are then lined with concrete. This allows use of conventional shipbuilding techniques, with the segments being launched after assembly in dry docks. Another method is to construct reinforced concrete box tube in a basin and the box is then flooded to allow their floating to tunnel site.

9.3.5 Jacked tunnels

Jacked tunnels are built using the method of jacking a large tunnel (box or tube) underneath certain obstructions, especially existing structures, such as roads, buildings, rail lines, etc. Jacked tunnels are an alternative for the shallow tunnels, where cut and cover method is unfavorable due to the environmental restriction. The application of jacked tunnels is increasing in recent years.

During the construction of a jacked tunnel, first jacking pits are constructed. Then tunnel sections are constructed in the jacking pit and forced by large hydraulic jacks into the soft ground, which is systematically removed in front of the encroaching tunnel section. If the surrounding rocks above the proposed tunnel is too poor, ground improvement, such as grouting or freezing, is required.

In the recent years, jacked pipes are well used in the constructions of the urban utility tunnels, which are usually larger in lengths and smaller in diameters, normally with a maximum size of 3.0 m. It is often that in pipe jacking hydraulic jacks are used for pushing specially made pipes through the ground behind a TBM or shield.

Box jacking is similar to pipe jacking, but instead of jacking tubes, a box shaped tunnel is used. Jacked boxes can be a large span, such as more than 20 m. A cutting head is normally used at the front of the box being jacked and excavation is normally by excavator from within the box.

9.4 Excavations in conventional tunneling

Tunneling means excavation. Tunneling is executed in a planned sequence. Decisions have to be made concerning the modality of excavation, material handling, and tunnel supports. In terms of excavation-supporting cycle, the designed profile in cross section can be driven in one step, two steps or even more. The modality of excavations is accordingly determined in accordance with the whole tunneling procedure.

9.4.1 Modality of excavations

In conventional tunneling, the designed excavation profile may be driven by full-face, top heading and bench, or partial face excavations, as shown in Figure 9-2. The choosing of the excavation sequence is mainly dependent on the stand-up time of the surrounding rocks. For example, in sound grounds the maximum round length is limited by the acceptable tolerance for overbreak, which is mainly an economic criterion when overbreak has to be filled up to the design profile of the tunnel circumference; however, in weak ground, selecting excavation sequence and the length of the individual excavation-steps/rounds is determined mainly by the stand-up time of the surrounding rocks.

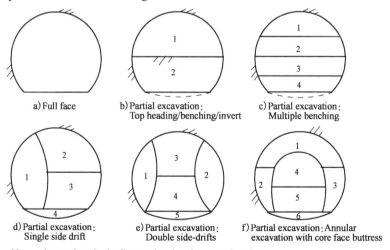

Note: the numbers in the figures showing the excavtions in sequence.

Figure 9-2 Typical excavation sequences in conventional tunneling

On the other hand, the features of the tunnel, especially the diameters of the tunnels are also influence factors on choosing tunneling modality and the sequence of excavations. For example, an important issue that has to be considered by designer is whether to specify excavation of the tunnel using a top heading and bench approach or a full face excavation method. In general, small diameter tunnels, with span less than 6 m, are often driven by full face method; while large underground caverns are almost always excavated in multiple stages starting from a top heading or side drifts.

9.4.1.1 Full-face excavation

Full-face excavation is often used for tunnel with smaller cross sections and in sound grounds with long stand-up time. Today full-face excavation is also becoming possible in difficult ground conditions, especially where proper pre-supports are applied in an effective way. Since a high degree of mechanization of the work and the use of large, high performance equipment become common, bigger cross sections (70-100 m^2 and more), even in difficult ground conditions (e.g., squeezing ground) are excavated with full-face method. In these cases, face stability shall be given serious consideration, such as with face reinforcement, shotcrete etc., if necessary.

Full face excavation has many advantages in terms of sequence simplicity and, in the ground of adequate strength, greater rates of tunnel excavation. Also full-face excavation allows the immediate closure of the primary support ring, close to the excavation face, and therefore, where possible it is the preferred method of tunneling.

9.4.1.2 Partial face excavation

Partial face excavation is used for big cross sections in bad or unfavorable grounds. There are several types of partial face excavation such as top heading, bench and invert excavation, side drifts, pilot tunnel. A partial face excavation allows the combination of the different excavation methods in the same cross section, e.g., blasting in the top heading and excavating the bench by using a mechanical excavator, e.g., a roadheader.

9.4.1.2.1 Reasons for partial face excavation

In tunneling, partial face excavation can be applied to tunnels in soft and hard rocks. However, the reasons are quite different. For a large span tunnel in soft ground, the stand-up time of the excavations is key factor to the design of the excavation sequence and the tunneling round length. The just excavated section must be stable in the period, which is necessary to carry out all the operations subsequent excavation, including mucking, scaling and support installation works.

The section, just behind the excavation face, where neither the walls nor the face is supported, is usually known as "unsupported span". The period, in which the unsupported section is stable and there is no adverse deformation in the surrounding rocks, is known as stand-up time. When the unsupported length or the stand-up time is too short to execute the following steps of the planned tunneling cycle, the excavation is often designed as partial face excavation, i.e., the designed tunnel excavation profile is made by several tunneling cycles.

As the mining face is smaller, the stand-up time is longer and the control of the excavation stability is easier. At the same time, the amount of mucking and supports to be installed decrease in the partial face excavation tunneling cycles. In general, the reasons for partial face excavation include: ①it enables early closure of part of the invert of the tunnel; ②with the excavation in each part taking place at different times, it helps to reduce the area of exposure of the tunnel face so that there is better control on tunnel stability; ③for unit advancement in any part of the tunnel excavation, the amount of excavation and supporting materials is reduced, and therefore the supports are readily provided in time.

In other situations, where the stand-up time of the excavations is not key factor to the design of the round length of the excavations in hard rocks, partial face excavations are used in large span tunnels or caverns in hard rocks mainly due to the considerations of construction efficiency, equipments available, and cost control, etc.

9.4.1.2.2 Classical methods

Partial face excavation method is an old mining method. Before the applications of rockbolts and shotcrete in tunneling, some partial face excavation methods were used for building relatively large span tunnels. In these tunnels, a series temporary supports, such as timbers arches, poles and posts, were first applied, and then was replaced by a permanent monolithic lining, such as masonry arch structures. The partial excavation methods used in these processes are called classical excavation method, which are also called traditional mining method. There are several classical methods are well known, such as American Method, old Austrian tunneling method, Belgian Method, etc.

Expansion reading 9-3

9.4.1.2.3 Top heading and bench

Top heading and bench excavation is often used in tunneling, especially with drill and blast method or manual excavation. In general, the excavations in a cross section are composed of three steps, i.e., top heading, bench and invert-excavation. For tunnels with specific site conditions with various stand-up times, the round length of each excavation, L_r, is accordingly designed as long bench ($L_r \geqslant 5B$), short bench ($B \leqslant L_r < 5B$) or micro-bench ($L_r < B$), where B is the span of the tunnel design profile.

9.4.1.2.4 Side drift

For a large span tunnel in soft grounds, the stand-up time is sensitive to the span of the excavations. The cross section of the planned tunnel, especially with horseshoe shape, is often excavated in sequence, such as side drift or two-side drift excavation, which is also called side galleries excavation.

The side drift method means the part of the excavation near a side wall is excavated ahead of the other parts. After the drifting part is supported with rockbolts and shotcrete system, and even temporary diaphragm wall to make the lining closed. Where the temporary diaphragm is generally at the center of the excavation, it is also called center diaphragm (CD) wall and the method is therefore called CD method, in terms of supporting. Where a temporary invert is applied between the side wall and center diaphragm wall, the temporary walls are indeed in a cross pattern, and is therefore named cross diaphragm wall method, i.e., CRD method. When the temporary center wall is composed of steel sets, shotcrete and reinforced with steel meshes, the wall is generally stiff supports.

Two-side drift excavation method is characterized by the two side drifts are alternately excavated in a designed round length, and the center part of the excavation is mined after the temporary center walls have been installed to close the tunnel lining system temporarily. Temporary inverts may be applied to reinforce the supporting capacity of the lining system. The shotcrete wall can be thichened at bench level to provide haunches for the crown arch, and may incorporate lattice wall plates to maintain adequate support to the arch during subsequent excavation for the invert.

Expansion reading 9-4

9.4.1.2.5 Annular excavation with core face buttress

Annular excavation with core face buttress starts with an annular excavation at crown of the tunnel, and then rockbolts and shotcrete system is applied in an arch form. The feet of the supporting arch are usually fixed or underpinned with micro-pipe or piles, before the excavation of the parts of ground around the sidewalls. The excavations at the crown and the parts around the sidewalls of the tunnel compose of an annular excavation in a sequence mode. This excavation sequence is indeed a kind of annular pilot excavation, with core remains or wedge stabilization at face. This method is analogical to the staked drift.

The core buttress at the face is often called soil core, core remains or wedge stabilization, to control deformation of the excavation face. In general, the core face buttress is a simple, cost-saving and effective restraint in face core extrusion deformation. Where the tunnel profile is large and the surrounding rocks is weak, the annular excavation is usually conducted in much small step, to give enough

Expansion reading 9-5

time to install both permanent and temporary supports.

In general, the arch shape supporting system after the annular excavation at both crown and sidewalls is a large span flexible support structure.

9.4.1.2.6 Sequential Excavation Method (SEM)

For the tunnels in hard soils or soft rocks, the strength of the surrounding rocks is such sufficient that the planned partial face excavation by equipment is possible without direct support. Following the excavation, rockbolts and shotcrete system is applied before the next round excavation. The tunnel design excavation profile is made with several round of partial face excavation in a planned sequence. This kind of partial face excavation method is called the sequential excavation method (SEM) in USA, where the term SEM is considered as the application of the NATM. In this method, pre-supports and ground improvement, as presented in Chapter 8, can be used for increasing the surrounding rocks strength and to reduce the permeability.

Where the SEM is applied in tunneling, the requirements smaller face excavation in a step means a low construction speed. As the principle of the NATM is applied, the instrumentation and monitoring on the behaviors of surrounding rocks and supports are vital to the success of the tunneling.

9.4.2 Factors to choosing excavation method

The general situations of the excavation method applications in conventional tunneling are: ① drilling and blast mainly applied in moderate to hard rocks; ② mechanical excavation mainly used in soft ground and in weak rocks (using roadheaders, excavators with shovels, rippers, hydraulic breakers etc.). Both excavation methods can be used in the same project in cases with a broad variation of ground conditions. In conventional tunneling, the round length generally varies from 4 m in good conditions to 1 m or less in soil and poor ground conditions (e.g., squeezing rock). The round length is generally the most important factor influencing the tunneling speed.

The choice of full-face, heading and benching, partial face excavation for tunneling is preferable and project unique. The factors for consideration include ground properties, environmental aspects and the features of the tunnels. All these three excavation methods can be used in a tunnel project, with various ground conditions.

In general, the factors considered for planning excavation method include the followings: ① the ground conditions; ② the features of the tunnel project, such as the shape and size of the tunnel; ③ the excavation method or tools available and the experience of application; ④ the planned modality of excavations and their round lengths, which is a function of the properties and stress state of the surrounding rocks, and the planned excavation method, supporting and ground reinforcement or improvement measures; ⑤planned intervention to reinforce, improve or stabilize the ground, which may be conservative (reinforcement of the core-face, sub horizontal jet grouting, mechanical precutting, end anchored radial rock bolting, etc.), or improvement (conventional injections, freezing, truncated cone "umbrellas" of drainage pipes ahead of the face, rings of ground reinforced with fully bonded rock bolts, etc.); ⑥the planned time schedule and cost; ⑦the environment and third party restrictions.

With the considering of the above factors as criteria for tunnel excavation modality choosing, the design engineer can exercise effective control on the tunnel construction design. In terms of project management, the design engineer generally prescribes or limits the choice of the excavation method only if there are compelling reasons based on project restrictions. The responsibility of the selection of the excavation method should be left to the contractor, based on the owner's description of the ground conditions and the limits set by the design engineer.

9.5 New Austrian Tunneling Method

The New Austrian Tunneling Method (NATM) is from Austria and is now used worldwide. The term NATM first used in a lecture by Rabcewicz at the Thirteenth Geomechanics Colloquium in Salzburg, in 1962. The international recognition of the NATM are mainly from the articles.[6]

Rabcewicz[6] stated: *A new tunnelling method—particularly adapted for unstable ground—has been developed, which uses surface stabilisation by a thin auxiliary shotcrete lining, suitably reinforced by rockbolting and closed as soon as possible by an invert. The systematic measurement of deformation and stresses enables the required lining thickness to be evaluated and controlled.* Rabcewizc stressed three key points, i.e., the application of thin shotcrete, closure of the ring as soon as possible and systematic deformation measurement. One of the key features of the NATM, in terms of design, is that the surrounding rocks *becomes a load bearing structural component through the activation of a ring like body of supporting ground*, as presented in the definition of NATM of the Austrian National Committee on Underground Construction of the International Tunneling Association in 1980.

In 2004, the Austrian Society of Engineers and Architects defined the NATM as *a method where the surrounding rock or soil formations of a tunnel are integrated into an overall ring-like support structure. Thus the supporting formations will themselves be part of this supporting structure.*

The application of the NATM means to take advantage of the inherent surrounding rocks strength available in tunneling. In comparison to the earlier methods, the NATM implies the potential of tunneling in an economic way. The technological development and the engineering practice in tunneling paved the way for new theoretical explanations to substantiate an economically beneficial design approach. Today, using the NATM, any required geometries for underground structures in almost all geotechnical conditions can be built in a safe and economic way[7]. This is mainly thanks to the introduction of the OM in the NATM application.

As Galler et al.[7] stated, when using the NATM, in order to achieve the required safety level, both a systematic geotechnical design and a fair contractual model for all involved partners have to be implemented into the design and construction process. Owners experienced in tunnel design and construction, together with specialized contractors, should develop an onsite decision making procedure, which is common practice in Austrian tunneling. This ensures an immediate and effective response to differing site, on the conditions that there is a good cooperation under a suitable contractual model among the qualified and experienced owners, designers and contractors, qualified and authorized engineers on site, as well as a qualified and experienced workforce.

9.5.1 Key elements of the NATM philosophy

The NATM is an approach or philosophy integrating the principles of rock mass behaviors and the monitoring of the behaviors during tunnel excavation. The word "method" is, to some extent, not a proper or exact word, as the NATM is not a set of specific tunneling techniques. A significant feature is that the NATM implies an effective application of many established tunneling ways, with the help of the monitoring and the revision of the tunneling to obtain the planned stable and the most economical results.

The NATM is often referred to as a "design as you go" approach, by providing an optimized tunneling measures based on the observed ground conditions. The design is based on the behaviors of surrounding rocks under load and will be tuned according to the monitored performance of surrounding rocks and supports during tunneling. Although there is no a set of specific excavation and support techniques, the NATM has seven elements, which are well accepted in the field of tunnel engineering, as the followings.

(1) Mobilization of strength of rock mass. The inherent strength of the surrounding rocks should be conserved through controlling the surrounding rocks deformation and mobilized to the maximum extent possible. The support is directed

to enable the rock to support itself. This means suitable supports, such as in terms of load-deformation characteristics, should be applied at a correct time.

(2) Primary support. Avoiding surrounding rocks loosening and excessive deformations are required and may be achieved in various ways, such as a primary support system consisting of systematic rock bolting and a thin semi-flexible shotcrete lining. What is important that the lining system should have a compact contact with the surrounding rocks, so that they deform in a harmony mode. Where the NATM is applied in tuneling, there is always shotcrete lining in the tunnel. This does not mean that the use of shotcrete constitutes the NATM.

(3) Flexible support. The appropriate surrounding rocks deformation and strength degeneration are generally achieved by the application of a flexible support system, which is characterized by versatility/adaptability, such as a combination of rockbolts, wire mesh, steel ribs and shotcrete. The primary support will partly or fully represent the total support required and the dimensioning of the secondary support will depend on measurement results.

(4) Instrumentation and monitoring. Instrumentation and monitoring are necessary in the NATM application and the results are used for tuning or revising the design and tunneling. For example, the instrumentation installation is generally at the time that the shotcrete lining is placed to monitor tunnel deformation and the build-up of load in the support. This provides information on tunnel stability and enables optimization of the load bearing surrounding rocks ring.

(5) Closing of invert. Closing of the invert to form a load-bearing ring is essential to control the surrounding rocks deformation and strength degeneration. In soft ground tunneling, the invert must be closed quickly and no section of the excavated surface should be left unsupported even temporarily. Otherwise, failure may occur. For example, HSE[8] stated, in most cases, the failure of tunnels, with NATM applied in construction, is a result of collapse at the face where the lining is still weak and not being closed.

(6) Excavation in sequence. Tunneling in soft ground, the disturbance to the surrounding rocks and the applied supports should be controlled to an acceptable level. So, where possible, the tunnel should be driven full face in minimum time with minimum disturbance to the surrounding rocks by excavation. Where the surrounding rocks is weak or the excavation profile is so large that the tunneling should be in sequence, such as partial face excavations or SEM. The above NATM tunneling principles should be adapted to each of the tunneling round for a planned section.

(7) Contractual arrangements. The principles of the OM are followed in the tuneling with NATM. During tunneling, there is great chance of tuning or adjusting

the construction details in an immediate mode. This project execution process requires a flexible contractual system to support such changes. The information to stimulate the start-up of the changes is from the observation on the surrounding rocks, and the behaviors of both surrounding rocks and supports. Since the decision-making on the changes should be in time, a quick response is required for all parties, involved in the execution of the project, such as client, design and supervisory engineers, the contractor's engineers and foremen. All the groups must understand and accept the NATM approach and adopt a cooperative attitude to decision making and the resolution of problems or dispute. These response mechanisms and procedures should be defined in the contractual system.

9.5.2 Variant names

NATM was originally developed for use in the Alps, where tunnels are commonly excavated at depth and in high in situ stress conditions. The principles of NATM are fundamental to modern-day tunneling and applied in various tunnels in mountains, urban and underwater. With the increasing of applications, various new techniques have been put into the tunneling practices, with NATM principles integrated. This has also led to confusion in terminology, such as NATM meaning different things among users.

The name of the NATM is still a controversial subject among experts or users worldwide. New terms have arisen and alternative names for certain aspects of the NATM have been adopted as its use spreading. On the other hand, when the NATM is applied in a tunnel project, the main focuses of the involved groups can be different[9,10]. And therefore, various meaning and terms appeared in the world. For example, SEM is named, when the NATM is applied in the design and construction of tunnels in soft ground in the USA. Similarly, Sprayed Concrete Lining is named in the UK, for this modern tunneling style. In Japan the terms Centre Dividing Wall NATM or Cross Diaphragm Method (both abbreviated to CDM), and Upper Half Vertical Subdivision method (UHVS) are used.

It is noted that the term NATM can be misleading in relation to soft-ground tunnels, since NATM can refer to both a design philosophy and a construction method[11].

9.5.3 Key features

The key features of the NATM design philosophy refer to that the strength of the tunnel surrounding rocks is deliberately mobilized to the maximum extent possible. The mobilization of ground strength is achieved by allowing controlled deformation of the surrounding rocks, such as through: ① to in install a support

Expansion reading 9-6

system having load-deformation characteristics appropriate to the ground conditions at the time, which is determined according the features of the surrounding rocks deformations;② to evaluate the support system and the surrounding rocks behaviors, which are illustrated by the instrumentation and monitoring during tunneling;③to tune and adjust tunneling, such as in terms of construction plan, support system and the time to apply in details.

9.6 Observational Method in design and construction

Terzaghi[12] presented this method "learn-as-you-go." Observational techniques for geotechnical engineering were recommended by Terzaghi and Peck[13] under the designation of the "Observational Procedure" and later formalized by Peck[2] as the OM in the 9th Rankine lecture. This method is recommended in Eurocode 7 for tunnel and geotechnical engineering, where a "design as you" execution procedure is required for a complex or high risk project.

Tunnel is of the features of specific site, which may be too complicated to describe exactly at design stage. For a tunnel in complex ground conditions, a "design as you go" execution procedure is often beneficial to all of the involved groups in a long run. In this procedure, observation is a key attribute of the involved excellent geotechnical and tunnel engineers[3]. The information from observation should be effectively shared among the groups, and therefore help the groups to make engineering decisions. In this way, the potential risks and opportunities in the project can also be understood and then shared among the groups.

Expansion reading 9-7

When the OM is applied to decision-making in tunneling, observation is associated with the assessment on the tunneling situation. The results of the assessment is a reasoned basis for the decision-making. Peck[2] recommended the procedural steps for the application of the OM in the design and construction of a tunnel.

In principle, the adequacy of the first phase of a construction procedure based on the OM is checked by specified observations to establish the need, if any, for further work to achieve the desired objectives. The application of the OM in tunneling is to make a rational modification to the design and construction plan in time. So that the adjusted plan suits the actual conditions. However, as the notion of the "most probable conditions" of Peck[2], is often interpreted as "unlikely to be exceeded", so that the modification to the original design becomes exceptional. For the exceptional conditions, based on the observational findings and the decision-making by the involved groups, the planned step ⑥, as Peck[2] recommended, is accordingly put in practice.

9.7 Instrumentation and monitoring in tunneling

For some simple tunnel projects, judgment based on experience and a conservative approach can successfully avoid failure, even where there is adverse differing site during construction. However, various case histories showed that the application of the OM is necessary and beneficial for a large tunnel project. When we apply the OM to tunneling, the observed behaviors of surrounding rocks and supporting system are used for verifying design assumptions and to tune or adjust the construction plan. The main objects of the instrumentation and monitoring (I & M) of a tunnel project are to: ①obtain "baseline" ground characteristics; ②provide construction control; ③verify design parameters; ④measure performance of the supporting system, e. g., lining, during, and after, construction; ⑤monitor environmental conditions (e. g., settlement, air quality and effects on the groundwater regime); ⑥carry out research to enhance future design. Instrumentation may also be installed to monitor mitigation measures and aid the quantification and management of risk to third parties.

Expansion reading 9-8

9.7.1 Value of instrumentation and monitoring

The application of I & M is usually required for a tunnel project with perceived hazards and the certain level of risk. But for well-established designs, such as tunnels in well-known grounds, the necessity for I & M is small. In high-risk environments, such as shallow tunnels in bad grounds, or where significant ground movements are predicted, contingency actions, such as alternative excavation, support and lining designs, should be designed together with a more rigorous I & M plan for the tunneling. A complete and rigorous monitoring system generally comprises in tunnel, borehole, surface and neighbor structures instrumentations.

In terms of design, the results of I & M are used for assessing the pre-construction conditions, the geotechnical parameters required for design, also for design verification and long-term post-construction monitoring. The process of analysis, design and site investigation continues during construction. For example, where a wide range of values of design parameters is feasible, the results of the I & M may be used for checking the response of the structure and the validity of the chosen values. In this context, the I & M becomes an integral part of the design verification and construction monitoring process.

Where the management of third-party issues is an important issue, the I & M is often required for, such as monitoring the response of the neighbor structures to the anticipated tunneling influence. Also, the pre-construction condition surveys, agreed to by all parties, are essential before work commences on site. In the post-construction period there may be a requirement for long-term monitoring, for example, on the rail and road tunnels, where public health and safety is dependent on the performance of the structures.

In terms of information recording, the data from instrumentation and monitoring is part of the final record of all "geo" information gathered during the course of the tunnel project. It will also constitute a living document, in which all future monitoring results are included and any modifications to the project are recorded.

9.7.2 Instrumentation and monitoring design

Tunnel is site specific and of structure features. The instrumentation and monitoring of a tunnel project therefore need a detailed plan, which is in accordance with the tunnel features and environmental restriction. The general guidelines or suggestions on the design of the instrumentation and monitoring of a tunnel project are presented in the design code and guidelines. For example, in China, the issues of a road tunnel project are suggested in the *Specifications* (JTG 3370.1—2018) and the *Guidelines* (JTG/T D70—2010), respectively.

Expansion reading 9-9

9.7.3 Data acquisition and management

9.7.3.1 General

In an I & M program, data sampling and recording are either manual or automated. In general, manual reading instrumentations is low costs in installation and data reading machines, but there is high potential for reading errors and a low frequency of data points obtained.

The advantages of using electronic transducers in conjunction with an automatic system are that real-time data and more detailed records (i.e., higher frequency of readings) can be obtained. This can be particularly valuable in research applications. On the other hand, automatic systems can also be programmed to adjust reading frequency in response to pre-set trigger values and to initiate alarms. Disadvantages with such an approach include higher initial installation costs and the potential to lose all data if the logger is damaged or fails.

For an existing tunnel and nearby structures, with the improvements in the accuracy of measurement, automated total stations are becoming an increasingly popular approach to monitoring distortions in existing structures and tunnel linings. This approach is also utilized for monitoring projects, where the area is extensive and the costs of using manual or data-logger based approaches alone is prohibitive.

Where the OM has been employed, the results of the I & M program should be reported, communicated and shared in a planned procedure. The response of the involved groups to the related results should be predefined in a contractual mode.

9.7.3.2 Trigger values

It is often to establish "trigger values" for key indicator parameters, which determine appropriate actions in response to these values being exceeded. Typical definitions of these trigger values can be presented such as Warning/amber and Action/red, respectively.

Warning/amber is a pre-determined value or rate of change of a parameter values that is considered to indicate a potential adverse result, but not of sufficient severity to require cessation of the present works. Exceeding this trigger level generally requires a check on instrument function, visual inspection on the structure being monitored, increase in monitoring frequency, the review of the design and modification of the tunneling.

Action/red is a predefined level, which may equate to a value above which an unacceptable deformation or damage is predicted to occur to the monitored structure or where safe operating thresholds for the tunnel structure or geometry are exceeded. If this value is surpassed an immediate check on instrument function and visual inspection of the monitored structure are required, as well as the initiation of a pre-determined response, which may include the temporary cessation of work, back analysis of the event and modification of the design and construction plan.

The selection of appropriate trigger values will depend on the particular requirements of the project and the governing "failure mechanism(s)" assessed by the designers. It is beneficial that the monitoring records are examined by experts in monitoring matters on a regular basis, to ensure that any untoward trends (pre-trigger) are identified and acted upon in a timely fashion. Even if serious anomalies are not indicated, it is always worth comparing predictions with observed values in order to understand the behavior of the structure and surrounding rocks.

9.7.3.3 Report

The report should ideally include: ①the as-observed records of geology and ground conditions; ②monitoring results both during and post excavation; ③the records of all investigations carried out during construction, including probe drilling and monitoring of performance; ④a record of construction experience, incidents and expedients; ⑤a full set of site investigation reports, plans, sections, and other records and documents, kept for reference purposes; ⑥the as-built records of the structure, including boreholes and temporary excavations, and of subsequent alterations made in the course of repairs or modifications.

Graphical output is generally preferred for some key parameters in the report.

9.8 Choice of tunneling methods

The choice of construction method for a tunnel project is generally considered at the planning of the project, specified in the detailed design, determined and adjusted during project construction. The choice of construction method mainly follows analogical method and regional experience at the planning stage, but is gradually dictated by the degree of certainty to which potential geological problems may be identified and located, in terms of the risk control of the tunneling.

A construction plan, in which the construction method is defined in details, is proposed as the starting of the tunneling. In this process, the benefits derived from innovation in construction method or from the experience obtained from test galleries or experimental tunnels are helpful to reduce uncertainty in an unfamiliar locality. For example, to determine the scheme of working, the stand-up time should be long enough to permit the results to contribute to the optimal solution, recognizing the period needed for observation and for the possible modification of tunneling techniques. Test tunneling is a direct way to get the stand-up time of the unfamiliar surrounding rocks.

During tunneling, the plan is put into practice. The construction method may need adjusting or altering where there appears significant site difference and original method could not accommodate the difference.

Here are the main points to be considered for choosing construction method for a tunnel project.

9.8.1 Factors to be considered

In general, tunneling is characterized by these features: ①extreme dependence on the ground conditions; ②the high degree of interdependence between project planning and design; ③the domination of construction methods on the design of the project; ④the effect of restrictions of access on logistics, particularly in dealing with construction problems; ⑤risk involved dynamic process in terms of design and construction; ⑥the necessary cooperation of the involved groups; ⑦probable adverse impact to the environment and the third party.

For a tunneling method option, factors associating the specific project with the means for its construction may include: ①surrounding rocks features; ②the features of the tunnel, such as, lengths of continuous tunnel of a particular size, taking account of any requirement for relative timing of sections of the work; ③extent of interconnection between tunnels; ④useful tunneled space in relation to practicable tunnel profiles; ⑤value of time or time limit for a project.

Other project-specific factors which may be significant are: ①requisite spacing between tunnels;②local experience and maintenance facilities;③the accessibility of project;④the likelihood of late variations in requirements;⑤environmental concerns.

For overall project economy and risk control, there needs to be a clear mutual understanding among the involved groups, arising from the discussion of the significance of the above factors. Only then can the optimal construction strategy be devised.

What should be noted that the tunnel is belonging to client and the requirements of client, e.g., time schedule, new techniques and materials introduce into a specific project, is therefore priority to the others. The main factors are generally considered in the choice of construction method for a tunnel project is shown in Figure 9-3. The possible significance of these factors is described below.

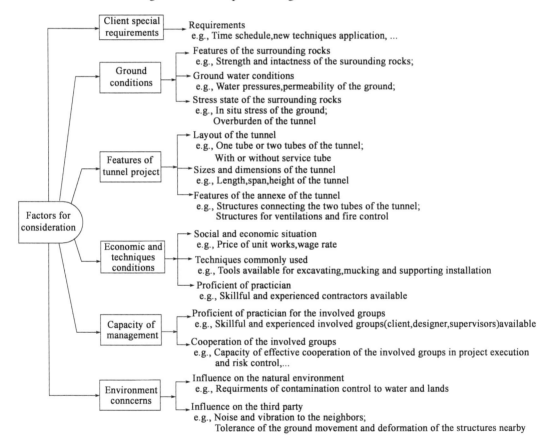

Figure 9-3 Factors considered in choosing construction method

9.8.1.1 Surrounding rocks features

The properties of the surrounding rocks have a strong influence on choosing construction method for a tunnel project, since the stability of the excavations is strongly related to the features of the surrounding rocks, which are the part of the tunnel structures. The features of the surrounding rocks are generally indicated by the intact rock strength and rock mass structures, stress state, groundwater conditions, as well as the features of the tunnel. For a designed tunnel, the surrounding rocks properties can be approximately shown by the stand-up time of the surrounding rocks during construction, such as excavating with conventional method. The stand-up time is one of the basic factor for the consideration in choosing construction method.

Another factor of great importance concerns the ground variability, which is considered for construction method choosing. For example, in sedimentary rocks, strata represent depositional layers or cyclothems, the coarser grained rocks (possibly sandstones) may be stronger and more permeable to water than the interleaved fine-grained layers (mudrocks or siltstones). The features of the surrounding rocks may change abruptly in a short chainage. The tunneling measures should be altered accordingly.

Where sharp geological change occurs within a length of tunnel, the optimization of the scheme of construction needs to pay attention to the particular features of the transition. If this transition occurs on an interface at low angle to the tunnel line, there may be appreciable lengths of mixed face presenting problems specific to the adopted means of tunneling. For example, the combination of hard and soft rock in the face of a TBM could make the tunneling difficult, such as throwing the machine off line while thrust pads sink into yielding ground.

9.8.1.2　Features of the tunnel project

The features of a tunnel project include the layout of the tunnel, the sizes and dimensions of the tunnel tubes and their supporting and reinforcement measures, as well as the annexes for tunnel operation and safety control.

The tunnel layout is related to the project features, such as the tubes of the tunnel, with or without service tube. The features of the tubes are of the location, alignment, length, span and height. The types of annexes, such as conduits caverns and shafts for ventilation, stop sites or lay-bays for emergency, and their relationship to the tunnel, will has influence on the construction method choosing.

In general, the length of the tubes has a strong influence on the alternative of conventional method and TBM. On the other hand, the span, connecting passages to the tubes and the enlarging sections due to lay-bays, together with the features of the surrounding rocks, are related to the choice of excavations and their sequences. The influence of the interconnections on the scheme of construction should also be considered. For example, the junctions between tubes may provide particular difficulties in construction; on the other hand, the passages between the tubes can provide access for working and logistic conditions.

The features of the layout of the tunnel project and the features of the tunnel structures may vary along the line. A classical example is that of a series of running tunnels and stations connecting the tunnels for a metro system. What is the best method for the metro system construction? There are uncountable case histories that the running tunnels and stations have been built with shield method and cut and cover method, respectively.

The accessibility of project, especially at the beginning of the construction, is also one of the considerations for construction method choosing. Particularly where there may be dependence on special expedients, requiring rapid mobilization or the risk of the compensation of long periods of waiting time, accessibility and interaction between different operations may be an important issue affecting practicability and tunneling cost.

9.8.1.3 Economic and techniques situation

It is generally right that modernized tools are widely used in industrial society while simple tools are applied in a developing country. The economic situation of a society is related to the development and application of tunneling techniques. Wage rate and unit price are indicative of the social leveling conditions and the supply of work force. The application of modernized tools, such as systemic machine, to some extent, is a cost saving and effective construction method in an industrial society.

On the other hand, techniques of tunneling also include the experts and technicians, who can apply the modernized tools in a skillful and effective way. In this aspect, experienced contractors and consultants are vital to the application of the construction techniques.

9.8.1.4 Management of the project

People are always key factors to the success of a project. For a complex tunnel project, where new techniques are introduced into the project, skillful and experienced involved groups, e. g. , as client, designer, supervisors, are one of the preconditions for a tunnel project execution in an effective way.

Tunneling requires cooperation between the involved groups, especially where the application of the OM is involved in a complex tunnel project, in terms of risk control and dispute settlement.

Social and corporation cultures and customs also have influence on the cooperation of the involved groups. Culture and custom can be lubricant to the execution of a tunnel project, provided they are skillfully blended with modern tunnel project management procedure. The factors of culture, familiarity and traditional ways of working should be considered in tunnel project management planning.

9.8.1.5 Value of time

For tunneling, there will be an optimal rate of working. The timing of a project should attempt to understand and respect this feature, such as by making special provision where causes of uncertainty may justify a contingency allowance. In general, an accelerated rate of construction requires a rigorous and robust contingency plan for the possibility of delays.

9.8.1.6 Environmental concerns

The environmental concerns of tunneling include the ground and nearby structures deformation, the groundwater table alteration, noise and vibration due to tunneling. The contamination related to tunneling and materials depositing is also consideration for tunnel construction choosing. In general, the tolerance of the a specific item related to environmental concern is more strict in an urban area than that in other regions. The industrial nations have a strict tolerance for the environmental concerns. For example, where drill and blast method is chosen, to control the vibration and noise to the environment, small trial charges are usually employed for calibration and to establish means for compliance with the national or other standards.

9.8.2 Features of conventional tunneling

Conventional tunneling[5] is carried out in a cyclic execution process of the repeated steps of excavation followed by the application of relevant primary support, both of which depend on surrounding rocks conditions and behaviors. An experienced team of tunnel workers (miners), assisted by standard and/or special plant and equipment, shall execute the cycles in a planned sequence of the tunneling.

Conventional tunneling method, mainly using standard equipment and allowing access to the tunnel excavation face at almost any time, is very flexible in situations or areas that require a change in excavation and support measures. A standard set of equipment for the execution of conventional tunneling may consist of[5]: ①drilling jumbo to drill holes for blasting, rock bolting, water and pressure release, grouting etc. ; ② roadheader or excavator in cases where blasting is not possible or not economic; ③lifting platform allowing the miners to reach each part of the tunnel crown and of the tunnel face; ④lifting equipment for steel sets installation; ⑤loader or excavator for loading mucks onto dump trucks; ⑥ dump trucks for hauling mucks; ⑦set of shotcrete manipulators for the application of wet or dry process.

In general, conventional tunneling is especially convenient for: ① difficult

Expansion reading 9-10

grounds with highly variable ground conditions; ② projects with highly variable shapes of cross section; ③ projects with a higher risk of water inflow under high pressure; ④ projects with difficult access; ⑤ short tunnels. However, it is the responsibility of experienced engineers to make the most appropriate choice according to the science of engineering and their personal experience for a safe and economic tunneling.

9.8.3 Features of TBM

TBMs are well used in tunneling. But the application of TBMs is not always the optimal plan for a tunnel project.

A number of factors, such as the ground conditions, features of the tunnel project, planned time schedule and cost, may have influence on the determination of the application of TBMs in the project.

In general, where a TBM is applied and the boring rate is higher the price per meter of tunnel is lower than that of conventional method[5], provided the ground conditions are of relatively low variability and excavation profile is almost same in the tunnel alignment. For rock tunnels, the application of TBM will induce less disturbance to the surrounding rocks than that by drill and blast method, and a regular and clean excavation profile is often produced by TBM.

Where a tunnel is located in soft grounds below groundwater table and in an urban area, the combination of ground improvement and conventional excavating of uniform cross-section tunnels would generally be more expensive than the application of a shield TBM, especially in the developed countries, where the cost of labor is high. In practice, there is a tendency of the increasing application of shield TBMs in the constructions of urban tunnels, especially the running tunnels of metro system.

However, TBMs are less flexible to a high variability in ground formations and properties, as well as tunnel shapes. Most of the TBM are produced to boring circle tunnels. The main adverse factors for the application of TBM in tunneling include the risks of un-predicted variations in ground and variable geometry structures required.

On the other hand. TBMs always mean a high capital cost, the tunnel length is a key issue that needs to be addressed. This means that shorter tunnels tend to be less economical in tunneling with a TBM in comparison to a conventional method.

The details of the TBMs tunneling will be presented in Chapters 11 and 12, respectively.

9.9 Critical thinking problems

C1: In terms of construction, tunnel project is generally different that of structures on ground. Consider: What are the main difference, in terms of: ①construction conditions? ②main risk? ③influence on the environment and the third party?

C2: Consider: ①What are the main features of tunneling? ②Commonly used construction methods and their applications in practice, respectively.

C3: Conventional method is well used in tunneling practice. Consider: ①The general construction procedure of a conventional tunneling cycle; ②The main factors to be considered to determine the round length of a conventional tunneling cycle in construction plan; ③The main factors to be considered to determine the modality of excavations, i.e., full-face, top heading and bench or partial face excavations, in construction plan; ④ Commonly used partial face excavation methods and their applications in practice, respectively.

C4: The NATM and OM are well used in tunnel design and construction. Consider: ① Key elements of the NATM philosophy, in terms of design and construction, respectively; ②Key features of the NATM; ③The procedural steps for the application of OM in the design and construction of a tunnel project; ④Why is a decision-making vital to the success of the application of the OM in a tunnel project and how a reasonable decision can be made in this process?

C5: Instrumentation and monitoring are often necessary and beneficial in tunneling. Consider: ①The values of instrumentation and monitoring in tunneling; ②Factors generally considered in instrumentation and monitoring design for a tunnel project and the main content of the design; ③ How are the results of the instrumentation and monitoring properly and effectively used in the tunneling, in which the NATM or OM is applied in the tunnel design and construction?

C6: The construction method should be planned at every stages of tunnel design and is the most dominating factor to be considered in the construction plan of the contractor of a tunnel project. Consider: As you are working for the contractor of a tunnel project, what are the factors you will consider in choosing construction method for the tunnel to be built?

9.10 References

[1] Flyvbjerg B. What you should know about megaprojects and why: an overview[J]. Project Management Journal, 2014, 45(2): 6-19.

[2] Peck R B. Advantages and limitations of the observational method in applied soil mechanics [J]. Geotechnique, 1969, 19(2): 171-187.

[3] Muir Wood A. Tunnelling: Management by Design[M]. Spon Press, 2000.

[4] Claudio Oggeri, Gunnar Ova. Quality in tunnelling: ITA-AITES Working Group 16 Final report[J]. Tunnelling & Underground Space Technology Incorporating Trenchless Technology Research, 2004, 19(3): 239-272.

[5] ITA Working Group Conventional Tunnelling. General Report on Conventional Tunnelling Method[R/OL]. ITA, 2009. http://tunnel.ita-aites.org/media/k2/attachments/public/ITA_Report_N2_WG19_P.pdf.

[6] Rabcewicz L V. The new Austrian tunnelling method[J]. Water Power, Part 1, 1964: 511-515, Part 2, 1965: 19-24.

[7] Galler R, Schneider E, Bonapace P, et al. The New Guideline NATM—The Austrian Practice of Conventional Tunnelling[J]. BHM Berg-und Hüttenmännische Monatshefte, 2009, 154(10): 441-449.

[8] Health & Safety Executive (HSE). Safety of New Austrian Tunnelling Method (NATM) Tunnels, A review of sprayed concrete lined tunnels with particular reference to London Clay[M]. HSE Books, 1996.

[9] Ma J Q, Berggren B F, Stille H. Concept of the NATM in China and its Influence on the Numerical Analyses on Tunnel Design and Construction with FEM[C]// The 12th IACMAG, 2008.

[10] Schubert W, Lauffer H. NATM—from a construction method to a system[J]. Geomechanics & Tunnelling, 2012, 5: 455-463.

[11] Brown E T. Putting the NATM into perspective[J]. Tunnels &Tunnelling International, 1981, 13(10):13-17.

[12] Terzaghi K, Peck R B. Soil mechanics in engineering practice[M]. New York: John Wiley and Sons, 1967.

[13] Nicholson D, Tse C-M, Penny C. The Observational Method in Ground Engineering: Principles and Applicclrions[M]. London: CIRIA, 1999.

[14] The British Tunnelling Soclety (BTS), the Institution of Civil Engineers. Tunnel lining design guide[S]. London: Thomas Telford Publishing, Thomas Telford Ltd, 2004.

10 Drill and Blast Tunneling

10.1 Introduction

Expansion reading 10-1

Drill and blast (D-B) method is popularly used in mining and tunnel engineering, mainly because it is not only versatile and effective in various ground, but also cost saving, especially for the tunnels, e. g. , with length less than 3 km. Before the advent of TBMs, D-B method is the only economical way of excavating long tunnels through hard rocks, where manual digging is impossible. At present, D-B techniques is still one of the most effective means of driving tunnels, especially in competent rocks.

The main disadvantages of the applications of D-B method include: ①environmental factors (e. g. , noise, vibration, nitrate contamination); ②high risk in the storage and transport of explosives; ③the low security of explosives; ④the large overbreak and support costs of blasted tunnels in comparison to that by TBM.

In modern tunneling, the surrounding rocks of the tunnel should not be significantly affected by mining. Considering blast is an intrinsically violent process, a particular concern with blast is its effect on the surrounding rocks, in terms of the degradation of the mechanical properties. Poor blast can produce intense local fracturing and the disruption of the integrity of the interlocked or jointed surrounding rocks. In high-stress settings, the disturbance associated with blast may trigger extensive instability around the excavations. To control the disturbance to the surrounding rocks, at present, controlled blasting is commonly used in rock tunneling.

In recent years, some improvements have been made in controlled blasting such as in the aspects: ①electronic detonators have eliminated delay overlap; ②bulk emulsion explosives reduce nitrate contamination; ③explosives energy can be varied to suit rock conditions; ④the reliability of emulsions virtually eliminates explosives failure in wet blasting conditions; ⑤some recently developed explosives can be safely delivered.

10.1.1 Drill and blast procedure in tunneling

As the name suggests, (D-B) method works as the following steps. ① A number of holes are drilled into the rock, which are then filled with explosives; ②Detonating the explosives causes the rocks to break to pieces; ③ Rubble is removed and the new surface is reinforced;④Repeating these steps will eventually create a tunnel.

In a D-B round in tunneling, the elements related are often as: drilling, charging, blasting and ventilation, scaling, broken rock removal, reinforcement or supporting. The efficient excavations require the proper combination of holes and explosive, which need to be well planned and controlled in the drilling and blasting. The positions and depths of the holes, and the amount of explosive each hole receives are determined by a carefully planned pattern, including the correct timing of the individual explosions, to guarantee that the tunnel will have an approximately designed excavation profile or cross-section.

10.1.2 Parameters of blasting

Expansion reading 10-2

The effect of the blasting of a blasthole is characterized by a number of parameters. The main parameters of a blasthole in tunneling are in similar to that in a bench blasting geometry, with parameters defined in the notes.

The main difference between tunnel blasting and bench blasting is that tunnel blasting is done towards one or two free surfaces while bench blasting is done towards two or more free surfaces.

10.1.3 Drill and blast plan

Reliable procedures for rock blasting are well established in tunneling practice, in which explosive charges are emplaced in blastholes suitably located relative to a free surface and detonated. Rock surrounding the holes is fragmented and displaced by the impulsive loading in the medium, generated by the sudden release of the explosive's potential energy. The control and routine application of such an intrinsically violent process represent significant feats in both chemical and tunneling technology.

A blast plan should be developed prior to the operations. The plan should depict the blast hole layout, the load factors and timing sequence for a given blasting operation. In general, it serves as an orderly guide to blast operations as well as a record to be followed by subsequent blasters. In general, a blast plan includes these parameters:①the number of holes;②hole diameter;③the average

Expansion reading 10-3

depth of hole;④the number of rows;⑤the space and burden of the holes;⑥the design powder factor;⑦the type of powder;⑧initiation method;⑨total caps; ⑩depth per hole; ⑪cubic meters per hole; ⑫powder (kilogram) per hole; ⑬powder units (sticks) per hole;⑭total powder (units and pounds);⑮estimated cubic meters to be shot.

10.2 Drill and blast in tunneling

Tunnel spaces are created incrementally by sequence of excavation and support rounds in a tunneling process. Where D-B method is applied in hard rocks, the tunneling rate is highly dependent on the successful execution of D-B procedures.

10.2.1 Driving steps of a tunnel face

For tunnel driving, the whole face may be driven in one step, e. g. , full face driving, two steps or even more, which are of split sections or multiple driving steps. The excavations are usually classified, according to the numbers of the steps of whole face driving, as full face driving, top-heading and bench, and multiple face (partial face) driving.

10.2.1.1 Full face driving

Expansion reading 10-4

If the whole face of a tunnel is driven in one step (Figure 10-1), the driving method is called full face driving. This method is effective for the tunnels in good rocks, such as, the surrounding rocks with long stand-up time. However, a tunnel, with large cross section, often requires large drilling jumbo. Where the cross section of the excavation profile is so large that a split section driving technique is effective, such as in terms of the cost of equipments and construction efficiency, partial face excavation may be an alternative.

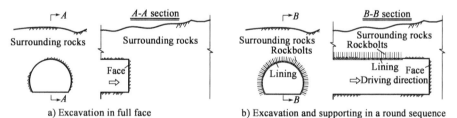

Figure 10-1　Sketch showing full face driving

10.2.1.2　Top-heading and bench

The top heading and bench arrangement is the most common of two steps process:①top heading and support installation or application;②benching and support installation or application. Where this method is used under sound rock conditions, the round length of the top heading and bench is determined in favor of

Expansion reading 10-5

construction speed and efficiency. In these situations, the top heading is much ahead of the benching face and the length of the bench, L, may be long enough, such as $L > 5B$, where B is the span of the tunnel excavation profile.

10.2.1.3 Multiple face driving

For a large tunnel or underground structure in sound rocks, with large cross section, the full face of a tunnel may be divided into multiple excavating faces or benches. The main advantages of building the tunnel in multiple faces excavation and supporting sequence are to use the benches as working stages and transportation ramps. Several sites can simultaneously mined in a large underground cavern or powerstation.

10.2.1.4 Applications in practice

In the past, when mucking was done by hand loading into mine cars and drill equipment was cumbersome, excavation was usually advanced in drifts or headings. In weak rock or for large-span tunnels, this method is still used. A top heading may be advanced first. This permits installation of crown supports if needed. The rest is excavated by benching down from the top heading. These different levels make transportation of excavated material inconvenient. Where a bench is to be excavated, legs of steel sets (supports for side walls and roof) or micropiles are first placed, where they are necessary. For large span tunnels, side headings (drifts) may be advanced. The side headings are followed by a top heading and erection of the arch supports. The remaining block can be attacked from the face or from the side drifts (Figure 10-2).

Expansion reading 10-6

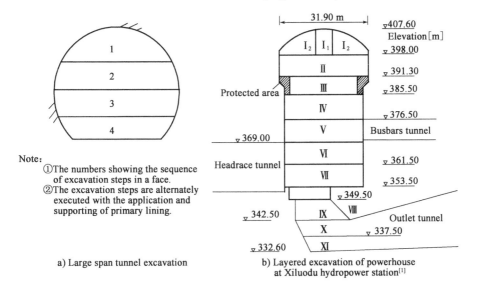

a) Large span tunnel excavation
b) Layered excavation of powerhouse at Xiluodu hydropower station[1]

Note:
① The numbers showing the sequence of excavation steps in a face.
② The excavation steps are alternately executed with the application and supporting of primary lining.

Figure 10-2 Commonly used multiple benches driving for a large span tunnel or underground structure

10.2.2 Drilling

10.2.2.1 Drilling process and tools

Drilling blastholes is the first step in tunneling with drill and blast method. A drilling system comprises two principal parts in terms of functions: ① the mechanical, electrical, and hydraulic components; ② the interactions between these components and the rock. The main parameters of a rotary percussive drilling include: the drill hammer, shank adapter, drifter or drilling rod, drifter feed, and drilling bit[2]. Percussion rotary air blast drilling is used most frequently in tunneling industry. The drilling uses a pneumatic reciprocating piston-driven "hammer" to energetically drive a heavy drill bit into the rock. The drill bit is hollow, solid steel and has 20-mm-thick tungsten rods protruding from the steel matrix as "buttons". The tungsten buttons are the cutting face of the bit. The cuttings are blown up the outside of the rods, such as air or a combination of air and foam.

Expansion reading 10-7

10.2.2.2 Cutting drilling deviation

Drilling accuracy is vital to the success of controlled blasting. The blasthole condition can impact on explosives choice and charge mass. In this term, increasing blasthole drilling accuracy can improve excavation productivity.

10.2.3 Explosives

Expansion reading 10-8

In early period, blast utilized black powder. In the later half of the 19th century, dynamite was used in blast. There are various explosives available today. Commonly used explosives in industry are ANFO (ammonium nitrate/fuel oil), slurries, and emulsions. Many factors, such as rock mass features, groundwater conditions and the density and strength of explosives, are taken into account in determining blast pattern or explosive choosing.

An explosive is any material or product which can produce a sudden outburst of gas, applying a high impulsive loading to the surrounding medium. Chemical explosives are widely used in tunneling. Industrial chemical explosives are of two main types: ①deflagrating explosives, such as black powder, which burn relatively slowly, and produce relatively low blasthole pressure; ② detonating (high) explosives, which are characterized by superacoustic reaction rate and high blasthole pressure. The latter is commonly used in tunneling.

The detonating explosives are themselves considered in three categories, reflecting their respective sensitivities to ease of initiation of detonation. ①Primary explosives, such as lead azide, lead styphnate, or mercury fulminate, are initiated by spark or impact. They are highly unstable compounds, and used industrially only in initiating devices such as blasting caps, as the top charge. ②Secondary explosives require the use of a blasting cap for practical initiation, and in some cases may require an ancillary booster charge. Explosives of this category are formulated from chemicals such as nitroglycerin (NG), ethyleneglycoldinitrate (EGDN), or pentaerythrotetranitrate (PETN), mixed with other explosive materials and stabilizing agents. ③Tertiary explosives are insensitive to initiation by a strength blasting cap. Most explosives of this category are the dry blasting agents (DBAs) or slurry explosives and blasting agents.

In tunneling, the fume properties of the explosive, i. e. ,the chemicals present in the detonation product gases, determine the air quality at site after blasting. The chemical properties of the explosive itself and its application conditions can present safety problems. For example, the explosive used in the lifters usually must withstand water. High concentrations of toxic fumes must be avoided for explosive choosing. Also, the small burdens used in the cut demand an explosive agent with properties precluding the occurrence of channel effects.

10.2.4 Controlled blasting in tunneling

Blasting is to break rocks in pieces in a planned mode, such as fracturing rocks by a calculated amount of explosive in a planned blastholes and detonating in sequence. Since the application of black powder, there have been steady developments in explosives, detonating and delaying techniques and in the understanding of the mechanics of rock breakage by explosives. Good blast design and execution are also essential to successful tunnel excavation. Improper or poor blasting can have a severely negative impact on the tunneling. For example, excessive explosives can result in damages to the surrounding rocks, caving or large overbreak and cost increase.

10.2.4.1 Controlled blasting

When a certain amount of explosive detonates at a specific depth in rock mass, approximately 20-30 percent of its energy is utilized in fragmenting the rocks[4]. Peak particle velocity (PPV) is the unit of measure used for determining the ground vibration effect of blasting. For example, in Japan the permitted vibration amplitude has to be between 0.5 mm/s and 1.0 mm/s in residential areas, whereas in New Zealand anything below 5 mm/s is acceptable[5]. Generally, higher frequencies generated from blasting have a smaller effect on buildings and people than low frequencies do, such as those created by earthquakes.

Expansion reading 10-9

To reduce the amount of overbreak and to control the ground vibrations, the two types of controlled blasting techniques are often used in practice. ①Pre-splitting is an old but highly recognized technique with the purpose to form a fracture plane, beyond which the radial cracks from blasting cannot travel. ② Smooth blasting (contour or perimeter blasting) is well used for mines and tunneling.

10.2.4.2 Types of blastholes

During tunneling, the damage around the excavation profile can seriously reduce the stability of the tunnel, sine the tunnel stability is much dependent upon the integrity of the surrounding rocks. In practice, blast damage can adversely extend several meters into the rocks, where has been poorly blasted, the halo of loosened rock can give rise to serious surrounding rocks instability problems, such as caving and rock blocks falling at the crown of the excavations.

10.2.4.2.1 Types

In general, the blastholes are named according to both their locations and functions, as shown in Figure 10-3. The burn cut, stoping holes, contour (perimeter) holes, and lifters are located in a specific section in a controlled blasting tunneling pattern. For the stoping holes, section B involves the holes breaking horizontally and upward; while section C is the holes usually breaking downward.

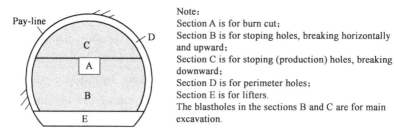

Figure 10-3 Types of balstholes and their locations in a controlled blasting tunneling pattern

Of tunnel blasting, the only available free surface, towards which initial breakage can occur, is the tunnel face. In a proper blast design in tunneling, the first requirement is to create a void, into which rock is broken by the blasting can expand. This is generally achieved by a wedge or burn cut, which is designed to create a clean void and to provide an initial free face for the following blastholes.

In tunneling, the burn cut is a pattern of carefully spaced parallel holes which are then charged with powerful explosive, with one or several large diameter holes lift empty, and detonated sequentially using millisecond delays.

Once a void has been created for the full length of the intended blast depth, the next step is to break the rocks progressively into this void. This is generally achieved by sequentially detonating carefully spaced stoping holes, such as using one-half second delays. The purpose of using such long delays is to ensure that the rock broken by each successive blasthole has sufficient time to detach from the surrounding rocks and to be ejected into the excavation, leaving the necessary void into which the next blast will break.

In a smooth blast process, lightly charged perimeter holes are detonated simultaneously in order to peel off the remaining half to one meter of rock, leaving a clean and designed excavation profile. Perimeter blasting is the process, in which closely drilled blastholes, lightly charged with special column charges, are applied to produce a geometrically precise and relatively undisturbed ultimate profile surface. The benefits of a well executed smooth blasting include controlled damage to the surrounding rocks and overbreak, and therefore controlling the effort in scaling, support cost. These consequences of effective perimeter blasting are expressed in the tunneling performance, such as in terms of safety, cost and time schedule.

The lifter holes at the floor are to make space for carriageway structure and invert building. Where there is no requirement of closing the support system in time, the lifters are generally much postponed in the process.

10.2.4.2.2 Cut patterns

The function of the burn cut is to create an opening in the rock face to serve as free face for the following blasting. The cut holes are arranged in such a way that the delay sequence permits the opening to gradually increase in size until the stoping holes can take over. The cut holes can be drilled in a series of wedges (V-cut), as a fan, or in a parallel geometry usually centered around an empty hole. The choice of the cut has to be made with respect to the type of available drilling equipment, the tunnel width and the desired advance.

Expansion reading 10-10

Various drilling patterns have been developed for blasting hard rock faces, such as: wedge cut or V cut, pyramid or diamond cut, fan cut and burn cut.

In burn cut mode, a series of parallel holes are drilled closely spaced at right angles to the face. One hole or more at the centre of the face are uncharged. The uncharged or empty holes are called the relief holes. The uncharged holes are often of larger diameter than the charged holes and form zones of weakness that assist the adjacent charged holes in breaking out the ground. The burn cut is particularly suitable for use in massive rock such as granite, basalt etc. However, in general, this blasting method requires an initial opening or uncharged void of approximately 25% which, in turn, forces the driller to have extremely close spaced blastholes in the burn cut area. It is not until the initial void is substantially opened that blastholes can be spaced at 1 m or more, depending on the blasthole diameter, to achieve effective energy use.

10.2.4.3　Sequence of detonation

Expansion reading 10-11

Detonation is a type of combustion involving a supersonic exothermic front accelerating through a medium that eventually drives a shock front propagating directly in front of it. Detonations occur in both conventional solid and liquid explosives, as well as in reactive gases. Detonation is an important element influencing the yield of the energy transmitted for both atmospheric over-pressure and ground acceleration. Most commercial mining explosives have detonation velocities ranging from 1800 m/s to 8000 m/s.

For both fragmentation and throw, blasting efficiency depends on the delay sequence of blasthole detonation. In tunneling, the burn area can be opened slowly to provide relief for later blastholes and the later stoping blastholes can be fired quickly to limit the blast duration and promote finer fragmentation in the muck pile for easy mucking. Delayed detonation improves loadability of the entire cut, contributes to a better strata control and reduction of blast-induced vibrations.

In order to control the damage to the surrounding rocks, as well as the installed supporting measures, the entire blast should be correctly designed and executed in tunneling. The controlling blasting, such as pre-splitting or smooth blasting, which involves the simultaneous detonation of a row of closely spaced, lightly charged holes, are designed to create a clean separation surface between the rock to be blasted and the surrounding rocks, as well as very clean profile face, with well controlled overbreak and disturbance.

10.2.4.3.1　Pre-split blasting

Pre-splitting is one of well used controlled blasting methods, which are based on the use of decoupled charges, with the objective to restrict the development of cracks around a hole. The controlled disturbance is sought by isolating the explosive charge from the blasthole surface, using a charge diameter appreciably less than the blasthole diameter, and using spacers to locate the charge axis along the blasthole axis.

Expansion reading 10-12[6]

In pre-splitting method, the perimeter holes are first detonated, then followed by the sequence of burn cut holes, stoping holes, lifters. With this method, a continuous fracture which will form the final surface of an excavation is generated in the absence of a local free face. The close-spaced parallel perimeter holes of the excavation are drilled in the direction of the fracture face advance.

It is noted that the above-mentioned crack development mechanism is for the ideal ground conditions. Real blasting settings may involve high in situ stress and in situ fractures in rock mass. In general, pre-split blasting will show variable results in a stressed medium, depending on the orientation of adjacent pairs of holes relative to the field stresses, and that the process becomes less effective as the field stresses increase; and as a result pre-split fractures may develop in anisotropic rocks parallel to a dominant fabric element[3].

10.2.4.3.2 Smooth blasting

Smooth blasting practice involves the development of the ultimate surface of the excavation by controlled blasting in the vicinity of a penultimate free face[3]. Holes are initiated with short delay between adjacent holes and the burden on holes exceeds the spacing.

Of the smooth blasting method in tunneling, the sequence of blastholes detonation is: ①burn cut holes; ②stoping holes; ③perimeter holes; ④lifters (hole). The lifters and perimeter holes may be detonated simultaneously in practice.

The mechanics of smooth blasting is examined by Brady and Brown[3], in terms of the the mechanism of the controlled fracture development around the penultimate boundary of the excavation under the local boundary stress state, as shown in Figure 10-4, where it is assumed that there is a compressive state of stress in the excavation boundary and adjacent rock. Considering a typical perimeter blastholes near the free face, shown in Figure 10-4b), the local stress field is virtually uniaxial and directed parallel to the penultimate surface. This generates tensile boundary stresses around the blast hole at points a and b, and compressive stresses at points c and d. Thus, the stress wave emitted by detonation of the charge in the hole initiates radial fractures at points a and b, and these propagate preferentially parallel to the local major field stress[3].

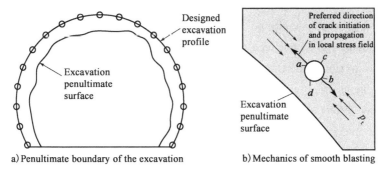

a) Penultimate boundary of the excavation   b) Mechanics of smooth blasting

Figure 10-4 Penultimate stage in the execution of a smooth blasting, and the mechanism of the controlled fracture development under the local boundary stress[3]

As indicated by the mechanics presented by Brady and Brown[3], a high local state of stress around an excavation, promotes more effective smooth blasting, i.e., smooth blasting is the preferred method of perimeter blasting at underground sites, where high states of stress are common.

10.2.4.4 Flyrock control

Blast area is the space, in which concussion (shock wave), flying material, or gases from an explosion may cause injury to persons. Flyrock can be considered as the broken rocks propelled from the blast area by the force of an explosion, or rock pieces forcefully displaced and sent hurling through the air by an explosives detonation.

Generally, flyrock is caused by a mismatch of the explosive energy with the geomechanical strength of the rock mass surrounding the explosive charge. Factors being responsible for this mismatch include: ①abrupt decrease in rock resistance due to joint systems, bedding layers, fracture planes, geological faults, mud seams, voids, localized weakness of rock mass, etc.; ② high explosive concentration leading to localized high energy density; ③inadequate delay between the holes in the same row, or between the rows; ④ inappropriate blast design; ⑤deviation of blastholes from its intended directions; ⑥improper loading and firing practice, including secondary blasting of boulders and toe holes.

Critical elements of any blast design are firing delays between adjacent holes in a row and also those between successive rows. The firing delay is a function of the burden, spacing, hole depth, rockmass features, and the quantity of charge fired per delay. Proper firing delay helps to achieve good fragmentation of the blasted material and to control ground vibration, air blast, and flyrock. In general, the rock fragmented by the previous hole must be given a chance to move out prior to firing subsequent holes.

10.2.4.5 Ground vibration control

In blast design, the influence of the planned blasting on the neighbor structures and grounds should be assessed, such as analysis of ground vibration effects. Ground vibration effects can be predicted with empirical constants and determining the maximum permissible charge weight per delay. For example, each individual delay as small as 8 ms is sufficient to separate two detonations so that their blast wave effects do not overlap. With a given explosive charge and a given distance, the intensity of vibration can be estimated using scaling laws. As suggested by EM 1110-2-2901[7], the intensity of the vibration is a function of the square root of the charge, W, and the peak particle velocity, V, is presented as:

$$V = H(D/W^{1/2})^{-B} \qquad (10\text{-}1)$$

where B is an empirically determined power. The quantity $D/W^{1/2}$ is called the scaled distance, and H is the peak velocity at a scaled distance of one. This relationship plots as a straight line on a log-log plot of velocity against scaled distance, with D in meters, W in kilograms of explosive, V in millimeters/second.

10 Drill and Blast Tunneling

Expansion reading 10-13

The quantity H varies with blast characteristics, confinement and rock mass features. A typical range for H is 100 to 800 (metric); for a given geologic medium, H can vary within a single blast: 250 for the V-cut, 200 for production (stoping) holes, and 150 for the trim holes. H is generally smaller for shorter rounds. The power B can vary from 0.75 to 1.75 and it is often taken as 1.60[7].

10.2.5 Case history

Expansion reading 10-14

Expansion reading 10-15

The blast design is important for tunneling with controlled blasting method. Along with the importance of selecting the proper blast system, other important factors that influence blast results should also be considered, such as: ①properties of explosives being used; ②the initiation systems; ③the distribution of the explosive in the blastholes; ④rock mass structure; ⑤the overall geometry of the planned tunnel. A case history of controlled blasting in tunnel excavation is presented by Hoek[8], where the blasthole pattern and charge details was used by Balfour Beatty-Nuttall on the Victoria hydroelectric project in Sri Lanka, as shown in Expansion reading 10-14.

The development of the burn cut is detonated by using millisecond delays in steps and half-second delay for the contour holes of the void excavated by the burn cut.

10.2.6 Experiences from Norway

Thanks to the development of shotcrete technology, in Norwegian tunneling, the application of conventional drill and blast technology is characterized as being highly mechanized and requiring a minimum of manpower[9]. The general features of tunneling with drill and blast method[9] are as the followings.

10.2.6.1 Contract execution

Contracts in Norway are unit rate contracts based on Bill of Quantity for relevant support and excavation elements. The contractor has to adapt to rapid changes and the decision making process is delegated to the tunnel site. The shift supervisor and the shift leader together with the client's resident engineer handle the daily tunneling matters.

10.2.6.2 Techniques of excavation and supporting

The drill and blast technique in Norway is characterized by the use of modern equipment and highly skilled and independent workers. Typical standard equipment includes: ①computerized drill jumbos, which is capable of drilling up to 3 m per minute, with computer controlled drilling and surveying of the previous excavated profile; ②mucking wheel loader and trucks; ③highly automated and computerized robots for wet process shotcrete; ④hydraulic hammers mounted on excavators for scaling; ⑤ computerized rock mass grouting units, which can deliver grout to several grout holes simultaneously.

10.2.6.3 Drill pattern and blasting techniques

The drill pattern in Norwegian tunneling is often based on parallel cut in combination with large diameter boreholes. The maximum contour hole distance is 0.7 m and the distance to the next helper row do not exceed 0.9 m. The charging of the contour holes and the helper row next to the contour is reduced, using specialized piped explosive or similar measures to reduce the charging, typically the charging would be 0.25 kg/m to 0.45 kg/m (78% ANFO by weight).

Expansion reading 10-16

A typical successful blast round in competent rock mass will display most of the drill holes in the tunnel contour. The Accuracy of the drilling of the contour holes can be controlled as: collaring within 0.1 m measured from theoretical drill pattern, and for alignment deviation, maximum 6% of the depth of the hole.

10.2.6.4 Typical figures for a 100 m² cross-section

Expansion reading 10-17

Typical figures for the drill and blast excavation of a tunnel with 100 m² cross-section[9] is shown, in terms of a full face excavation blast round.

10.3 Material handing

In tunneling, the volumes of materials to be moved are large and should be properly disposed in mucking. To make the mucking effective, individual pieces of material, often called muck, should be not too large, such as typically having dimensions up to several inches on a side. The features of a mucking system in tunneling include the followings.

(1) High-volume, reliable removal: With the volumes of muck removed in tunneling being hundreds of cubic meters per hour, current systems are marginal in their ability to keep up with a rapidly advancing mining operation, especially in small tunnels. Any breakdown in the material removal system may cause immediate cessation of tunneling operations.

(2) Compatibility with other functions: Workers and material must use the same work site. Safe and efficient shared facilities must be provided.

(3) Environmental disposal: Mucking or surface workings are often noisy and dirty operations handling large volumes of materials. Any mucking system and activities must be compatible with environmental requirements.

10.3.1 Belt conveyor system

A belt conveyor is the carrying medium of a belt conveyor system, which consists of two or more pulleys (sometimes referred to as drums), with an endless loop of carrying medium—the conveyor belt—that rotates about them. One or both of the pulleys are powered, moving the belt and the material on the belt forward. The powered pulley is called the drive pulley while the unpowered pulley is called the idler pulley.

The belt conveyors in tunneling is similar to those used for transporting large volumes of resources and agricultural materials, such as grain, salt, coal, ore, sand, overburden and more. Today there are different types of conveyor belts in PVC and rubber materials are available for mucking.

10.3.2 Tunnel mucking with loader and trucks

Tunnel mucking loader, e. g., crawler mucking loader and wheel mucking loader with fully hydraulic drive, working stable and reliable, is a kind of mechanization equipment mainly used in the tunnel blasting driving working. Haul trucks are commonly used in tunnel mucking transportation.

10.4 Critical thinking problems

C1: Drill and blast method is commonly used in tunneling. Consider: ①Why is this excavation method popular in rock tunneling? ②The general procedure of the drill and blast in rock tunneling; ③Why should the blasting in tunneling be planned? ④What are the main considerations in choosing driving mode, such as full face, top-heading and bench, multiple face, to excavate the planned tunnel profile?

C2: Where drill and blast method is applied in tunneling, the damage of surrounding rocks and the influence on the neighbors due to blasting should be controlled in a planned mode. To meet these requirements, controlled blasting is usually applied in tunneling. Consider: ① Types of commonly used controlled blasting method in tunneling and their main features, respectively; ② Why are different types blastholes designed in tunneling? ③Why is the detonating sequence different for the pre-split blasting and smooth blasting, respectively? ④Set a pre-split blasting or smooth blasting as example, list what are the key components in a controlled blasting implementation procedure.

C3: In tunneling practice, these factors, such as safety, cost and time schedule, are always factors to be considered in construction method choosing. In general, a well managed tunnel project is intended to be finished in a planned mode. Consider: ① As drill and blast method is under consideration for the excavation of a rock tunnel, what are the main factors, which will have influence on the decision-making to use this method? ②For a 1500-m-long, two-lane road tunnel in hard rocks, where all factors under consideration are favorable, try to estimate the time schedule for the excavation with drill and blast method.

C4: We can learn from history. For rock tunneling, the drill and blast method is well used in the world for a long period. Consider: ①What are the situations in the industrialized regions? ②What is the situation in China, at present? ③In your opinion, what will be the situation in China in the future?

10.5 References

[1] Lu W, Geng X, Chen M, et al. Study of selection of excavation procedure and contour blasting method for deep underground powerhouse[J]. Chinese Journal of Rock Mechanics & Engineering, 2011, 30(8):1531-1539.

[2] Thuro K, Spaun G. Introducing the 'destruction work' as a new rock property of toughness referring to drillability in conventional drill- and blast tunnelling[C]. ISRM International Symposium-EUROCK 96, Turin, Italy, 1996.

[3] Brady B HG, Brown E T. Rock Mechanics: For underground mining[M]. 3rd ed. Springer, 2006.

[4] Pesch R, Robertson A. Drilling and Blasting for Underground Space[C]. The EXPLO Conference, Wollongong, NSW, 2007.

[5] Rathore S S, Bhandari S. Controlled Fracture Growth by Blasting While Protecting Damages to Remaining Rock[J]. Rock Mechanics & Rock Engineering, 2007, 40(3):317-326.

[6] Kutter H K, Fairhurst C. On the fracture process in blasting[J]. International Journal of Rock Mechanics & Mining Sciences & Geomechanics Abstracts, 1971, 8(3):181-202.

[7] U. S. Army Corps of Engineers. Tunnels and shafts in rock-Engineer Manual[M]. Washington: U. S. Army Corps of Engineers, Department of the Army, 1997.

[8] Hoek E. Practical Rock Engineering[EB/OL]. 2007 ed. https://www.rocscience.com/assets/resources/learning/hoek/Practical-Rock-Engineering-Full-Text.pdf.

[9] Norwegian Tunnelling Society (NTS). Drill and Blast[M] // Introduction to Norwegian Tuunnelling, Norwegian Tunnelling Society, 2004.

11 Mechanical Tunneling in Rocks

11.1 Introduction

Expansion reading 11-1

Expansion reading 11-2

Following the definition of ITA[1], "mechanized tunnelling techniques", as opposed to the so-called "conventional" techniques, are all the tunneling techniques in which excavation is performed mechanically by means of teeth, picks or discs.

Since a cylindrical steel shield was first used for the construction of the Themes River Tunnel Crossing in England in 1823[1], and thanks to the industry and economy development in the world, mechanical excavation methods, such as with roadheaders and TBMs, are nowadays commonly used in tunneling, especially for long and super long tunnels. Where well planned TBMs are applied in relatively favorable ground conditions, the tunneling speed can be high enough to meet most of tunnel project plans.

The increasing needs of excavators and TBMs in mining and civil engineering fields have speeded the productivity and improvements of these machines. For example, in the recent years, TBMs for mixed ground of rock and soft material (mixed face) have been produced for varying ground conditions and have opened up new possibilities for machine tunneling in difficult grounds.

The advantages of mechanized tunneling are multiple, including the followings[2]: ① enhanced health and safety conditions for the workforce; ② the industrialization of the tunneling process, with ensuing reductions in costs and lead times; ③ the possibility of tunneling in complex ground conditions safely and economically; ④ the good quality of the finished product, including less disturbance to the surrounding rocks.

11.2 Types of mechanical methods

The applications of mechanical excavation methods have been steadily increased in tunneling. Nowadays, mechanical excavation methods can be applied in various types of grounds, with special reference to their stability and drillability. The types of mechanical excavation methods are accordingly increased with time. The mechanical excavation method designed for a specific tunnel is mainly referred to the methods for excavation (full face or partial face), the types of cutter head (rotation or non-rotation), and the methods of securing reaction force (from gripper or segment)[1]. For example, an open TBM is practically used for the mining of hard rock, where the face of the tunnel is basically self-standing, while a metal shield is primarily used for protective device for excavation works in soils or soft rocks. Where there is a need to stabilize the excavation face, such as tunneling through soft soils, much attention should be paid to the face supporting means. Under these situations, a slurry balanced or earth pressured balanced shield method may be chosen accordingly.

A machine is chosen when the excavation method for the tunnel is determined during tunnel design. The commonly used mechanical excavation methods in terms of the types of excavation machines, can be classified as partial face excavation with excavators and full face excavation with a TBM. The commonly used types of tunnel excavation machines are illustrated in Figure 11-1.

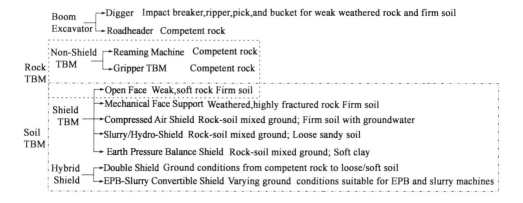

Figure 11-1 Classification of tunnel excavation machines for various ground

There are different classification schemes for tunnel excavation machines and is no unified classification system in the world. Here are the suggestions on the classification by AFTES[2] and ITA[1] presented, with special reference to the supporting and excavating modes in tunneling.

11.2.1 Classification of AFTES

Considering whether an immediate support are provided for the full face or partial face tunnel excavation with a machine, AFTES[2] classified tunnel boring machine into two groups: ①machines not providing immediate support; ②machines providing immediate peripheral support, as shown in Figure 11-2.

11 Mechanical Tunneling in Rocks 349

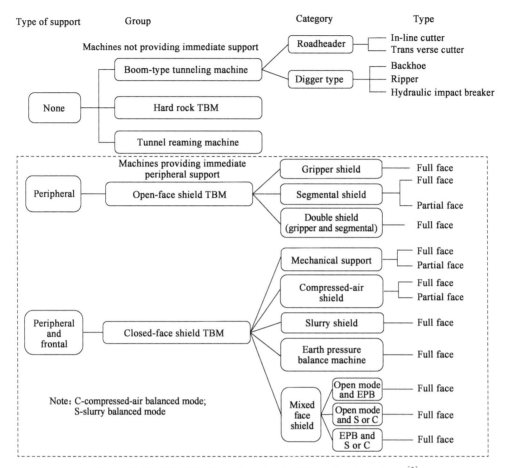

Figure 11-2 Classification of mechanized tunneling techniques[2]

11.2.1.1 Machines not providing immediate support

Machines not providing immediate support are those working in ground not requiring immediate and continuous tunnel support. These machines include boom-type units and hard rock TBM.

Boom-type units are machines with a selective excavation arm fitted with a tool of some sorts. This group of machines is fitted with one of two types of tool: ①backhoe, ripper, or hydraulic impact breaker; ② roadheaders, with in-line cutterhead or transverse cutterhead, respectively.

A hard rock TBM has a cutterhead that excavates the full tunnel face in a single pass. The thrust on the cutterhead is reacted by bearing pads (or grippers) which push radially against the tunnel surrounding rocks. The machine advances sequentially as: excavation while the gripper unit being stationary and regripping. Spoil is collected and removed rearwards by the machine itself. These TBMs do not provide immediate tunnel support.

Expansion reading 11-3

11.2.1.2 Machines providing immediate peripheral support

Machines providing immediate peripheral support are open-face shield TBMs or closed-face shield TBMs (Figure 11-2), depending whether the face being supported or not. The immediate peripheral support is provided by shield or shields, i.e., one-can shield and shield of two or more cans connected by articulations (e.g., articulated shield machines, steel tube articulated shield), respectively.

An open-face gripper shield TBM can be considered as a gripper TBM, mounted inside a cylindrical shield incorporating grippers. The shield provides immediate passive peripheral support to the tunnel surrounding rocks. The cutting or boring tools may be either a full-face cutterhead or an excavator arm like those of the different boom type units[2]. To advance and bore, the TBM's longitudinal thrust rams react against the tunnel lining, erected behind it by a special erector incorporated into the TBM.

A double shield TBM is a TBM with a full-face cutterhead and two sets of thrust rams that react against either the tunnel walls (radial grippers) or the tunnel lining. The thrust method used at any time depends on the type of ground encountered. With longitudinal thrust, segmental lining must be installed behind the machine as it advances to support the surrounding rocks. The TBM has three or more cans connected by articulations and a telescopic central unit, which relays thrust from the gripping/thrusting system in the front of the TBM.

11.2.1.3 Machines providing both peripheral and frontal supports

The TBMs that provide immediate peripheral and frontal support simultaneously belong to the closed-faced group. The TBMs excavate and support the tunnel walls and the face at the same time. Except for mechanical-support TBMs, they all have what is called a cutterhead chamber at the front, isolated from the rearward part of the machine by a bulkhead. In the chamber, a pressure is maintained in order to actively support the excavation and/or balance the hydrostatic pressure of the groundwater. The face is excavated by a cutterhead working in the chamber. The TBMs are jacked forward by rams pushing off the segmental lining erected inside the TBM tailskin, using an erector integrated into the machine.

A mechanical-support TBM has a full-face cutterhead, which provides face support by constantly pushing the excavated material ahead of the cutterhead against the wallrocks. Muck is extracted by means of openings on the cutterhead fitted with adjustable gates that are controlled in real time.

The confinement pressure in the cutterhead chamber may be provided through compressed-air, slurry or pressuring excavated soils. The shield TBMs are accordingly called a compressed-air shield TBM, slurry shield TBM and an earth pressure balance (EPB) shield TBM, respectively.

A compressed-air shield TBM can have either a full-face cutterhead or excavating arms like those of the different boom-type units. Confinement is achieved by pressurizing the air in the cutting chamber. Muck is extracted continuously or intermittently by a pressure-relief discharge system that takes the material from the confinement pressure to the ambient pressure in the tunnel.

A slurry shield TBM has a full-face cutterhead. Confinement is achieved by pressurizing boring fluid inside the cutterhead chamber. Circulation of the fluid in the chamber flushes out the muck, with a regular pressure being maintained by directly or indirectly controlling discharge rates.

An EPB shield TBM also has a full-face cutterhead. Confinement is achieved by pressurizing the excavated material in the cutterhead chamber. Muck is extracted from the chamber continuously or intermittently by a pressure-relief discharge system that takes it from the confinement pressure to the ambient pressure in the tunnel.

Mixed-face shield TBMs have full-face cutterheads and can work in closed or open mode and with different confinement techniques. For example, EPB shield TBMs can also operate in open mode or with compressed-air confinement as being specially equipped. Changeover from one work mode to another requires mechanical intervention to change the machine configuration. Different muck extraction means are used for each work mode.

11.2.2 Classification of ITA

Figure 11-3 shows the ITA[1] proposed TBMs classification scheme, of which the main indexes are the ground support system, excavation method and tools, and reaction force tool. TBMs are grouped into two machine categories: ① rock tunneling machines; ②soft ground tunneling machines.

11.2.3 Variant types of TBMs

From the 1980s then on, various innovations of shield tunneling machines have been used in urban tunneling. These innovated machines include TBMs with double-O-tube (DOT) shield, multi-circular face shield, rotating shield, and non-circular shield, respectively.

The cutterhead of a shield TBM is conventionally in the shape of circle. To meet the requirements of tunnel features and the efficient use of underground space in urban area, special-shaped shields, such as non-circular shield and multi-circular face shield, were developed in the 1980s. For example, to enable the construction of non-circular tunnels, several innovative shield tunneling methods have been developed in Japan, such as the DOT, triple face and four-circular-face types (Figure 11-3), which were equipped with computerized arms that can be used for digging a tunnel in virtually any shape[3].

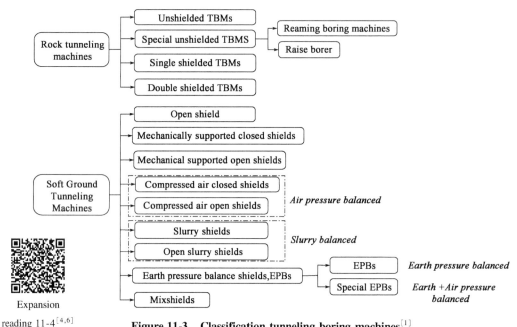

Figure 11-3 Classification tunneling boring machines[1]

11.2.4 Selection of mechanical methods

With the increasing applications of mechanical excavation methods, there is a tendency of fully mechanized tunneling. The creation of special methods such as face supporting with fluid or slurry as well as the successful utilization of cutter discs for removing rock-like intrusions and boulders have led to a considerable expansion of the TBM application and to an increase in the economy of these tunneling systems; and due to the continuous improvement of the various extraction techniques, some types of TBMs have the capacity to penetrate extremely heterogeneous subsoil, such as a mixture of soft ground and rock[7].

On the other hand, with the development in tunnel excavation machine types and the improvement in techniques, the clear distinction between TBM for hard rock and shield machines (SM) for soft ground, which resulted from their conceptual background, and the special engineering and extraction technology, has lost its original significance[7]. Some tunneling machines have the typical features of both techniques even in a single unit. There are generally various tunneling machines available and being suitable for the entire geotechnical spectrum.

However, in simplicity, a machine is a tool. A tool can be designed and made robust, but it is almost impossible to produce a tool to be proper for any job. The tunneling machines are generally considered complicated or assembled tools, which are designed and produced for a specific project. The machine choosing is characterized by the predicted performance of the mechanized tunneling with appropriate TBM or a roadheader, excavator for the planned tunnel project, such as tunneling in safe and economic way.

When a tunnel machine is planned for a tunnel, the considered features of the tunnel projects for the machine choosing, at least, include the followings: ①ground conditions, such as the strength and intactness of the rock mass, features of rock mass structures, variety of the rock mass along the tunnel axis, ground water conditions, in situ stress; ②the features of the tunnel project, including the length of the tunnel, the size and shape of tunnel cross section, features of tunnel alignment in terms of vertical and horizontal curves, overburden of tunnel; ③interaction between the ground and the tunnel, properties and stability of the surrounding rocks, the stability of the tunnel face, overburden and stress state; ④planned time schedule; ⑤ the conditions of social economy and techniques; ⑥experiences of the involved groups, especially the contractor, consultant and client; ⑦restrictions from the third party and environment.

These considered factors for tunnel excavation machine choosing are shown in Figure 11-4. The graphics with dash line border is intended to showing its changing feature.

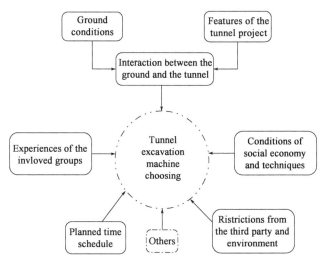

Figure 11-4 Factors related to tunnel excavation machine choosing

11.3 Excavation with a roadheader

In general, partial-face excavation machines are characterized by their robust adaptability to changing geological conditions. Partial-face excavation machines are also an economic solution in homogeneous and stable grounds with little or no groundwater.

Road headers available are commonly used partial face excavation machines in tunneling. The roadheaders are made in various sizes and shapes, and equipped for different purposes, such as to excavate tunnels in full face or partial-face pattern, and to excavate small or large underground chambers.

11.3.1 Components

A roadheader, also called a boom-type roadheader, is a piece of excavating equipment consisting of a boom-mounted cutting head, a loading device usually involving a conveyor, and a crawler travelling track to move the entire machine forward[8].

Expansion reading 11-5

Roadheaders generally include the following components: ①rotary cutterhead equipped with picks; ②hydraulically operated boom that can place the cutterhead at a range of vertical locations; ③turret permitting a range of horizontal motion of the cutterhead; ④loading device, usually an apron equipped with gathering arms; ⑤chain or belt conveyor to carry muck from the loading device to the rear of the machine for off-loading onto a muck car or other device; ⑥base frame, sometimes with outriggers or jacks for stabilization, furnished with electric and hydraulic controls of the devices and an operator's cab; ⑦propelling device, usually a crawler track assembly.

Expansion reading 11-6

The cutting head of a roadheader can be a general purpose rotating drum mounted in line or perpendicular to the boom, or can be special function heads such as jack-hammer like spikes, compression fracture micro-wheel heads like those on larger tunnel boring machines, a slicer head like a gigantic chain saw for dicing up rock, or simple jaw-like buckets of traditional excavators. According to the relationship between the rotational direction of the cutting header and the boom axis of a roadheader, the cutting heads of roadheader are classified as: ①longitudinal cutting heads, with rotation axis parallel to the cutter boom axis; ②transverse cutting heads, with rotation axis perpendicular to boom axis, respectively.

11.3.2 Applications

Roadheader booms are used in various hard rock tunnels. For example, the heavy duty roadheaders, with a weight more than 100tons, can utilized for

Expansion
eading 11-7[9,10]

excavating tunnels in hard rocks, with the uniaxial compressive strengths of up to 150 MPa. One of the features of roadheaders is their flexibility to various excavation shapes and sizes. The application range of roadhaeders can starts at around 1.5 m in diameter, as it is necessary to access the tunnel. Tunnelling operations with diameters of more than 10 m can be carried out cost effectively using additional support measures or grout injections to improve the ground.

The roadheaders in market are generally characteristics of: ①hydraulic pilot proportional valve controlled, also can be wireless remote controlled; ② the hydraulic system is variable pump system, which can both improve working efficiency and reduce the system heating, energy saving and environment friendly; ③the machine is with outer and inner water spray device for good dust suppression; ④ the unique system of separate motor to drive loading and transportation, respectively.

In general, the applications of roadheaders in tunneling are economic and effective under the following situations: ①rock strength below 120 MPa; ②short runs, one of a kind openings; ③odd, non-circular shapes; ④connections, cross passages, etc.; ⑤low to moderate abrasivity; ⑥preferably self supporting rock; ⑦no or small extra hard rock inclusions, such as chert interlayers; ⑧nominal water pressure.

On the negative side, roadheaders are much less efficient in longer drives in hard rock. The picks on the roadheader are something like 10% as efficient as TBM disks at removing rock and must be replaced very frequently. The tools are not effective in rocks with an unconfined compressive strength greater than 140 MPa. Changes and improvements in roadheader design are on-going, especially in these limitations.

11.4 TBM tunneling in rocks

The components of a TBM include: ①cutterhead, with cutting tools and muck buckets; ②systems to supply power, cutterhead rotation, and thrust; ③a bracing system for the TBM during boring; ④equipment for ground support installation; ⑤shielding to protect workers (if necessary); ⑥a steering system. Back-up equipment systems provide muck transport, personnel and material conveyance, ventilation and utilities.

11.4.1 Types and system of rock TBMs

Two general categories: gripper and segment TBMs are nowadays commonly used in rock tunnel excavations. Of the TBMs with rotational cutterheads, three general types of TBMs suitable for rock tunneling including open gripper/main beam, single shield and double shield TBM[11].

11.4.1.1 Open gripper/main beam TBMs

Expansion reading 11-8

The open gripper/beam TBMs are suited for stable to friable rocks with occasional fractured zones and controllable groundwater inflows. Main beam and open gripper are two common types of TBMs belong to this category.

Similarly, the major components of a Robbins open gripper main beam TBM include: cutterhead (with disc cutters) and front support, main beam, thrust (propel) cylinder, gripper, rear support, and conveyor.

Expansion reading 11-9

A trailing backup system is for muck and material transportation, ventilation, power supply, etc., in a TBM.

11.4.1.2 Single shield TBM

Single shield TBMs are mainly for tunneling through rock and other stable, non-groundwater-bearing soils, where the surrounding rocks cannot provide consistent support to the gripper pressure. The body of the machine is enclosed in a shield that is marginally smaller than the diameter of the tunnel. The shield of TBM protects workers from broken rock until the tunnel lining can be safely installed.

Shield TBMs can either be advanced by pushing against segment, or gripper. When tunneling with a single shield TBM, a rotating cutterhead equipped with disc cutters is pressed against the tunnel face. Due to the rolling movement of the discs, single pieces (chips) are broken out of the rock. Buckets installed at the cutterhead take up the broken rocks (muck). When the rock chips slide to the center of the machine through integrated muck chutes and then falls through the funnel-shaped muck ring onto the machine belt. At the end of the machine belt, the rock chips are passed on to belt conveyors or transport vehicles and removed from the tunnel.

Expansion reading 11-10

Boring and lining installation are performed sequentially. Nowadays, single shields are equipped with high-speed segment erectors for rapid tunnel lining installation. To steer, cylinders orient the articulated cutterhead in the required direction. The short shield length enables a small turning radius and minimizes exposure to squeezing ground forces that could potentially trap the machine.

11.4.1.3 Double shield TBM

A double shield TBM consists of a rotating cutterhead mounted to the cutterhead support, followed by three shields: a telescopic shield (a smaller diameter inner shield which slides within the larger outer shield), a gripper shield and a tail shield. Double shield TBMs consist of two main components: a front shield with cutterhead, main bearing and drive, and a gripper shield with gripping unit, auxiliary thrust cylinders and tailskin. The main thrust cylinders connect the two parts of the shield. They are protected by the telescopic shield where the shield skins of the front and gripper shield overlap. Thus, double shield TBMs are also called telescopic shields. In stable rock, the machine is braced radially against the surrounding rocks with the gripper shoes. This means that the front shield can be advanced independently for a gripper shield using the main thrust cylinders.

The reaction forces during the excavation process are transferred into the surrounding rocks by the extended gripper shoes. Simultaneously, the segments are installed in the tailskin section. The auxiliary thrust cylinders serve only to secure the position of the concrete segments placed. When the stroke is completed, the gripper shoes are loosened and the gripper shield is pushed behind the front shield using the auxiliary thrust cylinders. Since regripping lasts only a few minutes, the tunneling is almost continuous. In ideal rock formations, double shield TBMs can also operate without segmental lining.

Expansion reading 11-11

In double shield mode, the gripper shoes are energized, pushing against the surrounding rocks to react the boring forces just like the open gripper TBM. The main propel cylinders are then extended to push the cutterhead support and cutterhead forward. The rotating cutterhead cuts the rock. The telescopic shield extends as the machine advances keeping everything in the machine under cover and protected from the ground surrounding it. The completely enclosed shielded design provides the safe working environment.

11.4.2 Backup system

Tunnel boring productivity is often limited by the speed of muck removal and the supply of critical construction material to the TBM. The backup system or trailing equipment is as important as the machine itself. A backup system for a TBM can be short gantry systems to sophisticated, remote-controlled double-track systems. What is important that the system should match to the construction method and type of the TBM. The mucking of TBM tunneling may be a tracked system using muck trains or conveyors as well as rubber-tired vehicles.

A single-track backup system has the advantage of being short, simple to operate and simple to maintain. If the tunnel is small in diameter, relatively short in length, or the equipment assembly area is restricted, a single-track backup is often the best solution. Similarly, single-track systems are frequently used if the TBM must start from the bottom of a shaft. Depending on project construction schedule and requirements, single-track systems can be used with continuous conveyors or with muck trains. When using muck cars in large-diameter tunnels, double-track backup systems ensure the maximum productivity. This minimizes delays between trains and optimizes advance rates.

Rubber tired vehicle backup systems allow muck to be removed by conveyor or truck. This permits roadbed construction to be carried out simultaneously with tunnel excavation. As a result of this flexibility, they are often used in large diameter tunnels for rail, road and hydroelectric projects.

The commonly mounted equipments in the backup system of a TBM generally include: ventilation, ground support, water and compressed air, electrical facilities, as shown in Figure 11-5.

Ventilation:
    Dust scrubbers (wet or dry) with fans and silencers
    Fresh-air flexible ventilation duct cassettes
    Fresh air booster fans
	Water & Compressed Air:
	    Backup mounted compressors
	    Compressed air distribution system
	    Industrial fresh water distribution system
	    Cooling water recirculation systems
	    Compressed air and/or water hose reels

Ground Support:
    Shotcreting equipment, decks and robots
    Variable cutterhead speed
    Concrete segment transport and storage
    Back-filling systems for concrete segment lining
    Drill Systems for pattern bolting
	Electrical:
	    High voltage cable reels
	    Emergency generators

Figure 11-5　Commonly mounted equipment in the backup system of a TBM

11.4.3　TBM operation

Expansion reading 11-12

A TBM is a complex system with a main body and other supporting elements to be made up of mechanisms for cutting, shoving, steering, gripping, shielding, exploratory drilling, ground control and support, lining erection, spoil (muck) removal, ventilation and power supply. In terms of construction function, there are four system groups of facilities[12]: ①boring system, ②thrusting and clamping system, ③muck removal system, and ④support system.

11.4.3.1　Boring process

Modern TBMs have a closed cutterhead[12], generally with disc cutters are sit in it. Most of the disc cutters are simple disc and fixed between tracks. Disc cutters roll against tunnel face with the rotation of the cutterhead, as shown in Figure 11-6.

In terms of excavation, a TBM is a system that provides thrust, torque, rotational stability and steering. In most cases, these functions can be accomplished continuously during each boring cycle. Figure 11-6 is a sketch of a typical open or unshielded TBM for operation in hard rocks. The TBM cutterhead is rotated and thrust onto the rock surface, causing the cutting disc tools to penetrate and break the rock at the tunnel face. Reaction to applied thrust and torque forces may be developed by anchoring with braces (grippers) extended to the tunnel wall, friction between the cutterhead/shield and the tunnel walls, or bracing against segment lining installed behind the TBM.

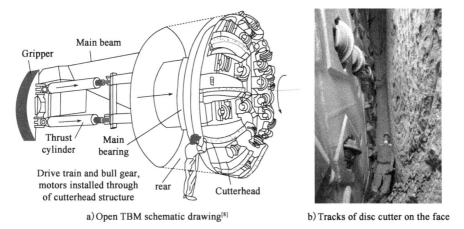

a) Open TBM schematic drawing[8]   b) Tracks of disc cutter on the face

Figure 11-6 Open TBM schematic drawing showing excavating and thrusting system

A cutterhead, rotating on an axis which coincides with the axis of the tunnel being excavated, is pressed against the excavation face; the cutters (normally disc cutters) penetrate into the rock, pulverizing it locally and creating intense tensile and shear stresses. As the resistance under each disc cutter is overcome, cracks are created as intersecting mode to break rocks in chips. Special buckets in the cutterhead allow the debris to be collected and removed to the primary mucking system.

Expansion reading 11-13

The working cycle is discontinuous and includes excavation for a length equivalent to the effective stroke, regripping and new excavation in a cycle. When a reaming boring machines is used, a TBM pilot tunnel is to be widened (reaming).

11.4.3.2 Cutterhead

The cutterhead of a TBM has multiple functions[12]: ① the carrier for the excavation tools; ② collecting and picking up the excavated materials by the muck bucket with the rotation of the cutterhaed and depositing them on conveyor; ③ supporting the face during both interruptions of normal operation and an accident; ④ carrying overcutters in special case.

In general, cutterhead should be closed, as short as possible, such that the rotating parts have a little contact with the tunnel walls. The types or shapes of cutterhead may be: ① fully open cutterhead mainly for small diameter tunnels in hard rocks; ② closed and domed cutterhead; ③ closed cutterhead of shield TBM with external bucket; ④ closed cutterhead of shield TBM with external and internal buckets.

In general, the larger a cutterhead is the more rolling cutters on it[20], especially for hard rock TBMs. The strong linear correlation between TBM

Expansion reading 11-14

diameter and the number of disc cutters implies that the arrangements of the cutters on a cutterhead are similar among the TBMs from different manufacturers.

For large diameter TBM, the capacity of the clearing muck at the excavation area may have a strong influence on the performance of the TBM, such as penetration rate. When the excavated materials are not cleared from the excavation area, a jam of the materials between the cutter head and the face may cause significant loss of the TBM's excavating torque, which indicates the smaller numbers of buckets, the more magnitude of torque loss, during the penetration of a TBM.

Similarly, the experience at the Superconducting Super Collider, for example, indicates that state-of-the-art tunnel boring machines may produce muck faster than the best available mucking system can remove it.

11.4.3.3 Performance of cutting tools

Many factors may influence on the performance of a TBM. The penetration of a TBM cutterhead in tunneling mainly depends on the geotechnical conditions of the surrounding rocks around the face, such as the strength and features of the fracture of rock mass, and the technical parameters of the TBM.

11.4.3.3.1 Penetration

Expansion reading 11-15

Robbins[13] gave the qualitative relationship of rock mass strength-cutter load-penetration of TBM with disc cutters. The results of Robbins[13] are in good agreement with nowadays experiences[12]. The strength of surrounding rocks has a strong influence on the penetration of cutting tool. The higher of rock strength, the lower of penetration cutting tools performance is and the higher cutter load is required. The operating limits of a TBM with 17 in (43 cm) disc cutters at different rock strengths are presented by Frenzel et al.[18].

The features of the rock mass fractures or joints may also have a strong influence on the performance of the cutter tools of a TBM. Penetration rates during excavation using TBMs are significantly influenced by the degree of fracturing in the rock mass, fracture type, fracture spacing, and the angle between fractures and the tunnel axis[15]. Where the space of the rock mass joints is lower than a critical value, certain safety measures may be required and penetration rate is therefore reduced sharply. The critical space for a small diameter TBM is about 10-20cm and 50-60cm for a larger gripper TBM[12], respectively. The penetration rate of TBM increases with the increase of the angle between tunnel axis and joint plane, as the angle is less than 60°; then decreases with increasing angle[16].

Recently, Hassanpour et al.[19] proposed Field Penetration Index (FPI) of rock mass to predict TBM penetration performance as:

$$FPI = F_n/P \tag{11-1}$$

where, *FPI* is Field Penetration Index in kN/cutter/mm/rev; *P* is cutter penetration in each cutterhead revolution, mm/rev; F_n is cutter load or normal force, kN; the *FPI* can be approximated with the rock mass parameters of *RQD* (%) and uniaxial compressive strength, *UCS* in MPa, and calculated with the following empirical equation:

$$FPI = e^{0.008UCS+0.015RQD+1.384} \tag{11-2}$$

Based on the empirical equation (11-2), Hassanpour et al. [19] presented a chart for estimating the penetration of a TBM under various rock mass properties. In practice, the ranges of the variations of TBM performance can be very wide, such as the range of *FPI* from 2.75(min) to 145.6(max) kN/cutter/mm/rev[19].

Based on the performance of rock TBM in case histories, Hassanpour et al. [19] summarized the general features of surrounding rocks and excavatability when a TBM excavation being executed.

Expansion reading 11-16

11.4.3.3.2 Wearing of cutters

To predict the life of the cutters are generally required in TBM choosing, since the wearing of the cutter tools of a TBM has a strong influence on the efficiency and economic situation of the tunneling. The main factors determine the wearing or life of cutters is the penetration and abrasiveness of the rocks to be bored. In order to increase the life of cutters, cutters with large diameter are produced, such as from 11 in (28 cm) to 19 in (48.3 cm). However, the large cutter means difficulty in change.

Expansion reading 11-17

The life of cutters is greatly changing for different types of rocks. Among the factors influencing the life of cutters, the rock strength is always dominating. The general relationship between rock strength and average disc cutter life measured in cubic meter rock excavated per cutter of 17 in (43.2 cm) in diameter, can be preliminarily used for approximating cutter life.

11.4.3.4 Advance rate

When ground conditions are sound, a TBM may be two or four times faster than drill and blast method[21]. However, the advance rate of a TBM depends not only the penetration of the cutterhead but also the other multiple factors, such as required rock support, changing cutters, machine repairs and the efficiency of the backup logistics for mucking and construction materials delivering. Any delay in these activities may have a strong influence on the performance of the TBM and the advance rate of the tunneling. Of the gripper TBM, the average time for boring is only about 30% the total excavation time. The time consumed in cutter changing or repairing and rock support occupies much part of the tunneling time. The improvement in the cutter repairing and rock support installing may propel the TBM advance in a specific project.

Expansion reading 11-18

In general, a small diameter TBM has a high advance rate in comparison to that of a large one. For example, using a 3.5 m diameter high performance TBM of Robbins, the 10 km transfer tunnel at Meraker Hydro Electric Power Project was bored six months ahead of schedule in Merkraft, Norway[14]. The surrounding rocks of this tunnel ranging from hard, massive meta-gabbro, with UCS of 300 MPa and greywacke and sandstone appeared as mixed face conditions to relatively soft phyllite. The features of the advance rate of the TBM are best shift (10 hrs.) 69.1 m, best day (two 10 hr. shift) 100.3 m, best week (100 shift hours) 426.8 m, best month (430 shift hours) 1358.0 m and average weekly advance rate 253.0 m, respectively.

In practice, the tunneling advance rate may much lower that of the penetration rate of the cutterhead. Various factors, including geotechnical risks and the activities, can solely or in a combination way have a strong influence on the tunneling advance rate. Barton[24] presented a synthesis of the general trends from 145 TBM tunneling projects to indicate the relationship between the tunneling advance rate and the cutterhead penetration rate. Where there is an unexpected events appearing, the actual tunneling advance rate can be much lower than that of expected or normal tunneling process. This feature is usually much significant in a tunneling process with large diameter TBM. There is a decreasing tendency of advance rate world records with increasing cutterhead diameter dimension. In general, the possibility of abrupt drop in productivity, in terms of TBM tunneling advance rates, increases with its cutterhead diameter dimension, especially the cutterhead diameter being over 7 m.

11.4.3.5 Thrust

Expansion reading 11-19

The thrust required by a TBM include the total forces of cutter loadings, friction forces caused by the body of the machine and the others. These thrust force are exerted axially, but transferred by clamping mechanism into the surrounding rocks or shield. In general, the thrust or force required by a TBM increases with the increasing magnitude of TBM diameter[17,20], as shown by the statistical results. In general, EPB TBMs have the highest installed cutterhead torque and TBM thrust, whereas the open TBMs have the lowest values for a given TBM diameter[20].

There are two types of clamping systems, i.e., single clamping system with the machine body sliding on one sliding shoe (e.g., Robbins and Herrenknecht); X-type gripping with the front and rear clamping grippers forming a unit with the main body (e.g., Jarva and Wirth).

In practice, the thrust of a applied TBM may be adjusted according to ground conditions. For example, to mitigate the effects of squeezing ground or collapses, custom-made gear reducers were installed and retrofitted to the cutterhead motors as a solution of increasing the TBM thrust capacity[28]. The gear reducers were installed between the drive motor and the primary two-stage planetary gearboxes. When the TBM boring in loose or squeezing ground the reducers are engaged, which results in a reduction in cutterhead speed but increased torque.

11.4.4 Tunnel supports

Expansion reading 11-20

Most ground support elements discussed in Chapter 8 can be specified with the use of hard rock TBMs, especially if the TBMs are manufactured specifically for the project. These support measures may include: ①rock reinforcement by roof bolting; ②spiling/forepoling for pre-supports; ③pre-injection or grouting; ④steel ribs or girders with or without lagging (wire mesh, timber, etc.); ⑤invert segment; ⑥shotcrete; ⑦precast concrete segmental lining. However, the implementation of supporting may mean decreasing the tunneling advance rate, especially where the supports should be installed at the machine area of an open TBM. In some cases, the working time in supporting takes about half of the construction time. One of the relevant effects of the lower tunneling advance rate is increasing tunnel cost[12].

11.4.4.1 Supports at the machine

In general, the implementation of supporting at the TBM has strong influence on the tunneling rate. However, where the ground conditions change from stable properties to that support should be applied in time, support installations at the machine are implemented. Nowadays, some additional equipment are also equipped, such as drilling facilities for investigation, grouting, rockbolts installation, steel sets and segment erectors.

The strength of shotcrete develops with time. So the supporting capacity of shotcrete is generally not fully counted on in the early age, such as in several hours. Shotcrete is not commonly used at the machine area as an immediate supporting measure. On the other hand, the rebounding of the concrete spraying has adverse influence on the TBM. Where the shotcrete is applied, the cutterhead should be retracted about 2 to 3 stroke length, such as the shotcrete application at the machine, in the Gossensass tunnel, Australia[12].

11.4.4.2 Supports in the backup area

The support applications in the backup area are generally same as the situation of conventional tunneling. The interfering effect of the supporting application in the

Expansion reading 11-21

backup area to the tunneling advance rate is generally acceptable. However, where there are more supports applications required, the longer of the backup system is needed.

The application of shotcrete is generally a separation of 30-60 m from the cutterhead[12]. This means the shotcrete should have high accelerator content. Same problem related to the application of shotcrete is also the rebounding and the dust in the working area.

11.4.4.3 Some innovated approaches in supporting systems

In the recent years, to control construction safety and to decrease excavation overbreak in difficult grounds, some innovated approaches have been applied to improve the supporting systems in TBM tunneling. Where a large diameter TBM is boring through a weak or broken zone, it is generally a tough and dangerous work to install the primary supporting system of the tunnel and to control the overbreak of the surrounding rocks. One of the main problems faced in tunneling is ground deterioration and the resulting falls of blocky ground. The majority of these events occurred just behind the tunnel face or just behind the cutterhead of the TBM, such as during the time taken for the newly excavated bore to pass behind the rear fingers of the roof shield, where steel sets and mesh are installed. On the other hand, under these situations, the rock support installation will require a very high ratio of the working time[28]. To improve these construction situations, some modifications were successfully made in TBM techniques to answer the practical challenges[29], such as through the improvements of pre-support and prospect, sealing system in a shield TBM and supporting system at excavation area.

For example, The McNally Support system, consisting of a curved assembly of pockets on the roof shield, are installed on the Robbins Main Beam, replacing the shield fingers on the TBM. With the McNally Support system applied, steel slats or meshes can be installed around the excavation face and the the required stand-up time of the excavation is therefore reduced[28].

Expansion reading 11-22

As the McNally support system holds loose rock in place, it is an effective measure to control working safety and excavation overbreak. The support installation in time and reduced overbreak in turn helps to mobilize the strength of the rock mass and maintain the inherent strength of the tunnel arch in the surrounding rocks. On the other hand, the McNally support system is also an effective measure to reduce the influence of surrounding rocks bursting events. As a result, the incorporation of the McNally support system and various other modifications to the TBM will be beneficial to a steady increase in tunneling rates[28]. Under the protection of the McNally support system, the other construction activities will also be safe and effective.

11.4.5 TBM steering

The steering is always required in TBM tunneling to lead the machine working as exactly as possible along the planned line or tunnel alignment. The various types of TBMs behave differently when they come to steering during tunneling[12].

11.4.5.1 Steering

TBM tunneling means full face boring and the planned tunnel alignment is made simultaneously as the machine moving ahead. One of the features of a TBM, together with its backup system, is long relative to their diameters and the machine tends to fit tightly onto the surrounding rocks. Under these situations, changing the direction of the excavation alignment is a matter of making the cutterhead cut sideways and getting the drive mechanism to follow.

TBMs generally excavate a tunnel of same cross section and the excavating head is not free to move sideways with respect to the main machine body. The excavation alignment direction can be changed either by exerting a sideways force on the rock cutting assembly or by tilting the cutting structure so that its axis is inclined to that of the existing tunnel[23].

For example, where an open TBM is applied, the body of the machine is held in the tunnel by one or more pairs of grippers, in addition to invert shoe. The vertical steering is realized with the invert shoe, which slides along the tunnel floor, to lift or lower the TBM. The side steering shoe, which is often linked to the invert shoe, can also serve to stabilize the TBM. It is a way to steer the movement of the TBM, through extension or withdrawal of the opposite side of the side steering shoe, in addition to the adjustment of the clamping unit. The side steering shoe is also called forward guide. The preferred method of steering consists of yawing the axis of the machine by displacing the main beam with respect to the rear gripper unit, and then the machine pivots about the forward gripped region. No sideways force is applied to the cutter head, so the machine axis is always tangential to the curve of the tunnel.

Expansion reading 11-23

To achieve a sharper turn, sideways force can be applied to the cutterhead by extending one of the forward side supports so that it bears against the tunnel wall[22]. In this way, the cutterhead is forced to cut sideways as well as forward. In this "crabbing" mode, the machine axis is no longer tangential to the curve, and care must be taken not to damage the machine by forcing it too hard into the side wall. Some TBMs are steerable by using a system of hydraulic jacks to tilt the cutterhead in the required direction.

For the TBM with special structures, such as the rotating shield tunnel machine, the steering of the driving is performed by the special structures for the relatively large rotation angle.

11.4.5.2　Guide

The precise position of a TBM is required to control and navigate the tunneling along the entire route, such as along the planned tunnel axis. This requires to determine the exact position and movement tendency of the TBM and display the data to all those involved in the project in real time. A tunneling navigation system is based either on tacheometry, laser or gyro technology. In general, a cost-effective navigation system is tailor-made to meet the specific requirements of each tunnel project, such as route geometry, diameter, machine type.

Expansion reading 11-24

In a laser theodolite-target system, the photo-sensory target unit is mounted in the shield or on the machine frame of the TBM and its position is accurately determined upon installation. A laser theodolite that is fixed to the tunnel wall continuously controls the position of the target unit and determines the position to the tunnel axis during the entire tunnelling process. The vertical position of the TBM is indicated by the data from the height sensor. For tunneling in curve section, the position of the TBM is determined by the data from the gyrocompass, fixed on the TBM.

11.5　Risks of TBM tunneling

The advantages of TBM tunneling are clear, such as higher advance rates, continuous operations, less surrounding rocks damage and support requirements, uniform muck characteristics and greater worker safety[8]. However, the disadvantages of TMB tunneling are also not to be sneezed at, such as fixed circular geometry, limited flexibility in response to the extremes of geologic conditions or changing grounds, longer mobilization time and higher capital cost. Risks associated with mechanized tunneling, for the choice of technique is often irreversible and it is often impossible to change from the technique first applied, or only at the cost of immense[2].

11.5.1　Risks in TBM tunneling

Hard rock TBMs can achieve remarkable advance rates only when overall conditions are favorable, otherwise, the TBM tunneling results may be less than what desired[24]. The foremost potential sources of geotechnical risk in rock tunnels include unexpected discoveries of, such as major fault zones, adversely oriented planar clay-coated joints, very weak rock, very hard massive rock, very abrasive rock, very low or high stress, high volumes of stored water and high permeability[25] in tunneling. In TBM tunneling, the main risks may be due to high rate of cutter wear, highly changing ground conditions, being blocked and so on. Where a TBM is blocked, long period of standstill of tunneling, the repair of the damage to the machine, measures of salvaging the machine and controlling the ground deformation are generally necessary. These results generally mean cost overrun and time schedule delay, which will be high burden to the project.

On the other hand, it is not the case that long tunnels are driven faster by one TBM than by drill and blast from both ends[24], as assumed by a general sense. Using Q-system based estimates of quality versus cycle time, and Q_{TBM} based prognoses for a similar size of TBM tunnel, Barton[21] presented a comparison of TBM prognosis and drill and blast prognosis results, as shown in Figure 11-7. Barton[24] stated that the case records likely show that it is the intermediate length tunnels that are faster by TBM; the TBM tunneling is much faster over short distances, with the proviso that rock mass qualities are not extreme, while as tunnel length increases, parts of the longer tunnels are more frequently outside the central rock quality region and need to maintain the obvious potential advantages of TBM.

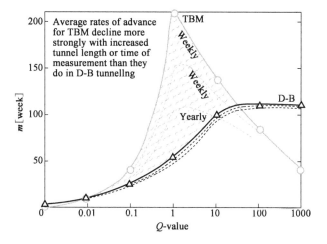

Figure 11-7 Comparing TBM and drill-and-blast over a full spectrum of rock classes[24]

In Figure 11-7, the rates of drill and blast tunneling change with the Q-values of the surrounding rocks. The rates of drill and blast tunneling frequently show average 40-60 m per week, though the world record is presently > 160 m/week on one face[24]. Where there is no significant rock support needed due to consistently high Q-values, the rates of drill and blast tunneling seems a maximum value, which is mainly determined by the cycle of drill and blast. Under these situations, such as where the surrounding rocks are so hard that the productivity of the cutterhead will decrease significantly with the increase of the Q-values of the surrounding rocks, the advantages of drill and blast tunneling can generally maintain in a wide range of the high Q-values. One of the reasons is that the parameters of drilling and blasting can be readily adjusted to the specific surrounding rocks features, while it is almost impossible to change the cutterhead and cutters of the TBM to favorable ones, respectively, in hard rock tunneling.

11.5.2　Risk control measures in TBM tunneling

The sources of the risk related to TBM tunneling are various. There is no simple measure to deal with this complicated situation. In a common sense, the main difficulty is to predict geotechnical risk due to the unexpected combination of adverse factors in an effective way. And therefore, the application of pre-face prospect, such as use of probe drilling and seismic logging ahead of the face can be a very powerful method for reducing TBM tunneling risk[25] through lower the chance of unpredictable 'unexpected events', together with efficient drainage and pre-injection ahead of the tunnel face. On the other hand, the importance of TBM tunneling method choosing is also vital to the risk control of a tunnel project. For example, double-shield TBMs, with robust elements that give the possibility of continued thrust while re-setting grippers, have good flexibility to variable rock conditions. It is also a way to reduce tunneling risk through the hybrid solution of using TBM and drill and blast method in a long deep tunnel project[26,27]. In the recent practice, some effective approaches have been innovated in the TBM tunneling risk control, such as through the modifications in TBM techniques to answer the practical challenges[29] in safety and overbreak control, such as by proper pre-support and prospect, sealing system in a shield TBM and well designed supporting system at excavation area, as discussed in Section 11.4.4.

11.6　Critical thinking problems

C1：There are several well used TBM classification systems, such as the classification scheme by ITA and AFTES. What are the key features or indexes of these schemes?

C2：Where a TBM is planned in a rock tunnel project, the features of TBM tunneling should be considered in a comprehensive mode, such as in terms of advantages and disadvantages. What are the main advantages and disadvantages as a TBM being applied in tunneling, respectively? Can the advantages and disadvantages be clearly pre-defined during the design process of the tunnel project?

C3：It is generally right to declare that there is always risks in TBM tunneling. What are the main reasons or situations of TBM tunneling risks and what are the commonly used measures to cope with these situations, respectively? Are the dominate reasons unique or project-specific for a planned tunnel?

C4: There is a tendency of the increasing applications of mechanical tunneling in the world, especially with the social and economic developments in a nation. Requirements make progress in mechanical tunneling. Various innovations have been made in tunneling machines in the recent years. What are the main achievements of mechanical tunneling method in the recent years, such as in terms of full face and partial face method?

11.7 References

[1] ITA WG Mechanized Tunnelling. Recommendations and Guidelines for Tunnel Boring Machines (TBMs)[M]. ITA-AITES, 2000.

[2] AFTES. 2005. New Recommendations on Choosing Mechanized Tunnelling Techniques [J]. TUNNELS ET OUVRAGES SOUTERRAINS, 2005, HORS-SERIE N° 1: 137-163.

[3] Koyama Y. Present status and technology of shield tunneling method in Japan [J]. Tunnelling & Underground Space Technology Incorporating Trenchless Technology Research, 2003, 18(2-3): 145-159.

[4] Chow B. Double-O-tube shield tunneling technology in the Shanghai Rail Transit Project [J]. Tunnelling & Underground Space Technology Incorporating Trenchless Technology Research, 2006, 21(6): 594-601.

[5] Fang Y S, Kao C C, Shiu Y F. Double-O-Tube shield tunneling for Taoyuan International Airport Access MRT [J]. Tunnelling & Underground Space Technology Incorporating Trenchless Technology Research, 2012,[30(4)]:233-245.

[6] Moria K, Abe Y. Large rectangular cross-section tunneling by the multi-micro shield tunneling (MMST) method[J]. Tunnelling and Underground Space Technology,2005,20 (2):129-141.

[7] DAUB. 1997. Recommendations for selecting and evaluating tunnel boring machines[J]. Tunnel 5/97, 20-35.

[8] U. S. Army Corps of Engineers Manual[J]. Design of Tunnels and Shafts in Rock,1991, 1110-2-2901.

[9] Bilgin N, Dincer T, Copur H, et al. Some geological and geotechnical factors affecting the performance of a roadheader in an inclined tunnel[J]. Tunnelling and Underground Space Technology,2004,19,629-636.

[10] Rostami J, Ozdemir L, Neil D M. 1994. Performance prediction: a key issue in mechanical hard rock mining[J]. Mining Engineering, November, 1263-1267.

[11] FHWA. Technical Manual for Design and Construction of Road Tunnels-Civil Elements [M].2009.

[12] Maidl B, Schmid L, Ritz W, et al. [M]. Hardrock Tunnel Boring Machines, Ernst & Sohn, a Wiley company, Berlin, 2008.

[13] Robbins R J. Economic factors in tunnel boring. Proc. fo South African Tunneling

Conference, Johannesburg, 1970.

[14] Norwegian Tunnelling Society. 2002. Drill and Blast. Norwegian Tunnelling Society Publication No. 14, Introduction to Norwegian Tuunnelling, 39-41.

[15] Macias F J, Jakobsen P D, Seo Y, et al[J]. Influence of rock mass fracturing on the net penetration rates of hard rock TBMs. Tunnelling and Underground Space Technology. 2014,44: 108-120.

[16] Gong Q M, Zhao J. Development of a rock mass characteristics model for TBM penetration rate prediction[J]. International Journal of Rock Mechanics & Mining Sciences,2009,46: 8-18.

[17] Farrokh E, Rostami J, Laughton C. Study of various models for estimation of penetration rate of hard rock TBMs[J]. Tunnelling and Underground Space Technology,2012,30: 110-123.

[18] Frenzel Ch, Käsling H, Thuro K. Factors influencing disc cutter wear. [J] Geomech. Tunnel,2008,1:55-60.

[19] Hassanpour J, Rostami J, Zhao J. A new hard rock TBM performance prediction model for project planning. [J] Tunnelling and Underground Space Technology,2011,26: 595-603.

[20] Ates U, Bilgin N, Copur H[J]. Estimating torque, thrust and other design parameters of different type TBMs with some criticism to TBMs used in Turkish tunneling projects. Tunnelling & Underground Space Technology,2014(40):46-63.

[21] Barton N. 1999. TBM performance estimation in rock using Q_{TBM}. Tunnels and Tunnelling International 31, 30-34.

[22] Robbins Co. 1993. Operating instructions for model 167-266/267 TBM: Robbins Co. Kent, Wash. ,p. 2.21-2.40.

[23] Karlsson H, Cobbley R, Jaques G E. New developments in short-, medium-, and long-radius lateral drilling[C] // SPE 18706, SPE/IADC Drilling conference, New Orleans, La. , Feb. 28-Mar. 3, Richardson, Tex. , SPE, p. 725-736.

[24] Barton N. 2009. TBM prognoses in hard rock with faults using QTBM methods[C] // Keynote lecture, Inst. of Min. Metall. International Tunnelling Conf. ,Hong Kong.

[25] Barton N. 2004. Risk and risk reduction in TBM rock tunnelling[C] // Keynote lecture, ARMS 2004 : 3rd Asian Rock Mechanics Symposium,Kyoto.

[26] Barton N. TBM prognoses for open-gripper and double-shield machines: challenges and solutions for weakness zones and water [C] // Fjellsprengningsteknikk-Bergmekanikk-Geoteknikk, 2013.

[27] Nick, Barton. Reducing risk in long deep tunnels by using TBM and drill-and: blast methods in the same project-the hybrid solution[J]. Journal of Rock Mechanics and Geotechnical Engineering, 2012, 04(2): 115-126.

[28] Clark J, Chorley S. Clark, J. & Chorley, S. 2014. The greatest challenges in TBM tunneling: Experiences from the field[C] // The North American Tunneling Conference, 2014.

[29] Home L. Hard rock TBM tunneling in challenging ground: Developments and lessons learned from the field [J]. Tunnelling & Underground Space Technology Incorporating Trenchless Technology Research, 2016, 57:27-32.

12 Shield Tunneling in Soft Ground

12.1 Introduction

Expansion reading 12-1

Expansion reading 12-2

As TBM tunneling in soft ground is planned, there are two problems should be dealt with first. One is to keep the excavations stable and the other is to support the TBM in an effective way. This situation means the chosen TBM should provide immediate peripheral and frontal support simultaneously. In general, the peripheral support is provided by the shield of a TBM. The measures of providing frontal support may through: ①mechanical support; ②compressed air application; ③fluid support; ④ earth pressure balance (EPB); ⑤ the combination of the above measures. Mainly based on the mode of face supporting measures, the types of the shield TBMs for soft ground are accordingly classified as: open shield, mechanically support shield, compressed air shield, slurry shield, EPB shield and mixshield. A similar classification system was recommended by the DAUB[1].

12.1.1 Features of shield TBMs

Expansion reading 12-3

There is general rule that larger span TBM tunnels are mainly built in urban areas. This is mainly attributed to the facts of large traffic volume and sometimes multiple utilizations (traffic modes) of the tunnels, such as for both road and railway or metro transportations. The features of urban tunnels, such as shallow and the short stand-up time of surrounding rocks, generally prefer a shield TBM to an open TBM. In practice, most of the mega TBMs are produced for urban tunnels. There is an increasing tendency of the diameter of shield TBMs to meet the market requirements in the recent 20 years, as shown by the increasing trend of the maximum diameters of the Herrenknecht TBMs with time (Figure 12-1).

As the diameters of shield TBMs is increasing, the total weight of a TBM, including backup system, is nearly proportionally increased[2] (Figure 12-2).

12.1.2 Choosing of a shield TBM

The choosing of a shield TBM for a planned tunnel is mainly controlled by the ground conditions and the diameter of the tunnel. Two main types of shield TBMs are commonly used in soft ground, i.e., slurry TBM and an EPB TBM. Both types operate with a sealed front compartment, which is kept under sufficient pressure to stabilize the face and minimize ground movement. In general, EPB shield TBM is first choice, provided that the requirements can be matched. Otherwise, adaptable dual purpose shield machines may be chosen for complicated ground conditions. For example, for soil tunnels, the feature of the grain size distributions of the soils are one of the decisive factors in selecting the type of shield TBM to be applied.

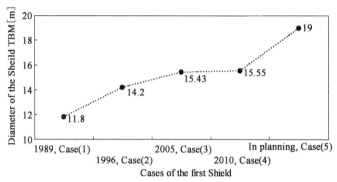

Figure 12-1 Increasing trend of the maximum diameters of the Herrenknecht TBMs with time

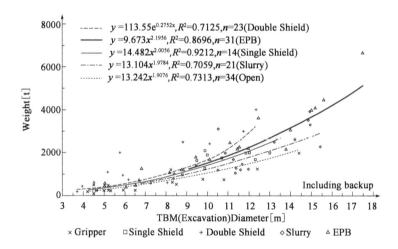

Figure 12-2 Relationships between TBM diameter and total TBM weight[2]

In general, the main geotechnical factors to be considered in shield TBM choosing for soft ground tunneling include the grain size distribution (Figure 12-3), shear strength and permeability of the soils. For example, an EPB shield can be used for the fine grain soils with permeability coefficient less than 10^{-7} m/s, while a slurry shield should be chosen for the ground with permeability coefficient more than 10^{-4} m/s.

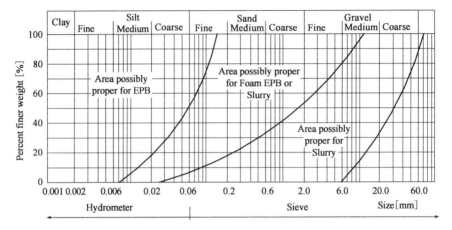

Figure 12-3 Selection of shield TBM based on soil grain size distribution

Where a tunnel is planned to pass through strongly varying subsoil conditions, tunneling methods have to be geared to the geotechnical prerequisites and shield machines, which are correspondingly adaptable[1]. For shield TBMs choosing, two situations may be under considerations: ①the case, of which the extraction method can be changed through mode change between earth pressure balance shield and compressed air shield, or between fluid shield and compressed air shield; ②another case, of which the extraction method can be changed through the combinations of, such as fluid shield + shield without support, fluid shield + EPB shield, EPB shield + shield without support and fluid shield + shield without support.

12.2 System of soft ground tunneling shield TBMs

12.2.1 Slurry shield TBMs

The slurry shield TBMs are of these machines with the face being supported by a fluid that is under pressure. Depending on the permeability of the soils, effective fluids must be used for supporting, such as in terms of the density and/or viscosity of the slurry. Bentonite suspension is often particularly effective. The working chamber is closed to the tunnel by a bulkhead. The pressure needed for supporting the face can be precisely regulated either by means of an air cushion or by controlling the speed of the delivery and feed pumps.

Figure 12-4 is a sketch of a mixshield used in Nanjing Yangtze River tunnel[4]. The pressure cabin of slurry shield TBM is divided into two chambers by submerged wall, and the chambers are connected by a gap designed at the bottom of submerged wall. During the advancement of the slurry shield TBM, the excavation chamber is filled with slurries (typical bentonite suspensions), meanwhile compressed air is pumped into the air cushion. And then the air pressure transferred into support pressure by the connected slurries, which is used for balancing the groundwater pressure and lateral earth pressure in the excavation face. In addition, the inspection and maintenance of cutters would be performed via a manlock or an airlock designed in the chambers. In general, the connection valves on the submerged wall could be opened before technicists accessed into excavation chamber, and the compressed air has been pumped into the slurry chamber. Meanwhile, the slurry level is lowered and more operations could be performed in the excavation chamber.

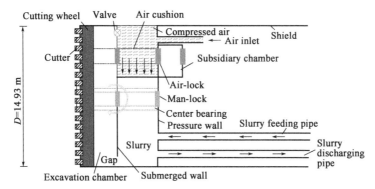

Figure 12-4 Sketch of the mixshield applied in Nanjing Yangtze River tunnel[4]

The cutterhead of the slurry shield TBM used in the Nanjing Weisan road Yangtze River tunnel is shown in Figure 12-4. The cutting wheel is faceplate disc and center supported, with 26% opening ratio.

The stabilizing effect of the slurry at a shield TBM face is sketched in Figure 12-5. Due to the excess pressure ΔP the so called filtercake is formed on the face surface as a membrane, which prevents the infiltration of the slurry into the ground. The formation of the filtercake requires the presence of sufficient fines in the ground and, depending on the applied excess pressure ΔP, a critical limit of the permeability of the soils.

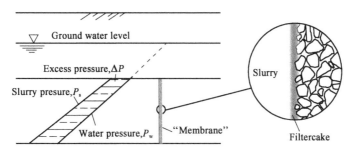

Figure 12-5 Sketch showing the stabilizing effect of slurry[5]

The supporting effect of the slurry is strongly different under various ground infiltration properties. If the slurry is allowed to infiltrate into the ground its supporting effect rapidly diminishes with increasing distance. For a given set of parameters, if the penetration of the slurry reaches half of the tunnel diameter, D, the value of the supporting force, S, falls to approximately 40 % of its initial value $S_0^{[5]}$. Appropriate conditioning of the suspension and reduction of excess pressure may prevent breaking through the filtercake or considerably reduce the infiltration of the slurry into the ground. The sudden loss of slurry may occur due to an unexpected high permeability of the ground, resulting in a drop in the excess pressure in the chamber.

In tunneling, the soil is removed full-face by means of a cutterhead equipped with tools. Stones or banks of rock can be reduced to a size convenient for conveyance through discs on the cutting wheel and/or stone crushers in the working chamber. Hydraulic conveyance with subsequent separation is essential in mucking.

If it is necessary to enter the working chamber, such as for tools change, repair work and removing obstacles, the fluid must be replaced by compressed air. The supporting fluid (e. g., bentonite or polymer) then forms a slightly air-permeable membrane at the face, whose life span is restricted. This membrane facilitates the supporting of the face through compressed air and should be renewed if need being[5].

When the shield TBM is at a standstill, mechanical supporting of the face is possible by means of segments, which can be shut, in the cutting wheel or through plates that can be extended from the rear.

12.2.2 EPB shield TBMs

EPB shield TBMs are specially designed for operation in soft grounds with high water content. For soft, cohesive soils, EPB shield TBM is a preferred option, such as the soils with high clay and silt contents and low water permeability.

Expansion reading 12-4

EPB shield TBMs turn the excavated material into a soil paste that is used as pliable, plastic support medium, which is possible to balance the pressure conditions at the tunnel face, to avoid uncontrolled inflow of soil into the machine and to create the conditions for rapid tunneling with minimum ground settlement. For example, Robbins EPB TBMs have an articulated shield that is sealed against the pressure of water inflows up to 1.0 MPa and control the stability of the tunnel face and subsidence of the ground surface by monitoring and adjusting the pressure inside the cutterhead chamber to achieve a balance with the pressure in front of the cutterhead, to realize "Earth Pressure Balance".

The special feature of EPB shield TBMs is using the excavated soil directly as support medium. A rotating cutting wheel equipped with tools is pressed onto the tunnel face and excavates the soils. The muck enters the excavation chamber through openings, where it mixes with the soil paste already there. Mixing arms on the cutting wheel and bulkhead mix the paste until it has the required texture. The bulkhead transfers the pressure of the thrust cylinders to the pliable soil paste. When the pressure of the soil paste in the excavation chamber equals the pressure of the surrounding soil and groundwater, the necessary balance has been achieved.

The screw conveyor for the discharge of the excavated material is the tunneling feature of EPB shield TBMs. A screw conveyor or auger conveyor is the mechanism that uses a rotating helical screw blade, usually within a tube, to move liquid or granular materials. The rotating part of the conveyor is sometimes called simply an auger. The screw conveyor's speed and discharge rate is controlled by the operator and is utilized for controlling the pressure at the working face and match the muck discharge rate to the advance rate of the EPB shield TBM as shown in Figure 12-6. The articulated joint between the forward shield and tail shield is equipped with a high pressure seal that allows angular movement between the shields and prevents water from seeping into the interior of the TBM.

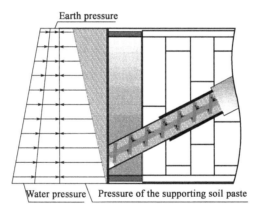

Figure 12-6 Sketch showing the balance between the TBM advance rate and screw conveyor speed through regulating the support pressure at the tunnel face

EPB shield TBMs erect the segmented tunnel lining sequentially after each push round. Specially designed high pressure seals in the tail shield effectively seal the machine to the outside of the tunnel lining and create a barrier against ground pressure.

Similar to slurry shield TBMs, when it becomes necessary to enter the cutterhead chamber to inspect the cutterhead or change cutting tools, the workers can safely enter the chamber through a manlock while compressed air is used for maintaining earth pressure balance to support the working face.

EPB shield TBMs can be steered through incredibly small turn radii by employing the articulation joint and the copy cutter mounted in the cutterhead. The amount of copy cutter extension and the articulation angle required for a tunnel should be specifically designed during the TBM choosing.

During EPB shield TBM tunneling, the frequently used countermeasures against the seepage of water into the working face may consist of the conditioning of soil both in the working chamber and in the screw conveyor, and/or of the installation of a thick matter pump at the end of the screw conveyor.

12.2.3 Mixshields

Expansion reading 12-5

Mixshields are developed for safe and efficient tunneling in heterogenous ground. The mixshield technology is generally developed from the conventional slurry technology. Here the main features of the mixshields produced by Herrenknecht are presented as example.

Thanks to the tunnel face support by an automatically controlled air cushion, sudden pressure and volume fluctuations can be balanced precisely. This ensures the maximum tunneling safety and minimum influence on the neighbors, such as in terms of heave and settlement. Since the support pressure in the excavation chamber can be precisely managed using an automatically controlled air cushion, the heterogeneous geologies and high water pressures of more than 1.5 MPa can be controlled safely even with very large excavation diameters.

A characteristic feature of Mixshields is an excavation chamber divided by a submerged wall. During excavation, the front section of the excavation chamber is completely filled with suspension for full tunnel face support during tunneling. In the rear section between submerged wall and bulkhead (working chamber) the suspension reaches up to only just above the machine axis. The counter-pressure needed at the tunnel face is supplied using a compressible air cushion in the upper section (Figure 12-4). Communication between the two chambers takes place through a submerged wall opening in the invert section.

In typical Mixshield tunneling operations in incohesive, heterogeneous soils, larger stones or blocks must be considered. Such boulders need to be crushed to a conveyable size so that hydraulic removal can be carried out smoothly. Mixshields often use a jaw crusher for this purpose, which is positioned in front of the intake screen. The size of the crushable stones varies according to the design of the crusher and the shield diameter. The intake screen is installed in front of the suction port of the slurry line to protect the machine against grain sizes that might cause problems. It holds up boulders until the crusher has crushed them sufficiently. If there are fine-grained, cohesive soils along the alignment, drum crushers are installed in front of the intake as an alternative. They carry out the intake screen function during the crushing process. Two lateral agitators support the flow of material in the invert.

Nowadays, for Herrenknecht mixshields, the maintenance of excavation tools is also optimized in structures. During mixshield tunneling, a filter cake forms at the interface between ground and bentonite suspension. This almost impermeable membrane enables the necessary support pressure and makes it possible to seal the tunnel face against streaming groundwater at the same time. During the tunneling process, the cutting wheel, excavation tools and a number of other components must be controlled, maintained or cleaned and obstructions must be removed. For this purpose, the suspension in the working and excavation chambers is partly lowered by introducing compressed air. By closing the submerged wall opening, the suspension in the working chamber can be lowered to a minimum, allowing work in the invert section. The maintenance personnel enter the pressurized chamber through an air lock. With chamber pressures of more than 3.6 bar (0.36 MPa), work under compressed air conditions is preferably carried out by professional divers, who haven be pre-trained or qualified, to keep work periods in the tunnel shorter.

On the other hand, accessible cutting wheel arms in nowadays Herrenknecht mixshield make it easier to replace excavation tools at site in large-diameter machines. Time-intensive hyperbaric interventions for the maintenance of excavation tools with large machine diameters have become obsolete due to a special development from Herrenknecht. The main arms of the cutting wheel are built in such a way that they can be accessed under atmospheric conditions. The worn excavation tools can be replaced from inside the cutting wheel without reducing the suspension level and without longer interventions in tunneling.

12.2.4 Backup system

In general, the backup system of a shield TBM is more complicated than an open TBM, since the segments of the lining system of the tunnel should be erected at the machine tail in time.

Expansion reading 12-6

The just-in-time supply of segments is an important prerequisite for non-stopshield tunneling operations. The formwork experts should calculate production cycles, develop optimum production concepts and set up a reliable logistics system[3]. In general, the segment production plants, which have a project-specific layout, are executed at a place out of the tunnel. The shield TBM formwork delivers and installs all the associated resources and equipment. At the same time, the facilities for applying seals and the surface finish to the segments also must be taken into account. It is general right with spare parts management, including professional storage, maintenance and repairs, to avoid production downtime and thus unnecessary costs.

Expansion reading 12-7

On the other hand, mucking is another important aspect of the backup system, such as conveyor and belt for mucking. Some of the equipments, such as trailers or mucking car produced by China Railway Engineering Equipment Group (CREC) Tunneling Equipment Manufacturing Co. LTD.

12.3 Tunnel segment lining

Segmental ring liners are often used in shield tunnels. The liners, used to be of cast iron, today are usually precast concrete. The segments of the lining should be first transferred to the TBM in the tunnel and then to the installation site and positioned correctly. The segments are generally transported to tunnel site by mine cars, unloaded by hoists mounted on the conveyor carriage, and deposited within reach of the erector arm. To ensure that these steps run smoothly, the handling devices used for demoulding and turning the segments, for attaching the seal and for storage both indoors and outdoors, are specifically designed in a shield TBM. For example, the erector arm is a telescoping, counterweighted arm pivoted on the center line of the tunnel for full rotation by a hydraulic motor. On the other hand, the shield TBM is usually moved forward using jacks pushing on the erected concrete lining.

12.3.1 Types of segments

The details of segments are selected to meet functional requirements, and for the practicality and economy of construction. For super long tunnels, placing a one-pass segmental lining is a practical solution, provided that lining erection does not significantly slow the advance of the shield TBM tunneling. Where the tunnel built below the groundwater table, the segments are bolted with gaskets for water tightness. Above the groundwater table, unbolted, expanded segmental linings are often used. If necessary, the segmental lining may be followed by a cast-in-place concrete lining and a water-or gas proofing membrane is placed before the cast-in-place concrete is placed, as in two-pass lining system.

Joint details are reinforced to resist chipping and spalling due to erection impact and the effect of uneven jacking on imprecisely placed segments. Tongue and groove joints (Figure 12-7) are particularly susceptible to spalling and the edges of the groove may require reinforcement.

A watertight lining is obtained by the applications of gaskets between neighbor segments. Fully gasketed and bolted linings may be used through the high groundwater ground zones. It should be considered that, since a gasketed and bolted segmental lining must be fabricated with great precision, such a lining is usually expensive to manufacture and to erection. In high groundwater grounds, it may be necessary to perform formation grouting to reduce water flows and sealing strips or caulking are employed in the segmental lining to retain grout filling.

12.3.2 Segments erection

The installation of the precast ring support is conducted by the the shield TBM erector system, which is a special crane that allows the installation of the complete ring during excavation. The erector is positioned just after the tail shield. With a full shield tail, the invert segment is placed on the shield surface at the bottom. When the shield passes, the invert segment falls to the bottom, unless it is bolted to the previous segment. The erector equipment must match the pick-up holes in the segments, be able to rotate the segment into its proper position, and have all of the motions (e. g., radial, tangential, axial, tilt) to place the segment with the tolerances required. Relatively high speed motion is required to bring a segment to its approximate location, but inching speed is for precise positioning. Unless each segment is stable as placed, holding devices are required to prevent them from falling out until the last segment (key stone) is in place(Figure 12-7).

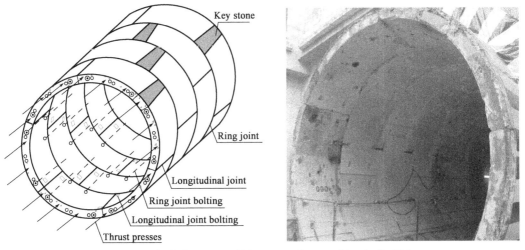

a) Block segment with keystone and staggered longitudinal joints

Figure 12-7

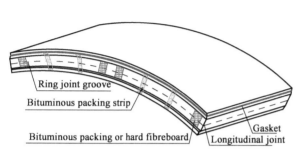

b) Segment equipment in the ring joint as tongue and groove system

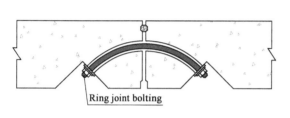
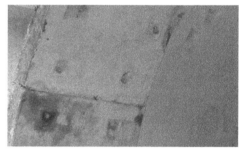

c) Flat ring joint

Figure 12-7　Structures of segments for shield tunnel

12.3.3　Packing

Expansion reading 12-8

Since the shield has a larger diameter than that of the lining, a void exists around the liner rings. This may cause a cave-in and ground settlement. The usual practice, where segmental liners are used, is to inject pea gravel into this void through grout holes in the liners immediately after the shield has been advanced. Just after the segment installation, the gap between the segment and the surrounding rocks is filled up with pea gravel using a pump installed on the backup system. Cement grout is later injected into the gravel to solidify it.

12.4　Ground displacements

The above shield TBM tunneling procedure shows that when the shield passing through ground, there is a space left between the ground and the shield lining rings. And therefore, unavoidable deformations will appear in the surrounding ground. Also, the disturbance of the excavation will induce a change in the state of stress in the ground, as well as displacements or deformations. In general, the settlements around the crown area are of the most significance. If these quantities become excessive, they may damage adjacent and overlaying facilities. These excessive damage or influence on nearby buildings, streets and utilities may be unacceptable or dangerous. To reduce or control the impact of such ground displacements, it becomes necessary to evaluate the displacements before tunneling, such as during design.

During shield TBM tunneling, there are two basic components of ground deformations[6]: ①immediate settlements, which are presented right after the pass of TBM and are a function of the tunnel face stability, the velocity of advance, the time necessary of lining installation and the time necessary to fill the tail-void; ②long-term settlements, due to the primary consolidation and secondary consolidation of the ground. The immediate settlement along the tunnel axis begins at a small distance ahead of the tunnel face and stops when the grout injection of the tail void has hardened enough to counteract any further radial displacement.

About the settlement of the greenland due to shallow tunnel driving, Peck[7] established that the transverse settlement trough caused by a tunnel can be described by a Gaussian error function (a bell shape), as shown in Equation (12-1). In simplicity, it is considered that the behavior of soft soils is undrained and the volume of surface settlement is equal to the excavated soil volume in excess to the theoretical volume of the tunnel, usually known as volume loss.

$$S_{(s,y)} = S_{max,s} \cdot e^{-\frac{y^2}{2i_s^2}} \quad (12\text{-}1)$$

where $S_{(s,y)}$ is the surface settlement at offset distance y from the tunnel center line, $S_{max,s}$ is the maximum surface settlement above the tunnel center line, and i_s is the distance from the inflection point of the trough to the tunnel center line. The parameter is commonly used for representing the width of the surface settlement trough.

Cording and Hansmire[8] reported that the maximum subsurface settlement was greater than the maximum surface-settlement, and the width of the subsurface settlement trough was narrower. As a result, the subsurface utilities above the tunnel probably would experience a larger angular distortion than surface facilities. This is the main reason why the magnitude and extent of subsurface settlement should be carefully investigated by the design engineer[9].

Mair et al.[10] suggested that the subsurface settlement due to shield tunneling could also be described with the normal probability curve, and the subsurface settlement trough at the depth, z, is approximated as follows:

$$S_{(z,y)} = S_{max,z} \cdot e^{-\frac{y^2}{2i_z^2}} \quad (12\text{-}2)$$

where $S_{(z,y)}$ is the subsurface settlement at offset distance y from the tunnel center line, $S_{max,z}$ is the maximum subsurface settlement above the tunnel center line at the depth of z, and i_z is the distance from the inflection point of the trough to the tunnel center line.

Expansion reading 12-9

Field measurements indicate that the width of the subsurface settlement trough decreases with increasing depth, and the subsurface maximum settlement increases with increasing depth[9]. Fang et al.[9] proposed a simple empirical method based on the normal distribution function and the subsurface to surface $S_{max,z}/S_{max,s}$ and i_z/i_s relationships to estimate the subsurface ground movement.

12.5 Risks of shield tunneling in urban areas

12.5.1 Risk related to shield tunneling in urban area

The main risks of shield TBM tunneling in urban area are related to the project situations, such as shallow overburden, relatively large tunnel diameter, soft ground, potential disturbance to the neighbor structures, probably unpredicted foreign objects in ground, as well as alignment and other constraints regarding material transport and TBM access.

Ground behavior is one of the most important features in urban tunneling, since stability and deformations due to tunneling may cause severe disturbance to the neighbor structures. Urban soft grounds, which are often of the features of soft soils, with frequently changing compositions and high water content, may have a significant influence on the nature of project risk. For example, where the ground is composed of filling, recent sediments, such as gravel, sand and clay, overlying on bedrocks, there are high chances of rock boulders in the soft layers. The relief of the top of the bedrocks are always rugged or of changing properties. The disturbance to the groundwater and pollution due to tunneling are generally required to be strictly controlled in urban area. A water table situated above the tunnel or crossing the tunnel profile requires particular attention, since significant disturbance to the groundwater level may cause serious environment problem and damage to neighbor structures.

The presence of hidden foreign objects in the ground is also one of the specific features of urban tunneling. These structures seem frequently including historical wells, ground anchors, sheet-piles, abandoned utilities, such as for gas and sewage, as well as tree trunks, artificial fillings, etc. In practice, a relatively small piece of hidden foreign object may cause serious damage to the machine and delay to the project schedule. For example, the failure of the $\phi = 17.48$m Hitachi Zosen EPB shield TBM Bertha's main bearing seal system❶, possibly due to the buried steel

---

❶ Kenyon, P. STP management changes enable Bertha restart 23 Feb 2016. http://tunneltalk.com/Seattle-SR99-Alaskan-Way-15Mar2016-TBM-Bertha-reaches-Safe-Haven-3.php.

pipe casing or a large boulder, caused the TBM to shut down on December 6, 2013. The damage to the TBM bertha caused about two years delay of the 2.6 km double-deck highway tunnel in Seattle.

In general, the neighbor structures and facilities, ground activities and environments are much sensitive to the disturbance due soft ground tunneling in urban area. The tunneling is always the focus of publics. Any accident or risk due to tunneling may be linked to a political affair.

12.5.2 Counter measures

One of the measures to reduce the risk related to shield TBM tunneling is to execute an appropriate planning and geotechnical exploration. This is also related to shield TBM choosing. Choosing a proper or robust shield TBM is key step for shield tunneling. For example, in recent years, mixshield TBMs seem a safe tunneling technology for heterogeneous ground. Also in construction planning, these factors are often under consideration, such as: ①ground conditions; ② the features of the planned tunnel project and shield TBM to be applied; ③construction environments; ④ the prediction of ground displacements and measures to control ground behavior.

It is almost always right that there is uncertainty in tunnel design. To control the risk of the shield TBM tunneling to a acceptable level, a systematic monitoring of ground deformations, the behavior of the neighbor structures, the groundwater table and the machine performance should be an integral part of any safety plan. The application of the observation method is always necessary for a shield tunneling project in urban area.

In practice, the risk control in shield TBM tunneling in soft ground may be realized through these constructional measures[5]: ① ground improvement; ② prepared stations for TBM; ③grouting for block stabilization; ④special structures.

Expansion reading 12-10

For the shield TBM tunneling in a densely urbanized area, especially under difficult geotechnical conditions, it is generally inevitable to stop the TBM for maintenance purposes. Prepared stations for TBM at predetermined locations and in good time can provide safe conditions even without pressurized air for rapid maintenance work in the chamber and avoid a time delay in construction[5].

12.6 Critical thinking problems

C1: As a shield TBM is planned for the tunneling in soft grounds, choosing a proper machine is always first under consideration. Consider: ①What are the main factors to be considered in this work? ②Commonly used types of shield TBMs for the tunneling in soft grounds and their main features; ③ Ground conditions for the applications of slurry shield TBMs and EPB shield TBMs, respectively.

C2: During a mixshield TBM tunneling in soft grounds, the system of the shield TBM will work in a planned mode, which is changing with the variation of the ground conditions. Consider: ①How will the face support mode alter from slurry shield mode to EPB shield mode, and vice versa, respectively? ②The operation of maintaining the cutterhead.

C3: Precast concrete segmental lining is often applied in shield TBM tunnels. Consider: ①Features of the structures of precast concrete segmental lining, such as in terms of structures of a segment, connection structures between neighbor segments; ②Waterproof measures of a concrete segmental lining; ③Operation of the erection of a segment ring in shield TBM tunneling.

C4: Where a shield TBM is applied in urban area, risks due to the tunneling is often key factor under consideration in both the design and construction planning of the project. Consider: ①Why is this situation always necessary? ②Where a shallow shield TBM tunneling under the greenland in urban area, what are the general features of the ground settlement? ③What are the commonly used measures to control the risks related to shield TBM tunneling in soft grounds in urban area?

12.7 References

[1] DAUB. Recommendations for selecting and evaluating tunnel boring machines[J]. Tunnel, 1997, 5: 20-35.

[2] Ates U, Bilgin N, Copur H. Estimating torque, thrust and other design parameters of different type TBMs with some criticism to TBMs used in Turkish tunneling projects[J]. Tunnelling and Underground Space Technology, 2014, 40(2): 46-63.

[3] Maidl B, Schmid L, Ritz W, et al. Hardrock Tunnel Boring Machines[M]. Berlin: Ernst & Sohn, a Wiley company, 2008.

[4] Min F, Zhu W, Lin C, et al. Opening the excavation chamber of the large-diameter size slurry shield: A case study in Nanjing Yangtze River Tunnel in China [J]. Tunnelling & Underground Space Technology, 2015, 46:18-27.

[5] Kovári K, Ramoni M. Urban tunnelling in soft ground using TBM's[C] // International Congress on Mechanized Tunnelling: Challenging Case Histories, 2004.

[6] Guglielmetti V, Grasso P, Mahtab A, et al. Mechanised Tunnelling in urban areas[J]. Tunnels & Tunnelling International, 2007, 12:21-23.

[7] Peck R B. Deep Excavations and Tunneling in Soft Ground-State-of-the-art reports[C] // The 7th International Conference on Soil Mechanics and Foundation Engineering, Mexico, 1969.

[8] Cording E J, Hansmire W H. Displacements around soft ground tunnels-general report[C] // The 6th Pan-American Conference of Soil Mechanics and Foundation Engineering, Buenos Aires, 1975.

[9] Fang Y S, Wu C T, Chen S F, et al. An estimation of subsurface settlement due to shield tunneling [J]. Tunnelling & Underground Space Technology Incorporating Trenchless

Technology Research, 2014, 44(44):121-129.

[10] Mair R J. Subsurface settlement profiles above tunnels in clays[J]. Geotechnique, 1995, 43(2):361-362.

13 Cut and Cover Tunnels

13.1 Introduction

Expansion reading 13-1

When cut and cover method is applied in tunneling, the structures of the planned tunnel are generally built inside an excavation or trench and covered over with backfill materials at the completion the structures. Cut and cover method is used where the tunnel is shallow or where it is advantageous to construct the tunnel at a shallow depth[1] and where the excavation from the surface is possible, economical and acceptable. Nowadays, this method is well used for metro stations, underpasses to overcome urban constraints, such as existing roads, railways and other structures, or to overcome environmental constraints; the approach sections to mined tunnels and immersed tunnels. In the recent years, some tunnels have been built mainly due to the features of being environment favorable. For example, a 306-m-long cut and cover tunnel was built to mitigate the high speed railway's impact on the environment close to residences[2].

Expansion reading 13-2

For depths of about 10 m to 12 m, cut and cover method is usually more economical and practical than mined or bored tunneling[1]. The cut and cover tunnel is often designed as a rigid frame box structure. Of the construction in details, especially the features of the trench cutting and retaining system to maintain the excavation are strongly dependent on the construction conditions or environmental restrictions. For example, wherever construction space permits and in greenland, it is economical to employ open cut method; in urban areas, due to the limited space available, the tunnel is usually constructed within a neat excavation, which should be supported with braced or tied back retaining walls.

Where the tunnel alignment is beneath a street in downtown, the conventional cut and cover construction may cause unacceptable interference with traffic and other urban activities. This disruption can be lessened through the use of decking over the excavation to restore traffic[3] and a modified cut and cover method, i.e., cover and cut method in a sequence of top-down, can be applied.

13.2 Construction methodology

In terms of the construction sequence of a cut and cover tunnel, two construction methods, namely, bottom-up (Figure 13-1) and top-down, are well used in practice. In the recent years, there are variations for them.

13.2.1 Bottom-up construction

In a conventional construction sequence, a cut and cover tunnel is built from the bottom of a trench or excavation to the top slab of the tunnel in a sequence of bottom-up activities. The trench can be formed using open cut, of which the sides are sloped or vertical retaining walls. The sides of a slope excavation may be in steps, with or without protection and retaining supports. In simplicity, a conventional bottom-up construction sequence (Figure 13-1) generally consists of the following steps[1].

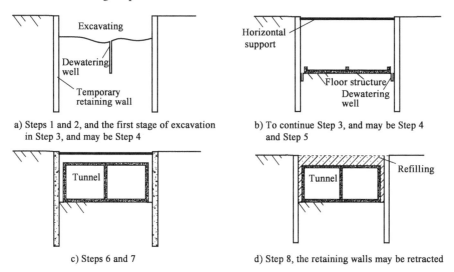

Figure 13-1 **Bottom-up construction sequence of a cut and cover tunnel**

Step 1: Cleaning and working site preparation.

Step 2: Installation of excavation retaining walls, such as soldier pile and lagging, sheet piling, slurry walls, tangent or secant pile walls.

Step 3: Excavation and the installation of wall horizontal support elements, such as struts or tie backs.

Step 4: Dewatering within the trench if required.

Step 5: Construction of the foundation of the tunnel structure.

Step 6: Construction of the tunnel structures in a bottom-up sequence.

Step 7: Completing the construction of the walls and then the roof, apply waterproofing as required.

Step 8: Backfilling to final grade and restoring the ground surface.

In practice, the excavation can be much deep. The Steps 2 and 3 are executed in alternant steps, such as excavating down to a planned level and then installing struts or tie backs in an alternation mode[4].

Expansion reading 13-3

Where the bottom-up construction sequence is applied, the following advantages are always assured[1]: ①waterproofing can be applied to the outside surface of the structure; ②drainage systems can be installed outside the structure to channel water or divert it away from the structure; ③the inside of the excavation is easily accessible for the construction equipment and the delivery, storage and placement of materials.

The main disadvantages of bottom-up construction include: ①relatively long period of interrupting to the ground activity; ②relatively high risk of environmental disturbance, such as the ground water table decreasing of the retained soils and inducing large deformation.

13.2.2　Top-down construction

The construction of a tunnel may be strongly restricted by the requirements of the third party or environmental articles. For example, the building of metro stations in downtown, where the least possible disruption of traffic is often required, "cover and cut" method, i.e., top-down construction, may be chosen to alleviate the disturbance to the ground activities.

In top-down construction of a cut and cover tunnel, retaining walls, such as slurry walls and concrete pile walls, are constructed first and followed by the roof or top slab, which is tied into the walls (Figure 13-2). The surface is then temporarily reinstated before the completion of the construction. The remainder of the excavation and construction is completed under the protection of the top slab. Upon the completion of the excavation, the floor is completed and tied into the walls. Secondary finishing walls are often provided upon the completion of the construction. For wider tunnels, temporary or permanent piles or wall elements are sometimes installed along the center of the tunnel to reduce the span of the roof and floors of the tunnel. The steps of the top-down construction of a cut and cover tunnel generally consists of the following steps[1].

Step 1: Cleaning and working site preparation.

Step 2: Installation of excavation support/tunnel structural walls, such as slurry walls or secant pile walls.

Step 3: Dewatering within the excavation limits if required.

Step 4: Excavation to the level of the bottom of the tunnel top slab.

Step 5: Construction and waterproofing of the tunnel top slab tying to the excavation support walls.

Step 6: Backfilling the roof and restoring the ground surface.

Step 7: Excavation of tunnel interior, bracing of the support of excavation walls is installed as required during excavation.

Step 8: Construction of the tunnel floor slab and tying it to the support of excavation walls.

Step 9: Construction of the center wall and completing the interior finishes including the secondary walls.

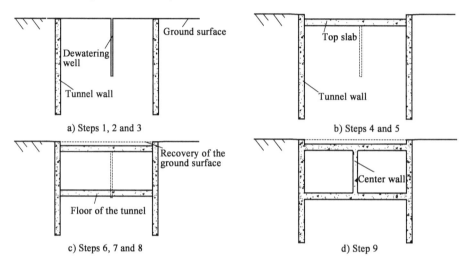

Figure 13-2　Top-down construction sequence of a cut and cover tunnel

The above-mentioned sequence (Figure 13-2) is only simply presented the case, of which the retaining walls are also used as sidewalls and no inside structures are built. Where there is additional sidewall or inside structures are designed for the tunnel, the inside structures may be built from the top slab down to the bottom slab, or alternatively in the sequence of the bottom slab, sidewalls and connection to the top slab. In practice, the construction activity is mainly dependent on the features of the tunnel structure and the requirements of horizontal supports by the retaining walls.

The main advantages of top-down construction, in comparison to the bottom-up construction, include[1]: ①it allows early restoration of the ground surface above the tunnel; ②the temporary support of excavation walls are used as the permanent structural walls; ③the structural slabs will act as internal bracing for the support of excavation thus reducing the amount of tie backs required; ④easier construction of roof since it can be cast on prepared grade rather than using bottom forms; ⑤it may result in lower cost for the tunnel by the elimination of the separate, cast-in-place concrete walls within the excavation and reducing the need for tie backs and internal bracing.

The main disadvantages of top-down construction are also related to the features of the "covered" construction activities and using retaining walls as permanent tunnel walls. These disadvantages[1] should be considered, such as: ①inability to install external waterproofing outside the tunnel walls; ② more complicated connections for the roof, floor and base slabs; ③ potential water leakage at the joints between the slabs and the walls; ④risks that the exterior walls (or center columns) will exceed specified installation tolerances and extend within the neat line of the interior space; ⑤access to the excavation is limited to the portals or through shafts through the roof openings; ⑥limited spaces for excavation and construction under the top slab.

13.2.3 Variations

The construction environment restrictions and the requirements of shallow tunnels may be various. The typical construction procedure of bottom-up and top-down may not meet the requirements of a specific project. The mixture of these two methods is often used in practice and therefore the variations of construction method appear.

13.2.3.1 Vault method

The "cover and cut" method can be used in tunnel portal construction[5] in soft ground, where a shallow excavation is first performed, and then followed by the construction of a concrete "vault", which is supported by the pre-installed pile walls. The vault acting as a retaining structure provides full protection to the main excavation activities below. The tunnel structures are built under the vault protection. The last stage is to backfilling or recovering the ground surface.

Expansion reading 13-4

In this method, the fundamental concept of the "cover and cut" method consists of minimizing the extent of the non-retained cutting and providing full cover to the tunnel bore underneath. The construction process comprises six distinct stages, including earthwork operations, drilling and casting of piles, slab construction, earth removal and backfilling. The space of piles is usually equal to $2D$, where D is the pile diameter. Also fiber-shotcrete may be applied onto the ground surface at inter-spaces between piles.

In practice, the height of the excavation space under the vault is determined according the requirements of both tunnel structure and construction activity.

13.2.3.2 Island method

Island method is a multiple-stage construction method, which is executed by first forming a slope on soils beside retaining wall, then cutting the center of the ground and building a solid body or structure; and the structure is used as the base for struts to control the soil retaining wall, then cutting the remainder of the slope.

Island method is applied to relatively shallow cases with wide cut area. The cutting in the center is first done easily by mechanized execution. But the work period is long because the work is performed in stages. It is noted that if the cut ground is soft, maintaining the stability of the slope may need special consideration in design.

Expansion reading 13-5

13.3 Excavation method and supporting system

13.3.1 Excavation method

Where a trench is excavated, the lateral supports of the trench side walls are usually required, if the excavation is deep or the retained soils are weak. In practice, where the depth of the trench or excavation is more than 6 m, certain measures, such as retaining walls and horizontal supports are always required to keep the trench stable or to control the deformation of the nearby ground. The design of excavation support systems requires the consideration of a variety of the factors that affect the performance of the support system and the impacts on environments due to the cut and cover tunnel construction.

Expansion reading 13-6

In general, the excavation method and the required supporting system are determined on the features of the tunnel, ground conditions and environmental restrictions. The excavations may be executed under open cut slope or (and) supported situations.

The open cut slope is used in the areas where sufficient room is available to open cut the area of the tunnel and to slope the sides back to meet the adjacent existing ground line. The slopes are designed similar to any other cut slope taking into account the natural repose angle of the in-situ material and the global stability. The commonly used supporting measures in open cut slope include soil nails, shotcrete and rock bolts or dowels and anchors.

Where there is no sufficient room available to open cut, or the excavation is such deep that supported excavation is required to provide a safe working space, including providing access for construction activities and protecting structures, utilities and other infrastructure adjacent to the excavation, especially for the constructions of cut and cover tunnels in soft ground in urban area.

Where the excavations are shallow or the movements of the retained soils are not strictly limited, unbraced retaining system may be used. Otherwise, braced retaining system is applied at a deep excavation for cut and cover tunnels.

13.3.2 Retaining walls

13.3.2.1 Soldier pile wall

Soldier pile wall is made by forming gaps by placing H-steel or I-steel and inserting lagging in the gap (Figure 13-3). It is the most widespread and economical soil retaining wall in small scale cutting. Because the water cutoff property of a soldier pile wall is low, the fall of the groundwater level may be a problem and the simultaneous use of auxiliary water tight work is a premise for its application. The embedded parts are not continuous and this limits its application to soft ground. On the other hand, a gap tends to form between the lagging and the ground, the displacement of the retained soils may be greater than that the case of other soil retaining wall used[6].

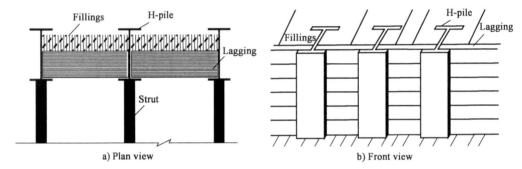

Figure 13-3 View of a typical completed soldier pile wall

Soldier pile wall is often a temporary retaining wall and is commonly used for excavations in urban areas. The construction of a soldier piles wall consists of: ①drilling regularly spaced boreholes in which metal beams are sunk or vibrating main beams into the ground; ②installing cladding (timber sleepers, shotcrete, steel plates, cast-in-place concrete or precast concrete panels) between the beams as the excavation progresses. Sometimes, a concrete foundation may be applied for each of the steel piles.

The stability of the retaining wall is often provided by struts or anchors except in shallow excavations, where the wall may be self-supporting.

In general, soldier piling is proper for the ground of cohesive nature, with minimal or nil groundwater present. Under these situations, soldier pile walls are a cost effective alternative to sheet piling or other systems.

13.3.2.2 Steel sheet pile wall

Steel sheet piles may be broadly divided into three types, i.e., lightweight steel sheet piles, steel sheet piles, and steel pipe sheet piles. Steel pipe sheet piles are mostly used for permanent structures, while lightweight steel sheet piles and steel sheet piles are used for permanent or temporary structures. The thickness of the steel sheet is generally from 3 mm to 8 mm.

Steel sheet piles are available in various designs, such as the commonly used U-shaped, Z-shaped, H-shaped, and straight (Figure 13-4), which are used according to different application needs to form retaining wall by continuously placing these piles and engaging their joints.

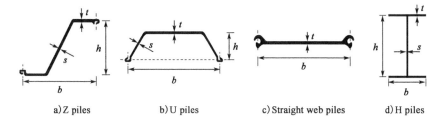

a) Z piles b) U piles c) Straight web piles d) H piles

Figure 13-4 Typical section profiles of steel pile units

The Z-shaped steel sheet piles, which are chiefly used for permanent structures, feature the joints located outside in the right and left when fit with neighbor units.

The U-shaped steel sheet piles feature the most available types. In the curved application, a standard turning angle is six degrees in either side, right and left, in relation to the neutral axis.

The straight steel sheet piles feature very high mechanical strength of engaged joints, thus are ideally suited for cell structures.

The steel pipe sheet piles are made up from a single pipe with joints, and used for stand-alone permanent structures. The joints are available in three types, i.e., L-T, P-P, and P-T, as shown in Figure 13-5.

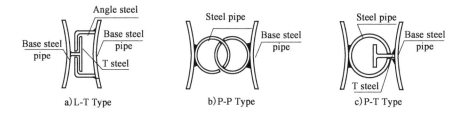

a) L-T Type b) P-P Type c) P-T Type

Figure 13-5 Joints of steel pipe sheet pile

There are many cases where U-steel or plates are used in practice, but their stiffness may be inadequate for large-scale cutting. In practice, various sheet pile walls can be formed with U-shaped, Z-shaped, H-shaped, straight and pipe piles, according to specified arrangements of different piles combinations. For example, the cases of pipe/AZ combined wall system and a special arrangement of AZ combinations are shown in Figure 13-6.

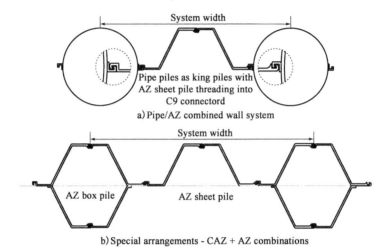

Figure 13-6 Arrangements of piles combinations

In general, the water cutoff property of a steel sheet pile wall is good and the embedded part under the bottom surface of the cut maintains continuity. So it is generally used in ground where the groundwater level is high or in soft ground. But if the noise and vibration produced by the placing will cause problems, it is necessary to take care to adopt a low noise and low vibration execution method.

Steel sheet piling is able to penetrate depths of up to 24 m depending on the geotechnical conditions of the site. Steel sheet piles can be installed by means of using a water jet system, a free fall hammer, a pneumatic hammer, a vibrator, or by pushing it in with an excavator. At greater depths or in soils with a high resistance, a steel guiding sheet pile is used. Steel sheet piles can easily be combined with or connected with other building materials. The sheets can be sawn or drilled. Wood, concrete, steel or plastic can be used as cap and wale system. A combination with a tie back system is also a possibility.

13.3.2.3 Concrete pile wall

Concrete pile wall is also called column pile wall, which is constructed either cast-in-place pile method or precast pile method. Precast methods commonly use pre-stressed concrete piles or steel pipes placed into soil by static pressing, pre-boring or striking. The retaining walls at deep excavations are often built with cast-in-place pile method, through continuously constructing cast-in-place reinforced concrete piles.

The arrangements of column piles include the independent pattern, the staggered pattern, the line pattern, the overlapping pattern, and the mixed pattern, to meet various requirements of supporting capacity and water cutoff in a specific geotechnical conditions. Figure 13-7 shows the commonly used patterns of concrete piles. The relationship between the neighbor piles may be independent, tangent and secant, respectively.

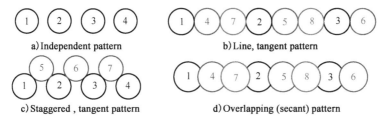

Figure 13-7 Typical arrangements of column piles

The main advantages of cast-in-place pile walls include: ①the work produces little noise and vibration; ②adjustable pile depth; ③greater stiffness than soldier piles or steel sheet piles; ④easier construction on sandy ground[7].

Cast-in-place piles provide substantial section performance and the work produces little noise and vibration so this method is often used in place of sheet pile soil retaining walls in urban districts. However, in many cases, the disadvantages of a concrete pile wall, including poor water cutoff performance, high cost and long work period, should be considered in wall type choosing.

13.3.2.4 Diaphragm wall

Diaphragm wall, also called slurry wall, is built by the method of constructing a continuous soil retaining wall underground by using the ground stabilization action of bentonite slurry or polymer slurry to cut a trench in the ground and inserting steel material or rebar columns, then filling the trench with tremie concrete (Figure 13-8).

The first stage of the construction of a diaphragm wall is to divide the whole length into several panels according to the construction conditions. For each of the panel, the construction steps are as followings: ①construction guided walls; ②the excavation of trenches; ③placing steel cages; ④tremie concrete casting.

In general, the function of water cutoff is required for a slurry wall, so the connection construction is vital to the wall. There are various types of connections used in practice. The connection pipe method (Figure 13-8) and the end-plate method are the commonly used methods. In general, the pipe connection is good in water tight, but it is relatively weak in transmitting bending moments and shear forces[7].

The water cutoff property of a diaphragm wall is generally good, provided that the embedded part under the bottom surface of the cut maintains continuity. Also, the section performance of a diaphragm wall is large, so it is used for large-scale excavations, near important structures and for work in soft soils. On the other hand, diaphragm walls can be used as part of the main structure and the construction of the wall produces little vibration and noise.

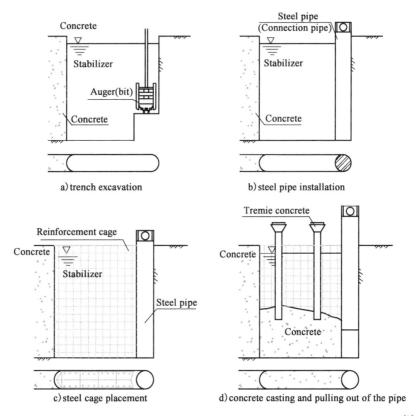

Figure 13-8　Construction procedure of a diaphragm wall with pipe connection[7]

The main disadvantages of the diaphragm walls include the relatively high work cost and long work period.

There are several modified diaphragm walls used in practice, such as slurry solidified diaphragm wall, which is made by inserting steel piles or precast concrete panels into the slurry trench then mixing a hardener with the stabilizing fluid to solidify the stabilizing fluid. The main value of this method is to dispose the unnecessary stabilizing fluid by solidifying the stabilizing fluid to use it as part of the soil retaining wall. However, execution conditions may have a big impact on work costs and its adoption must be studied in details.

13.3.2.5　Soil mixed wall

A soil mixed wall(SMW) is formed using soil cement in place of mortar. The cement or binder is mixing with soft soils in ground and is also called deep mixing. The mixed soils are developed by using a special chopping bit to drill a hole with the cement (or concrete mortar) or binder sent out from the front of the bit to be mixed with the soils. When the designed depth is reached, lift the bit a little, keeping swirling and grouting simultaneously, and let the cement or binder mix with soil thoroughly. After pulling out the drilling rod, put steel cages or H-piles into the hole if necessary. The H-piles may be inserted in every mixed pile, or in alternate piles (Figure 13-9). Since the soil mixed walls are always used as a water cutoff measure, secant pattern of the piles are commonly applied in practice (Figure 13-9).

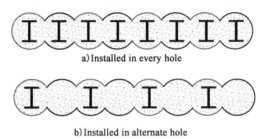

a) Installed in every hole

b) Installed in alternate hole

Figure 13-9 Sketch of soil mixed wall

The section performance of a SMW is generally not quite as good as that of the column type diaphragm wall, since the unconfined compressive strength of the mixed soils is often designed as about unit MPa, but its water cutoff property is good. For SMW construction, the soil from the existing ground is used as material for soil cement. So, where the ground is inadequate for use as material for soil cement, the method is generally not improper in application. And also in terms of layers, large variations in the section performance may appear in the depth direction of the SMW. It is clear that relatively uniform section performance in the depth direction is generally required in terms of retaining capacity and water cutoff.

The performance of a SMW is related not only to features of the mixed piles, such as the diameter of the mixed pile and the space between neighbor piles in a row, the pattern of the inserted steel H-piles, but also to the the lateral assembly pattern of the mixed piles. The performance of a SMW will be improved by increasing the lateral rows of the mixed piles, in terms of supporting capacity and water cutoff property.

13.3.3 Support methods

There are various kinds of soil retaining walls, horizontal support structures and excavation methods. The considerations for selection from these include safety, construction conditions, cost and environmental restrictions. The support method of an excavation is of importance. Where a soil retaining structure is applied in urban area and close to lines in particular, the impact of the retained soils deformation on surrounding structures, noise, vibration, the requirements from third party and other restrictions must be fully clarified, and corresponding countermeasures should be designed to control the risks related to the tunneling to an acceptable level.

13.3.3.1 Unbraced retaining works

Unbraced excavation means the excavation being supported by an unbraced retaining wall, which provides lateral supporting pressure by the passive resistance of the embedded part of the retaining wall. Where an unbraced soil retaining work is used at an excavation, the construction is generally easily executed, with good cutting efficiency, because there are no supports in the cut area. On the other hand, because only the passive resistance of the part embedded in the soil retaining wall provides resistance, this method is only applicable to shallow cutting in relatively good soil. In general, wall displacement is large because of a lack of horizontal support works.

Expansion reading 13-7

In practice, to resist the lateral earth pressure, an earth berm may be remained in alternate steps along the longitudinal direction of the retaining wall. The earth berm is usually made by removing the soils in the central area while retaining earth berms to support the retaining walls. The berm remains are also used as a supplemental measure to an island excavation method.

13.3.3.2 Strut type retaining works

Where the excavations are deep and the retained soils are soft, the deformation of the retaining wall at the deep excavations should be limited to meet the pre-defined magnitude, with horizontal supports, such as struts and anchors, as shown in Figures 13-10 and 13-11, respectively. In general, where the bedrock or stiff layers are far down from the toe of the retaining wall, strut type retaining works are often used at deep excavations. Figure 13-10 shows a case of deep excavation supported with strut type retaining works for a cut and cover tunnel in soft soils, with high groundwater table.

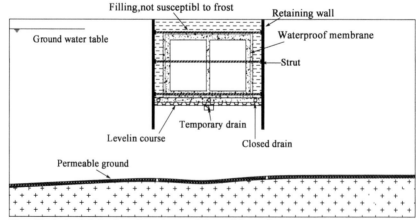

Figure 13-10 **Deep excavation with strut support**

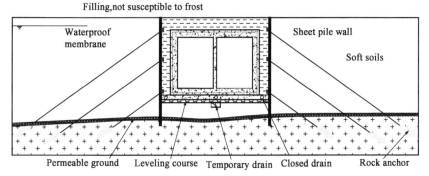

Figure 13-11 Deep excavation with tied back support

Strut type retaining works are composed of struts, retaining walls and the embedding part of the retaining walls, wales, or other support works. The materials of struts may be timbers, steel pipes or H-shaped steels and concrete beams.

Strut type retaining works are flexible. For example, the number of horizontal supports works and their layout are easily adapted to site conditions. The horizontal supports are usually perpendicular to the walls in the middle sections of the excavation, but in a diagonal pattern at the corners of the excavation. On the other hand, the struts may be installed in an inclined mode, as rakers, which are generally shorter than horizontal struts and used in island excavation method.

One of the drawbacks of the strut type retaining works is the struts tends to obstruct machine cutting and tunnel construction. This situation is unfavorable to the rate of the construction. There may be more than one working sites for a large cut and cover tunnel to meet the requirement of time schedule, provided the conditions available. On the other hand, if the struts and wales are not fully connected with the wall, large lateral displacement will occur, and it is not effective for pre-stress application to the struts, in comparison to an anchor tied-back retaining system.

13.3.3.3 Ground anchor soil retaining works

Where the bedrock or stiff layers are not far down from the ground surface and underground conditions are favorable to anchors installation, ground anchor soil retaining works are usually applied at a deep excavation, probably with the toes of the retaining walls down into bedrocks or stiff layer (Figure 13-11), for a cut and cover tunnel construction. Ground anchor soil retaining works are composed of anchors, retaining wall and the embedding part of the retaining wall, wales, or other support works.

There are no struts or similar obstructions inside the cut area. So mechanized cutting is simplified and effective. This type retaining works are often applied for large-scale cutting.

The main disadvantages of the ground anchor soil retaining works may include: ①the anchors are generally long, and may do harm to nearby underground structures; ②the installations of the anchor system may cause soils loss; ③if the anchors remain after execution, problems may occur, so it may be necessary to study using removable type anchors.

13.3.3.4 Reinforced soil type retaining works

To avoid the interference to the neighbor underground structures due to such as ground anchors installations, and also the struts obstruction to machine activity in the excavation area, reinforced soil type retaining works may be an alternative and effective supporting system for relatively shallow excavations[8].

Reinforced soil type retaining works provide support by tensile reinforcing materials placed to increase the integration with the ground based on the principle of reinforced soil and by wales or similar support works. Similarly to the anchor retaining works, there are no struts or similar obstructions inside the cut surface, so mechanized cutting is simplified.

In general, reinforced soil type retaining works require more building activities than the ground anchor method, but the length of the reinforcement elements is much shorter than that of a ground anchor, so the work is rarely obstructed by nearby structures or buried structures. Because pre-stressing is not done, the wall and wales are simplified.

13.3.4 Auxiliary measures

Where the deep excavations are executed in an urban area or the excavation is nearby to existing structures, the disturbance due to the excavation of the planned cut and cover tunnel is always restricted to certain limits. The protection of surrounding structures is under the consideration of the supporting work and tunneling designs. Under these situations, the deformation of the retaining system, the retained soils and nearby structures caused by the cutting must be predicted, and their allowed displacements must be appropriately set. To control the deformation, as well as the disturbance to the neighbors and environments, to an acceptable level, some auxiliary measures may be required accordingly.

13.3.4.1 Commonly used measures

When it is predicted that the quantity of displacement of the structure will be equal to or higher than the allowed displacement, or the disturbance to the neighbors and environments is unacceptable, the protective work for the construction method must be studied. Sometimes, auxiliary methods, such as ground improvement, water cutoff, the under-pinning and reinforcement of existing structures, may be used at the planned deep excavations.

During deep excavations, the area inside the retaining system is usually dewatered, such as the ground water level is lowered about one meter below the excavation bottoms. At the same time, the ground water level should be maintained about same as the original situation in the retained soils. For example, it is generally required that the fluctuation of the ground water level in the retained soils should be around one meter. The ground water control is always one of the main jobs of deep excavations.

13.3.4.2 Groundwater control

13.3.4.2.1 Construction dewatering

The dewatering is always required in deep excavations. During tunneling, the groundwater level in the excavation area should be gradually decreased with the excavation proceeding while the groundwater level in the retained soils should be maintained. Dewatering is of lowering the groundwater level in sandy or gravelly grounds rather than in clayey grounds. Generally speaking, the goals of lowering the groundwater level are: ① to keep the excavation bottom dry; ② to prevent leakage of groundwater or soils; ③ to avoid sand boiling; ④ to forestall the upheaval failure; ⑤ to keep the basement from floating. The details of these goals are discussed in the reference Ou[7]. It is clear that these goals could not be realized without the help of the other auxiliary methods. For example, groundwater can be controlled during construction either by using impervious retaining walls, such as concrete slurry or secant pile walls, steel interlocking sheeting, etc., by wellpoints drawing down the water table, chemical or grout injection into the soils, or by pumping from within the excavation.

Commonly used dewatering methods for cut and cover tunnel construction are open sumps or ditches, well points and deep wells. The methods, as recommended in the Technical Code for Groundwater Control in Building and Municipal Engineering, can be preliminarily used for designing dewatering measures for a deep excavation in urban area.

In practice, the dewatering systems will generally depend on the permeability of the various soil layers exposed. In terms of experience, for example, where the area of excavations is not too large, an economical method of collecting water is through the use of ditches leading to sump pumps, and provisions to keep fines from escaping into the dewatering system should be made. In larger excavations in permeable soil, either well points or deep wells are often utilized for lowering the water table in sand or coarse silt deposits, but are not useful in fine silt or clay soils due to their low permeability. It is recommended that test wells be installed to check the proposed systems. In practice, multiple stages of well points, deep wells with submersible pumps or an eductor system would be needed.

For important project, pumping tests for dewatering plan for an excavation is always required for the selection of dewatering methods.

13.3.4.2.2 Groundwater cut-off curtain

Expansion reading 13-8

To control the groundwater level in the retained soils at a deep excavation, groundwater cut-off curtain is always necessary for the cases, where groundwater level is much higher than the formation level of the deep excavation. In general, a groundwater cut-off curtain can be formed by grouting, deep mixing, ground freezing, retaining walls with watertight features.

A planned groundwater cut-off curtain method should meet the following requirements: ①to be suited with the supporting system of the tunnel; ②to provide the stability of excavation bottom in terms of anti-uplifting by groundwater flow; ③to be relatively impermeable, with a permeability coefficient of no more than 1.0×10^{-6} m/s. The practicability of the measures, such as jet grouting, deep mixing and freezing method, for a groundwater cut-off curtain at deep excavation in urban area, should be checked with the help of site test during design in details.

13.3.4.2.3 Potential impact of dewatering and countermeasures

Dewatering at an excavation may lower the groundwater outside the excavation, and cause settlements and damage to adjacent structures and utilities. So, it is important that the method selected is suitable for the proposed excavation. Furthermore, where lowering groundwater exposes wooden piles to air, deterioration may occur. Adjacent structures with a risk of settlement due to groundwater lowering may require underpinning. Precautions should be taken when dewatering the area outside the excavation limits. Within the excavation, dewatering can be accomplished with impermeable excavation support walls that extend down to a firm, reasonably impermeable stratum to reduce or cut-off water flow. The lowering of the external groundwater can be reduced by the use of slurry walls, secant pile wall, or steel sheet pile wall. The auxiliary measures, may be chosen to control the potential impact of dewatering.

On the other hand, the construction water will require testing and possibly treatment before it can be discharged. Settling basins, oil separators, and chemical treatments may be required prior to disposal. Local regulations and permitting requirements often dictate the method of disposal.

To minimize any lowering the water table immediately outside the excavation, water pumped from the excavation can be used for recharging the water bearing strata of the groundwater system, such as using injection wells.

After construction is completed, if the permanent excavation support walls above the tunnel might be blocking the cross flow of the groundwater or may dam up water between walls above the tunnel, the designer may need to consider to breach the walls above the tunnel at intervals or remove the walls to an elevation to allow movement of groundwater[1], such as using granular backfill around tunnels to maintain equal hydrostatic heads across underground structures.

13.3.5 Selection of retaining system

A retaining system may consist of retaining walls and horizontal supports. The selection of retaining walls should consider the features of the project, such as the excavation depth, tunnel structure type and its shape and size, construction time schedule, geotechnical and ground water conditions, environmental and the third party restriction on the project, together with the features of the retaining walls, especially the supporting capacity and construction condition pre-requirements and the cost of the walls.

On the other hand, the relationship between the retaining walls and the tunnel structures sometimes is also considered in the selection of retaining walls. The retaining walls are often applied to just supporting the excavations during construction as temporary structures. Under these situations, the durability of the retaining walls generally does not dominate the selection of the retaining walls, and the relationship between the tunnel structures and the retaining walls is relatively simple, such as in a separated mode.

The retaining walls may be used as parts of the tunnel sidewalls. For example, where the top down method is planned for the tunneling, diaphragm walls are usually chosen as retaining walls and also used as tunnel sidewall structures, such as in terms of single wall, composite wall, and integrated wall, as shown in Figure 13-12.

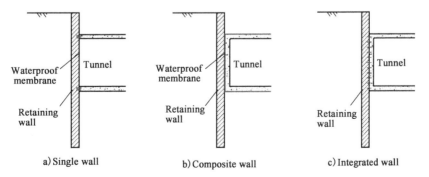

Figure 13-12 Relationship between retaining walls and tunnel

Expansion reading 13-9

Of the general situations of the selection of retaining walls for design and construction considerations, Ou[7] listed the application ranges of the commonly used system. The selections of the horizontal supports are discussed in Section 13.3.3.

13.4 Design considerations

Expansion reading 13-10

The design of a cut and cover tunnel include determining the structures of the tunnel and the construction method, especially the retaining system at deep excavations. The safety of the deep excavations is generally required as same as the permanent tunnel structures.

In terms of structure requirements, the inner section of the tunnel should be appropriately determined, with the considering the clearance, tunnel structures, the installations of electrical equipment, drainage system, disaster prevention equipment, maintenance equipment, as well as reserved ground displacement and construction space.

The construction method is often selected by making a comprehensive judgment based on ground conditions, construction environment, safety and costs. It is essential to adopt the most appropriate type of soil retaining work method, the type of excavation method and the type of auxiliary methods for the tunnel project.

13.4.1 Basis of design

It is often difficult to repair, reinforce or reconstruct a cut and cover tunnel. This is why it is important to fully study the ground conditions, state of groundwater, materials used and the construction method to accurately predict the limit states that may occur during the tunnel design lifetime and to design a tunnel that is durable and easily maintained.

13.4.1.1 Limit states

All limit states, at which the tunnel and its structural members fail to fill their functions or will no longer satisfy the stipulated safety, serviceability, and durability during the design lifetime, should be considered, including: ultimate limit state, serviceability limit state and fatigue limit state.

Ultimate limit state, where members of the structure fail, the structure is no longer stable, such as under settlement, movement, leaning, or lifting, or is excessively displaced, losing its functions.

Serviceability limit state, where the structure or a member is excessively cracked, deformed, displaced, or leaks, prevents structure normal use and reduces its durability.

Fatigue limit state means fatigue failure of a structure under cyclic action of variable loads. For example, fatigue failure caused by the cyclic action of trains or vehicles loads.

13.4.1.2 Loads

A cut and cover tunnel is generally a statically determinate structure. In design load consideration, appropriate loads and their combinations, load factor and the state of action are set to perform the study. Design loads include permanent load, variable load and accidental loads that act during construction and the design service life, and may be combined according to limit states and study items.

Permanent loads are loads that act continuously and with variations small enough that they can be ignored. They include vertical and lateral earth pressures, water pressures and dead load due to structure gravity.

Variable loads act frequently or continually with variations that cannot be ignored and include trains or vehicles and the impacts of shock and temperature change.

Accidental loads are loads that act during the design lifetime at extremely low frequency, but have extreme effects, such as load by earthquakes.

An example of structural analysis model, with the considerations of various loads in cut and cover tunnel structure design, is quoted from the RTRI[8], as shown in Figure 13-13. Similarly, FHWA[1] also presents cut and cover structures design load considerations.

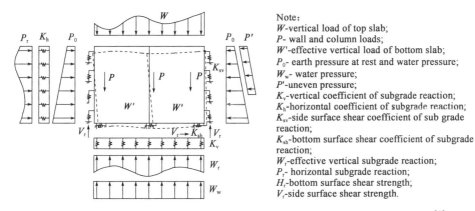

Note:
W-vertical load of top slab;
P- wall and column loads;
W'-effective vertical load of bottom slab;
P_0- earth pressure at rest and water pressure;
W_w- water pressure;
P'-uneven pressure;
K_v-vertical coefficient of subgrade reaction;
K_h-horizontal coefficient of subgrade reaction;
K_{sv}-side surface shear coefficient of sub grade reaction;
K_{sh}-bottom surface shear coefficient of subgrade reaction;
W_r-effective vertical subgrade reaction;
P_r- horizontal subgrade reaction;
H_r-bottom surface shear strength;
V_r-side surface shear strength.

Figure 13-13 Example of structural analysis model for a cut and cover tunnel[8]

13.4.1.3 Safety factors

Expansion reading 13-11

Seven safety factors are generally used, i. e., load factor γ_f, structural analysis factor γ_a, material factor γ_m, member factor γ_b, ground investigation coefficient γ_g, ground resistance coefficient γ_r, and structure factor γ_i, in cut and cover tunnel design and tunneling plan, respectively.

The values of the safety factors applied in a project may vary according to the

Expansion reading 13-12

project features, especially the importance of the structure and the potential influence of the failure of the structure on the project and neighbors, as well as the risk of the uncertainty of the parameters. The recommended values of the safety factors for the design parameters may be different in the standards, codes and guidelines in the world.

13.4.2 Design of main structures

13.4.2.1 Considerations

When the main structure of a cut and cover tunnel is designed, the structural form and construction method should be considered according to actual ground conditions and construction restrictions at site. Also, the structures is often designed, together with the retaining system design. Three basic methods are often used in the design of cut and cover tunnel structures[1].

(1) Service load or allowable stress design, which treats each load on the structure equally in terms of its probability of occurrence at the stated value. The factor of safety for this method is built into the material's ability to withstand the loading.

(2) Load factor design accounts for the potential variability of loads by applying varying load factors to each load type. The resistance of the maximum capacity of the structural member is reduced by a strength reduction factor and the calculated resistance of the structural member must exceed the applied load.

(3) Load and Resistance Factor Design (LRFD) takes into account the statistical variation of both the strength of the structural member and of the magnitude of the applied loads.

The LRFD is usually used in design calculation. For example, where the R_r is the calculated factored resistance of the member or connection, the factored load force effects (Q_i) should be no more than the resistance R_r, as presented in the following equation[1]:

$$\sum \eta_i \gamma_i Q_i \leq \varphi R_n = R_r \qquad (13\text{-}1)$$

where η_i is a load modifier relating to the ductility, redundancy and operation importance of the feature being designed; γ_i is a load factor applied to the force effects (Q_i) acting on the member being designed.

Values for γ can be found in the referenced design codes and guidelines. The load modifier η is comprised of three components[1]: ① η_D = a factor relating to ductility = 1.0 for cut and cover tunnels constructed with conventional details and designed in accordance with the AASHTO LRFD specification; ② η_R = a factor relating to redundancy = 1.0 for cut and cover tunnel design, for example, typical

Expansion reading 13-13

cast in place and prestressed concrete structures are sufficiently redundant to use a value of 1.0 for this factor, and typical detailing using structural steel also provides a high level of redundancy; ③ η_1 = a factor relating to the importance of the structure, often η_1 = 1.05 for cut and cover tunnel design. Tunnels are usually major links in transportation systems. The loss of a tunnel will usually cause major disruption to the flow of traffic, hence the higher importance factor.

13.4.2.2 Structures

Structural study is often used for determining the most suitable structure, with special consideration on the construction method, during the design of a cut and cover tunnel. The main factors to be considered include shape and size of the proposed tunnel, the planned tunnel structures and support system and the construction method. Each of these elements is interdependent upon the other and should be considered in a holistic approach, taking into account the effect that one option for an element has on another element[1].

13.4.2.2.1 Shape and size

The shape of a cut and cover tunnel is generally rectangular. The basic requirements to be met are the clearance for operation and facilities installation. The depth of the roof and floor combined with the clearance requirements will define the vertical height of the tunnel structure, the depth of excavation required and the height of the associated support of excavation[1]. In general, a shallower alignment profile results in shorter approaches and the approach grades are more favorable to the operational characteristics of the vehicles using. As a result, the tunnel will be in lower costs for the users of the tunnel.

The relationship between the retaining walls and the tunnel structure is also a consideration in design. Without considering the temporary support of excavation, the tunnel section would be considered a frame with fixed joints. When support of excavation walls are to form part of the tunnel structure, fixed connections between the support of excavation walls and the rest of the structure may be difficult to achieve in practice; partial fixity is more probable, but to what degree may be difficult to define[1]. A range of fixities may need to be considered in the design analysis. On the other hand, when the retaining wall will be part of the tunnel structures, the physical keying of the structural top and bottom slabs into the support of excavation walls is essential for any transmission of moments and shear[1], which usually needs special consideration in design.

13.4.2.2.2 Materials of structures

Cut and cover tunnels are commonly cast-in-place concrete structures, but other materials such as precast prestressed concrete, post tensioned concrete and

Expansion reading 13-14

structural steel are also used in practice[1].

13.4.2.2.3 Waterproof system

Expansion reading 13-15

A tunnel should be dry in its operational space and facilities installation rooms. The existence of a high groundwater table in ground or probable water percolating down from ground surface requires that tunnels be waterproof. Durability is also improved when the tunnel is waterproof. Leaking tunnels are unsightly and can give rise to concern by users. In colder climates, leaks can become hazardous ceiling icicles or ice patches on roadways. The waterproofing system is selected based on the required performance and its compatibility with the structural system, and is often composed of waterproof membrane, water stop belt and the tunnel concrete structures.

When tunneling protected by temporary supports, the tunnel section is constructed totally within them, often with a layer of waterproofing completely enveloping the section. In contrast, when the support of excavation walls become part of the final structure, an enveloping membrane is difficult to achieve. Therefore, provisions for overlapping, enveloping and sealing the joints are needed.

13.4.2.2.4 Foundations

The foundations of a cut and cover tunnel is often design to resist against flotation, to reduce differential settlement along the tunnel alignment, especially at the transitional sites, in terms of structures and geotechnical conditions.

Buoyancy is a major concern in shallow tunnels that are under or partially within groundwater table. Buoyancy should be checked during the design. The structural system selected should take into account its ability to resist buoyancy forces with its own weight or by providing measures to deal with negative buoyancy. In cases where the structure and backfill are not heavy enough to resist the buoyancy forces, flotation can occur. Measures to resist the forces of flotation must be provided and accounted for in the design.

The resistance against flotation can be achieved by a variety of methods. Typical methods used for increasing the effective weight of the structure include[1]: ①connecting the structure to the excavation support system and thus mobilizing its weight and/or its friction with the ground; ②thickening structural members beyond what is required for strength in order to provide dead load to deal with the flotation forces; ③widening the floor slab of the tunnel beyond the required footprint to key it into adjacent soil and thus to include the weight of soil above these protrusions; ④using steel or concrete tension piles to resist the uplift forces associated with flotation; ⑤using permanent tie-down anchors; ⑥permanent pressure relief system beneath the base of the structure, by allowing water to be collected from under the bottom slab and removed from the tunnel. It should be noted that the last measure requires maintenance and redundancy in addition to the life cycle costs associated with operating the system. It can also have the effect of lowering the local groundwater table which may have negative environment consequences.

In a long run, tie-down anchors to resist flotation forces may have the risk of corrosion of these tension elements and the consideration of their connection to the tunnel structure, and the use of an invert pressure relief system and backup system must include provisions to address the risk of the long-term operation and maintenance requirements. So the design of tension piles and increased dead load of the structure and/or weight of fill above the structure are generally applied to resist buoyancy forces[1].

13.4.3 Design considerations of retaining system

The design of soil retaining works is usually analyzed with the beam elastoplastic spring method, or a conventional design method based on regional custom. The design procedure should include document surveys, ground surveys and construction environment surveys.

Although the soil retaining work of a cut and cover tunnel is generally temporary structure, the safety margin of the retaining system is same as a permanent structure. Because, if soil retaining work collapses, the work at that location will be disrupted and surrounding structures can be severely damaged, and also workers may be injured or killed. On the other hand, the cut and cover tunnel temporary structures have a great impact on overall costs and time schedule. The soil retaining work and auxiliary work must be rationally selected. The main considerations of the retaining system design include[1,8]: ①studying the stability of bottom of excavation; ②clarifying surrounding environmental conditions to select a construction method; ③clarifying the construction conditions; ④fully understanding the soil retaining work method; ⑤considering safety and costs; ⑥considering risk control measures.

13.4.3.1 Loads

The geotechnical conditions, ground water level, the features of cutting, surrounding structures, work period are considered to set the loads, which usually include dead load, live load, shock, lateral earth pressure, overburden load. Under the standard, the lateral earth pressure is set for a design method.

13.4.3.1.1 Active lateral pressure

Following the suggestions by RTRI[8], the active lateral pressures thrusting on the retaining walls can be estimated with beam elastoplastic spring method and

Expansion reading 13-16

customary computation method, see the Expansion reading 13-16.

13.4.3.1.2 Passive earth pressure

Passive earth pressure acting on the retaining wall is often calculated with application of the Coulomb's theory[8], in which the angle of wall friction δ is often set as $\delta = \varphi/3$ to calculate the Coulomb's coefficient of earth pressure, where φ is internal friction angle of the soils.

The equal lateral pressure used for the beam elastoplastic spring method is the lateral pressure that acts on the passive side as lateral pressure that does not contribute to the deformation of the wall[8]. Accordingly, the computation is done based on the effective active lateral pressure and the effective passive lateral pressure obtained by subtracting the equal lateral pressure from the active and passive lateral pressures (Figure 13-14). The lateral pressure produced by overburden load is set, such as 10 kN/m² in normal cases and more for special case.

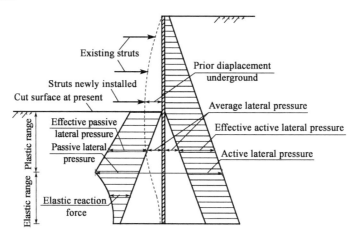

Figure 13-14 Explanatory diagram of lateral pressure used for the beam elastoplastic spring method[8]

The calculation model of the lateral pressures thrusting on the retaining wall is shown in Figure 13-14, in which the interaction between the ground and the retaining wall is also shown in terms of the beam elastoplastic spring method.

13.4.3.2 Stability of excavation bottom

13.4.3.2.1 Heaving caused by background loads

Where soft clay ground is excavated, the progress of cutting is accompanied by remarkable imbalance of forces beside and behind the retaining walls. Depending on the circumstances, the bottom surface of the excavation may heave remarkably as the soil retaining wall is deformed and the retained soils settle. In some cases, the soil retaining wall may collapse due to sliding along a circle failure surface, as shown in Figure 13-15.

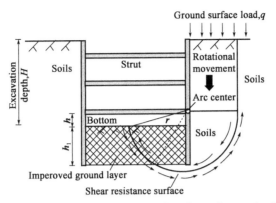

Figure 13-15   Sketch showing the bottom heaving safety evaluation model

In Figure 13-15, the failure surface of the basal heaving is considered a combination of a circular arc, with radius of r, which centers at the lowest level of strut and a vertical plane above the lowest level of struts. When the shear strength on the vertical failure plane is ignored, and the retaining wall and soil below the lowest level of struts and above the circular arc are as a free body, as well as the soil weight and surcharge on the ground surface are the driving force ($\gamma \cdot H + q$), the study of safety is performed according to a study method based on Peck's stability coefficient as the following[8]:

$$N_b = (\gamma \cdot H + q)/c \quad \text{(in principle } N_b \leq 5\text{)} \tag{13-2}$$

where, N_b is safety factor; γ is wet unit weight of soils at and above the ground water level, kN/m²; H is cut depth, m; q is overburden load, kN/m²; c is cohesiveness of clay deeper than the bottom surface of the cutting, kN/m².

The limit value of the stability coefficient N_b that can ensure stability from heaving caused by ground surface loads can be assumed to be 5[8]. But if it exceeds 3, ground is severely deformed. To increase the stability of the bottom area, ground improvement may be applied, especially for the soils below the excavation bottom or formation level, as shown in Figure 13-15.

Where the soils have been improved, the cohesiveness of clay increases. The safety factor of resisting bottom heaving, F, can be preliminarily evaluated as:

$$F = \frac{\left[\dfrac{90 + \cos^{-1}(h/r)}{180}\right] \cdot \pi \cdot c_e}{\gamma \cdot H + q} \tag{13-3}$$

where h is distance from the bottom to the lowest strut and c_e is the equivalent cohesion strength of the soils, as shown in Figure 13-15, the other parameters are same as the above-mentioned.

Considering $N_b \leq 5$ is required in principle for Equation (13-2), $F > 1.6$ should be a basic provision, provided that the mechanism is as shown in Figure 13-15. When the Equation (13-3) is applied to evaluate the safety of the bottom, the increase of the cohesion strength of soils should be evaluated according to the weight of the soils, where ground improvement has been applied, in the total shear resistance surface, with the cohesion strength (c_1) and the depth (h_1) of the improved soils (Figure 13-15). For example, the equivalent cohesion strength of the soils, c_e, can be calculated as:

$$c_e = \frac{90(c+c_1) - [\sin^{-1}(h/r) + \cos^{-1}(h/r + h_1/r)]c_1}{90 + \cos^{-1}(h/r)} \quad (13\text{-}4)$$

13.4.3.2.2 Study of soil boiling

In fine-grained soils, such as sand, silts or clayey silts, differential water pressure across the support of excavation may cause sufficient water flow (piping) for it to carry fines. This causes material loss and settlement outside the retaining wall. In extreme cases, the base of the excavation may become unstable, causing a blow-up and failure of the excavation support, as an upward seepage flows from behind to the ground near the bottom surface of the excavation bottom. If this seepage force is greater than the effective weight of sand submerged in water, the sand particles are suspended in the water and cause soil boiling. The safety factor of resisting soil boiling can be calculated by the following equation[8]:

$$F = \frac{W}{U} = \gamma' \cdot \frac{D_b}{\gamma_w} \cdot h_a \geq 1.5 \quad (13\text{-}5)$$

where, F is safety factor; $W = 0.5 D_b^2 \cdot \gamma'$; $U = 0.5 D_b \cdot h_a \cdot \gamma_w$; $h_a = \lambda \cdot a \cdot (B/D_b)^{-b} \cdot h_w$, $a = 0.57 - 0.0026 h_w$, $b = 0.27 + 0.0029 h_w$; γ' is unit weight of sandy soil submerged in water, kN/m^2.

This situation may be mitigated by ensuring that cut-off walls are sufficiently deep, by stabilizing the soil by grouting, or freezing, or by excavating below water (without dewatering inside) and making a sufficiently thick tremie slab to overcome uplift before dewatering[8].

13.4.3.2.3 Study of heaving by water pressure

Where there is a permeable layer with artesian water below an impermeable layer, the progress of the cutting is accompanied by the soil mass above the piezometric surface declining until the weight of the soil mass is smaller than the upward water pressure. It then begins to float and finally breaks through the impermeable layer, harming the stability of the excavation work. For impermeable ground, such as a clay or silty clay layer near the bottom surface of a cut, the resistance factors include the weight of the soil mass, the friction between the impermeable layer and soil retaining wall, and the cohesiveness of the impermeable layer. The heaving tendency of the excavation bottom can be evaluated as[8]:

$$\frac{W}{F_1} + \frac{C_1}{F_2} + \frac{C_2}{F_3} \geq U \quad (13\text{-}6)$$

where, W is weight of soil mass shallower than the piezometric surface ($\Sigma B \cdot \gamma \cdot t$); C_1 is friction resistance of embedded part of the soil retaining wall and the ground ($2\Sigma f \cdot t_1$); C_2 is shear resistance of impermeable layer ($2\Sigma \tau \cdot t_2$); U is water pressure ($H \times B$); B is cut width, m; t is thickness of weight resistance layer, m; f is friction strength with wall surface, kN/m^2; τ is shear strength of ground, kN/m^2; t_1 is friction resistance thickness, m; t_2 is shear resistance thickness, m; γ is wet unit weight of weight resistance layer, kN/m^3; H is piezometric head acting on the bottom surface of impermeable layer, kN/m^2; F_1, F_2, F_3 is safety factors, with value of 1.1, 6.0 and 3.0, respectively.

Expansion reading 13-17

The shear strength of the impermeable layer [kN/m^2] is calculated as: $K_0 \cdot \sigma'_v \cdot \tan\varphi' + c'$, where effective overburden pressure at the focus is greater than or equal to 50 kN/m^2, and coefficient of earth pressure at rest $K_0 = 1 - \sin\varphi'$, where φ' is the effective internal friction angle.

Methods to stabilize the excavation bottom may be realized by increasing embedding length, lowering the groundwater level, forming a cutoff wall by the ground improvement method, or forming an impermeable layer by the ground improvement method.

13.4.3.3 Retaining walls

13.4.3.3.1 Embedding length

When to determine the embedding length of the retaining walls at a deep excavation, the following requirements should be met in checking calculation, as suggested in the design guideline by RTRI[8]:

(1) Embedding length at which the resistance moment produced by the lateral pressure on the passive side is 1.2 times the acting moment produced by lateral pressure of the active side, at the completion of cutting and before the lowest support work is installed.

(2) Embedding length necessary to stabilize the ground against heaving caused by background loads and, boiling and heaving by water pressure, respectively.

(3) Embedding length stipulated based on the stress and deformation of the soil retaining wall and the strength of struts.

(4) Embedding length obtained based on the bearing capacity of the soil retaining pile and soil retaining wall in the cases of vertical load action.

13.4.3.3.2 Bending stiffness of retaining wall

The beam elastoplastic spring method can be used in the evaluating the bending stiffness of the retaining wall. The bending stiffness used for obtaining the section force and deformation of the retaining wall is stipulated, such as by RTRI[8], with the maximum section forces being determined for both cutting and backfilling

Expansion reading 13-18

processes. Shallow cutting less than 15 m may be done by customary computation method.

13.4.3.3.3 Stiffness of supporting system

The effect of system stiffness for a propped retaining wall system on the maximum lateral deformation has been a subject for deep excavation project in soft soil for a long time. Since Rowe studied this problem with structural engineering principles, different definitions for wall system stiffness were developed by others, such as Goldberg et al.[11], Mana and Clough[12] and Clough et al.[10]. Recently, Yoo and Lee[13] using numerical method investigated the effects of the wall stiffness, unsupported depth and soil stiffness on the wall and ground movement characteristics at deep excavations. The combination effect of the parameters wall stiffness, unsupported depth and soil stiffness was presented in terms of a flexibility ratio:

$$F \approx \frac{E_s L^3}{EI} \qquad (13\text{-}7)$$

where E_s is the soil stiffness, L is the unsupported excavation length below the last support, and EI is the wall flexural rigidity.

Yoo and Lee[13] showed that L and over excavation have a greater influence on the wall deformations of a given excavation than EI does, provided that the basic stability is assured for the excavation work.

For a retaining wall-anchor (or strut) system, another well accepted definition of a retaining wall system stiffness (Clough et al.)[10] as:

$$k_s = EI/(\gamma_w h_{avg}^4) \qquad (13\text{-}8)$$

where γ_w is the unit weight of water and h_{avg} is the average vertical spacing of the anchors (or struts), E is the Young's modulus of the wall and I is the structural internal moment of inertia per unit length of the wall, EI is wall flexural rigidity.

Similarly, the magnitude of the average vertical spacing of the anchors (or struts), k_s, would have significant influence on the stiffness of the retaining wall system, since there is four to the power of h_{avg} in the Equation (13-8). For example, where the designed average vertical spacing of horizontal supports is 2.0 m and the retaining wall system stiffness with is presented as k_{s0}, the practical average vertical spacing of horizontal supports is 4.0 m in deed and the other parameters are same as what designed. From the Equation (13-8), the practical retaining wall system stiffness is calculated as 0.06 k_{s0}.

13.4.3.4 Ground movement and impact on nearby structures

In general, the tunneling of cut and cover tunnels is much more disruptive than that of bored tunnels[1]. The evaluation and mitigation of the tunneling impacts on adjacent structures, facilities and utilities are necessary for the design and construction of a cut and cover tunnel.

13.4.3.4.1 General features of ground movements

During tunneling of a cut and cover tunnel, the movement of the retained soils can be due to deflection of the support walls of the excavation and ground consolidation, provided the excavation work is stable. The general features of ground movement and retaining wall deformation is presented in Figure 13-16. Walls will deflect into the excavation as the excavation proceeds prior to the installation of each level of struts or tiebacks supporting the wall. The deflection is greater for flexible support systems than that for rigid systems. The deflections are not recoverable and they are cumulative (Figure 13-16), unless that re-prestress is applied to the horizontal supports, such as struts or anchors. At the same time, the settlement of the retained soils behind the walls increases with the accumulation of the lateral displacement of the retaining wall and the retained soils.

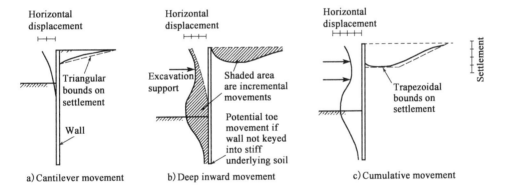

Figure 13-16 General profiles of ground movement and retaining wall deformation[14]

Where the dewatering during excavation leads to a drop in the hydrostatic pressure outside the cut, this can also lead to ground consolidation and settlement.

13.4.3.4.2 Measures

The influence of the ground movement due to excavation on the existing buildings and facilities at the excavation must be evaluated in the design and construction plan. The factors considered in the evaluation are the type of existing structure, its distance and orientation from the excavation, the soil conditions, the type of foundations of the structure and others. The analysis in the evaluation is project specific and can be very complex. In general, empirical methods available are first applied to characterize the potential impacts. Also, numerical analysis, as well as instrumentation and monitoring, is required for the sensitive buildings and facilities at the excavations during construction.

In terms of design and construction planning, measures to control the impact of tunneling on the nearby structures, such as to an acceptable level, generally include: ①to increase the wall system stiffness, such as through applying a stiffer and more watertight excavation support walls, such as by providing more closely spaced and stiffer excavation support braces and/or tiebacks; ②the application of pre-excavation soil improvement, underpinning of existing structures or auxiliary measures, to control the ground movement or protect the buildings; ③ the application of the OM[9], such as through instrumentation and monitoring during tunneling and the execution of mitigation plans if movements approach allowable limits.

13.5 Risks of construction

13.5.1 General

Cut and cover method is well used in shallow tunnel constructions. The successful case histories are countless. However, it seems also not an easy job to count out all of the failure cases of tunneling. In general, most of the accidents related to cut and cover tunnel constructions are from the origins of excavation failures or collapses. For example, the braced excavation collapse of the Nicoll highway, Singapore, on the 20th of April 2004, occurred during the trench excavation of the cut and cover tunnel section construction. The collapse started from the failure of the temporary lateral support system at a panel section, which had been excavated to the depth around 30 m, and then induced the collapses of nearby sections. The accident left a collapse zone 150 m wide, 100 m long, and 30 m deep. One of the chief reasons for the failure of the temporary lateral support system is due to the overestimation of the undrained shear strength capacity of the soil in design. This means that the mistake in the design would have contributed to the failure.

Although there may be one or two main factors, which induced construction accidents in some case histories, most of the failures of cut and cover tunnel construction are the results of the coupling functions of a few mistakes in the design and construction. For example, according to the Committee of Inquiry report on the collapse of the Nicoll highway, "The Collapse did not develop suddenly. A chain of events preceded the collapse that in retrospect appeared to be a warning of the problems that were developing". There were many warnings of approaching collapse but most of the warnings were either not taken seriously or ignored. Some of the incidents that happened prior to the collapse shed some light on the critical error in the design methodology that is the use of effective stress approach for the design of the diaphragm walls of the temporary retaining wall systems.

Expansion reading 13-19

The risk related to cut and cover tunnel construction is generally from trench excavation and the following tunnel structure building. The excavation stability is therefore the focus of both design and construction considerations. On the other hand, the unacceptable deformation of the retained soils and its influence on the neighbor structures are also the risk origins to be considered in a serious mode. For example, the push-in and the basal heave are two main overall failure mode of deep excavations and the failure of the stability of the excavation is mainly due to overall shear failure, which is the result of series of local shear failure and then these local failures develop into a continuous plane[7].

Push-in mechanism also can cause soil near the wall to heave. Similarly, when basal heave occurs, the soil around the excavation bottom will mostly heave. The failure surface may pass through the bottom of the retaining wall, or through soil below the bottom of the wall. Where the earth pressures on both sides of the wall reach the limiting state, push-in failure may follow. Under these situations, the large deformation of the retaining wall may induce unacceptable settlement and lateral displacement of the retained soils and neighbor structures.

13.5.2 Application of the observational method

For a large cut and cover tunnel project, various factors related to the improper design and construction may induce an unacceptable result or accident during construction, such as due to differing site, mistake in design analysis, improper construction or supporting materials, bad workmanship. Considering most of the unacceptable events did not occur suddenly but develop in a construction process, the application of the OM[9] is always beneficial to reduce the risk level of a project, provided the instrumentation plan is well designed and implemented during the tunnel construction.

Expansion reading 13-20

The following presents the instrumentation and monitoring for cut and cover tunnels, which are commonly applied in urban metro system. Although exact number of arrays and the spacing between them depends upon the ground conditions and the detail design of the station box or tunnel section, the instruments installed for monitoring generally include: deformations, pressures, stress/strain, groundwater level changing.

The implementation of the instrumentation and monitoring program, with the OM in application, should be started with a well designed plan, as discussed in Chapter 9, which includes the planning, execution, data management and application in tunneling. The success of the risk control in the tunneling depends on a successful implementation of the well designed instrumentation and monitoring program.

It is noted that some of the accidents may occur in a sudden way. For example, serious soil loss can occur in a sudden mode, especially where ground water seepage and leakage induce sand boiling in the excavation or water and soil inflow into the excavation. For these situations, much care should be taken in design and an emergency plan is required for the construction in the risk control planning.

13.6 Critical thinking problems

C1: Cut and cover tunnels are built under various situations and for different reasons. Consider: ①The applications of cut and cover tunnels in transportation lines; ②The typical construction sequences of a cut and cover tunnels, in terms of bottom-up and top-down constructions, respectively; ③ What are the main advantages and disadvantages of the applications of bottom-up and top-down constructions, respectively? ④Why are there variations developed for the cut and cover tunnel constructions?

C2: Where a cut and cover tunnel is planned, the excavation and supporting system is to be chosen. Consider: ①Types of excavations in practice and their main applications; ②Types of retaining walls in practice and their main applications; ③Types of horizontal support methods in practice and their main applications; ④Commonly used auxiliary measures in cut and cover tunnel construction and their applications at deep excavations; ⑤ Why are dewatering and groundwater level control important to cut and cover tunnel construction? ⑥What are the factors generally considered in supporting system choosing for a large cut and cover tunnel in urban area?

C3: Where a cut and cover tunnel is planned, there are various factors under considerations. Consider: ①Safety factors often considered in cut and cover tunnel design and why is the magnitude of a safety factor for different limit states probably changing? ②What are the main considerations for the main structure design of a cut and cover tunnel? ③Of the design considerations for retaining systems, what are the main aspects to be analyzed, in terms of the stability of excavation bottom and the supporting capacity of retaining system, respectively?

C4: Where a deep excavation is to be cut for the tunneling of a large cut and cover tunnel in urban area, risk control is always one of the main tasks. Consider: ①What are probable risks to be considered in the design and tunneling plan? ②What are the countermeasures usually used for controlling the risks to an acceptable level? ③Why is the application of the OM necessary, helpful and beneficial for the risk control of the tunnel project?

13.7 References

[1] U. S. Department of Transportation, FHWA. Technical Manual for Design and Construction of Road Tunnels-Civil Elements[M/OL]. Books Express Publishing, 2009. http://www.fhwa.dot.gov/bridge/tunnel/pubs/nhi09010/tunnel_manual.pdf.

[2] Twine D. Cut-and-cover tunnels[J]. The Arup Journal, 1/2004, 29-32.

[3] Bickel J O, Kuesel T R, King E H. Tunnel Engineering Handbook[M]. 2nd ed. Chapman & Hall, 1996.

[4] Ma J Q, Berggren B, Bengtsson P-E, et al. Behavior of anchored walls in soils overlying rock in Stockholm[J]. International Journal of Geoengineering Case Histories, 2010, 2(1): 1-23.

[5] Mouratidis A. The "cut-and-cover" and "cover-and-cut" techniques in highway engineering [J]. EJGE, 2008, 13, Bund E: 1-15.

[6] Long M. Database for Retaining Wall and Ground Movements due to Deep Excavations[J]. Journal of Geotechnical & Geoenvironmental Engineering, 2001, 127(3): 203-224.

[7] Ou C-Y. Deep Excavation: Theory and Practice[M]. Taylor & Francis, 2006.

[8] The Railway Technical Research Institute (RTRI). Design Standards for Railway Structures and Commentary (Cut and Cover Tunnel)[M]. Japan, Maruzen Co., Ltd., 2008.

[9] Peck R B. Advantages and limitations of the observational method in applied soil mechanics [J]. Geotechnique, 1969. 19(2): 171-187.

[10] Clough G W, Smith E M, Sweeney B P. Movement control of excavation support systems by iterative design[M] // Geotechnical Special Publication 22, ASCE, Vol. 2, c1989: 869-884.

[11] Goldberg D T, Jaworski W E, Gordon M D. Lateral support systems and underpinning, Volume Ⅲ: Construction methods [R/OL]. Federal Highway Administration, Washington, D. C. 1976. https://rosap.ntl.bts.gov/view/dot/14531/dot_14531_DS1.pdf?download-document-submit = Download.

[12] Mana A I, Clough G W. Prediction of movements for braced cuts in clay[J]. J. Geotech. Engrg., 1981, 107(6), 759-777.

[13] Yoo C, Lee D. Deep excavation-induced ground surface movement characteristics-A numerical investigation[J]. Computers & Geotechnics, 2008, 35(2):231-252.

[14] Clough G, O'Rourke T. Construction Induced Movements of Insitu Walls[C] // Design and Performance of Earth Retaining Structures, ASCE, 1990.

14 Immersed Tunnels

14.1 Introduction

Expansion reading 14-1

The words immersed tunnel imply where and how a tunnel is built. In the definition by the ITA WG Immersed and Floating Tunnels, an immersed tunnel consists of several prefabricated tunnel elements, which are floated to the site, installed one by one and connected to one another under water[1,2]. An immersed tunnel is generally installed in a trench that has been dredged previously in the bottom of a waterway during the tunnel elements being constructed in the dry docks. The space between the trench bottom and the soffit of the tunnel can be a previously prepared gravel bed, or sandbedding pumped or jetted underneath the tunnel. Piled foundations are sometimes used, where soil conditions require them. As construction proceeds, the trench is backfilled. The completed tunnel is usually covered with a protective layer over the roof.

The history of immersed tunnel practice began in 1910, with the construction of a two-track railway tunnel across the Detroit River between the United States and Canada[1]. The first concrete box immersed tunnel, the Maas Tunnel in Rotterdam (the Netherlands), was built in 1941, and considerable number of tunnels were constructed in Europe with this method[2]. In general, the steel shell method is commonly used in the United States and the concrete box method in Europe. Of the two basic techniques, each has unique advantages and limitations, depending on the site. For example, Japan built tunnels of both types[2]. Also, the multiple-lane requirements of a road tunnel lead usually to the concrete box scheme.

The immersed tunnel method has been used for about 100 years and around 200 immersed tunnels have been constructed worldwide[4]. They mainly serve as road or rail tunnels, but immersed tunnels are also used for water supply and electric cables. In recent years, immersed tunnels have become wider (2 × four-lane or 2 × five-lane, multimodal rail and road), deeper and conditions more challenging (off-shore or close to off-shore). Long tunnels, such as the 6.7 km immersed tunnel of the Hong Kong-Zhuhai-Macao Bridge (HZMB) in China and the 17.6-km-long Fehmarnbelt Fixed Link (FFL) between Denmark and Germany, require special approaches in terms of operation, tunnel safety and construction, such as the production of tunnel elements at the factory, including cast and launch. On the other hand, some tunnels have been built in very challenging ground conditions, where soil treatment on a large scale was applied, such as sand compaction piles in the HZMB project and cement deep mixing piles of the Busan-Geoje Fixed Link in South Korea.

Expansion reading 14-2

14.2 Features and applications

14.2.1 Features of immersed tunnels

An immersed tunnel does not suit every situation. However, whenever there is a need to cross a body of water, it is beneficial to consider an immersed tunnel as an option. In the pre-design phase there is commonly a choice to make between a bridge, bored tunnel or immersed tunnel. The final choice of crossing method will of course depend on many factors. The main advantage of the immersed tunnels is that they can be considerably more cost effective than alternative options, i.e., a bored tunnel beneath the water being crossed (if indeed this is possible at all due to other factors such as the geology and seismic activity) or a bridge. The other advantages of an immersed tunnel may include the followings.

(1) *Economic use of shape (cross section)*. The cross section of an immersed tunnel does not have to be circular as it does for a bored tunnel, such as with TBM. A wide variety of cross section demands can be accommodated, making immersed tunnels particularly attractive for wide road and combined road/rail tunnels, for example, the cross section of the Oresund tunnel between Denmark and Sweden. The Oresund tunnel includes two railway tubes, two motorway tubes and an escape gallery. The outer dimensions of the cross section are 8.6 m × 41.7 m.

Expansion reading 14-3

(2) *Economic length*. Immersed tunnels can be placed on the bed of a waterway or just below it, while a bored tunnel normally must be placed at least a one diameter below the bed of the waterway. Under this situation, immersed tunnels may have special advantages over bored tunnels for water crossings at some locations since they lie only a short distance below water bed level. Approaches can therefore be relatively short and/or approach gradients to be flatter.

(3) *Minimal disruption to the waterway and environment*. Tunnels offer an unlimited vertical clearance for shipping compared to a bridge. During tunneling, the impact of immersed method on daily shipping life is relatively low, as tunnel elements can be produced outside the congested areas and can dramatically reduce the hindrance to the environment.

(4) *Flexibility of profile*. Although the shape of the tunnel profile is often partly dictated by what is possible for the connecting tunnel types, the flexibility of

profile is often one of the advantages of an immersed tunnel. The tunnels can be round, oval or rectangular in shape. In general, for a large strait crossing, a wider rectangular shape is cost effective for wider tunnels.

(5) *Safety and speed of construction*. In general, immersed tunneling consists of four operations, i. e., dredging, tunnel ramp/entrance construction, tunnel element construction and tunnel installation, which can take place concurrently and can generally be completed in less time than a bored tunnel. Safety of construction is always assured for the element building work in a dry dock as opposed to the situations of boring beneath a water body, especially mining in the soft and permeable ground.

(6) *High adaptability to ground condition or seismic conditions*. The elements of an immersed tunnel can be constructed in ground conditions, which would preclude bored tunneling or render it unfeasibly expensive, such as under the conditions of the soft alluvial deposits characteristic of large river estuaries. Immersed tunnels can also be designed to handle the forces and movements associated with earthquakes.

Every coin has two sides. The main disadvantages of an immersed tunnel include the followings: ①immersed tunnels are often partly exposed on the river/sea bed or shallow-buried, risking a sunken ship/anchor strike; ②direct contact with water necessitates careful waterproofing design around the joints; ③the segmental approach requires careful design of the connections, where longitudinal effects and forces must be transferred across; ④environmental impact of tube and underwater embankment on existing channel/sea bed. On the other hand, immersed tunnels have potential disadvantages in terms of environmental disturbance to the water body bed, such as the impact on fish habitats, ecology, current, and turbidity of the water. In addition, many of the water bodies such as harbors or causeways have contaminated sediments requiring special handling. The use of immersed tunnel techniques might encounter such contaminated ground and would require its regulated disposal.

14.2.2 Applications

Immersed tunnels (or immersed tubes) are often used for crossing a body of shallow water. As the above discussed, immersed tunnels may have special advantages over bored tunnels for shallow water crossings at some locations, since they lie only a short distance below water bed level. Approaches can therefore be relatively short. For example, where the waterway to be crossed is an important shipping channel, a high and wide clearance is needed for large ships in the navigational channel. This requirement will increase the costs of a bridge.

Compared with high level bridges or bored tunnels, which should be deeper than the immersed tunnels, the approaching of the immersed tunnel will be shorter than that of the bridge or bored tunnel. Figure 14-1 shows how the length of the crossing of a waterway differs in each case scheme. This allows immersed tunnel approaches to be shorter especially for rail tunnels where the required gradients are low. The beneficial of an immersed tunnel is clear in this term.

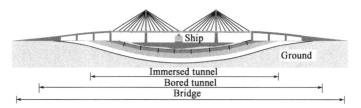

Figure 14-1   Immersed tunnels can be shorter than other types of crossing[3]

If a high and wide clearance is needed for large ships in the navigational channel, the bridge piers may have adverse effect on the water body bed or changing of embankments of a watercourse. Hydraulic impact and blockage effects become more and more an issue in a lot of places when it comes to the realization of a crossing. Especially in rivers with large discharges and substantial sediment transport, the presence of obstacles in the river (such as bridge piers) may result in serious scouring and sedimentation, resulting in banks or even small islands and the changing of embankments during periods of high discharge.

Expansion reading 14-4

The ground conditions do influence immersed-tunnel design, but the impact is less than for bored or mined tunnels. Immersed tunnels can be built in any shape of cross-section so the space can be optimized, especially in comparison to circular bored tunnels. Immersed tunnels can be made to suit horizontal and vertical alignments, since the tunnels can be constructed in soils, which would be a real challenge to a long-span bridge structure. Also, the construction of immersed tunnels will cause relatively less impact on the water body bed. As a result, an immersed tunnel may be very cost competitive.

14.3   Structures of immersed tunnels

Immersed tunnels are applied in crossing water, such as river, lake, strait, bay or a channel of sea. The immersed tunnel can be the man structure of a project, or part of a hybrid solution, which often combines an immersed tunnel at the deepest section of the crossing, or the main sea-route, with bored "approach" tunnel or cut and cover tunnel, bridge. The structures of the approach sections to the immersed tunnel mainly depend on the geotechnical and geographical conditions of the coast or bank area. For example, where the immersed tunnel is the main structure of the project and the coast slope is of wide beach, the immersed tunnel is always connected to cut and cover approach tunnels, such as Fehmarnbelt Fixed Link between Denmark and Germany. Otherwise, a bored approach tunnel is often an optimization.

Where the immersed tunnel is part of a hybrid solution and the tunnel is connected to a bridge, the transition between the immersed tunnel and its approach structures may be located in an artificial island. One of the famous recent examples is the building of the artificial island in the project of the Oresund Link. A more recent example, the island and immersed tunnel project of the HZMB in China, in which the two artificial islands, each approx 625-m-long, have been constructed for the transition between the bridges and the approach tunnel. The tunnel cross section comprises two traffic tubes (a separate tube for each traffic direction) and an escape/service gallery in between the traffic tubes. The length of the standard element is 180-m-long, with 8 m × 22.5 m segments.

Expansion reading 14-5

14.3.1 Fabrication

Immersed tunnels consist of large pre-cast concrete or concrete-filled steel tunnel elements fabricated in the dry dock and installed under water. Concrete tunnel elements are fabricated inside dry decks or specially constructed casting basins. Sometimes the cofferdam for the approach ramp structure is first used as a basin for the fabrication of the tunnel elements[1]. Occasionally elements have been fabricated on semi-submersibles or launched using a marine lift[2]. Steel tunnel elements are usually fabricated in a shipyard. After the element is launched, most of the interior concrete is installed while the element is floating. The element is then placed in the trench. Steel shell tunnels have also been fabricated and partly concreted in drydocks[1].

Tunnel elements are fabricated in convenient lengths on shipways, in dry docks, or in improvised floodable basins, sealed with bulkheads at each end, and then floated out. They can be towed successfully over great distances. For example, of the Busan-Geoje Fixed Link, Busan, South Korea, the construction of the tunnel elements is carried out in a temporary precast yard on the western side of the Jinhae Bay, about 40 km from the immersion area. The casting of the tunnel elements is carried out in two batches of four and two batches of five tunnel elements, respectively. The tunnel elements are 180-m-long, 10-m-high, 26-m-wide and weigh about 48000 t. The tunnel elements are closed off with steel, reusable bulkhead panels on both ends.

14.3.1.1 Tunnel cross-section

In most cases, the selection of the typical cross-section is determined by preferences based on successful previous experience in the specific region or country, as well as local site constraints. For example, the listed practices[2] show that steel shell tunnels are often designed in the USA, concrete tunnels are usually selected in northwest Europe, and in Japan, where both concepts are applied.

The structure of a steel shell tunnel consists of relatively thin-walled composite steel and concrete rings. The steel shell provides the water barrier. The ballast concrete is placed outside the shell in pockets formed between the structural diaphragms. Concrete tunnels are monolithic structures, of which most of the final weight is incorporated in the structural components.

There is a wide range of cross-sectional configurations, mainly depending on the intended use of the tunnels. In determining the ultimate shape and size of the tunnel cross-section, the designers must consider, for example, whether the tunnel is to be used for railway or road traffic; how many tracks or lanes are required; whether it will be a single tube, double tubes, or multiple tubes; what the ventilation requirements will be; and what construction practices will be applied.

Low-point drainage sumps have to be provided within the confines of the structure. In binocular double-steel shell tunnels, the sump can be placed between the tubes. In single-steel-shell and concrete tunnels, the sumps have to be placed underneath the roadway. The presence of service galleries is helpful in positioning the pumps. Generally, for given cross-sectional requirements for vehicular space and ventilation, the concrete box section can be made shallower than the steel shell section. However, for the same conditions, the steel section is generally a narrower section.

14.3.1.2 Steel shell tunnels

For steel shell tunnels, a circular-shaped section for a single tube or a binocular shape for a double-tube cross section are the most economical for external pressure loading, as the sections of the structural rings are in compression at all times. An additional benefit is that the space between the roadway slab and the invert and the space above the suspended ceiling, if applied, can be used for air supply and exhaust for transverse ventilation. These spaces can also be used for services. Steel immersed tunnel elements can be categorized into three subtypes[4]: single shell, the double-shell tunnel and sandwich.

The single-steel-shell concept is used for tunnels with one or two relatively narrow tubes, such as tunnels for metro rail transportation. The steel shell is on the outside and acts compositely with the internal ring concrete. The ballast concrete, which is proportionately less than for a larger double-steel-shell highway tunnel, is placed on top of the element to keep the shell as small in section as possible (Figure 14-2). For single tubes, a circular shape is preferable and sharp corners are avoided.

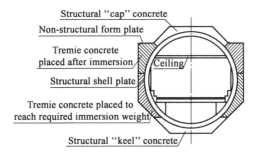

Figure 14-2 Circular double-shell steel immersed tunnel design[4]

Expansion reading 14-6

A double-steel-shell tunnel may be applied in larger vehicular tunnels. The usual configuration involves one or two tubes, each having two roadway lanes. The structure consists of a circular steel shell stiffened with steel diaphragms. A reinforced concrete ring installed inside the shell is tied to the shell and acts composite with the shell and the diaphragms. The main structures are designed to resist applied hydrostatic and soil loadings. Steel elements welded to the exterior flange plates of the diaphragms is a second shell, the form plate, which acts as a container for the ballast concrete, partly placed as tremie. The ballast weight provides the required negative buoyancy.

Expansion reading 14-7

A sandwich structure is where internal steel diaphragms connect internal and external structure steel plates, to form closed cells that are subsequently filled with unreinforced non-shrink self-compacting concrete (Figure 14-3). This type of tunnel is a relatively recent development in Japan, where it has been used for the Osaka South Port and Kobe Port tunnels[4].

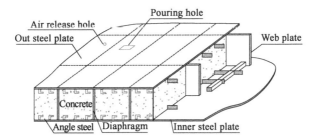

Figure 14-3 Sketch showing the steel sandwich used in Naha Port & Kobe Port tunnel, Japan[6]

14.3.1.3 Concrete tunnels

For concrete tunnels, circular shapes have sometimes been used for single tubes (in combination with transverse ventilation) and for relatively narrow service tunnels. For railway tunnels with two single-track tubes, the near binocular shape is often used because of the obvious advantage for transverse load transfer. However, the shape most often used for double- and multiple-tube concrete traffic tunnels is the rectangular box, which may have to be widened with extra cells for ventilation air supply and services. The box shape best approaches the rectangular internal clearance for traffic, with good conformity between resistance and weight. The box shape also permits practical concrete construction practice. When longitudinal ventilation would be sufficient, all of the services can be kept within the traffic tubes-that is, along the roof and inside the ballast concrete underneath the roadway or walkway. Often, however, a special services gallery is preferred or may be required by the fire department for emergency escape.

Of the concrete tunnels, the Oresund Link is special and in a number of ways extending the possibilities for the immersed tunnel technique for major sea crossings. The tunnel includes two railway tubes, two motorway tubes and an escape gallery. The outer dimensions of the cross section are 8.6 m ×41.7 m. In terms of elements fabrication, the total length of the 3500 m immersed part of the tunnel is divided into 20 elements, each 176-m-long; and an element is made up of 8 segments of 22 m each. The design of the elements are referenced by the following sea crossing immersed tunnel projects, such as the Busan-Geoje Fixed Link, Busan, South Korea and the immersed tunnel of the HZMB in China. For example, the structures of the immersed tunnel of the HZMB consist of 33 tunnel elements. With the cross sectional dimensions of 11.5 m × 37.95 m (Figure 14-4), the element self-weight is almost 80000 tons.

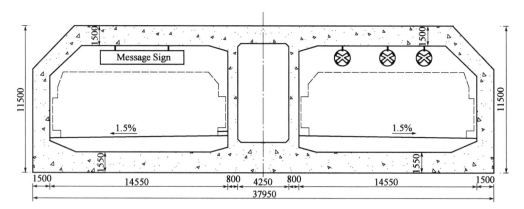

Figure 14-4 Cross section of the element of the immersed tunnel of the HZMB in China(unit:mm)[9]

For special cases, the length of the elements of an immersed tunnel may be short and the center wall of the element structure is not in a continuous form. For example, the immersed tunnel in the North/South Metro line in Amsterdam[8] is for the platform tunnel, which is underneath the railway station, 130-m-long, 21-m-wide and 8 m in height. The tunnel is designed as a segmental tunnel, consisting of 7 segments with lengths varying from 14.5 m to 21 m. In the sake of public safety and surveillance during operation, the centre support of the tunnel cross section is designed as a row of columns with heavy longitudinal beams at roof and floor slab level.

For long tunnels, service facilities for both operation and safety control are also the key factors of the tunnel element design considerations. For example, in the immersed tunnel for the 17.6-km-long FFL between Denmark and Germany, the tunnel elements consist of a combined road and rail cross-section all at one level, contained within a concrete structure. Two types of tunnel elements are designed as standard elements and special elements[7], respectively. The standard elements represent the major part (> 95% in length) of the immersed tunnel section. Each standard element has a maximum length of approximately 217 m. The elements have the same geometric layout and are, to a high degree, interchangeable. The high degree of standardization will allow an industrialized construction method, as developed for the Oresund project.

Expansion reading 14-8

Of the FFL tunnel, the special elements, which are about one every 1.8 km along the length of the immersed tunnel, will provide space within the tunnel dedicated for mechanical and electrical equipment. The concentration of the tunnel installations and access facilities for maintenance staff in these special elements resulted in a further optimization of the standard elements. Underneath the road and rail tubes there will be access to all areas of the tunnel in order to reduce the disruption of the traffic to a minimum.

14.3.1.4 A composite steel-concrete tunnel

A composite steel-concrete immersed tunnel was used for the Marmaray tunnel in Turkey, crossing the Bosporus between Asia and Europe[9]. The Marmaray tunnel project comprises 9.8 km long underground tunnel, 2.4-km-long cut-and-cover and 1.4-km-long immersed tube connecting Asia and Europe under the Bosphorus Strait with railway crossing. The Marmaray immersed tube crossing is the deepest tunnel in the world with its unique depth of 58 m.

The elements of the Marmaray immersed tunnel consist of sandwich steel end shells[6] and concrete tube. The steel end shell consists of nine prefabricated sections. The open ends of the tube elements were wrapped with bulk head. The end shells were designed to accommodate gasket beam. The gasket beam serves to hold rubber gasket as a temporary seal. The function of the rubber gasket is to ensure smooth connection and watertightness between two tube elements during the period from the sinking of the elements to the completion of the permanent works[9].

Expansion reading 14-9

14.3.2 Joints

Joints applied in immersed tunnels are classified as immersion joint (or typical joint), closure or final joint, earthquake joint, construction joint and segment or dilatation joint[1,2]. All joints are gasketed and tightly closed for waterproof.

All immersed tunnel joints must be watertight throughout the design life and can accommodate expected movements caused by differences in temperature, creep, settlement, earthquake motions, method of construction, etc[6], respectively. Displacements in any direction should be limited so that the waterproof limits of a joint are not exceeded. In design, joint shear capability should take into account the influence of normal forces and bending moments on the shear capacity of the section. Joints must be ductile in addition to accommodating longitudinal movements. The design should also take account of shear forces generated where the faces of the joints are not normal to the tunnel axis. Tension ties may be used for limiting movement so that joints do not leak or break open, especially during a seismic event. The axial compression of tunnel elements and bulkheads due to the depth of immersion should be taken into account in determining joint dimensions at installation.

14.3.2.1 Immersion joints

The immersion joints, also called typical joint, between the tunnel elements can be permanent flexible rubber compression gaskets, as is often the case for concrete tunnels[1]; also can be made rigid, as is usual with steel tunnels[2]. These gaskets are pre-installed at one end of each tunnel element. The watertight joint is dewatered when an element is installed at the seabed.

The immersion joint is usually formed when a tunnel section is joined to the section that is already in place on the seabed. After placing the new element and joining it with the previously placed element, the space between the bulkheads of the two adjoining elements is then dewatered. In order to dewater this space, a watertight seal must be made. A temporary gasket with a soft nose such as the Gina gasket [Figure 14-5a)] is often used. In addition an omega seal [Figure 14-5b)] is provided after dewatering the joint from inside the joint.

For immersion joints, the primary immersion seal is usually made of natural or neoprene rubber compounds. For a "Gina" type, it consists of a main body with designed load/compression characteristics and an integral nose and seating ridge. The materials used should have a proven resistance to the specific corrosive qualities of the water and soils and an expected life no shorter than the design life of the tunnel unless the gasket is considered temporary. For flexible joints, a secondary seal is usually required in case of failure of the primary seal. It is usually manufactured from chloroprene rubber to an overall cross-section corresponding to that known as an "Omega" type [Figure 14-5b)].

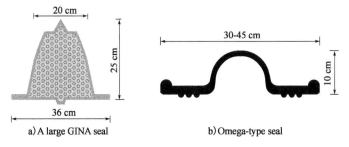

a) A large GINA seal   b) Omega-type seal

Figure 14-5 Types of watertight seals applied in immersion joint

For rigid joint of immersed tunnel, the space between the elements at the joint is filled with cast-in-place concrete, under the protection of the installed outer waterproof formwork around the joint. After immersion, permanent seal of the joint section is provided by a watertight (steel) plate that is to be covered by rigid reinforced concrete joint member.

Expansion reading 14-10

It is essential that immediately after dewatering of the chamber between the two bulkheads, an inspection of the primary seal is made so that any lack of watertightness can be remedied. Similarly, the secondary seal of a flexible joint should be pressure tested up to the expected maximum service pressure via a test pipe and valve to ensure that it too can function as required. After a successful testing, the chamber between the seals is de-watered.

14.3.2.2 Closure or final joint

Where the last element has to be inserted between previously placed elements rather than appended to the end of the previous element, a marginal gap will exist at the secondary end. This short length of tunnel sometimes is completed as cast-in-place concrete and is known as the closure or final joint.

Intermediate joints can also be made rigid. This is done at the inside of the temporary immersion seal by welding lap plates to the shells of steel tunnels or by placing concrete for concrete tunnels. The final joint must always be made in-situ[1].

The form of the closure or end joint is dependent on the sequence and method of construction. Closure joints may also be similar to the immersion joints, although details may need to be different. Potential options for the closure joints include the followings[6].

(1) Place the last element between two previously placed elements and dewater one joint between the newly placed element and the one of the previously placed

elements. Then insert under water closure form plates and place tremie concrete around the closure joint to seal it. The joint can then be dewatered and interior concrete can be completed from within the joint. Other methods such as telescopic extension joints and wedge joints have been developed to make the closure joint similar to the immersion joint.

(2) Construct both end (terminal) joints first, lay the tunnel elements outwards from these and complete the immersed tunnel with a special closure (final) joint.

(3) Construct one terminal joint first and lay all the immersed tunnel elements outwards from that side and backfill over the top of the final element, using a soil-cement mixture (or other reasonably watertight material) in the vicinity of the second terminal joint, and then construct the structures abutting the second terminal joint after the immersed tunnel is complete.

(4) Lay and complete the immersed tunnel with or without a special closure joint and backfill at the terminal elements using a soil-cement mixture (or other watertight material) in the vicinity of both terminal joints, and then construct the structures abutting the both terminal joints after the immersed tunnel is complete.

14.3.2.3 Earthquake joint

Earthquake joint is a specially designed immersion joint to accommodate large differential movements in any direction due to a seismic event. It is also applied to a semi-rigid or flexible joint strengthened to carry seismic loads and across which stressed or unstressed prestressing components may be installed[2].

In order to achieve the performance requirements, the structural elements generally have to be designed in such a way that in the post-elastic range damage and deformations are controlled and the structural elements are ductile, and the immersed tunnel elements and joints shall remain watertight.

Upon the completion of the compression phase, the secondary Omega seal is installed[5], because the Gina gasket requires a minimum compression to achieve water-tightness while the Omega seal does not. Since none of them can transmit substantial shear or tension, shear keys and tendons are installed. A shear key at the bottom of the tunnel will transmit transverse shear forces, while two similar shear keys in the side-walls will transmit vertical shear. The tendons could transmit a limited amount of tension if necessary. It is hoped that given the initial compression of the Gina gasket, it will be unlikely for net tension to take place, as this would imply excessive decompression. To resist the anticipated strong seismic shaking, the installation of tendons is as a second line of defense. Tendons are connected through couplers, which is adjusted to allow some decompression before being activated.

Expansion reading 14-11

14.3.2.4 Segment or dilatation joint

Moveable segment joints must be able to transmit shear across the joint, allowing dilatation and rotation. So it is also called expansion joint[2]. Expansion joint is a special moveable watertight joint between segments of a tunnel element. The joints contain an injectable rubber-metal waterstop as well as neoprene and hydrophilic seals. The segmental joint uses Omega seal and injectable rubber-metal gasket to seal water. The 2 mm polyurea waterproofing paint covered by 1.5 mm PVC isolating membrane will be sprayed externally within 1.2 m on the segmental joint. Four vertical and horizontal reinforced concrete shear keys, respectively, are designed to transfer shear forces caused by longitudinal bending and twisting.

Expansion reading 14-12

14.3.2.5 Construction joint

Construction joint is a horizontal or vertical connection between monolithic parts of a structure, used for facilitating construction. A waterstop is commonly placed in such a joint.

14.3.3 Watertightness

The structural concrete should be designed to be watertight. Immersed tunnels have a few in-situ joints. With regard to watertightness, this is quite an advantage over most bored tunnels. Immersed tunnels are designed to be watertight. Steel shell tunnels are watertight by virtue of the quality of the many welds of the shell made in the fabrication yard, by virtue of the quality of the in-situ joints, and on the quality of the flexible joints. The watertightness of concrete tunnels depends on the quality of the joints, on the absence of full-depth cracks in the concrete, and on the quality of the waterproofing, such as watertight enveloping membranes.

Expansion reading 14-13

For the immersed tube element of the Marmaray tunnel in Turkey[9], the contractor is intending to use a steel membrane for the sides and base, and an adhering waterproofing sheet on the roof covered with protective concrete. The top slab may be waterproofed using San-A Sheet, made of Ethylene Vinyl Acetate (EVA) that has napped (hairy) layers on both sides. The concrete structure is first formed and then a layer of polymer cement paste is applied as adhesive for the EVA sheet. The protection concrete will also adhere to the napped upper surface. The edges are sealed to the steelwork using epoxy adhesives. In lieu of anchoring ribs for the steel waterproofing, strips of the same material will be used for dividing the surface of the steel waterproofing membrane into the required 10 m² panels.

Depending upon the type of waterproofing applied, the protections on the sides and top of the tunnel elements are often required to ensure that the waterproofing system remains undamaged during all operations up to final placement and during subsequent backfilling operations.

14.4 Construction

Immersed tunnels consist of large pre-cast concrete or concrete-filled steel tunnel elements fabricated in the dry dock and installed under water. The construction of an immersed tunnel mainly includes the activities of elements fabrication, trench and foundation preparation, floating, towing, elements placement, backfilling. Tunnel elements are fabricated in convenient lengths on shipways, in dry docks, or in improvised floodable basins, sealed with bulkheads at each end, and then floated out. The elements can be towed over great distances to their final locations. Then they are immersed into a prepared trench, and joined to previously placed tunnel elements. The tunnel elements can be installed on a pre-installed gravel bed or after the immersion of the tunnel element on temporary supports, the gap between the tunnel base and the trench is filled with sand using the sand flow method. After additional foundation works have been completed, the trench around the immersed tunnel is backfilled and the water bed reinstated. The top of the tunnel should preferably be at least 1.0-1.5 m below the original bottom to allow for sufficient protective backfill. However, in a few cases where the hydraulic regime allowed, the tunnel has been placed higher than the original water bed within an underwater protective embankment[4].

The traditional European method for constructing an immersed tunnel is to establish one or more casting basins as open excavations, where the individual tunnel elements are constructed. When the elements are completed, they are sealed with temporary bulkheads and the casting basin is flooded with water. The elements are floated one by one to their intended location, immersed into their final position on the seabed, and linked together. The tunnel is normally placed in a pre-dredged trench in the seabed of the waterway. The connection to the land surface is normally connected to a cut and cover tunnel to overcome the level between the water and the land surface. Variations in the construction method deal primarily with materials and the location of the fabrication site, where the elements are constructed.

The construction activities of an immersed tunnel will be briefly presented, in terms of elements fabrication, tunnel element towing, immersion and installation of tunnel elements at sea bed.

14.4.1 Tunnel element fabrication

The element fabrication of a steel tunnel is usually done by modules, with each module being in the range of 5m long and spanning between diaphragms. The modules are then connected and welded together to form the completed shell of the tunnel element.

Concrete tunnel elements are usually constructed in a number of full-width segments to reduce the effects of shrinkage and the placing of keel concrete should be done in such a way that it avoids any overstressing or excessive deflections in the bottom shell and its stiffeners[6]. The segment joints may be construction joints with reinforcement running through them, or they may be movement joints. Where concrete segments are with movement joints, they are joined together using temporary or permanent post-tensioning to form complete elements at least during transportation and installation.

The techniques of tunnel element fabrication have been greatly improved in the recent years, mainly due to the success of some famous immersed tunnels. One of the examples is the immersed tunnel of the Oresund Link, in which a number of ways extending the possibilities for the immersed tunnel technique for major sea crossings. To meet the tight time schedule, an industrial production method, with 2 production lines (Figure 14-6), was used in the production of elements. This method has been followed by the recent immersed tunnels, such as tunnel of the Busan-Geoje Fixed Link in South Korea and the tunnel of the HZMB in China. In the more recent FFL between Denmark and Germany, 8 production lines are applied at a working site of elements fabrication in order to meet the planned time schedule (Figure 14-7), in which the other logistic facilities are also illustrated in a sketch mode.

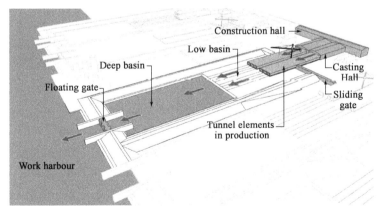

Figure 14-6 Sketch showing the production of elements using an industrial production method, Oresund tunnel, Denmark

14.4.1.1 Fabrication in an industrial production method

In an industrial production method, each element is cast in short sections called segments. One segment is expected to be cast at each production line every 7-8

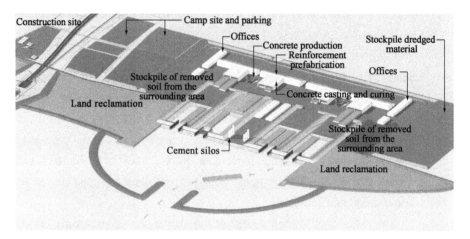

Figure 14-7 Sketch showing the working site of the element fabrication of the Fehmarnbelt Fixed Link

days. Each segment is cast in formwork on a fixed casting bed. After a minimum curing period, the segment is pushed free of the casting bed and out into the shallow launching basin by hydraulic jacks to give space for the next segment to be cast (Figure 14-7). Once sufficient segments for one element have been made, they are joined by tension cables. The construction method applied in the Oresund tunnel by casting each tunnel segment in a single pour (2600 m^3 in about 30 hrs) can effectively avoid concrete cracking during fabrication. However, careful consideration is still needed for early age stress management. This included concrete mixture selection, pour sequence, ambient temperature control in the factory, selective insulation of the concrete and timing of the all aspects of the production of a segment, including pour, strip and jack sequence[9].

Once a complete tunnel element has been produced, it is pushed the last part of the way into the shallow part of the launching basin, where watertight bulkheads are mounted at each end of the element. The basin is then cut off from the production area by a sliding gate and from the sea by a floating gate. The launching basin, surrounded by dikes and gates, is then filled with water in a controlled process until the tunnel elements float (Figure 14-8). Then the tunnel elements are pulled into the deep section of the launching basin and moored, after which the water level is lowered down to the initial level, such as in the Fehmarnbelt Link project by pumping water out of the basin. Subsequently the sliding gate and floating gate can be opened. The upper shallow basin is now dry again and ready for the next tunnel elements.

From the deep basin, the elements are then towed to a fixed holding area, from where they are ready for immersion into the tunnel trench. Prior to towing, a system of ballast tanks has been installed inside the element, and when it reaches the holding area, the element is connected to the pontoons needed for the immersion operation.

a) Steel bar framework for a segment

b) The finshed reinforcement concrete segment

c) Overview of the elements fabrication working site

Figure 14-8 Elements fabrication for the immersed tunnel of the HZMB in China❶

14.4.1.2 Finishing the fabrication in two stages

It is noted that a factory production method for tunnel elements is beneficial to the high quality concrete works by using full section casting and meeting construction schedule. But the concrete immersed elements are constructed in a large excavation basin. The excavation has to be below the water level, so that it can be flooded once the tunnel elements are complete, to allow them to be floated out to their final location. For a tunnel like the Oresund tunnel, this method would have involved a huge excavation and extensive water level lowering for a period of years[9]. A basin large enough would be also expensive.

In the construction of the immersed tunnel of the Marmaray Crossing in Turkey, a new and unique construction method was developed[9]. The immersed tube elements were fabricated in two stages and therefore no deep and large basin was required during fabrication. The first stage was undertaken in two dry docks, including the base slab casting (Phase 1) and the following castings of lower part outer walls and inner wall (Phase 2) in full length. The casting time interval between Phase 1 and Phase 2 concretes was limited to 14 days since increasing

---

❶ http://en.ccchzmb.com

stiffness of the base slab by the time was a significant factor causing external restraint stress during hydration of the wall concrete[9]. In the second stage, the half-cast tunnel element was towed out to the temporary jetty area. The upper part of the wall elements and top slab were cast together in a single operation under floating condition, as shown in Figure 14-9, by dividing the element into six casting sections (Phase 3). Using floating pontoons as working platforms, this procedure enables new tunnel elements to be started when the tunnel elements are only half finished and then shortens the overall construction time.

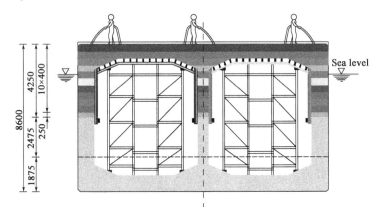

Figure 14-9　Sketch showing the element fabrication in two stages as casting of side, inner wall and top slab under floating condition of the immersed tunnel of the Marmaray Crossing in Turkey (unit:mm)[9]

14.4.2　Tunnel element towing

Before towing, a system of ballast tanks should be installed inside the element. The tunnel element is always first towed from the construction site to a holding area near the tunnel trench, through connecting to four tug boats. Figure 14-10 shows the transportation of a tunnel element to its final position, connecting to the East island of the immersed tunnel in the HZMB Project, China. The transportation distance of the tunnel elements of an immersed tunnel mainly

a) The E33 was towing to be connected to the East island　　　b) Immersion pontoon "Jinan 2"

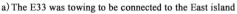

Figure 14-10　Element towing of the immerse tunnel, HZMB Project in China

depends where the element construction conditions are available around the tunnel location. For example, in the Busan Geoje Fixed Link in South Korea, tunnel elements were transported about 40 km and immersed under adverse off shore conditions[7].

Floating would be prevented by the dead load of the tunnel. Before immersion, the tube is designed to be just floatable (factor of safety against floating $F_{\text{float}} \approx 1$). For the transportation and handling of tunnel elements, the stability of tunnel elements must be ensured by checking tunnel elements for stability while floating. The considerations for this checking include the followings[6].

(1) Sufficient freeboard for marine operations, so that tunnel elements are relatively unaffected even when waves run over the top. A positive buoyancy margin exceeding 1% is recommended to guard against sinking due to variations in dimensions and the densities of both tunnel materials and the surrounding water.

(2) Lateral stability of the element using cross-curves of stability analysis should have a factor of safety in excess of 1.4 of the area under the righting moment curve against the heeling moment curve. A positive metacentric height (static stability) exceeding 200 mm is also recommended.

On the other hand, an emergency plan is also required, especially for storm conditions. Storm moorings or shelters are often included in the design of the tunnel. When a storm warning is issued, or forecast wave heights are expected to exceed operational limits, all marine operations should be ceased temporarily; marine plant and floating tunnel elements should be sent to their designated storm moorings or shelters[6].

14.4.3 Immersion and installation of tunnel elements

14.4.3.1 Trench preparation

Before the immersion of the tunnel elements, trench and foundation preparations are often conducted during the element fabrication. The most common method of excavation for immersed tunnels is the use of a clamshell dredger. The applied type of the dredger should meet the project requirements. For example, sealed buckets should be used for contaminated materials and/or to reduce turbidity in environmentally sensitive areas. Cutter suction dredgers have also been used and are able to remove most materials other than hard rock. Blasting may be required in certain areas, though it is highly environmentally undesirable[6].

Expansion reading 14-14

Before the tunnel trench to be dredged, a designed longitudinal profile and bottom widths, with specific slope ratios should be planned, such as according to the geotechnical conditions of the ground. Excavations should be evaluated for stability using appropriate limit state methods of analysis. Temporary slopes offshore should be designed for a minimum factor of safety of 1.3. Side slope ratio of the trench should not be larger than 0.5 in soils, nor larger than 0.25 in rock provided the minimum specified factor of safety is achieved[6]. The design should ensure that the bottom of any excavation is stable. Otherwise, remedial measures such as ground improvement may be required to provide stability of the excavation base against heave in any cohesive soils.

Dredging should be carried out in at least two stages[6], i. e. , the removal of bulk material and trimming. The trimming should involve the removal of at least the last 1.0 m above final dredge level. All silt or other material that may accumulate on the bottom of the trench should be cleared immediately before placing the element. Over-dredged areas should be refilled with materials conforming to design requirements for foundation materials. Methods, materials, and mitigation measures should be used for reducing the impacts of excavation, filling and other operations on the marine environment to acceptable levels. Figure 14-11 show the general situation of the tunnel trench cross section of the immersed tunnel of the HMZB in China.

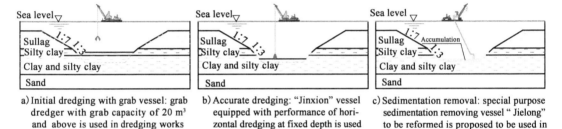

a) Initial dredging with grab vessel: grab dredger with grab capacity of 20 m³ and above is used in dredging works

b) Accurate dredging: "Jinxion" vessel equipped with performance of horizontal dredging at fixed depth is used in dredging

c) Sedimentation removal: special purpose sedimentation removing vessel "Jielong" to be reformed is proposed to be used in this dredging works

Figure 14-11 Foundation trench dredging of the immersed tunnel of HMZB in China❶

A dramatic increase in dredging and disposal costs over the past three decades due primarily to continually tightening environmental restrictions present significant challenges to the disposal of unwanted material. For example, an unique solutions were developed for various projects including: the use of the dredged materials to construct a manmade island such as for the Second Hampton Road Tunnel in Virginia or to reclaim a capped confined disposal facility as a modern container terminal such as the case of the Fort McHenry Tunnel in Baltimore[6].

14.4.3.2 Tunnel foundation

The foundation design of an immersed tunnel involves the foundation bed that is installed between the tunnel structure and the original sea bed. Settlement analyses for the immersed tunnel should be performed, with the consideration of the compression of the foundation course. The analyses should also include the estimating

❶ http://en.cccchzmb.com/P47-124.biz.

the longitudinal and transverse differential settlement within each tunnel element, between adjoining tunnel elements, and at the transitions at the ends of the immersed tunnel. Measures should be taken to prevent sharp transitions from soil to rock foundations, such as by varying the thickness of the continuous bedding[6]. Once the trench excavation is complete, the installation of the foundation should begin. Two types of foundations are often used in immersed tunnel construction, i.e., continuous bedding (screeding foundation or pumped sand) or individual supports[6].

Continuous bedding should consist of clean, sound, hard durable material with a grading compatible with the project conditions. The foundation thickness should not be less than 0.5 m and preferably less than 1.5 m. The gap between the underside of the tunnel and the trench bottom should be filled with suitable foundation material. The foundation can be prepared prior to lowering the elements, or it can be completed after placing the elements on temporary supports in the trench (pumped sand), such as by sand jetting, sand flow and grout. For a screeding foundation, the bedding is fine graded with a screed to the line and grade required for section placement, or a stone bed may be placed with a computer-controlled tremie pipe.

A gravel bed is most applied in case of an offshore tunnel. A gravel bed can be installed in berms and with a high accuracy from a pontoon by means of fall pipes in advance of the tunnel element immersion (Figure 14-12). The gravel bed foundation of the tunnel elements can be installed in individual berms. The basic principle for placing the bed is to feed the gravel down a pipe directly into position on the trench floor. The lower end of the pipe is equipped with a screeding plate, leaving the top level of the gravel at the correct level as it is placed. The process is continuous and there is no secondary screeding operation. The feeder pipe is

Figure 14-12 Sketch showing the gravel bed installation for a immersed tunnel [9]

mounted on a multi purpose pontoon, fixed temporarily in position by spuds. The system appeared capable delivering an overall level accuracy of +25 mm from the design line throughout, such as with the help of a laser leveling system linked to hydraulic cylinders on the feeder pipe[7]. This method is applied at the Oresund tunnel, the Busan Geoje tunnel, the tunnel of the HZMB and the FFL.

Individual supports usually consist of driven piles[6]. Pile foundations should be designed in accordance with generally recognized procedures. Since in most cases, the weight of the tunnel section being placed is less than the weight of the soil it is replacing, pile foundations are rarely used. Foundation piles may be used in case the ground is too weak or too unpredictable.

Where an immersed tunnel is planned under relatively poor ground conditions, which mean that various relatively adverse ground support scenarios had to be considered, ground improvement has to be carried out over some part of the tunnel alignment to improve the foundation conditions. In this way the settlements and differential settlements can be limited and therefore also the internal forces in the tunnel. In the recent, various ground improvement of the ground properties in terms of strength and stiffness are applied to increase the uniform behavior of the ground, such as: ① the replacement of soft soils by mean of sandy gravels or gravel; ② settlement reduction piles in soft cohesive layers; ③ cement deep mixing piles in soft cohesive layers; ④ sand compaction piles. For example, ground treatment of cement deep mixing piles and sand compaction piles are applied in the foundations of the immersed tunnel of the Busan-Geoje Fixed Link, South Korea[7]. In the immersed tunnel of the HZMB, which is placed mainly on muck and silty clay at both ends and on silty clay or sand in the middle, in order to control the differential settlements along the tunnel alignment, various foundations have been used.

Expansion reading 14-15

14.4.3.3 Immersion of tunnel elements

The immersion operation involves all activities concerning the preparation, immersion and connection of the tunnel elements under water. Before immersion, the tunnel element is connected to immersion pontoons that are positioned over the tunnel trench and moored to anchors and is then ready for immersion. In near-shore area tug boats or crane may need to be used for helping guide the elements into place.

The immersion starts by the ballast tanks being filled with water until the freeboard of the floating element is reduced to zero. The ballast tanks are then further filled to create the required weight for the element to sink. During the immersion operation, the tunnel element is lifted by the two immersion pontoons using suspension wires. The position of the pontoons is controlled by mooring wires connected to anchors onto the seabed.

Expansion reading 14-16

In general, the tunnel elements should be installed at an elevation that considers an allowance for settlement such that after completion of the foundation works and all backfilling, they will be expected to be located within a tolerance of 50 mm laterally and vertically from their theoretical or design location. The relative location difference laterally and vertically should not be more than 25 mm across any joint. The relative location vertically across the terminal joints to other structures should not exceed 50 mm. For example, to create a more controlled situation of the immersion, the contractor (Mergor of the Busan-Geoje Fixed Link) in South Korea, developed an alternative system, the External Positioning System (EPS). With this system the tunnel element is placed on a gravel bed on a safe distance of the previously immersed tunnel element, and the tunnel element is lifted and moved forward in a fully controlled situation with its underwater jacking system. After emptying the immersion chamber, horizontal jacks can be used for re-aligning the tunnel element[7].

Of the survey of an immersion operation, the measuring techniques include, such as GPS system on the immersion pontoons during transport, a taut wire system which reads the position between the primary side of the tunnel element and the previously immersed tunnel element, an acoustic survey system which consists of a transducer and several transponders, and distance sensors which are mounted on the bulkheads and touches the previously immersed tunnel element after the tunnel element is positioned on its foundation.

14.4.3.4 Backfilling and covering the tunnel

Once a tunnel element has been installed on the foundation bed, subsequently alignment adjustments are made if needed. As the tunnel element is correctly positioned, locking fill is placed around the element, such as by using a hydraulic fall pipe. The thickness of the top protection layer varies depending on the location on the alignment. It is necessary to backfill the trench with suitable materials and to provide a protection layer of approximately 1.2 m on top. The protection layer ensures against any damage from grounded ships, or falling and dragging anchors.

Expansion reading 14-17

In navigable waters, anchor release protection should be provided, if required, and if the tunnel cover extends above the bed[6]. Rock armor for anchor release bands should be of sound, dense, newly quarried rock in clean angular pieces and well graded. The material needs to be durable for at least the design life of the tunnel.

14.4.3.5 Completion works

When the backfilling around an element has been completed and the protective layer has been laid out, water is pumped out of the ballast tanks inside the tunnel element while ballast concrete is cast along the full length of the tunnel floor. Then the ballast tanks and the steel bulkheads separating the tunnel elements are removed and finally the joints between the elements are completed.

The immersion and installation of an immersed tunnel is finished by the construction of the final joint, which is the last connection point of the element, such as with the application of one of the techniques presented in Section 14.3.2.2. For example, the final joint of the immersed tunnel of the HZMB is designed between the elements No. 31 and No. 30. The construction of the final joint is under the protection of specially designed steel framework cover, by placing tremie concrete around the final joint to seal it. The joint is then dewatered and interior concrete is completed from within the joint.

14.5 Critical thinking problems

C1: An immersed tunnel may be planned, where there is a need to cross a body of water for an infrastructure project, such as railway or roadway line. Consider: ①What are the advantages and disadvantages of the application of an immersed tunnel, respectively? ②What are the commonly used types of tunnel element fabrications and the their main features, such as in terms of construction, respectively? ③What are the main factors to be considered when an immersed tunnel is planned and designed, respectively? ④ The general process of the construction of an immersed tunnel, such as at sea.

C2: Watertight is required for an immersed tunnel. Consider: ①Waterproofing measures commonly used in the built tunnels; ② Types and structures of the waterproofing measures applied at joints of an immersed tunnel, respectively.

14.6 References

[1] ITA Working Group 11. State of the art report in immersed and floating tunnels [J]. Tunnelling and Underground Space Technology, 1993, 8(2): 119-285.

[2] ITA Working Group 11. State of the art report in immersed and floating tunnels [J]. Tunnelling and Underground Space Technology, 1997, 12(2): 83-354.

[3] ITA Working Group 11. Immersed Tunnels-a better way to cross waterways [M/OL]. ITA tribune-special edition, 1999. https://about.ita-aites.org/publications/wg-publications/download/126_c6f7ea51f64df9b928231995ecce5ea7.

[4] Ingerslev L C. Innovations in resilient infrastructure design: immersed and floating tunnels. Proceedings of the Institution of Civil Engineers - Civil Engineering, 2012,165(6): 52-58.

[5] Anastasopoulos I, Gerolymos N, Drosos V, et al. Nonlinear Response of Deep Immersed Tunnel to Strong Seismic Shaking [J]. Journal of Geotechnical & Geoenvironmental Engineering,2007,133(9): 1067-1090.

[6] U. S. Department of Transportation, FHWA. Technical Manual for Design and Construction of Road Tunnels-Civil Elements [M/OL]. Books Express Publishing, 2009. http://www.fhwa.dot.gov/bridge/tunnel/pubs/nhi09010/tunnel_manual.pdf.

[7] De Wit J C W M, Van Putten E. Immersed Tunnels: Competitive tunnel technique for long (sea) crossings[C] // UNDER CITY 2012 Dubrovnik, 2012.

[8] De Wit J C W M, Dorreman J, Van der Ploeg R M. Technical challenges in immersed tunnelling and pneumatic caissons in the North/South Metroline in Amsterdam[EB/OL]. (2018-7-12). http://tec-tunnel.com/wp-content/uploads/2012/11/Paper-ABS0503-Technical-Challenges-in-immersed-tunnelling-and-pneumatic-caissons-in-NSL.pdf.

[9] Su Q, Chen Y, Li Y, et al. Hongkong Zhuhai Macao Bridge Link in China Stretching the limits of Immersed Tunnelling [EB/OL]. (2018-7-12). http://tec-tunnel.com/wp-content/uploads/2012/11/Abstract + paper-1615119-Hong-Kong-Zhuhai-Macao-Link.pdf.

15 Tunnel Operational Facilities and Management

15.1 Introduction

Expansion reading 15-1

Tunnels are nearly closed underground ways and differ from open roadway or railway, mainly due to: ①limited space for entrance and exit; ②limited influence from the light conditions of the sun; ③the difficulty of judging rising or falling gradients; ④difficult to estimate the distance to vehicles in front; ⑤the difficulty of exchange of the air in tunnel with that of open area; ⑥constrained access for safety, emergency services etc. The risk of a long road tunnel may be high in terms of safety, especially due to fires incidents in tunnels. For example, between March 1999 and October 2001, total 62 people died in 3 tunnel fires, i.e., 39 in the Mont Blanc tunnel fire(March 1999), 12 in the Tauern tunnel fire(May 1999) and 11 in the Gotthard tunnel fire (October 2001), in Europe's main international traffic arteries[1]. Similarly, fires in railway tunnel, for example, the Channel tunnel fire in 1996[2], caused serious damage to 50 m tunnel lining in length and services in the vicinity of the fire, including high-voltage cables, low-voltage cables, communications, lighting systems, traction and junction boxes over 800 m. As a result, 500 m track had to be replaced, as did 800 m of overhead line, 800 m of refrigeration pipe and signal equipment over a length of 1500 m; four escape cross-passages and five pressure relief ducts had to be refitted with new doors and dampers.

The case histories of tunnel disasters[4] show that the likelihood of the escalation of the accidents in tunnels into major events is low. However, the consequences of some accidents in road tunnels[4] can be severe in terms of victims, damage to the structure and impact on the transport economy. This cognition implies the awareness of the importance of safety control during tunnel operation.

During tunnel planning and design, the potential risk of driving through a tunnel should be assessed to determine which sorts of operational facilities are needed for the safety in tunnels. However, when considering the relevant issues, it is imperative that one should not simply consider the worst conceivable situations[3]. When these extreme incidents are considered in a strict mode, the consequence would be that tunnel traffic in general would be banned or at least, it would become too expensive to be a practical application. It is clear that an absolute zero risk can never be technically and financially attained in our everyday lives.

The facilities and safety of a tunnel should be designed in a proper way, in terms of a well functioning and reliable infrastructure. The measures to improve the safety of tunnel during an accident, such as a fire, a degree of protection should be determined for the most probable cases, with a defined residual risk being accepted. For the operational facilities and safety control of new and in-service tunnels, there is a need an integrated approach, in which all relevant aspects of tunnel safety are taken into account in an "holistic" way[4].

15.2 Facilities for a road tunnel in general

The safety in tunnels is important to the efficient operation of a road network in a society. In this term, a set of road tunnel safety requirements implies the standardization of the tunnel operational facilities and management. For example, modern road tunnels and their approach roads may require a centralized tunnel safety management system (TSMS) to maintain safety[5,6]. While requirements vary among tunnels, the facilities in Table 15-1 are generally required for tunnels.

Table 15-1 Commonly applied facilities for tunnel operation and management

Facilities for the requirements	Functions
Traffic flow monitoring	To monitor traffic flow and identify impending congestion from breakdowns or accidents
Safe environment	To maintain a safe tunnel environment responsive to traffic density and travel speed
Communications	To communicate traffic restrictions to motorists
Emergency response	To mobilize required emergency response to clear accidents within the tunnel
Emergency systems operations	To initiate required emergency systems operations
Service equipment monitoring	To monitor status of tunnel service equipment

Of the safety requirement of road tunnels, there is always a standard or guideline on the minimum safety requirements. For example, the EU (European Union) Directive[7] is for the Trans-European Road Network to harmonize the tunnel safety standards across EU and achieve the optimal level of safety in road tunnels, with two safety goals: ① the prevention of critical events that endanger human life, the environment and the tunnel infrastructure; ② the mitigation of the potential incident/accident consequences.

In general, the tunnel safety goal involves[5,6] the: ①efficient evacuation of the people involved in the incident/accident; ②immediate intervention of road users to prevent greater damage;③provision of efficient and effective emergency response actions;④protection of the environment;⑤reduction of damages.

To realize these objectives, a plan, such as in terms of a TSMS, is required for long and super long tunnels, as well as tunnels with large traffic volume. The minimum tunnel safety design requirements are usually defined by national standards. For example, the Austrian tunnel infrastructure encompasses the following minimum safety tunnel equipment[5,6]:①a control center;②lighting (emergency exits lighting, lighting inside and outside the tunnel);③physical environment sensors(e. g., smoke sensors, toxic fumes detectors, temperature sensors);④ventilation and smoke extractors(all longitudinal ventilation);⑤energy supply;⑥incident detection sensors;⑦signaling;⑧fire detection sensors;⑨communication equipment.

Tunnel safety management processes are often classified according to:①the basic elements of tunnel safety management, i. e., infrastructure, operation, and emergency response management;②the tunnel safety management stages, i. e., planning, implementing, evaluating, regulating/reforming. For example, a tunnel control center coordinates the following categories of emergency response operations: incident detection and verification, the utilization of emergency response actors and on-scene actions, post-incident clearance action, evacuation, travelers/public information and traffic management.

The tunnel emergency response plan usually includes the following categories of operations[5,6]:①incident detection and verification practices;②crisis communication plan;③emergency command plans for serious accidents;④routing plans for the emergency response units;⑤on-scene actions per incident type;⑥post-incident action;⑦evacuation;⑧travelers/public information;⑨the rerouting options of the incoming traffic;⑩cooperation plan between the operators and the emergency response units.

Concerning the contribution of each emergency response actors to the incident response procedure, the tunnel operator is responsible for detecting and verifying an incident and performing the post-incident operations (e. g., damage analysis, incident investigation), and the fire brigade, police, roadway assistance services provide the on-scene operations and the civil protection measures.

The vehicles that carry hazardous materials are in general restrained from using long road tunnels, or are conditionally allowed, for example, under the following circumstances:①with escort vehicles equipped with signal lamp;②special training and knowledge of the driver of the escort vehicle;③the existence of voice communication;④fire extinguisher.

15.3 Design of operational facilities for a tunnel

15.3.1 Factors to be considered

In general, the design of the installed equipment and the operation of road tunnels should meet the national codes or guidelines for a specific task. The major factors to determine the equipment requirements include the length and traffic features of tunnels, structure features of the tunnel, operational plan and facilities. Sometimes, the traffic features, e. g., traffic volume, composition and mode, have a key influence on the tunnel space requirements, such as tunnel cross section, overhead clearance and traffic space. The operational equipments and the plan of management and safety control are considered, together with civil engineering structures, by tunnel designer.

For a long road tunnel, the operational facilities generally include lighting system, ventilation, communication facilities, fire alarm systems and extinguishing installations, fire emergency lamp and escape route marking, central control systems and service rooms. For a super long tunnel or vital tunnel in a road system, the traffic safety features of the tunnel should be designed with special consideration, e. g., in terms of safety control, central control technology and contingency organization.

The civil engineering equipments include hard shoulder, breakdown bays, emergency exits, escape and rescue routes, emergency footpaths, the formation of walls, overhead clearance control, service routes, the control facilities and elements of visual guidance, and drainage system.

The tunnel operation and management is not only responsible for ensuring the continuous and safe traffic flow through tunnels, but also for developing a tunnel maintenance plan of the tunnel. In general, the responsibilities are allocated during tunnel operation and safety control planning. For example, the emergency response procedure is coordinated by an established control center. The relevant emergency response plan refers to the types of tunnel incidents: ① vehicle break-down; ②crashes between vehicles;③crashes with infrastructure elements;④objects on the road;⑤fire;⑥the accident of isolate vehicle.

The tunnel operation and safety control is a complex decision making process, which is related to the applications of appropriate technological tools, such as decision systems and information communication and management systems, and the actions of personnel, involved in the tunnel operation and management. Similarly, with the help of monitoring system, such as to detect or alarm an accident, the verification of the accident and making response or reaction to the accident should be performed by the tunnel operator. For example, the tunnel on-scene actions generally involve the following organizations: ①the fire department which provides all necessary fire repression measures and is also assigned to rescue people in the tubes; ②the ambulance for rescuing injured people; ③maintenance companies for providing urgent equipment repairs; ④the roadway assistance which is responsible for cleaning the road from stopped or damaged vehicles. Also, traffic monitoring and control, personnel training, and emergency response planning are usually provided by the tunnel operator. The tunnel operator executes the restriction plan with regards to the use of tunnels by heavy goods vehicles and vehicles that carry hazardous materials.

In practice, the task for a designer is to identify and specify the minimum requirements for construction and facilities for a specified or planned tunnel. For example, in China, the configuration and classification of traffic engineering and affiliated facilities for a planed tunnel can be preliminarily determined according to the tunnel facilities and equipment requirement grade, A+, A, B, C and D, which is mainly based on the annual average daily traffic[pcu/d] and length of the tunnel[m] in the *Specifications* (JTG D7012—2014), as shown in Figure 15-1. The tunnel surveillance and control system can also be planned with reference to the related requirements in the specification.

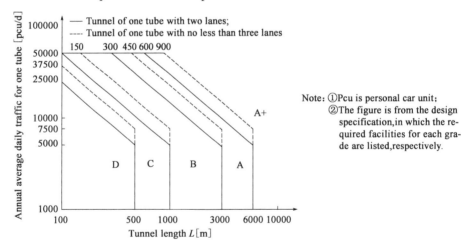

Figure 15-1　Grade of the facilities and equipment requirement of a road tunnel

15.3.2　Design of the equipment and operation of tunnels

The proposed structures and facilities for tunnel operation and safety management system generally includes infrastructure and emergency preparedness, as well as the tunnel operation and management plan of achieving an acceptable level of safety. The necessary elements and considerations include[5,6]: ① electromechanical equipment; ② tunnel geometry and structure; ③communication technologies; ④emergency planning; ⑤ repressive equipment; ⑥maintenance and operational plan;⑦traffic management plan;⑧risk assessment.

15.3.2.1　Civil structure planning

15.3.2.1.1　One-way or two-way traffic for a tunnel

A frequently discussed question is the permissibility of operating a long tunnel with bi-directional traffic. There is no doubt that two parallel tubes with one-way traffic constitute a considerably lower potential risk on account of their better escape and rescue possibilities than a single tube with two-way traffic. For example, in Germany, motorway tunnels generally have two tubes and provide a high safety standard in conjunction with their furnishing, which has to comply with the RABT guidelines.

The demand for operating tubes is closely related to the traffic situation and the construction conditions of the planned tunnel. For example, a 10-km-long or 15-km-long tunnel with high rock overburden and a relatively low planned traffic volume is always designed two-way traffic through a single tube in economic terms, though two-way traffic may exacerbate the traffic situation, such as being an absolute ban on overtaking and a relatively low speed restriction. This design concept has been generally applied in the Alpine countries in the last half century. For some cases, to enhance the rescue concept, a parallel ventilation tunnel, which can also be used for escape purposes, is built, such as the situation at the Mont Blanc tunnel between France and Italy.

In general, the safety criteria applied in a bi-directional tunnel is much more restrictive than those used for open roadways or one-way tunnels with similar traffic density and geometric conditions. When a bi-directional tunnel is planned, the safety criteria for the prevention of accidents, especially accidents or incidents that result in head-on collisions, or a fire, should be seriously considered, because of the worsening of the resulting conditions due to the confinement of a tunnel. In general, a bi-directional tunnel must be designed so that the users themselves can act to ensure their safety in the event of an emergency.

15.3.2.1.2　Tunnel geometry of road tunnels

Concerning the tunnel geometry issues, the important factors are the cross-section geometry and horizontal and vertical alignment of a tunnel and its access roads. For example, it is clearly stated that for new tunnels the longitudinal gradient should not exceed 3% while for already existing tunnels, with gradient exceeds 3%, additional risk reduction measures should be enforced. Furthermore, if the width of the lane is less than 3.5 m then additional risk reduction measures should also be taken.

In the recent years, the safety criteria applied in a bi-directional tunnel tend to increase the tunnel section, in terms of wide hard clearance, comfortably wide walkways, facilities for disabled people, long visibility distances, the possibility of overtaking a stopped vehicle at any point, etc.

15.3.2.1.3　Tunnel structure

The design of the tunnel should include emergency exits, such as direct exits from the tunnel to the outside, cross-connection between tunnel tubes, exits to an emergency gallery, shelters with an escape route separate from the tunnel tube, in case a relevant risk analysis on the speed of the smoke expansion indicates that the existing ventilation system is insufficient to ensure the safety of the users. For example, in some countries, for new road tunnels with two tubes, emergency exits should be constructed in case the expected traffic volume per lane exceeds 2000 vehicles. In addition, for existing tunnels longer than 1000 m with a traffic volume higher than 2000 vehicles/lane/hour, the construction of emergency exits should be considered and evaluated. At the same time, the distance between two emergency exits should not exceed a specific limit, such as 500 m or more.

The escape routes should be protected from smoke and heat. Road tunnels should also be provided with emergency walkways and signs for use by the tunnel users in case of a breakdown or an accident.

Other design considerations may include the establishment of access inside road tunnel for emergency services; and the construction of lay-bys, which should be constructed every 700 m to 1000 m for new bi-directional tunnels, which are longer than 1500 m and the expected traffic volume exceeds 2000 vehicle per lane. If hazardous materials are allowed passing the tunnel, the drainage system of flammable and toxic liquids should be designed.

15.3.2.1.4　Case history

Expansion reading 15-2

In practice, the civil engineering structures of a tunnel are often planned according to the main features of the tunnel project. For example, the longest underwater tunnel, the Seikan Tunnel in Japan, one tube, with double-track, was built for the main tunnel. With the geological and hydrological conditions under considerations in design, in the seabed section of the Seikan Tunnel, a pilot tunnel and construction (service) tunnel were designed and built. Seven inclined shafts and two vertical shafts were also built for construction and operation purposes.

15.3.2.2　Communication technologies

The communication system refers to the establishment of communication between the tunnel manager and the tunnel users in emergency situations. For example, radio rebroadcasting equipment for emergency services use and loudspeakers within shelter facilities for communication should be considered in design for super long tunnels.

15.3.2.3 Electromechanical equipment

In general, the electromechanical equipments to provide the tunnel lighting and ventilation systems are usually designed for long tunnels. It is often imperative for tunnels to be equipped with emergency power supply for evacuation, such as safety lighting for the users to evacuate the tunnel in case of an emergency situation and evacuation marker lights to guide tunnel users to shelters or exits.

15.3.2.4 Emergency preparedness

Concerning emergency preparedness, the EU Directive[7] addresses emergency planning, stations and water supply. The minimum equipment requirements of an emergency station may include an emergency telephone and fire extinguishers. It is mandatory for a long or super long tunnel to provide a water supply, such as hydrants placed at the portals or inside the tunnel at a specific interval.

The major factors that influences the tunnel safety include tunnel structural components, the ventilation system and the electromechanical equipment, such as[5,6]: ①the number of tubes and lanes; ②the emergency exit, escape routes and ventilation; ③fire extinguishing systems; ④the fire resistance of tunnel equipment; ⑤cross connections in twin-tube tunnels. In general, the construction of escape routes is essential unless a relevant fire scenario analysis proves that a high level of safety for road users can be achieved even without this structural component[7].

Another major factor that influences tunnel safety is the behavior of people in tunnels. Improper behavior of road users could be attributed to psycho-pathological causes. In general, it is an effective measure to establish a correct behavior when driving through tunnels, such as through safety control instruction to the tunnel users with the communication system in the tunnel.

Fire can be a disaster in a tunnel. Special attention should be placed on fire detection system, fire fighting equipment and fire resistant materials used for the tunnel construction, especially for long tunnels.

To sum up, the emergency preparedness of a long or super long tunnel should be planned and executed in terms of the integrated view of the TSMS[5,6], which includes the four stages of total quality management(plan, do, check and act) covering the whole lifecycle of the tunnel (design, construction, operation, maintenance and refurbishment).

15.3.2.5 Tunnel operation planning

Tunnel operation planning includes the development of maintenance, operation and traffic management plans.

15.3.2.5.1 Operation & maintenance plan

According to the EU Directive[7], tunnels should be provided with the essential operating means that ensure the safety of the traffic flow inside the tunnel. In addition, proper traffic arrangements should be applied when maintenance works are performed. The arrangements include the traffics inside and nearby the tunnel.

15.3.2.5.2 Traffic management plan

Traffic management plans, e. g. , the plan of the procedures of closing the tunnel in case of an emergency situation, should be developed. The tunnel closure should be performed with the activation of tunnel closure specific equipment. The traffic management plan in emergency situations is designed so that the vehicles inside the tunnel would efficiently evacuate the tunnel while alternative roads would be proposed for the incoming traffic.

It is well accepted that the drivers' erroneous behavior is the major cause for road accidents. Any measures that contribute to the avoidance of human error while driving through a tunnel will be recommendable for design consideration.

15.4 Safety control of a tunnel

Tunnel designer should make special reference to the tunnel security in terms of safety control, such as under emergency or disasters. The main scenarios for consideration in a tunnel design and operational management plan may include: ①recommending policies and actions to reduce the probability of catastrophic structural damage that could result in substantial human casualties, economic losses, and socio-political damage; ②designing preventative constructional, operational fire protection as well as combating fire measures; ③ developing strategies and practices for deterring, disrupting, and mitigating potential attacks.

15.4.1 Safety control in general

15.4.1.1 General principles

The objectives for road tunnel safety design and operational management include[4]: ①preventing accidents or incidents, especially critical events that may endanger human life, the environment and tunnel installations; ② reducing the consequences of accidents, such as fires by creating the prerequisites for: a. helping people involved in the incident to rescue themselves; b. helping road users to intervene immediately to prevent greater consequences; c. ensuring efficient action by emergency services; d. protecting the environment; and e. limiting damage due to the accidents.

The safety in a tunnel is the result from many factors, including tunnel structure features, operation, vehicles in the tunnel and the tunnel users. In terms of tunnel operation safety, the tunnel features are mainly related to the dimensions (the number of tube, length and width of the tube), traffic management in the tunnel and the facilities installed in the tunnel, and are often considered as infrastructure. It is necessary to take into account all the aspects of the system formed by the infrastructure itself to ensure safety as well as its operation, interventions, vehicles and users, through parallel concerning[8]: ①organization, human and material means, the procedures of operation and intervention; ②the training of operating staff; ③the emergency services' equipment with efficient material and the training of their staff; ④communication with users.

PIARC[4] proposed integrated approach for tunnel safety. This approach is presented as a "safety circle", which implies that it is inefficient to focus on improving the safety performance of only one element in the sequence, without considering the safety performance of the other elements, since the safety control is a chain of the involved elements. Any failure or break of an element can lead to unacceptable results of the tunnel safety.

The accidents in road tunnels can lead to severe victims, and damage to the structure and impact on the transport economy. It is beneficial to improve preparation as well as preventing and mitigating tunnel accidents. This can be achieved by the provision of safe design criteria for new tunnels, as well as effective management and possible upgrading of in-service tunnels, and through improved information and better communications with tunnel users. PIARC[4] proposed integrated approach to the safety of new and in-service tunnels, in which the considerations include the infrastructure, operation, emergency services, tunnel users and vehicles. The key elements for an integrated approach to road tunnel safety include[4]: ① safety level criteria (regulations and recommendations); ②infrastructure and operational measures for tunnel safety; ③socio-economic and cost-benefit criteria; ④ safety assessment techniques (safety analysis and safety evaluation); ⑤road tunnel utilization; ⑥the stage of the tunnel life (planning, design, construction, commissioning, operation, refurbishment or upgrading); ⑦operating experience; ⑧tunnel system condition.

Expansion reading 15-3 [9]

15.4.1.2 Measures for safety control

In general, the safety problems in a tunnel are directly or indirectly related to the traffics passing through the tunnel. It is a way to manage and control the traffics in the tunnel to realize the safety control. Traffic control signal lights may be one of the most simple, low cost and effective measures in the safety control of a transportation line. Traffic control signal lights generally are mounted at the portals of a tunnel and at intervals in the interior such that at least one traffic light is plainly visible within a safe stopping distance. For example, in a tunnel with two-way traffic, the signals facing traffic may incorporate red, amber, and green lights. Lights on the reverse side of those signals may be red and amber, to permit lane alternation in an emergency.

The safety control measures in a new designed long or super long tunnel is usually programmed for computer operation. To permit surveillance of tunnel traffic by personnel in the control room, monitors may be installed in that room to display the views of the entire length of the roadways as transmitted by television cameras mounted in the tunnel. The computers may be bypassed for manual operation in an emergency, such as the sequence is interrupted to permit a specific camera to focus on the region of concern.

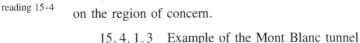
Expansion reading 15-4

15.4.1.3 Example of the Mont Blanc tunnel

The Mont Blanc tunnel was built jointly by France and Italy and opened to traffic in 1965. The tunnel is 11.6-km-long and is operated by ATMB (Autoroute et Tunnel du Mont Blanc) in France and SITMB (Societa Italiana del Traforo di Monte Bianco) in Italy. The roadway of the tunnel is 7-m-wide, with a 0.8-m-wide walkway at each side. After the fire on March 24, 1999, the present tunnel safety management system constitutes a complete super set of tunnel safety management processes for the existing tunnels across EU. The tunnel has Centralized Technical Management (CTM), a computer system that checks and keeps the tunnel under constant surveillance along its entire length and processes data coming from over 35000 control points. The system is designed to detect any anomaly and suggest to the operator the scenario that will allow him to use the appropriate road signs, adjust the ventilation, inform users (e.g., with FM radio, variable message boards), give the alarm to emergency teams and give the alarm to and communicate with outside intervention teams.

Expansion reading 15-5

The established traffic control measures include: ① the minimum distance between the vehicles moving inside the tunnel should be 100 m (200 m apply for the trucks carrying hazardous materials); ② the maximum and minimum speed limits inside the tunnel are 80 km/h and 50 km/h respectively, and by-passing inside the tunnel is prohibited; ③ the traffic inside the tunnel is controlled by three-colors traffic lights that are located at the sides every 1200 m.

15.4.2 Fire control in a tunnel

The methods of preventing, responding to, and controlling fires in existing and future road tunnels are key tasks of a tunnel designer. There is no straightforward route to follow in fire control design. But the objective of the design is clear, such as including to reduce damage, injuries and fatalities. Fire safety design is to achieve the best outcome in the event of an incident[10]. In general, a consideration of several factors, such as the type of traffic allowed, the ventilation system, tunnel geometry and fire mitigation systems are to be taken into account. The design should also be based on the recent findings and recommendations of the evaluations of: ① experimental tunnel fire tests; ② significant tunnel fires; ③observations on tunnels;④interviews with major tunnel operators;⑤the accident risks of unrestricted transit of hazardous materials.

In fire control design, the "Design Fire", such as defined in terms of its magnitude, growth rate and duration, is the basis for sizing the required systems and anticipating the operational measures that need to be in place. In practice, the "Design Fire" in different countries varies from 20 to 300 MW[10]. However, a prescriptive approach has generally been adopted with design fires, formerly in a range up to a peak heat release rate of 30 MW.

15.4.2.1 Facilities

In general, the factors influencing the determination of safety equipment and systems to be installed in a tunnel include: tunnel length, traffic volume and compositions, tunnel location(urban area, outside an urban area, underwater), the number of traffic lanes, the magnitude of heavy-goods traffic and regulations in force for the transit of dangerous material through the tunnel. In practice, the published standards, codes, recommended practices, and guides for fire and safety issues should be referenced in detail design. In general, ventilation system with a fire/emergency operating mode is recommended for a long tunnel.

The significance of time in a tunnel fire can best be identified by the sequence of events in a fire situation depends on the total times of:①time to detect a fire; ②time to send an alarm; ③ time to verify the source of the fire; ④ time to implement the planned emergency response procedures. Automatic fire detectors are often required for a long or super long tunnel.

Once a fire is detected by the automatic fire detectors, an effective response system to the information should be provided in a fire control system. For example, when a fire occurs, they indicate the location and send an alarm to an operator who alerts an emergency crew. If the operator verifies the alarm, an emergency program can be started, such as the emergency crew and vehicles are mobilized. For traffic moving toward a fire, signal lights are turned to red, while for traffic moving away from the fire, signals remain green, to permit evacuation. The ventilation system for the affected part of the tunnel is converted to exhaust.

The commonly used fire fighting measures installed in a tunnel include fire extinguisher, hydrants, water sprayer or water curtain. For example, hydrants generally are installed in niches in tunnel walls, to provide water for fire fighting. Water may be obtained from municipal water supplies, if available. Otherwise, the water mains may be connected to tanks. The tanks may be located near each portal and supplied by pumps from local sources or from groundwater. Booster pumps may be installed to provide at least 0.9 MPa pressure for the application of water on fires. Fire alarms and fire extinguishers for the control of minor fires may be installed next to the hydrants.

15.4.2.2 Requirements of tunnel structures

For some tunnels, special structure for fire protection may be required as integral parts of the main load-bearing systems. When designing the fire protection, the heating as well as the cooling phases of the fire cycle should be taken into consideration. For example, a tunnel should be designed so as to prevent the propagation of highly inflammable or explosive gases and fluids to side spaces. The installations that are parts of the safety system of the tunnel should be protected against fire in the planned time. Installations should be designed so that excessive effects on an individual structural member will not result in other subsequent damages.

It is required that the materials in main load-bearing systems, fittings and installations must not contribute to the spread of fire and fire combustible gases. For example, plastic materials in fittings and installations should be free from chlorine. A material should be non-combustible unless the contribution to the spread of fire by the material can be considered negligible. For example, the requirements should be based on an estimate of the damage that the client considers to be acceptable.

The fire resistance capacity should be verified by means of testing, calculation or a combination of these alternatives. For rock tunnels, the verification of the resistance capacity is required only for the main load-bearing system, provided that the capacity is ensured by a supporting construction. Structures that separate escape routes and chambers and access routes and escape routes should also comply with the requirements on integrity and isolation. For example, it must be proved that main load-bearing systems, fittings and installations have enough capacity to resist fire effects during the time required for evacuation and rescue operations without the risk of falling parts that can cause local damage. Installations should comply with this requirement at temperatures below about 300 ℃. However, it should be remembered that the chipping of concrete structures starts at a surface temperature of 150-200 ℃. The speed of heating, the strength and impermeability of the concrete are also significant influential factors.

15.4.2.3 Fire protection

Mainly due to a number of catastrophic fires in tunnels[11], the tunnel authorities in the world has thoroughly reviewed their fire safety assumptions. The fire protection practices for road and railway tunnels have been undergoing significant changes in the last decade[12,13]. In the wake of that catastrophic fire in tunnel can result in loss of life, large property losses and relatively long business interruption periods[11], tunnel authorities tend to focus their efforts on fire safety issues. In the recent years, loss prevention solutions including fire protection engineering have been recommended or suggested, such as in standards, design codes and manuals, and PIARC documents.

In general, the measures of fire protection include the installation of "active" and "passive" fire protection systems to mitigate fire risk in tunnels. Passive fire protection measures include the use of fire resistive construction materials which help protect the critical structural elements from damage due to high temperatures; active fire protection systems include fixed piping systems to deliver water sprays, such as deluge sprinklers and water mist, or other water-based agents such as compressed air or high expansion foam[12], such as compressed air foam(CAF) and high-expansion (Hi-Ex) foam. There is a tendency that active fire protection systems for tunnels are referred to as water based fixed fire fighting systems (FFFS), which have the potential to reduce the impact of a severe fire on the tunnel structure from catastrophic to manageable at an affordable cost[12]. For example, water mist systems may involve less complex piping and agent storage than CAF or Hi-Ex foam, and may provide equivalent or superior performance with less water and smaller pipes than conventional sprinkler deluge systems.

To improve safety in tunnels, the FFFS are designed to meet the general requirements. Of the FFFS, the main functions of high-pressure water mist systems have been well tested in both practice and full-scale fire tests throughout the world[12,13]. For example, in the Eurotunnel[13], to cope with the significantly larger potential fire load in the truck shuttles, the establishing of FFFS is designed as four SAFE stations, which are located at the ends of interval 4 of both tunnel tubes, around 18 km from the portals. Each SAFE station is 870-m-long and divided into 29 sections of 30 m length each. In the event of a fire, 3 sections are activated. The total pumping capacity, including redundancy, is 4000 L/min at 115 bar in one SAFE station. The test results from Eurotunnel SAFE project indicated that the heat release rate (HRR) developing in excess of 200 MW were brought under control using FFFS[13]. In these tests, the temperatures around the fire with 200 MW HRR were reduced from 1100 ℃ to below 50 ℃ within 2

Expansion reading 15-6

minutes after triggering the system, and fire was brought under control.

The protection targets for FFFS are to improve self-rescue conditions and access by fire services, and to prevent fire spread and limit damage to the tunnel. In terms of the design of FFFS, the design criteria for the fixed and manual fire protection systems should be presented for different levels, such as by Schütz[11].

It is noted that the applications of FFFS are still not widespread in road tunnels in the world. Where there is a plan of FFFS installation in a tunnel, the advice on the design and selection of appropriate FFFS by PIARC[14] are helpful, to be sure that they are correctly designed, installed, integrated, commissioned, maintained, tested and operated.

15.4.2.4 Management plan

Emergency plans should be prepared and the plan should include the instructions that state how different fire scenarios should be handled, as well as schemes for regularly training the involved personnel. The fire control management plan, which should include explosion scenarios, is part of the safety control system of the tunnel. For example, where a FFFS is installed, it is recommended that they are activated in the early stages of a fire to minimise fire growth and to provide the desired effectiveness[14].

15.4.2.5 Case history: the Gotthard base tunnel

The 57-km-long Gotthard base tunnel is the longest tunnel in the field of transportation. Mainly due to its length and modern safety control considerations on the tunnel operation, the tunnel auxiliary facilities are complicated. The general alignment of the tunnel main tubes and operational facilities are shown in Figure 15-2.

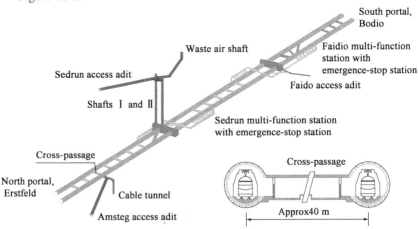

Figure 15-2 General alignment of the Gotthard base tunnel and its operational facilities

For operation safety, the tunnel was designed with two single-track bores. Approximately every 325 m, the two tubes are linked with 30-m-long to 60-m-long cross passages. With special consideration of fire and safety controls, two Multifunction Stations (MFS) in Sedrun and Faido, respectively, were designed and built. The whole tunnel is divided into three sections of almost equal length by the MFSs, which contain emergency stopping points and other installations (Figure 15-3), and there is access adit to the main tunnel, respectively. Each MFS consists of caverns, galleries and shafts. The technical rooms are located in the main caverns and in the ventilation stations.

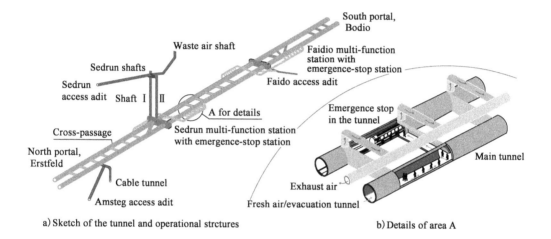

Figure 15-3 Safety concept in the Gotthard base tunnel

In terms of fire control and emergency management, the main cavern of each MFS is connected with an emergency station in each tube via a parallel tube and six access galleries. The aerodynamic separation between the MFS and the emergency station is achieved by 6 emergency doors located at the junction of the access galleries with the parallel gallery. During normal operation the doors are closed. Near each MFS trains can switch over to the opposite tube through crossovers. Under normal operation, these crossovers are closed by large doors.

Expansion reading 15-7

Primarily for an emergency but also for maintenance operation, smoke or air can be extracted out of the emergency station through up to 7 exhaust points uniformly distributed along the roof of the emergency station. During normal operation the exhaust network is separated from the tubes by remotely actuated mechanical dampers at each exhaust point.

15.5 Case histories

15.5.1 Case One: the facilities and management system in Hsuehshan tunnel

The following information is mainly from the paper[15]. The operation facilities and management system of the Hsuehshan tunnel(in Chinese: 雪山隧道) is presented as a case history for a long highway tunnel, in terms of tunnel characteristics, traffic control response plan, system equipment and operation situation.

15.5.1.1 Tunnel characteristic

The 12942-m-long Hsuehshan tunnel, opened on June 16, 2006, is located on the Taipei-Yilan freeway and is the longest tunnel in Taiwan, in China. The tunnel, with two tubes and each with two lanes in single direction, was bored through the Hsuehshan Rang. One of the key aims of constructing the tunnel is to connect the western coast of Taiwan, where 95% of the population lives, to the eastern coast of the island and to tackle the unbalanced development in the island. Although one pilot tunnel was constructed, during tunneling, engineers encountered difficult geological problems like fractured rock and massive inflows of water, which caused severe delays. In the 15 years construction, the ground collapsed 98 times, underground water inundated the tunnel 36 times, tunnel boring machines were trapped inside 26 times and 25 workers lost their lives❶. One of the three TBMs on the westbound tunnel was buried by a ground collapse. In order to speed up the tunnel boring, an additional working interface in Interchange Station No. 2 (under Ventilation Shaft No. 2) was built.

15.5.1.2 Tunnel operation and safety control system

15.5.1.2.1 Traffic control response plan

The main objective of the establishment of traffic control system is to monitor the road conditions and to implement the traffic control strategy. The traffic control strategy was studied and stipulated in accordance with the characteristics of control road conditions and various incidents. Based on the study on the traffic control strategy, traffic control facilities were designed and installed.

The traffic control system of the Hsuehshan tunnel is part of the traffic control system of Taipei-Ilan Expressway. The control system includes control road sections, incident detection and bad weather. The control road section covers road

---

❶ Discovery to air documentary on Hsuehshan Tunnel, http://www.taipeitimes.com/News/front/archives/2006/08/19/2003323765(2016-5-7).

section of Taipei-Ilan Expressway under area of traffic control in central region. Incident Detection Road section in the Hsuehshan tunnel, considering where incident happens frequently, is designed as the control road sections: 27K + 320-40K + 245 in the eastbound line and 27K + 297-40K + 251 in the westbound line, respectively. Bad weather road section in the area of control road section as: the road section from south portal of the Hsuehshan tunnel to Toucheng Interchange covering mileage 40K + 250-42K + 858 is considered as fog area; the road section from Pengshan tunnel to north portal of Hsuehshan tunnel covering mileage 25K + 450-27K + 250 is considered as fog/rain/wind area.

The traffic control system adopts the traffic control strategy as follows to minimize the congestion of recurrence and non-recurrence that happens in the congested road sections frequently and in the bad weather road sections. The traffic control strategy is realized mainly through: ①road user's information display; ②main line speed limit control; ③tunnel traffic control; ④ramp metering signal.

15.5.1.2.2　Equipments

The main equipments include the followings:

(1) Ventilation Building: three places including one for fresh air and one for waste exhaustion in distance of 50 m.

Expansion reading 15-8

(2) Ventilation Machinery Room: one underground machinery room for each ventilation place.

(3) Ventilation through stop: three stops to complete the ventilation cycling networks between two tunnel areas, for ventilation efficiency.

(4) Communication tunnel: emergency communication walks per 350 m with total of 18 are built to connect east and west tunnels for escape and to link with pilot tunnels.

(5) Vehicle Communication Roads are set per 1400 m with total of 14 to connect east and west tunnels for escape and hazard control, and to link to pilot tunnels for staff use.

(6) Security facility: hydrants are installed per 50 m, emergency phones per 175 m, and emergency parking curve on outside of emergency vehicle communication roads per 1400 m.

(7) Pilot tunnel: the Hsuehshan tunnel is huge construction and in complicated geology. The detecting pilot tunnel of 4.8 m in diameter is built between two separated tunnels for overall understanding along geological characters as design and construction references and for control risks on ground water and weak geology problems. The pilot tunnel is used for assistant path during main tunnel construction, and for maintenance and emergency during tunnel operation.

15.5.1.2.3 System interface

To make the application of tunnel control systems services package effective, operating manual, maintenance manual and training were planned to supply a management staff for a specified period during start-up and the warranty that ensures responsibility for a specified period. For the execution of the tunnel operation and safety control system, there are hardware and software interfaces between the traffic control system and electrical mechanics system of the tunnel.

For a hardware interface, the tunnel electrical-mechanic monitoring system provides a router interface by a control center or the traffic control system. The purpose of this interface is to communicate and interlock high level system events and related vehicle detection, fire alarm and tunnel ventilation data. The definition of "high level system events" is "a traffic event that has to be synchronously proceeded and concurrently controlled by both tunnel electrical mechanics and traffic control systems".

Expansion reading 15-9

The traffic control system provides data to the electrical mechanic system through the hardware and software interfaces. Basically, the electrical mechanics system and traffic control system shall exchange through TCP/IP communication protocol. Both systems have to obey the TCP/IP communication protocol and the further application driver of each system is developed by an individual system, such as in terms of required data and time to transmit.

15.5.1.3 Operation situation

When traveling through the Hsuehshan Tunnel, vehicles must not exceed the 70 km/h limit and the usual minimum speed limit is 50 km/h, with a separation distance of 50 m under normal situations. Even when the speed is less than 20 km/h due to congestion, a separation distance of 20 m must still be maintained. Double solid lines prohibit lane changes. Automated road-rule enforcement cameras are used for monitoring speeders, tailgates, and those who unlawfully change lanes.

The Hsuehshan Tunnel broadcasts a dedicated radio station on two FM channels inside the tunnel. Drivers can tune to either of the two FM stations to hear announcements regarding the Hsuehshan Tunnel, rules for driving inside the tunnel, and music.

As of May 1, 2008, the speed limit has been raised to 80 km/h with a 10 km/h tolerance. At this speed a trip through the 12.9 km tunnel takes 8.6 minutes. As of Nov 1, 2010, the speed limit was raised to 90 km/h to alleviate traffic jam.

15.5.2 Case Two: the smart operational and safety systems in Seattle SR99 highway tunnel

The double-deck Seattle SR99 highway tunnel, also called Alaskan Way Viaduct replacement tunnel, is about 3200-m-long and is built to replace the elevated section of State Route 99 in Seattle, built in the 1950s, in the U. S. state of Washington. The tunnel is a shield TBM bored tunnel under the downtown of Seattle and is planned to carries 110000 vehicles per day. The tunnel is designed to meet modern safety standards and to withstand natural disasters, such as earthquake and flooding. The SR99 tunnel, which has smart operational and safety system[1], opened to traffic on February 4, 2019.

15.5.2.1 Structure features

In the large diameter double-deck Seattle SR99 highway tunnel, the southbound travel lanes are stacked above the northbound lanes, with ducts, emergency exit corridors and access at the roadway sides (Figure 15-4). On each deck, there are two 11-foot (2 × 3.35 m) travel lanes in each direction, with an eight-foot (about 2.5 m) safety shoulder and a two-foot (0.6 m) shoulder to the lane sides, respectively. The tunnel is in long, gentle curves, which will allow for safe sight distances.

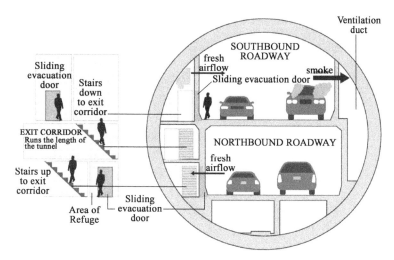

Expansion reading 15-10

Figure 15-4 Sketch showing the roadways, ducts, emergency exit corridors and access to the exits

15.5.2.2 Operational and safety systems

The facilities in Seattle SR99 highway tunnel for normal operation and safety

---

[1] https://www.tunneltalk.com/USA-24May2018-Seattle-SR99-highway-tunnel-safety-features.php.

Expansion reading 15-11

systems include ventilation, lighting, real-time traffic technology, traffic and security monitoring, control center, emergency exits and refuge areas, fire extinguishers, sprinkler systems, emergency power and so on. These components will work as an integrated system, with the function as a single integrated operational network. In terms of design, the public safety is a top priority in the SR 99 tunnel, with the following features❶.

15.6 Critical thinking problems

C1: To make the safety of the operation of a tunnel to meet planned requirements, operational facilities are designed and should be managed in a planned mode, especially for super long or important tunnel in a transportation line. Consider: ①Why are operational facilities generally required for a tunnel? ②What are the main operational facilities in a super long road tunnel for normal operation and safety control under accidents, respectively? ③What are the considerations for the facilities design of a long road tunnel?

C2: To control the risk of tunnel operation to acceptable level, safety control is often required in tunnel design and tunnel management planning. Consider: ①General principles of safety control of for a tunnel operation; ②Commonly used measures of the safety control; ③Why is fire control important? ④What are the commonly used measures of fire control for super long or important tunnels?

15.7 References

[1] Voeltzel A, Dix A A. Comparative Analysis of the Montblanc, Tauern and Gotthard Tunnel fires. Routes/Roads, 2004,10: 18-34.

[2] Kirkland C J. The fire in the Channel Tunnel[J]. Tunnelling & Underground Space Technology Incorporating Trenchless Technology Research, 2002, 17(2): 129-132.

[3] Haack A. Current safety issues in traffic tunnels[J]. Tunnelling & Underground Space Technology Incorporating Trenchless Technology Research, 2002, 17(2): 117 – 127.

[4] Technical Committee 3.3 Road Tunnel Operation, PIARC. Integrated Approach to Road Tunnel Safety[R/OL]. PIARC, 2007. https://www.piarc.org/ressources/publications/4/5709, 2007R07-WEB.pdf.

[5] Zografos K G, Androutsopoulos K N. Development and Implementation of an Integrated Tunnel Safety Management System[C]// International Symposium "safe and Reliable Tunnels", 2006.

[6] Kuen H, Lönnermark K A, Ingason H. Comparison of Road Tunnel Design Guidelines [C]// the 3ird International Symposium on Tunnel Safety and Security, 2008.

[7] The European Parliament and the Council of the European Union. Directive 2004/54/EC of

---

❶ https://www.tunneltalk.com/USA-24May2018-Seattle-SR99-highway-tunnel-safety-features.php.

the European Parliament and the Council on minimum safety requirements for tunnels in the Trans—European Road Network[J]. European Union Official Journal, 2004, L167, 31-91.

[8] Technical Committee 3.3 Road Tunnel Operation, PIARC. Road Tunnels Manual[M/OL]. PIARC, 2015. http://www.piarc.org/en/knowledge-base/road-tunnels/tunnels-manual/.

[9] Technical Committee 3.3 Road Tunnel Operation, PIARC. Assessing and improving safety in existing road tunnels [R/OL]. PIARC, 2012. https://www.piarc.org/ressources/publications/3/17100,2012R20-EN.pdf.

[10] Technical Committee 3.3 Road Tunnel Operation, PIARC. Design fire characteristics for road tunnels[R/OL]. PIARC, 2017. https://www.piarc.org/ressources/publications/9/26494,2017R01EN.pdf.

[11] Schütz D. Fire protection in tunnels: Focus on road & train tunnels[J/OL]. SCOR Global P&C-Newsletter technique, 2014, 7: 1-12. https://www.scor.com/en/file/15583/download? token = ecWF7clB.

[12] Mawhinney J R. Fixed Fire Protection Systems in Tunnels: Issues and Directions[J]. Fire Technology, 2013, 49(2): 477-508.

[13] Lakkonen M, Bremke T. Fixed Fire Fighting Systems for Road and Rail Tunnels[J]. Tunnel, 2012, 1: 40-46.

[14] Technical Committee 3.3 Road Tunnel Operation, PIARC. Fixed fire fighting systems in road tunnels: Current practices and recommendations. PIARC, 2016. https://www.piarc.org/ressources/publications/8/24177,2016R03EN.pdf.

[15] Lin B-P. Introduction of Hsuehshan tunnel traffic control system[C]// The World Long Tunnels 2005, Taipei, 2005.

16 Ventilation in Tunnel Engineering

16.1 Introduction

Expansion reading 16-1

In tunnel project, ventilation is the intentional introduction of outside fresh air into the tunnel, such as to control tunnel air quality by diluting and displacing pollutants in tunnel with the fresh air. The introduction of outside air can also be used for purposes of thermal comfort or dehumidification to achieve desired working conditions in tunneling, and even in operation. Smoke control can also be the main object of tunnel ventilation, especially when there is a fire in the tunnel.

The introduction of outside air may realized by mechanical ventilation or/ and natural ventilation. The latter refers to the passive methods of introducing outside fresh air into a tunnel without the use of mechanical systems. Mechanical ventilation generally uses fans to drive the flow of outside air into a tunnel, or displace pollutants out of the tunnel. For example, the intentional introduction of outside fresh air into the tunnel can be accomplished by pressurization or by depressurization in the tunnel with a supply or exhaust ventilation system, respectively. A long tunnel may use a combination of both systems.

Natural ventilation is the intentional passive flow of outside air into a tunnel through planned openings(e. g. , louvers, portals and windows). The movement of the air relies entirely on passive physical phenomena, such as wind pressure, piston effect of the moving vehicles, or the stack effect❶. It is noted that the natural component can be affected by unpredictable environmental conditions and it may not always provide an appropriate amount of ventilation or fresh air for a tunnel.

In tunnel engineering, ventilation is applied in both construction and operation

---

❶ Stack effect is, also referred to as the "chimney effect", the movement of air into and out of tunnels, resulting from air buoyancy. Buoyancy occurs due to a difference in tunnel-to-out tunnel air density resulting from temperature and moisture differences. The result is either a positive or negative buoyancy force. In general, the greater the thermal difference or the height difference between the portals or openings exists, the greater the buoyancy force is, and thus the stack effect.

periods. Accordingly, the ventilations are classified as: construction ventilation and operation ventilation. For the latter, ventilation for safety control, such as ventilation for fire control is also included.

16.2 Ventilation for construction

In the old times, the working condition at tunneling and mining site is generally poor. Numbers of the people, who lost their lives in tunneling and mining, are inestimably counted in the world. Of the people died in tunneling, some were killed at the working sites, such as by falling rocks, by water bursting into the tunnel, or maimed through incorrect handling of explosives; while some others died later of silicosis, an insidious, incurable disease of the lungs caused by unprotected inhalation of quartz dust. The latter reason is indeed a question of health in working conditions. In the recent years, the driving concepts used on the project, as well as the ventilation and cooling systems, give the maximum attention to the question of health at working sites.

In general, high quality products are made in a safe and comfort environment. In a long run, good working conditions are also beneficial to the development of society in a sustainable mode. For tunnel construction, good sanitary conditions for all workers at working sites are generally required by the standards, regulations, guidelines, established by an occupational safety and health administration, or similar branches. For example, ITA Working Group of Health and Safety in Works published Guidelines[1] for good occupational health and safety practice in tunnel construction. Employers are required not only to initiate and maintain programs that will prevent accidents, but also to instruct and train employees, to recognize and avoid unsafe, unsanitary conditions, including prevention and spread of fires.

In general, the concentration of oxygen, dust, toxic or potentially explosive fumes or harmful gases in the tunnel atmosphere should be routinely monitored. Steps should be accordingly taken as necessary to ensure that the contaminant levels do not exceed those laid down by national legislation or guidance. For example, for the fresh air requirements, the minimum quantity of fresh air for personnel is suggested as $1.5 \, m^3$ per minute per man and $4 \, m^3$ per minute per kW rated power for diesel machines[1], respectively. Additional air may be required for cooling purposes. After blasting, smoke and fumes should be immediately exhausted out the tunnel before work is resumed in affected areas. For a long tunnel or a tunnel driven by drill and blast method, a ventilation system for construction is always required accordingly.

Of the ventilation system applied in construction, the direction of air flow should be reversible. Ventilation air entering a tunnel should be free from dust, smoke or other impurity. On the other hand, where there is a specific work activity known to generate significant contamination, local monitoring should be undertaken.

Followings are some of the environmental requirements applicable to the ventilations in construction.

16.2.1 Oxygen deficiency

Accidents may occur when workers enter unventilated tunnels due to a lack of oxygen in the air. It is imperative when entering underground works, which have not been mechanically ventilated, to keep this risk in mind. Fresh air should be supplied to all underground work areas in sufficient quantities to prevent dangerous or harmful accumulation of dusts, fumes, mists, vapors or gases. Unless natural ventilation meets this requirement, mechanical ventilation should be supplied. In general, the quantity of air supplied or extracted from tunnel face should be such that the average flow in the full cross section of the tunnel or shaft should be between 0.3 m/s and 2 m/s during working period[1].

Ventilation should be such that in every underground working area, healthy conditions exist and fumes or gases shall be diluted to harmless extent. At normal atmospheric pressure sites, the air should contain at least 19.5% but not more than 22% oxygen in concentration. The minimum oxygen concentration of 19% should be maintained at all times when persons are at the work sites. Otherwise, ventilation is applied to restore the oxygen concentration to above 20%. No-one should remain there when the ventilation system is not operating as planned.

During freezing operations, where liquid nitrogen is used, it is essential to continuously monitor the oxygen concentration in the air as the fracturing of a freezing pipe can increase the nitrogen content in the air and result in oxygen deficiency.

16.2.2 Control of contamination

The air in tunnels should be continuously tested for oxygen concentration and the presence of toxic gases. Tests for dust levels should be conducted at regular intervals in tunneling. Dust levels in working areas should be controlled within healthy limiting values. In the absence of national limits those from another country may be adopted.

Test should be made frequently first for oxygen, then for carbon monoxide, nitrogen dioxide, hydrogen sulfide, and other pollutants. If hydrogen sulfide concentration reaches 20×10^{-6}, or 20% or more of the lower explosive limit for flammable gases is detected, precautions should be taken to protect or evacuate personnel. It is essential to adequately ventilate the working sites and test the return air flow before entering.

Where the tunneling is interrupted for a long time, no one should enter the works without being equipped with both CO and CO_2 detectors and also an oxygen monitor.

16.2.3 Control of temperature

In good tunneling environment, the wet globe bulk temperature should not exceed 27 ℃. Ventilation can be used as a means of removing excess heat from the working sites, together with spraying water.

16.2.4 Control of explosive atmospheres

When methane and oxygen are mixed in certain proportions they form an explosive gas called firedamp. Since 4% of methane in the air is already sufficient to cause an explosion, firedamp is a feared hazard in tunnel construction. Generally, ventilation to dilute the concentration of methane gas to below 1% is the only countermeasure.

It is strongly recommended that ventilation should be used for maintaining the concentration of methane or other explosive gas below 10% of the lower explosive limit. Underground operations are classified as gassy if the air monitoring discloses for three consecutive days 10% or more of the lower explosive limit for methane or other flammable gases, measured about 30 cm from work-area enclosure surfaces. Where such conditions occur, the planned countermeasures should be executed to correct the conditions. Ventilation systems should be made of fire-resistant materials. Controls for reversing air flow should be located above ground.

If more than 20% of the lower explosive limit of the gas is detected in the tunnel atmosphere, all persons must be withdrawn, and all non-explosion protected electric and mechanical power switched off until a competent person has supervised the venting of the gas.

Checks using electronic atmospheric monitoring equipment should always be made to ensure that methane or other potentially explosive gas is not present in the ground to be traversed. Tests for potentially explosive gas should be specifically carried out before charging a face and after blasting.

16.2.5 Case histories from the Gotthard Base tunnel

The Gotthard Base tunnel is a railway tunnel through the Alps in Switzerland and is opened on 1 June, 2016. With the route length of 57 km and a total of

151.84 km of tunnels, shafts and passages, it is the world's longest and deepest traffic tunnel. The tunnel bypasses the Gotthardbahn, a winding mountain route opened in 1882 across the Saint-Gotthard Massif, and establishes a direct route usable by high-speed rail and heavy freight trains.

The tunnel has special aspects in construction conditions, mainly due to the tunnel length of 57 km and the great depth of overlying rock in some places up to 2300 m, which cause exceptional rock pressure and climatic conditions. One of the key factors for ensuring health and safety in the tunnel are ventilation and air cooling[2].

A complex mechanical ventilation system is applied in tunnel construction. The ventilation system uses one of the railway tubes to supply fresh air and the parallel tube to extract used air. In most sections worked by AlpTransit Gotthard Ltd., fresh air is sucked in at the portals and intermediate headings, and blown through ducts to the tunnel-face workplaces. Pollutants in diluted form are carried by the stream of air through the tunnel cross-section back to the portals either automatically or assisted by fans. The functions of the ventilation system include the followings.

(1) Ventilation dilutes the pollutants which are released by blasting and by the mucking vehicles. The permissible values of the pollutants are clearly defined by the national law.

(2) Controlling the concentration of methane gas. Gas sensors at the tunnel face ensure that any occurrence of gas can be detected and monitored immediately. Ventilation to dilute the concentration of methane gas to below 1% is the only countermeasure.

(3) Controlling the temperature of the atmosphere in tunnel during construction. The temperature of the rocks increases with increasing depth below ground. Since the Gotthard Base tunnel has more than 2000 m of overlying mountain, rock temperatures up to 45 ℃ are expected. Additional heat is generated by the increasingly numerous and powerful machines used for constructing the tunnel. It would therefore be unacceptably hot for the tunnellers unless measures to cool the workplace are implemented. A certain amount of heat is removed by the ventilation system. However, to reduce temperatures to the level allowed by the Swiss Accident Insurance Fund (SUVA), extra cooling has to be installed at the tunnel faces. This takes the form of water which is circulated in a system of pipes to remove heat from the rocks and machines. Using this method the atmosphere can be cooled to 28 ℃.

Expansion reading 16-2

16.3 Tunnel operation ventilation

In terms of tunnel operation and safety control, ventilation may be required to dilute or remove contaminants, control temperature, improve visibility and to control smoke and heated gases in a fire. In general, the design of the ventilation system should comply with the following requirements on: ① air quality; ②discharge to the environment in the vicinity;③noise and vibrations;④visibility; ⑤protection against propagation of combustible gases and fire;⑥the control of heat and smoke movement during a fire.

16.3.1 Emission contaminants and environmental criteria in road tunnels

16.3.1.1 Vehicle emissions

Exhaust gases of gasoline internal combustion engines contain deadly carbon monoxide (CO) and irritating smoke and oil vapors. Diesel engines will also produce dangerous nitrogen oxides (NO_x) and aldehydes. The components of exhaust gases vary over a wide range for different vehicles with internal combustion engines.

The major constituents of the gasoline passenger cars exhaust are CO, carbon dioxide(CO_2), sulfur dioxide (SO_2), oxides of nitrogen (NO_x), and unburned hydrocarbons; while the major components of diesel engine exhaust are NO_x, CO_2, and SO_2. The vehicle emissions should be considered for a road tunnel ventilation system design. The PIARC reports[3,4] present as an example of the emission standards for passenger cars with gasoline engines valid for the European Union, and emission standards for heavy vehicles, respectively.

16.3.1.2 Environmental criteria

Expansion reading 16-3

CO is traditionally taken as reference emission for the assessment of the toxicity of the exhaust gases by vehicles. The concentration of diesel-smoke is the reference for visibility and odour in the tunnel, for example, in the case of particulate matter (PM) emitted by diesel engine vehicles when the tunnel traffic stream contains on an average more than 15% diesel engine vehicles. In a few countries NO_x is now taken into account and threshold values as in WHO-recommendations for the Environment[6] are to be considered. Depending on the situation either NO_2 (or NO_x) inside the tunnel or NO_2 outside can be the design parameter for ventilation sizing.

CO is ubiquitous pollutant in tunnels and the concentration of CO in a tunnel is often specified according to related situations. For example, the limits of the concentration of CO in air is determined on time-dependent exposure to CO.

The PIARC reports[3] gives CO and extinction coefficient K design-values for different traffic situations. The 100 cm^3/m^3 value corresponds to the WHO recommendation for short term-exposures[6]. In order to avoid excessive fresh air demands for rarely occurring congestion, a higher CO-concentration may be allowed.

Haze from vehicle exhaust gases, particularly from diesel engine vehicles, does reduce visibility in the tunnel. The admissible extinction coefficients for different traffic situations are as: ① $K = 0.003 m^{-1}$, clear tunnel air (visibility for several hundred meters); ② $K = 0.007 m^{-1}$, a haziness of the tunnel air; ③ $K = 0.009 m^{-1}$, a foggy atmosphere; ④ $K = 0.012 m^{-1}$, limiting value which presents most uncomfortable tunnel atmosphere but enough visibility for a vehicle to stop safely at an obstacle.

The design values of extinction coefficient K are determined according to the consideration of the factors, such as the features of tunnel and traffic situations. The limiting values for extinction coefficients are to be calculated as an average over the ventilation section, while the threshold value for tunnel closure is the maximum allowable value at the measurement location. For example, strong fluctuations in the K-value cannot be avoided. Annoying peak values can occur when several diesel-trucks move as a group, when some unusually smoky vehicles are in the tunnel, or when the ventilation control reacts too slowly to emission peaks.

In China, in the "guidelines for design" of ventilation of highway tunnels, the limit values of CO concentration for normal operation ventilation sizing are 150 cm^3/m^3 and 100 cm^3/m^3 for tunnels with length of no more than 1000 m and more than 3000 m, respectively. When there is congested traffic, or standstill on all lanes, the design CO concentration is allowed to 150 cm^3/m^3, provided that the lasting time is less than 20 minutes.

For tunnels in which traffic may incorporate a high percentage (10% or more) of diesel vehicles, the ventilation requirements for dilution of NO_x particles of nitrogen and particulates (smoke) become significant. The NO_x emitted by vehicles consists mainly of nitric oxide (NO), which oxidizes in the atmosphere to form nitrogen dioxide (NO_2). Based on exposure limits recommended by the ACGIH❶ and a typical 4-to-1 ratio for NO to NO_2, the maximum permissible concentration of NO_x is about 10 cm^3/m^3. In China, the maximum permissible concentration of NO_2 is 1 cm^3/m^3, as suggested in the *Guidelines* (JTG/T D7012-02—2014). For most of the cases, a tunnel passage generally only lasts a few minutes, stringent NO_2 threshold values should only be considered either in combination with traffic conditions and/or ambient conditions at the ventilation outlets[3]. The PIARC

---

❶ American Conference of Governmental Industrial Hygienists. http://www.acgih.org.

report[3] proposed to permit an average in-tunnel NO_2 concentration of 10^{-6} along the length of the tunnel at any time as the design value.

16.3.2 Types of ventilation in tunnels

To limit the concentration of pollutants or dangerous contaminants to acceptable levels during normal operation, and to remove and control smoke and hot gases during fire emergencies, tunnel ventilation may be provided by natural means, traffic-induced piston effects or (and) mechanical ventilation equipment, according to tunnel operation situation. A tunnel may require mechanical ventilation when the tunnel is sufficiently long, has heavy traffic flow, or experiences adverse atmospheric conditions.

The classification of a ventilation system applied in tunnels is often based on the direction of airflow in the traffic space. The airflow of longitudinal ventilation is in the direction of the tunnel axis whereas that of transverse ventilation is perpendicular to the tunnel axis. Tunnel ventilation systems can be categorized into five main types, i.e., ①natural ventilation; ②longitudinal ventilation; ③semi-transverse ventilation; ④full-transverse ventilation; ⑤the any combination of these four types or with other ventilation systems, e.g., single-point extraction.

The ventilation system applied to a specific tunnel depends on many factors including: ①tunnel location, with particular regard to the potential impact on the local environment; ②design year in respect of forecast traffic volume and composition; ③tunnel geometry and location environment, such as altitude and local topography, temperature, features of natural wind; ④fire safety considerations; ⑤the service level of the tunnel.

In general, the parameters of a suitable and economical ventilation system for a particular tunnel layout will be determined by: ①the purpose, length, gradient, cross-section and the general configuration of the tunnel; ②polluted air discharging location and general impact on the local environment, such as environmental considerations at portals and shaft outlets (if provided); ③predicted traffic conditions, taking into account the number of lanes, one way or two way traffic, or tidal flow, design flows, traffic speed and its composition, dangerous goods traffic; ④the nature and frequency of traffic congestion in the tunnel including any requirements for contraflow working during maintenance periods; ⑤the influence of road layouts either side of the tunnel; ⑥vehicle emission levels; ⑦fires and their likely severity; ⑧capital investment and running costs, maintainability.

For most of short tunnels, with length, $L \leqslant 300$ m, the piston effect of vehicles induced air flow will provide satisfactory natural ventilation for normal environmental needs. For tunnels, with $300 \text{ m} < L \leqslant 400 \text{ m}$, mechanical ventilation will need to be considered with respect to fire smoke control, for example, where the traffic is relatively light and/or gradients are not steep, the length of tunnel where mechanical ventilation is unlikely to be required may be increased to 400 m. Mechanical ventilation may be required for all longer tunnels, with $L > 400$ m, especially for the tunnels on steep gradients or those subject to frequent congestion, either due to high utilization or external traffic conditions, where it is self evident to be unacceptable to close the tunnel to traffic for short periods to clear pollution levels naturally.

In general, ventilation systems are more applicable to road tunnels due to high concentration of contaminants. In practice, rail transit tunnels often have ventilation systems in the stations or at intermediate fan shafts, but during normal operations rely mainly on the piston effect of the train pushing air through the tunnel to remove stagnant air. The ventilation system also must be capable of controlling smoke and hot gases in case of fire, especially for the long and super long road tunnels with large traffic volume. Many rail transit tunnels have emergency mechanical ventilation that only works in the event of a fire.

16.3.2.1 Natural ventilation

A naturally ventilated tunnel is as simple as the name implies. The movement of air is controlled by meteorological conditions and the piston effect of vehicles pushing the stale air through the tunnel. The piston effect is minimized when bi-directional traffic is present. The meteorological conditions are related to the elevation and temperature differences between the two portals, and wind blowing into the tunnel. Figure 16-1 shows a typical profile of a naturally ventilated tunnel. Another configuration would be to add a center shaft that allows for one more portal by which air can enter or exit the tunnel. Natural ventilation will not provide control of smoke etc in the event of a fire. In Europe, many naturally ventilated tunnels, such as over 200 m in length, have mechanical fans installed for use during a fire emergency.

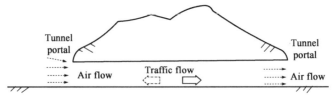

Figure 16-1 Sketch showing the flows of air and traffic in tunnel under natural ventilation

For a tunnel project, whether a natural ventilation system can meet the environmental requirements is not only related to the features of the tunnel(e. g., length, alignment), but also the traffic features passing through the tunnel. In straight tunnels up to about 250 m in length, natural air flow is usually sufficient, particularly with one-way traffic. If a tunnel is exposed to heavy traffic congestion at times, the installation of exhaust fans in a shaft or adit near the middle of the tunnel for emergency ventilation is advisable if the length exceeds, such as 500 m.

The main disadvantage of the natural ventilation is the uncertainties of the natural wind at the portal areas. With a steady natural air flow through a one-way tunnel, in the direction of the traffic flow, the exhaust emission concentration increases from the entrance (ambient air or background value) up to a maximum value near the exit portal. However, if the combined resultant force on the tunnel air changes direction, an oscillating movement of the air can result the maximum pollutant concentration to be nearer the centre of the tunnel. Because there will be no certain control of air direction or velocity, natural ventilation cannot be fully relied upon to prevent the build up of unhealthy fumes, obscuration or contamination occurring in a tunnel during adverse wind and still or slow moving traffic conditions.

On the other hand, since there is no certain control of air direction or velocity in the tunnel, movement of the smoke by a fire can not be controlled with a planned mode. This situation may be unfavorable to the evacuation of the tunnel users, trapped between the incident and the portal.

For urban tunnels, which are shallow-buried, for example, cut and cover tunnels, using large gaps or open slots in the tunnel roof provide an opportunity to vent a tunnel by natural ventilation. This indeed separates the tunnel into sections with the gaps or slots in the tunnel roof, as shown in Figure 16-2. The role of the slots or gaps is analogical to the shafts in a deep tunnel, built in mountain or under water. It is noted that the position and dimensions of the slots should result in acceptable air quality near each slot and the tunnel portals. On the other hand, the large openings in the tunnel roof provide opportunities for large volumes of air to be exchanged in a fire. The performance of the tunnel in terms of fire safety is vastly superior to a conventional tunnel[7].

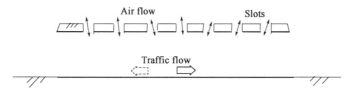

Figure 16-2　Natural ventilation by using repeating gaps or slots in the roof of a long tunnel

16.3.2.2　Longitudinal ventilation

The airflow in a tunnel, with longitudinal ventilation, is similar to that of natural ventilation, but with the addition of mechanical fans, either in the portal buildings, the center shaft, or mounted inside the tunnel. Longitudinal ventilation systems ensure a longitudinal airflow along the axis of the tunnel. Air may be introduced into or removed from the tunnel at a limited number of points, such as portals or ventilation shafts.

Longitudinal ventilation is the simplest form of tunnel mechanical ventilation and often is the first choice because of its lower capital in facilities and operational cost benefits.

16.3.2.2.1 Jet fan longitudinal ventilation

Jet fan longitudinal ventilation is a popular mode of using ceiling mounted jet fans to produce the required airflow through the tunnel [Figure 16-3a)], which is basic longitudinal ventilation for one-way or two-way traffic tunnels. The jet fans can be reversible and are used for moving air into or out of the tunnel at the portals, respectively.

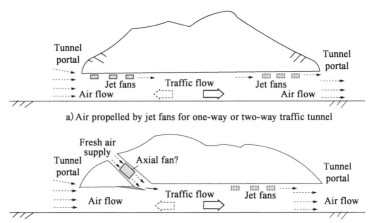

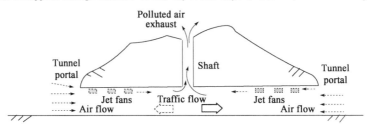

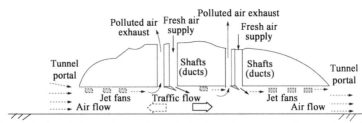

Figure 16-3 Sketch showing the flows of air and traffic in tunnel under longitudinal ventilation

Jet fan longitudinal ventilation has been installed in most of tunnels worldwide. Longitudinal ventilation is achieved with specially designed axial fans (jet fans) mounted at the tunnel ceiling. Such a system eliminates the spaces needed to house ventilation fans in a separate structure or ventilation building. However, jet installations may require a tunnel of greater height or width to accommodate the jet fans, which should be out of the envelope of the tunnel structure gauge.

With normally moving traffic, longitudinal ventilation with jet fans, moving air from portal to portal, is feasible for tunnel length up to 5 km, depending on the design criteria for traffic density and emissions. The reversible jet fans would operate in the same direction as the main traffic flow. The designed maximum allowable longitudinal air velocity in the tunnel by forced ventilation is usually 10 m/s and and 8 m/s for one-way and two-way traffic, respectively.

As the length of the tunnel increases, however, the disadvantages of jet fan longitudinal systems, such as increasing air speed required in the roadway and smoke being drawn the entire length of the roadway during an emergency, become apparent.

16.3.2.2.2 Injection longitudinal ventilation

Injection longitudinal ventilation is frequently used in rail tunnels and is also found in road tunnels. Air injected at one end of the tunnel mixes with air brought in by the piston effect of the incoming traffic. This type of ventilation is effective in tunnels where traffic is one-way. The air speed remains uniform throughout the tunnel and the concentration of contaminants increases from zero at the entrance to the maximum at the exit.

The point-flow injectors, which are directing jets of fresh air into the tunnel, induce a secondary flow through the entry portal and enhance the longitudinal air flow. Without imposing a flow direction on the point-flow injection, a longitudinal flow may develop in both directions, e.g., towards both tunnel portals. Alternatively, the Saccardo nozzle injects the flow at a flat angle into the traffic space in order to support one predefined flow direction in the tunnel, as shown in Figure 16-3b).

16.3.2.2.3 Central exhaust shaft ventilation

Massive point extraction is obtained by extracting high quantities of air at one fixed point directly from the tunnel. Point-flow extraction may lead to longitudinal flow from both sides towards the extraction point [Figure 16-3c)]. Additional jet fans at ceiling might be necessary to ensure the desired flow pattern and airflow speed.

16.3.2.2.4 Multiple shafts air exchange system

In longitudinal ventilation with air exchange ducts or shafts, there are push-pull arrangements of axial type/jet fans, where a longer tunnel can be split into two or more ventilation sections, with discharge and inlet shafts forming the junction of each section [Figure 16-3d)]. Multiple stacks are an option to spread the load of pollution over several dispersion points avoiding very high concentrations at one place. However, complicating factors such as terrain and high rise buildings can severely limit the location of shafts[7]. On the other hand, environmental factor can also be a key consideration for the shaft location choosing, especially for an exhaust duct in urban area or nearby residents.

16.3.2.2.5 Features of longitudinal ventilation

Generally, longitudinal ventilation is the most economical type of mechanical ventilation system since it places the smallest operating burden on the fans and does not require separate air duct provision. However, power consumption can become significant where longitudinal ventilation is provided by jet fans which are needed to operate more or less continuously. With one-way traffic flow, longitudinal ventilation with jet fans is the normal solution. The strategy is to make use of natural longitudinal ventilation if it is possible and then to supplement this for short periods by jet fans. In comparison to semi-transverse or full-transverse ventilation, this means reduced operation and construction costs.

In the tunnels, with longitudinal airflow, the degree of pollution rises progressively along the length of the tunnel to the maximum at the point of discharge (Figure 16-4). The polluted air is normally discharged directly through the tunnel portal, but this may be unacceptable in certain urban conditions and a discharge shaft and extract fan may be necessary.

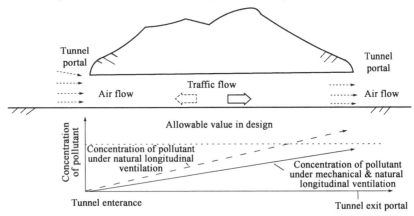

Figure 16-4　Conceptual concentration profile in a longitudinal ventilated tunnel

In the tunnel with two-way traffic, "the piston effect" is largely lost. Exhaust shafts may need to be located at intermediate points of long tunnels. In its simplest form, where a single shaft is located centrally, the system shall create inward air flows from each portal to this central point.

In terms of smoke control in a fire, a longitudinal ventilation system must generate sufficient longitudinal air velocity to prevent the backlayering of smoke, which is the movement of smoke and hot gases contrary to the direction of the ventilation airflow in the tunnel roadway. The required air velocity to prevent backlayering of smoke over the stalled vehicles is the minimum velocity needed for smoke control in a longitudinal ventilation system and is known as the critical velocity.

For a highway tunnel, with two tubes, the traffic flow may vary significantly. The rush periods of the two tubes may be not at the same time. The pollutant concentrations in the two tubes are therefore different. The capacity of the ventilation in the tube with larger traffic volume may be fully used while there is affluent power in the tube with lower traffic volume. It may be an economic way to partially direct the air flow in the tube with lower traffic volume into the neighbor tube through a horizontal connection, as shown in Figure 16-5.

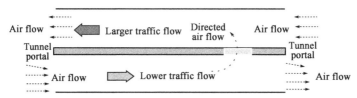

Figure 16-5 Conceptual mode of directing partial airflow into the reverse tube

16.3.2.3 Semi-transverse ventilation

Traditionally semi-transverse ventilation systems are referred to when, in normal operation, airflow is either extracted or injected in a distributed fashion over the length of the tunnel, as shown in Figure 16-6a). In semi-transverse ventilation system, a separate plenum or ductwork is added either above or below the tunnel roadway with flues that allow for uniform distribution of air into or out of the tunnel. The plenum or ductwork is typically located above a suspended ceiling or below a structural slab within a tunnel with a circular cross-section.

A semi-transverse system typically uses a supply duct along the tunnel and the whole traffic space acts as the exhaust duct, discharging either at a portal or through one or more extract shafts. The distribution of exhaust pollutants is reasonably even throughout the tunnel, provided the fresh air supply along the tunnel is proportional to the exhaust gas produced at each location. This is achieved by baffle plates which can adjust, as necessary, the apertures of the fresh air inlets into the road space. However, semi-transverse systems of this kind, in exhaust, are not efficient for smoke control[8], especially under a big fire as the fresh air being supplied.

In the recent years, there are many variations of a semi-transverse system. For example, the ventilation system may have half the tunnel being a supply-air system and the other half an exhaust-air system, or have supply-air fans housed at both ends of the plenum that push air directly into the plenum, towards the center of the tunnel.

Recent developments in semi-transverse systems apply remotely controlled dampers enabling point extraction of smoke[8], as shown in Figure 16-6b), where only the dampers near to the fire are opened and the remaining ones are closed. In this system, reversible fans are used allowing flow injection in normal mode and flow extraction in case of a fire. Clearly, the efficiency of the smoke extraction is greatly increased if the longitudinal air velocity in the tunnel can be controlled from the beginning of the fire, e. g., by jet fans, thus avoiding extensive smoke spread along the tunnel. Smoke can then be extracted over a short distance near to the fire. This overcomes the shortcoming of traditional semi-transverse systems where extraction is performed over longer sections of tunnel. However, the pre-condition of the time taken to reverse the fans in an emergency and the overall system efficiency for smoke control should be fully considered in ventilation design[8].

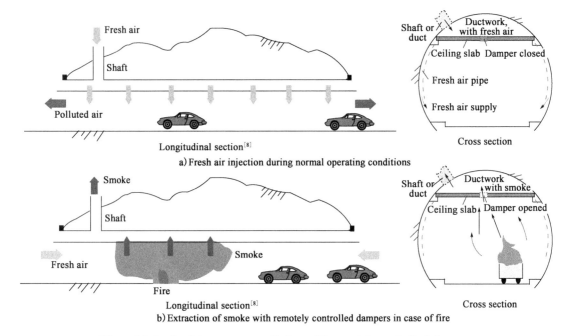

a) Fresh air injection during normal operating conditions

b) Extraction of smoke with remotely controlled dampers in case of fire

Figure 16-6　Semi-transverse ventilation with remotely controlled dampers

The main disadvantage of a semi-transverse ventilation system is the low longitudinal air velocity, particularly at the centre of the tunnel length, and care must be taken to ensure that the velocity does not fall below the requirements for efficient smoke movement in the event of fire. Exhaust semi-transverse ventilation installed in a one-way tunnel produces a maximum contaminant concentration at the exit portal. In a two-way tunnel, the maximum level of contaminants is located near the center of the tunnel. The mid-point null effect should be offset by boosting fresh air supply to the road-space at the null location. Care must also be taken to eliminate local stagnant areas of air and build up of pollutant concentrations on uphill gradients.

16.3.2.4　Full-transverse ventilation

Full-transverse systems use both supply and exhaust air ducts to uniformly distribute fresh air into and remove air from a tunnel[8]. Typically, air is supplied at low level near the roadway and extracted along the tunnel ceiling, as shown in [Figure 16-7a)]. This is advantageous for exhausting hot smoke in the event of a fire [Figure 16-7b)]. This method is used primarily for long tunnels, with large amounts of fresh air requirements due to heavy traffic producing high levels of contaminants. This system may also incorporate supply or exhaust ductwork along both sides of the tunnel instead of at the top and bottom, especially for a cut and cover tunnel or immersed tunnel.

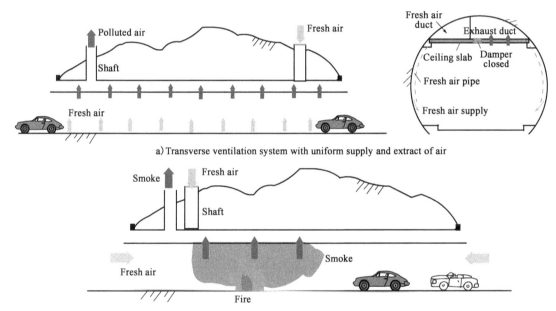

a) Transverse ventilation system with uniform supply and extract of air

b) Extraction of smoke with remotely controlled dampers in case of fire

Figure 16-7　Transverse ventilation with remotely controlled dampers[8]

The recent developments of transverse systems incorporate remotely controlled dampers enabling point smoke extraction, similarly as shown for the semi-transverse ventilation [Figure 16-6b)], where only the dampers near to the fire are opened and the remaining ones are closed. The longitudinal air flow can be controlled either by additional jet fans in the tunnel or by using the ventilation system in adjacent ventilation sections to establish an airflow in the required direction by applying different pressure regimes. During a fire the fresh air supply is sometimes reduced along the tunnel length to preserve stratification and to create a longitudinal velocity towards the fire. In some transverse ventilation systems the fresh air duct might have a reversible fan in order to provide additional extraction capability in the fire mode[8].

In a transverse ventilation system, the maximum allowable air velocities do not impose limits on the duct lengths. For example, using controlled dampers, localized requirements at increased pollution sections along gradients, can be met by increasing supply and exhaust rates at that section. The pattern of transverse ventilation is not affected by the direction of traffic flow.

Transverse ventilation systems may be classified as upward, lateral, or downwards(extracting) according to the positions of the supply and exhaust ducts. The upward air flow, i. e. , inlet air at low level with exhaust at high level is the most effective layout both for normal pollution control and for smoke control in an emergency. In the event of a fire, smoke is extracted directly, aided by its buoyancy, and thus the longitudinal spread of smoke and hot gases is effectively limited. Downwards extraction is not suited to smoke control as it would interfere with stratification(smoke etc in the upper layer with cooler fresh air below) and draw smoke down to the evacuees. Lateral extraction is a compromise between upward and downward extraction and may be acceptable for smoke control if extraction is effectively achieved in the upper reaches of the tunnel bore.

Fully transverse ventilation is, in theory, the ideal system for long tunnels for two-way traffic and for smoke control and removal. However, fully transverse ventilation is the most comprehensive form of mechanical ventilation. Also because of its high capital and operational costs, full-transverse ventilation is seldom adopted for new tunnels. Because separate ducts must be provided for supply and exhaust, as a rule of thumb, operational energy costs increase in proportion to the duct length[8]. On the other hand, soot accumulations in the exhaust duct makes cleaning necessary.

16.3.2.5 Hybrid(Combination) ventilation systems

In terms of operational cost and safety, the maximum acceptable air velocities both in the ducts and in the traffic space impose limitations on the length of tunnel able to be ventilated from each station. Various combinations of the three basic systems, natural, longitudinal and transverse ventilation may be measures for a long tunnel. Such arrangements may be designed to suit particular conditions. For example, a long tunnel may require a central section with transverse or semi-transverse ventilation to provide fresh air input to a longitudinal ventilation system. Similarly, for subaqueous tunnels(of circular section) a ventilation station, on land at the quarter point on each side of the crossing, supplies fresh air along the mid section of the tunnel through the space under the roadway. The fresh air is usually fed into the traffic space by regulated apertures at kerb level[8].

Ventilation system enhancements and contaminant removal technologies are also used in some tunnel ventilation system, as a combination ventilation system.

16.3.2.5.1 Ventilation system enhancements

The two major enhancements applied in a ventilation system are single point extraction and oversized exhaust ports. Single point extraction is an enhancement to a transverse system that adds large openings to the exhaust duct. These openings include devices that can be operated during a fire emergency to extract a large volume of smoke close to the fire. This concept is effective in controlling the temperature and smoke in the tunnel under big fire.

Oversized exhaust ports are simply an expansion of the standard exhaust port installed in the exhaust duct of a transverse or semi-transverse ventilation system. Two methods are used for creating such a configuration. One is to install on each port expansion a damper with a fusible link; the other uses a material that when heated to a specific temperature melts and opens the airway.

16.3.2.5.2 Contaminant removal technologies

In the late 1980's, contaminant removal technologies were developed for cleaning tunnel air, mainly in Norway, Austria, Germany and Japan. Initially these technologies were used for assisting solely with internal air quality (specifically visibility) and have been used more recently to help achieve external air quality objectives[7]. However, today the use of these technologies remains rare. The electrostatic technology, one of the particle removal technologies, has been used for visibility improvement and to improve an external air quality. Another technology is focused on the removal of NO_2^-[7].

The electrostatic technology is to filter out some of the smoke and soot by electrostatic precipitation. Basically a precipitator consists of high voltage emitters and adjacent collecting electrodes. Most particles in the gas stream become ionized negatively and are therefore attracted to the positive collecting plates. Collected material has to be removed from the plates by either rapping the plates with flail hammers(if the material is dry), or by air or water blast. In the Norwegian tunnels is by hot water while by compressed air in Japan.

The efficiency of particle removal technologies has significantly improved in maintenance, pressure loss, particle removal efficiency and longevity of equipment service[7]. In both Norway and Japan the operation of air particle removal technologies is on an as needed basis. The "needs" are determined in Japan by actual air measurements, while in Norway it is usually on a time clock which corresponds with peak hour traffic. The technology is best used when air quality is at its worst and hence the benefit is greatest.

The particle removal technologies may be used as particle removal filters mounted into the stack or installed in by-pass tunnels, as shown in Figure 16-8. Since the full volume flow is filtered, filters mounted in the extraction stacks of tunnels is the most effective mode[7].

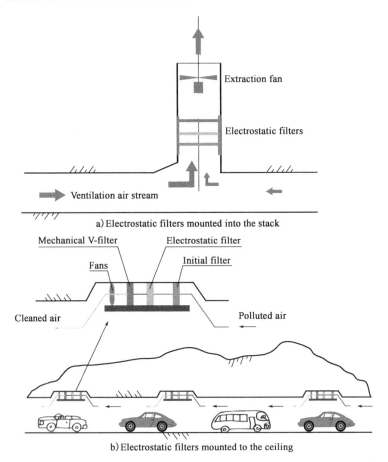

Figure 16-8 Example electrostatic particle removal filters for a tunnel[7]

The energy consumption of air cleaning technologies is generally high. On the other hand, the removal of emission components from tunnel air may creates a lot of chemical waste. In a word, the technology can lower concentrations near a tunnel, but will not prevent the traffic polluting in the environment.

16.3.2.6 Case history: the ventilation system of the Lærdal tunnel

When a ventilation system is planned for a tunnel, various factors, such as tunnel features, geology and geography features at the tunnel site, traffic volume and composition in the planned tunnel, should be considered in a comprehensive way. The main features of the Lærdal tunnel are of extra-long one tube, bi-direction mountain road tunnel, with a traffic volume of about 1000 vehicles/day. The design of the ventilation system of the Lærdal tunnel in Norway is one of the case histories of extra-long road tunnel.

The ventilation system of the tunnel is a combination type, which is composed of conventional longitudinal ventilation system and air cleaning devices. The tunnel and the access ventilation tunnel are in the Precambrian gneiss (Figure 16-9), which is mainly hard rocks, with broken and fracture zones. In the northeast of the tunnel site, there is a side valley Tynjadal, where the 2.1-km-long access tunnel is also designed for the transportation of the excavated materials to the deposition site[1].

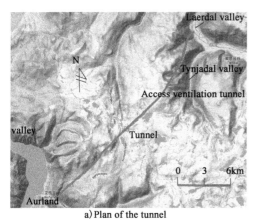
a) Plan of the tunnel

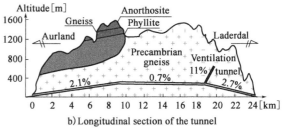
b) Longitudinal section of the tunnel

Note: The tunnel and the access ventilation tunnel are in the Precambrian gneiss, which is mainly hard rocks, with broken and cracked zones.

Figure 16-9 Geology and geography of the Lærdal tunnel in Norway

The air quality in the tunnel is rigorously required, such as the concentrations of CO, haze, NO_x and PM10. The air in the tunnel required such clean that the visibility is designed as 1000 m. High air quality in the tunnel is achieved in two ways: ventilation and purification. Large fans draw air in from both entrances and polluted air is expelled through the 2.1-km-long ventilation tunnel, which is 18 km from the Aurland portal. Jet fans are installed in the tunnel.

The Lærdal tunnel is the first in the world to be equipped with an air treatment plant, located in a in a 100-m-long side tunnel[2], which is about 9.5 km northeast of Aurland svangen. The plant removes both dust and nitrogen dioxide from the tunnel air. Two large fans draw air through the treatment plant, where dust and soot are removed by an electrostatic filter; and then the air is drawn through a large carbon filter which removes the NO_2[3]. The gas cleaning process is based on catalytic reactions which decompose the undesirable gases into nontoxic elements like N_2, NO and CO_2.

---

[1] http://www.roadtraffic-technology.com/projects/laerdal-tunnel.

[2] http://www.engineering.com/Library/ArticlesPage/tabid/85/articleType/ArticleView/articleId/60/Laerdal-Tunnel.aspx.

[3] https://en.wikipedia.org/wiki/Lærdal_Tunnel.

The running of the electrostatic precipitator is automatically managed into operation, which is based on the information of the continuously monitored air quality in the tunnel. When it is required for air quality reasons, the electrostatic precipitator will be automatically quenched for de-dusting at regular intervals. The maintenance (de-dusting) of the gas filtration catalyst is expected to be required only at intervals of several years❶.

16.3.2.7 Comments on the types of ventilation

In general, the commonly applied ventilation systems, i. e., natural, longitudinal, semi-transverse and full-transverse ventilations, have their advantages and disadvantages, respectively. For example, Figure 16-10 presents the features of pollutants distribution, velocity of air flow and fire smoke-controlling in a tunnel with different ventilation systems. On the other hand, the air flow in a tunnel is also strongly influenced by the features of the tunnel and the environment of the tunnel location. And therefore, a ventilation system, chosen for a specific tunnel,

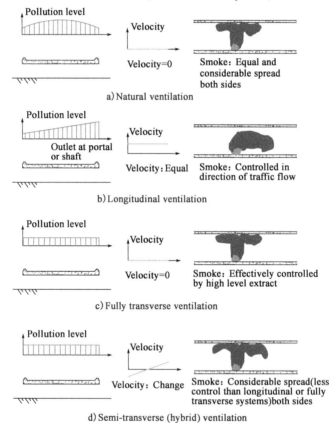

Figure 16-10   Features of the smoke spread and fire control of tunnel ventilation systems[9]

---

❷ http://www.engineering.com/Library/ArticlesPage/tabid/85/articleType/ArticleView/articleId/60/Laerdal-Tunnel.aspx.

should be designed with the consideration of the factors including:①the location of the tunnel with particular regard to the potential impact on the local environment, especially the requirements on pollutant concentration, noise and vibrations; ②design year in respect of forecast traffic levels and its composition; ③tunnel geometry, altitude and local topography;④fire safety considerations.

The ventilation system should meet the specified criteria for both normal and emergency operations, and should be the most economical solution, considering both construction and operating costs. For example, the ventilation system may be based either on longitudinal ventilation or cross ventilation or a combination of these principles(so called semi cross ventilation). When selecting ventilation system and designing it, the fact that the required air flow in the planned tunnel may decrease in the future, should be taken into consideration, as a result of reduced emissions from vehicles. The reduced air velocity in the tunnel and chimneys will affect the dispersion of pollution in the surrounding.

16.3.3 Equipments

The equipments of a tunnel ventilation system mainly depend on the length, traffic volume and the safety requirement of the tunnel. The equipments may be installed in the tunnel and at auxiliary buildings, such as power plant and shaft. For short-and-medium-length tunnels, one building at either portal is sufficient. Longer tunnels may have a building at each portal. Super long tunnels may have three or four buildings. For underwater tunnels, ventilation buildings may be at the water's edge, each building controlling a land and a water body section of the tunnel. The major components of ventilation systems commonly used for road tunnels, including fans and supplemental equipments, are described in the following.

16.3.3.1 Fans

A fan generally consists of electrical transformers and switchgear, control board, and auxiliary equipment. Two types of fans are available, i. e. , centrifugal fans and axial fans, for tunnel mechanical ventilations. The efficiencies of well designed fans of either type are about the same.

16.3.3.1.1 Axial fans

An axial fan is a type of a compressor that increases the pressure of the air flowing through it. The blades of the axial flow fans force air to move parallel to the shaft about which the blades rotate. For an axial fan, the flow is axially in and axially out, linearly, hence their name is called. If the propeller is exercising propulsion, the parameters of interest, include power, flow rate, pressure rise and efficiency.

An axial fan consists of much fewer blades i. e. , two to six. The reason is that axial fans operate at high specific speed i. e. , high flow rate and low head and hence adding more blades will restrict the high flow rate required for its operation. Also the blades are made relatively long with varying blade sections along the radius. Reverse flow may be achieved by reversing the direction of rotation of the motor. An axial fan with blades set to be optimized for a specific flow direction will produce a reduced volume when the motor is reversed. When reversed, the fan can provide 80% of its maximum capacity. Axial fans may be adjusted from 0 to 100% of capacity for supply and exhaust, thus permitting adjustments to meet variable demands for ventilation with fewer fans.

Axial flow main fans are used in ventilating major road tunnels. Capacities are typically in excess of 100 m^3/s. The large diameter fans are mounted in inlet or exhaust shafts, or in a plant room (Figure 16-11), supplying air ducts of a full or semi transverse system, or shafts of a longitudinal ventilation system. Such fans can supply or extract air for a complete tunnel section, or work together with jet fans.

Figure 16-11 Axial fans in a plant room connecting to a ventilation shaft at the Qinling Zhongnanshan highway tunnel

Axial fans are to mount horizontally at a plant room or to mount vertically within a ventilation shaft that exits to the surface. If the space for installation is limited, the jet fans may be fitted with adjustable air flow directors for setting the optimum jet effect.

The noise level of axial fans at maximum speed is somewhat higher than that for centrifugal fans because of greater tip speed. In sensitive surroundings, the noise from fans should be dampened, such as by sound baffles.

16.3.3.1.2　Jet fans

Jet fans are relatively small in airflow output and size and can be housed in groups in tunnels (Figure 16-12), spaced lengthwise in series, to give a multi-fan longitudinal airflow or at the tunnel entrance, as blowers. The fans are horizontally mounted, axial impulse type and maintain a longitudinal velocity of air in a tunnel.

A jet fan increases the velocity of the air mass as it passes through. The subsequent exchange of momentum between the high velocity jet (typically between 30 m/s and 35 m/s) and the slow moving air within the traffic space is utilized to maintain the required overall air velocity for ventilation and smoke movement. The following features should be considered in fan choosing for a tunnel ventilation system[9].

(1) Jet fans are not as efficient (10% loss over still air conditions) as the axial fans operating in a ducted system. However, low capital cost and simplicity of installation and maintenance justifies their use, especially as a control system is not required to regulate the number of fans in use. Developments in new blade forms have efficiencies in excess of 70%.

(2) The distance between fans in the longitudinal direction of the tunnel requires careful consideration. To prevent the flow from one fan reducing the performance of another they will normally be mounted at a minimum (without fan blade deflectors) of 10 times hydraulic tunnel diameters (4 × ratio of cross sectional area and tunnel perimeter) apart or 6 to 8 diameters with 5 to 10 degree fan blade deflectors which allow more rapid momentum transfer. The installation of signing boards close to these distances should be avoided.

a) Conventional jet fans mounted on the ceiling of a tunnel

b) The Banana Jet with the bent outlet airflow directs the impulse jet slightly towards the centre of the tunnel

Figure 16-12 Jet fans mounted on the ceiling of a tunnel

(3) Fans shall be provided with anti vibration mountings, which shall fail safe, e. g., by the provisions of safety chains, to prevent the fans falling onto traffic in the event of failure of a fixing. Vibration monitoring for determining service requirement purposes shall be considered. Care shall be taken to avoid galvanic and other corrosion of any fixings. Water entering a jet fan from washing activities etc will need to drain out and sealed for life bearings shall also be considered. Self cleaning blade shapes may be beneficial in reducing maintenance needs.

(4) Jet fans act by the combined effect of many fans. The design shall make

provision, as described, for a loss of output from a certain number of fans (in maintenance and fire conditions) without jeopardising the overall minimum airflow.

(5) Jet fans can be located at various places in the tunnel cross-section. They are most efficient when located at 3 fan diameters from a continuous surface. Fans in ceiling or wall recesses are not desirable for loss of ventilation efficiency (17% loss) reasons, and particularly at corner locations (31% loss) but may be justified economically compared with the alternative of higher civil construction costs, particularly for immersed tube tunnels. Deflector blades at the air jet exit can be beneficial in reducing energy losses at such locations. Inclining fans at a small angle (around 5°-10°) increases efficiency [Figure 16-12b)]. For reverse flow, a facility to reverse the inclination angle would be required.

(6) The number of fan groups, their transverse alignment or staggering, together with details of any niche recess shapes, efficiency losses, ensuring local re-circulation not to occur, cabling and maintenance requirements and any functional loss during a fire shall be assessed in a comprehensive ventilation study to balance initial, maintenance and operational costs for a given traffic flow and the probabilities of each critical scenario occurring simultaneously, such as collective fan noise.

The recently developed jet fans, for example, the Banana Jet [Figure 16-12b)], with the bent outlet airflow, directs the impulse jet slightly towards the centre of the tunnel, and therefore frictional losses due to swirls at the ceiling are negligible. So with the Banana Jet® tunnel installation loss factors such as the Kempf-Factor can be ignored in most of the cases.

For the installation of jet fans, the following requirements should be met.

(1) The relative longitudinal distance between the jet fans should be determined to obtain an even and stable air velocity profile from one fan or group of fans to the next.

(2) Supplementary jet fans should be installed in low level zones of the tunnel if there is a need to extract polluted air caused by cold down-draughts[9].

(3) Jet fans should normally be designed for reversible operation. They should preferably be designed as axial flow fans with direct drive. The design of the flow rate regulation must be determined in each individual case.

(4) Jet fans are normally installed hanging from the ceiling. The jet fans should be mounted to the frame supports using a uniform system in order to facilitate maintenance, replacement and stock-keeping of spare parts. Jet fans should be installed with static and dynamic balancing. The fans should be mounted on absorbers.

16.3.3.1.3 Centrifugal fans (mainfans)

Centrifugal fan (mainfan) outlets the air in a direction that is 90° to the direction at which air is obtained. Air enters parallel to the shaft of the blades and exits perpendicular to that. For tunnel applications, centrifugal fans can either be backward-curved or airfoil-bladed. Centrifugal fans are predominantly located within ventilation plants or portal buildings and are connected to supply or exhaust ductwork. They are commonly selected over axial fans due to their higher efficiency with less horsepower required and are therefore less expensive to operate, as well as less noisy in operation.

Centrifugal fans are operated by squirrel-cage motors through chain or multiple V-belt drives. The latter eliminate lubrication problems and wear on a multiplicity of parts (inherent in chain drives), give excellent service, and can be easily replaced. Chains are enclosed in solid housings and belts are protected by wire guards. For flexibility, the load of the ventilation is divided between several fans, at least two, sometimes six for each system.

Centrifugal fans have given excellent service since 1934 at Mersey tunnel and are used in the major Boston Central Artery project USA in recent. However, they are not normally suitable for modern tunnel airflow control as they require more space than axial fans of the same duty and reverse airflow can only be achieved by use of dampers and a reversing duct arrangement.

16.3.3.2 Auxiliary equipments

The auxiliary equipments of tunnel ventilation system mainly depend on the types of the planned ventilation system and of the fans, as well as the locations of the tunnels. For example, when a long urban tunnel is located in a downtown area, dust separation plants should be installed if an investigation based on the requirements on air quality and visibility shows that there is a need. The following supplemental equipments may be required for a long tunnel, such as electric power, electric motors, fan drives, fan control system, sound attenuators, dampers, outdoor air intakes, air extraction outlets, the control of combustible gases, dust separation plants, carbon monoxide analyzers and haze control.

16.4 Fresh air requirement

Good ventilation is an essential part of modern tunnel, where passenger safety and comfort is under consideration. The ventilation system should provide enough fresh air in normal operation and be able to work as designed mode during emergency situations. Fresh air requirements are basic factor to be determined in tunnel design.

16.4.1 General considerations

The designed ventilation system should meet the requirement for fresh air to control the concentrations of the pollutants emitted by vehicles, and to control smoke and heat in the event of fire. The choice and design of a ventilation system for a road tunnel depend mainly on the factors[4]: ①the length, number of tubes, location of the tunnel (urban or rural); ②traffic volume passing the tunnel and vehicle fleet segmentation; ③fresh air requirement under normal and special traffic situations; ④ admissible air pollution around tunnel portals; ⑤ fire safety considerations. In the recent years, there is a steady tightening of emission laws for vehicles and changes in the risk assessment of a tunnel fire, and therefore, some design data need constant updating.

With the fresh air requirements under consideration, the design of ventilation system should be based either on calculation of the necessary air flow rate to maintain air quality, or the control of the design fire; whichever controls. The contributions to the air flow rates of the natural ventilation and the mechanical ventilation, respectively, should be analyzed in design scenario. In general, the parameters, such as airflow rates and directions, pressure drops and pollution levels for each ventilation sector, should be determined in design calculation. The level of utilization of the ventilation power and fans should also be shown in the design.

In general, a tunnel longer than 1000 m in length, with the respective daily traffic volume more than 2000 vehicles per lane, should be equipped with a mechanical ventilation system. In preliminary design, as suggested in the "guidelines" in China, the following empirical criteria can used for determining whether mechanical ventilation is required for a proposed tunnel:

For tunnels with two-way traffic,
$$L \cdot N \geqslant 6 \times 10^5 \tag{16-1}$$

For tunnels with one-way traffic,
$$L \cdot N \geqslant 2 \times 10^6 \tag{16-2}$$

where L is the length of the tunnel in meter; N is tunnel traffic flow in veh/h.

If mechanical ventilation is deemed not necessary, this must be proved by means of calculation, in which the need for the control of smoke under fire must be taken into consideration.

In ventilation design calculation, except the above listed factors, the following factors should also be considered and presented: ①the effects of air flow rates that can occur both at the openings of adjacent tunnel tubes or chimneys, and at the connecting points of ramp tunnels; ②the influence of wind against tunnel openings as well as other meteorological conditions; ③the influence of suspended road signs;

④piston effects generated by vehicles;⑤the distribution of traffic in both directions in the case of two-way traffic tunnels with longitudinal ventilation systems.

In designing the fire control system it should be considered that a number of fans near the seat of the fire may be eliminated due to the heat effect.

When designing a ventilation plant with jet fans, the target should be that the air velocity in traffic spaces will not exceed 10 m/s in one-way traffic tunnels and 8m/s in two-way traffic tunnels. Where pedestrian is considered as a common traffic, air velocity should be no more than 7 m/s in the tunnel space.

16.4.2 Fresh air requirement

The major factors affecting the extent of vehicle pollution within and from road tunnels are as[3]:①the ventilation system of the tunnel;②pollution control limits within the tunnel, i.e., for CO, NO_x (a mixture of nitric oxide and nitrogen dioxide gases) and visibility;③tunnel geometry, e.g., gradients, length and cross section of bores;④evolving laws on fuels and permissible vehicle emissions and the age of vehicles;⑤average distance vehicles travel from a cold start before reaching the tunnel;⑥wind direction and strength in respect of both the influence on the ventilation system and the dispersal of polluted air from the tunnel;⑦traffic flow characteristics and risk of congestion leading to inefficient combustion, loss of piston effect and reduced air flow from blockage caused by large, slow moving vehicles;⑧the altitude of the tunnel location.

16.4.2.1 Fresh air demand

For a road tunnel, the required amount of fresh air, V, for a given traffic situation in the tunnel depends on the number of vehicles in the tunnel, n_{veh}, the average emission per vehicle, Q, and the admissible concentration for this particular emission, C_{adm} and the ambient air concentration, C_{amb}. The fresh air demand is calculated as the maximum of the air volumetric flow rates needed to dilute each of the contaminants to the admissible magnitude. These air volumetric flow rates, for each contaminant, can be obtained using following equation adding up the individual contribution for each type of vehicle[3]:

$$\dot{V}_{cont} = \frac{\sum_{veh\text{-}type}(n_{veh\text{-}type} \cdot Q_{cont}^{veh\text{-}type})}{C_{adm} - C_{amb}} \quad (16\text{-}3)$$

(cont: CO, NO_x, PM; veh-type: PC-gas, PC-diesel, LDV, HGV)

where $\dot{V}_{cont}$ is air volume flow rates for each type of contaminant, m³/h; $n_{veh\text{-}type}$ is number of vehicles in tunnel for each type; $Q_{cont}^{veh\text{-}type}$ is emission for CO, NO_x[g/(h · veh)] and emissions of particle matter [m²/(h · veh)]; C_{adm} is admissible concentration of each type of pollutant (CO, NO_x), g/m³; C_{amb} is ambient (background) concentration of each type of pollutant (CO, NO_x), g/m^3; K_{adm} is admissible extinction coefficient m^{-1}.

For the opacity due to diesel smoke and non-exhaust PM, $C_{adm} - C_{amb}$ is replaced by K_{adm}.

Number of vehicles in tunnel, n_{veh}, is calculated as[3]:

$$n_{veh} = \frac{M \cdot L}{v} \text{ for } v > 0 \text{ km/h}; \quad n_{veh} = D_0 \cdot L \text{ for } v = 0 \text{ km/h}$$

where v is vehicle speed, km/h; D_0 is traffic density for $v = 0$ km/h, pcu/km; L is Length of tunnel, km; M is traffic volume for $v > 0$ km/h, pcu/km.

For example, in the case of CO, the required air volume flow for its dilution is determined by PIARC[3]:

$$\dot{V}_{CO} = \frac{n_{\text{PC-gasoline}} \cdot Q_{CO}^{\text{PC-gasoline}} + n_{\text{PC-diesel}} \cdot Q_{CO}^{\text{PC-diesel}} + n_{LDV} \cdot Q_{CO}^{LDV} + n_{HGV} \cdot Q_{CO}^{HGV}}{C_{adm} - C_{amb}}$$

(16-4)

where $\dot{V}_{CO}$ is air volume flow necessary for CO dilution, m^3/h; $n_{\text{PC-gasoline}}$ is number of passenger car vehicles with gasoline engines in tunnel; $n_{\text{PC-diesel}}$ is number of passenger car vehicles with diesel engines in tunnel; n_{LDV} is number of light duty vehicles in tunnel; n_{HGV} is number of heavy goods vehicles in tunnel; $Q_{CO}^{\text{PC-gasoline}}$ is passenger car with gasoline engines emission for CO, $g/(h \cdot veh)$; $Q_{CO}^{\text{PC-diesel}}$ is passenger car with diesel engines emission for CO, $g/(h \cdot veh)$; Q_{CO}^{LDV} is light-duty vehicle emission for CO, $g/(h \cdot veh)$; Q_{CO}^{HGV} is heavy goods vehicle emission for CO, $g/(h \cdot veh)$; C_{adm} and C_{amb} are admissible and ambient concentrations of CO, g/m^3, respectively.

16.4.2.2 Traffic and operation situations

For an important tunnel project, each possible traffic situation must be defined by the traffic planner. The main points to be considered are the followings[3].

(1) Traffic density: Is each traffic lane used for its capacity, or may a reduced flow be assumed due to a low traffic density or to traffic control, especially under congested conditions? Does congested traffic occur daily or is it a rare event?

(2) Unidirectional or bi-directional tunnel: In some cases, a unidirectional tunnel is occasionally also operated in bi-directional mode. The number of lanes in this case must be determined.

(3) Vehicle fleet: For the emission calculation it is necessary to split the vehicle fleet into the segments passenger cars (PC) and heavy goods vehicles (HGV). Very often the number of HGV is given as a percentage of the total traffic volume. It has to be noted that the heavy duty fleet may vary in its age distribution

depending on the type of traffic. For example, on international routes (long haul traffic) modern vehicles are operated, while distribution traffic (urban areas) is managed with older vehicles.

(4) Traffic speed: Usually the traffic speed in the tunnel is restricted by law. On gradient, trucks have a reduced speed. The higher values represent the speed of newer trucks the lower values represent those of older trucks.

(5) Peak traffic flow: The maximum traffic flow per lane is possible at velocities around 60 km/h, depending whether it is a rural or an urban tunneltraffic. Average peak values are suggested by PIARC[3]. In a heavily used urban tunnel peak values in fluid traffic may be 10% to 20% higher[3]. The hourly free flowing peak traffic of a day is generally about 10% of the daily average traffic volume. With little daily traffic the capacity of the lane will not be used. However, under certain circumstance the number[3] can be exceeded.

Expansion reading 16-4

(6) Congested traffic and standstill: In ventilation calculations for congested traffic vehicle speeds from 10 km/h and standstill normally define the design case. In a heavily used urban tunnel these values may be 10% to 20% higher[3]. To avoid oversizing the ventilation equipment in a long tunnel, it is advisable to prevent congestion or standstill over the full tunnel length by a traffic control system. So in design, for example, as suggested in the "guidelines" in China, the length of congested condition and standstill for traffic data consideration is 1000 m, respectively, for long and super tunnels.

(7) Passenger car units [pcu]: For converting pcu into number of vehicles (passenger cars, trucks, buses) a truck/bus may be assumed to occupy the space of 2 passenger cars in free flowing traffic and up to 3 passenger cars in slow moving traffic and at upgrades. With a given HGV percentage "a", the vehicle density per lane km "D" is calculated as[3]:

$$D_{pcu}[\text{pcu/km}] = D_{veh}[\text{veh/km}] \cdot \left[\left(1 - \frac{a}{100}\right) + \frac{a}{100}(2 \text{ or } 3)\right] \quad (16\text{-}5)$$

(8) Trucks and buses: For the emission calculation the number of trucks and buses, especially those powered by diesel engines, must be known. Often this data is given as an average percentage of the total traffic flow, but this value is normally too high when applied to the peak traffic flow. The actual average mass of the trucks must also be known. In the PIARC[3] trucks and buses are referred to as heavy goods vehicles (HGV). HGV could be solo trucks, truck-trailer combinations, articulated trucks/semi-trailers or buses.

(9) Passenger cars: Passenger cars (PC) can be powered by gasoline or diesel engines. It has to be noted that light duty commercial vehicles (LDCV) up to 3.5 t are dealt with as passenger cars.

(10) Emission-laws (emission standards): The vehicle emission regulations of the country must be matched to the emission factors.

(11) Design-year: The design-year of a tunnel ventilation system is often the opening year, but it may be up to 10 or more years later, when traffic development is expected. The traffic composition and its average emission must be estimated for the design year. The design has to be based on the maximum airflow needed.

16.4.2.3 Admissible concentrations

CO is traditionally taken as reference emission for the assessment of the toxicity of the exhaust gases. The concentration of diesel-smoke is the reference for visibility and odour in the tunnel.

In a few countries NO_x is now taken into account and threshold values following national and/or WHO-recommendations for the Environment[6] are to be considered. Depending on the situation either NO_2 (or NO_x) inside the tunnel or NO_2 outside can be the design parameter for ventilation sizing.

16.4.2.3.1 Carbon monoxide

The admissible concentrations of CO for a tunnel may vary among nations[3]. The 100 ppm value corresponds to the WHO recommendation for short term-exposures[6]. In order to avoid excessive fresh air demands for rarely occurring congestion, a higher CO-concentration can be allowed. The limiting values are to be calculated as an average over the ventilation section, while the threshold value for tunnel closure is the maximum allowable value at the measurement location.

16.4.2.3.2 Visibility

A light beam decays in intensity as it passes through smoky air. This process can be described by the formula:

$$E = E_0 \cdot e^{-KL} \quad (16\text{-}6)$$

where, E_0 and E are initial light beam intensity and the light beam intensity after passing through tunnel air in length of L, respectively; K is constant varying with tunnel air condition, such as in tunnel ventilation, K is customary called extinction coefficient to express visibility.

The extinction coefficient (K) is defined as the loss of intensity (E) after traveling the distance L through the tunnel air relative to the source intensity E_0. From Equation (16-6) the extinction coefficient is expressed as:

$$K = -\frac{1}{L} \cdot \ln \frac{E}{E_0} \quad (16\text{-}7)$$

Another definition of visibility is the transmission ratio, s, the light beam intensity E after traveling the distance L relative to the source strength E_0, as $s = E/E_0$. It is defined on the basis of Equation (16-6) as:

$$s(\%) = 100 \cdot e^{-KL} \quad (16\text{-}8)$$

Expansion reading 16-5

The admissible extinction coefficients are therefore in corresponding to different traffic situations. The designed extinction coefficient for a tunnel is mainly dependent on the grade of the road, design speed, the traffic feature in the tunnel, and the types of lights installed in the tunnel.

16.4.2.3.3　Limit values for ventilation sizing

The fresh air requirement for a tunnel may be determined by the admissible concentrations for the design values, such as for CO, visibility, NO_x. The concentration of diesel-smoke as well as of non-exhaust particle emissions is the reference for visibility in the tunnel[3]. In the recent years, usually the fresh air demand for diesel-smoke dilution is higher than for the CO-dilution, but in countries where the NO_2 limits will be adopted, the fresh air demand for NO_2-dilution may be even higher than for diesel smoke dilution. For example, the PIARC[10] proposes 1ppm NO_2; France proposes 0.4 ppm as the limiting concentration inside a tunnel(average 15 min); Belgium sets 1000 $\mu g/m^3$ (0.5 ppm) NO_2 as the short term average(<20 min), and 400 $\mu g/m^3$ (0.2 ppm) as 60 min average in both Belgium and Sweden[3].

16.4.2.4　Ambient air concentrations(C_{amb})

The outside air, taken in as fresh air for the tunnel, has a background level of CO, NO_2 and soot(PM). These ambient levels are normally quite low, but they should be checked for a city tunnel(CO, e.g., about 1 ppm to 5 ppm). Likewise, the concentrations of NO_2 up to 200 $\mu g/m^3$ are typical peak values, but can be exceeded in dense urban areas[3].

The situation is modified further when air from the portal of one bore recirculates and enters the portal of the adjacent bore as "fresh air". Simple structural design features can minimize or avoid recirculation of tunnel air.

16.4.2.5　Minimum air exchange

In general, the minimum air exchange rate is determined using the threshold values. In order to have a ventilation installation which has sufficient fresh air capacity for a sudden demand, it is recommended in some countries as a design criterion to size the fresh air exchange capacity at least 3 times per hour, or a minimum longitudinal air velocity of 1.5 m/s in the long tunnels, such as with their length more than 1800 m.

16.4.2.6　Smoke control

Smoke is the most mortal factor in the fire case, where a huge quantity of toxic gases is released. The smoke from a fire in a tunnel poses problems for the tunnel users and the firefighters[5]. There are two ways to deal with smoke from a fire: extract the smoke or control the smoke. Demands on smoke control or dilution of chemical releases may mean that the ventilation system has to move larger air volumes than those required for the dilution of exhaust gases. This must also be considered in design.

In general, of the facilities installed for the planned smoke extraction for a tunnel, the larger of the capacity of the facilities, the more chance of choosing a proper solution to the smoke extraction problem in a tunnel under fire. However, as the installed facilities are designed according to design criteria or plan, there are no facilities enough as same as what they are needed for the smoke extraction under a catastrophic or big fire. In practice, the effective way is to extract the smoke as close to the fire site as possible. As a result, there is high likelihood to permit tunnel user evacuation and firefighter ingress.

For the strategy of emergency planning and smoke control, based on the longitudinal ventilation, the minimum ventilation velocity, generally designated by the critical velocity, is simply the velocity by which all the smoke is pushed from one side. Below this velocity, a backlayering layer goes against the fresh air current produced by tunnel ventilation. Smoke control is often realized by the development of a sufficiently high velocity (critical velocity) to prevent backlayering. Thus the smoke is contained in the portion of the tunnel beyond the fire incident and unless there is an extraction system present, it will exit at the downstream portal. One of the foremost criteria for the design of longitudinal ventilation system of tunnel is the critical velocity value[11].

An empirical relationship between the critical velocity, v_{cr} (in m/s) and the heat release rate of fire, Q (in kW), is then presented as follows equation[12]:

$$v_{cr} \approx \left(\frac{gHQ}{\rho_0 T_0 C_p A}\right)^{1/3} \quad (16\text{-}9)$$

where H is tunnel height, m; Q is heat release rate from fire, kW; ρ_0 is ambient density, kg/m³; T_0 is ambient temperature, ℃; C_p is specific heat capacity, kJ/(kg·K); A is cross sectional area of the tunnel, m²; g is gravitational acceleration, m/s².

Based on their small-scale experiments, Oka and Atkinson[13] have inspired a "supercritical ventilation velocity" from which the critical velocity does not increase with the one-third power of the heat release rate. The experimental results can be expressed in a simple correlation in dimensionless form Equations (16-10) and (16-11):

$$v_{cr}^* = k_v (0.12)^{-1/3} (Q^*)^{1/3} \quad \text{for } Q^* < 0.12 \quad (16\text{-}10)$$

$$v_{cr}^* = k_v \quad \text{for } Q^* > 0.12 \quad (16\text{-}11)$$

With v_{cr}^* and Q^* are the dimensionless critical ventilation velocity and the dimensionless heat release rate respectively, and k_v is a constant that varies from

0.22 to 0.38. They are given by:

$$v_{cr}^* = \frac{v_{cr}}{\sqrt{gH}} \quad (16\text{-}12)$$

$$Q^* = \frac{Q}{\rho_0 C_p T_0 g^{1/2} H^{5/2}} \quad (16\text{-}13)$$

Wu and Bakar[14] have identified, by experimental investigation and numerical simulation, a new model to predict the critical ventilation velocity for tunnels with various cross sectional geometry. The presented model confirms the model proposed by Oka and Atkinson[13]. This model shows clearly that there are two regimes of variation of critical velocity with heat release rate of the fire. Their suggested model is given as:

$$v'_{cr} = 0.40 \left(\frac{Q'}{0.20}\right)^{1/3} \quad \text{for } Q' \leq 0.20 \quad (16\text{-}14)$$

$$v'_{cr} = 0.40 \quad \text{for } Q' > 0.20 \quad (16\text{-}15)$$

where v'_{cr} and Q' are the dimensionless critical ventilation velocity and the dimensionless heat release rate respectively. They are defined as follows:

$$v'_{cr} = \frac{v_{cr}}{\sqrt{g\overline{H}}} \quad (16\text{-}16)$$

$$Q' = \frac{Q}{\rho_0 C_p T_0 g^{1/2} \overline{H}^{5/2}} \quad (16\text{-}17)$$

with $\overline{H}$ is the hydraulic tunnel height.

Recently, Li et al.[15] carried out experimental tests and theoretical analyses to study the critical velocity together with the backlayering length in tunnels fires. Based on experimental tests, Li et al.[15] proposed:

$$v_{cr}^* = \begin{cases} 0.81 Q^{*1/3} & \text{for } Q^* \leq 0.15 \\ 0.43 & \text{for } Q^* > 0.15 \end{cases} \quad (16\text{-}18)$$

In general, there is significant difference among the magnitude of the calculated critical velocity with the Equations (16-9) to (16-18). This implies that the foremost criteria for the design of a tunnel longitudinal ventilation system is the critical velocity value in terms of fire control. For example, for a two-lane tunnel, with $A = 90 \text{ m}^2$, $H = 8.0 \text{ m}$, $\overline{H} = 10.7 \text{ m}$, the air environment of $\rho_0 = 1.29 \text{ kg/m}^3$, $T_0 = 25\ ℃$, $C_p = 1.40$, under the fire of the heat release rate, Q varying from 10 MW to 200 MW, the calculated the critical velocities are much different, as shown in the Expansion reading.

Expansion reading 16-6

16.4.3 Emissions

Emission values are generally determined according to the emission standards of a nation. In general, the emission regulations seem much more stringent in the emission standards for passenger cars (PC) as well as for heavy goods vehicles (HGV). In practice, there is often a big gap between emission reductions given in the emission standards and those achieved during real world driving. Many factors may have influence on the emission values of a vehicle, such as real driving conditions relative to the standardized test conditions, maintenance level, ageing of the vehicles and their engines conditions.

A new situation has arisen concerning visibility in tunnels. As the tail pipe emissions have decreased progressively, the non-exhaust particulate matter emissions are now playing a more important role.

16.4.3.1 Emission standards

The emission standards for the vehicles in a tunnel usually follow national or international recommendations, such as by PIARC[3,4]. As the emission factors given in the report[3,4] should correspond to the national or regional regulations, the user of the recommended values has to adjust the vehicle fleet composition according to the model year and the date when the specific emission standard is applied for the tunnel under consideration. Before using the recommended values, the application of the emission standards to the local situation should be checked.

On the other hand, the emission calculation requires the knowledge of the fleet segmentation according to the vehicle category (i.e., HGV, PC-gasoline, PC-diesel, etc.) and the model year segmentation (i.e., emission standards) of each of the respective categories. This data is in general available from national design code or guidelines.

16.4.3.2 Emission of passenger cars (PC) and light-duty vehicles (LDV)

According to the suggestion[3], the calculation of the emission of PC and light-duty vehicles (LDV), for CO, NO_x [g/(h·veh)] and diesel particles [m²/(h·veh)], has to be performed for PCs with gasoline and PCs with diesel engines and for LDVs separately, using the following equation:

$$Q = q_{ex(v,i)} \cdot f_h \cdot f_t \cdot f_e + q_{ne(v)} \qquad (16\text{-}19)$$

where Q is emission for CO, NO_x [g/(h·veh)] and emissions of particle matter [m²/(h·veh)]; $q_{ex(v,i)}$ is base emission factor for PC/LDV with gasoline or diesel engines, depending on average speed and road gradient for the base year 2010, g/(h·veh) or m²/(h·veh); $q_{ne(v)}$ is emission factor for non-exhaust particulate emissions, m²/(h·veh); f_h is altitude factor; f_t is influence factors years differing from the base year; f_e is influence factor for other technology standards. The values for the factors f_h, f_t and f_e can refer to the recommended values in the PIARC report[3] or national design code and guideline.

Expansion reading 16-7

For the PCs, the basic emission factors, $q_{ex(v,i)}$, recommended values are given, as a function of the average vehicle velocity in a tunnel, and of the road gradient in the PIARC report[3]. The values given for a vehicle speed of 0 km/h represent idling conditions. The emissions are given per hour. By dividing the value with the corresponding vehicle velocity, the emission per km is obtained.

For the LDVs, the base emission factor quantifies the vehicle specific tailpipe emission for specific pollutants as a function of average vehicle speed and road gradient. In the PIARC report[3], the factor given is a mix for diesel and gasoline LDVs according to the provided proportion.

To convert the emission given in grams g into a volumetric emission, the emission values have to be divided by the specific weight of the particular gas, such as the average values for CO and NO_2 are ρ_{CO} = 1200 g/m^2, ρ_{NO_2} = 1900 g/m^3, respectively.

Nitrogen oxide emissions (NO_x) in the car exhaust consists predominantly of NO, which has a lower specific weight than NO_2. When giving NO_x-emission data by weight, it is the convention to express the NO_x volume as NO_2 in order to have comparable NO_x emission values.

The conversion factor between particulate matter (PM) emissions in mass (gram) to the turbidity effect is given by 1 g which is corresponded to 4.7 m^2. This factor is based on the MIRA-correlation factor 6.25 m^2/g and a reduction factor of 0.75 for the reduction in optical activity due to the strong dilution of the diesel smoke in the tunnel[3].

At sea level, the altitude factor f_h is always unit for each component. The altitude influence on the different exhaust components varies with the type of engine. The altitude factor is taken into account to be on the safe side in ventilation design. Up to a height of 700 m it is assumed there is no change in the emission behavior of gasoline cars with three-way catalytic converters.

For gasoline cars with catalytic converters, thermal ageing of the catalyst affects its performance. This effect is taken into account by applying the appropriate ageing factors, f_a. Consideration should be given to the ageing factors in relation to the year of implementation and the emission standards those where current at that time.

16.4.3.3 Heavy-goods vehicles and buses with diesel engines (HGV)

The method for the calculation of HGV specific emissions is similar to that for PCs. However, contrary to the PC procedure, the emissions for HGV are almost proportional to the vehicle mass to be moved. Hence, the actual vehicle mass is included into the calculation, as the following[3]:

$$Q = q_{ex(v,i)} \cdot f_h \cdot f_t \cdot f_e \cdot f_m + q_{ne(v)} \quad (16\text{-}20)$$

where Q is emission for CO, NO_x [g/(h · veh)] and emissions of particle matter [m²/(h · veh)]; $q_{ex(v,i)}$ is base emission factor for HGV with diesel engines, depending on average speed and road gradient for the base year 2010 [m²/(h · veh)]; $q_{ne(v)}$ is emission factor for non-exhaust particulate emissions, m²/(h · veh); f_h is altitude factor; f_t is influence factors years differing from the base year; f_e is influence factor for other technology standards; f_m is influence factor for vehicle gross masses.

In the PIARC report[3], the recommended base emission factors for diesel HGV are given in the tables refer to an average vehicle mass of 23 t (mix of lorries, lorry-trailer combinations, semi-trailers). Buses can be calculated using the HGV tables, using a lower mass factor. A mass of 15 t is proposed for buses and coaches. In this case, the values must be adjusted to compensate for the reduced mass.

In the PIARC report[3], mass is defined as the average total vehicle weight of the HGV inside the tunnel and is given for 15 t and 32 t relative to 23 t. Mass factor, f_m, is applied to the HGV with different weight. For the HGV with weight 15 t and 32 t, the mass factors, f_m, are given 0.7 and 1.9, respectively.

The altitude factors, f_h, for CO and PM are more significant than for passenger cars with diesel engines. The factor has to be interpreted as a relation to the basic emission values, i.e., a factor for the height 2000 m means that the basic emission values have to be multiplied by the respective factor[3]. Up to a height of 700 m, it is assumed there is no change in the emission behavior.

16.4.4 Comments on the fresh air requirements

The above fresh air requirements calculation procedure is mainly based on the recommendation of the PIARC report[3]. Dependent on the availability of vehicle fleet data, two methodologies for calculation vehicle emissions are described. One offers a simple approach based on the emission estimations for the year 2010 and the application of different correction factors for the year of operation, altitude of the tunnel, and vehicle mass (for HGVs only). In cases where the vehicle fleet data are known in detail, a more accurate calculation can be performed using the detailed emission factors for single vehicle model years (i.e., emission standards).

As noted in the PIARC report[3], the emission factors and correlation factors given in this document are based on the emissions of vehicles within the European Union. So, it is always in the responsibility of the designer of the ventilation system to check the appropriateness of the emissions factors for their project, such

… as with reference to the specific national codes or guidelines.

16.5 Choice of ventilation system

16.5.1 Requirement of fresh airflow

Based on the calculation results of the fresh air requirements in section 16.4, the maximum fresh air requirement, V_{req} [m³/s], can be determined to meet the following limits.

(1) Admissible concentrations for the design values, such as for CO, visibility, NO_x, PM in the tunnel, based on which the maximum magnitude of the required amount of fresh air is determined following the method of Equation (16-3), presented in Section 16.4.2.1.

(2) The minimum air exchange, based on which the minimum magnitude of the required amount of fresh air, such as in terms of the airflow velocity of a longitudinal ventilation system, $v_{min} \geq L/1200$, m/s, where L is the length of the tunnel in meter, or $v_{min} \geq 1.5$ m/s, for the long tunnels, with their lengths more than 1800 m.

(3) Fire smoke control, if required, such as for the critical velocity, v_{cr}, as presented in Section 16.4.2.6.

(4) Velocity limit of the air in the tunnel, v_{max} [m/s], for different traffic mode or composition, such as presented in Section 16.4.1.

Using the geometrical and size parameters of the planned or existing tunnel, as the area of the tunnel clearance cross section is A_r [m²], the hydraulic diameter of the tunnel D_r [m] can be determined as: $D_r = 4A_r/C_r$, where C_r is the circumference of the tunnel clearance profile in meter. In assumption, as a longitudinal ventilation system is applied, the required airflow velocity is calculated as the following:

$$v_{req} = V_{req}/A_r [\text{m/s}] \quad (16\text{-}21)$$

To meet the basic requirement of the velocity limit of the air in the tunnel, v_{max} [m/s], the v_{req} should be no more than the v_{max}, i.e., $v_{req} \leq v_{max}$. Otherwise, the tunnel should be divided into sections, such as by ventilation shaft, provided a longitudinal ventilation system will be built in the tunnel.

On the other hand, where the calculated v_{req} is small, the requirement of the fresh airflow will be determined by the criteria: $v_{req} \geq \max\{v_{min}, v_{cr}\}$, which is the larger one of the two velocities.

It is noted, longitudinal ventilation system is the most commonly used type of ventilation in tunnels, as discussion in Section 16.3 in this Chapter and in Chapter

15, respectively. However, when selecting a ventilation system and designing it, many factors should be taken into consideration, including civil engineering construction and its cost, the environmental and operational factors, as well as safety in tunnel. The other types of ventilation system may be an alternative for the tunnel.

16.5.2 Pressure evaluation of a longitudinal ventilation system

The airflow in a tunnel, with longitudinal ventilation system, can be simply considered as being propelled by the installed mechanical fans, possibly together with the help of the piston effect of the moving vehicles in the tunnel. As the airflow moving in the tunnel or ducts, the airflow pressure losses due to the friction along the lining surface. This resistance force is usually called on-way resistance. Mainly due to the changeable feature of the natural wind at the tunnel location, the pressure from the natural wind is usually considered as resistance for a tunnel with mechanical ventilation system.

Consider a simple case of a road tunnel with jet fan longitudinal ventilation system, the design velocity of airflow in the tunnel is v_{req} [m/s]. To maintain the required airflow of v_{req} in the tunnel, the following force balance is needed:

$$\Delta p_r + \Delta p_m = \Delta p + \Delta p_t \qquad (16\text{-}22)$$

where Δp_r is the on-way resistance of the airflow in the tunnel, N/m²; Δp_m is the airflow pressure of natural wind in the tunnel, N/m²; Δp_t is the airflow pressure due to the piston effect of the moving vehicles in the tunnel, N/m²; and Δp is the mechanical ventilation pressure, such as provided by the jet fans, N/m².

The following calculation is mainly based on the method suggested in the *Guidelines*(JTG/T D7012-02—2014) in China.

16.5.2.1 Airflow pressure of natural wind

The airflow pressure of natural wind in the tunnel, Δp_m, is calculated as:

$$\Delta p_m = \left(1 + \xi_e + \lambda_r \cdot \frac{L}{D_r}\right) \cdot \frac{\rho}{2} \cdot v_n^2 \qquad (16\text{-}23)$$

where v_n is the assumed airflow velocity in the tunnel due to the natural wind at the tunnel location, usually v_n = 2.0 m/s or 2.5 m/s; ξ_e is the resistance coefficient of the airflow at the tunnel entrance, usually ξ_e = 0.5; λ_r is the resistance coefficient of the airflow along the tunnel, with λ_r = 0.02 for cast-in-place concrete lining; L is the length of the tunnel, m; D_r is the hydraulic (equivalent) diameter of the tunnel clearance cross section, m; ρ is the density of the air at the tunnel portal, usually as $\rho = 1.2$ kg/m^3 at the sea level.

16.5.2.2 Airflow pressure due to the moving vehicles

The airflow pressure due to the piston effect of the moving vehicles in the tunnel (Δp_t) is dependent on the traffic situation in the tunnel. The Δp_t in a tunnel is propulsion or resistance, which can be determined, such as according to the following two cases.

(1) Resistance, under condition of bi-directional traffic in the tunnel.

(2) Possibly propulsion, under condition of uni-directional traffic in the tunnel, provided that the presenting velocity of the vehicles, v_t, is more than the design airflow velocity, v_{req}; otherwise, it is resistance.

16.5.2.2.1 Airflow pressure of bi-directional tunnel

The airflow pressure due to the moving vehicles in a bi-directional tunnel, $\Delta p_{t,B}$, is calculated as:

$$\Delta p_{t,B} = \frac{A_m}{A_r} \cdot \frac{\rho}{2} \cdot n_+ \cdot [v_{t(+)} - v_{req}]^2 - \frac{A_m}{A_r} \cdot \frac{\rho}{2} \cdot n_- \cdot [v_{t(-)} + v_{req}]^2$$

(16-24)

where n_+ and n_- are the number of the vehicles in the forward and negative directions of the designed airflow, veh; and can be calculated with $n_+ = \dfrac{N_+ \cdot L}{3600 v_{t(+)}}$ and $n_- = \dfrac{N_- \cdot L}{3600 v_{t(-)}}$, respectively; N_+ and N_- are the design peak hourly traffic volume in the forword and negative directions of the designed airflow, respectively, veh/h; ρ and L are same as in Equation (16-23); v_{req} is the design velocity of airflow in the tunnel, m/s; $v_{t(+)}$ and $v_{t(-)}$ are the presenting velocities of the vehicles in the forword and negative directions of the designed airflow, respectively, m/s; A_r is the area of the tunnel clearance, m^2; A_m is equivalent impedance area of the vehicles, m^2 and can be calculated with the following equation:

$$A_m = (1 - r_1) \cdot A_{cs} \cdot \xi_{c1} + r_1 \cdot A_{cl} \cdot \xi_{c2} \quad (16\text{-}25)$$

where A_{cs} and A_{cl} are the frontal projected areas of small cars and large cars, respectively, m^2, such as $A_{cs} = 2.13$ m^2 and $A_{cs} = 5.37$ m^2; r_1 is ratio of the large cars in the total vehicles; ξ_{ci} is the air resistance coefficient of the of small cars and large cars and can be presented as $\xi_{cs} = 0.5$ and $\xi_{cl} = 1.0$ for small cars and large cars, respectively, or calculated with the following equation:

$$\xi_{ci} = 0.0768 A_{ci} + 0.35 \quad (16\text{-}26)$$

where A_{ci} is the front face area of the the vehicle, type i.

$\Delta p_{\mathrm{t,B}}$ should be calculated for different traffic situation, such as for $v_{\mathrm{t(+)}}$ and $v_{\mathrm{t(-)}} = 10, 20, 30, \cdots$ design speed, respectively, to find the most adverse situation for the designed mechanical ventilation. Also, standstill for traffic data consideration is 1000 m for (super) long tunnels, as suggested in the "guidelines".

16.5.2.2.2　Airflow pressure of uni-directional tunnel

For a uni-directional tunnel, the direction of the airflow is same as that of traffic flow. The airflow pressure due to the moving vehicles in a uni-directional tunnel, $\Delta p_{\mathrm{t,u}}$, is calculated as:

$$\Delta p_{\mathrm{t,u}} = \pm \frac{A_{\mathrm{m}}}{A_{\mathrm{r}}} \cdot \frac{\rho}{2} \cdot n_{\mathrm{c}} \cdot (v_{\mathrm{t}} - v_{\mathrm{req}})^2 \quad (16\text{-}27)$$

where n_{c} is the number of the vehicles in the tunnel and can be calculated with $n_{\mathrm{c}} = \frac{N \cdot L}{3600 v_{\mathrm{t}}}$; N is the design peak hourly traffic volume in the tunnel, veh/h; v_{req} is the design velocity of airflow in the tunnel, m/s; v_{t} is the presenting velocities of the vehicles, m/s; A_{m}, A_{r}, ρ and L are same as in Equation (16-24).

For Equation (16-27), the " + " and " - " are for the traffic situations of $v_{\mathrm{t}} > v_{\mathrm{req}}$ and $v_{\mathrm{t}} < v_{\mathrm{req}}$, respectively. The traffic velocities for consideration may be $v_{\mathrm{t}} = 10, 20, 30, \cdots$ design speed, and standstill in (super) long tunnels.

16.5.2.3　Resistance of the airflow along the tunnel

The resistance of the airflow along the tunnel, $\Delta p_{\mathrm{r}}(\mathrm{N/m^2})$, is calculated as:

$$\Delta p_{\mathrm{r}} = \Delta p_{\lambda} + \sum \Delta p_{\xi i} \quad (16\text{-}28)$$

where the on-way resistance of the airflow along the tunnel, $\Delta p_{\lambda}(\mathrm{N/m^2})$, is calculated as:

$$\Delta p_{\lambda} = \left(\lambda_{\mathrm{r}} \cdot \frac{L}{D_{\mathrm{r}}}\right) \cdot \frac{\rho}{2} \cdot v_{\mathrm{req}}^2 \quad (16\text{-}29)$$

and the local resistance of the airflow, such as at the tunnel entrance, exit and other sites in the tunnel, $\sum \Delta p_{\xi i}(\mathrm{N/m^2})$, is calculated as:

$$\sum \Delta p_{\xi i} = \sum \xi_i \cdot \frac{\rho}{2} \cdot v_{\mathrm{req}}^2 \quad (16\text{-}30)$$

where the parameters of v_{req}, λ_{r}, L, D_{r} and ρ are same as in Equations (16-23) and (16-24), respectively; ξ_i is the local resistance coefficient of the airflow, such as at the tunnel entrance and exit, $\xi_{\mathrm{e}} = 0.5$ and $\xi_{\mathrm{ex}} = 1.0$, respectively, and the other resistance coefficients as presented in the "guidelines".

16.5.2.4　Requirement of the mechanical ventilation pressure and jet fans

From Equation (16-22), the required mechanical ventilation pressure for the tunnel, Δp, is

$$\Delta p = \Delta p_{\mathrm{r}} + \Delta p_{\mathrm{m}} - \Delta p_{\mathrm{t}} \quad (16\text{-}31)$$

16 Ventilation in Tunnel Engineering

For a tunnel with jet fan longitudinal ventilation system, the required mechanical ventilation pressure is provided by jet fans. The pressure of high-velocity airflow induced by each jet fan, $\Delta p_j [\text{N/m}^2]$, is calculated as:

$$\Delta p_j = \rho \cdot v_j^2 \cdot \frac{A_j}{A_r} \cdot \left(1 - \frac{v_{req}}{v_j}\right) \cdot \eta \qquad (16\text{-}32)$$

where v_j is velocity of the airflow at the exit of the jet fan, m/s; A_j is the areas of the jet fan exit, m^2; η is the friction reduction coefficient for the mounted position of the jet, such as $\eta = 0.7$ to 0.91, or following the magnitude in the *Guidelines*; the parameters of v_{req}, A_r and ρ are same as in Equations (16-23) and (16-24), respectively.

And therefore, the required number of the jet fans, i, can be determined as:

$$i = \frac{\Delta p}{\Delta p_j} = \frac{\Delta p_r + \Delta p_m - \Delta p_t}{\Delta p_j} \qquad (16\text{-}33)$$

In general, the fans are mounted in groups of two or more, so the practical jet fan number should meet the installation requirement.

16.5.2.5 Case history

16.5.2.5.1 Conditions and requirement

A road tunnel is planned to apply jet fan longitudinal ventilation system. The features of the tunnel geometry, traffic situation, parameters for ventilation design and planned jet fan are determined first, seen the Expansion reading. To determine the number of jet fans for the tunnel, the other parameters can follow the presentation in Section 16.5 or the suggestion in the *Guidelines*.

16.2.5.2.2 Calculation and results

Expansion reading 16-8

Based on the calculation results, 10.47 jet fans are required for the jet fan longitudinal ventilation of the tunnel. For two fans in each group for installation, the number of the total fans are 12 for the tunnel.

16.5.3 Fan installation

The airflow in the tunnel, with jet fan longitudinal ventilation system, is induced by the high-velocity impulse of jet fans, possibly with the help of the piston effect of the moving vehicles. The fans are usually mounted at the tunnel ceiling in groups of two or more and spaced longitudinally in the tunnel at about 100 m to 120 m intervals. The general requirements for the installation of jet fans are presented in Section 16.3.3.1.2.

The first group of the jet fans may be mounted about 80 m to 120 m to one of the tunnel portals. The choosing of entrance or exit portal for the reference point of installation will depend on the specific characters of the tunnel, such as the features of the tunnel longitudinal alignment and its slope grade, traffic situation in the tunnel and meteorological conditions at the tunnel location. For example, where there is a tendency of stack effect of the air in the tunnel, such as in terms of natural wind, the jet fans will usually be mounted in favorable to the pollutants or PM exhausting.

16.6 Critical thinking problems

C1: For tunnel construction, ventilation is always required, especially for long and super-long tunnels. Consider:①Why are the ventilations important in tunneling? ②What are the main functions of the ventilations in tunneling?

C2: In terms of tunnel operation and safety control, ventilation may be required to dilute or remove contaminants, control temperature, improve visibility and to control smoke and heated gases in a fire. Consider:①Why is a ventilation system always required for a long road tunnel, in terms of tunnel operation and safety control, respectively? ② Types of the tunnel ventilation systems in road tunnels; ③ Why are longitudinal ventilation systems commonly applied in road tunnels? and what are the main advantages and disadvantages of a longitudinal ventilation system applied in road tunnels, respectively? ④ What are the main factors to be considered during the choosing of a ventilation system for tunnel ventilation design?

C3: Major components of ventilation systems commonly used for road tunnels, including fans and auxiliary equipments. Consider:①The types and main features of fans commonly applied in tunnels;②Why are jet fans commonly applied in road tunnels?

C4: A road tunnel may need mechanical ventilation system to make the pollutants and PM within their admissible concentrations, respectively, such as by supplying enough fresh air into the tunnel or exhausting the polluted air out of the tunnel, or to control the smoke from a fire in the tunnel. The air in the tunnel should be exchanged with the fresh air in time. Consider:①In terms of fresh air requirement, how to determine the magnitude of traffic data in the tunnel, vehicle emissions in the tunnel, the requirement of fresh air for the tunnel operation, critical velocity for smoke control; ② How to determine the magnitude of the fresh air requirement for the ventilation design of a planned tunnel?

C5: Jet fan longitudinal ventilation system is usually applied in tunnels. Consider:①The general procedure of the feasibility analysis for a planned tunnel; ②To determine the number of jet fans for the following planned tunnel.

Description of the planned tunnel and design parameters for ventilation

Features of the tunnel			
Length of the tunnel	1588 m	Area of the clearance cross section	70.57 m^2
Hydraulic diameter of the tunnel	8.76 m	Grade of the roadway alignment	2.2%, −2.2%
Traffic situation			
Traffic flow	Bi-direction	Design peak hourly traffic volume in the tunnel	360 veh/h
Ratio of the large cars in the total vehicles	56%	Ratio of the traffic volume in upward direction	55%
Design parameters			
Design fresh air requirement	146.77 m^3/s	Design speed	16.67 m/s
Velocity of the airflow in the tunnel due to the natural wind	2.0 m/s	Density of the air at the tunnel portal	1.07 kg/m^3
The other parameters can follow the presentation in Section 16.5 or the suggestion in the *Guidelines* (JTG/T D7012-02—2014)			
Parameters of jet fan, type SDS-9-4P-6-27°			
Velocity of the airflow at the exit of the jet fan	25 m/s	Area of the jet fan exit	0.636 m^2

16.7 References

[1] ITA Working Group 5. Guidelines for good occupational health and safety practice in tunnel construction [R/OL], ITA, 2008. https://about.ita-aites.org/publications/wg-publications/download/105_e7f3cfe919f4dacf7513e2e2a071d962.

[2] Unterschütz P. The new Gotthard Rail Link[M]. AlpTransit Gotthard Ltd., Switzerland, 2004.

[3] Technical Committee 3.3 Road Tunnel Operation, PIARC. Road tunnels: vehicle emissions and air demand for ventilation [R/OL]. PIARC, 2012. https://www.piarc.org/ressources/publications/7/16655,WEB-2012R05-EN-revise.pdf.

[4] Technical Committee 3.3 Road Tunnel Operation, PIARC. Road tunnels: vehicle emissions and air demand for ventilation [R/OL]. PIARC, 2004. https://www.piarc.org/ressources/publications/2/4482,05-14-VCD.pdf.

[5] Bendelius A G. Tunnel Ventilation[M]// Tunnel Engineering Handbook, 2nd ed. Chapman & Hall, c1996: 541-544.

[6] World Health Organization. Air Quality Guidelines for Europe[M]. WHO Regional Publications, European Series 1988 No. 23.

[7] Technical Committee 3.3 Road Tunnel Operation, PIARC. Road tunnels: a guide to optimising the air quality impact upon the environment[R/OL]. PIARC, 2008. https://www.piarc.org/ressources/publications/4/5891,2008R04WEB.pdf.

[8] Technical Committee 3.3 Road Tunnel Operation, PIARC. Road tunnels: operational strategies for emergency ventilation [R/OL]. PIARC, 2011. https://www.piarc.org/ressources/publications/6/6941,WEB-2011R02.pdf.

[9] Design of Road Tunnels(BD 78/99)[M/OL]// Design Manual for Roads and Bridges, Highways England, 1999. http://www.standardsforhighways.co.uk/ha/standards/dmrb/vol2/section2/bd7899.pdf.

[10] Technical Committee 5 Road Tunnels, PIARC. Pollution by nitrogen dioxide in road tunnels[R/OL]. PIARC, 2000. https://www.piarc.org/ressources/publications/1/3874,05-09-e.pdf.

[11] Tsai K-C, Lee Y-P, Lee S-K. Critical ventilation velocity for tunnel fires occurring near tunnel exits[J]. Fire Saf. J., 2011, 46: 556-557.

[12] Gannouni S, Maad R B. Numerical study of the effect of blockage on critical velocity and backlayering length in longitudinally ventilated tunnel fires [J]. Tunnelling and Underground Space Technology incorporating Trenchless Technology Research, 2015, 48: 147-155.

[13] Oka Y, Atkinson G T. Control of smoke flow in tunnel fires[J]. Fire Saf. J., 1995, 25: 305-322.

[14] Wu Y, Bakar M Z A. Control of smoke flow in tunnel fires using longitudinal ventilation systems-a study of the critical velocity[J]. Fire Saf. J., 2000, 35: 363-390.

[15] Li Y Z, Lei B, Ingason H. Study of critical velocity and backlayering length in longitudinally ventilated tunnel fires[J]. Fire Saf. J., 2010, 45: 361-370.

17 Tunnel Lighting

17.1 Introduction

Expansion reading 17-1

Roadway and traffic conditions in tunnels can differ considerably from those that prevail on open road, especially during daytime, in terms of luminance. For a long tunnel without lighting, there occurs significant luminance contrast between portal area under daylight and roadway in tunnel. When vehicle drivers arrive from the external environment with a natural lighting level, which can be very high during daytime, they look at a tunnel like at a "black hole". This situation is known as the "black hole" effect. On entering a tunnel from the brightness of daylight surroundings, it takes a short time for drivers' eyes to adapt to the relatively dimly lit tunnel interior. As a natural way, motorists should slow down as they approach the tunnel entrance. On the contrary, as motorists could see a "white hole" or "dark frame" as they drive in a long tunnel to the tunnel exit.

Both of the these situations of "black hole" effect and "white hole" appearances can be minimized by providing enough light at the immediate tunnel entrance, or the threshold zone, to help drivers' eyes adapting smoothly. The goal of tunnel lighting design is to create a lighting system that facilitates a constant traffic flow and speed from the open road into the tunnel entrance, and then passing through safely a tunnel in a designed speed during daylight hours.

In general, the lighting of a tunnel should be sufficient to:①avoid the "black hole effect" when a driver is unable to see into the tunnel;②reduce the likelihood of a collision with another vehicle(or bicycle or pedestrian);③enable a driver to react and stop within the safe stopping distance (SSD) if an unexpected hazard appears;④provide visual guidance in both normal operation and accident situations.

17.2 Lighting of a road tunnel in general

17.2.1 Lighting situation of a road tunnel

Good visibility enables motorist to quickly discern the details of the roadway. In general, the factors that directly influence driver's visibility are:①the brightness of an object on or near the roadway;②ambient light;③the size of objects and identifying details;④the contrast between an object and its surroundings;⑤the contrast between pavement and its surroundings as seen by the observer;⑥the time available for seeing the object;⑦glare(both disability glare and discomfort glare); ⑧the quality of the driver's vision. As vehicle drivers arrive from the external environment with a natural lighting level, which can be very high during daytime or even due to the daylight reflected by the snow, "black hole" effect may appear as they look at a tunnel, in which they are supposed to perceive the presence of dangerous situations, such as obstacles, queues or traffic stops. As a result, the visibility of the drivers may be impaired due to the contrast difference in luminance between the access road and the carriageway in the tunnel. The difficulty of the driving task when approaching and passing through a tunnel is also influenced by the speed, the volume(flow) and the composition of the traffic, and by the layout of the approach and the tunnel, as well as their immediate surroundings.

The "black hole" effect at the entrance and the "dark frame" effect at the exit can have a strong influence on the safety of driving task. The higher percentage of accidents mainly occur in the transition areas around entrance and exit[1], as shown in Figure 17-1 as zones 1, 2 and 3, respectively, where efficient lighting is needed to avoid drivers' visibility impairing and allow the driver to safely approach and pass the tunnel.

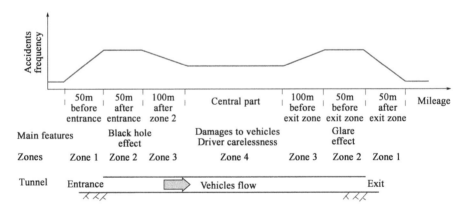

Figure 17-1 Tunnel longitudinal partition according to levels of danger[1]

The lighting requirements of a tunnel are totally different during daytime and night. At night the problem is relatively simple and consists in providing luminance levels on lit routes inside the tunnel equal to those outside the tunnel. The design of the lighting during daytime is particularly critical because of the features of human visual adaptation in varying lighting environments. As a driver approaching a tunnel, where the lighting situation is a highly illuminated exterior and a relatively dark interior, the driver outside the tunnel cannot simultaneously perceive details on the road at design speed. This means the transient adaptation being difficult. The adaptation process takes a certain time, depending on the amplitude of the lighting reduction from the open road to the tunnel. The greater the difference in lighting level between the tunnel approach and roadway in the tunnel, the longer the adaptation time needs for the driver. At a given speed, this means that the greater the difference between the lighting level outside and that inside the tunnel, the longer will be the distance over which the visual system of the driver has to adapt.

In general, driving from the approach and entrying into the inner section of a tunnel, drivers' eyes will get adapted to the darker surroundings, where the lighting level is provided for the diver to see obstacles on the roadway at design speed. This adaptation should be a continuous process. In terms of cost saving, the lighting level should be steadily reduced until it reaches the constant level in the tunnel interior zone. On emerging from a tunnel into daylight, the eye adapts far more quickly to the higher luminance level. However, similarly, rearward visibility should be maintained when leaving a tunnel to facilitate safe within the parting zone.

In terms of the compliance with the safety and cost saving requirements referring to artificial lighting, both the progressive adaptation of the eye and the different levels of luminance required along the tunnel are the main factors to be considered in tunnel lighting design. The contribution of lighting is to enable the road user to perform his visual tasks by ensuring a sufficient visibility of objects[2]. A well deigned tunnel lighting system must guarantee adequate safety conditions both at night and during daytime, with the aim of providing the driver with the best visual comfort. For example, the visual conditions have to be at least equal to those of the previous or subsequent open roads. The photometric features meeting the safety requirements, at least, include the followings[2]: ① adequate luminance, uniformity and distribution levels on the road surface and tunnel walls; ② the reduction of glaring effects; ③ the reduction of flicker effect.

17.2.2 Traffic and visual tasks

In tunnel lighting design, the visual task to be considered comprises the detection of the presence and movement of objects on the road in front of the driver. The objects depend on the type of tunnel in question, e.g., urban tunnel, road tunnel, highway tunnel and on the type of traffic mainly incorporated, e.g., motorized vehicles, cyclists, pedestrians. Following the suggestions by CIE[2], a reference task on the visibility of an object is a target of 0.2 m × 0.2 m, having a specified reflection factor of 0.20, which is a very dark object to represent the smallest potentially dangerous obstacle which could be found on the roadways. This object is similar to that often taken into consideration in road lighting studies. The lighting condition in a tunnel should not impair diver's visibility to detect the obstacle from a distance of a safe Stopping Sight Distance (SSD) as approaching the tunnel entrance. Norms, such as CIE[2], take account of what the driver sees from the SSD within a visual field of ±30° horizontally and ±20° vertically for a dry road.

The design of tunnel lighting is generally based on the visibility of objects. In this respect, the design speed of the vehicles is a fundamental element. The SSD of vehicles defines not only the point at which the observing driver must be able to detect the presence of an object but also, as shown later, the length of the entrance zone of the tunnel lighting. In general, an increase in the design speed will generally result in an increase in the lighting requirements and consequently in the cost of the installations and operation. For the continuity of the traffic flow, it is desirable to have the same design speed in the tunnel as on the adjacent open road. And therefore, the aims of tunnel lighting are: ①firstly, to allow traffic to enter, pass through and exit the enclosed section safely; ②secondly, to do so without impeding the through-flow of traffic. These aims are achieved by the adequate illumination of the tunnel, which allows drivers to smoothly adapt to the light within the tunnel and identify possible obstacles under designed speed.

17.2.3 Lighting of tunnels with different features

The objective of road tunnel lighting is to ensure that traffic can enter, pass through and leave the tunnel, with the same level of safety as on the adjacent roads. So it is necessary for the carriageway to be clearly visible throughout the length of the tunnel and that the carriageway and tunnel walls give a clear picture of the road.

The ability of a driver to see through a tunnel in straight line depends primarily on the length of the tunnel, although other design parameters, such as width, height and vertical curvatures of the tunnel, also have an effect. The critical factor is whether approaching drivers can see vehicles, other road users or obstacles when their distance from the entrance portal is less than or equal to the SSD. When the exit portal is a large part of the scene visible through the entrance, other road users and objects can easily be seen silhouetted against the lighter scene behind the exit portal. On the other hand, artificial lighting is needed when the exit portal is in a relatively large (thick) dark frame, in which objects can be hidden. This can happen when a tunnel is relatively long in relation to width, or when a tunnel is curved in such a way that only a part of the exit can be seen or the exit cannot be seen at all. And therefore, the lighting design of the tunnels, with different feature, such as in length and curvatures, should be determined according to the degree to which an approaching driver can see through the tunnel to the exit portal from a point at a distance equal to the SSD, in front of the entrance portal.

In terms of lighting, CIE[2] define a short tunnel as one where, in the absence of traffic, the exit and the area behind the exit can be clearly visible from a point, a SSD ahead of the entrance portal. For lighting purposes, the length of short tunnel is limited to 46 m(150 ft); tunnels up to 122 m(400 ft) long may be classified as short if they are straight, level, and have a high width(height) to length ratio.

Some tunnels—where the drivers cannot see the exit from a reference point in front of the tunnel—need to be illuminated like a long tunnel, even if their lengths would seem to make them a "short" one. These tunnels are designated as "optically long tunnels", contrary to those "optically short tunnels" where approaching motorists can see through the tunnels clearly.

The reference point is in principle the point located in the centre of the approaching lanes, at a height of 1.5 m and at a distance from the entrance of the tunnel equal to the SSD at the design speed. This stopping distance is the distance necessary to stop the vehicle moving at the speed in question in total safety. It comprises the distance covered during the reaction time and during the braking time. The reaction time of the average driver is generally assumed equal to 1.5 seconds.

With regard to daytime lighting, tunnels are subdivided into three classes[2]: ① geometrically long tunnel; ② optically long tunnels; ③ short tunnels. Both the long tunnels need lighting. The distinction can be made on the basis of the diagram given in Figure 17-2, which offers a first approximation in design, with the parameters of the length, geometrical feature, sunlight condition at the portal, sidewall reflection condition and traffic situation of the planned tunnel, under

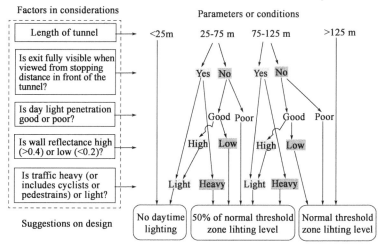

Figure 17-2 Daytime lighting of tunnels for different tunnel lengths[2]

consideration. At night only the recommended value for night-time lighting is needed.

Short tunnels appear to the approaching driver as a black frame, as opposed to the black hole experienced in long tunnels. A lighting system is generally not required in short tunnels, as daylight penetration from each end and the silhouette effect of brightness at the opposite end, assure satisfactory visibility.

Expansion reading 17-2

In practice, the classification of tunnels in terms of lighting can vary among nations. For example, it is recommended in British code[3] as followings. ①Tunnels shorter than 25 m do not normally need daytime lighting; ②Tunnels longer than 200 m should always have artificial daytime lighting, to avoid adaptation problems for road users; ③For tunnels of length between 25 m and 200 m, specified method should be used for determining if daytime lighting is needed.

If full daytime lighting is not needed for tunnels of length between 25 m and 200 m, some limited daytime lighting can be provided for tunnels where the traffic flow is classified as "high", when luminance levels within the tunnel are low, and during the periods immediately before dusk and after dawn, particularly on overcast days. The decision to provide such limited daytime lighting is a matter for the road or tunnel authority.

In China, the requirements of a artificial daytime lighting for a tunnel are determined on the factors of length and structure features of the tunnel, traffic composition of the tunnel, grade of the road, to which the tunnel is belonging, such as the *Guidelines*[4] presents the followings. ①The geometrically long tunnels or tunnels with length longer than 200 m in motorway or class-1 road need daytime lighting; ②The optically long tunnels or tunnels with length longer than 100 m but no longer than 200 m, in motorway or class-1 road, need daytime lighting; ③The geometrically long tunnels in class-2 road, with length longer than 1000 m, need daytime lighting; ④The geometrically long tunnels in class-2 road, or tunnels with length longer than 500 m but no longer than 1000 m, should provide daytime lighting.

17.2.4 Tunnel lighting zones

Tunnel can be considered a covered structure, which restricts the normal daytime illumination such that the driver's capability to see is substantially diminished. To ensure that driver's vision is not impaired, and also to minimize installation and energy costs of lighting, the luminance is reduced progressively from the entrance portal into the tunnel inner section. A similar provision is made at the exit to assist the reverse transition back into daylight. It is practical to distinguish different zones in the tunnel in order to determine the longitudinal lighting level of daytime lighting[2], i. e., the access zone, the threshold zone, the transition zone, the interior zone and the exit zone, as shown in Figure 17-3, along the traffic flow direction from the tunnel entrance to the exit portal. The high lighting levels in the threshold and transition zones of the tunnel are to give a safe adaptation from external high level to internal level. The exit zone is shorter than the entrance zone because drivers' eyes adapt from darkness to brightness more quickly than from brightness to darkness. Allowance needs to be made for the tunnels of an east to west orientation, when the sun is low.

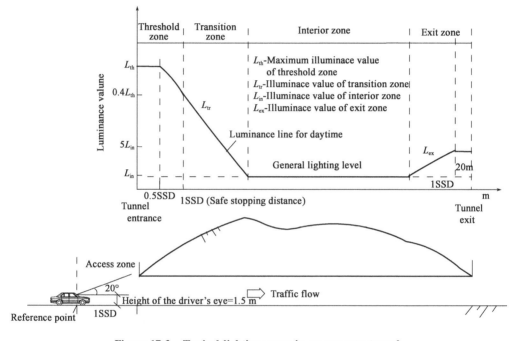

Figure 17-3 Typical lighting zones in an one-way tunnel

Access zone: the part of the open road immediately outside (in front of) the tunnel portal, covering the distance over which an approaching driver must be able to see into the tunnel. The access zone begins at the safety stopping distance point (reference point) ahead of the portal and it ends at the portal.

Threshold zone: the first part of the tunnel, directly after the portal❶. The threshold zone starts either at the beginning of the tunnel or at the beginning of the daylight sun screens when occurring. The length of the threshold zone is at least equal to the SSD.

Transition zone: the part of the tunnel following directly after the threshold zone. The transition zone begins at the end of the threshold zone. It ends at the

---

❶ Entrance portal: the part of the tunnel construction that corresponds to the beginning of the covered part of the tunnel, or-when open sun-screens are used-to the beginning of the sun-screens.

beginning of the interior zone. In the transition zone, the lighting level is decreasing from the level at the end of the threshold zone to the level of the interior zone.

Interior zone: the part of the tunnel following directly after the transition zone. It stretches from the end of the transition zone to the beginning of the exit zone.

Exit zone: the part of the tunnel where, during the daytime, the vision of a driver approaching the exit is predominantly influenced by the brightness outside the tunnel. The exit zone begins at the end of the interior zone. It ends at the exit portal❶ of the tunnel.

Parting zone: the first part of the open road directly after the exit portal of the tunnel. The parting zone is not a part of the tunnel, but it is closely related to the tunnel lighting. It is advised by CIE[2] that the length of the parting zone equals two times the SSD, but a length of more than 200 m is not necessary.

17.2.5 Influence of visual environment

The human eye can only perceive surfaces, objects and people through light that is emitted from them. Surface characteristics, reflection factors, and the quantity and quality of light determine the appearance of the target. In this term, the lighting features of a tunnel affect safety, task performance and the visual environment. For example, safety is ensured by making any hazards visible; task performance is facilitated by making the relevant details of the task easy to see; the effect of the environmental luminance is the generation of a veiling luminance, which reduces the contrasts of an obstacle and consequently also its visibility.

Road tunnel lighting installation must generate a good visual environment, which may be created by changing the relative emphasis given to the various objects and surfaces. In general, the required lighting level at the tunnel entrance for making a possible(reference)obstacle visible is proportional to the veiling luminance.

On the other hand, the subjective visual appearance will depend upon eye adaptation. The eye can adapt to a wide range of lighting conditions. For example, headlines in a newspaper can be read under moonlight(which provides some 0.2 lux), or by daylight(where the illuminance may be of the order of 100000 lux). However, the eye cannot adapt to the whole of this range at one time. At night the headlights of an oncoming car will dazzle a dark-adapted viewer, whereas on a sunny day these lights will be barely noticeable. In this term, sharp shadows, sudden large changes in luminance, and excessively bright and frequent highlights

---

❶ Exit portal: the part of the tunnel construction that corresponds to the end of the covered part of the tunnel, or-when open sun-screens are used-to the end of the sun-screens.

should be avoided in a tunnel. With a uniform electric lighting system and medium to high reflectance of the main surfaces of tunnel interior, the range of luminance will usually be satisfactory for a road tunnel.

17.3 Daytime lighting levels of long tunnels

In terms of safety, the tunnel lighting must always guarantee that the visual perceptions of drivers are maintained by avoiding sudden variations in lighting levels when entering, passing and exiting a tunnel. During daytime, where there is a high level of external light, it is necessary to increase the level of luminance at the entrance of the tunnel mainly to avoid a black hole effect and thus a reduction in visual perception. At the tunnel exit, the level of luminance should also be increased to avoid drivers being subjected to glare effects by the high sunlight outside. On the other hand, energy saving is always the consideration of tunnel lighting design. In general, the design of tunnel lighting should be based on the features and environment of the tunnel. At night, the level of luminance in a tunnel should be constant and equivalent to the level on the road leading into the tunnel.

17.3.1 Tunnel lighting classification

Expansion reading 17-3

The tunnel lighting classification should be based on the characteristics of tunnel utilization. For example, in the British code [3], according to the main influencing factors of traffic flow, traffic type and mix, and visual guidance, the class of lighting for a tunnel can be determined following the procedure, as shown in Figure 17-4. The factor of traffic flow intensity should be classified as high, medium or low. It is clear that the higher of the grade of a tunnel, in terms of lighting class, the higher lighting level is required in design and operation.

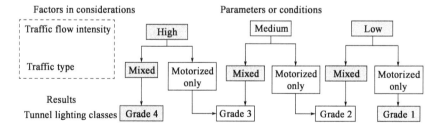

Figure 17-4 Tunnel lighting class selection[3]

Similarly, in the *Guidelines*[4], the requirement of tunnel lighting mainly depends on the factors of road grade, the traffic volume and its compositions, and the length of a tunnel.

17.3.2 Determination of access zone luminance

In order to determine the necessary daytime lighting levels within a tunnel, the access zone luminance, the luminance L_{20}, should first be determined, and then the threshold zone luminance and the luminance in the transition zone are calculated accordingly.

The luminance L_{20} in the access zone is defined as the average of the luminance values measured in a conical field of view, subtending an angle of 20° ($2 \times 10°$), by an observer located at the reference point and looking towards a centered point at a height equal to one quarter of the height of the tunnel opening, which is generally considered as the height of the driver's eyes about 1.5 m. The sky percentage in the 20° field is key parameter for determining the magnitude of the L_{20}. This average luminance is conventionally considered as representative of the state of adaptation of the eye of a driver approaching the entrance of the tunnel when he finds himself at the reference point[2] and is used as a basis for computing the luminance in the entrance zone.

The evaluation of lighting levels and transition time for the the access zone should consider the following factors: ① tunnel orientation; ② latitude; ③geographical location; ④approach grades; ⑤terrain. There are several methods of determining access zone luminance L_{20}. For example, direct measurement at the site as described in the Annex A1 in CIE[2], the grid method as described in the Annex E and the method of estimating L_{20} presented in the Annex F of the code[3], respectively. In China, empirical values for the estimating of L_{20} are also given[4].

Expansion reading 17-4

A method of estimating L_{20} may be used for providing an interim value for provisional design purposes, but should not be used for the final design. The preliminary result should be checked with that of other method. The method given in the Annex D by the code[3], is recommended, particularly when it is likely to produce different results from each approach.

17.3.3 Lighting in the threshold zone

To help drivers eyes adapt smoothly and comfortably, the first part of the tunnel, called the threshold zone, is strongly lit over a distance equal to the SSD of the tunnel. It is clear that the higher the design speed, the longer the threshold zone. The high level lighting in the threshold zone of the tunnel should meet the condition requirement that a driver can see a possible obstacle situated inside the tunnel from outside the tunnel.

17.3.3.1 Threshold zone luminance

The road surface luminance of the threshold zone should be derived from the daytime luminance of the access zone. The length of the threshold zone is equal to the SSD of the tunnel. The threshold zone luminance, L_{th}, should be provided during daytime from the beginning of the threshold zone for a length of 0.5SSD. The threshold zone luminance L_{th} can be calculated as:

$$L_{th1} = k \cdot L_{20} \qquad (17\text{-}1)$$

Expansion reading 17-5

where, k is reduction factor value, which should be selected from the recommended values in a referenced design code or guideline. Similarly, a series of recommended values of k are also presented in the *Guidelines*[4].

From half the SSD onwards, the lighting level should gradually and linearly decrease to a value, at the end of the threshold zone, equal to $0.4L_{th1}$, i.e., $L_{th2} = 0.4L_{th1}$[2], or to $0.5L_{th}$, i.e., $L_{th2} = 0.5L_{th1}$, as suggested by the *Guidelines*[4]. The gradual reduction over the last half of the threshold zone may also be in steps. However, the luminance level should not fall below the values corresponding to a gradual linear decrease. The general feature of a tunnel daytime lighting luminance curve is shown in Figure 17-5.

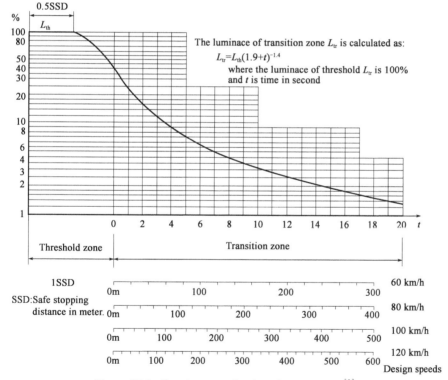

Figure 17-5 Luminance reduction along a tunnel[2]

17.3.3.2 Length of threshold zone

Where the design speed is low, the length of the threshold zone is nearly equal to the SSD. The value of SSD should be evaluated for the tunnel lighting design. The SSD is considered that the sum of two stretches of road: ①the distance covered during the reaction time of driver; ②the distance covered during the braking time, as suggested in CIE[2]. The values of the SSD are usually presented in design codes or the *Guidelines*[4].

Expansion reading 17-6

The length of the threshold zone is can be considered as same as the SSD (Figure 17-5), or following the *Guidelines*[4], calculated as:

$$D_{th1} = D_{th2} = \frac{1}{2}\left(1.154D_s - \frac{h - 1.5}{\tan 10°}\right) \qquad (17\text{-}2)$$

where D_{th1} and D_{th2} are the half length of the threshold zone, m; D_s is the length of SSD, m; h is the height of the tunnel clearance cross section profile, m.

17.3.4 Transition zone

The threshold zone is followed by a transition zone, in which the level of luminance is gradually reduced over a distance that is always determined according to the design speed. The level of luminance in the transition zone is to support the curve of acceptability for the reduction in luminance perceived by the driver's eyes and thus control the temporal adaptation[2].

In the transition zone, the average road surface luminance should be gradually reduced from the end of the threshold zone towards the interior zone. The lighting level of the transition zone, L_{tr}, can be calculated as[2]: $L_{tr} = L_{th}(1.9 + t)^{-1.4}$, where L_{th} is the threshold zone luminance in 100%; t is traveling time in seconds.

The curve determined by the equation $L_{tr} = L_{th}(1.9 + t)^{-1.4}$ can be replaced by a stepped curve with levels that should never fall below the continuous curve. The maximum luminance ratio permitted on passing from one step to another is 3. The last step should not be greater than 2 times the interior zone luminance. As suggested in the *Guidelines*[4], where the curve is presented by three-step sections, the luminance of each section, L_{tr1}, L_{tr2} and L_{tr3}, can be calculated as:

$$L_{tr1} = 0.15 L_{th} \qquad (17\text{-}3\text{-}1)$$

$$L_{tr2} = 0.05 L_{th} \qquad (17\text{-}3\text{-}2)$$

$$L_{tr3} = 0.02 L_{th} \qquad (17\text{-}3\text{-}3)$$

In corresponding to the luminance calculated using Equation (17-3), the length of the sections, D_{tr1}, D_{tr2} and D_{tr3}, respectively, of the transition zone can be determined as:

$$D_{tr1} = \frac{D_{th1} + D_{th2}}{3} + \frac{v_t}{1.8} \qquad (17\text{-}4\text{-}1)$$

$$D_{tr2} = \frac{2v_t}{1.8} \qquad (17\text{-}4\text{-}2)$$

$$D_{tr3} = \frac{3v_t}{1.8} \qquad (17\text{-}4\text{-}3)$$

where v_t is the design speed, km/h; $v_t/1.8$ is the traveling distance in two seconds.

As the view field of the driver is made up by the tunnel interior, a longer transition zone may be advisable in order to counteract a second black hole effect. For additional driving comfort, in the case of the stepped luminance curve, the length of the transition zone may, at its end, is extended for 1-2 seconds over the length as suggested in the CIE-curve (Figure 17-5).

17.3.5 Interior zone

The average luminance of the road in the interior zone of the tunnel is given as a function of the SSD and of the traffic flow. Very long tunnel's interior zone consists of two different sub zones. The first sub zone corresponds to the length which is covered in 30 seconds traveling and should be illuminated with the "long tunnels" levels; and the second sub zone corresponds to the remaining length and should be illuminated with the "very long tunnels" levels[2]. The luminance of the second sub zone can also be reduced to a certain percent of that the first sub zone, such as in the *Guidelines*[4].

Expansion reading 17-7

The average value of interior zone road surface luminance L_{in} should be not less than the value. For a tunnel, its lighting class[2], such as low or heavy, is related to the features of the traffic flow in the tunnel. The features of traffic flow used may be defined as: ① For one-way traffic flow, the values > 1500 in vehicles/hour/lane is heavy and the values < 500 in vehicles/hour/lane is low; ② For two-way traffic flow, the values > 400 in vehicles/hour/lane is heavy and the values < 100 in vehicles/hour/lane is low.

The luminance values of emergency lanes, where they are provided, are generally larger that of the average luminance of the road in the interior zone. For example, the luminance values of emergency lanes are recommended no less than 4.0 cd/m^2 in the *Guidelines*[4].

17.3.6 Exit zone

During the daytime, the tunnel exit appears as a bright hole to the motorist. Usually, all obstacles will be discernible by silhouette against the bright exit and will be clearly visible. This visibility by silhouette can be further improved by lining the walls with tile or panels having high reflectance and thus permitting greater daylight penetration into the tunnel, through improving the contrast of the obstacle.

At the exit, the adaptation of the driver's eyes to the higher luminance is very rapid and extra lighting is not needed to assist this adaptation. However, in order to give direct illumination of smaller vehicles, which can otherwise be inconspicuous behind larger vehicles because of the glare effect of the exit; and to enable drivers who are leaving the tunnel to have sufficient rear vision via their mirrors, the exit zone should be illuminated in the same way as the interior zone of the tunnel. In situations where additional hazards are expected near the exit of the tunnel and in tunnels where the interior zone is long, CIE[2] recommends that the daytime luminance in the exit zone increases linearly over a length equal to the SSD (before the exit portal), from the level of the interior zone to a level five times that of the interior zone, $5L_{in}$, at a distance of 20 m from the exit portal.

In China, the exit is recommended by the *Guidelines*[4] as two sub zones, E_{X1} and E_{X2}, with length of 30 m for each. The luminance of the sub zones, L_{ex1} and L_{ex2}, respectively, are calculated as:

$$L_{ex1} = 3L_{in} \quad (17\text{-}5\text{-}1)$$
$$L_{ex2} = 5L_{in} \quad (17\text{-}5\text{-}2)$$

In a two-way tunnel, the threshold and transition zones lighting for the opposing traffic provides the recommended luminance, as presented above.

17.3.7 Parting zone lighting

Expansion reading 17-8

In case the tunnel is part of an unlit road and the speed of driving is higher than 50km/h, night-time lighting of the parting zone is recommended[2]: ①if the night-time lighting level in the tunnel is more than 1 cd/m^2; ②if different weather conditions are likely to appear at the entrance and at the exit of the tunnel.

CIE[2] recommends road lighting in the parting zone shall be provided over the length of 2 times SSD with road luminance not lower than 1/3 of the night-time luminance in the interior zone of the tunnel. The *Guidelines*[4] give lighting Luminance and length of the parting zone for road tunnels.

17.3.8 Quality of lighting

For all zones, the average road surface luminance values, such as being designed, should be provided for the total carriageway width of the tunnel, including emergency lanes, if they are provided. The luminance values given are maintained values. The quality of lighting in a tunnel is often evaluated with the features of luminance and uniformity values, flicker and glare.

17.3.8.1 Luminance and uniformity

Good uniformity of luminance must be provided on the road surface and on the sidewalls up to a height of 2 m. The lower parts of the walls act as a background for traffic, as does the carriageway. For all dimming steps of the lighting installation, CIE[2] recommends that: ①overall uniformity (U_0), a ratio of 0.4 for the minimum (L_{min}) to the average value (L_{av}) of luminance on the road surface and on the walls up to 2 m in height in clean conditions of the tunnel, i.e., $U_0 = L_{min}/L_{av}$; ②longitudinal uniformity, a ratio of 0.6 for the minimum to the maximum value (L_{max}) of luminance along the centre of each lane for the road, i.e., $U_1 = L_{min}/L_{max}$.

The requirement of luminance uniformity is also considered the function of tunnel lighting class, e.g., in the *Code*[3] in UK or traffic features in a designed tunnel, as recommended in the *Guidelines*[4].

Overall uniformity should be calculated for the full road width, i.e. for the driving lane(s) and for the emergency lanes if they are provided in the tunnel. Longitudinal uniformity should be calculated for each lane separately, including emergency lanes where they are provided. In the transition zone and the second half of the threshold zone(and in the exit zone if existing), the luminance uniformity should be calculated and measured in the central part of each step replacing the continuous variation curve. The required values of uniformity shall be reached, respectively and independently, on the length of the step[1].

17.3.8.2 Lighting of tunnel walls

Expansion reading 17-9

Tunnel walls are part of the background for the detection of obstacles in the tunnel. Good lighting onto the low part of the walls(Figure 17-6) contributes to the adaptation level and to the visual guidance. The luminance of the walls is considered an important component for the quality of the tunnel lighting. The average luminance of the tunnel walls, up to at least a height of 2 m, must be atleast 60% of the average road surface luminance at the relevant location as recommended in CIE[2]. As required in the *Guidelines*[4] or *Code*[3], the average luminance of the walls up to a height of 2 m should be not less than the average road surface luminance at the corresponding location.

17.3.8.3 Flicker

The sensation of flicker (impression of fluctuating luminance or color) can cause visual discomfort to drivers. It is induced by periodic changes in luminance within the field of vision. Driving under incorrectly spaced luminaires within the tunnel or through an entrance zone with daylight louvres can give rise to this effect.

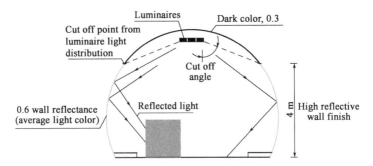

Figure 17-6 Sketch showing light distribution for a tunnel[7]

Visual flicker of between approximately 2.5 Hz and 15 Hz, caused by spacing luminaires at certain intervals may lead to discomfort or distress for drivers passing through the tunnel[6]. The degree of discomfort is dependent on: ①total duration of the flicker experience; ②contrast between the flicker source luminance and its background; ③flicker frequency; ④the rate of change of luminance.

The effect of flicker should be minimized. This can be done by ensuring that[2,3]: ①flicker duration is no greater than 20 s; ②unlit length between adjacent flashed areas in a luminaire row is less than the flashed length of a luminaire; ③flicker frequency falls outside the band 2.5 Hz to 15 Hz.

Flicker frequency can be calculated by dividing the speed, in meters per second by the luminaire spacing (centre-to-centre, in meters). For example: for a vehicle speed of 60 km/h(= 16.6 m/s) and luminaire spacing of 4 m, the flicker frequency is 16.6/4 = 4.2 Hz, which may cause visual discomfort to drivers, since this value is in the range of 2.5 Hz to 15 Hz.

17.3.8.4 Glare

Glare occurs whenever one part of a tunnel is much brighter than the general brightness in the tunnel. The most common sources of excessive brightness are luminaires, seen directly or by reflection, in comparison to the general background brightness. However, no glare occurs during daytime when the luminaire is on, because the background lighting is much high during daytime.

Glare can have two effects. As a glare impairs vision, it is called disability glare; and as it causes discomfort, it is called discomfort glare. Disability glare is more harmful than discomfort glare. The former should be minimized while the latter should be decreased or alleviated to a acceptable level, in terms of lighting design.

17.3.8.4.1 Disability glare

Disability glare is most likely to occur when there is an area close to the line of sight that has a much higher luminance than the object of regard. Then, the

Expansion reading 17-10

scattering of light in the eye and changes in local adaptation can cause a reduction in the contrast of the object. This reduction in contrast may be sufficient to make important details invisible, and hence may influence task performance. Alternatively, if the source of high luminance is viewed directly, noticeable afterimages may be created.

Disability glare reduces visibility and should be minimized. Following the suggestion of CIE[2], the threshold increment *TI* of luminance should be less than 15% for the threshold zone and the interior zone of the tunnel during the daytime and less than 15 % for all tunnel zones during night. The *TI* can be calculated with the method suggested in CIE 31-1976 "Glare and uniformity in street lighting", as the following[2]:

$$TI = 65(L_v/L_r^{0.8}) \qquad \text{for } L_r \leqslant 5 \text{ cd/m}^2 \qquad (17\text{-}6\text{-}1)$$
$$TI = 95(L_v/L_r^{1.05}) \qquad \text{for } L_r > 5 \text{ cd/m}^2 \qquad (17\text{-}6\text{-}2)$$

where L_r average road surface luminance; and L_v veiling luminance created by all luminaires in the visual field within 20° above the horizontal. Unfortunately, at present, it is not possible to give a numerical value for the restriction of the glare control in the transition zone[2].

17.3.8.4.2 Discomfort glare

Discomfort glare occurs when some elements of a tunnel have a much higher luminance than others. A high source luminance, large source area, low background luminance and a position close to the line of sight all may increase discomfort glare. As a general rule, discomfort glare can be avoided by the choice of luminaire layout and orientation, and the use of high-reflectance surfaces for the low part of tunnel walls.

17.4 Determination of night-time lighting levels

If a tunnel is in a section of illuminated road, the night-time luminance inside the tunnel should be at least equal to the access road luminance, but not more than three times this value. If the tunnel is on a section of unlit road, the British code[3] recommend that:①tunnels shorter than 25 m do not normally need to be lit;②for tunnels between 25 m and 200 m in length the decision to provide night-time lighting is a matter for the highway authority, taking account of matters including tunnel lighting class, type of utilization at night and environmental considerations; ③tunnels longer than 200 m should be lit at night to a luminance level of not less than 1.0 cd/m².

As suggested in the British code[3] and CIE[2], where night-time lighting is provided to a tunnel on an unlit road, the decision to provide lighting on the access zone and parting zone is a matter for the road authority. However, where such lighting is provided, the length of this section should normally be not less than the SSD of the tunnel, unless there are particular reasons such as environmental reasons for a reduced length.

The luminance uniformity of night-time lighting of a tunnel on unlit road should be not less than the value given in a design code for the appropriate tunnel lighting class[2].

17.5 Design of lighting system

Tunnel lighting is determined by the satisfaction of the luminance requirements, in terms of safety. On the other hand, costs and energy saving are also factors to be considered in design. The daytime luminance curve from the threshold luminance at the entrance to the interior zone is designed for a tunnel. Sometimes, visual comfort is also required, providing that the users of the tunnel with a feeling of well-being, which generally also contributes to a high safety level.

For tunnel lighting design in terms of lighting system determination, factors should be taken into consideration generally include the shape of the portal, type and density of traffic, contribution of wall luminance, orientation of tunnel, and luminous environment, which is mainly related to these parameters, including: ①luminance distribution; ②illuminance; ③glare; ④the directionality of light; ⑤the color rendering and color appearance of the light; ⑥flicker; ⑦daylight at the tunnel.

17.5.1 Lighting systems

To provide a good lighting environment in a tunnel, luminaires are normally aligned with their long axis parallel to the tunnel. There are three artificial lighting systems in common use, i. e., symmetrical, counterbeam lighting and pro-beam lighting❶. Pro-beam lighting and counter beam lighting are of asymmetrical and directional feature. In general, symmetrical lighting provides a mixture of negative and positive contrast; counter beam lighting provides negative contrast; and pro-beam lighting provides positive contrast, respectively(Figure 17-7).

17.5.1.1 Symmetrical lighting

Symmetrical lighting is the lighting where the light equally falls on objects in directions with and against the traffic. Symmetrical lighting is characterized by using luminaires that show a luminous intensity distribution that is symmetrical in relation to the plane normal to the direction of the traffic, as shown Figure 17-7a).

---

❶ The terms "symmetrical" "counterbeam" and "pro-beam" refer to the luminous intensity distribution of the luminaires in relation to the oncoming divers on the tunnel roadway.

The linear symmetrical lighting using fluorescent luminaires distributes similar patterns in all directions to create a uniform luminescence throughout the tunnel. Figure 17-7a) shows the shape of distribution with low contrast values[6].

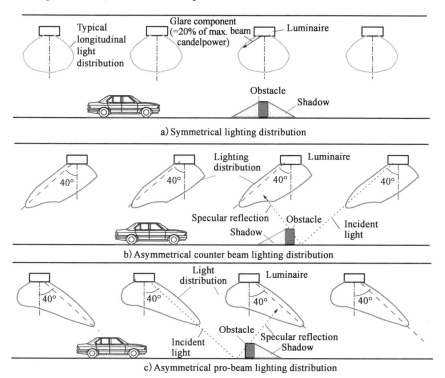

Figure 17-7 Lighting system and lighting distribution features

Symmetrical lighting systems can provide good contrast between objects on the road and the background road surface, and assist the visibility of other vehicles moving in the same direction. It is beneficial when tunnels are bi-directional, either in normal use or during maintenance operations.

17.5.1.2　Asymmetrical lighting

Asymmetrical (directional) lighting such as counter beam and pro-beam lighting distributes patterns only in one direction, either with or against traffic [Figure 17-7b),17-7c)].

17.5.1.2.1　Counter beam lighting

The counter beam lighting system uses luminaires with the luminous intensity distribution being mainly directed towards oncoming traffic [Figure 17-7b)]. The aim of a counter beam lighting is to illuminate vertical surfaces as little as possible, to give the maximum contrast with the carriageway surface[8]. By minimizing glare, drivers can clearly see the contours of the vehicle ahead[6].

To reinforce the luminance level and at the same time to accentuate the negative contrast of potential obstacles, counter beam lighting is achieved with asymmetrical light distribution facing into the traffic flow, both in the direction of the on coming driver and in the run of the road. The beam lighting stops sharply at the vertical plane passing through the luminaire. No light is directed with the flow of traffic. This generates negative contrast and enhances visual adaptation.

In general, using the increased contrast implies a reduction of the required level of carriageway luminance. This gives a choice of energy saving through lower installed power and is also the reason that counter beam lighting in widespread use[8], especially in the threshold and transition zones of an one-way tunnel.

It is noted that the counter beam lighting can have the following disadvantages[6]: ①it might not be appropriate for a tunnel entrance with high daylight penetration; ②it can be less effective for tunnels with very high traffic flows or for tunnels with a high percentage of heavy goods vehicles; ③it might not be appropriate for bi-directional tunnels; ④ it can be difficult to achieve the necessary luminance on the tunnel walls; ⑤it can reduce drivers' rearward visual performance when looking in driving mirrors.

Also, as stated in the road tunnel lighting code[8], counter beam lighting has a number of disadvantages that may outweigh the above-mentioned advantages, such as①counter beam lighting reduces the contrast between road markings and the road surface; ②when the road surface is humid or wet, it reflects the luminaires and the uniformity of the carriageway luminance is low; ③sizeable objects, seen against the much darker background of the carriageway further into the tunnel, have a lower visibility than with normal lighting. So, counter beam lighting directed towards the oncoming traffic is not recommended for traffic safety reasons, where contrast has not been sufficient to distinguish obstacles reliably[6].

17.5.1.2.2 Pro-beam lighting

Pro-beam lighting [Figure 17-7c)] directs the maximum candlelight with the traffic away from the driver providing high object luminance and low road luminance, creating a positive contrast[6]. In general, pro-beam lighting is not recommended where the road luminance is low.

17.5.2 Choice of light source

17.5.2.1 Photometric curve

The whole of the measures of luminous intensities emitted by a luminaire in all directions forms the "photometric solid". Luminous intensity values represented in polar co-ordinates on a plane define a line that is called "photometric curve". They are generally expressed as cd/klm, i.e., referred to a source emitting a luminous flux equal to a 1000 lm. Usually not all information regarding the photometric solid is given, but only as regards two vertical planes normal to each other, crossing the optical center of the luminaire, as shown in Figure 17-8.

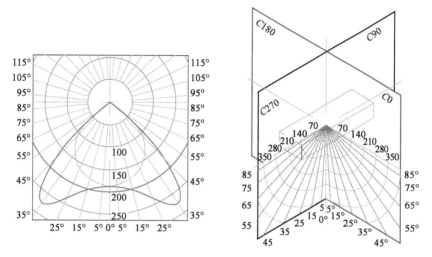

Figure 17-8 Sketch showing the photometric curve of a luminaire[cd/klm]

17.5.2.2 Types of luminaires

A wide variety of tunnel lights are available, such as mercury, low pressure sodium, high pressure sodium (HPS), LED (Light Emitting Diode) and fluorescent. The last three types are commonly used in tunnels.

Fluorescent lamps are of the discharge type where fluorescent material is excited by ultraviolet radiation. They are most suitable for the interior zone and night time lighting. Lengths of 1.5 m to 1.8 m are preferred, and lamps and starting gear shall be suitable for starting in temperatures below 0 ℃. The main features of a fluorescent lamp include:①its restrike times and flicker are minimal; ②light distribution is even with good color control; ③lamps are dimmable for energy saving.

Sodium vapor lamps are of high pressure(10000 Pa)partial vapor types. They are suitable for the higher lighting level zones. Louvres shall be used in the high pressure luminaires to reduce glare. Dimming is possible with special equipment. However, flicker and restrike time shall be considered for the use of sodium vapor lamps in interior zones. The sodium vapor lamps are most popular before the LEDs get their positions in tunnel lighting.

LEDs are semi-conductor diodes that convert electrical energy to visible light and are able to produce many colors without color filters. LED tunnel lights get popular in recent years. The main reasons include:①quality white light, luminous flux directionality and great uniformity contribute to a significant increase of the safety conditions within the covered section; ②they operate on low voltage, with high energy efficacy and instantly turning on.

LED tunnel lights are dimmable luminaires, which offer greater flexibility of control for energy saving but with relatively lower capital and maintenance costs in the recent years. One of the advantages of LED technology, in addition to the reduction of energy consumption and maintenance costs, is the possibility of optimizing the threshold lighting dimming according to the external lighting conditions. The results from the AEC Illuminazione Srl[1] show that LED technology optimizes the dimming levels up to 15%-20% of their initial flux, maintaining the necessary perceptive conditions and guaranteeing a significant consumption reduction with an estimated 10%-15% energy saving, while the conventional HPS lights is impossible for dimming the sources below 60% of their initial flow (with a ferromagnetic power supply unit). On the other hand, the improvement of the LED luminaires has made their high power factor under low dimming. For example, AEC Illuminazione Srl LED luminaires for tunnel lighting reach a power factor of more than 0.9, even with a 30%-40% dimming. The use of LED devices allows reducing the power consumption of the whole installation in a tunnel.

Choice for a particular application and performance shall offer the minimum whole life cost, taking into account energy consumption, lamp replacement intervals and the costs of luminaires and lamps. The main parameters in considerations for tunnel lights choosing[7] are lamp circuit luminous efficacy, lumen maintenance (the average number of operating hours from new when light output will have dropped to 80% of the initial value), lamp survival (the number of operating hours from new when 20% of lamps in an installation will have failed), restrike time, color rendering index, shape and whether being dimmable.

Expansion reading 17-11

The choice of luminaires shall be related to tunnel profile, systems of support, ease of access and vulnerability from traffic. Luminaires shall be of robust construction, sealed to IP65 requirements to prevent the ingress of moisture, and adequately protected against the harsh conditions of the tunnel environment, i.e., the combined corrosive effects of vehicle pollution, dust, chemicals used in tunnel cleansing, and road salts thrown up by traffic.

In conjunction with the lighting system, a highly reflective surface on the walls and ceiling, such as tile or metal panels, may be considered in light source choosing.

17.5.3 Luminaire arrangement

The luminaires for lighting in a tunnel can be installed in the following types of arrangement: ①central line luminaire arrangement; ②single side luminaire arrangement; ③double side (bilateral) luminaire arrangement; ④staggered luminaire arrangement, as shown in Figure 17-9. For each installation pattern, the most economic solution has to be considered on the basis of the energy, lamp and labor cost, as well as the convenience of maintaining.

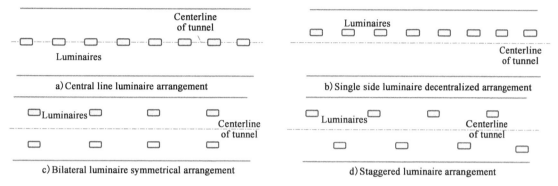

Figure 17-9　Commonly used luminaire arrangement

The luminaires of in a tunnel can be installed in a horizontal or diagonal mode. Figure 17-10 shows the installation mode in a cross section for bilateral arrangement.

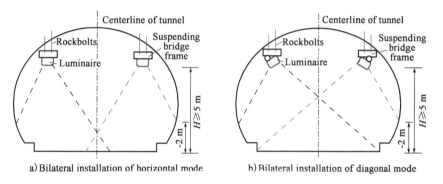

Figure 17-10　Sketch showing the installation mode of luminaries

In terms of energy efficiency, the centerline arrangement is generally better than that of two side arrangement; and for the two lines arrangement, the staggered luminaire arrangement is better than that of the symmetrical one.

Of a tunnel with a (modified) horseshoes shape in cross section, the luminaires can be mounted onto the ceiling or crown walls. In the recent years, the mounting mode is modified in order to improve the energy utilization efficiency. For example, the luminaires can be installed onto a suspending bridge frame, which is supported by rockbolts mounting into tunnel lining. The height of the luminaires are therefore to be less than that of mounting directly onto lining ceiling, as shown in Figure 17-10.

Where tunnel alignment is in curve, there is always more luminaires installed in comparison to that of a tunnel in straight line. The sharper the curve is the more luminaires required for a tunnel. Similarly, a tunnel, with steeper grades, especially at the crests of hills, a closer spacing of luminaires is applied in order to provide higher pavement luminance and improved uniformities. This is mainly because headlighting of the vehicle is not effective in these situations, where a tunnel is in a geometry of abrupt curves, and silhouette seeing cannot be provided in some instances, such as a condition where the target, or obstacle, has a lower luminance than the background. In this situation, luminaires should be located to provide ample illumination on vehicles, road curbing and berms, guard rails and so on. Proper horizontal orientation of luminaire on curves is important to assure balanced distribution of the light flux on the pavement. When luminaires are located on grade inclines, it is desirable to orient the luminaire so that the light beams strike the pavement equidistant from the luminaire. This assures the maximum uniformity of light distribution and keeps glare to a minimum.

In general, where the interior zone of a tunnel is in a curve, the following luminaires arrangement are proper[4]: ①where the radii of the curve of the tunnel is no less than 1000 m, the luminaires is designed same as the luminaires arrangement of a tunnel in straight line; ②where the radii of the curve is less than 1000 m, symmetrical mode is proper for bilateral luminaire arrangement, or the luminaires are on outside of the curve where single side luminaire decentralised arrangement is planned and the spacing is about 0.5-0.7 times that of a tunnel in straight line; ③where the tunnel is in a reverse curve, the luminaires should be installed along one side, with additional luminaires installed on the outside of the curve. This is favorable to the maintenance of the luminaires and to the guiding efficiency of lighting.

Expansion reading 17-12

17.5.4 Daylight variation and lighting control

As the access zone luminance varies with changes in daylight conditions. A lighting system must be designed and managed to achieve good control of energy use under different daylight conditions, for both daytime and night.

As the luminance levels in the threshold and transition zones are designed constant percentages of the access zone luminance, it is possible to provide the control of the lighting in these zones, to realize an energy saving plan. The control may be done through continuously dimming devices or by switching in separate steps. Many modern tunnels have up to 6 steps, including those for night-time operation, as shown in Figure 17-11. In these lighting reduction design, an instantaneous reduction by a factor of not more than 3 is recommended because of economic and comfort reasons[5].

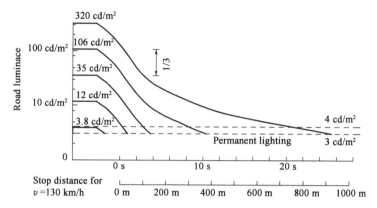

Figure 17-11 Luminance levels with subsequent switching off without regulators[5]

For adequate light control, the access zone light level must be monitored continuously, to realize that the difference between the actual and the preferred luminance in the threshold zone is as small as possible.

The lighting installation should assure the required road luminance both with the maximum external sunlight in summer time and/or in winter with snow and sun. When the daylight level decreases during the day or the seasons, also the luminance generated by the installation should decrease proportionally, in terms of energy saving. Traditionally, without regulators the decrease of the road luminance can be obtained by switching out a number of luminaries and to realize a number of fixed luminance levels. Automatic control can be used, such as a timer control system may switch the whole lighting installation on and off at predetermined times, or it may be programmed to send signals at certain times during the day to switch off selected luminaires. However, if some luminaries are switched off, the lighting on the road can be patch-wise and go under the minimum for general and/or longitudinal uniformity, with severe dangers for the traffic. To avoid these problems, in the installations number of luminaries must be higher. In general, a higher number of luminaries require the higher costs of cables and electrical components for supplying the higher number of supply circuits. On the other hand, equipped moreover with lower power lamps also means lower efficiency of energy utilization, since smaller lamps have lower luminous efficiency[5].

In the recent years, with the application of LED lights, which have good dimmable feature, as well as the development of automatic controller, the luminance of the lights can be reduced in a continuous mode. For example, the application of the regulators (Intelux)[5] permit to reduce the luminance of each level to 20% before going to the lower one by switching off some lamps, as shown in Figure 17-12, in which the field of actions of the regulators is hatched.

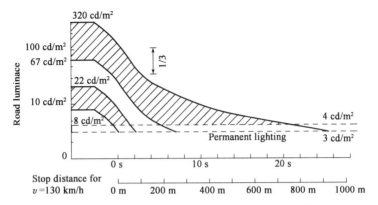

Figure 17-12　Luminance levels with regulators[5]

In Figure 17-12, the luminance level reducing implies huge economic savings. At the same time, the risks to slip under the uniformity values of the norms are much lower, since between two subsequent levels a lower number of luminaries must be switched off.

17.5.5　Flicker control

Point lighting source is often the preferred system for tunnel lighting. Discontinuity of the lighting may create the flicker effect, which is caused by periodic luminance changes and the spacing of luminaires. This can be reduced by adjusting the luminaire spacing outside of the annoyance range[6].

Expansion reading 17-13

To prevent light flicker, the recommended intervals[3] between light sources can be reference for the interior zone lighting design. Also luminaires shall be located so as to permit simple and easy access for cleaning, re-lamping and complete replacement when required. The selected location has a significant impact on the light distribution within the tunnel and should be determined at an early stage in design.

17.5.6　Use of daylight-screens

It is generally effective to reduce the amount of direct sunlight reaching the road surface and walls at the portal section using daylight louvre or screen structures over the tunnel entrance, and then it is a means of reducing energy consumption of threshold zone lighting. For lighting design, the position of the portal is considered at the beginning of the screens. The contribution of the inter-reflected light shall be included in the calculation. In practice, the daylight screens can be part of the tunnel ceiling or of the walls, or both.

Where a screen is planned for a tunnel, the following aspects shall be considered[3]: ①the possible effect on drivers of any flicker induced by passing through alternating bands of bright sunlight and shade; ②the frequency of cleaning required to maintain performance; ③ the possible effects of strong winds or the accumulation of snow and ice; ④the effect on dispersal of polluted air from the tunnel.

In general, sun-tight louvres are not suggestion for daylight screens in the tunnel ceiling[2]. A light transmission of non-sun-tight louvres usually used for reducing the lights installation in the threshold zone.

However, daylight louvres or screen structures have the following disadvantages[3]: ①the degree by which the screens exclude natural daylight will vary according to the position of the sun and the amount of diffusion of sunlight by cloud and the actual performance of the screens is therefore very difficult to predict; ②the presence of screens can promote icing of the road surface beneath from water drips, icicles, and areas in shadow; ③ structures requiring maintenance are introduced at critical points of the tunnel.

17.5.7 Calculations

17.5.7.1 Surface light density

When calculating the number of luminaires necessary to obtain a chosen average illuminance on the horizontal reference plane (roadway), two methods suggested in the Road Lighting Calculations[9] are applicable.

17.5.7.1.1 Using the utilization factors

The average illuminance over the reference surface, E_{av}, can be calculated with the "lumen method"[2]:

$$E_{av} = \frac{\eta \cdot \Phi \cdot M \cdot N}{W \cdot S_0} \quad (17\text{-}7)$$

where Φ is the luminaire luminous flux (lumens); N is the number of luminaires, where the luminaires are in opposite arrangement, $N = 2$, otherwise, $N = 1$; M is the maintenance factor (maintained illuminance), which is defined according design code, such as $M = 0.6\text{-}0.7$; η is the utilization factor for the reference surface and is usually provided by luminaire producer in form of table or figure, such as $\eta = 0.35\text{-}0.50$; W is the width of carriageway [m] and S_0 is spacing of luminaires [m], as shown in Figure 17-13a).

In practice, the E_{av} is determined using the relationship with the designed average luminance, L_{av}, i.e., $E_{av} = K \cdot L_{av}$, where K is a constant which is related to the material of the roadway, such as $K = 10\text{-}13$ lux/(cd $\cdot$ m^{-2}) for cement concrete and $K = 15\text{-}22$ lux/(cd $\cdot$ m^{-2}) for asphalt concrete. Using the Equation (17-7), the spacing of luminaires, S_0 [m], is calculated as the following:

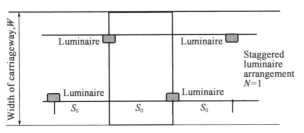 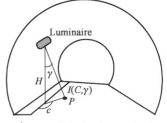

a) Calculation area in the CIE method (2000)   b) Surface light density at point P

Figure 17-13 Sketch showing calculation of surface light density

$$S_0 = \frac{\eta \cdot \Phi \cdot M \cdot N}{W \cdot E_{av}} \quad (17\text{-}8)$$

17.5.7.1.2 "Point-by-Point" method

In the "Point-by-Point" method, the illuminance of point P on a reference surface (horizontal plane) by a luminaire, E_{pi}, is calculated as the following:

$$E_{pi} = \frac{I(C,\gamma)}{H^2} \cos^3\gamma \times \frac{\Phi}{1000} \times M \quad (17\text{-}9)$$

where E_{pi} is horizontal surface light density at point P (lux), as shown in Figure 17-13b); $I(C,\gamma)$ is intensity in candles in the direction of the point in question; γ is angle between the luminaire vertical and the point in question; H is distance of the light source from the plane where the surface light density is to be calculated; the Φ and M are same as in Equation (17-8).

$I(C,\gamma)$ is determined from the luminaire intensity (I)-table after corrections have been made for the orientation, tilt, and rotation of the luminaire and linear interpolation, if necessary, applied.

The total illuminance of the point P, E_p, is calculated as:

$$E_p = \sum_{i=1}^{n} E_{pi} \quad (17\text{-}10)$$

where n is the number of the luminaires contributing illuminance to the point P.

The average illuminance of the calculated area, E_{av} (lux), is calculated as the following:

$$E_{av} = \frac{\sum_{p=1}^{m} E_p}{m} \quad (17\text{-}11)$$

where m is the point number being calculated in the area.

17.5.7.2 Surface luminance

Luminance is a photometric measure of the luminous intensity per unit area of light travelling in a given direction. In tunnel lighting, the carriageway surface luminance is referred to reflected lights, which can be from a luminaire or sunlight at the portal. In general, the carriageway surface of a tunnel is considered as flat diffuse surface. The luminance indicates how much luminous power will be detected by an eye looking at the surface from a particular angle of view. Luminance is thus an indicator of how bright the surface will appear. In this case, the solid angle of interest is the solid angle subtended by the eye's pupil, since the obstacles are to be discerned by drivers' eyes.

The calculation of the carriageway surface luminance is more complicated than that of the illuminance, as presented in the above section. Besides illuminance over a reference surface, the carriageway surface luminance is also related to other parameters, including the position and direction of the observer, reflection features of the carriageway surface. Mainly due to the height of a driver's eyes, drivers usually clap their eyes on the area about 60 m to 160 m ahead[2].

17.5.7.2.1 Luminance at a point

Following the method[9], the luminance at a point can be calculated with the following equation:

$$L = \sum \frac{I(C,\gamma) \cdot r \cdot \Phi \cdot M \times 10^{-4}}{H^2} \qquad (17\text{-}12)$$

where, L is the maintained luminance in cd/m^2; Σ indicates the summation of the contributions from all the luminaires; $I(C,\gamma)$ is the luminous intensity in the direction(C, γ), as indicated in Figure 17-13b), in cd/(k·m); r is the reduced luminance coefficients of the road surface for a light ray incident with angular coordinates(β, ε); Φ is the initial luminous flux (klm) of the sources in each luminaire; M is the luminaire maintenance factor; H is the mounting height of the luminaires above the road surface, in meter.

Expansion reading 17-14

The reduced luminance coefficients of the road surface, r, are conventionally expressed in terms of the reduced luminance coefficient multiplied by 10000 (for convenience of presentation), at the angular intervals and in the directions, such as indicated in Table 2 of the Road Lighting Calculations[9], and the Tables A.0.1-1 and A.0.1-2 in the *Guidelines*[4], which give the reduced luminance coefficients according to the angles. The value of r for the appropriate value of β and tan ε is determined with the use of quadratic interpolation, if necessary[9].

17.5.7.2.2 Field of calculation for luminance

Expansion reading 17-15

As suggested in the Road Lighting Calculations[9], the field of calculation should be between two luminaires in the same row, the first luminaire being located 60 m ahead of the observer. For a conventionally used eye height of 1.5 m and a range of viewing angles lying between 0.5° and 1.5°, the r-table is applicable to points lying between 60 m and 170 m ahead of the observer. In the transverse direction, it should cover the whole carriageway width on roads without a central reservation, or the width of one carriageway on roads with a central reservation.

The calculation points in the field should be evenly spaced and located.

17.5.8 Emergency lighting

Expansion reading 17-16

Emergency lighting is intended for application when standard lighting fails and it is divided into the following two types. ①Standby lighting, in case of failure of standard light sources, should allow to go on or, where possible, achieve a work cycle in progress under safety conditions; ② safety lighting that, in case of accidental lack standard light sources, should be provided to identify and guide escape routes under extremely critical conditions. The former is applied in some long and super long tunnels, while the latter is required for the tunnels with a lighting system.

17.5.9 Installation of luminaires in a lighting system

17.5.9.1 General lighting and enhanced lighting

A road tunnel is lit with luminaires for the entrance, interior zone (possibly including emergency lanes), exit and emergency lighting. Based on the calculation, the spacing of the luminaires for each zone in a tunnel lighting luminance profile under design can be determined, and therefore, the number for each type of the planned luminaires can be designed.

In practice, for the installation of the luminaires in a road tunnel, the lighting levels in the tunnel are usually designed in two steps, i. e., for general lighting and enhanced lighting, respectively.

First, the tunnel is lit with general lighting, of which the lighting level is same as that of the interior zone. Half of the luminaires for the general lighting is often designed for emergency lighting.

On the level of the general lighting, the enhanced lighting is to provide enhancing lighting to meet the requirements of entrance lighting, exit lighting and emergency lanes lighting.

In general, no luminaire is installed in the first 10 m from both entrance and exit portals, since enough sunlight can penetrate onto the tunnel roadway at the portal.

17.5.9.2 Case history

17.5.9.2.1 Conditions and requirement

A long road tunnel is planned to apply LED luminaires for daytime and emergency lighting. The features of the tunnel geometry, traffic situation, parameters for lighting design and the planned LED luminaires are the required parameters to be considered. To determine the number of luminaires for the tunnel, the other parameters can follow the presentation in Sections 17.3 and 17.5, or the suggestion in the *Guidelines*[4].

17.5.9.2.2 Calculation and results

Expansion reading 17-17

The spacing of luminaires is determined with the "lumen method"[2] or using the utilization factors, applying Equation (17-8), with $\eta = 0.47$ and $N = 1$. Following the method presented in the section 17.3 and 17.5, the lighting levels and the spacing and number of luminaires for each of the lighting zones can be calculated and determined, respectively. In this case, the first luminaire is mounted 9 m from the portal.

Expansion reading 17-18

In practice application, the above case seems too simple. As the luminance value for the second threshold sub-zone, L_{th2}, is only half of that of L_{th1}; and the luminance value for the transition zone, $L_{tr1} = 5.6$ cd/m², is less than one third of the value of $L_{th2} = 18.8$ cd/m². i.e., $5.6 < 18.8/3 = 6.26$ cd/m². Where the luminaires are mounted following the above calculation, there is an abrupt decrease in the magnitude of the luminance from first threshold sub-zone to the second sub-zone; and so is from the threshold zone to the transition zone. To meet the requirement of the magnitude of the luminance, such as suggested by the CIE[2], or the Figure 17-5, for the entrance lighting level, more enhanced lighting luminaires should be installed in the second threshold sub-zone and transition zone, to improve the lighting environment.

17.5.10 Lighting for special niches

It's a ideal situation, when a driver came into a tunnel, the views in his or her sight are almost same along the tunnel routine. On the other hand, the environment in the tunnel is generally not as good as that in open road, such as, in terms of noise, lighting, visibility and air quality. Drivers may feel monotonous or even strained where the tunnel is so long that it will take long period, such as more than 15 minutes, to reach the exit portal. This tunnel situation can give driver the experience of claustrophobia, which is typically thought to have two key symptoms: being fear of restriction and fear of suffocation. To reduce the chance of the experience of claustrophobia in a super long road tunnel, special niches, which are lighted with special scene, have been designed in some tunnels, such as the Lærdal tunnel in Norway, which is 24.5 km in length.

Expansion reading 17-19

In the design of the Lærdal tunnel, with the mental strain on drivers under consideration, the 24.5-km-long tunnel is divided into four sections, separated by three 30-m-wide large mountain caves at 6 km intervals. Different from the white color lighting in the main tunnel, the caves are lighted blue with yellow lights at the fringes to give an impression of sunrise, to break the routine and provide a refreshing view and allowing drivers to take a short rest. The caverns are also used as turn around points and for break areas to help lift claustrophobia during a 20-minute drive through the tunnel.

In the recent years, the design of special lighting niches have been followed by the extra-long road tunnels in China, such as the Qingling Zhongnanshan highway tunnel and Baojiashan tunnel in the line from Xi'an to Ankang.

On the other hand, special lights are also used for showing regional or national features in some metro stations. One of the world famous cases is the lighting at the metro stations in Stockholm, where unique arts are shown by special lights in the stations of structural characteristics, which is of single lining or unlined hard rock tunnels.

17.6 Remarks on tunnel lighting

Tunnel lighting is part of lighting public areas and is generally required to be: ①high-quality, uniform lighting to increase the level of safety, sometimes comfort and well-being; ②energy saving; ③optimized maintenance schemes. In a word, providing the right amount of lighting, where and when it is needed, is the preferred practice. For example, a correct adaptation of the lighting levels, depending on traffic density, is strongly supported[2,8]. A lower density of traffic does not require the same quantity of light to ensure the safety of the users as long as the uniformity is maintained. Intelligent dimming scenarios and new technologies for the luminaires, including: light sources (e.g., LED), optical systems, electronic control gears and control systems provide the necessary tools to achieve these high-quality and energy saving lighting installations. Luminaires can be equipped either with fixed dimming schemes or more intelligent adaptive lighting, integrated into a powerline or wireless controlled network. In general, an intelligent adaptive lighting system enables an overall energy reduction that outperforms savings, such as by switching off inefficient lighting systems according to traffic density, day and night and weather conditions etc.

17.7 Critical thinking problems

C1: There is always a lighting system in a long road tunnel. Consider: ①Why is a lighting system always required for a long road tunnel? ②What are the main objectives of lighting at a tunnel? ③The main types of lighting, in terms of function, in a long road tunnel or urban tunnel.

C2: The lighting level of a road tunnel is changeable along the tunnel longitudinal alignment. Consider: ①The zones of the daytime lighting level of a tunnel; ②Why are the lighting levels of the zones in a daytime lighting luminance curve different? ③ How to determine the lengths and lighting levels of the zones, respectively? ④The main factors to be considered in determining the magnitude of L_{20}.

C3: There are various luminaires available for tunnel lighting. Consider: ①Commonly used types of luminaires in road tunnels; ② Why are LED tunnel lights popularised in the recent years?

C4: In simplicity, the luminaires in a tunnel is lit with electrical power. In terms of energy saving, what are the commonly used measures in road tunnels?

C5: Where a long road tunnel is designed, lighting system is included in the project. Consider: ①The general procedure of lighting design for a planned tunnel; ②Following the suggestion in the *Gguidelines*, or the "lumen method" using the utilization factors, to determine the lighting system for the following tunnel.

Description of the planned tunnel and design parameters for lighting system

Features of the tunnel				
Length of the tunnel	1250 m	Width of the cement concrete roadway		10.8 m
Height of the tunnel clearance cross section profile	7.10 m	Grade of the roadway alignment		2.2%, -2.2%
Traffic situation				
Design hourly traffic volume in the tunnel	≤180 veh/(h·ln)	Traffic flow		Bi-direction
Design speed	60 km/h	Safety stop distance, SSD		59.2 m
Design parameters				
Luminaire arrangement	Single side luminaire decentralized arrangement	Maintenance factor		0.7
Luminance level in the emergency lanes	≥4.0 cd/m²	Luminance level in the tunnel interior		≥2.0 cd/m²
Access zone luminance	L_{20} = 2500 cd/m²	Values of reduction factor		k = 0.015
Parameters of LED luminaires				

Type of lights	Power	Luminous flux	Type of lights	Power	Luminous flux	Type of lights	Power	Luminous flux
50 W LED	50 W	5000 lm	100 W LED	100 W	10000 lm	150 W LED	150 W	15000 lm

The results of the lighting system evaluation are as presentation in the following table.

Results of the evaluation of the lighting levels and required LED luminaires

Lighting level (cd/m²)		Length(m)		Spacing and number of luminaires							
				50 W		50 W(E)		100 W		150 W	
				Spacing	Number	Spacing	Number	Spacing	Number	Spacing	Number
Threshold zone	L_{th1}	?	D_{th1}	?	?	?	?	?			?	?
	L_{th2}	?	D_{th2}	?	?	?	?	?			?	?
Transition zone	L_{tr1}	?	D_{tr1}	?	?	?	?	?	?	?		
	L_{tr2}	?	D_{tr2}	?	?	?	?	?	?	?		
	L_{tr3}	?	D_{tr3}	?	?	?	?	?	?	?		

continue

Lighting level(cd/m²)			Length(m)	Spacing and number of luminaires							
				50 W		50 W(E)		100 W		150 W	
				Spacing	Number	Spacing	Number	Spacing	Number	Spacing	Number
Interior zone	L_{in}	≥ 2.0	?	?	?	?	?				
Emergency lanes	L_{em}	≥ 4.0	80	?	?	?	?	?	?		
Total number for luminaires					?		?		?		?

Note: Find the magnitude for the blank space with mark of "?", if it is needed; The utilization factor $\eta = 0.52$; The enhanced lighting of threshold zone and transition zone is provided with 150 W and 100 W LED luminaires, respectively.

17.8 References

[1] AEC. AEC Tunnel Lighting[M]. AEC Illuminazione Srl, 2014.

[2] CIE (the International Commission on Illumination). Guide for the Lighting of Road Tunnels and Underpasses[M]. 2nd ed. CIE, 2004.

[3] Code of practice for the design of road lighting-Part 2: Lighting of tunnels[S]. The British Standards Institution, 2016.

[4] Guidelines for Design of Lighting of Highway Tunnel (JTG D70/2-01—2014)[S]. China Comminications Press, 2014. (in Chinese).

[5] Reverberi Enetec. Road Tunnel Lighting: Lighting power controllers[M]. Reverberi Enetec srl, 2006.

[6] Buraczynski J J, Li T K, Kwong C, et al. Tunnel Lighting Systems[C]// The Fourth International Symposium on Tunnel Safety and Security, 2010.

[7] Design of Road Tunnels(BD 78/99)[M/OL]// Design Manual for Roads and Bridges, Highways England, 1999. http://www.standardsforhighways.co.uk/ha/standards/dmrb/vol2/section2/bd7899.pdf.

[8] NVF (Nordisk Vejteknisk Forboud) Committee 61. Road tunnel lighting[M]. Nordisk Vejteknisk Forbund, 1995.

[9] CIE (the International Commission on Illumination). Road Lighting Calculations[M]. CIE, 2000.

18 Risk Management in Tunnel Engineering

18.1 Introduction

Expansion reading 18-1

Tunneling may impose risks on all parties involved, and also possibly on those not directly involved in the project. For example, the risks requiring an unexpected time, work and cost due to collapses during tunnel construction, can result in major cost overrun and time delays in the construction, and then can have a strong adverse impact on the building and operation plan of the project. To control the risk of a tunnel project in an acceptable level, risk management is always beneficial. By using risk management, potential problems can be clearly identified such that appropriate risk mitigation measures can be implemented in a timely manner[1].

In the ITA Guidelines for tunneling risk management[1], risk in a tunnel project is defined as a combination of the frequency of the occurrence of a defined hazard and the consequences of the occurrence, and hazard is a situation or condition that has the potential for human injury, damage to property, damage to environment, economic loss or delay to project completion.

Of the principles and the main points of risk management in a tunnel project, BTS[2] stated as the followings. ①Hazard identification and the management of risk to ensure their reduction to a level "As Low As Reasonably Practicable" (ALARP) shall be integral considerations in the planning, design, procurement and construction of tunnel works; ② Responsibility for risk management shall be explicitly allocated to relevant parties to a contract so that they are addressed adequately and appropriately in the planning and management of a project and that appropriate financial allowances can be made; ③ A formalized risk management procedure shall be employed as a means of documenting formally the identification, evaluation and allocation of risks.

18.2 Risk management in general

18.2.1 Risk and risk management

There are various definitions on risk. For example, Antunes and Gonzalez[3] defined risk as the potential of gaining or losing something of values, such as physical health, social status, emotional well-being or financial wealth, which can be gained or lost when taking risk resulting from a given action or inaction, foreseen or unforeseen. On the other hand, risk can also be defined as the intentional interaction with uncertainty or a consequence of action taken in spite of uncertainty, which is a potential, unpredictable, unmeasurable and uncontrollable outcome. The Oxford English Dictionary defines risk as: exposure to the possibility of loss, injury, or other adverse or unwelcome circumstance; a chance or situation involving such a possibility.

In the Joint Code of Practice for Risk Management of Tunnel Works in the UK[2], risk is defined as the combination of the consequence(severity) of a hazard and its likelihood, that is:

Risk = *Consequence(severity) of a hazard* × *Likelihood of occurrence of the hazard*

where a hazard is defined as an event that has the potential to impact on matters relating to a project which could give rise to consequences associated with: ①health and safety; ②the environment; ③the design; ④the programme for design; ⑤the costs for the design; ⑥the construction of the project; ⑦the programme for construction; ⑧the costs associated with construction; ⑨third parties and existing facilities, including neighbor buildings, utilities and all other structures/infrastructure that shall be affected by the carrying out of the works.

In the ITA guidelines[1], hazards are presented in two groups: ① general hazards, which include contractual disputes, insolvency and institutional problems, authorities interference, third party interference and labor disputes; ② specific hazards related to accidental occurrences, unforeseen adverse conditions, inadequate designs, specifications and programmes, the failure of major equipment, substandard, slow or out-of-tolerance works.

In general, the nature of the hazards(and hence their consequent risks) will be dependent on the stage of a project under consideration. Hazards should be identified and evaluated on a project-specific basis and their consequent risks shall be identified and quantified by risk assessments through all stages of a project.

In the ISO 31000: 2009, risk is defined as the effect of uncertainty on objectives. An effect is a deviation from the expected-positive and/or negative. Objectives can have different aspects (such as financial, health and safety, and environmental goals) and can apply at different levels (such as strategic, organization-wide, project, product and process). Uncertainty is the state, even partial, of deficiency of information related to, understanding or knowledge of an event, as well as its consequence or likelihood. Risk is often characterized by reference to potential events and consequences, or a combination of these, and often expressed in terms of a combination of the consequences of an event and the associated likelihood of occurrence.

The above discussion shows that risk is a probability or threat of damage, injury, liability, loss, or any other negative occurrence that is caused by external or internal vulnerabilities, and that may be avoided through preemptive action. So it is reasonable that risk should be reduced through appropriate actions, such as reasonable design and project implementation procedures, which include risk management.

Risk management is the systematic process of[2,4]: ①identifying hazards and associated risks that impact on a project's outcome in terms of costs and programme, including those to third parties; ②quantifying risks including their programme and cost implications; ③ identifying pro-active actions planned to eliminate or mitigate the risks; ④identifying methods to be utilized for the control of risks; ⑤allocating risks to the various parties to the Contract.

Also in the ISO 31000: 2009, risk management is coordinated activities to direct and control an organization with regard to risk. Risk management framework is a set of components that provide the foundations and organizational arrangements for designing, implementing, monitoring, reviewing and continually improving risk management throughout the organization. The foundations for risk management include the policy, objectives, mandate and commitment to manage risk. The organizational arrangements include plans, relationships, accountabilities, resources, processes and activities. The risk management framework is usually embedded within the organization's overall strategic and operational policies and practices.

In a word, risk management is the identification, analysis, assessment, control, avoidance, minimization, or elimination of unacceptable risks. An organization may use risk assumption, risk avoidance, risk retention, risk transfer, or any other strategy(or combination of strategies)in a proper management of future events.

18.2.2 Probable risks in a tunnel project

Project risk is an uncertain event or condition that, if it occurs, has an impact on at least one project objective. The probable risks in a tunnel project depend on the features and scope of the project. Also the building activities would have influence on the third parties and environment. In general, the risks of a tunnel project may include: ①harm to the project and its involved groups; ②harm to the third party and the environment; ③loss of goodwill.

18.2.2.1 Harm to the project and its involved groups

When a tunnel is planned and designed, it is hoped to be built as a high quality structure in planned time and proper expending. The risk due to the harm to the project and its involved groups may include: ①harm to the quality of the tunnel project; ②injury to workers or emergency crew; ③time delay; ④economic loss to owner and others.

These risks can be closely related to each other. For example, where there is a large collapse, the quality of the tunnel construction may be adversely influenced and the collapse would have done harm to the workers or emergency crew. As a result, the unit price would have been increased and time schedule could be delayed. An extreme situation may occur, such as when activities of the project contractor lead to bankruptcy or abjuration, the owner would pay for not only the economic loss of the collapse, but also the remedy works by a new contractor.

Of the economic loss to the owner, in practice, if it cannot readily be established whether additional costs are to be covered by the owner or by other parties, it should be assumed that the loss is paid by the owner[1]. On the other hand, the risk related to the tunnel operation due to increased maintenance or operation costs due to substandard works may also cause economic loss to the owner. So, in the recent years, there is a tendency that the cost of tunnel operation in design life should be considered in the planning and design period.

18.2.2.2 Harm to the third party and the environment

In a simple logic, the third party generally has no benefit from the construction work and should not be subjected to a higher risk than that if the construction work were not being carried out. So the risk due to the injury to third parties and damage to third party property should be much strictly controlled and the risk tolerance is normally decreased. However, the practice, as stated by Eskesen et al.[1], is that the clients of large civil engineering contracts are usually exposed to economic risks in excess of what is considered reasonable to third parties who, in many cases, are not the direct beneficiaries of the project.

Harm to the environment may come from: ① conventional construction activities, such as noise, vibration, spoiling due to mucking; ②pollution due to mucking, grouting with poisonous materials; ③disturbance to the ground water circulating system, such as due to excessively draining ground water during tunnel excavation. In terms of sustainable development and building an environmental favorable tunnel, environmental issues are of key factors considered in risk management. It is proposed to assess the likely harm to the environment in relation to the potential permanency and severity of the potential damage[1].

18.2.2.3 Loss of goodwill

Where tunnels are main parts of infrastructures, the cost of the project is paid by tax payers at last. The public will have goodwill to use the tunnel in planned time. So the tunnel projects are politically, economically or environmentally sensitive, and public opinion can be expected to have a severe impact on the project development[1]. On the other hand, a tunnel may be the only major infrastructure project in a region for a long period. The dimensions of risk related to the tunnel project are more or less correlated to the public goodwill both from a temporal point of view and from a geographical point of view[5].

In general, the loss of goodwill should be considered from the standpoint of harm to the owner, third parties and the environment, which are normally assessed to rank high on the political agenda. Any hazards, leading to bad press, may have a significant impact on the public and political goodwill to the project. In this term, during tunnel construction, the harm to the third parties, such as material damage and bodily injury to third parties or damage to third-party property, i. e., telecommunications lines, electricity cables, water pipes, which are closely related to daily life and activities, may cause the loss of the public goodwill to the project.

18.2.3 Objectives of risk management in tunnel project

In simplicity, the management of risk is to ensure their reduction to a level of ALARP[2]. The application of risk management in a tunnel project is to minimize the physical loss or damage and associated delays in time schedule of the tunnel project. Risk management activities should be implemented throughout the tunnel project from the early planning stage to the start of operation[1].

The risk management objectives may be given as general objectives supplemented by specific objectives for each type of risk. For example, proper risk management throughout a tunnel project can be ensured at all stages of the project by[1]: ①the identification of hazards; ②the identification of measures to eliminate or mitigate risks; ③the implementation of measures to eliminate or mitigate risks, where economically feasible or required according to the specific risk objectives or health and safety legislation. To realize these objectives, the hazard identification and the management of risk should be integral considerations in the stages of the planning, design, procurement and construction of the tunnel works. Since the features and main points of the tasks in these stages are various, the responsibility for risk management shall be explicitly allocated to relevant parties, such as in a contract form, so that the tasks are adequately and appropriately addressed in the execution of the project and that appropriate financial allowances can be made[1].

In a tunnel project, various risks may be related to its construction and operation. For each type of risk, specific minimum risk objectives should be defined in addition to the general risk objectives. For example, the level of risk sharing is a major factor in deciding the type of procurement practice to be implemented. Other issues that influence the type of procurement include the size and the complexity of the project, the definition of its scope, and the identification of imposed constraints. Clients need to weigh various factors in reaching a decision regarding the procurement system.

It is noted that the risk management of a tunnel project is not a simple and predefined straight line process. Risk control, which is often components of the risk management, should be executed in the project development, design, construction contract procurement and building in a tunnel project. The main purpose of the implementation of risk control in tunnel engineering is to secure best practice for the minimization and management of risks associated with the design and construction of the tunnels.

18.3　Main components of risk management in a tunnel project

18.3.1　Origins of risk in a tunnel project

The origins of hazards in a tunnel project may be much different from that of the others and of specific project features. This is mainly because a tunnel is a unique structure, generally with site specific features, which should be considered in the design, construction and operation of the tunnel. In general, the related risks in a tunnel project may be from: ① uncertainties in ground conditions; ②uncertainties in investment; ③the features of the tunnel project; ④the quality of project management, as shown in Figure 18-1[6].

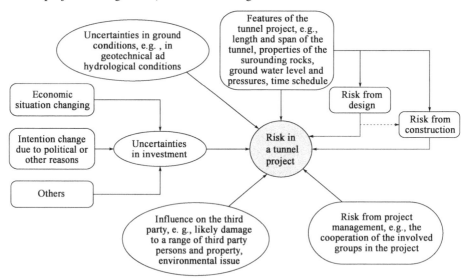

Figure 18-1　The probable contributors of the risk in a tunnel project

The ground conditions are of inherent nature. But uncertainties are always involved in the prediction of the ground conditions during site investigation and design. This situation may have a strong influence on the risk of a tunnel project. Of the features of a tunnel project, where the ground conditions are same, it is generally true that the larger of the magnitude of the tunnel, such as length and span, the higher risk of the tunnel project, especially in terms of construction. Also, the risk of a tunnel in the downtown of a city is generally more significant than that of a tunnel in rural area.

A tunnel is mainly built in ground, as an linear structure, the influence of the tunnel construction and operation on the third parties, for example, the influence to the existing structures nearby, the disturbance to the ground water system and pollution to the environment due to vibration, noise, exhausting gas, may be significant. Any of these key factors should be considered in risk management.

On the other hand, a tunnel is often parts of an infrastructure system, which is often fully or mostly invested by public finance. The political issue or even the public point of view on the tunnel project may have strong influence on the procedure of the project, in terms of public investment and support. In this term, the any factor that lead to the loss of goodwill should be identified and the related risk should be controlled to a level of ALARP[2].

Several groups, including, owner(client), designer, contractor, consultant, supervisor and monitor, will be involved in a tunnel project. The behaviors of these groups also can have influence on the risk of a tunnel project. An effective cooperation among these groups are required in risk control[6].

18.3.2 General procedure of risk management

Risk management in a tunnel project is a systematic process, which should be conducted from the planning to the operation. For a new tunnel project, it is required and also beneficial, to consider the operational issues, such as safety and cost during operation, at the stages of planning and design. Risk control is one of the considerations. However, the main features of the risk management from the stages of planning and design to the stage of construction, are much different from that during the operation, in terms of main points and their objectives, involved groups and the origins of hazards. In practice, the risk management is usually implemented for tunneling and operation, respectively, to meet the natures of risk management, which is of project specific. For example, a tunnel in operation may be built one hundred years age. The operational situation of the tunnel, such as the traffic volume and its compositions, state of the tunnel structures, the requirements of safety standards and the tunnel users, is significantly different from that of being planned and designed. At the same time, the roles of the groups of the involved people are also different from these, who were involved in planning, design and construction of the tunnel project. The risk management in tunnel operation has been discussed, in terms of safety control, in chapter 15. Here is the risk management of tunneling presented in the following sections.

Risk management is implemented in tunnel project is incorporated in tunneling activities, which generally include planning, early design stage (feasibility and conceptual design), tendering and contract negotiation, and construction. The ITA guidelines[1] show the application of risk management in tunnel project from the early planning stage to the start of operation. The main points of the risk management procedure are presented in Figure 18-2.

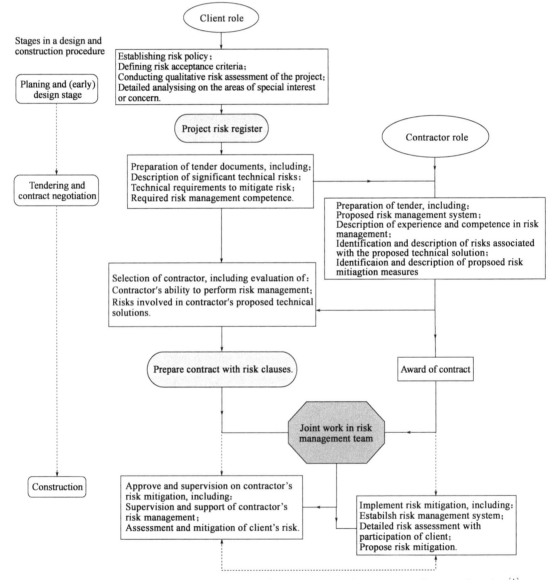

Figure 18-2 Risk management activity flow for the owner and contractor of a tunnel project[1]

18.3.2.1 The involved groups and their roles

The organization of the project execution is highly dependent on the selected contract model. In general, the involved groups include client (owner), designer, contractor, site supervisor, specialists and experts, and dispute review board. For example, where a design-build contract is applied, the designer and contractor are in same group. In some project management model, the site supervisor may also work for the design-build contractor. The dispute review board only works for the settlement solution of dispute between the client and contractor. In terms of risk control, the main role of the site supervisor and experts is to check, identify, evaluate workmanship and site conditions. Here are the roles of client, contractor and designer briefly shown in risk management.

Expansion reading 18-2

18.3.2.2 Risk policy and acceptance criteria

The risk policy is a common reference for all parties involved, e. g., the owner, designers, insurers and contractors. The specific minimum risk objectives may be defined in addition to the general risk objectives for each type of risk[1]. The risk policy of a tunnel project is usually established by the tunnel owner, according to the risk objectives. For example, a construction risk policy for the project should indicate the scope, objectives, and strategy of the risk management; and the identification of risks resulting from design and construction is an essential early task in a project.

In risk management, the owner's risk policy should clearly show the risk control objectives of the tunnel project. These objectives are usually expressed as risk acceptance criteria, which should be suitable for use in the risk assessment activities in the planned procedure. The risk policy document should give an explanation on how the risk acceptance criteria being established, because the criteria will be used in qualitative and quantitative risk assessment. For example, risk criteria can be expressed as[1]: ①a limit above which the risk is considered unacceptable and thus must be reduced regardless of the costs; ②a limit below which it is not required to consider further risk reduction; ③an area between the two limits where risk mitigation shall be considered and mitigation measures implemented according to the circumstances, e. g., using the ALARP principle.

18.3.2.2.1 Risk acceptability

In terms of actions to be carried out for each hazard, the related risk level of a tunnel project is classified in the ITA guidelines[1] as unacceptable, unwanted, acceptable or negligible levels.

Unacceptable: The risk shall be reduced at least to the unwanted regardless of the costs of risk mitigation.

Unwanted: Risk mitigation measures shall be identified. The measures shall be implemented as long as the costs of the measures are not disproportionate with the risk reduction obtained.

Acceptable: The hazard shall be managed throughout the project. Consideration of risk mitigation is not required.

Negligible: No further consideration of the hazard is needed.

In practice, whether the related risk is acceptable or not is of project specific features[10]. For example, 30 mm differential settlement of the ground may acceptable for the portal section of a mountain tunnel, while it is usually unacceptable for a tunnel undercrossing downtown area, on which a sensitive building is founded or nearby.

The acceptability for each hazard considered is usually evaluated with the parameters of frequency and consequence. A risk matrix for the determination of risk level is proposed in the ITA guidelines[1], as quoted in Table 18-1.

Table 18-1　Risk matrix for the determination of risk level[1]

Frequency	Consequence				
	Disastrous	Severe	Serious	Considerable	Insignificant
Very likely	Unacceptable	Unacceptable	Unacceptable	Unwanted	Unwanted
Likely	Unacceptable	Unacceptable	Unwanted	Unwanted	Acceptable
Occasional	Unacceptable	Unwanted	Unwanted	Acceptable	Acceptable
Unlikely	Unwanted	Unwanted	Acceptable	Acceptable	Negligible
Very unlikely	Unwanted	Acceptable[a]	Acceptable	Negligible	Negligible

Note: Depending on the wording of the risk objectives it may be argued that risk reduction shall be considered for all risks with a consequence assessed to be "severe", and thus be classified as "unwanted" risks even for a very low assessed frequency.

18.3.2.2.2　Classification of frequency

In general, it is right that the higher of the frequency of hazard events the lower of the acceptability of the considered risk. And therefore, a frequency assessment is usually needed in risk assessment. However, it is not an easy job to define the frequency of occurrence and extent of consequences for each hazard, since there is often no enough published statistics available for reference. Sometimes, expert judgement, drawn from a number of sources, may be base of the risk frequency assessment. Eskesen et al.[1] proposed to have a risk assessment team, consisting of experienced tunnel engineers to formulate their own guidelines for frequency classes. The data for reference should include the number of events experienced by the participants, the number of events they have heard of, the number of experienced near-misses and the number of near-misses they have heard of; all in relation to the number of projects they have been involved in or are aware of.

Expansion reading 18-3

There are various expressions for the frequency of the hazards occurring, such as in a conventional way of occurring a unit, "per year" or "per km of tunnel". Eskesen et al.[1] suggested a five grade classes or intervals as a practical way of classifying frequency and using the potential number of events during the whole construction period as evaluating base.

18.3.2.2.3 Classification of consequence

Expansion reading 18-4

The consequence of a hazard is one of the parameters to be considered in risk assessment. The acceptability of the consequence varies according to the scope and nature of the tunnel project. And then the selection of consequence types and potential severity will depend on project features. For example, Eskesen et al.[1] presented a case of the classification of consequence for a project value of approximately 1 billion Euro and duration of approximately 5-7 years. Using a five classes or intervals system, Eskesen et al.[1] defined the grade of: ①injury to workers or emergency crew; ②injury to third parties; ③damage to third party property; ④harm to the environment; ⑤delay; ⑥economic loss to owner.

18.3.2.3 General procedure of risk management in tunneling

Risk management is a continuous process, which should ①identify risk; ②analyze risk and its impact, and prioritizes risk; ③develop and implement risk mitigation or accept; ④track risks and risk mitigation implementation plans; ⑤assure risk information is communicated to all project/program levels, as shown in Figure 18-3. Each of these activities is implemented in the procedure of the tunnel project, which is usually executed in stages of planning and design, tendering and contract negotiation, and construction, as shown in Figure 18-2. The main points of risk management in these stages for a tunnel project can refer to the related code or guidelines, e.g., BTS code[2], ITA guidelines[1] and ITIG code[11].

In the implementation of the risk management, based on the project features and risk policy, the actions are executed in a planned process and the related main points are presented in documentations and figures, or other forms, which should be easily available and readily understood by the involved groups of the project. With the project executing, modification and feeding back of the actions are always required, as new data and information are available. The whole process should be based on the communication and documentation extending throughout all of the related activities in the tunnel project.

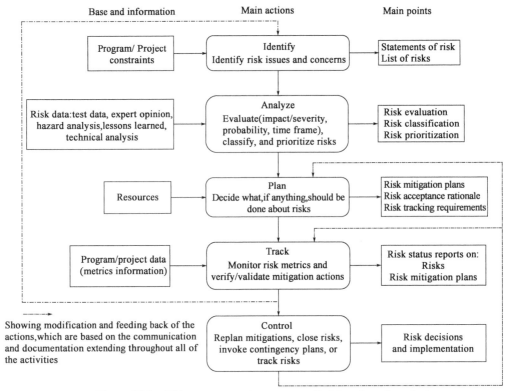

Figure 18-3　Risk management process applied in a tunnel project

18.4　Risk control in tunneling

The objectives of risk management in a tunnel project are to control the risk of the project in a planned mode, at least to an acceptable level, such as through contract management system including risk identification, analyzing, evaluating, monitoring and reviewing. To realize the planned objective, the risk control of a tunnel project is usually based on a risk sharing contract management.

18.4.1　Features of the risks in tunneling

In general, a risky environment is considered as situations, in which probability distributions are known, whereas uncertainty corresponds to situations, in which probabilities, and possibly the list of potential outcomes, are unknown. Under a situation of uncertainty, the decision maker should rely on some well-established procedures, methods, experiences, and revise the decision once there is new relevant information available.

For the risk management in tunneling, the risky environment under uncertainty situation may be due to the tunnel project scope and the project environment, as well as the adverse interaction between these two factors. For example, the designer and client of a tunnel project are often confronted with geotechnical uncertainty of the tunnel surrounding rocks. The risks due to the uncertainty of the ground conditions are often of features of project specific. Where the influence of the uncertainty of the ground conditions on the design and construction of the tunnel is not properly and skillfully dealt with, a damage to the tunnel construction quality will occur, such as collapse or cave-in of the excavation, large deformation of the surrounding rocks and supporting system. Sometimes, these adverse situations can also induce significant adverse influence on the third parties and environments. The results will significantly decrease the goodwill of the project, especially in the public views.

In general, where there is hazard in environment issue in a tunnel project, the adverse effect of the environment hazard may cause great loss of the goodwill of the project, especially to the local public. For example, during the construction of the Hallandsås tunnel in Sweden, series of adverse events happened starting from the uncertainty of the ground conditions. The construction of the Hallandsas Tunnel, a two-tube 8.7-km-long railway tunnel, with rock cover of 100-150 m along most of the tunnel alignment, began in 1992 and the traffic opening was originally planned for 1995. However, the tunnel opened for traffic on 13 December, 2015. Except the time schedule delay, there are several main risk issues and their consequences in this tunnel project are significant and generally unacceptable.

Expansion reading 18-5

As shown in Section 18.2.1, there are various sources of hazards in a tunnel project. The specific features of the hazards of a tunnel project may be unique. However, the following features should be considered in risk management, such as with the objectives of project quality, cost and time schedule controls.

(1) For a tunnel project, the uncertainty in geotechnical and hydrological conditions of the tunnel surrounding rocks may be the most significant hazard source, which can induce other hazard sources.

(2) The risk of a tunnel project due to the uncertainty in geotechnical and hydrological conditions can develop from a usual and unwanted one into an unacceptable and large event of disaster, if the hazard will not be coped with in a proper mode at its initial stage.

(3) When the hazard of a tunnel project has been such severe that the harm to the third parties and environment is unacceptable, the failure of the risk control will usually have strong and adverse influence on the results of the project, especially in terms of cost overrun and time schedule delay.

18.4.2 Risk control measures

18.4.2.1 Risk management tools and techniques

Risk management is the systematic process including identifying hazards and risk assessments, quantifying risks, risk control and mitigation implementation. This process is in corresponding to the different phases of a tunnel project from planning and through the construction to the operation. These activities may be difficult to track without tools and techniques, documentation and systematic information.

Expansion eading 18-6[12,13]

Risk management tools allow planners to explicitly address uncertainty by identifying and generating metrics, parameterizing, prioritizing, and developing response measures, and tracking risk. Various tools and techniques have been introduced from the industries outside the tunnel engineering into the applications of risk identification, analysis and response planning in risk management in a tunnel project. In general, simple risk management tools present in documentation while more sophisticated tools provide a visual display of risks.

Expansion reading 18-7

18.4.2.2　Contract options for tunnel risks control

Contract option is a valuable tool in risk management. As stated in the ITA guidelines[1], the risk management should be performed in an environment of good cooperation between the parties, such as by the application of partnering in contract management. The process of "partnering" may therefore be seen as a risk mitigation measure for the owner and contractor, by risk sharing contract and the application of GBR. Similarly, the BTS code[2] requires allocating risks to the various parties in the contract.

18.4.2.2.1　Risk sharing in contract management

Risk sharing is based the cooperation among the involved parties of a tunnel project. The partnering of the involved groups in the tunnel contract management is therefore required in encouraging good communications between the groups. In terms of the cost paid by the owner and the profit for the contractor, it may be a formula for minimizing cost to the owner while maximizing profit for the contractor, such as through joint planning and problem solving, scheduling, mitigation of delays and value engineering[1]. The ideal case is a two parties accepted balance measure having been found through the joint activities.

In practice, tunneling contracts are various among projects. The relationship between client and contractors varies in terms of management, cost and price defining, as well as risk allocation. The mode of contract management in a tunnel project may have strong influence on the result of the risk management. For example, for the risk due to unexpected ground conditions, i.e., differing sites, there may be three situations as the followings.

(1) Case Ⅰ: client takes all risks means low risk for contractor. Contractor is paid the cost of completing project in full. No incentive for the contractor to resolve problems cost effectively when they arise. This situation is similar to the contract mode of client directly employs labor in Figure 18-4.

Figure 18-4　Risk level in tunneling contracts delivery[14]

(2) Case Ⅱ: contractor takes all risks means high risk for contractor. Contractor is likely to be unable (or unwilling) to price the risks—and so can go badly wrong. This situation is similar to the contract mode of contractor execute the contract of lump sum with fixed price in Figure 18-4. In a simple and clearly defined contract, lump sum with fixed price means that the contractor is responsible for site investigation, design and construction of the project for a fixed price. The risk level for the contractor is the highest, while for the client is the lowest, provided that the contractor can afford the total risks of the project.

(3) Case Ⅲ: compromise alternatives, which may be executed through ① agreed upon reference ground conditions at start, ② clause allowing additional payment, ③ partnering, allowing either gain or loss to both parties if conditions are better or worse than anticipated. These situations are similar to the contract modes between the case Ⅰ and Ⅱ, the cost reimbursable, admeasurement and lump sum escalation contract modes in Figure 18-4, of which there is a general increasing tendency of risk from low to high for a contractor, while is contrary to client.

In general, for a design-bid-build contract, the design team is impartial and looks out for the interests of the owner; whereas, a design-build contract is beneficial to minimize the project risk for an owner and to reduce the delivery schedule by overlapping the design phase and construction phase of a project.

Expansion reading 18-8

18.4.2.2.2　Disputes review board

The common causes for disputes in tunneling occur where the project has changed, or has appeared to change, in such a way that the rates or terms for undertaking the work are alleged as being no longer applicable[15]. Where the inherent uncertainty in tunneling is a major cause for disputes, the settlement of those disputes are usually expensive and time-consuming[15] and may lead to a result of "how-do-you-do" or internecine. For example, litigation is a traditional disputes resolution in tunnel project. This may lead to friction and ill-will among the involved parties. The result will divert the objectives of the project. On the other hand, jury or judge has limited construction experience and the conflicting expert witness testimony will complicate resolution. In the court, factual data may get obscured in deed. As a result, there will be an immeasurable argument between the owner and the contractor in a litigation procedure. In a long run, the lawyers may be the only party of being lossless and rich picking.

To settle down the disputes in tunneling in a risk sharing mode, Disputes Review Board (DRB) can be a beneficial way. This dispute settling down mechanism was first successfully used in the Eisenhower tunnel second tube construction in Colorado, USA, in 1975, to resolve any disagreements between the owner and the contractor that could not be settled through the claim process of the contract[16]. And then the type of DRB was advocated by the American Society of Civil Engineers (ASCE) Committee on Contract Administration. The result of Menassa and Peña Mora[17] showed that there was growth in number of projects with DRB in the field of building, highway and tunnel engineering, and also in construction volume category, from 1975 to 2007.

During 1990s, the application cases of DRB increased in tunnel projects and other construction industry in USA[16], because of the advantages for both the owner and the contractor, since it ① provides a forum to foster cooperation between the client and contractor; ② can be prompt and equitable resolution; ③ is beneficial to dissuade frivolous disputes and claims. In comparison to the litigation resolution mode, the application of DRB procedure has the effect of reduction in the cost and time[16]. The benefit of the application of DRB procedure is also because that the recommendations of professional experts are more likely to be based on practical considerations than on abstruse points of law[16]. This situation was also suggested by Muir Wood[15] as the essence of the formula for success throughout a tunneling project depends on the appreciation of the professional demands made upon the participants.

When a DRB is applied in practice, a three member board is first proposed. Of the three members in the board, one is selected by the owner and another by the contractor. And then the third member selected by the first two. All of the members are experts in tunnel engineering and approved by the owner and contractor. In general, the third member will be the leader of the board. In theory, the activities of the leader will be unbiased. The DRB should be organized early in the contract and will meet regularly throughout the contract. The disputes between the client and the contractor may be raveled out in a cooperation mode. In principle, as a kind of arbitration, DRB procedure is best suited to disputes of a factual nature and where there are few overriding issues of the law[18].

In an ideal way, all parties of DRB must understand that board members are not representatives or advocates of the party that selected them and the board should be organized before there are any disputes[19].

Figure 18-5 shows the general procedure of conflict resolution, with DRB application in the construction phase of the project. The conflict resolution may be settled down at the one of the probable three phases, i. e., Prevention-Conflict Resolution, Alternative Dispute Resolution and Litigious Dispute Resolution[17]. When the parties do not agree to solve the conflict within the contract provisions in phase 1, DRB hearing sessions are undertaken whenever all interparty negotiations have been exhausted without successful resolution of the dispute[20], as shown in the second phase of the conflict/dispute resolution process in Figure 18-5. The end result of a DRB hearing session is a recommendation rendered by the DRB members and communicated to the disputing parties in writing form. The details of the practices and procedures of the application of DRB in a construction project is available from the DRBF Manual[20].

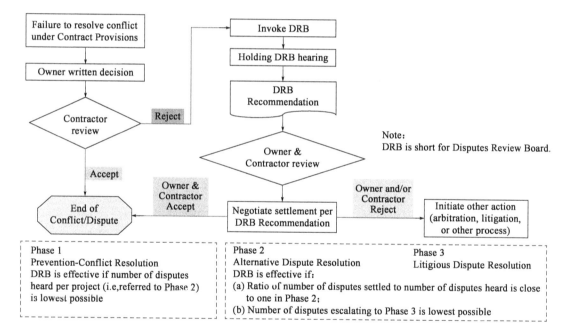

Figure 18-5 Conflict/dispute resolution process with a DRB involved[17]

It is assumed that the higher the rate of settlement of any given disputes based on a DRB recommendation, the more effective the DRB is, because it assisted the parties in resolving their disputes without the need of further escalation to the third phase of resolution, such as arbitration or litigation[17]. For example, in Figure 18-5, the effectiveness of the DRB process at phase 1 can be measured by the number of conflicts that actually escalated to a dispute that required a DRB hearing. The lower the number of conflicts that escalate to a dispute, the higher the probability is that adopting a DRB has encouraged project participants to resolve their issues at this initial phase among themselves. As the project procedure is smoothened by the contributions of the DRB and then the execution efficiency of the project is improved accordingly.

It is noted that a tunnel project is unique. Considering advantages and disadvantages of using a DRB, there need a deliberate decision on whether or not a DRB is right for a project[21]. One way is learning from the case histories, such as the DRBF database from the internet website: www.drb.org, where the data is updated timely.

18.4.2.2.3 Application of GBR

Many infrastructure projects run out of time and/or budget, because of unforeseen behaviors of the ground. Numerous case histories indicate that for over a century there has been a repetition of common reasons, which have led to project failures[22]. Differing site conditions are a main source of construction risk and the related claims are about 28 % of the contract price in average[23].

A key factor for effective risk management is related to the contractual allocation of risks arising from differing site conditions. The main objective of the application of Geotechnical Baseline Report (GBR) in tunnel project risk management is to provide a clear contractual arrangement for the allocation of the risks arising from differing site conditions. The underlying philosophy of GBR is a contractual statement. It states that the owner is ultimately responsible for any geotechnical conditions, which are materially different from the anticipated geological conditions in geotechnical reports. The geological conditions can be contractually defined by geological profiles or geotechnical baseline parameters for the planned tunnel surrounding rocks. Where differing site conditions clauses[7,8] are included in contracts, the responsibility for the differing site conditions can be clear.

GBR can create risk awareness and contractual transparency about the differing sites. This is a promising tool for the allocation of geological risks between owner and contractor. If GBR becomes a true document for contract negotiation in the future, the reduction of costs is possible. This is beneficial to both client and contractor in a long run, since the project can be executed in a planned procedure, and then the risk of the project related to the differing site is under control.

Figure 18-6 shows a concept procedure of developing a GBR, with geological risk allocation involved. In a GBR developing, basic types of site conditions are materially different, by the definition of baselines for the key risk factors of the ground. Risks associated with conditions consistent with or less adverse than the baseline are allocated to the contractor. Those risks more adverse than the baselines are accepted by the owner.

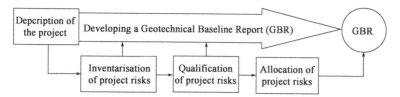

Figure 18-6　Development of GBR with risk allocation involved[14]

When developing a GBR, the geological risk analysis is from a qualitative mode to quantitative one. In order to determine whether risks are acceptable or not, one has to qualify the project risks. This is possible by qualifying the probability of occurrence and consequences. The allocation of project risks is the focus of the GBR writing. In a GBR, it should be clear who is responsible for unexpected events dealing with the ground. As a beneficial result, the GBR is an effective prevention against time consuming and expensive legal and claim procedures.

As the above shown, the purpose of a GBR is to establish a realistic, common basis for evaluating any contractor claims for differing site conditions that appear during construction. The GBR is the basis for equitable contractual risk sharing and risk allocation between the project owner and their selected contractor. The GBR is charged with portraying a realistic interpretation of the ground conditions that are anticipated in the proposed construction. A GBR should include not only the mean conditions of ground behavior and groundwater conditions anticipated, but should also address the range of variances that is expected, with aims to establish a contractual understanding of the ground conditions and risks associated with the conditions being specified.

Expansion reading 18-9

18.4.2.3　Application of the observational method

Expansion reading 18-10[25]

The application of the Observational Method (OM)[9] in tunnel project risk management can be classified as two types: ① identification of the ground conditions; ② assessment of the behavior of the ground and tunnel construction activities. The former is mainly used for suppressing disputes between the owner and the contractor; the latter application is to risk control.

18.5　Comments on risk management

As Eskesen et al.[1] stated that the practice of performing risk management requires much experience, practical and theoretical knowledge. Here are only some general points presented, with the intention of providing some basic knowledge and indicate what is recommended industry best practice for tunneling risk management.

In a long run, the overriding purpose of the risk management in tunnel project is to protect public benefit, since most of the tunnels are parts of infrastructures.

However, to realize this objective, the tunnel project should be a constructed product at least cost to the owner, with an appropriate profit to both the sponsor and constructor[24]. A contract with the feature of equality is required for the effective cooperation among the involved parties.

As Muir Wood[15] noted that the most likely single cause for disputes arises from claims for unforeseeable conditions of the ground, affecting the costs of construction and possibly of consequential remedial work, is the inherent uncertainty in tunneling which demands the high degree of professionalism. The essence of risk sharing project management formula for success, such as the application of risk management tools and techniques in risk control, depends on the appreciation of the professional demands made upon the participants, who should further an equitable adjustment of disputes rather than allow it to escalate to litigation[24]. The lawyer's approach is contrary to this objective and will not make for good engineering[15].

18.6 Critical thinking problems

C1: Risk always exists, low or high, in a tunnel project. Risk management activities should be implemented throughout the tunnel project from the early planning stage to the start of operation. Consider: ① Why is risk management always needed or beneficial to a tunnel project? ② What are the main origins of risk in a tunnel project? ③ What are main objectives of the risk management in a tunnel project?

C2: As risk management is applied in a tunnel project, consider: ① The general procedure of risk management implementation in a tunnel project; ② The main points of risk control implementation, in terms of contract option and the application of the OM, respectively.

C3: A tunnel is built by the involved groups in the tunnel project. The behavior of the groups will have a strong influence on the success of a complex tunnel project, especially with high risk included. Consider: ① Why is risk sharing among the involved groups important and beneficial? ② What are the commonly applied approaches in the implementation of risk sharing in the risk management of a tunnel project?

18.7 References

[1] Eskesen S D, Tengborg P, Kampmann J, et al. Guidelines for tunnelling risk management [J]. Tunnelling and Underground Space Technology, 2004, 19 (3): 217-237.

[2] The Association of British Insurers and the British Tunnelling Society. The Joint Code of Practice for Risk Management of Tunnel Works in the UK[M]. The British Tunnelling

Society (BTS), 2003.

[3] Antunes R M S. A Production Model for Construction: A Theoretical Framework [J]. Buildings, 2015, 5(1): 209-228.

[4] Fouladgar M M, Yazdani-Chamzini A, Zavadskas E K. Risk evaluation of tunneling projects[J]. Archives of Civil & Mechanical Engineering, 2012, 12(1): 1-12.

[5] Palma A D, Picard N, Andrieu L. Risk in Transport Investments[J]. Networks & Spatial Economics, 2012, 12(2): 187-204.

[6] Ma J Q. Risk Control in the Deep Excavations with the Application of the Observational Method[C]// Advanced Materials Research, 2011, 243-249:3403-3410.

[7] Technical Committee on Contracting Practices of the Underground Technology Research Council, ASCE. Geotechnical Baseline Reports for Underground Construction: Guidelines and Practices[M]. New York, ASCE, 1997.

[8] Essex R J. Geotechnical Baseline Reports for Construction: Suggested Guidelines[M]. New York, ASCE, 2007.

[9] Peck R B. Advantages and limitations of the observational method in applied soil mechanics [J]. Geotechnique, 1969. 19(2): 171-187.

[10] Vanem E. Ethics and fundamental principles of risk acceptance criteria[J]. Safety Science, 2012, 50(4): 958-967.

[11] ITIG. A Code of Practice for Risk Management of Tunnel Works[M]. ITIG (the International Tunnelling Insurance Group), 2006.

[12] Nerija Banaitiené, Audrius Banaitis, Arturas Norkus. Risk management in projects: peculiarities of Lithuanian construction companies[J]. International Journal of Strategic Property Management, 2011, 15(1):60-73.

[13] Reilly J, Brown J. Management and control of cost and risk for tunneling and infrastructure projects[C]// International Tunneling Conference, Singapore, 2004.

[14] Ma J Q. Cost Control in a Systematic Procedure for Tunnel Project[J]. Advances in Information Sciences & Service Sciences, 2013, 5(8): 222-230.

[15] Muir Wood A M. Tunnelling: management by design[M]. London: E & FN Spon, 2000.

[16] Kuesel T R. Tunnel Construction Contracting[M]// Tunnel Engineering Handbook. 2nd ed. Chapman & Hall, USA, c1996: 541-544.

[17] Menassa C C, Mora F P. Analysis of Dispute Review Boards Application in U. S. Construction Projects from 1975 to 2007 [J]. Journal of Management in Engineering, 2010, 26(2):65-77.

[18] Hester W T, Kuprenas J A, Randolph T H. Arbitration: A Look at its Form and Performance[J]. Journal of Construction Engineering & Management, 1987, 113(3): 353-367.

[19] Treacy T B. Use of Alternative Dispute Resolution in the Construction Industry[J]. Journal of Management in Engineering, 1995, 11(1): 58-63.

[20] Owen G, Totterdill, B. Dispute boards: procedures and practice[M]. Gwyn Owen: Brian Totterdill and Thomas Telford Limited, 2008.

[21] Harmon K M J. To Be or Not to Be—That Is the Question: Is a DRB Right for Your Project? [J]. Journal of Legal Affairs & Dispute Resolution in Engineering &

Construction, 2011, 3(1): 10-16.
[22] Fookes P G, Baynes F, Hutchinson J N. Total Geological History: A Model Approach to the Anticipation, Observation and Understanding of Site Conditions[C]// EngGeo 2000, Melbourne, 2000.
[23] Smith R. Allocation of risk—the case for manageability[J]. The International Construction Law Review, 1996, 4: 549-569.
[24] Gould J P. Geotechnology in dispute resolution[J]. Journol of Geotechnical Engineering, 1995, 121(7): 523-534.
[25] Hoek E. Putting numbers to geology-An engineering viewpoint[J]. Quarterly Journal of Engineering Geology & Hydrogeology, 1999, 32(1):1-19.

19 Appendix-Frequently Used Tunneling Terms

QR code 1

QR code 2

Terms with the initial letter alphabet A (QR code 1)
Terms with the initial letter alphabet B (QR code 2)
Terms with the initial letter alphabet C (QR code 3)
Terms with the initial letter alphabet D (QR code 4)
Terms with the initial letter alphabet E (QR code 5)
Terms with the initial letter alphabet F (QR code 6)
Terms with the initial letter alphabet G (QR code 7)
Terms with the initial letter alphabet H ~ M, respectively (QR code 8)

QR code 3

QR code 4

Terms with the initial letter alphabet N, O, P and Q, respectively (QR code 9)
Terms with the initial letter alphabet R (QR code 10)
Terms with the initial letter alphabet S (QR code 11)
Terms with the initial letter alphabet T, V, W and Y, respectively (QR code 12)

QR code 5

QR code 6

References

This glossary relies heavily on the standards listed below. Many of the terms are defined directly from the following references.

QR code 7

QR code 8

[1] Basic terms in mechanized tunnelling. https://www.herrenknecht.com.

[2] BS 5489-2:2003, Code of practice for the design of road lighting-Part 2: Lighting of tunnels. For the purposes of this part of BS 5489, the terms and definitions given in BS EN 12665, BS EN 13201-2, BS EN 13201-3 and the following apply.

QR code 9

QR code 10

[3] Caldecott Improvement Project: Geotechnical Baseline Report, prepared by Jacobs Associates, June 2009. 100pp.

QR code 11

QR code 12

[4] California Department of Transportation. 2003. Project Risk Management Handbook. California Department of Transportation, Office of Project Management Process Improvement, Sacramento, CA.

[5] Engineer Manual 1110-2-2901, CECW-EG, Engineering and Design, Tunnels and Shafts in Rock-Appendix B, Department of the Army, U.S. Army Corps of Engineers, 30 May 97.

[6] Project Management Institute. 2004. A Guide to Project Management Body of Knowledge (PMBOK® Guide). Project Management Institute, Newton Square, PA.

[7] The U. S. Department of Transportation-Federal Highway Administration's online Technical Manual for Design and Construction of Road Tunnels. http://www.fhwa.dot.gov/bridge/tunnel/.

[8] U. S. Department of Energy. 2003. Project Management Practices: Risk Management. U. S. Department of Energy, Office of Management, Budget and Evaluation, Office of Engineering and Construction Management, Washington, DC.